Praise for A History

'Marr's writing is persuasive, liberal politics and economics is superbly authoritative, never better than when discussing our changing relationship with the United States'   *Observer*

'Marr excels at brief, droll pen portraits of the major players. His language is vivid and powerful, enlivened with a sparky wit . . . Despite its great size, this is a stimulating and witty account of the forces that made our age by a man who somehow manages to be a well-informed insider without sacrificing the perspective of those outside the Westminster village. It's written from the perspective of someone who travels around the country, who thinks and who listens'   *Scotland on Sunday*

'Richer and deeper than television commentary can ever hope to be. As popular history, it is a lively and enjoyable, as well as a solid, achievement. He is fair and humane in his judgement of men and events'   *Daily Mail*

'As in the days when he was the BBC's chief political editor, it is the clarity of his judgements, the arresting insights and the irrepressible wit that keep us hanging on to his words . . . It is a measure of Marr's professionalism that his judgements inspire the kind of trust which Tony Blair and his allies squandered through spin and outright lies'   *Literary Review*

'Marr is shrewd enough to know that yet another irenic trot through what is in outline an overly familiar story may risk what he himself calls "autistic repetitiveness". So his invigorating method is to adopt what you might call the Ben Schott approach to history, piling up interesting detail, often through quotation, and hoping, quite correctly, that it will do more work than windy generalisation'   *Guardian*

'Marr is, predictably, at his best when discussing politics, with his keen understanding of economic policy and his feel for the Westminster world of ambition, conspiracy and rivalry . . . he excels in providing compelling summaries of leading political figures'   *Sunday Telegraph*

'Marr has a gift for narrative and précis, a pithy turn of phrase and an ability to unearth the unfamiliar, and he is passionately engaged with his subject'   *The Times*

A History of Modern Britain

Andrew Marr was born in Glasgow. He graduated from Cambridge University and has enjoyed a long career in newspaper journalism, working for the *Scotsman*, the *Independent*, the *Economist*, the *Express* and the *Observer*. From 2000 to 2005, he was the BBC's political editor. He presents the imaginatively titled *Andrew Marr Show* on BBC1 on Sunday mornings. His broadcasting includes BBC2's series *A History of Modern Britain*, political documentaries for Channel 4 and BBC Panorama, and Radio 4's 'Start The Week'.

Also by Andrew Marr

MY TRADE
A Short History of British Journalism

Andrew Marr

A HISTORY OF
MODERN BRITAIN

PAN BOOKS

First published 2007 by Macmillan

First published in paperback 2008 by Pan Books
an imprint of Pan Macmillan Ltd
Pan Macmillan, 20 New Wharf Road, London N1 9RR
Basingstoke and Oxford
Associated companies throughout the world
www.panmacmillan.com

ISBN 978-0-330-43983-1

7 9 8

A CIP catalogue record for this book is available from
the British Library.

Typeset by SetSystems Ltd, Saffron Walden, Essex
Printed and bound in the UK by
CPI Mackays, Chatham ME5 8TD

Contents

Introduction to the Paperback Edition ix

Prologue xv

Part One

HUNGER AND PRIDE: BRITAIN AFTER THE WAR

1

Part Two

THE LAND OF LOST CONTENT

113

Part Three

HAROLD, TED AND JIM: WHEN THE MODERN FAILED

229

Part Four

THE BRITISH REVOLUTION

379

Part Five

NIPPY METRO PEOPLE: BRITAIN FROM 1990

475

Notes 603

Index 613

Acknowledgements 631

Introduction to the Paperback Edition

One Year On

A year has passed since this book was first published in hardback. How much has changed? How do the judgements stand up? The big theme of the story that follows is the defeat of politics by shopping. The surging consumer economy has been by turns exhilarating, wasteful, liberating and narrowing. Nobody who escaped the grey years of rationing, queues and shortages should snootily dismiss the triumph of shopping; yet nobody who looks at our dead-eyed obsession with buy and-throw newness can be comfortable either. Britain's shopping economy, shorn of most of its industry, has produced a country which is more crowded, cleaner and richer (far richer) than it used to be, but which is also more vulnerable to shocks from outside. Consumerism has shouldered aside other ways of understanding the world – real political visions, organized religion, a pulsing sense of national identity.

Yet during 2007, the biggest change was a darkening of the national mood. It is not just global warming, but a sense that the good times are not, after all, forever. The decade-long Blair–Brown boom has been based on cheap imports from China, on very high levels of borrowing secured by upward-spiralling house prices, and on cheap, skilled migrant labour from Eastern Europe. None of these things are indefinitely sustainable. As this book shows, our recent prosperity is partly the achievement of politicians who are now almost forgotten. But after ten years in which New Labour had enjoyed the political fruits of strong, low-inflationary growth, many of us think we can see the buffers looming out of the mist.

This is recent. Early in 2007 house prices were still strongly rising. The stock market was at a six year high. Economists and opposition parties were warning about the government being overborrowed, and about private debt. But nobody paid much attention. In the City the big banks still reported huge profits. There were mysterious characters called private equity investors and hedge fund managers. Few people really understood what they were up to, except that it was all very clever and complicated. The banks were paying astronomical bonuses to their managers. And for the majority, in the shops, clothes and gizmos were ludicrously cheap. A Western economy based on high debt, both private and public, ensured cash was there to keep the spree going. But the intricate and always-shifting tangle of loans, bets, guesses and 80-proof, chill-filtered optimism that is modern global finance, was about to suffer a reality check. And if 'reality check' is an ugly American phrase, then it is perhaps not as ugly as another which entered the Queen's English in 2007. 'Sub prime' is jargon for bad loans – the mortgages and other pricey money offers to ordinary Americans who had no proper security and in many cases no way of paying it back. This overborrowing, mere greed by the banks, had been causing worries on Wall Street as early as February 2007. We have known since the Great Crash of 1929 that a global economy transmits problems from one country to another through the banking system very fast. We are supposed to have a stabler world trading system these days. But what has also changed is that bad debts have been bundled up and sold around like sacks of plastic casino counters between banks so many times that nobody knows just who is in trouble, and for how many billion dollars. In great US institutions like Merrill Lynch, Morgan Stanley and Citigroup, the one-time wizards started to lose their jobs.

Meanwhile back in Britain, its prime minister lost his. Tony Blair carried on working at strategic plans almost until the day he finally left Downing Street. It was as if he was still waiting for a final vindicating victory in Iraq or believed that if he could only nail down one last element of his programme to the cabinet table, his domestic legacy would be secured. But at last he went, in June 2007, telling the Commons: 'I wish everyone, friend and foe, well. And that is that. The End.' Gordon Brown took over without the bloodbath or recriminations that had been so widely predicted. He promised to govern differently, to take the cabinet more seriously, and to be more inclusive, bringing in outsiders with police, military and business careers to advise him – and Liberal Democrats too. To start with, all this was popular. Under Brown, Labour rose sharply in the polls and many Conservatives were dejected. Perhaps he would not turn out to be the disaster they had predicted. Their new leader David Cameron was attacked for being lightweight, 'the heir to Blair' just when the country had had enough of Blair. There was muttering about replacing him. So there was too about Sir Menzies Campbell, who was attacked not for being in his sixties, but for looking as if he was. A sequence of crises, including terrorist attacks in Glasgow and London, widespread summer flooding and an outbreak of foot and mouth disease, seemed to show Brown as a decisive, rather traditional leader; and his position strengthened further.

Then, in the autumn of 2007, it all started to go wrong for him. By far the most ominous event was the revelation than an adventurous building society, based in the north-east of England, had been forced to go to the Bank of England for emergency support. What had happened to Northern Rock, Britain's fifth-largest provider of mortgages, was the direct consequence of those 'sub-prime' problems in America earlier in the year. Mud and ice were spreading through the Western banking system as banks, wondering how much bad debt others were exposed to, stopped lending readily to one another. The lubrication began to fail, and because Northern Rock had lent so much money so aggressively, it was first in trouble. Its bosses resigned, but not before the world had watched huge queues of people across Britain waiting to get their money out.

It was the first run on a bank in this country for 140 years. The new chancellor, Alastair Darling, promised to guarantee all savers' funds in Northern Rock – though not elsewhere – in order to shore up the stability of the banking system. The Bank of England injected money into the system to provide some more lubrication. A search began to find a private buyer who would take over Northern Rock without being completely underwritten by the taxpayer. And another search began to find who was to blame. The management of Northern Rock? American banks? The Bank of England, which had reacted slowly to the early signs of trouble? Most attention focussed on the prime minister, who had created the new system of banking regulation early in his time as chancellor. In the end, the building society had to be nationalised – a whiff of the Seventies.

The Northern Rock crisis began just when pressure was mounting on Brown to call an early general election. Things came to a head at the Labour party conference at Bournemouth. Some of the cabinet ministers closest to him were convinced that by going to the country in October 2007, capitalizing on his summer successes, he could win a clear and substantial majority over the Tories. But he hesitated. The following week, as the Tories gathered for their conference at Blackpool, their mood was grim and there was open talk in the bars about forcing out yet another leader. Then came a speech by the shadow chancellor, George Osborne, in which he promised to abolish inheritance tax on estates worth under £1 million and scrap the stamp duty for first time buyers on homes worth up to £250,000. This would be paid for by a new tax on foreigners living and earning in Britain but not paying tax here. It was a brilliantly targeted political counter-strike, which caused an abrupt shift in the polls, confirmed after an assured speech by Cameron. Assuming that Brown really was in a strong position in September 2007, as the polling suggested, and this author believes, then Osborne's speech will go down as one of the most significant moments at a party conference in recent political history. It persuaded Brown not to call an election. Rarely do party conferences have any impact on the real world; this one did.

In a BBC interview calling off the election, Brown repeatedly denied that the opinion polls were the cause, but the impression was given of indecision, or lack of nerve. He was not helped by maladroit political counter-thrusts nor by a series of serious failures which followed. These were, in a weary way, familiar – another Labour party funding scandal, more embarrassing losses of data, above all the personal details of a mere 25 million people involved in applying for or getting child benefit, and 600,000 who had wanted to join the Navy or the marines. The initiative had, for the time being, gone to the Conservatives who were now sounding more traditional on tax and immigration and riding so high in the polls they could dream of a clear victory in a future election. The Liberal Democrat leader was more or less pushed into resigning once it was clear there would be no election for a while. His job was taken by another young and telegenic leader, Nick Clegg. The country prepared for an eighteen-month slog in parliament, over the new European treaty, civil liberties, the problem of violent youth crime and pay – politics as usual, or at least as it had often been during the seventies and eighties. People had grown fed up of Blair, regarding his television skills and vision as lightweight:

remarkably quickly, they seem to have concluded that Brown, welcomed as dour and cautious, was worse. He put his head down and resolved to batter his way back to popularity with hard work and more initiatives.

Many British people would barely have noticed. The papers were obsessed by the disappearance of a young girl, Madeleine McCann, from her parents' apartment during a holiday in Portugal, and an inquest into the death of Princess Diana. A hard-shopping, hard-drinking pleasure economy continued to thrust ahead, even as evidence of a looming recession piled up. House prices slowed, then stuttered, then fell. Rumours about other banking problems flickered and hissed. The stock market has some terrible lurches, including its biggest one-day fall since the attack on the Twin Towers. Only a hard effect on wallets, jobs and security will really make most people think about politics at all seriously. So an obvious question is whether the triumph of consumerism, that big story of British life from 1945 until today, is about to be halted. It seems most unlikely that the country is going to be transformed merely by the economic cycle. Britain and America may well be heading towards recession, perhaps some very hard years by modern standards. But these will feel at worst more like a return to some of the earlier tough times in the seventies, eighties or nineties, than a great change of direction as happened after the war or in the Thatcher revolution. It will teach another generation that nothing goes up forever, that there are no final answers in economics and that, perhaps, we have been a little too smug in dismissing earlier generations of politicians and economists as ignorant.

More important for our shopping economy will be the effects of carbon addiction. Distinguished scientists are beginning to confront the notion that to save the planet, an age of hair-shirted austerity is now necessary. Instead there is a renewed enthusiasm for technological fixes, from nuclear power and offshore windfarms, to electric cars and sun-deflecting mirrors in space. Such optimism is urgently needed because one of the most important effects of the global warming debate is that it has so disheartened people, they simply turn away. We are flinching. This is too big, too frightening to think about. Many people felt just the same way about the rise of Hitler, or the likelihood of nuclear holocaust in the sixties. 'You can't just turn your back,' some say. Oh yes you can. Without hope, without a clear sense that, beyond the struggle, there are blue skies and a life worth living, then most of us will turn away and try not to look. So far, all the main parties are sending mixed messages (to put it politely) about global warming. One day it is wind turbines on the roof, or new taxes to force more recycling; the next it is a major expansion of airports so we can fly even more often, and promises that cheap holidaymaking overseas will remain a human right. In the end, it may be the scientists, the engineers and the investors who lead the politicians, not the other way about. As a political observer myself, I cannot pretend that the past year has seen politics at its best. But is the challenge ahead so big that it dwarfs the problems already confronted? Absolutely not. The history of modern Britain tells us we have had some narrow squeaks, but also that we have done some extraordinary things – even more extraordinary than going shopping and worrying about house prices. This gives no alibi for pessimism. At the risk of sinking to sales patter, I would say – don't panic about the crystal ball when you can settle down and read the book.

Andrew Marr

2008

Prologue

The play starts on the afternoon of 28 May 1940, at a meeting of the war cabinet in the Prime Minister's office in the old House of Commons. There are only a few players. There is Winston Churchill who has become the nation's leader only eighteen days earlier. He is seen by most of the Establishment and many Conservatives as a rather ridiculous, drunken and dodgy man with a penchant for wild speeches and silly hats. Behind their gloved hands they call him the 'rogue elephant', even 'the gangster'. Among those lukewarm about him becoming the King's first minister less than three weeks before, had been the King. In Labour circles he was widely regarded as an enemy of the working class, the pink-faced toff who, years ago, had ordered in the army against strikers. Now Churchill has just ordered British troops at Calais to fight without hope of evacuation to try to protect the 200,000 left on the beaches at Dunkirk, who might be saved. He regarded it as a stand-and-die order which he said left him 'physically sick'. He had also been trying to barter with the Americans for desperately needed destroyers. So far they had been no help. With thousands of British troops making it back across the channel every hour, there was still some hope of rescuing the bulk of the army. But German invasion loomed and without heavy weapons, that seemed a hopeless prospect. Churchill had just been asked to approve plans for the evacuation of the Government and the Royal Family, as well as the Bank of England's gold, to Canada. Like the King and Queen, he refused to contemplate this.

Around the table with him were two men ever afterwards associated with appeasement. There was the former Prime Minister Neville Chamberlain whose 'peace in our time' negotiations in Germany with Hitler had made him a national hero until, very quickly, Hitler turned him into a national fool. He was dying. There was the Conservative Foreign Secretary, Lord Halifax, who on earlier visits to Germany had found Hitler 'most sincere' and Goering 'frankly attractive', a composite character like 'a great schoolboy . . . film star, great landowner . . . party manager, head gamekeeper at Chatsworth.' Much favoured by the Court, a lanky, wry, religious and reactionary man, Halifax had been expected to become Prime Minister himself. But in the Lords, he was the wrong kind of Tory for these dark days and would soon be packed off to be ambassador in Washington. In this government of national unity, along with the Liberal leader Archibald Sinclair, were two Labour men. Clement Attlee had become leader of his party almost by accident and was little known in the country. Terse, patriotic, rather colourless, the idea that he would one day be remembered as a great Prime Minister would in 1940 have seemed outlandish. Then there was Arthur Greenwood, a former teacher who had stood in for Attlee during his recent illness. Greenwood is little remembered today. He was a much-loved Labour figure before the war but proved to be a poor minister. In his lifelong fight with the bottle, the bottle won every round. But many second-rate people find themselves called to a moment when history turns, and this was Arthur Greenwood's day.

In front of the war cabinet was a simple question. After the devastating success of Hitler's armies in slicing through Belgium, the Netherlands and France, was it time to try to cut a deal? Halifax and Chamberlain were both in favour. The Italian dictator Mussolini had been touted as a go-between and various bribes for his good offices had been discussed. The Italians might take Gibraltar, Malta, Suez, Kenya and Uganda as part of their payment to stop the invasion of the British Isles. The terms might be these. Britain would accept Hitler as overlord of Europe but would be allowed to keep her Fleet and the rest of her Empire, including India. Churchill had not yet rejected any deal, on any terms, but he was acutely aware that if talk of talks leaked out, the effect on national morale would be devastating. Churchill also believed that any terms offered by Berlin would include handing over the Royal Navy and the creation of a pro-Nazi puppet government in London. Half American himself, he believed that in the end the United States would come into the fight even if Britain was invaded. Surrounded by dim hopes, fears and question-marks, this was 'make your mind up time'.

Had the gathering been only of Conservative politicians Winston would have been outvoted. Attlee and Greenwood, however, were solid for fighting on and for refusing to negotiate or surrender. So by a squeak Churchill had his majority. Fortified by this, his mood revived and he quickly summoned the full cabinet, where in true Churchillian English he told them: 'I am convinced that every man of you would rise up and tear me down from my place if I were for one moment to contemplate parley or surrender. If this long island history of ours is to end at last, let it end only when each one of us lies choking in his own blood upon the ground.' Or that at least is how he recorded it later. Ministers jumped up, shouting approval and thumped the old man on the back. Later he said he would have been dragged from office if he had tried to surrender; every minister was ready, with his family, to be killed 'quite soon'.

As we have seen this was an exaggeration. Quite a few British politicians would have done a deal. Washington had been privately told by its London ambassador that the British would surrender. Looking back, such a thing may seem impossible unthinkable. But it was quite possible and it was seriously discussed. This was the moment when Britain was on the edge and her modern story begins. From that decision on that day, everything follows. First, there was the war, from the Battle of Britain, through Pearl Harbor to the final defeat of Germany and Japan. So, second, the world was differently shaped. The end of the British Empire, once the world's greatest, and the rise of the United States as ruler of the free world occurred for complicated reasons. But they can be plausibly traced back to what Winston, Clem and Arthur agreed was the right thing to do on that difficult day in May. That decision made contemporary Britain, with her weaknesses and strengths, which are the subject of this book. Many unexpected and surprising things followed. Neither Churchill nor Attlee got the Britain they wanted. Instead, unwittingly, they made us.

The Second World War was such a shattering, overwhelming experience for Britain that it is tempting to isolate the country we became afterwards from the pre-war Britain, as if a huge blade fell across the national story. In obvious ways this is true. The war changed Britain physically and industrially, destroying city centres; it ultimately changed who lived here by encouraging both immigration and emigration. It changed Britain's political climate and our attitude to government. It even changed, through a subsequent jump in the birth rate, relations between the generations. Yet in other ways post-war Britain was simply a continuation of the Britain of the thirties. When it was all over, and before Churchill was voted out of power, the Parliament of 1945 was the same one elected in 1935, a Commons frozen from another time. Deference and respect for the Royal Family, belief in the superiority of the white man, a complacent assumption that British manufacturing was still best . . . all that survived seemingly unaltered through the years of danger.

Britain still believed herself to be in her imperial heyday, mistress of the seas. Though we think of it as essentially Victorian, the British Empire, declaring itself the first 'world state' had continued to grow right up until the mid-thirties. At the beginning of the Second World War there were some 200 colonies, dominions and possessions connected to London, covering more than 11 million square miles. The Empire embraced Pacific tribesmen and Eskimos, ancient African kingdoms and the rubble of the great Mughal empire, Australian farmers and the gold-miners of South Africa. It ran from the Scottish Highlands to the Antarctic, from the French-speaking villages of Quebec to the mosques of the Middle East. For a comparatively small nation of fewer than 50 million people to have acquired all this might seem a global absurdity, a large joke in the history of humankind.

Relatively few of those square miles helped the British economy thrive yet the empire was considered the essence of British power, a global financial and trading system independent of the rising might of the United States. 'The Empire on which the sun never sets' was not poetic, but factual. Imperial feeling still suffused the Britain of the forties and fifties. Schools displayed the famous red-splattered maps and taught the history of Clive's battles in India and the achievements of missionaries in Africa. Children's encyclopedias brimmed with information about the calico industries of the subcontinent, or those useful rubber trees in Malaya. Middle-class bookshelves groaned with Kipling, Somerset Maugham, Henty and T. E. Lawrence. The Empire was everywhere, inside the home and out, in street names and statues, to the Indian knick-knacks and elephant-foot umbrella stands, Bombay gin and Imperial Leather soap, the rhododendron bushes from the Himalayas, words like tiffin and bungalows and the eating of kedgeree for breakfast by all those retired Indian civil servants and administrators in the Home Counties. There were the names of the major companies

– Imperial Chemical Industries, Home and Colonial Stores, British Imperial Airways, the Imperial Rubber Company. Empire Day was celebrated until 1958. More seriously there was continuing large-scale emigration from the British Isles to Africa, Canada, Australia and New Zealand. Until the sixties, one in five emigrants were heading from the UK to the old 'Crown Commonwealth' countries and more than a million Britons went to Australia alone during 1946–72. On wet days, back home, there were the endless Pathé and Movietone newsreels of Royal visits to New Zealand or some dependent territory.

Twenty years earlier the Royal Navy, like the British Empire, had seemed at its zenith, a world-dominating power. By the end of the First World War, it had no fewer than 61 battleships, more than the American and French fleets put together, plus 120 cruisers and 466 destroyers.[1] Without this awesome force, and the scores of naval bases and coaling stations, all controlled by the superbly organized Admiralty in London, the Empire would have been impossible to defend.

The navy was for the British what the roads and legions had been for the Romans, the thin, steely web holding together many different lands and people. By the twentieth century, with a quarter of the world under British rule, no country had ever claimed power over so many people and so much land. It had been made possible by a centuries-old British love affair with salt water, and by the Victorian enthusiasms for steam power and the appliance of science. In the twentieth century these traits, which had made Britain Great, were in decline. Even so, the navy continued to enthral the British in the first half of that century in ways we now struggle to remember; sea shanties on music-hall stages, the books of Marryat and Forrester for boys, the great Spithead reviews, the Dreadnoughts on cigarette cards, the blue-and-gold uniforms at Court. Drake and Raleigh, Cook and Nelson, were the subjects of ten thousand history lessons in almost every school in the country. To be British was to thrill at the sight of a White Ensign.

Many post-war trends had started long before the war and to understand post-war Britain we must take a bird's-eye view of an earlier, only half-familiar country. One way to do this is to travel with some of the talented writers who set out to discover their own nation between the wars. Part of the aftershock of the First World War, which had made people look again at just what they had been fighting for, it was a great time for such journeys of reportage. Not since Boswell and Johnson had heaved themselves onto ponies and into jolting carriages to visit Scotland in the eighteenth century, and the great radical newspaperman William Cobbett had set jogging off on his 'rural rides' through the depressed countryside of England in the 1820s, had journeys round Britain been so popular. The twenties and thirties were a golden age of road travel. While most roads had been like thin twists of twine following ancient routes, bumpy, frayed and narrow, now there were new trunk roads with bright 'roadhouses' and restaurants awaiting the traveller. Rural roads, empty by modern standards and almost unpoliced, made car travel for those who could afford it a moderately dangerous delight. For those who could not, the boom in motor-coaches, or buses as we would call them, and in the open-topped charabancs, made rural and coastal Britain available as it had never been before.

Some of the travellers, such as H. V. Morton, who went 'in search of England' in a bull-nose Morris car in 1927, were looking for a lost, green land. He was a little late. The real Britain was heavily industrialized and urban by then, and had been for nearly a century. Morton knew this perfectly well and defended himself by claiming that 'the village and the English countryside are the germs of all we are and all we have become.' In this, he stands for an ancient tradition of English writing, running back through Thomas Hardy, Kipling and Chesterton, right the way to the poets of Jacobean times. The real England is green, remote, local, wild, ancient and with a wisdom of her own. Perhaps, as well as being a little late, he was just in time, for this was before the urbanites had moved in and finally finished off the traditions that reached back to the Middle Ages. His tour matters because it stands for an idea of Britain which keeps its hold on many people well into the post-war period. His book was hugely popular, capturing post-industrial rural Britain before our current economy of supermarkets and super-roads finally killed it off during the seventies and eighties.

Looking for quaintness, Morton finds it everywhere, from old gallows left on remote hills, to ladies taking tea in ancient church premises. He finds the 'Furry', or floral, dancers of Helston in Cornwall, jigging in their top hats, flint-chippers in Norfolk, the last almshouse in England and even the last bowl-turner, making wooden bowls with Anglo-Saxon technology. There are ghosts, cobbles, eaves, lanes, Roman ruins, ancient pubs serving mahogany-coloured beer and in general more quirk than any normal person could consume at one sitting. Birmingham, where Morton grew up and worked successfully as a journalist, is dismissed without a visit as 'that monster' and Manchester is only distantly glimpsed as 'an ominous grey haze in the sky'. On the rare occasions that Morton is roused to genuine anger it is, like Cobbett, on behalf of the declining and disregarded farming community.

Green England's grip on the national imagination should not be underestimated. Comic novels by P. G. Wodehouse and brain-teasing crime novels by Agatha Christie were set in its timeless villages, peopled by ancient families, vicars and well-educated old maids whose lovers had died in the trenches. The cartoons of *Punch* portrayed England's cricket greens, church halls, peasant-crowded lanes and stables, interrupted by the modern world through charabanc tours, but still somehow essential. At the start of the war the Ministry of Labour sent a group of artists, mainly conscientious objectors, off round the country to draw and paint the barns, parish churches and country houses of old England before the Nazi bombers and housebuilders could destroy them: the scenes chosen look like a visual version of Morton's journey.

Yet British agriculture and therefore the British countryside, an early casualty of the global economy, had been in a long slump which lasted from the 1870s until 1940, with only the interruption of the Great War to lift prices. The opening up of the great prairies of North America, the easier transportation of grain and meat with steamships, refrigeration and railways, and even the use of barbed wire to extend the farms of Canada and New Zealand, all badly hurt home producers. From the middle years of Queen Victoria to the beginning of Hitler's war, two-fifths of arable land had gone out of use, and millions of farm workers left the countryside for ever, a trend mildly ameliorated in the mid-thirties by the arrival of tariffs and labour-saving technology. Much of the upland areas had been abandoned to thistles and weeds and were only returned to productive use, along with abandoned arable land, in the extraordinary circumstances of the Atlantic blockade. Some 7 per cent of the great country houses were demolished between the wars. Many more were converted into hotels, hostels, asylums and schools. The reality was far removed from the nostalgic, muzzy haze through which Morton blissfully pootled but the haze was what Whitehall thought worth recording when the nation's future was threatened by Germany.

A few years later another prolific successful literary journalist and writer set out on a tour. John Boynton Priestley was brought up in Bradford, and moved south. A large, intensely patriotic, lugubrious-looking pipe-smoking man, Priestley complained that his bestselling novels made people think of him as 'a bovine, hearty sort of ass' producing 'watery imitations of Dickens'. Sneered at and disregarded by university academics and posher writers, Priestley's book about England had a great influence on how people understood their own country. He was loquaciously political and when he set out on his 'English Journey' in 1933 almost a quarter of the British workforce was unemployed; in some areas, nearly everyone was unemployed. Priestley wanted to rub the nose of southern middle-class Britain in the reality of the other nation. Rattling around in buses and trams, the heart of his journey was in places like Wolverhampton, St Helens, Bolton, Liverpool, Gateshead, Jarrow and Shotton, where he searched out slums and blighted shipyards, grim factories and desperate mining villages. He found wastelands, industrial decline so bad that it made him question whether the whole nineteenth-century industrial revolution had been worth it.

No expert in industry, Priestley had a sharp eye. He describes the Blackburn Technical College, full of 'industrious, smiling young men from the East, most anxious to learn all that Lancashire could tell them about the processes of calico manufacture'. They missed nothing, says Priestley, but smiled at their instructors and then disappeared into the blue. 'A little later – for we live in a wonderfully interdependent world – there also disappeared into the blue a good deal of Lancashire's trade with the East. Most of those students came from Japan.'

In the potteries of Staffordshire's Stoke on Trent, Priestley found craftsmen repeating designs which had been fashionable in Victorian times, and still more astonishingly, working on treadles and lathes introduced by Josiah Wedgwood in 1763. Each town in Britain looked different, smelt different and were full of different words, shapes, noises – because they did different things. Leicester was boots and socks, and typewriters; Nottingham was lace (its female workers were also famous for their lack of sexual puritanism); Bradford was wool, and strongly influenced by German Jews; Coventry was cars; Sheffield, cutlery; Dundee, jute – and so on. In 1933, there was a strong variation, a texture, to the nation that the decline of industry, together with the growth of consumerism and broadcasting, would soon wash away. Priestley understood this. Eventually globalization and capital's search for cheaper labour which Priestley had spotted would wipe out the Britain he knew.

Priestley inspired other writers, notably George Orwell who famously took the road to Wigan Pier (it does not exist) on foot, three years later, as well as photographers and early documentary film-makers who followed him deep into wrecked Britain. The grim condition of old industrial Britain was only tentatively addressed before the war. The coalmining industry, still key to Britain's economy, was a mass of independent, under-invested companies, using technology which was hilariously old-fashioned by American or German standards. Britain's miners worked with picks, wearing only trousers in stifling heat and near darkness, for low wages and without any kind of job security. Back in the thirties, there seemed neither possibility nor prospect of any real change. This was just how things were. Yet evidence of catastrophic decline was piling up. Once, investment and innovation had been at the heart of British heavy industry. No longer. British ships, two-thirds of the vessels afloat before the First World War, were riveted by hand, outdoors, by a hyper-unionized and strike-prone workforce in virtually the same way as they had been put together in Edwardian times to take on the Kaiser. While other countries had changed, Britain had not. Protection and cheap money, then rearmament, helped in the short term. But the industrial problems of seventies Britain from Japanese competition to under investment were primed well before the Germans invaded Poland.

As Priestley saw films, to his despair, replacing music halls, he predicted a country which would seem much the same wherever you are. Once inside a cinema, he pointed out, you could be anywhere from Iowa City to Preston. But it wasn't just the films. Young people were experimenting with cocktails in the new American bars springing up across England. Old English songs were being pushed out by the American blues. 'This is the England of arterial and bypass roads, of filling stations . . . of giant cinemas and dance-halls and cafes, bunga-lows with tiny garages, cocktail bars, Woolworths, motor coaches, wireless . . .' It is comparatively classless, with its cheap and uniform chain stores and its new industries – the electronics, synthetic fibres, light engineering and aircraft factories spreading around London and through the Midlands. Slough, a byword for the new, suburban, light-industrial and rather monotonous country taking shape, provoked one of Betjeman's angriest poems. 'Come, friendly bombs, and fall on Slough / It isn't fit for humans now.' What had he against it? 'Those air-conditioned, bright canteens / Tinned fruit, tinned meat, tinned milk, tinned beans / Tinned minds, tinned breath . . .' Betjeman was a great snob and nostalgist but even J. B. Priestley, the self-described democrat and socialist, found something a bit too cheap about the new Britain: 'Too much of it is simply a trumpery imitation . . . There is about it a rather depressing monotony. Too much of this life is being stamped on from outside . . . this new England is lacking in character, in zest, gusto, flavour, bite, drive, originality.' Priestley calls it a third England and this global-culture England is far nearer the country that survives today.

Many of the same trends were obvious in Wales, Northern Ireland and Scotland – but less so, since these did not have the fast-growing new industries of southern England and were even more buried in the dirt and stagnation of Victorian industrialism. South Wales with her archaic coalfields and steel industry was as badly hurt by the mid-war slump as anywhere in the United Kingdom, and considerably more militant than most of England. Scotland's decline was equally obvious, from the shipyards of the Clyde to the sudden silence in Dundee's mills. The Scottish poet Edwin Muir bitterly describes the small industrial town of Cathcart, now effectively part of Glasgow, in his *Scottish Journey*. He found 'a debased landscape in which every growing thing seemed to be poisoned and stunted, a landscape which involuntarily roused evil thoughts and seemed to be made to be the scene of murders and rapes'. He comes across abandoned coal pits where along black slag paths 'one would see stunted naked boys bathing in the filthy pools, from which rose a smell of various acids and urine'. In common with Priestley and Orwell, for Muir the answer was socialism and, like Priestley, he notes the Americanizing influence of film and radio on the people of better-off cities, such as Edinburgh. It is a commercial 'bus-driven, cinema-educated' age making the immediate environment – this town, that industry – matter less to how people behave. 'The inhabitants of all our towns, great and small, Scottish and English, are being subjected more and more exclusively to action from a distance,' he argues. It is a brilliant insight which well describes what will happen to Britain after the war was over.

So, as the travellers of the thirties demonstrate, Britain was changing fast before the war. While the look of fifties Britain, with long 'ribbons' of semi-detached houses spreading out from the old cities, had been set in the age of Stanley Baldwin, American music and films were here long before the GIs arrived. There was a lightness and a brightness about thirties architecture and design that would be picked up, rediscovered and taken forward after the war into the fifties. Teenagers may not have existed as a named group in Britain, though the term was already being used in pre-war America, but people in their teens with money to spend on records and clothes and increasing independence from their parents were already a phenomenon in British cities. Chain stores were selling brighter clothes. Television sets were on sale, and starting to spread among the London middle classes. The texture of the country was changing. Britain was already becoming a slightly flimsier, less varied nation, a little more American and a little less British. This will be a major part of the story to come.

Britain in her imperial heyday was a country which believed in small government, at least at home. Planning was the kind of thing sinister Germans and funny Italians got up to. Despite the pleas from writers the thirties were not a time when the majority really thought government could make things better. It is easy to feel appalled and bemused by the enthusiasm of so many reasonably intelligent British people for Mussolini and Hitler but there was more to it than cowardice and racism. There was an impatient yearning for government that actually worked – that ended unemployment, built big new roads, developed modern industries and, yes, made the trains run on time. Politicians as far apart as the socialist John Strachey, the Tory Churchill, the fascist Oswald Mosley and the old Liberal Lloyd George, all at one time or another found the dictatorial style something to be at least half-admired. The war made such errors so embarrassing they were quickly forgotten. The most fundamental thing the war changed was the political climate: it made democracy fashionable.

But it did more. It convinced the British that their government could reshape the nation too. Like most victorious wars it raised the reputation of the state. If the government could throw an army into Europe and defeat the most well-organized and frightening-looking military machine of modern times, then what else could it do? Was all the waste and lack of planning and general amateurism really the best the British could achieve? In the first of a series of famous BBC radio broadcasts during the war, given on 5 June 1940 after the chaotic near-disaster and last-minute escape of Dunkirk, Priestley called for the amateurism to stop: 'Nothing, I feel could be more English . . . both in its beginning and its end, its folly and its grandeur . . . We have gone sadly wrong like this before and here and now we must resolve never, never, to do it again.' It was time to 'think differently'. That resolution, to do things differently in future, was the biggest domestic change brought by Britain's victory. As we shall see, it was implemented in the worst possible conditions and had most unexpected effects.

It didn't, however, mean that we stopped fighting. The world after the war was still a world of war. From Greece and Cyprus to Korea and Malaya; from Kenya to the Falklands, Ireland to Iraq, Britain would always be fighting somewhere. The most serious enemy became world communism but shooting wars very rarely involved communist armies directly because of the risk of nuclear conflagration. They were more directed at rival forms of nationalism, liberation armies led by African, Asian or Arab leaders who would be idolized until they turned with depressing regularity into dictators themselves. Many of the colonial wars have almost slipped out of British public memory, though they were bloody enough.

Today the country likes to see itself as a peacekeeper, an armed ambulance service, social workers with machine guns, rather than a natural belligerent in the old way. Yet the fighting has gone on even as the armed forces have shrivelled in size. Some of the 'post-war' wars caused huge political interest and argument, out of all proportion to their size, both making and destroying reputations. Suez, in which British casualties were just twenty-one, is rightly seen as a post-war turning point, proving how dependent and weak Britain had become. Without the reconquest of the Falkland Islands the Thatcher era might have lasted just a few years. The second Iraq war split Britain and ravened Tony Blair's reputation. But Britain's modern military history has been paradoxical. We cut back because the age of warfare is always about to end, yet in practice we keep fighting. We withdraw to barracks, mothball warships, announce a peace dividend; and then jump back out again. In spite of this, and in spite of the abandonment of National Service conscription in 1963, Britain has spent disproportionately more on defence than other countries of a similar size and economic strength. Only France has rivalled us. Money which could have gone on education, industrial support or more modern infrastructure has gone on aircraft carriers, nuclear submarines and tank regiments in Germany. This has been done to keep Britain as a world player, which she still just is, though in almost every war actually fought, and certainly throughout the Cold War, she fought in the larger shadow of the United States.

Throughout the post-war age Britain maintained an inner 'security state' hidden from public view, a living, unseen structure behind bland brick and stone buildings with a vast electronic ear to the ground at Cheltenham GCHQ. The work of MI5 and MI6 has been of unhealthy fascination to novelists, film-makers and conspiracy theorists, a continuing metaphor for Britain itself. In the late fifties and early sixties it was the uncomplicated pride of the 007 confections, followed by the seedy, betrayal-strewn wilderness of John le Carré's novels and more recently the politically-correct, scrubbed young television drama *Spooks*. Behind the fiction, the secret state kept her counsel through the Cold War and has only recently let the mask slip a little. MPs, BBC employees, civil servants, judges and political activists were monitored, many having filed reports kept about them. The prime ministers, with the monarchical authority inherited from the seventeenth century, kept decisions and information away from cabinets and Parliament. These included the original decision to develop atomic weapons, and the incredibly complex and detailed network of bunkers and tunnels prepared for in case of nuclear attack. Inevitably, from the first atom spies and the first Aldermaston marches to the second Iraq war and the role of intelligence in the 'dodgy dossier', the security state has injected mistrust and worry into public life.

Less often discussed is that the post-war wars also maintained a level of patriotism and an interest in things military among many British people – the 'silent majority', far from the media world. There has been a larger proportion of people connected to the armed forces than would otherwise have happened. National Service involved nearly two million men. The Territorial Army along with the various cadet corps in schools spread military influence far beyond barracks or dockyards. Something of the atmosphere of the Second World War lasted through decades of blanco'd belts, .303 rifles, air displays and the roar of V-bombers and English Electric Lightning fighters in the skies above us. The tone, the fabric, of life in post-war Britain has been more affected by war than perhaps we like to admit.

History is either a moral argument with lessons for the here-and-now or it is merely an accumulation of pointless facts. The story of the British in the immediate aftermath of the Second World War is a morally attractive one with much to learn from – a time of optimism and energy, despite apparently crippling difficulties. Politicians on both sides of the political divide believe that Britain will be important in the new world to be built and a great force for good. Returning soldiers and millions of civilians are determined to make up for lost time, to live happier lives. Patriotism is not narrow, there is such a thing as society, and the common good is not laughed at. Labour is promising a New Jerusalem and though no one is entirely sure of what that magical city might feel like to live in, it clearly involves a new deal in health, schooling and housing. In British film there is great energy and ambition. Designers and architects have brought over here plans originally drawn in Europe between the wars to create a brighter, airier and more colourful country. In science and technology Britain seems to have achieved great things which augur well for peacetime.

There is a general and justified pride in victory, not yet much tainted by fear of nuclear confrontation to come. If people are still hungry and ill housed, they are safe again. If they are grieving, they also have much to look forward to, for the baby boom is at full pitch. There is much in the Britain of the later forties that would surprise or even disgust people now. It was not just the shattered cities or the tight rations that would arch modern eyebrows, but the snobbery and casual racism – even, despite the freshly shocking evidence of the concentration camps, widespread anti-Semitism. Yet overall, this was a country brimming with hope. In history, no quality rubs up as brightly.

The great debate about the meaning of our post-war history has been, roughly, an argument between left and right. There are historians of the centre left such as Peter Hennessy who are generally impressed by the country's leaders and get under their skin as they wrestled with dilemmas. Then there are those led by Corelli Barnett who emphasize failure and missed opportunities, at least until Margaret Thatcher arrives to save the situation in 1979. Everyone else struggles between these force-fields. And so what is my view? That we grumpy people, perpetually outraged by the stupidity and deceit of our rotten rulers, have (whisper it gently) had rather a good sixty years. Britain suffered a crisis in the seventies, a national nervous breakdown, and has recovered since. Britain in the forties and fifties was a damaged and inefficient country which would be overtaken by formerly defeated nations such as France, Germany and Japan. But the longer story, the bigger picture, is that Britain successfully shifted from being one kind of country, an inefficient imperialist manufacturer struggling to maintain her power, to become a wealthier social democracy, and did this without revolution.

And shift she did, in the greatest scuttle in the world. British governments, Labour and Tory, duly got rid of the Empire. This meant the deaths of untold numbers in other continents – Muslims and Hindus caught up in ethnic cleansing, the African victims of massacre and dictatorship, civil war and famine for the Arabs, Cypriots and many nationalities of the Far East. Britain, meanwhile, refocused on her new role as a junior partner in the Cold War, close to Europe but never quite European, speaking the same language as Americans, but never meaning exactly the same.

Always, we have been a country on the edge. We moved from being on the edge of defeat, to the edge of bankruptcy, to the edge of nuclear annihilation and the edge of the American empire, and came out on the other side to find ourselves on the cutting edge of the modern condition, a post-industrial and multi-ethnic island, crowded, inventive and rich. The years before Thatcher were not a steady slide into disaster. Nobody has put this relative British success better than an American historian George Bernstein, who called his account of post-1945 Britain *The Myth of Decline* and who said of the years before the crisis of the seventies that 'Britain's performance in providing for the well-being of its people – as measured by employment, a safety net that kept them out of poverty, and improved standards of living – was outstanding.'[2] And this despite ferocious economic conditions.

There is a danger of distorting real history with false endings. If one decides that the breakdown of the seventies was the single most important thing to have happened to post-war Britain, which shadows everything before and since, then inevitably the story of the forties, fifties and sixties becomes darker. Humdrum events dutifully rearrange themselves as ominous warnings. All the things that went right, all the successful lives that were lived during thirty crowded years, the triumphs of style and technology, the better health, the time of low inflation, the money in pockets, the holidays and the businesses that grew and thrived, are subtly surrounded with 'yes, but' brackets . . . guess what's coming next. But this is a strange way of thinking. In personal terms it would be like defining the meaning of a life, with all its ups and downs, entirely by reference to a single bout of serious illness or marital breakup in middle age.

Does this mean we should cheer our leaders? Certainly not. For most of the modern period politics has served Britain less well than our self-congratulation about parliamentary democracy might suggest. Good people, acting honourably, failed to lead well. We have been run by cliques of right and left who did not understand the direction the country was taking. Hennessy is right: the political class was intelligent and faced terrible choices which are easy to brush aside afterwards when the dangers have passed. But Barnett is also right: we could have had a better country, had we had clearer-minded leaders who did not shrink from telling hard truths, or from treating the voters like adults. So, Labour did not build a New Jerusalem. So, the Tory cabinets of the fifties and early sixties failed to create the restored great power, the New Elizabethan Age they dreamed of. The Wilson and Heath years were supposed to be a time of modernization, a refitted, retooled Britain. They ended with trade unions rampant and the lights flickering out. John Major set out promising to create a country at ease with itself and ended up with a country ill at ease, above all with John Major. Tony Blair's New Labour Britain was never as cool or efficient as he told us it would be, even before the Iraq war. Nor was it whiter than white. Each failure occurred on its own terms.

The exceptions were the Labour government of 1945, which developed a Welfare State even if it did not achieve the social transformation it wanted, and Margaret Thatcher's first two administrations, which addressed the British crisis head-on. Both set templates for what followed. But even these two counter-examples are not completely clear. Post-war Labour ran out of popularity and momentum within a couple of years, while Mrs Thatcher's vision of a remoralized, hard-working nation of savers and strong families was hardly what the partying, divided, 'loadsamoney', easy credit, big-hair eighties delivered. What follows is a story of the failure of political elites. Often the famous political names, those faces familiar from a thousand cartoons and newsreels, seem to me like buzzing flywheels with broken teeth, failing to move the huge and complex structures of daily life.

If that was all, it would be a depressing tale. But it is not. Opening markets, well-educated and busy people, a relatively uncorrupt and law-abiding national tradition, and an optimistic relish for the new technologies and experiences offered by twentieth-century life all make the British experience generally better than political history alone would suggest. In the more recent decades the retreat of faith and ideology, and their replacement by consumerism and celebrity may have made us a less dignified lot. Yet modern Britain has made great advances in science, culture and finance which have benefited, and will benefit, the world. Among the puzzles facing humanity at the beginning of the twenty-first century are global warming; the mystery of consciousness; and how ageing Western societies adapt to the new migrant cultures they require to keep them functioning. British people have been important in bringing answers, just as they were seminal in the development of the Web, and in creating modern music and television. We have become a world island in a new way. In the period covered by this book, the dominant experience has been acceleration. We have lived faster. We have seen, heard, communicated, changed and travelled more. We have experienced a material profusion and perhaps a philosophical or religious emptiness that marks us off from earlier times.

If, by an act of science or magic, a small platoon of British people from 1945 could be time-travelled sixty or so years into the future, what would they make of us? They would be nudging one another and trying not to laugh. They would be shocked by the different colours of skin. They would be surprised by the crammed and busy roads, the garish shops, the lack of smoke in the air. They would be amazed at how big so many of us are – not just tall but shamefully fat. They would be impressed by the clean hair, the new-looking clothes and the youthful faces of the new British. But they would feel shock and revulsion at the gross wastefulness, the food flown here from Zambia or Peru then promptly thrown out of houses and supermarkets uneaten, the mountains of intricately designed and hurriedly discarded music players, television sets and fridges, clothes and furniture; the ugly marks of painted, distorted words on walls and the litter everywhere of plastic and coloured paper. They would wonder at our lack of church-going, our flagrant openness about sex, our divorce habit, alongside our amazingly warm and comfortable houses. They would then discuss it all in voices that might make us in turn laugh at them – insufferably posh or quaintly regional. Yet these alien people were us. They are us. The cropped-haired urchins of the forties are our pensioners now. The impatient lean young adults of 1947 with their imperial convictions or socialist beliefs are around us still in wheelchairs or hidden in care homes. It was their lives and the choices they made which led to here and now. So although they might stare at us and ask, 'Who are these alien people?' we could reply, 'We are you, what you chose to become.'

Part One

HUNGER AND PRIDE:
BRITAIN AFTER THE WAR

The Democratic Bombshell

Many of us find our innermost fears or hopes take arms while we sleep, ready to strike at the moment of wakening. Churchill recorded that, on the morning of 26 July 1945, he woke up with 'a sharp stab of almost physical pain' to find himself sure that he and the Conservatives had just lost the general election. There was a long delay for the votes to be brought back from battlefields around the world. Few people thought the war leader could lose power. Most Labour leaders assumed he would be returned. So did the apparently well-informed City experts, the in touch trade union bosses, the self-certain press, the diplomatic observers passing back the latest intelligence to Washington and Moscow. Churchill was at the very peak of his personal triumph, outshining the King and Royal Family when he appeared on the famous balcony to wave. Never in British history has military success been so personally associated with a civilian leader – not the two great Pitts, not Disraeli at his peak, not David Lloyd George, could rival Churchill's radio age charisma. True, 1945 had been a most unusual election. The Parliament it ended had begun in the middle of the thirties – nine years, six months and twenty days earlier, making it the longest UK Parliament ever, a Parliament of old men unused to raw party conflict. Churchill would have liked it to go on longer, at least until Japan was defeated. Never quite a party man, he had a coalition cast of mind. It had been Labour which insisted on the election. Now, no one knew what was coming: the scattered and disrupted nature of the electorate meant accurate polling was impossible. The new electoral roll was inaccurate, too, having been based on ration book records. Among those who found they had no vote because of clerical errors was the Prime Minister himself.

For those with ears to hear, there were intimations of what was about to happen. During the war a high-minded religious socialism had become fashionable at home. As the carnage ground on overseas, an almost Utopian determination to build a more Christian country took root. As early as 1940 the great wartime Archbishop of Canterbury, William Temple, had called for 'extreme inequalities of wealth to be abolished'. Going rather further, his Council of Clergy and Ministers for Common Ownership declared private ownership of industry 'contrary to Divine Justice'. In the forces compulsory discussions about Britain after the war had been led by the Army Bureau of Current Affairs, ABCA, organized by a left-leaning educationalist called W. E. Williams. Conservative-minded officers complained about the tone of the pamphlets sent round the army and that Williams had 'smothered the troops in seditious literature'. One general burned 10,000 of the 'wretched pamphlets' in front of his men and warned that they were 'rank treason'.[1] To this day many Conservatives believe that socialist propaganda foisted on the troops was to blame for their defeat in 1945. In fact, the numbers do not add up; the minimum voting age was 21, which cut out many of the more malleable troops and in any case, there were fewer than two million service votes cast in a total electorate of 33 million.

The change was happening among civilians. A strong sense that it was time for a fresh beginning had been reflected in a series of by-election defeats of Tory candidates when vacancies were caused in the Commons by the deaths of sitting members. (Twenty-two MPs were killed fighting, all but one of them Conservatives.) At Maldon in Essex, the left-wing journalist Tom Driberg had won, standing as an independent. By 1943 candidates for the piously socialist Common Wealth movement, founded by our English traveller J. B. Priestley and by Sir Richard Acland, were winning upset victories up and down England. In April of that year the Battle of Britain pilot John Loveseed won a Cheshire seat; Lt Hugh Lawson won Skipton in the Yorkshire Dales. Most sensationally of all, in April 1945 in Tory Chelmsford, Wing Commander Ernest Millington, a pre-war pacifist and socialist who had then joined the RAF and turned his attention to bombing Germany, defeated the Conservative candidate. Millington, standing for Common Wealth and supported by local vicars, had fought a remarkably aggressive campaign whose tone can be summarized by a banner he put up in the middle of the market town which read, 'This is a Fight between Christ and Churchill.' By 1945, there was a whiff of Oliver Cromwell in the air.

The Labour conference which kick-started the election campaign one hot afternoon in Blackpool is still remembered for the youth of the delegates. Denis Healey was there, in battledress and beret, fresh from the battlefront in Italy, preaching red-hot socialist revolution. Across Europe the upper classes were 'selfish, depraved, dissolute and decadent' he told the cheering hall. Roy Jenkins, who had helped crack the German codes at Bletchley Park, was there too, a slim and dapper soldier. There was even a socialist Rear Admiral. Labour's manifesto, well written and snappily designed, would be distributed to nearly two million people, backed by powerful posters, 12 million leaflets and huge numbers of party volunteers. Its most popular passages could hardly have come as a shock. They relied on the blueprint for a fairer, more planned country which had been worked out by the coalition government before the war ended. Labour had the support of only a minority of the national press. Apart from the *Daily Mirror* and its in-house *Daily Herald*, the big-circulation papers were all pro-Tory and the two upmarket leftish newspapers, the *Manchester Guardian* and the *News Chronicle*, both backed the lost-cause Liberals. Different parts of the country found very different audiences for Labour's meetings. Attlee was rushing about in his little Standard car, rapping out around eight speeches of a terse twenty minutes apiece every day. He thought his reception was excellent. In some towns the election seemed quiet. In others, huge and attentive crowds turned up to listen and argue back. In Birmingham Roy Jenkins recalled 'seas of faces looking up in the twilight, a mixture of exhaustion, hope, some kind of doubt. A sea of tired faces looking up in hope, that's the best phrase I can make of it.'[2]

Churchill meanwhile was fighting one of the bad campaigns of his life. His theme was that Labour was a sinister socialist conspiracy. In a badly misjudged radio broadcast kicking off his campaign, he let his florid wartime language loose and struck entirely the wrong note. No socialist system, he said, could be established without some form of political police, a British Gestapo. Instead he offered a vision of bucolic good cheer which would have seemed dated in the aftermath of the Boer War: 'Let us make sure that the cottage home to which the warrior will return is blessed with modest but solid prosperity, well-

fenced and guarded against misfortune . . .' Attlee answered him with
gentle irony. The Gestapo suggestion was grossly offensive but the
Labour leader disarmingly replied that it was no doubt Churchill's way
of demonstrating the gulf between his qualities as a great war leader
and those of a mere party leader, and that the attack had probably
been devised by the press baron Lord Beaverbrook. It was in fact all
Churchill's own work. His wife Clemmie had strongly warned him
against it and his party's chief whip had commented that 'it is not my
idea of how to win an election'. A second line of Tory attack was that
Attlee was the mere frontman for extremists. The Labour chairman
Harold Laski was portrayed by Conservative candidates as hell-bent on
revolution. Laski did use wild language and was on the left of the
party, though his father campaigned for Churchill and had recently
suggested that a public fund be raised to show Churchill the nation's
gratitude. (The Prime Minister said a better monument for him would
be a public park for the children of London on the south bank of the
Thames 'where they suffered so grimly from the Hun'.[3] This was
never followed up.)

Churchill had based himself in Claridge's Hotel in London and
used a private train and a cavalcade of cars to make his speeches
around the country. Mostly he won an enthusiastic enough reception,
though he was dumbfounded to find himself booed by a large section
of the crowd in his final rally at Walthamstow. This was not quite
the respectful British nation of myth. Despite these warning signs, the
brutal rejection of Churchill for Attlee caused amazement around the
world. Before the election result was declared the two men had been
together at Potsdam in Germany negotiating the future of post-war
Europe with Joseph Stalin and President Harry Truman. Where would
Poland's borders be? How hard should defeated Germany be squeezed?
Whose was Greece? Returning to London for the results, Churchill
had not even bothered to say goodbye to the Soviet dictator or
Washington's new man. He did not properly pack. He would be back.

Attlee was by then somewhat more optimistic. He thought it
would be close. About that, at least, he was wrong. In 1935 the
Conservatives had won 585 seats. In 1945 they won just 213. Labour
won more votes that the Tories for the first time ever, giving
them 393 seats and a majority of 146. When Attlee returned to
Potsdam alone without Churchill, Stalin's right-hand man, Molotov,

was incredulous. He suspiciously cross-questioned the Labour leader about why he had not known the result in advance. Such democratic sloppiness would not have been tolerated further east. Churchill, brooding at home, found it a terrible personal shock. When Clemmie tried to cheer him up with the thought that it might be a blessing in disguise he grunted that, just at the moment, it seemed quite effectively disguised. Yet he quickly spirited a silver lining out from the cloud. The years ahead would be a terrible trial to the British people, Churchill believed. Might not Labour be better left to cope with the disappointments to come? At last, discovering the generosity of spirit that had gone absent without leave during his election campaigning, the old man rebuked one of his aides: 'This is democracy. This is what we have been fighting for.'

What had Labour been fighting for? The party's new MPs arriving in London by train, car and bus were a mixed bunch. Most were inexperienced in the ways of Parliament, as they would soon show by giving a raucous rendition of the Red Flag in the temporary chamber – the historic one having been demolished by the Luftwaffe. There were Fabian intellectuals, wartime rebels, trade unionists and civil servants such as the podgy, moustachioed Harold Wilson, soldiers and teachers, cautious moderates and – so the Communist Party believed – at least nine secret communist plants. All of them had stood on a manifesto written by Herbert Morrison and a young idealist called Michael Young who would go on to found the Consumers' Association. It called for the establishment of 'the Socialist Commonwealth of Great Britain – free, democratic, efficient, progressive, public-spirited'. It contained a long list of ideas but it was as realistic as (in private) Churchill had been about the difficulties ahead: 'The problems and pressures of the post-war world threaten our security and progress as surely as – though less dramatically than – the Germans threatened them in 1940. We need the spirit of Dunkirk and of the Blitz sustained over a period of years.' In the years ahead this fighting bulldog tone would quickly grate.

Some of the new Labour MPs felt they had been elected to overturn the class basis of the country, others that they simply had a difficult list of domestic reforms to get through. As they introduced themselves to one another for the first time, gossiping and exchanging campaign stories, a sizeable minority also believed they had better get rid of the conventional-sounding Attlee and elect a proper leader while there was time. Herbert Morrison, a popular minister who had organized London's defence against the Blitz, had warned Attlee that he would stand against him in a party contest. The plot gathered force in the corridors and urinals of Westminster Central Hall. At the same time, Attlee, Morrison, the burly ex-trade union leader Ernie Bevin and the party secretary met at Transport House, the party headquarters a few hundred yards away. As Morrison nipped out to make a call to another supporter, Bevin leaned across to Attlee and growlingly gave him the best advice of his life: 'Clem, you go to the Palace straight away.' Clem did. He took tea with his wife Vi and family at Paddington, hopped into their little car and was driven to Buckingham Palace where the King, a staunch conservative taken aback by the turn of events, duly handed him control of the British Empire. Morrison and the other Labour plotters left half a mile to the east had underestimated Attlee. Many people had. He would go on to become one of the two genuinely nation-changing prime ministers of modern British history.

Hiroshima and Keynes: the Limits of Wit

The Labour government of 1945–50 is remembered today as among the greatest British administrations ever. Some of the glory is justified. As we will see, it changed the health and welfare structure of the country, nationalized sections of the economy and managed to survive a series of terrible external shocks. But if its aim was to create a British socialist commonwealth with different values and different people in charge – to make a social revolution – then Labour failed. No significant changes to the British class system came about as a result of the work of the Attlee government. Nor was there any loosening of the ties to Washington, ardently desired by many on the left who thought Labour could deal better with Moscow on the dubious principle that 'left can speak to left'. Labour hoped to keep Britain free and independent, going her own way between the Great Capitalism on the other side of the Atlantic and the Great Communism now in possession of half Europe. Yet under Attlee Britain became dependent on the United States. She could not match America's overwhelming military power around the world, symbolized by an atomic bomb that Britain had helped create but was not allowed to share. The weakness of Britain's dying imperium meant her world role would have to shrink dramatically. Attlee understood this much faster than most of his colleagues.

Britain had arrived blinking into a new world still cloaked in the archaic nineteenth-century grandeur of imperialism. The Americans were busy creating their own commercial empire, moving into markets vacated by defeated or exhausted rivals. The Soviet Union was equally busy extending its political empire, funding local dictators and occasionally lurching towards more dramatic confrontation. These two new empires were very different. America's empire came informally dressed talking about freedom and equality. Outside its Asian wars and its support for vicious South American regimes these words did not ring hollow – but those are large geographical exceptions. Moscow, meanwhile, was busy repressing and imprisoning in the name of History and the working class, one eye always on the even more bloodthirsty tyranny of Mao's China challenging it for Third World leadership. Against these new empires, the moth-eaten pretensions of a mild-mannered king-emperor, a few battleships and a modest number of colonial governors in baggy shorts barely seemed relevant.

Britain's dilemma from 1945 until today has been easy to state, impossible to resolve. How do you maintain independence and dignity when you are a junior partner, locked into defence systems, intelligence gathering and treaties with the world's great military giant? At times Britain has had real influence in Washington, above all in the talks with the Labour government which produced the North Atlantic Treaty Organization, NATO, and in the first Gulf war when Margaret Thatcher urged George Bush senior not to wobble. At other times her dependence has been embarrassing, in big ways such as the Suez fiasco; and small ways, such as the American refusal to share intelligence assessments in Iraq, even when the raw intelligence was gathered originally by British agents and passed on. Yet when one country, the United States, is both leader of a large alliance of other countries, and has strong national interests which may conflict with those of her allies, there is bound to be friction. Periodic bouts of anti-Americanism inside the Foreign Office and in Whitehall generally have been the result. Anti-American feeling has been the Establishment's secret vice.

In public, successive foreign secretaries and mandarins spoke reassuringly of the British 'punching above our weight' and the vital importance of the Churchill-hallowed 'special relationship'. In practice this meant sharing intelligence with the Pentagon and CIA, the intertwining of nuclear strategy, large US bases on British soil, the leasing of British bases to America, and a posture towards American presidents that is nearer that of salaried adviser than independent ally.

For there was another reason for Britain's new dependency politics. The country was broke. Attlee's government had little time to contemplate all this. The military and economic weaknesses of the country were tested with devilish symmetry just a fortnight after the new government was formed. On 14 August 1945, eight days after the atomic bombing of Hiroshima and five after the attack on Nagasaki, Japan surrendered. A week after that President Truman reached across and briskly placed his signature on a paper ending the wartime Lend-Lease agreement with Britain and other countries. Lend-Lease, which dated from 1941, had allowed the US government to lend, sell, lease and give countries fighting Germany and Japan whatever they thought was needed. Britain was by far the largest recipient, getting more than $30 bn of the $50 bn spent. She had become dependent on the huge pipeline of aid, and not only for fighting. About a fifth of people's food needs came from America. When the pipeline was suddenly cut off, and a bill presented for whatever was still being used, it was brutal cold turkey indeed. Truman, acting in strict accordance with American law, stopped Lend-Lease without warning his allies and without, it seems, realizing the implications of what he was doing.

The effect on Attlee's new government was instant. Britain did not have enough dollars left to feed the country. Nor was there any way to earn the money quickly. The shattered economy was exporting only around a fifth of what it had before the war, yet non-military imports were five times higher than in 1938. In the words of one historian Britain had by now declined into 'a warrior satellite of the United States, dependent for life on American subsidies' and had, by waging total war, destroyed the basis of her economy on which she had flourished for the previous hundred years. Through the war years America had been open-handed but Britain, fighting also to prevent a German victory which would have threatened the global influence of the United States, spent proportionately far more of her energy on the common struggle. The official historians of the wartime economy, writing in the dark post-war years, allowed their feelings to show: 'In a war allegedly governed by the concept of the pooling of resources among Allies, the British had taken upon themselves a sacrifice so disproportionate as to jeopardise their economic survival as a nation.'[4]

In his memoirs Truman said he had learned the lesson from his signature of the ending of Lend-Lease 'that I must always know what is in the documents I sign'. But the economic crisis which the action caused in Britain in many ways served American interests. At the time, with the victory celebrations a recent memory and patriotic films pouring from the British cinema industry, pessimism about the future would have seemed outlandish to most people, a kind of moral treason. This after all was the Britain of – to quote Labour's 1945 election manifesto – 'scientists and technicians who have produced radio-location [radar], jet propulsion, penicillin and the Mulberry Harbours', the Britain whose Empire had mostly survived, the Britain occupying swathes of Germany and Italy, the Britain whose leaders sat with those of the new superpowers, apparently shaping the world.

The historian Correlli Barnett summarized the situation with brutal clarity: the post-war British people had 'the psychology of the victor although their material circumstances approximated more to those of a loser'.[5] That was a perception gaining ground in Whitehall at the time, where they had the figures. In August 1945, the economist John Maynard Keynes told Attlee that the country 'is virtually bankrupt and the economic basis for the hopes of the people non-existent'.

Attlee's cabinet duly sent Keynes, the world's most famous economist, to Washington to get help. What followed was as important in the history of modern Britain as any minor war to be fought in the decades to come. As beggar, Keynes may not have been a good choice. He was over-optimistic about his powers of persuasion, indeed startlingly arrogant, a trait not unknown among Bloomsbury intellectuals. He sailed off assuring Attlee that he believed he could get a free gift of some $6 bn from the Americans, a large proportion of what was left in the Federal Reserve. Once in Washington, he ran into a stodgy defensive line of conservative bankers, bolstered by public opinion which was 60 per cent against giving the British a loan, never mind a gift. Keynes responded by dazzling but also irritating the American negotiators with wit, high-minded arguments and occasional mockery.

One US banker retorted, 'He is too brilliant to be persuasive with us Americans . . . how many trust him? How many will accept his sales talk? No one.' Up against Keynes, who arrived ill via a troopship to Canada, was William Clayton, a gangling cotton manufacturer from Texas, and Fred Vinson, a former professional basketball player and lawyer. For four solid months, based in his Washington hotel and supported by the British ambassador Lord Halifax, Keynes haggled and chiselled. Keynes's biographer said this of their marathon argument: 'The Kentucky lawyer and the Bloomsbury intellectual were like chalk and cheese . . . Vinson and Clayton were no match for Keynes in argument. But they always held the whip-hand. It was a case of brains pitted against power.'[6]

London had a completely unrealistic notion of what might be won. Attlee's cabinet refused the early US offers and held out, vainly, for better ones. Keynes, ill with a heart complaint and surviving on ice-packs and sodium amytal capsules through a sweltering autumn, was trapped by the exuberance of his earlier self-confidence. He described the mood as 'absolute hell'. The core of the trouble was that the Americans did not quite believe how broke the British Empire really was. Nor did they much care. Powerful players in Washington may have been sentimental about the common struggle that had just ended but were unsentimental about empires and the new world that must now be built. This was not a game of equal players. Every time the British turned down an American offer, the next offer was worse. An angry Keynes wrote back to his mother: 'They mean us no harm but their minds are so small, their prospects so restricted, their knowledge so inadequate, their obstinacy so boundless and their legal pedantries so infuriating. May it never fall to me to *persuade* anyone to do what I want, with so few cards in my hand . . . I am beginning to use up my physical reserves.'[7]

Eventually, though the effort would contribute to his death early the following year, Keynes's hoped-for gift or interest-free loan of around $6bn had shrunk to a 50-year loan of $3.75bn, at 2 per cent interest. In addition, the Americans required that within a year of the loan starting, pounds should be freely exchangeable for dollars, so removing a traditional protective wall from London. Alongside British agreement for the new Washington-dominated international financial system, this placed the country firmly under the economic control of the United States, which through the later forties and early fifties would also be steadily advancing into former British markets round the world. It was a moment of truth for the country as stark as the fall of Singapore, or Dunkirk. The loan was not finally paid off until 2006, well into Tony Blair's time at Number Ten. So part of the story of post-war Britain was set. The new financial system made future financial crises inevitable and they duly followed under Attlee, Eden, Macmillan, Wilson and Callaghan. Each time, Britain's weak economy meant another 'run on the pound' as the world, and particularly the United States, sold Sterling, causing inflation and a slump in investment. Neither the starkness of the crisis nor the inevitable long-term repercussions were ever fully grasped by the country. This was the moment when the British government could have honestly explained to the people how grave the country's situation really was.

Instead, Attlee and his ministers hid their dismay about the underlying weakness of Britain's hand – the brutal treatment of Lord Keynes in Washington and, later, the equally brutal repudiation of Britain's claim to nuclear cooperation. War-trained, and proud, they put on a good face. The new Chancellor, Hugh Dalton, claimed that he valued the settlement 'very highly' and instructed MPs to 'welcome' it. *The Economist*, generally the most pro-American British publication, retorted: 'We are not compelled to say we like it. Our present needs are the direct consequence of the fact that we fought earlier, that we fought longest, and that we fought hardest.' But in Parliament, after the devastating events of the past few years, it seemed there was little energy left for outrage or debate.

One action was taken immediately. Within months of the end of the war the characteristic sounds of the Royal Navy changed. The thunder of guns and the pounding of turbines gave way to a great clanging, from Portsmouth to the Clyde, a smashing of hammers and hissing of flame, the thud and the sparks of destruction as, one by one, the great ships were destroyed. By 1946, when the Russians were beginning to build an even bigger surface and submarine fleet than they had had during their 'Great Patriotic War', 840 British warships had already been struck off the Navy List, and a further 727 in various stages of construction had been abruptly cancelled.[8] By the time the new Admiral of the Fleet, Lord Fraser, took over in 1948 a total of 10 battleships, 20 cruisers, 37 aircraft carriers, 60 destroyers and 80 corvettes had been sent to the scrapheap. This was an extraordinary rate of destruction. Fraser, who had worked with the US Navy in the Pacific and survived a kamikaze attack and who therefore understood the need for modernization, now had to deal with a demoralized and stunned Royal Navy. Battleships whose names read like a history lesson – *Nelson, Rodney, Valiant* – were broken up. New battleships and aircraft carriers whose names read like an optimistic prospectus for a revived empire, which had been ordered to project British power around the world into the sixties, ships such as *Lion, Malta, New Zealand, Eagle, Gibraltar* and *Africa*, were abruptly cancelled. Britain's very last battleship, HMS *Vanguard*, was completed on the Clyde. Too late for the war, she survived to take the King and future Queen Elizabeth to South Africa for an unsuccessful Commonwealth-boosting trip, and then functioned as a training ship before she too was towed away and broken up.[9] Ninety British warships were towed out to sea and used for target practice until they broke up and sank. Hundreds more were taken to the breakers' yards and painstakingly disassembled back into piles of torn, rust-softened steel.

Some were sold to small countries which had hardly had navies before. The US Navy had proved that aircraft carriers were an indispensable part of modern global war, but Britain could afford only a few, relatively small ones. So one British carrier was given to the French as a free loan until they could pay for her. Another was loaned to the Dutch and two were offloaded at half price to the Australians. The inaptly named *Terrible* ended as an uncompleted hulk sitting in the Gare Loch, near Glasgow. Some smaller ships were 'mothballed' – shrouded with nets, which were then sprayed with plastic and treated with electrolysis to stop their bottoms rotting. Initially, seagulls proved worryingly keen to eat the plastic. Meanwhile, inside their cocoons, the ships' poor-quality wartime steel rotted anyway.[10] Vessels which had protected the convoys which helped keep Stalin's Russia fighting, or shepherded food and fuel convoys across the Atlantic, or had rescued the British army from Dunkirk, or which had been in at the kill in the Pacific, ships whose names went back to Nelson's navy and whose captains came from West Country families which could trace their service just as far – almost all of them went, and very quickly. This is little remembered. It is as if the nation engaged in a giant act of smashing, the quiet murder of its nautical self, out of sight, out of mind. Of the 880,000 men and women serving in the Royal Navy towards the end of the war, nearly 700,000 had left two years later.

The admirals fought back. 'If we are to hold our world position, we must maintain our sea power,' said the Admiralty. Using an argument already hopelessly out of date, the deputy director of naval planning, Captain Godfrey French, protested that a force of two major fleets, with battleships and carriers, was vital to sustain the British Empire's status as 'a first class power'. Battleships, he said, were needed to counter the Soviet fleet and, in the future, rather more bizarrely, the French. The Labour government was not impressed. Attlee argued forcefully that Britain was no longer America's rival on the high seas and could not maintain large fleets. Hugh Dalton, his Chancellor, ordered the dockyards to give up the electricians and woodworkers he needed for the post-war home-building programme. By 1948 the defence statement said that it was necessary for manpower to be brought down as quickly as possible, even though this meant 'a degree of disorganisation and immobility' Naval campaigners in the Commons were horrified to discover that the Home Fleet was down to a single cruiser and a few lesser ships.

Reports came into the Admiralty of 'strangely apathetic crews' and occasions of 'outright disobedience'. In time, of course, the navy readjusted to a far smaller role, particularly once the nuclear deterrent was based in its submarines, not on the RAF's airfields. But finally, the 336-year history of the Admiralty itself ended, when it was swallowed up by the Ministry of Defence. On 31 March 1964 the Queen saved a salary by becoming her own Lord Admiral. The Admiralty's historian expresses institutional hurt as eloquently as it can be told:

> No department of state survived so long, through so many metamorphoses and vicissitudes, as the Admiralty. When most of the great departments of state were born, it was already ancient . . . Monarchs and dynasties, statesmen and ministers, came and went, the tides of war and revolution washed over and around, constantly altering but never submerging the Admiralty, and it survived them all, counter, original, spare and strange to the last.[11]

It was the last act in the ruthless liquidation of the organization that had been central to British identity for as long as Britain had been a single nation.

Falling behind in military technology and without the strength to keep hold of her empire, the Royal Navy's time had gone. What might have happened without the extremity of the financial crisis after the American cancellation of Lend-Lease is unknowable. The government's failure to involve the country in the full grimness of the situation was made more palatable two years later with the generous American Marshall Plan aid, as Washington finally realized how far Soviet Communism might advance over bankrupt and demoralized Western European nations. Britain got the largest share of that, and the immediate crisis eased. The Marshall Plan helped put all Europe back on its feet. It is still remembered as Washington's 'most unsordid act'.

Optimism about the British economy's ability to export its way back to health returned. There was a great national drive for more exports at the expense of consumption at home. The post-war world, in which so many industrial countries had been devastated, was starved of goods, so it was not hard to find export markets, even for outdated British cars and unsuitable British clothing. But the politicians' habit of embarrassed deception about how things really stood would continue. Successive British prime ministers treated the country's weakness as a personal failing which could be hushed up.

A Meeting of Remarkable Men

Keynes's deal bought Labour time. Yet the Attlee government was not well prepared to use it. In London in 1945 there was nobody with experience of how to take over and then organize a peacetime economy. Ministers agreed that central planning was the way to create a more efficient economy but the way British administration was structured made efficiency a distant dream. There was a vast sprawl of overlapping Whitehall committees which meant slow decision-making and fudged choices. By one count the Attlee administration employed just ten fully qualified economists – and this from a government which promised 'rule by experts'. It is often and rightly said that the problems Labour had to grapple with were awesome and so they were – the demolished housing and the archaic economy, the demand for swift Indian independence, the crises in Palestine and Greece, the need to demobilize so many people, the danger of starvation on continental

Europe and the need for some kind of new world order, even as the first intimations of the Cold War began. But the eventual failure of New Jerusalem's architects and orators, remarkable men and women that they were, was also caused by their inability to agree what it was they really wanted to do.

The people who took charge of Britain in 1945 were as mixed a bag as any democratic government has seen. First comes Attlee himself, the model of suburban Pooter, speaking so little and so tersely it drove everyone around him mad. He was the butt of some often retold Churchillian insults: 'an empty taxi drew up at the House of Commons, and Attlee got out' (though Churchill later denied that one) and 'a modest little man with much to be modest about'. Yet if Churchill had been formed by imperial dreams and his grand family history, Attlee was just as determined a product of Edwardian England. He had merely taken a different course, good works and mean streets, not cavalry charges and country houses. His father was a hard-working lawyer of advanced Liberal views. He grew up surrounded by prayers and poetry. After his rough public school, Haileybury near Hertford, he studied law but was diverted by the chance of being asked to help out at the Haileybury boys' club in the sooty, impoverished east London borough of Stepney. He stayed and eventually joined the Independent Labour Party. Never a great speaker he was a dogsbody and organizer, cutting up bread for children, helping suffragettes, distributing leaflets and carrying banners on marches. After brave service in the First World War, he returned as Major Attlee and threw himself into London politics again, becoming Mayor of Stepney and then an MP. He became Labour leader in 1935 almost by accident. There were so few other plausible candidates in the wake of Labour's shattering election defeat of four years earlier, he was almost the last plausible leader left standing – a stopgap.

He would become the most effective stopgap in British political history. No intellectual, he was a man who held things together, the ultimate chairman. He was reassuring, thoroughly English, addicted to the *Times* crossword, cricket and as fond of his old public school as Churchill was of his. Before the war he had steered the Labour Party towards moderation and away from pacifism. During the war he tolerated Churchill's long-winded egotism and quietly directed the civilian ministries. After it he became the watchful ringmaster for elephantine egos roaring and bellowing around him. He was never a charismatic character – one sympathetic historian judges him to have had 'all the presence of a gerbil'[12] – but that was part of his attraction. He defended himself against the charge that he was too moderate, quietly insisting that practical measures to boost employment, share resources fairly and plan the economy were as socialist and radical as any revolutionary could wish. Yet he was weak on economics, and when his cabinet was arguing over deep practical problems, such as the troubled programme for steel nationalization, he had a tendency to pull back and let ministers struggle without his support. He had shafts of clear analytical insight, into Britain's overstretched military commitments, and the importance of house-building. But his analysis of domestic change, above all what nationalization was really meant to achieve, was pretty thin.

He did not offer the cheering-up that ministers sometimes require and his put-downs became legendary. When one hapless minister was summoned to be sacked and asked, appalled, what on earth he had done wrong, Attlee looked up, pulled out his pipe and remarked, 'Not up to the job.' Interviewed at the start of the 1951 election campaign, he told the journalist just that he hoped to win and now was off to a committee meeting. The interview finished thus: 'Interviewer: Is there anything else you'd like to say about the coming election? Attlee: No.'[13] This was an entirely characteristic exchange and there are literally hundreds of similar examples. Yet despite all this, Attlee has gone down as a great man, loved for his limitations, not despite them. He was a staunch believer in the monarchy and if he had misgivings about the class system he rarely voiced them. His political conservatism is well described in a touching limerick he wrote long after losing office. Though he embodied the opposite of spin, sleaze, self-importance or swank, he did allow himself a famous pat on the back:

> Few thought he was even a starter
> There were many who thought themselves smarter
> But he ended PM
> CH and OM
> An earl and a knight of the Garter.

What is touching about this is, of course, that it could equally well have been written by a hostile satirist. Clement Attlee was a strange mix of radical and paternalist; he would have made a good Liberal reformer under Gladstone. Yet half a century on, he was the right man for the time. Wartime magnifies some personalities. Similarly, peace discovers its own people. Attlee was the chairman of the peace party, but what about the rest?

There were the class rebels. Sir Stafford Cripps was an intensely religious vegetarian, brilliant lawyer and sometime Marxist. Obstinate, politically naive and worryingly convinced that he was, at any given time, doing God's work, he was the most controversial upper-class socialist until the heyday of Tony Benn. In the thirties Cripps had fallen under the spell of the charismatic leader of Britain's Communists, Harry Pollitt. A colleague said of him that he started to go wild in 1931. Then stimulated by attacks from the Tory press 'and by eager cheers from our own lunatic fringe, he went wilder and wilder'.[14] He had advocated emergency powers to deal with the coming 'capitalist dictatorship' and zigzagged over whether rearmament would be a betrayal of the workers. In 1939 he was thrown out of the Labour Party for advocating a Popular Front with the Communists. Yet a year later the same Cripps was sent as Churchill's special envoy to the real Communists in Moscow. He was brought into the war cabinet, then put in charge of aircraft production, sent to negotiate the end of British rule in India and by the end of 1947 was Chancellor – a job he performed with great grit, patriotism and determination. It was about as strange a change as any in natural history. Throughout the war, as a former rebel, he was not even in the Labour Party but was already famous for his rimless glasses, regime of cold baths and doctrinaire views. He got the Churchill treatment too, famously in the cutting remark, 'There but for the grace of God, goes God.' In ruder mood, Churchill was said to have been approached while in the toilet by an official, knocking on the door and nervously insisting that Cripps, then Lord Privy Seal, needed to see him immediately. The Prime Minister is said to have replied: 'Tell Sir Stafford I am in the lavatory and can only deal with one shit at a time.'[15] He may have been affected by rumours that Cripps was plotting to replace him, the war being at a low ebb then; Cripps would later go on to suggest to Attlee that he too should quit as Prime Minister but was quickly bought off.

Then there was the loud, haw-hawing Hugh Dalton, a useful reminder of how small and interwoven Britain's political class was in the middle of the twentieth century. He was the son of the canon at Windsor, a clergyman so ferocious he was said to have terrified even Queen Victoria. He tutored the King-Emperor, George V. His son, George VI, loathed Dalton and begged Attlee not to make him Foreign Secretary. This was probably a service to the nation because of the extreme nature of Dalton's anti-German feelings but the King saw merely Dalton as a turncoat, an Etonian who rebelled against his class and monarch. Dalton had started out as a Tory and switched, partly as an act of rebellion against his father. He was sexually repressed and easily depressed. The poet Rupert Brooke had been one of those he adored. 'My love', he said much later, 'is the Labour movement and the best of the young men in it.' Beyond anything, though, Dalton loved conspiracies. As Chancellor he paused on his way to deliver the crucial 1947 Budget and told a lobby correspondent some of its key points, allowing a London paper, the *Star*, to scoop his speech. This indiscretion – in Dalton's customary ear-splitting whisper – led instantly to his resignation, a blow from which he never really recovered. But Dalton had had a difficult and unsettling day until he leaked the Budget, having just come from unpleasant and confrontational talks at the Palace about how much money Philip and Elizabeth, the new Royal couple, should get from the Civil List. Perhaps he simply saw the journalist concerned – a man he knew very well – as the first friendly face of his day.

The silent, anti-intellectual Attlee, the Christian ex-Marxist Cripps and the confused Dalton do not sound like the core of a coherent vision for the new Britain of 1945. But alongside them were some remarkable figures who had known rather more of life at the coalface. Attlee apart, nobody was as important in the new government as the hulking figure of Ernest Bevin, the most influential man British trade unionism has ever produced. Orphaned at eight, 'Ernie' began as a Somerset labourer and worked his way up to become the organizer of dockworkers, until in 1921 he helped merge those men into the new Transport and General Workers' Union. A powerful figure in the General Strike, he ran the union until he was brought into the Churchill cabinet in 1940, a parliamentary seat being hurriedly found for him in Wandsworth. As the most powerful trade union leader of the inter-war years, Bevin was a passionate anti-Communist and a patriot who believed 'my boys' in the T & G were the very best of

Britain. In the wartime government he had almost dictatorial powers to direct workers into factories, mines and fields. If total war consisted in gathering together a country's total human and physical resources and then directing them at the enemy, Bevin was the Great Director. Described by one newspaper of the time as 'a bad mixer, a good hater, respected by all', he could be rude enough, even to Stalin who once hilariously whined that Mr Bevin was 'no gentleman'.

In the post-war government Bevin ruled almost in alliance with Attlee, both of them describing the other in fond, almost devoted terms. Attlee called it 'the deepest relationship of my political life'. Bevin chortled about Attlee, after he had shrewdly seen off another attempted coup against the Prime Minister, 'I love the little man.' After cabinet meetings, they would stay on together, charting the government's course. He always mistrusted intellectuals, particularly socialist ones. Reportedly, when he bumped into the famous Kingsley Martin, editor of the *New Statesman*, after the 1945 victory celebration, he greeted him: 'Ullo gloomy, I give you about three weeks before you stab us all in the back.' When Bevin died right at the end of the Attlee years, the loss was more than symbolic. He was probably the only person who could have stopped the party splitting over the rows which engulfed it because of the Korean War and military expenditure, but by then he was too sick to help.

His achievements as Foreign Secretary were enormous and controversial. The North Atlantic Treaty Organization, NATO, founded in 1949, depended on America's military power to provide a shield against Stalin for the shattered European democracies. Something like it would have happened, given the United States' growing fear of Soviet expansion, but the timing, precise form of the treaty and its basic principles owed a lot to Bevin. In 1948 he began calling in private letters for 'an Atlantic approaches pact of mutual assistance'. Its purpose was clear: 'to consolidate the West against Soviet infiltration and at the same time inspire the Soviet government with enough respect for the West to remove temptation from them and so ensure a long period of peace.'[16] And so it would be. Now, it all seems inevitable but at the time Bevin was particularly clear about the nature of the Soviet threat and withstood a storm of bitter attack from the USSR and its allies at home. More than a hundred Labour MPs abstained when the Commons voted first on NATO, and only a year before Bevin's first proposal Cripps, for instance, had been telling officials that 'we must be ready at any moment to switch over our friendship from the US to Russia.'

Bevin is less happily remembered for his role in the bitter arguments and fighting that led to the creation of the state of Israel. Most unfairly, he is still traduced as an anti-Semite. He had in fact been numbered as a friend of Zionism during the war, until faced with the impossible contradictions in Britain's position in the Middle East afterwards. There, the UK was both in charge of Palestine under international mandate, and had wider links to surrounding Arab countries. British officers ran the Jordanian Arab Legion, one of the instruments of Arab anger against Jewish migration; yet British officials were in charge of the Jewish homeland too. There is no doubt that the desperate migrations of Jewish refugees were handled very badly by Britain, determined to try to limit the settlement to a level that might be acceptable to Palestinian Arabs. The worst example was the turning-round of a refugee-crammed ship, *Exodus*, as she tried to land 4,500 people in 1947, and the eventual return of most of them to a camp in Hamburg, an act which caused Britain to be reviled around the world. This was followed by the kidnap and murder of two British soldiers by the Irgun terrorist group, which then booby-trapped their bodies. But Bevin was pressed very hard by the United States, which wanted far larger migration, and his instinct for a limited two-state solution now seems sensible. The British forces in Palestine were entirely ill equipped for the guerrilla and terrorist campaign launched against them by Jewish groups; in the circumstances of the later forties, Bevin's position was entirely impossible. It is worth recalling, if only for a bleak balance, that Bevin was reviled by Arab opinion as vigorously as by Jewish opinion.

The key to Bevin, from NATO to directing the British fight against Communist insurgents in Greece, was that he believed in liberty as essential to the building of a fair society. He believed in a welfare system to keep the wolf from the door, and full employment for unionized workers, which could be delivered by taking some of the economy into public ownership. Because of his huge wartime powers, he was a great believer in the State. He once told some American correspondents that he believed it was possible to have public ownership and liberty: 'I don't believe the two things are inconsistent . . . If I believed the development of socialism meant the absolute crushing of liberty, then I should plump for liberty because the advance of human development depends entirely on the right to think, to speak, and to use reason, and allow what I call the upsurge to come from the bottom to reach the top.'[17] He was a wonderful man, on a huge scale. He had faults too, of course: he was as easily entranced by the old Britain of smooth mandarins and Palace receptions as anyone.

This was not, on the whole, the weakness of the next of the extraordinary men who made up the 1945 government. Aneurin, or Nye, Bevan was wild, rebellious, radical, and above all, Welsh. Not since the days of Charles James Fox, champion of the French Revolution, had the British public been confronted by a minister as divisive and flamboyant as Bevan. Like Bevin, he had been a trade union leader. Born in Tredegar in South Wales into a mining family, he too was largely self-taught, in his case mopping up thrillers and Marx in workmen's libraries and at college in London. Like Bevin, he had been an excellent organizer during the 1926 General Strike. But there the comparisons between the two near-namesakes end. After entering Parliament a few years later, Bevan established himself as one of the few truly great orators of the time, rare in being a worthy opponent of Churchill – who Bevan described as 'suffering from petrified adolescence'. Unlike Attlee, Cripps, Bevin or Dalton, he had been outside the wartime coalition government and on many issues had seemed like a one-man opposition to it. Partly because of this, he had a far fiercer attitude to the Tories than his colleagues, and a clearer determination that Labour must build a completely new world. The nationalization and public control of almost the whole economy was his aim.

Nye Bevan spoke for the grassroots of the Labour Party, the people who expected a genuine socialist takeover of Britain. He did not believe there could be any compromise between capitalism and 'democracy'. The Commons was 'an elaborate conspiracy to prevent the real clash of opinion which exists outside from finding an appropriate echo within its walls. It is a social shock absorber placed between privilege and the pressure of popular discontent.'[18] Unlike most of the other leading figures, Bevan was, at least in theory, dangerous to the established order, even if in office he would turn out to be shrewder and subtler than his ranting public performances suggested. People prejudiced against him often came away from a first meeting seduced and bewitched. Like Bevin, he showed that a trade unionist could turn into a successful national leader. Unlike Bevin he had a vision of what Britain ought to become which went far beyond better pay and free spectacles. He would eventually be destroyed by the hard choices and compromises ahead, resigning when spending cuts were needed and dividing himself from most of his natural supporters over the issue of nuclear weapons. Beautifully dressed, witty, sibilant, wide-ranging, sarcastic, poetic and at times very alarming indeed, Nye Bevan represented everything that the old upper classes most feared after the 1945 election.

The final great shaper of post-war Labour Britain is Peter Mandelson's grandfather. Herbert Morrison was a Cockney policeman's son, the third working-class boy to set against the Labour 'aristocrats'. Like Gordon Brown he was blind in one eye and an obsessive reader. He started out working in a shop, weighing out the tea and sugar. His devotion to politics took him up through the London party machine until he eventually became the minister in the first Labour government, responsible for the capital's early integrated transport system. Had he not lost his seat in 1931 he would probably have become leader instead of Attlee (and hence Prime Minister), a loss he never ceased to regret. Instead he went on to become the first Labour leader of the London County Council and the most prominent voice of the rising new class of public servants, small traders, teachers and shop-keepers who would become key to Labour's successes. This meant that he was a moderate – enough of a moderate for the young Tory MP Harold Macmillan to suggest that he lead a new Centre Party in the late thirties. None of this, and his long career as an organizer and fixer, endeared him to the romantics in the party. Nor was he exciting. He lived a quiet suburban life with a quiet wife he rarely spoke about and pootered around in a small car. Michael Foot described him as a 'soft-hearted suburban Stalin'. In government Morrison was responsible for directing the astonishing torrent of legislation – seventy bills in the first year alone. He was not, however, a great economic planner and was far too obsessed with his reputation in the press, keeping great piles of cuttings to complain about when he met editors. He was also, like his grandson, a rotten intriguer, the boy always spotted and called to the front of the class the minute he starts whispering. Yet he was popular, passionate about his voters and hugely admired by Labour members. Had Morrison become Prime Minister, he might have been a good one.

Patriots First, Socialists Second

These were the six men who set Britain on its post-war course, a chaotic platoon, sentimental, reactionary, revolutionary, patriotic, moderate and extreme all at once. A small book could be devoted just to the disobliging things they said about each other. They believed in a socialist society but few of them seemed able to agree in detail what that meant – whether widespread nationalization was really needed, what should be done about the public schools, whether rationing was basically a good thing or a bad thing. Marching behind them was an equally divided crowd of intellectual socialists, practical middle-class people who believed in planning, trade unionists who thought it was time for the workers to get their share, and a few committed Marxists. And behind them, watching, there were millions of Labour voters who merely hoped for a better life. This meant, in practice, welfare plus nationalization, a consolidation and extension of the wartime directed economy and the 'fair shares' of the previous few years. Labour would apply the lessons of the war to the peace. After so many later disappointments it is hard to recapture quite the sense of hope that was clearly present in the mid-forties. Nor is it easy to recall how openly and passionately proud of Britain people were.

This was a government of patriots first and socialists second. In this Attlee set the tone. The historian Peter Hennessy said of him that he was 'certainly the most understated and, perhaps the most deeply, almost narrowly, English figure ever to have occupied Number Ten'. Bevin, rooted in his union and its members, ran Attlee close. He had a deep understanding of British political history and his predecessors in government, as the American Secretary of State Dean Acheson later recalled:

> He talked of them as slightly older people whom he knew with affectionate respect. In listening to him, one felt strongly the continuity and integrity of English history . . . 'Last night', he said

to me, 'I was reading some papers of Old Salisbury. Y'know, 'e had a lot of sense.' 'Old Palmerston' too came in for frequent and sometimes wistful mention . . . With George III he was very companionable. When sherry was brought in, he would twist around to look at the portrait. 'Let's drink to him,' he would say. 'If 'e 'adn't been so stoopid, you wouldn't 'ave been strong enough come to our rescue in the war . . .'[19]

Like Dalton, Bevin hated the Germans and thought little of the Russians and, though no imperialist, profoundly believed that Britain should take a lead role in the post-war world. The rulers of post-war Britain were far keener on the Empire than one might expect of socialists. While Attlee was sceptical about the need for a large British force in the Middle East, his government thought it right to maintain a massive presence sprawling across it, in order to protect both the sea-route to Asia and the oilfields Britain worked and depended on. Restlessly active in Baghdad and Tehran, Britain controlled Gibraltar, Malta, Cyprus and, at the tip of the Red Sea, the world's second-busiest port after New York, Aden. Throughout the forties and fifties, British conscripts and professional soldiers baked and sweated to little purpose in garrisons which bled the British Treasury. When they finally went home, they left behind an unstable, unhappy part of the world, with borders like wounds scored across it.

When it came to Indian independence the whole government agreed there was no holding back. Beyond that, the Labour ministers felt strong kinship with Canadians, Australians and New Zealanders and assumed that most of the African colonies were decades away from self-government. They were dubious about European integration, above all because it might compromise Britain's freedom to set her own political destiny. Attlee, in characteristically terse mode, later explained his feelings about Western Europe coming together: 'The so-called Common Market of six nations. Know them all well. Very recently this country spent a great deal of blood and treasure rescuing four of 'em from attacks by the other two.' Herbert Morrison, for his part, declared that the new socialist government of Britain was 'friends of the jolly old Empire; we are going to stick to it'.

Such views were widely shared. The left dreamed of a distinctly British socialism which would in turn become a beacon to other nations, a fantasy almost imperial in its ambitious assumption. It falls oddly on the ear now but it touched great writers such as George Orwell, fine journalists like the young Michael Foot and many idealistic Labour footsoldiers. Virtually all the Labour family, from Attlee to the radicals at *Tribune* believed that the Empire should be eventually be turned into a free association of democratic countries; but they assumed this could become the basis for a different kind of British power. The sterling area of countries using the pound included about 1,000 million people and was therefore seen by Whitehall as roughly equivalent to the areas of the world under American influence. There was talk of a new Commonwealth airways system, linking the social democratic worldwide web of the future. (An echo of this lost dream can be found in the writings of the fantasy novelist Michael Moorcock, who speculated about a liberal, anti-racist British commonwealth linked by huge fleets of airships.)

The question was how aggressively socialist was the government's post-war agenda to be? After 1940, many local Labour branches had wanted to retain robust party politics in pursuit of class war. Even as the German armies drilled on the coast of Normandy, the Labour conference had a unanimous motion sent to it from the Halifax branch calling for a negotiated peace with Germany because this would be less disastrous 'for the workers' than a military victory 'by this or any other capitalist government'.[20] Such sentiments were mostly squashed by the mood of national crisis, but there was a lively debate about what should happen after the war which could not be subdued. The centrist PEP (Political and Economic Planning) pressure group said with evident pleasure that wartime conditions 'have already compelled us to make sure, not only that the rich do not consume too much, but that others get enough . . . new measures for improving the housing, welfare and transport of the workers . . . the end of mass unemployment.' In the debate about the country's war aims in 1940, the generally understated Attlee complained that while the Germans were fighting 'a revolutionary war for very definite objectives' Britain was fighting a conservative war: 'We must put forward a positive and revolutionary aim admitting that the old order has collapsed and asking people to fight for the new order' – a view much modified by the time he came to power. But he was not alone in 1940 in thinking that the stronger government needed for fighting total war could usefully lead a peacetime revolution afterwards. As the New Statesman put it, 'We cannot actually achieve socialism during the war, but we can institute a whole series of Government controls which after the war can be used for Socialist ends.'

For Labour, there had been no conflict between the inspiring story of an old nation rallied against Hitler, and the rational organization of a future society; they were the same thing. As Orwell had written in 1941, in a famous essay describing England as a family with the wrong members in control, 'This war, unless we are defeated, will wipe out most of the existing class privileges. There are every day fewer people who wish them to continue.' But it would not become Russianized or Germanized: 'The Stock Exchange will be pulled down, the horse plough will give way to the tractor, the country houses will be turned into children's holiday camps, the Eton and Harrow match will be forgotten, but England will still be England, an everlasting animal . . .'[21] Orwell put it far more beautifully and persuasively than most others and of course the Stock Exchange, the Eton match and the country houses survived. But his dream of a third way, building on British parliamentary traditions, plus a national instinct for restraint and fair play to make a new kind of socialist society, unknown in Russia or elsewhere, was widely shared among Labour supporters.

A vision of Britain as an almost ungoverned, self-regulating place, whose people got on with their lives without interference, had survived from the eighteenth century, through Victorian liberalism to the instincts of many of the National government politicians of the thirties. But by 1945, in a Britain of identity cards, ration books, regulations and high taxation, it seemed to be dead. The mood was for big government, digging deep into people's lives to improve them. Yet the extraordinary thing was that, within a couple of years, Attlee's 'peace-time revolution' had lost momentum too. The optimism shrivelled under economic and physical storms, and though much of the Attlee legacy survived for decades, it was nothing like the social transformation Labour socialists had hoped for.

In Deepest Secret

On the morning of 11 December 1941 over the Gulf of Siam, a stretch of sea between Malaya and Vietnam, a single Japanese torpedo-bomber flew out of the cloudless sky. Piloted by Lieutenant Iki, it dipped down towards the waves and dropped not a bomb but a single wreath of leaves and flowers, left floating amid the oil stains and debris. Nothing like this would happen again in the bloody Far East war. The wreath was a rare sign of Japanese respect for nearly a thousand dead British sailors, blown to pieces or drowned when two great warships, the 'unsinkable' new *Prince of Wales* and the rather more elderly *Repulse*, had gone to the bottom in less than two hours, thanks to brilliantly precise and lethal torpedo attacks by the Japanese. The defeat had shocked Britain and plunged Churchill into despair. These ships were, in the words of one naval historian, 'symbols of the men and nation that had dominated the sea lanes of the Pacific since the days of Anson and Cook'.[22] The fall of Singapore, the psychological death-blow to the British Empire and the single worst defeat in the war for British forces, followed swiftly. But Lt Iki's gallant action was not simply a tribute to the sunken ships, the Royal Navy generally, or even to that expiring British Empire the Japanese had long admired. It was also a tribute to an Aberdeenshire aristocrat, William Francis Forbes, the Master of Semphill.

Semphill is one of those Britons forgotten here, remembered over there. He had been a pioneer aviator who served in the Royal Flying Corps in the First World War and made a once-famous early solo flight to Australia. When the two warships were sunk he was serving with Britain's Fleet Air Arm. A child of the British Establishment, the son of an aide to George V, Sempill would live on until 1965, honoured as a veteran of air warfare. So why the Japanese wreath? A quick inspection of the honours Semphill received after the war would have turned up the Order of the Rising Sun. The fact was that Semphill can be blamed or credited for some of Japan's awesome skill in destroying warships with torpedo-carrying aircraft, not only off Malaya but at Pearl Harbor. He had been sent to Japan on a British mission in the twenties to help build the Japanese naval air force, teaching the latest torpedo bombing techniques and advising on the design of aircraft carriers. Another British engineer had obligingly helped design one of the aircraft, which eventually developed into the feared Mitsubishi Zero. Semphill was impressed by the determination of the Japanese pilots and was thanked by the then Japanese Prime Minister who called his work 'almost epoch-making'. By 1942 it certainly was. When Semphill had trained his Japanese friends the two countries were linked by a treaty of friendship. More recently it has been revealed that Semphill went on to spy for the Japanese as well. He was not a one-off, nor was the passing over of a vital technology from Britain a rare event. Repeatedly in the past century Britain was involved in the early development of a breakthrough in military or industrial thinking which went straight to enemies or rivals who developed it further and used it better. The sinking of those battleships should have caused even more soul-searching than it did.

In the early years of the twentieth century the Royal Navy had been well ahead of the Germans, Americans and French in developing a modern submarine with guided torpedoes, despite the objection of one admiral who found it 'underhanded, unfair and damned un-English'. The Second Sea Lord, Jack Fisher, a brilliant, restless, terrifying man, widely rumoured to be half-Asiatic himself, pressed ahead. Yet it was Germany, first under the Kaiser and then under Hitler, which developed the U-boat to its logical and lethal conclusion, coming very close to starving Britain into submission in both world wars. Again, it was a Royal Navy engineer and a British company, Fosters, who produced the first workable tank in 1915 (they were originally called 'landships' but to keep their purpose secret, factory workers in Lincoln were told they were mobile water-tanks for the desert and this was shortened to simply, tank). Yet it was the Germans who turned the tank two decades later into an instrument of a new kind of warfare, by which time British tanks were comparatively outdated. As Semphill demonstrated, Britain had also once been ahead with torpedo-attack aircraft. In the mid-forties Britain was far advanced with jet engines, too. But again and again, deploying the new idea, actually getting it to work, was something that foreigners seemed better at.

The greatest example of all is the atomic bomb. We now know that Hitler's scientists were working hard on this new doomsday weapon, and hoped to test it as early as 1944. Scientists from Italy, France and Hungary were struggling with the physics throughout the thirties. The anguished private warning of Albert Einstein to President Roosevelt in a letter of 1939 about 'extremely powerful bombs of a new type' has gone down in history. Less well known is the work of two émigré scientists a year later in a laboratory at Birmingham University. Otto Frisch and Rudolf Peierls were working on the effects of using the isotope uranium 235 for a nuclear weapon. They made the theoretical breakthrough for building an effective bomb and in 1940 hurriedly typed out a memo for the British government, an obscure paper which has been described as one of the most significant documents of the century. The government, as governments will do, set up a committee of scientists and military advisers and reported back that 'the scheme for a uranium bomb is practicable and likely to lead to decisive results in the war.' This was shrewd enough. Thanks to Hitler's persecution of the Jews Britain had the know-how to get ahead of Germany. But this was the year when the Blitz was at its height and the threat of invasion very real. Britain's economy was already vastly overstretched. The huge effort needed to create a nuclear industry, to turn the mathematics into metal, was beyond the country's technical and economic strength. So the news about the bomb was passed to the Americans. Out in the New Mexico desert, they soon leapt ahead. A new world order would swiftly follow.

For a short while after the war it looked as if Britain would stay out of the nuclear race, which seemed to the Attlee government expensive and difficult. Key ministers argued against trying to join it. Had Ernest Bevin, Britain's post-war Foreign Secretary, not been a prickly patriot, perhaps Britain would have stayed non-nuclear. But after being patronized by his American opposite number, Bevin told his colleagues that he wanted no British Foreign Secretary to be treated that way again. It was a matter of national status, said Ernie. 'We've got to have this thing over here, whatever it costs. We've got to have the bloody Union Jack on top of it.'[23] This was an agonizing struggle, far harder than was admitted. Churchill had had a private wartime deal with President Roosevelt. Both countries would seek the other's permission before using nuclear weapons. Information would be shared. Britain would not develop civil nuclear power without Washington's agreement. This was effectively torn up by the Americans in 1946 with the McMahon Act, which prohibited the sharing of nuclear information or technology. When Attlee tried to revive nuclear cooperation after the war, the White House ignored his letter and the US copy of the secret Churchill–Roosevelt agreement was conveniently lost in the wrong file. A few years after that early breakthrough by the refugees in Birmingham, Britain was far behind the Americans, without access to their work.

The decision to develop the first A-bombs had been a secret even from Churchill in opposition, who later told the Commons: 'I was not aware until I took office that not only had the Socialist Government made the atomic bomb as a matter of research, but that they had created at the expense of scores of millions of pounds the important plant necessary for its regular production.' Though private assessments of the threat posed by the Soviet Union were drawn up within months of the end of the war, right from the start in the cabinet committee papers there is the curious and unmistakeable fact that the Soviet menace is rarely at the top of the argument about the British bomb. It is all about the Americans. First, in the Bevin years, it is about status and old-fashioned bulldog pride.

Then it becomes a matter of global strategy, something needed as leverage to influence US policy. Answering the appeal of the defeated Admiralty after the war, the mandarins bluntly admitted: 'The UK has ceased to be a first-class power in material terms. The United States and Russia already far outstrip us in population and material wealth, and both have vast untapped resources. Canada, India and China, to name only three . . . in time will certainly outstrip us.' But, they pointed out, the much more powerful hydrogen bomb was transforming the military situation around the world: 'If we possess these weapons, the Americans will be prepared to pay attention to our opinions in a way they would otherwise not. The same applies to our standing in the eyes of other countries, such as Germany. And our lesser potential enemies, such as Egypt, will feel that we might, if pushed too far, use nuclear weapons against them.' 'These', concluded the mandarins rather chillingly, 'are great advantages . . .'[24]

From early on, Whitehall intelligence reports to ministers identified the peril of war being triggered by a pre-emptive strike from America, hitting the Russians, before they had devised their own nuclear systems at a level which would allow them to properly retaliate. With British troops on the vulnerable front line in Germany, Britain would be thrown into the midst of the new war for which she was not prepared.

Persuading the Americans to stay their hand might be easier, the British policy-makers suggested, if Britain was herself an independent nuclear power. In the summer of 1947 work began in deepest secret to build a plutonium-producing plant at Windscale, a little place on the coast of Cumbria, and work started on designing a bomb under the guidance of one of the British scientists who had been at Los Alamos, William Penney. A few years later, the tiny Berkshire village of Aldermaston, with its twelfth-century church, brick labourers' cottages and ancient Roman defences, which had been looking forward to quieter times with the closure of an airbase, was chosen as the site for Britain's nuclear weapons programme. More money spent on defence and status was of course less money available for a New Jerusalem.

A Winter Landscape

The winter of 1947 has gone down in history and personal memory as a time of almost unendurable bleakness. For three months, Britain seemed more like one of the grimmer scenes in a medieval Flemish painting. It was not only the shortages of almost everything in the shops, and what was described as a virtual peasant diet, heavily based on potatoes and bread – though by then even the bread had now been rationed, and potatoes ran short. It was not only the huge state bureaucracy still interfering in so much daily life, controlling everything from how long you could turn your heater on, to what plays you could see and whether or not you could leave the country. It was not the 25,000 regulations and orders never seen in peacetime before, administered by a government which though anti-Communist, still urged people to learn from the 'colossal' industrial achievements of Soviet Communism.[25] It was not the smashed and broken homes. It was not even all those war dead – for this war had involved far fewer soldiers than the First World War, and far fewer dead – 256,000 as against nearly a million, as well as the 60,000 British civilians who had died in air-raids. Relief at the final victory was still strong across the country, and pride in Britain's part in it. No, the crisis of 1947 was set off by that most humdrum of British complaints – the weather.

At the end of January with an efficiency the Red Army could not have mustered, a great freeze had swept across from Siberia and covered the country in thick snow, a bitter cold which brought the exhausted British very nearly to their knobbly, ill-clad knees. The country still ran on coal. But at the pits, the great piles of coal froze solid and could not be moved. The winding-gears ceased to function. Drifting snow blocked roads and closed the rail lines. At the power stations, the remaining coal stocks ran swiftly down until, one by one, power stations began to close. Lights flickered off. Men dug through snowdrifts, tramping for miles to find food to carry back to their neighbours and homes. Cars were marooned on exposed roads. With shortages of power, factories across the South and Midlands of England had to stop work and within a week two million people were idle. Attlee suspended that still unusual middle-class diversion, television. Much worse, electric fires were banned for three hours each morning and two each afternoon.[26] Everywhere, people shivered, wrapped in blankets in front of barely smoking coal fires, or those rationed electric ones. Around London, commuters were completely unable to reach the capital. Scotland was cut off from the rest of the country. Then things deteriorated further. It was the coldest February for 300 years. Another half million people had to stop work. One young office worker from Slough, Maggie Joy Blunt, recorded herself sitting in her house, the water in washbasins frozen, looking out at the ice-blue sky: 'I am wearing thick woollen vest, rubber roll-on, wool panties, stockings, thick long-sleeved wool sweater, slacks, jacket, scarf and two pairs of woollen socks – I am just about comfortable.'[27] The sun was so little seen that when it came out briefly, a man rushed to photograph the reassuring sight for the newspapers. Green vegetables ran out in the shops. 'CHRIST ITS BLEEDING COLD' howled the future novelist Kingsley Amis to the poet Philip Larkin, from his Oxford student rooms.

After a short thaw March had brought terrible storms and snow-drifts thirty feet high. People talked about snowflakes the size of five-shilling coins. There were ice-floes off the East Anglian coast. Three hundred main roads were unusable. Still to come were the worst floods in memory, cutting off towns, inundating huge areas of low-lying England, and destroying the crops in the fields. On the hills the sheep were dying. Their carcasses would be piled into pyres, causing foul-smelling smoke to hang over rural Wales, a precursor to the foot-

and-mouth and BSE episodes of later decades. It was, in short, about as near as this country has been to experiencing at first hand a truly Siberian winter, though without the sturdy boots, furs and vodka that help the Russians get through. It would be followed by the real political storm – the run on the pound made inevitable by the Keynes deal in Washington, and a balance of payments crisis. As people were digging out frozen vegetables from fields and despairing of the empty shops, the Treasury was finally running out of dollars to buy help from overseas. This was the moment when the optimism of 1945 shivered and died among many voters.

Summer did come, as summer does, and it was a good summer. The sun shone, cricketers blazed away at Lords and a nation sweltered. Economically, though, Hugh Dalton's year of misery continued. The clauses negotiated by Keynes insisting that sterling should become freely convertible to American dollars were triggered, and the inevitable happened. The world rushed to change pounds into greenbacks, and such was the outflow that convertibility had to be hurriedly stopped. The economy was simply too weak – a message that echoed round continental Europe's finance ministries too. British housewives might have been more worried still had they known of a secret plan during the sterling crisis drawn up by the civil servant Otto Clarke (father of the later New Labour minister Charles Clarke). With Britain running out of dollars to buy food from America, Clarke drew up preparations for a 'famine food programme', including taking children out of school to help in the fields.[28] It never came to that but the rationing of bread, which had not been necessary during the war was now in place. There was not enough cash left to buy wheat supplies from the United States, yet British ministers had to ensure there was no actual famine in other parts of the world for which they were responsible, including India and defeated Germany.

The answer, bread rationing at home, was hugely unpopular and long remembered. Along with the sterling crisis and the subsequent devaluation of 1949, a further but necessary humiliation, it gave Churchill's Tories the essential ammunition they needed to turn Attlee out. Their manifesto would later remind voters that 'In 1945, the Socialists promised that their methods of planning and nationalization would make the people of Britain masters of their economic destiny.

Nothing could be more untrue. Every forecast has proved grossly over-optimistic. Every crisis has caught them unawares. The Fuel Crisis cost the country £200 millions and the Convertibility Crisis as much.'

The next year, though, the government did try to cheer the country up, holding the 1948 London Olympics. Cost over-runs were trivial. Security was barely an issue. The games were a triumph of determination in a war-scarred, rubble-strewn city, during which the athletes were put up in old army camps and hospitals, and the Union Jack was missing for the opening parade. And though the medal toll for British competitors was very meagre, holding the games was a genuine sign that Britain was back. For all its weaknesses, this was still a country that could organize itself pretty well.

The Sun Also Sets

The deep nostalgic vision of Empire was dented too in 1947. The King ceased to be Emperor. The jewel in the imperial crown, India, was moving towards independence long before the war. Gandhi's brilliant insight that through non-violence the British could be embarrassed out of India more effectively than they could be shot out, had paid off handsomely in the inter-war years. London was dragged to the negotiating table despite the attempts by Churchill and others to scupper every deal from the thirties to the late forties. The war delayed independence but showed how much goodwill there was on the subcontinent, if Britain was wise enough to withdraw gracefully. During the conflict some two million Indians fought on Britain's side or served her forces directly, their contributions being particularly strong in the campaigns in North Africa against the Italians and defeating a pro-German regime in Iraq. Gandhi himself was sentimentally fond of Britain and saddened by the Luftwaffe attacks on London. While Nehru was in prison, he kept a picture of his old school, Harrow, in his cell.

Yet many Indians had become frustrated by endless delays and the watering-down of plans for more autonomy. Leaders out of jail organized a massive wartime protest involving the burning of police stations, the beating of British residents, the cutting of telegraph lines and the blowing up of a railway line. For a while, British control of

India hung in the balance, though the true story of what was happening was kept out of newspapers at home. Less dangerous if more spectacular, was the formation of an anti-British Indian National Army under Subhas Chandra Bose, armed and supported by the Japanese. Indians were used to guard captured British troops, a humiliation designed to spread the Japanese line that this was essentially a war of Asian people against colonial Westerners. When the pro-Japanese Indians returned home after the defeat of Japan, Britain wanted them prosecuted as traitors but they were greeted as heroes by Gandhi's Congress Party.

As soon as Attlee took power, his government organized talks on withdrawal. Anti-imperialism had been a genuine strand in Labour thinking since the party's formation, but now there were other motives too. There was gratitude for Indian support for the Empire at its worst moment. There was also fear – the clear evidence that delaying independence would result in mass and probably uncontrollable protest. Attlee wanted a united, independent India, Muslims and Hindus in one vast state connected by trade and military agreement with Britain. Apart from anything else, he believed this would function as a major anti-communist bulwark in Asia, at just the time when the Russians were looking south and China was in revolutionary turmoil.

Attlee would get some of what he wanted, but not all. Sir Stafford Cripps led the first Labour delegation to post-war India but it was not socialist politicians who negotiated the end of British control in India. That job was begun by Field Marshal Wavell, a veteran of the Boer and First World Wars who had served with the Czarist Russians before fighting the Italians (successfully) and Rommel (less so) in the desert. He had come to India as commander-in-chief just ahead of the most decisive Japanese advances, and had succeeded as Viceroy in time to free the Congress leaders from prison. But this poetry-loving and mildly pessimistic soldier was unsuccessful in trying to reconcile Hindus and Muslims. Sectarian mobs began to attack one another, the first flickers of the communal violence which would soon ravage the subcontinent. Early in 1946 there was a major mutiny by the Royal Indian Navy, when about a quarter of its strength aboard ships off Bombay, Calcutta and Madras raised Congress flags. It was put down, with hundreds dead, but trouble spread to the Royal Indian Air Force and the police, and it looked as if authority was finally crumbling.

Wavell's last-ditch plan involved British withdrawal without any political agreement, evacuating whites from the country and handing it over to local state governments. This was regarded in London as likely to lead to civil war and fundamentally dishonourable.

Attlee passed the job to Lord Louis Mountbatten, who had been supreme commander in South-East Asia, organizing the reconquest of Burma. It was a wily choice. Mountbatten was a member of the Royal Family and his nephew, a naval officer, Prince Philip of Greece, was about to marry the young Princess Elizabeth, so he was a hard man for the imperialists at home to attack. Dashing and arrogant, he shared Attlee's determination to get a swift deal with the leaders of the Muslim and Hindu peoples, which meant with Mohammed Ali Jinnah's Muslim League and Nehru's Congress Party. Jinnah was always hard for the British to deal with or like, and was by now close to death; but Nehru proved an easy partner, forming a famously close attachment to Mountbatten's wife, Edwina. Partitioning the subcontinent was by now inevitable. Muslims would not accept overall Hindu domination and yet across most of India the Hindus or Sikhs were in the majority. British India was duly split into Muslim Pakistan (a made-up name, an anagram of Punjab, Afghania, Kashmir, Sind and Baluchistan, the key provinces) and Hindu-dominated India. The line was drawn up by a British lawyer, Sir Cyril Radcliffe, and kept secret until after the handover of power.

Mountbatten announced to widespread surprise and shock that independence would happen ten months earlier than planned, on 15 August 1947. Churchill was so appalled that his former Foreign Secretary and friend Anthony Eden had to keep him away from the chamber of the Commons. Having listened to the parliamentary statement, Enoch Powell was shattered enough to wander the streets of London all night, squatting in doorways with his head in his hands. No doubt millions of other British people felt equally that their familiar world was coming apart. And while the speed of British withdrawal may have been a political necessity, the consequences were appalling. By some counts a million people then died, many of them women and children as Muslims and Hindus caught on the wrong side of the new border fled from their homes. Sikhs rose against the Muslims in the Punjab, Muslims drove out Hindus. Rather as in Yugoslavia after the collapse of Communism, it turned out that the old central power had merely frozen and held in suspension older religious and ethnic rivalries which revived at a moment of crisis. As some 55,000 British civilians returned home, the Indian Army was hurriedly divided into two. Mountbatten had hoped for a close military alliance to continue and Karachi had even been earmarked as a base for British atomic bombers to use in attacking Russia. But no military deal could be agreed. Eventually, Pakistan broke up, with Bangladesh declaring herself independent, and succumbed to a history of coup and dictatorship. Today India and Pakistan face each other with nuclear weapons and large armies across their Kashmiri frontier.

Britons have been told that as compared to the war in Algeria which tore post-war France apart, or the Americans' desperate war in Vietnam, Britain managed decolonization rather well. It is too comfortable a conclusion. Who was to blame for the horrifying number of Indian deaths – far more, for instance, than have died during the mayhem in Iraq? British post-war weakness probably meant that it would have been impossible to impose a single state at the time of independence. Yet Jinnah's Muslim League and Congress had been nearer to a mature deal before the war; had Churchill and others not stymied independence in the thirties by cynically supporting the cause of the semi-independent Indian princes, then perhaps the slaughter would have been averted. Against that, the story of the Second World War would have been very different too. And today's India, linked by English and a growing democratic superpower, stands as one of the more successful of Britain's old imperial possessions. Indian independence was a trauma to some, a relief to many more.

Labour ministers were less enthusiastic about dismantling the Empire in Africa. Officials wrote minutes to Attlee's ministers informing them it might take many generations before some of the colonies were ready for independence. Herbert Morrison, the deputy leader of the Labour Party, agreed. He said that to give the African colonies their freedom would be 'like giving a child of ten a latch-key, a bank account and a shotgun'. Attlee himself speculated about creating a British African army, on the lines of the lost Indian one, to help project British power around the world. The Colonial Office described Africa as the core of Britain's new world position, from where she could draw economic and military strength. In the early fifties, the Colonial Office itself grew in numbers and was even hoping for a large new headquarters opposite Parliament Square, promised to it by Churchill. There was a grand scheme for growing groundnuts in Tanganyika, to provide cheap vegetable oil for Britain – though that was a swift and embarrassing failure. For a while it seemed that the Raj would be transplanted, in fragmented form, to Africa.

White People

Back in the mother country in 1947, who were those people who were just beginning to adjust to a post-imperial world? They were sparser and whiter. In the years after the war Britain contained about ten million fewer inhabitants than live here today. The thirties had seen a fall in the birthrate and there was much official worry about another kind of national shrinkage. In William Beveridge's famous 1942 report launching the modern Welfare State, he suggested that a bit of fast breeding was needed: 'with its present rate of reproduction, the British race cannot continue.' To Beveridge and his generation 'the British race' meant white natives of these islands. Before the war, around 95 per cent of people in Britain had been born here, and the other 5 per cent was mostly made up of white English and Scots whose parents had happened to be serving the Empire in India, Africa or the Middle East when they were born. There were black and Asian people in Britain but very few. In the thirties the Indian community numbered perhaps 8,000 at most – a tenth of them doctors, intriguingly – and there were a few Indian restaurants and grocery stores in the biggest cities. There had been a tiny West Indian presence. No detailed surveys were done, but there were at most a few thousand, many of them students. Black sailors and mixed-race Lascars, along with Chinese, had been settled in dockland areas of Liverpool, Cardiff, Bristol and London for a long time. Again, though, the numbers were small.

During the war, men from the Caribbean began to arrive, serving with the British forces. There was a Jamaica Squadron and a Trinidad Squadron in the RAF and a West Indian Regiment in the British Army. Others came to work in factories, in the countryside and on radar stations. But once the war was over, most were sent straight home leaving an estimated permanent non-white population of about 30,000. It had been the 130,000 black American troops who made the most impact on British public opinion during the war. Despite official worries about 'fraternization' with coloured soldiers, they were widely welcomed and lionized. There are well-attested incidents of white GIs who tried to apply the American colour bar being mocked and challenged.[29] After the war, almost unnoticed by the general public and passed in response to Canadian fears about the lack of free migration around the Empire, the 1948 British Nationality Act dramatically changed the scene. It declared that all subjects of the King had British citizenship. This gave some 800 million people around the world the right to enter the UK. Though it seems extraordinary now after so many decades of new restrictions on immigration, this was uncontroversial at the time for a simple reason – it was generally assumed that black and Asian subjects of the King would have no means or desire to travel to live in uncomfortable, crowded Britain. Travel remained expensive and slow. Why would they want to come, anyway? Until the fifties so few black or Asian people had settled in Britain that they were often treated as local celebrities and officially it was not even considered worth while trying to count their numbers.[30]

There were other immigrant communities. A Jewish presence had been important for a long time, in retailing, the food business and banking – everything from Marks & Spencer to Rothschild's Bank. But in the five years before the war, some 60,000 more Jews from Germany and Eastern Europe arrived here, many of them highly qualified, helping transform the scientific, musical and intellectual life of forties Britain. When Hitler came to power in 1933 it was agreed at cabinet level to try 'to secure for this country prominent Jews who were being expelled from Germany and who had achieved distinction' in science, medicine, music and art. Beveridge himself helped set up an organization to help Jewish refugees, the Academic Assistance Council, which, using public donations, helped 2,600 intellectuals escape. No fewer than twenty of them later won Nobel prizes, fifty-four were elected Fellows of the Royal Society, and ten were knighted for their academic brilliance.[31] In their invasion plans for 1940, the German SS reckoned the Jewish population of Britain to be above 300,000, and hugely influential.

Then there were the Irish, a big group in British life after a century of steady immigration, the vast majority of it from the south. It continued through the war, despite government restrictions, as Irish people came over to fill the labour shortage left by mobilization. Ireland's stony neutrality and her expression of sympathy at Hitler's death at the end of the war, had made Eire very unpopular with the British. Popular prejudice against the Irish continued, as it always had, and would for a long time to come. Yet none of this seemed to affect immigration, which carried on at a great rate through the forties and fifties, running at between 30,000 and 60,000 during any given year. Whenever cabinet committees turned to the issue of migration, the Irish were excluded from debate because they were regarded as effectively indigenous. There were other more exotic groups. By the end of the war, Britain was home to 120,000 Poles who had fled the Soviets and Nazis, many of them then serving in the British forces, notably the RAF. Most chose to stay on and by the end of 1948, with the energetic help of government settlement officers, 65,000 had jobs, in everything from coal-mining to factory work. Similar tales can be told of Czechs and many other nationalities. All these, of course, were white.

It would be wrong to portray Britain in the forties as relaxed about race. Despite the horror of the concentration camps, widely advertised in the immediate aftermath of the war, anti-Semitism was still present. The assumption that 'they' dodged queues or somehow got the best of scarce and rationed goods, erupts from diaries and letters of the time. After Jewish terrorist attacks on British servicemen in Palestine in 1947, there were anti-Jewish disturbances in several British cities, including attacks on shops and even the burning of a synagogue, mimicking the actions of Nazis in the thirties. More widely, trade unions were quick to express bitter hostility to outsiders coming to take British jobs – whether they be European Jews, Irish, Poles, Czechs or Maltese. The government itself spoke without self-consciousness or embarrassment about the central importance of 'the British race'.[32] The multilingual, multi-hued Britain of today, with its greengrocers selling baskets of yams and its scents of turmeric and incense, in which more than 90 per cent of us do not think you have to be white to be properly British, would have left a visitor from the immediate post-war years utterly astonished. Then, Jews and passing American service-men apart, the composition of the country in 1945 was not much different from late medieval times.

Proper Drains and Class Distinction

Patriotic pride cemented a sense of being one people, one race, with one common history and fate. But to be British in the forties was to be profoundly divided from many of your fellow subjects by class. By most estimates, a good 60 per cent of the nation was composed of the traditional working class – that is, they were factory workers, agricultural labourers, navvies on the roads, riveters, miners, fishermen, servants or laundrywomen, people in a thousand trades, using their muscles; and all their dependents. The workers were paid in cash, weekly – cheque-books were a sign of affluence. People did not move, much. War aside, most would spend all their lives in their home town or village, though the thirties had produced modest migrations such as from industrial Scotland and Wales to the English Home Counties The sharp sense of class distinction came from where you lived, how you spoke; and it defined what entertainments you might enjoy. The war had softened class differences a little and produced the first rumblings of the coming cultural revolution. Men and women from widely different backgrounds found themselves jumbled together in the services. On the home front, middle-class women worked in factories, public schoolboys went down the mines and many working-class women had their first experiences of life beyond the sink and the street. In uniform or in factories, working-class or lower middle-class men could find themselves ordering former well-spoken toffs around. 'Blimps' – the older, more pompous upper-class officers – became a butt of popular humour, a symbol of dying old Britain.

With skill shortages and a national drive for exports, wages rose after the war. The trade unions were powerful and self-confident, particularly when the new Labour government repealed the laws that had hampered them ever since the General Strike of 1926. Three years after the war, they achieved their highest ever level of support. More than 45 per cent of people who could theoretically belong to one, did so, and there were some 8.8 million union members. In other European countries at this time, trade unions were fiercely political, communist, socialist or Roman Catholic. In Britain, they were not. The Communist Party, deprived of any real part of parliamentary politics, spent much of its energy and money building support inside the unions, and was beginning to win elections for key posts, but in general British trade unionism remained more narrowly focused on the immediate cash-and-hours agenda of its members. This did not mean British trade unions were quiet. Because so many of their most experienced and older shop stewards and organizers had effectively gone to work for the government during the war, or had joined up to fight, a new generation of younger, more hot-headed shop stewards, men in their twenties or even teens, had taken control of many workplaces. The seeds of the great British trade union battles of later decades were sown and watered during the forties.

The core of the old working class which had depended for jobs on coal, steel and heavy manufacturing would eventually have a grim time as these industries first struggled, and then failed, in the decades to come. But this was not obvious after the war. The shipyards of the Clyde, Belfast and the Tyne were hard at work, the coalfields were at full stretch, London was still an industrial city, and the car-making and light engineering areas of the West Midlands were on the edge of a time of unprecedented prosperity. We were a nation of brick terraces. It was not until the next two decades that many of the traditional working-class areas of British cities would be replaced by high-rise flats or sprawling new council estates. The first generation of working-class children to get to university was now at school, larger and healthier than their parents, enjoying the dental care and spectacles provided by the young National Health Service. But for the most part working-class life was remarkably similar to working-class life in the thirties. No televisions, cars, foreign holidays, fitted kitchens, foreign food, service sector jobs had yet impinged on most people's lives. Politicians assumed most people would stay put and continue to do roughly the same sort of job as they had done before the war. Rent acts and planning directives were the tools of ministers who assumed that the future of industry would be like its past, only more so – more ships, more coal, more cars, more factories.

The class who would do best out of the wartime changes was be the middle class, a fast growing minority. Government bureaucracy had grown hugely and would continue to do so. Labour's Welfare State would require hundreds of thousands of new white-collar jobs, administering national insurance, teaching, running the health service. Even the Colonial Office vastly expanded its staff as the colonies disappeared, giving one of its officials, C. Northcote Parkinson, the idea for 'Parkinson's Law' – that work expands to fill the time available. Studies of social mobility, such as the major one carried out in 1949, are notoriously crude and have to be taken with a pinch of salt. But they suggest that while working-class sons generally followed their fathers into similar jobs, there was much more variation among middle-class children. Labour might have intended to help the workers first, but education reform was helping more middle-class children get a good grammar school education. A steadily growing number stayed at school until fifteen, then eighteen.

So, perceptibly, the old distinctions were softening. The culture was a little more democratic. Increasing numbers would make it to university too, an extra 30,000 a year by 1950. The accents of Birmingham and Wales, the West Country and Liverpool would challenge the earlier linguistic stamp of middle-class respectability. The culture of public radio would bring literature and music to much wider audiences; the post-war humour of Tommy Handley and *Round the Horne* would be as enjoyed by the suburbs as by the palaces. Churchill himself had told Harrow schoolboys that one effect of the war was to diminish class differences. Sounding almost like a New Labour politician, he said to them as early as 1940 that 'the advantages and privileges that have hitherto been enjoyed by the few shall be far more widely shared by the many.'

The Old Order

But not quite yet. The ruling class was still the ruling class. Despite the variety of the 1945 cabinet, Britain in the forties and fifties was a society run mostly by cliques and groups of friends who had first met at public schools and Oxbridge. Public school education remained the key for anyone hoping to make a career in the City, the Civil Service or the higher echelons of the Army. Schools such as Eton, Harrow and Winchester might educate only some 5 per cent of the population, but they still provided the majority of political leaders, including many of Labour's post-war cabinet. Parliamentary exchanges of the period are full of in-jokes about who was a Wykehamist and who an Etonian. Briefly, it had seemed such schools would not even survive the war:

boarding schools had been in enough of a financial crisis for some to face closure through bankruptcy. Churchill's own Harrow was one, along with Marlborough and Lancing, though all struggled on. More generally there was a belief that public schools had contributed to failures of leadership in the thirties and right up to the early defeats of the war. When the Tory minister R. A. Butler took on the job of education reform during the war, he contemplated abolishing them and folding them all into a single state school system. Had that happened, post-war Britain would have been a very different country. But Butler, intimidated by Churchill, backed off. A watered-down scheme would have seen Eton and the rest obliged to take working-class and middle-class children, paid for by the local authorities, but this quickly fizzled out too. The public schools stayed. Attlee, devoted to his old school, had no appetite for abolition. Grammar schools were seen as a way of getting bright working-class or middle-class children to Oxbridge, and a few other universities, so that they could buttress the ruling cliques. One civil servant described the official view as being that children were divided into three kinds: 'It was sort of Platonic. There were golden children, silver children and iron children.'[33]

The problem for the old ruling order was whether the arrival of a socialist government was a brief and unwelcome interruption, which could be sat out, or whether it was the beginning of a calm but implacable revolution. The immediate post-war period with its very high taxation was a final blow for many landowners. Great country houses like Knole and Stourhead had to be passed over to the National Trust. It was hardly a revolutionary seizure of estates, yet to some it felt that way. Tradition was being nationalized, with barely a thank-you. In 1947 the magazine *Country Life* protested bitterly that the aristocratic families had been responsible for civilization in Britain: 'It has been one of the services of those currently termed the privileged class, to whom, with strange absence of elementary good manners, it is the fashion not to say so much as a thank you when appropriating that which they have contributed to England.' Evelyn Waugh, an *arriviste* rather than a proper toff, sitting in his fine house in the Gloucestershire village of Stinchcombe, struggled with the dilemma. In November 1946 he considered fleeing England for Ireland (many richer people did leave Britain in the post-war years, though more often for Australia, Africa or America). Why go? Waugh asked himself. 'The certainty that England as a great power is done for, that the loss of possessions [he is talking of the colonies], the claim of the English proletariat to be a privileged race, sloth and envy, must produce increasing poverty . . . this time the cutting down will start at the top until only a proletariat and a bureaucracy survive.'

A day later, however, he was having second thoughts. 'What is there to worry me here in Stinchcombe? I have a beautiful house furnished exactly to my taste; servants enough, wine in the cellar. The villagers are friendly and respectful; neighbours leave me alone. I send my children to the schools I please. Apart from taxation and rationing, government interference is negligible.' Yet the world felt as if it was changing somehow. Why, he wonders, is he not at ease? Why does he smell 'the reek of the Displaced Persons Camp'?[34] Many more felt just the same; Noël Coward said immediately after Labour's 1945 win, 'I always felt that England would be bloody uncomfortable in the immediate post-war period, and it is now almost a certainty.'[35] These shivery intimations of change would have some substance, though it would happen more slowly and have little to do with Attlee or Bevan. The old British class system, though it retained a medieval, timeless air, much exploited by novelists, depended in practical terms on the Empire and a global authority Britain was just about to lose. 'Disgusted of Tunbridge Wells' would soon become shorthand for the returnees from Malaya or Rhodesia. A pervasive air of grievance and abandonment would hang about the right of British politics for decades.

Meanwhile, old society events like the 'Varsity' rugby match, the Boat Race, the Henley Regatta and Ascot, quickly returned after the war and indeed reached the height of their popularity. Young Conservative dances were where the better-off went to find partners. The most famous actors and actresses were able to carry on a lavish lifestyle, hidden from the taxman. London clubland carried on almost as in the twenties. The capital's grandest restaurants, some which are still going, such as the Savoy Grill and the Ivy, were again crowded with peers, theatrical impresarios, exiled royalty and visiting American movie stars. In the upper-class diaries of the day there are complaints about a rising tide of 'common' behaviour, the end of good taste and the regrettable influence of Americans and Jews.

Under Attlee, Britain remained a country of private clubs and cliques, ancient or ancient-seeming privileges, rituals and hierarchies.

In the workplace, there was a return to something like the relationships of pre-war times, with employers' organizations assuming their old authority and influence, at least some of the time, in Whitehall. Inside the new nationalized industries the same sort of people continued to manage and the same 'us and them' relationships reasserted themselves remarkably easily. In the City, venerable, commanding merchant bankers with famous names would be treated like little gods; stiff collars, top hats and the uniforms of the medieval livery companies were still seen, even among the grey ruins of post-Blitz London; younger bankers and accountants deferred utterly to their elders. Newspaper owners would sweep up to their offices in chauffeured Rolls-Royce cars and be met by saluting doormen. *The Times* was soon full of advertisements for maids and other servants. Lessons in speaking 'the King's English' were given to aspiring actors and broadcasters; much debate was had about the proper way to pour tea, refer to the lavatory and lay the table. Physicians in hospitals swept into the wards, followed by trains of awed, indeed frightened, junior doctors. At Oxford colleges, formal dinners were compulsory, as was full academic dress, and the tenured professors hobbled round their quads as if little had changed since Edwardian times. All of this was considered somehow the essence of Britain, or at least of England.

Gnasher George and his Girls

So too was the last grand monarchy in Europe, the only remnant of the extended family of former German princelings which had once enjoyed power from Siberia to Berlin, Athens to Edinburgh. After the national trauma of the Abdication crisis, George VI had established a reassuringly pedestrian image for the family which now called itself simply the Windsors. In private the King expressed fiercely right-wing views, falling into rages or 'gnashes' at the pronouncements of socialist ministers. In public he was a diffident patriarch, much loved for his tongue-tied stoicism during the Blitz, when Buckingham Palace received several direct hits. There had been cautious signs of Royal modernization, with Princess Elizabeth being used to make patriotic radio broadcasts and later joining the ATS, photographed in battledress and even mingling anonymously with the crowds on VE Day. The

King and Queen, though, ran what was in all essentials an Edwardian Court well into the fifties. Every March teenage virgin girls from aristocratic or merely wealthy families would be presented to the Queen wearing three ostrich feathers in their hair. Then they would begin 'The Season', a marathon four-month round of balls and dinners during which, it was hoped, they would find a suitable man to marry. These debutantes would often have been sent to 'finishing school' in Switzerland where they would have learned how to walk properly, speak French and run a household according to the old manner. The Royal presentation dated back to 1780 and would eventually be ended by the Queen in 1958: Prince Philip opined that it was 'bloody daft' while Princess Margaret complained. 'We had to put a stop to it. Every tart in London was getting in.' It continued at a nearby hotel where, in eccentric British fashion, the girls still arrived to curtsy to a six-foot-tall birthday cake, rather than the monarch.[36]

Initially, it was unclear how well the monarchy itself would fare in post-war Britain. The leading members of the family were popular and Labour ministers were careful never to express any republicanism in public — indeed, there is almost no sign of it in their private diaries either — but there were many Labour MPs pressing for a less expensive, stripped down, more contemporary monarchy, on Scandinavian lines. Difficult negotiations took place over the amount of money provided by cash-strapped taxpayers. Yet the Windsors triumphed as they would again, with an exuberant display which cheered up many of their tired, drab subjects. The wedding of the future Queen Elizabeth and the then Lieutenant Philip Mountbatten in 1947 was planned as a public spectacle. Royal weddings had not been so organized in the past. This was an explosion of colour and pageantry in a Britain that had seen little of either for ten years, a nostalgic return to luxury. Presents ranging from racehorses to cigarette cases were publicly displayed, grand cakes made and a wedding dress by Norman Hartnell created out of clinging ivory silk 'trailed with jasmine, smilax, seringa, and rose-like blossoms,' encrusted with pearls and crystals.

There had been interesting arguments before the wedding about patriotism, complaints about the silk having come from Chinese worms, and a rather over-effusive insistence on Philip's essential Britishness. The nephew of Lord Mountbatten was sold to the public as 'thoroughly English by upbringing' despite his being an exiled Greek

prince, a member of the Greek Orthodox Church, and having many
German relatives. In the event, Philip's three surviving sisters were not
invited to the wedding, all of them being married to Germans. He
showed himself wryly prepared to accept all this, though he was
reported to have annoyed the King by curtsying to him at Balmoral
when he saw him wearing a kilt.[37] The wedding was a radio event,
still, rather than a television one, though newsreel films of it packed
out cinemas around the world, including in devastated Berlin. In its
lavishness and optimism, it was an act of British propaganda and
celebration for bleak times, sending out the message that despite
everything Britain was back. The wedding and the later Coronation
reminded the club of European royalty how few of them had survived
as rulers into the post-war world. Dusty uniforms and slightly dirty
tiaras worn by exiles were much in evidence: the Queen's younger
sister Princess Margaret remarked that 'people who had been starving
in little garrets all over Europe suddenly reappeared'.

The Look of the Forties

History is mostly written about wars and politics and then, after that,
about the lives of people as expressed through schools, employment
and so on. Outside official history are the lives we actually lead, more
marked by births, love affairs, illnesses, deaths, friendships and coinci-
dences, than by public events. Those are the personal histories depicted
in novels, films and poems. But something is missing, because we also
live surrounded by stuff – rooms, chairs, plates, curtains, bags of pasta,
bowls, televisions, and beyond that, offices, shopping centres, roads
cluttered with signs, adverts and cars – all of which changes constantly
and colours or shapes the world in which our smaller histories happen.
For the consumer society, changing brands and ads are the scents
which suddenly bring back a moment in childhood or later: we walk
through life marking it off with a new rug, or the tune for a drinks
commercial.

In the forties, there were far fewer brands and a glaring insuffi-
ciency of 'stuff'. There was a shortage of furniture, cups, plates, lights,
curtains, towels, bicycles, radios – you name it, you couldn't find it.
The famous brands from before the war, whether for soap, cooking

materials, clothes or cars, were rather desperately still reminding people that they would return, as soon as possible. There was a natural tug back to the lost world of pre-war Britain, the designs and flavours people had been familiar with – art deco moulds from ten years earlier were pressed back into manufacturing service; old pot and pan designs were given a lick of cheerful paint and put back on sale; the vacuum cleaners and toasters which did arrive in shops had a sturdy, clunky, almost defiantly ugly look. But there was a strong push in the other direction, towards a new Britain that would look and feel brighter, cleaner, more rational, more open. This was partly driven by politics. Ministers wanted the slums replaced by airy communal housing and schools which would be three-dimensional expressions of a less fusty, cluttered nation. Labour believed in the public sphere and in planning; that meant straight lines and big spaces. In these years, public housing far outpaced private housing; and taste followed the money.

Changes in technology and the shortages of traditional materials like wood after the war drove architects and designers to express those political beliefs through brick and concrete, steel-framed windows and flat roofs. The prefab homes being hastily built in former aircraft factories may have been a stop gap, but something about their simplicity chimed with the mood; it was the coming, cut-price British version of the modernist architecture, sculpted from the new concrete and steel-rod systems developed on the continent before the war, and brought here by refugee, generally left-wing, architects. But what would go into these flats and houses? The designer Robin Ray, a key figure at the time, noted that the Council of Industrial Design had been formed in 1944, but its power remained until the early fifties, partly because of tax incentives: 'We naively felt that modern town planning and enlightened design of buildings and products would transform the environment and enhance the lives of people. Progress was made in many areas, helped by the socialist government.'[38]

This meant a stream of new-looking furniture, fabrics, crockery and rugs designed to fill the new-looking homes. There was not a surplus of much after the war, but there were surpluses of materials intended for warplanes or landing-craft, or indeed troops. So perspex, developed for gun-turrets in bombers, was tried out for table tops and even women's shoes. Royal Air Force uniform material was dyed green or brown and used to cover sofas and armchairs. There was a great amount of aluminium which could be effectively used for lightweight chairs and tables. Laminated wood techniques, steel rods and latex became popular. After the drab colours of wartime, there was a yearning for brightness; designers responded with abstract, whimsical and cubist patterns in primary colours.

Better-looking cooking pots, mugs, lights and cutlery were advertised, the first of them in the 1946 *Britain Can Make It* exhibition at the Victoria and Albert Museum, which had been emptied of its treasures during wartime. The show was quickly nicknamed 'Britain Can't Have It' by disgruntled citizens but its design work was hugely influential, not least on Scandinavians, who returned home and started manufacturing similar designs which would be bought in large quantities by the British over the next decade – a less familiar version of a story that would be repeated with cameras, motorcycles and aircraft. The result of the new designs, on show again in the Festival of Britain in 1951 at the end of Labour's era, was to decorate austerity with a sharp-edged, spindly, brittle and optimistic look, one that is now as securely of its era as lava-lamps or beanbags stamp the seventies. Some of the design now looks rather cold; perhaps it never truly caught on. But some of it, from the Roehampton flats overlooking Richmond Park, to the famous Jason stacking chairs, just like some of the young designers, including Terence Conran, would last.

What Did We Look Like?

Study photographs or film of a reasonable number of Britons of the mid-forties, and you are likely to notice striking physical differences; above all, bulky, creased clothes, tired-looking faces and bad teeth. From working-class women with great gaps and sharp edges in their smiles, to landed politicians with buck-toothed smirks, this was not a country able to take care of its appearance in the modern way. For good practical reasons, the male 'short back and sides' was almost universal. Women struggled to put on a show. American troops coming over here during the war had been warned that English girls would be a bit grubby and 'often cannot get the grease off their hands or out of their hair'. Women were advised to rub their hair with dry towels when they could not get shampoo, or to steam it over boiling water. Spongeing with lukewarm water had replaced regular baths for millions of people. To put it bluntly, many British people in the forties would, by our sensitive standards, have smelt a little. Cosmetics were hard to get, too. Women had used everything from cooking fat and shoe polish to soot and baby powder to make themselves up – though bought cosmetics were still regarded as a little racy by many older women and men.[39] Others put up with squints, semi-blindness or ugly, heavy-rimmed spectacles, which were not yet free. Buck-toothed, squinting and not overly clean: we were, in the mid-forties, very far from the scented, freshly dressed and sometimes surgically enhanced narcissists of modern Britain. People looked older at any given age than they would today – except the children who, dressed in shorts, dresses and buckle shoes, looked younger.

The dirtier air of coal-fuelled city life, and long traditions about respectability meant coats and umbrellas were much more often worn. In the City, on the football terraces and among women shopping, hats were almost universal. Photographs are a vivid reminder of how creased and rumpled the clothes of even quite well-off people looked. It was not only the war. These were still the days before easy dry cleaning and almost universal washing machines at home. In a country whose workforce was overwhelmingly manual, men's clothes were a straightforward marker of class and occupation; heavy jackets, thick wool trousers, leather boots for most; three-piece suits, also heavy by today's standards, with detachable collars, for the middle classes. Leisurewear was hardly known for most – simply a matter of using an older shirt, or swapping a suit jacket for a tweed one. Clothes had to last longer, so were inevitably patched and mended more frequently. During the war, most of the civilian clothes produced were so-called 'utility clothes', with special labels, and designed to save material; they had fewer pockets, seams and buckles. Turn-ups on men's trousers, then fashionable, were banned. The result of utility designs could be seen on every British street well into the fifties. Richer people still had their well-made clothes from before the war, but for the working classes, clothing rationing, which arrived in 1941, meant a struggle to stay warm and decent.

Because rationing affected the quantity of clothes you could have, but not their quality, it hit the poor harder. Government campaigns about how to reinforce or reshape old clothes, ranging from well-meant advice about reinforcing 'underarm areas', to unravelling old woollens and re-knitting them as something else, did not improve the mood. For women, faced with an almost impossible struggle to replace laddered stockings or underwear, the wartime fashions felt boxy and unattractive – service-style caps, or flat bonnets, with short skirts and masculine jackets, what was called 'man-tailored'. The dominant colours were dull, greys or dark blues or dark browns. On their feet women wore the heavy soled, heavily-strapped 'wedgie', or laced-up black leather shoes, endlessly repaired. If pregnant, they were encouraged to adapt their ordinary clothes – the ethos of 'make-do and mend'. Their children, they complained, tended to grow far too fast for the coupons. It was a time of ankles protruding from short trousers, jackets that would barely do up, mottled wrists hanging from outgrown jerseys. It wasn't that the post-war British did not know how to look smart. The imported American films showed immaculately dressed icons and the newspapers showed the richest, flashiest Britons, from Anthony Eden to the King, still beautifully tailored. But they could not afford to look smart. Some men found themselves avoiding invitations to drinks parties because they were ashamed of the state of their clothes. Women avoided brightly lit restaurants when their stockings had gone, and been replaced with tea-stains and drawn-on seams.

Under the hats or umbrellas, below the coats and suits, the British of the forties were also considerably leaner. Wartime rationing had actually increased the health and strength of the working classes whose diets had been nutritionally dreadful before it. By 1945, children were growing measurably taller. Fair and effective rationing of food and clothing was a prime domestic achievement of the wartime government. Organizationally, it was as complex and difficult as moving armies around the world, building instant harbours and invading Europe. Though there was some experience from the very end of the First World War to recall, it had been done almost from scratch, replacing the market with the queue and the ration book, distributing the same amounts of protein and starch to families on hill farms, in industrial Northern terraces and in Home Counties villages. If wartime opinion-polling is to be believed, it was even popular in the first few years. Some 44 million ration books, in buff, green or blue, were distributed. Regional offices were set up across the country and

1,400 local food control committees were organized. Everyone had to register with a local shopkeeper, who would get supplies of the rationed meat, ham, sugar, butter, margarine and the rest from centrally bought supplies accumulated by the newly formed Ministry of Food. With more people working away from home, more people ate out too, though in a frugal and strictly controlled way. There was a huge expansion of school meals; children were allocated free orange juice and codliver oil; works canteens and 'British Restaurants' were opened throughout urban Britain, serving plain and limited but nourishing food. A system of 'points', which allowed people to get tinned foods, dried fruits and other extras when they were available, had proved one of the great successes of wartime rationing.

For socialists, of course, this was more than sad necessity. It showed what could be done to achieve a fairer country. Yet if Labour thought rationing provided any kind of popular lesson for peacetime this would soon seem a great mistake. For though rationing was fair, it was also dull, monotonous, time-consuming and by the end infuriating. A portion of meat each week little larger than an iPod was not an existence the beef-eating British could endure for ever. During the war people had resorted to all sorts of bizarre concoctions to keep up their interest, everything from haricot beans flavoured with almonds making do as marzipan, to mashed parsnips masquerading as bananas, 'mock goose' made of potatoes, cooking apples and cheese, or jam made from carrots. The rich, particularly in London or when they had access to country estates, managed to avoid some of the effects of rationing: Boodles Club in London, for example, enjoyed a steady supply from hunting-and-shooting members of venison, hare, rabbit, salmon, woodcock and grouse – none of these things was rationed – though it failed to sell many portions of a stuffed and roasted beaver served on one occasion.[40] For most, rationing was the prime example of the dreary colourlessness of wartime life. After the guns had stopped, it went on unbearably long. It was still biting hard at the end of the forties. Meat was still rationed until 1954. And though the poor were better fed, most people felt hard done-by. Many doctors agreed. Shortly after that horrific 1947 winter was over, the *British Medical Press* carried a detailed article by a Dr Franklin Bicknell which argued that available foods were 400 calories short of what women needed each day, and 900 calories short of what men required: 'In other words, everyone in

England is suffering from prolonged chronic malnutrition.'[41] This was angrily disputed by Labour politicians, keen to point out the effect of all that free juice, codliver oil and milk on Britain's children. But people were on the side of Dr Bicknell.

Under the Skin: Belief

Below the skin, though, were the British of the forties fundamentally different to the British of today? This was then a religious society, though less so than in any previous time. In surveys people overwhelmingly described themselves as Christian, but communal worship and knowledge of the Bible was falling away. The Church of England saw one of the sharpest declines in membership in the decade from 1935 to the end of the war, losing half a million communicants, down to just under three million. (Another half million would be lost by 1970 and more than a million by 1990.) The Roman Catholics rose in numbers after the war, perhaps because of Polish, Irish and other European immigration, while the Presbyterians and the smaller churches also suffered decline. Though the first mosque in Britain had been built in Woking, Surrey as early as 1889, there were few Muslims or Hindus. North of the border, the Church of Scotland, which had only finally won full independence from the British State in 1921, was more popular than the English established church, and continued to grow until the early sixties. In the absence of a Scottish parliament, debates at the Kirk's ruling body, the General Assembly, had an authority and produced a level of newspaper interest unthinkable today. Scotland's higher religiosity – for the Catholics were strongly represented too – had its darker side in the persistence of Orange marches, bigotry and mutual suspicion on a scale which almost matched that of Northern Ireland. To the visitor, Britain would have seemed a very obviously Christian nation, with its State and Royal ceremonies, its famous and often controversial bishops, its religious broadcasting and above all its spires and towers in every suburb and village. The churches below those spires were at least thronged for marriages, funerals and the special services such as Christmas and Easter. Girls and boys were likelier to be in the Christian Scouts or

Guides; schools had prayers at morning assembly; Sunday schools were busy; the Army had its Sunday parade.

Some of the most eloquent cultural moments in the life of post-war Britain had religious themes, from the rebuilding of Coventry Cathedral, with its tapestries by Graham Sutherland, to the popularity of Benjamin Britten's wartime choral work *A Ceremony of Carols*. Perhaps Britain's best-loved serious painter was Stanley Spencer, who was turning out work in the forties and fifties based on his own idiosyncratic interpretations of biblical events – the Resurrection, Christ calling the Apostles, the Crucifixion. John Piper was famous for his watercolours and etchings of medieval churches; John Betjeman celebrated later, Victorian ones. Post-war Britain's major poet, the American-born T. S. Eliot, was an outspoken adherent of the Church of England. His last major book of poetry, *Four Quartets*, is suffused with English religious atmosphere, while in his verse drama *Murder in the Cathedral* he addressed an iconic moment in English ecclesiastical history. He would win the Nobel Prize for Literature in 1948. C. S. Lewis had become a nationally known Christian broadcaster during the war, with his *Screwtape Letters*, and for children there was soon to be the religious allegory of the Narnia books, the first of which, *The Lion, the Witch and the Wardrobe*, appeared in 1950. It could fairly be said that in this period, there still existed an Anglican sensibility, a particularly English, sometimes grave, sometimes playful, Christianity, with its own art and thought. It may have been wispy and self-conscious but it was also alive and argumentative, as it is not today. It was of course a limited and elite movement. Already, saucy revelations in the Sunday papers were where most people turned when they thought of immorality, not to sermons.

Were the British of the forties any more moral, or at any rate any more law-abiding, than the modern British? This is one of the hardest questions to answer. Conventions and temptations were just so different. On the surface, it was certainly a more discreet, dignified and rule-bound society. Divorce might have been becoming more widespread, but it was still a matter for embarrassment, even shame. Back in the early thirties, the average number of divorce petitions filed was below 4,800 a year. During the war, it jumped to 16,000. By 1951, with easier divorce laws, it was more than 38,000. In the forties and fifties, it still carried a strong stigma, across classes and reaching to the highest. As late as 1955, when Princess Margaret wanted to marry Group Captain Peter Townshend, the innocent party in a divorce case, a Tory cabinet minister, Lord Salisbury, warned that he would have to resign from the government if it allowed such a flagrant breach of Anglican principles. Divorced men and women were not welcome at Court. Homosexuality was illegal and vigorously prosecuted. Pornography was, for most people, almost unknown – 'dirty books' were on sale in a very few bookshops but 'smut' was still considered something mostly available for foreigners.

The censorship of the theatre, dating back to Walpole's time, was taken extremely seriously. Playwrights had to submit their plays to the Lord Chamberlain's Office at St James's Palace, which would strike out double entendre or vulgar language. John Osborne had a letter back about his play *The Entertainer* in March 1957, with sixteen alterations, such as 'Page 6, alter "turds". Page 9, alter "camp" . . . The little song entitled, "The old church bells won't ring tonight 'cos the Vicar's got the clappers". Substitute: "The Vicar's dropped a clanger".' Yet behind the firewall of censorship and law, there is plenty of evidence of a country just as sex-obsessed as it is now, and probably always was. The scatological outpouring in private letters and diaries is amazing, presumably the flip-side of public discretion. The war had involved years of disruption to family life, broken relationships, a lot of quiet domestic adultery, and a boom in homosexual activity, as tens of thousands of young, frustrated servicemen were let loose in darkened cities. One thing which would shock many people now, if they could be transported back, was the huge number of prostitutes working openly on the streets in the 'red light' areas of the cities, around Manchester city centre, Edgbaston in Birmingham and Edinburgh's Leith Walk. In London, the so-called Hyde Park Rangers and Piccadilly Commandos were gangs of prostitutes working almost unmolested by the police and earning small fortunes from horny soldiers.

Street crime had boomed particularly in London and in the words of one of the capital's historians by 1945 'the country was awash with guns, illegally sold by American servicemen for £25 for a handgun, or brought back by British servicemen from abroad'. Over the war years, though the population of London had dropped by some two million, the number of serious offences per head had doubled.[42] The immediate post-war years saw real problems, partly because of the size of the black market, armed racketeers, and the continued presence of deserters, of whom many thousands were hiding out, including an estimated 19,000 from the US Army. Because of frustration at the slow pace of demobilization, desertions increased after hostilities ceased. Films of the time sometimes reveal a semi-anarchic wilderness territory of bombed-out homes and urban wasteland, which may be policed by gangs. Memoirs confirm that many children and adolescents, lacking parents or simply profiting from the shaky administration of a great city returning to life, more or less ran wild.

Yet to get the tone of the times right, it is important not to forget that, among the rebellions against rationing and official incompetence, Britain was basically law-abiding. In a country awash with cheap handguns, struggling with profound resentments about shortages and a thriving black market, and still containing many deserters on the run, by virtually every count available, serious crime then fell. The guns did not lead to spates of shootings. Croydon did not become Chicago. Armed crime in London involving guns fell from a high of forty-six incidents in 1947 to just four cases in 1954. The number of people sentenced to prison fell by 3,000 between 1948 and 1950. The murder rate fell.[43] Indeed, overall serious crime fell by nearly 5 per cent per head of population in the five years after the war. One historian of British crime concludes: 'Perhaps the most peaceful single year was 1951, with a low level of crime, especially violent crime, following a brief increase in bad behaviour following the war.'[44] Bearing out the tricksiness of all statistics, this year is cited by others as a post-war crime peak, yet the general picture holds up. People respected the police and came across serious crime rarely. The various scares about violent racketeers in London, or lawless youths, were mostly confined to the papers. Foreign observers talked about the orderly, calm, law-abiding nature of British society as something rare in Europe or around the world. All of this matters enormously to Britain's self-image now, since commentators and politicians often point to the post-war era as a time of Edenic peace and order, far removed from the world of machine-gun-toting police and drug gangs. Why was Britain so well-mannered and lawful?

Some argue that tougher penalties are the most obvious reason. It is true that from 1946 until the year hanging ended, 1964 (though it was legally abolished two years later), some 200 murderers were executed. Other grim punishments, notably flogging, were on the wane; they were ordered infrequently in the fifties. The last judicial birching was approved by the Conservative Home Secretary, R. A. Butler, as late as 1962, though the practice continued in the Isle of Man and very occasionally in Scotland. Yet violent crime was on the increase again well before hanging was abolished. Its abolition cannot be the only reason. One obvious factor is that so many young men, the people who commit most crimes, were in the Armed Forces, latterly doing National Service. This did not simply take people off the streets. It provided discipline and the habit of obeying – and issuing – orders. Two generations of boys were marched off for short haircuts and taught to polish their shoes by fathers who had been in the services. Then there was the relative lack of opportunity. A society in which people barely have enough to eat and possess few movable goods is rather less prone to street crime than one in which every teenager totes an expensive mobile phone, and every urban street is lined with parked cars. Finally, not to be underestimated simply because it cannot be measured, there was the spirit of the times. The war had shaken everyone's sense of security – not just serving troops but the bombed and the evacuated and the bereaved as well. The Cold War would not diminish an underlying sense that life had become fragile. In these circumstances, it is hardly surprising that there was a profound post-war turn towards hearth and home and a yearning for security, order, predictability – in the street, in the neighbourhood, if it could not be there in the wider world.

These then, in all their variety, patriotism and hope, were the people whose fate was now in the hands of Clement Attlee and his ministers. We have looked at the difficulties facing the country and at the confused hopes of the new government. We know that the dream of a New Jerusalem, a socialist commonwealth, was never realized and that some historians see the 1945 government as a wasted chance. It is time now to look at what this government actually did.

What the Romans Did For Us

The post-war Labour government did the following things. It created the National Health Service. It brought in welfare payments and state insurance 'from the cradle to the grave'. It nationalized the Bank of England, the coal industry, which was then responsible for 90 per cent of Britain's energy needs, and eventually the iron and steel industry too. It withdrew from India. It demobilized much of the vast army, air force and navy that had been accumulated during the war. It directed armament factories back to peaceful purposes and built new homes, though not nearly enough. It oversaw a rationalization and shake-up in the school system, raising the leaving age to fifteen. It kept the people fed, though, as we have seen, not excitingly fed. It started to fight Communism in Korea and to develop the atomic bomb. It did these things against the background of the worst financial crisis that could be imagined, at a time when its own civil servants were drawing up plans for starvation rationing if the money ran out, and while meeting its obligations to the malnourished people of other countries, left bereft by war or crop failure. It harangued people to work harder and consume less. In its dying months it did its best to amuse and entertain them too, with the Festival of Britain. This combines to form the most dramatic tale in our peacetime history of a State organization doing things it actually meant to.

Without the war, clearly, there would have been no 'Attlee government' as we remember it. With the war, though, some major social reform programme became inevitable; wars shake up democracies violently, whether they win or lose. France and Italy saw a huge rise in Communist influence after the war. Britain did not. But had a post-war British government tried to shrug off the hopes for a brave new world shared by so many and encouraged by everyone from archbishops to newspaper editors, what damage would have been done to Britain's political system? There could have been no return to the thirties. After the privately run chaos and underinvestment of pre-war Britain people from almost all parts of the political spectrum thought central planning essential. Churchill's Tories would have done many of the things Labour did, just a little less so, and more slowly. By the time the old man returned to power again in 1951, he was promising to do more in some areas, such as housing. The historian of the Welfare State puts it like this: 'A country which had covered large tracts of East Anglia in concrete to launch bomber fleets, and the south coast in Nissen huts to launch the largest invasion the world had ever seen, could hardly turn round to its citizenry and say it was unable to organise a national health service; that it couldn't house its people; or that it would not invest in education.'[45] What was done after the war to remake Britain was not inevitable. There were lots of battles and individual decisions on the way. But some such quiet revolution, some big grab of state power, or extension of political will, was bound to have occurred.

Beveridge: Spin Doctor and Sage

If there is one man who deserves a place in the pantheon of reform, outside party politics, it is that cadaverous, white-haired, publicity-mad, kindly, harsh, determined and entirely impossible man, William Beveridge. He had left his wealthy upper-class circle to become a social worker in the East End of London, just like Clement Attlee. He then became a journalist and a civil servant before the First World War, a friend of intellectual socialists. He worked with the young Winston Churchill in the Liberal government, was one of the architects of rationing in 1916 and was later a Liberal MP. He knew Whitehall inside-out but left to become an academic, using the young Harold Wilson as his dogsbody. This was a hard life. Beveridge was fanatically hard-working, rising at six for a cold bath before spending the rest of his day icily wallowing in cold statistics, writing and dictating. When war came again, Beveridge decided that government could not properly function without him and pestered the Churchill team for a job. He was bitterly disappointed when Bevin, who disliked him intensely, finally shut him up with the offer of a review into the confusing array of sickness and disability schemes for workers. It was hardly glamorous or central to the war effort and Beveridge apparently wept tears of rage and frustration when he was told. He set to work, however, and quickly decided there could be no coherent system of work benefits without looking too at the plight of the old, women at home and children. Workers were not alone, self-sufficient. They had families.

They aged. He would have to devise a system to include everyone, while keeping the incentive to work. There would have to be family allowances, and a National Health Service, but all this would be undermined if Britain returned to the era of mass unemployment; so the State would have to manage the economy to keep people in work. Giving Beveridge a limited remit and telling him to get on with it was like giving Leonardo da Vinci some paper and telling him to doodle away to pass the time.

Earlier we noted that the spirit of Oliver Cromwell was abroad in the England of the mid-forties. Beveridge was urged by his helper, soon to be his wife, Jessy Mair, to adopt the language of Cromwell too. Soon he was stomping around telling anyone who would listen that he intended to slay five giants – Want (he meant poverty), Disease, Ignorance, Squalor and Idleness. Beveridge was addicted to what a later Britain would call 'spin'. He used his position as a well-known broadcaster, and his contacts with the press, to drip out advance hints of the great report he was preparing, which he clothed in millennial language. He was also lucky in his timing. After the bleakest of the war years, Britain's fate was on the turn. There were, inevitably, plenty who were nervous or hostile. Leading industrialists protested that Britain was fighting Germany to keep the Gestapo out of our houses not to build a costly Welfare State. The Conservative Chancellor, Sir Kingsley Wood, briskly told Churchill that Beveridge's plan would be unaffordable. Whitehall mandarins resented his egotism and self-promotion. But he had the wind at his back. Popular expectations were too high and memories of the thirties were too vivid for the white-haired giant-killer to be stopped.

Beveridge's was a long, detailed, number-filled report, longer than this book, with no pictures and very few adjectives. Yet there were queues in London on the day of publication waiting to grab copies. It sold like no government report before, and very few since. Within a month, 100,000 copies had been bought; eventually six times as many were sold. It was distributed to British troops, snapped up in America, and dropped by Lancaster bombers over occupied Europe as propaganda – 'Look, here's the kind of thing a democratic society promises its people.' A detailed analysis of the Beveridge Report was discovered in Hitler's bunker at the end of the war, ruefully describing it as 'superior to the current German social insurance in almost all points'.[46]

At home, unaware of the impact he was making in the unlikeliest places, Beveridge lectured. He wrote columns. He filled halls. He broadcast. A few months later the cautious Churchill acknowledged that, far from distracting attention from the war effort, the Beveridge Report was greatly boosting morale. He gave his first broadcast on domestic issues, accepting 'a broadening field for state ownership and enterprise' in health, welfare, housing and education, noting that Britain could not have 'a band of drones in our midst', whether aristocrats or pub-crawlers; and in a splendidly Churchillian twist announcing that 'there is no finer investment for any community than putting milk into babies.'

The inevitable tumble that follows a Report and White Paper – the watering-down, haggling, legislating and organizing – had to take place before the new National Insurance system was finally brought into being in 1948. Yet it was a fantastic feat of organization which puts modern government to shame in its energy and speed. A new office to hold 25 million contribution records was needed, plus 6 million for married women. It had to be huge and to go up quickly. Prisoners of war were used to build it in Newcastle; meanwhile a propeller factory in Gateshead was taken over to run family allowances. The work of six old government departments was brought into a new ministry. More than half the staff who were transferred were still working away with typewriters and fountain pens in the bedrooms of 400 Blackpool hotels and boarding houses where they had been sent for the war. Forms were printed, box files assembled, new teams picked. Jim Griffiths, the Labour minister pushing it all through and refusing to take no for an answer, wanted a thousand local National Insurance offices ready around the country, decently decorated and politely staffed. After being told a hundred times that all this was quite impossible, he got it. Britain has been a subtly different and slightly less dangerous place to live in ever since. The level of help given was rather less than Beveridge himself would have wanted, and married women in particular were still treated as dependents; there was a lot to be argued about over the next fifty years. Still, from Beveridge's first rough notes in an office where he was thought to be safely out of harm's way, to a revolution in welfare, sweeping away centuries of complicated, partial and unfair rules and customs, it had been just six years' work.

The NHS: Nye's Simple Idea

The creation of the National Health Service, which Beveridge thought essential to his wider vision, was an angrier task. Britain had had a system of voluntary hospitals, raising their own cash, which varied wildly in size, efficiency and cleanliness. Later, it also had municipal hospitals, many growing out of the original workhouses. Some of these, in go-ahead cities like London, Birmingham or Nottingham, were efficient, modern places whose beds were generally kept for the poor. Others were squalid. Money for the voluntary hospitals came from investments, gifts, charity events, payments and a hotchpotch of insurance schemes. Today we think of ward closures and hospitals on the edge of bankruptcy as diseases of the NHS. The pre-war system was much less certain and wards closed for lack of funds then too. By the time the war ended most of Britain's hospitals had been brought into a single national emergency medical service. The question was what should happen now – should they be nationalized or allowed back to go their own way? A similar question mark hung over family doctors. GPs depended on private fees, though most of them also took poor patients through some kind of health insurance scheme. When not working from home or a surgery, they would often double up operating in municipal hospitals where, as non-specialists, they sometimes hacked away incompetently. And the insurance system excluded many elderly people, housewives and children, who were therefore put off visiting the doctor at all, unless they were in the greatest pain or gravest danger. The situation was similar with dentistry and optical services, which were not available to anyone without the cash to pay for them. Out of this Labour was determined to provide the first system of medical care, free at the point of need, there had been in any Western democracy.

Simplicity is a great weapon. Nye Bevan's single biggest decision was to take all the hospitals, the voluntary ones and the ones run by local councils, into a single nationalized system. It would have regional boards but it would all come under the Ministry of Health in London. This was heroic self-confidence. For the first time, a single politician would take ultimate responsibility for every hospital in the land, bar a tiny number of private ones. Herbert Morrison, the great defender of municipal power, was against this nationalization but was brushed aside by Bevan.

A more dangerous enemy by far were the hospital doctors. What followed was the most important, most difficult domestic fight of the post-war Labour government's life. The doctors, organized under the Conservative-leaning leadership of the British Medical Association, had it in their power to stop the NHS dead in its tracks by simply refusing to work for it. They were worried about their standing in the new system – would they be mere state functionaries? And they were suspicious of Bevan, quite rightly. He had wanted to have the doctors nationalized too, all employed by the state, all paid by the state, with no private fees allowed. This would mean a war with the very men and women trusted by millions to cure and care for them. But Bevan, the red-hot socialist, turned out to be a realist and diplomatist. He began by wooing the top hospital doctors, the consultants. The physicians and surgeons were promised they could keep their lucrative pay beds and private practice. Bevan later admitted that he had 'stuffed their mouths with gold'. Next he retreated on the payment of the 50,000 GPs, promising they could continue being paid on the basis of how many people they were treating, rather than getting a flat salary. This wasn't enough. In a poll of doctors, for every one who said he would work in the new National Health Service, nine said they would refuse to take part. As the day for the official beginning of the NHS drew closer, there was a tense political stand-off. Bevan continued to offer concessions while also attacking the doctors' leaders as 'a small body of politically poisoned people' sabotaging the will of Parliament. Would the old Britain of independent professionals, with their cliques, status and fees, accept the new Britain of state control? They did, of course. More concessions and more threats brought them round. In the end, Bevan was backed by a parliamentary majority and they were not. But it had been a long, tight, nasty battle.

When the NHS opened for business on 5 July 1948, there was a flood of people to surgeries, hospitals and chemists. Fifteen months later, Bevan announced that 5.25 million pairs of free spectacles had been supplied, as well as 187 million free prescriptions. By then 8.5 million people had already had free dental treatment. Almost immediately there were complaints about the cost and extravagance, the surge of demand for everything from dressings to wigs. There was much anecdotal evidence of waste and misuse. There certainly was waste. The new bureaucracy was cumbersome. And it is possible to overstate the change – most people had had access to some kind of affordable health care before the NHS, though it was patchy and working-class women had a particular difficulty in getting treatment. But the most important thing it did was to take away fear. Before it millions at the bottom of the pile had suffered untreated hernias, cancers, toothache, ulcers and all kinds of illness, rather than face the humiliation and worry of being unable to afford treatment. There are many moving accounts of the queues of unwell, impoverished people surging forward for treatment in the early days of the NHS, arriving in hospitals and doctors' waiting rooms for the first time not as beggars but as citizens with a sense of right. If there was one single domestic good that the British took from the sacrifices of the war, it was a health service free at the point of use. We have clung to it tenaciously ever since and no mainstream party has dared suggest taking it away.

The People's Economy?

The same cannot be said of some of Labour's other nationalizations. The first, that of the Bank of England, sounds dramatic but had almost no real impact. Exactly the same men stayed in charge, following just the same policies. Nationalization of the gas and electricity industries, themselves already part-owned by local authorities as well as many small private companies, caused few ripples. Labour had talked about nationalizing the rail system from 1908, almost from the moment it became a party. The railway system had been rationalized long before the war into four major companies – London & North-Eastern; Great Western Railway; Southern Railways; and London, Midland & Scottish. By the mid-forties there was almost no real competition left in the system and periodic grants of public money had been needed for years to help the struggling companies out. The distance between rationalized and nationalized is longer than a single letter, of course, but since the government had taken direct control of the railways from the beginning of the war it was an easy letter to replace.

This did not produce a transport system of delight. Labour had the ultimate Fat Controller world-view. It wanted everything from lorries and ships to trains and barges under one giant thumb. The new British Rail would be only one part of an empire comprising the London Underground, canals slicing through the England of the industrial revolution, the grimy trucks of thousands of road haulage companies, the major ports and harbours and even travel agents and hotels. All this came under a single British Transport Commission. For the railway system, which had been the glory of the country, this meant a subsidiary position, answering to a new Railway Executive and his regional managers who would oversee the 632,000 staff, 20,000 steam locomotives and more than 4,000 electric commuter trains in the country. Among the stock were battered, rackety gas-lit carriages from the days of Queen Victoria and 7,000 horses used to pull rolling stock around shunting yards.[47] The post-war train system was more powerful than the pre-motorway road network, but it was now in dreadful condition and, because of the economic crisis and the shortage of steel, it would be starved of new investment. Unpainted bridges and dripping tunnels nearly a century old, creaking and failing signalling systems, clapped-out locomotives, rusted and broken lines, the lack of electrification and cold, uncomfortable carriages – none of that was the fault of nationalization. But nationalization without new investment was no answer to it either. The only people who did well out of rail nationalization were the original shareholders of the railway companies who were, to their surprise, rather well compensated.

In the forties, coal and steel stirred up more emotion even than transport. Coal provided nine-tenths of Britain's energy. Its smoke and smell hung heavily over every town and city. When the coal industry fell behind its quotas, or was interrupted by bad weather, the factories closed and the people shivered. Coal was also central to Labour's story. The 1926 General Strike had begun and ended with the miners and 'hard-faced colliery owners' were the group most despised by Labour MPs. Coal was red-hot. The ambitious young Harold Wilson, looking for a way to make a mark, wrote a book about how to modernize the industry. Socialist writers such as Priestley and Orwell used the awful conditions of the miners to rub readers' noses in what was wrong with Britain. So for Labour MPs, nationalizing the coal industry was what they were in politics for, as well as sweet revenge. The job was given to one of the government's older and more ideological members. Manny Shinwell had been a tailor's boy in

London's East End before moving to Glasgow and emerging as a moving force on 'Red Clydeside'. He was a stirring speaker and veteran MP but when handed the task of nationalizing coal and electricity, he found there were almost no plans or blueprint to help him. All anyone could dredge up was a single Labour pamphlet written in Welsh.

Shinwell managed the job by the due day, 1 January 1947. But his timing was catastrophic. As we have seen it was just then that the freezing weather stopped coal being moved and the power stations began to fail. You can hardly blame socialism for snow but, along with the food minister, John Strachey, Shinwell became a demonized figure for promising that there would be no power cuts. 'Shiver with Shinwell and Starve with Strachey' said the papers. More important in the longer term was the lack of planning about how to modernize the industry that kept Britain working, warm and fed. Many mines, operated under Victorian conditions by families which had owned them for decades, simply needed to be closed. In other parts of the coalfield, new mines needed to be sunk for, by 1947, Britain was producing a lot less coal than before the war. Modern cutting and winding gear was desperately required everywhere. So was a better relationship between managers and miners to end the history of mistrust and strikes. The miners got new contracts and a five-day week but the first major strikes spread within months of nationalization. On inauguration day, signs had gone up outside most collieries proudly announcing that they were now managed by the National Coal Board 'on behalf of the people'. In some cases, 'people' was scored out, and 'miners' written in. Over time, relations between local managers, most of them from the pre-nationalization era, and the miners did improve a little. Over time, investment did come in, and the worst pits were shut down. But the naive idea that simply taking an industry into public ownership would improve it had been punctured early. What matters is the quality of the managers. The historian Correlli Barnett was unkind, not unfair, to complain that Whitehall chose for the nationalized boards 'administrators of their own kidney, sound chaps unlikely to rock boats, rather than innovative leaders strong in will and personality'.[48] Coal was under Viscount Hyndley, a 63-year-old marketing man from the industry, an Etonian ran the gas boards and transport was overseen by Sir Cyril Hurcomb from the Ministry of

War Transport, 'a man whose entrepreneurial experience and knowledge of engineering were nil'. The political symbolism of taking over great industries on behalf of the people was striking but as politicians discover anew, every few years, talking about change and actually imposing it are very different things.

By the time the last big struggle to nationalize an industry was underway, the steel debates of 1948–9, the public mood was already turning. Labour did nationalize the iron and steel industry, which differed from coal and rail in being potentially highly profitable and having good labour relations. But it did so with a nervousness that showed the government felt a change in the weather. Labour had worked itself up, proclaiming that 'the battle for steel is the supreme test of political democracy – a test which the whole world will be watching.' Yet the cabinet agonized and went ahead only because of a feeling that, otherwise, they would be accused of losing their nerve. In the debates in the Commons, bright young Labour backbenchers rebelled. The steel owners were organized and vigorous. Labour had a torrid time and the Tories seemed to be regaining their spirits.[49] An over-excited Cripps told the Commons: 'If we cannot get nationalization of steel by legal means, we must resort to violent methods.' They did get it, but the industry was little shaken. Steel needed new investment almost as much as the coalmines and railways did – new mills, coke ovens, new melting furnaces. Again, though, nationalization helped not at all. Within just a few years more, it was largely returned to private ownership.

Nationalization would give Britain a kind of modernization, but a thin, underfunded and weak variety, nothing like the second industrial revolution its planners hoped for. Reversing it would give Margaret Thatcher some of her greatest victories, in the programme of privatization that followed some forty years after Attlee's government. The coal industry would virtually disappear after catastrophic strikes. The railways under BR would become a national joke, but then fall further after a botched privatization. The whole notion of state planning would fall from fashion.

Squatters and Prefabs

The first stories began to appear in newspapers in July 1946. Out of the blue, fed up with having nowhere decent to live, around forty-eight families had marched into disused army camps at Scunthorpe. Then it happened again, in Middlesborough when thirty families moved into a camp. Homeless people in Salisbury took over thirty huts there. At Seaham Harbour, just up the coast from Newcastle, eight miners and their families chalked their names on empty huts and began unrolling bedding. Then squatting began in Doncaster. In picturesque Chalfont St Giles in Buckinghamshire, a hundred families declared themselves the 'Vache Park Estate committee' and took over a military base. They elected a Mr Glasspool as chairman, who declared in best Ealing comedy mode, 'by sticking together, we can do it. If the local authorities try to move us out, they will have a bit of a job now.' Through August, the squatting gathered pace – Ashton, Jarrow, Liverpool, Fraserburgh in Aberdeenshire, Llantwit Major, one of the oldest towns in Wales. In Bath, an RAF aerodrome was seized. At Ramsgate, miners and their families took over gun emplacements. Families marched into an unoccupied Cardiff nurses' home. A London bus conductor and his family occupied an empty nursery in Bexleyheath. Some 500 people took over camps outside Londonderry. A Sheffield anti-aircraft battery was taken over. Most of the invasions were peaceful, but the squatters were determined. At Tupsley Brickworks army camp outside Hereford, where German prisoners had been housed, *The Times* reported that 'A British corporal refused them admission, but he was overpowered, the gates were forced and a party of about twenty men and a number of women entered the camp. They found ten empty huts, which were promptly allocated.' Six couples moved into a Royal Artillery camp in Croydon. At Slough, where thirty-two empty Nissen huts stood in the football stadium, squatters waited until the guards were distracted and infiltrated through hedges. Birmingham people took over flats.

By early autumn it was estimated that 45,000 people had illegally taken over empty huts, flats or other shelters. It was only then, however, that the spreading revolt really hit the headlines.

On the wet Sunday afternoon of 8 September, about a thousand people began to converge on Kensington High Street in London. They were mainly young married couples with children, including babies. Most carried suitcases. Taxis piled with bedding, and the odd furniture van, joined them. A carefully choreographed operation, it was organized by London Communist Party officials such as Tubby Rosen of Stepney and Ted Bramley, the party's London boss. They had been identifying and marking up empty properties in the capital. A reporter from *The Times* takes up the story: 'Those who could not find accommodation stood patiently in the rain while the scouting parties were sent out to inspect neighbouring property . . . Consultations were held under lampposts in the rain and there appeared to be an elaborate system of communications by messengers.' Around town, properties were duly taken over: Lord Ilchester's former London home and Abbey Lodge in Regent's Park, a building just round the corner from Buckingham Palace and flats in Weymouth Street, Marylebone, Upper Phillimore Gardens and further afield, in Ealing and Pimlico.

The authorities' initial reaction was superbly British. The Women's Voluntary Service (WVS) brought hot drinks, and the police, rather than trying to evict the families, supplied tea and coffee from Kensington Barracks. The press was sympathetic and so, it seemed, was much of the public. As the squatting continued, crowds gathered outside and formed human chains to pass food and drink through windows. In some streets, the police picked up the food parcels and brought them to the squatters themselves. Blankets, money, food, chocolates and cigarettes were collected for the families. Students from London University marched through the streets with banners declaring 'Homes for Everybody before Luxury for the Rich'. Some squatted properties soon had too much food to cope with. But as the rebellion went on, the official mood hardened. Electricity supplies were cut to some of the seized properties, local authorities were warned not to help them and mounted police were used to disperse sympathetic crowds. Squatters in Buckingham Palace Road wrote to the King to protest. A deputation went to Number Ten but was met by the Prime Minister's housekeeper, who told them Attlee was too busy to see them. The cabinet had decided the revolt had to be stopped. Nye Bevan, in charge of housing, announced that this was now a confrontation to defend social justice and led the government response against 'organized lawlessness'. The Communist leader Harry Pollitt retorted that 'If the

Government wants reprisals, they will get them. The working class is in a fighting mood.' In the end, the squatting revolt fizzled out and the Communists led the retreat. The clinching argument seems to have been a threat that people who squatted would lose their position in the queue for new council homes.

Housing was the most critical single post-war issue, and would remain near the top of the national agenda through the early fifties. Half a million homes had been destroyed or made uninhabitable by German air-raids, a further 3 million badly damaged and overall, a quarter of Britain's 12.5 million homes were damaged in some way. London was the biggest single example. Films of the post-war years, such as the Ealing comedies *Hue and Cry* and *Passport to Pimlico*, show vividly a capital background of wrecked streets, a cityscape of ruins, inhabited by feral urchins. But the problem was nationwide. Southampton lost so many buildings that during the war officials reported that the population felt the city was finished and 'broken in spirit'. Coventry lost a third of her houses in a single night. Over two nights, the shipbuilding town of Clydebank, which had 12,000 houses, was left with just seven undamaged.[50] Birmingham had lost 12,000 homes completely, with another 25,000 badly damaged. By the time people began to pour out of the armed forces to marry or return to their families, the government reckoned that 750,000 new houses were needed quickly. This was far more than a country short of steel, wood and skilled labour could possibly manage, at least by ordinary building. Worse, though there had been slum clearances, the old industrial cities, including London as well as Glasgow, Manchester, Liverpool and Newcastle, still contained hideous slums, blackened grimy terraces lacking proper sanitation, and in some cases lacking any gas or electric power supply too.

This was about a lot more than bricks and mortar. The war had separated husbands and wives, deprived children of their parents and in general shaken the family fabric of the country. Some 38 million civilians had changed address, a total of 60 million times. Many marriages had broken up under the strain of the war. Yet people wanted a return to the warmth and security family life can offer. There were more than 400,000 weddings in 1947 and 881,000 babies born; the beginning of the 'boom' that would reshape British life in the decades ahead.

With both marriages and births, these were really big increases on the pre-war years, a million extra children in the five years after the war. There were not nearly enough individual homes to go round, so hundreds of thousands of people found themselves living with their in-laws, deprived of privacy and locked in inter-generational rows. It was, admittedly, a time when people were prepared to live more communally, more elbow-to-elbow, than they would be later. Wartime queuing had revived a kind of street culture, as women spent hour upon hour standing together, inching forward, sharing their grumbles as they waited for the shutters to snap up. Cinemas and dance-halls were crammed with people trying to escape the cold and monotony of their homes. Without television, or central heating, and severely short of lighting, people were in it together. It was the least private time of all. With wartime requisitioning, evacuation and the direction of labour, many were lodging in unfamiliar rooms. So the sharing of toilets and squeezing past each other in small kitchens that so many new families had to put up with in the late forties, was not a shock. It was just a disappointment, like the dreary and meagre food, and the ugly, threadbare clothing. Some believe the popularity of the mother-in-law joke in British variety and television comedy, well into the seventies, was forged in the cramped family homes of the immediate post-war period. Public support for the squatters was perhaps not so surprising. What could ministers do?

The most dramatic response was factory-made instant housing, the 'prefabs'. They were designed for a few years' use, though a few of them were still being lived in sixty years later. Between 1945 and 1949, under the Temporary Housing Programme, a total of 156,623 prefabs went up, far fewer than the total of new homes needed, but a welcome start. They were a lot more than mere huts; the prototype 'Portal' bungalow, shown outside the Tate Gallery and in Edinburgh in 1944, came with a cooker, sink, fridge, bath, boiler and fitted cupboards too. Though, at £550, it cost fractionally more than a traditional brick-built terraced house, it used a fraction of the resources – it weighed, for example, just under two tons, as compared to about 125 tons for a brick house.[51] The houses were typically built in hastily converted aircraft factories – the Bristol Aeroplane Company made many – and then loaded onto lorries, with bags of numbered screws, pipes and other fittings. When they arrived at cleared sites, ready-painted, they would be unloaded and screwed together on a concrete plinth, often by German or Italian prisoners of war. Within a couple of days, they could be ready for moving into. The thirteen designs, such as Arcons, Spooners and Phoenixes, had subtly different features – some had larger windows, some had porches, some had curved roofs, some looked almost rustic – but they were all weatherproof, warm and well lit. People did complain about rabbit hutches or tin boxes but for many they were hugely welcome. The future Labour leader Neil Kinnock lived in one, an Arcon V, from 1947 until 1961, and remembered the fitted fridge and bathroom causing much jealousy: 'Friends and family came to view the wonders. It seemed like living in a spaceship.' As they spread around the country, in almost all the big cities and many smaller ones too, they came to be regarded as better than bog-standard council housing. Communities developed in prefab estates which survived cheerfully well into the seventies.

Dirty Stubs to Rich Spikes

The great grey stubs of the tower-block boom which ran from the fifties to the late sixties litter most of urban Britain. Never has newness turned dark so quickly. Rarely has revolutionary optimism been so quickly and abjectly confounded. This revolution was born, like others, on the European continent and imported to Britain a generation after the prophets of concrete modernism had spoken. Mies van der Rohe, Le Corbusier, Auguste Perret and Walter Gropius were idealists of the twenties and thirties who dreamed a new world of light, tall, glass-covered buildings springing up to free humanity. This was about more than architecture. It was to be social revolution accomplished with concrete and prefabricated steel, bringing hygiene and sunlight to the masses who had lived and worked in the dark, grimy and above all messy streets of industrial Europe. With the arrival of the Nazis many of the idealists fled, particularly to the United States, where their towers would glorify not socialism but American capitalism in its age of triumph. Some, however, came to Britain. Berthold Lubetkin designed beautiful white modernist structures for London, early multi-storey concrete flats, a famous health centre and the Penguin Pool and Gorilla House at London Zoo. Erno Goldfinger on the other hand went for vast towers to house human gorillas and managed to offend Ian Fleming sufficiently to be used as a Bond villain's name.

In other circumstances, avant-garde artists from Germany, Russia, France and Switzerland might have had limited impact in Britain, a country whose architecture had see-sawed between classicism and revivalism, and where the prefix 'mock' was not a term of mockery. But from the end of the Second World War through to the seventies, the shortage and foul quality of much older working-class housing meant a desperation for speed and short-cuts. Scotland alone had 400,000 homes without indoor toilets in the mid-fifties. Glasgow's slums were so bad they had been formally denounced by the Roman Catholic church as inhuman. The great industrial cities of the Midlands and the North of England were in almost as bad a way. Politician after politician promised more new houses, ever faster. Britain would end up building a higher proportion of state-subsidized houses than almost any comparable country – beating, in fact, most of the Communist-run countries of Eastern Europe. The idealist architects offered scale and speed – huge streets in the sky, thrown up fast. The local bosses of British cities seized these foreign dreams with both hands. There is a photograph from the late fifties and sixties endlessly reproduced. Actually, it is many photographs, taken in different cities at different times. But they all show the same thing: eager, powerful men in suits staring down, or pointing, at a small-scale model with cardboard blocks set across it.

The architectural visionaries and the scores of ambitious, modern-thinking British architects who worshipped them, drew their towers set against rolling fields, surrounded by trees, on sunny spring days. In Britain's cities, the municipal bosses were generally hostile to decanting populations out beyond their borders to entirely new settlements where they might have more space. People would want to stay in their own communities, they reasoned. Also, they wanted to keep the tax base and the votes. So instead, the towers tended to go up right in the middle of towns, on waste ground, or where old Victorian terraces had just been bulldozed. From 1958 councils got a central government subsidy for every layer over five storeys, a straightforward bribe to build up, not out. The new towers, which were only ever a minority of the total new housing, offered working-class families real benefits, though – fitted kitchens, underfloor heating, proper bathrooms, enough space for children to be able to stop sharing beds. The more ambitious and refined tower-block plans rarely got built: shortage of money and haste, plus a lot of local corruption, favoured quick-build thrown up by local companies.

Once, the different regions, counties and countries of Britain had boasted their own architectural traditions. Glasgow had her red sandstone tenements, London her ornate dark crimson brick apartments, Manchester her back-to-backs. Now, under the influence of a single modern aesthetic, identical-looking towers appeared, often bought off-the-peg from builders. The architect Sheppard Fidler recalled a boozy day out with Birmingham's Labour boss, the 'little Caesar' Harry Watton, when they went to inspect a prototype tower-block by the builder Bryant. It gives a flavour of the time: 'in order to get to the block we passed through a marquee which was rolling in whisky, brandy and so on, so by the time they got to the block they thought it was marvellous ... As we were leaving, at the exit, Harry Watton suddenly said, "Right! We'll take five blocks" – just as if he was buying bags of sweets! "We'll have five of them ... and stick them on X" – some site he'd remembered...'[52] Watton was a right-wing, anti-immigrant, pro-hanging Labour boss (not lord mayor, but chairman of the key committee in Birmingham). He was not corrupt but he was autocratic and self-righteous. There were Wattons everywhere. Some, like Newcastle's T. Dan Smith, working with the massive architectural practice Poulsons, were corrupt. Others, like the puritanical socialist Bailie David Gibson of Glasgow, were certainly not. One of Gibson's colleagues remembered him as frightening: 'white-faced, intense, driving idealist, absolutely fanatical and sincere ... He saw only one thing, as far as we could see: how to get as many houses up as possible, how to get as many of his beloved fellow working class citizens decently housed as possible.'[53]

Scotland and the North of England saw the most dramatic examples of the prefabricated mania. On the outskirts of Dundee, under the city's controversial Bailie J. L. Stewart, more new housing was thrown up per head than anywhere in Europe, including the vast hexagonal nightmare of the Whitfield estate, built by Crudens. Under Gibson in Glasgow, the huge thirty-one-storey Red Road flats went up, the tallest in Europe, and at astonishing speed. As time went on, lessons were learned and more dispersed, varied and decorated concrete developments appeared. Newcastle had a late example, the giant wriggle of the Byker Wall, as if the emperor Hadrian had turned residential developer. Mostly, though, the stubby blocks were much the same everywhere. West Ham or Kidderminster, Blackburn or Edinburgh – who could tell? And everywhere the same problems quickly began to crop up. Dispersed local communities did not easily reform when stuck vertically in the air. The entrance halls and lifts, so elegantly displayed in architects' watercolours, were vandalized and colonized by the young and the bored. Asbestos, it was discovered too late, was dangerous. Hideous condensation problems appeared. Walls were too thin for decent privacy. Shops were too far away.

In many cases, blocks were popular and well run in the early days, when people were proud of their new homes. The deterioration was human as well as concrete. A single drunken, fighting family could spread misery throughout many floors of a block. Two or three could wreck it. Councils who simply crowded tenants in, without considering problems such as those caused by having large numbers of children high up in the blocks, were at least as much to blame as Le Corbusier or Mies van der Rohe. It is true that some of the prefabricated, hurriedly flung-up blocks were dangerous. In May 1968 part of the Ronan Point tower block in east London, built with concrete panels, simply collapsed. Since the four deaths then, nobody else has been killed by a collapsing tower block and the craze to condemn them as inherently unstable matches the original craze to throw them up everywhere. Just as the slimy brick slums of the forties and fifties were blamed for producing hooliganism, so the new vertical slums were blamed for the vandalism of the sixties and seventies – even though some were being vandalized well before they were finished and open. Perhaps the bleakly uncompromising shadows they cast did have a demoralizing effect. You would have to be a very naive rimless-glassed modernist to love those dully repetitive lines.

Opinion began to turn against the towers, even among architects. Smaller-scale projects came into fashion during the seventies except in a few isolated and well-managed cities, such as Aberdeen. Tower blocks began to be blown up. Rochester destroyed all of its blocks to improve the look of the town. Later, Birmingham promised to do the same. Even Glasgow's Red Road flats were being discussed for demolition. In other places, such as Wandsworth in London, the blocks were repackaged, covered with brightly coloured panels and given a more decorative silhouette. Left-wing councils, which in the sixties had championed the blocks, began to champion cottage-style housing instead. Council house sales meant blocks in the most favoured areas began to be improved from the inside, by their new owners. Many were sold to housing associations, others were left to house asylum seekers, drug addicts and the most desperate of the poor. Through her history, Britain has seen many building crazes, most notably the vast sprawl of brick terraces during the industrial revolution and then the ribbon-development suburbia of the interwar years. Yet not even they have marked so much of the look of Britain as quickly and nastily as the tower block revolution. The concrete jungles have become the most easily despised, most universally rejected aspect of the British experiment in modern living.

So it is worth remembering that some survived with contented tenants. It is worth recalling that even some graffiti-stained tower blocks, if they have heating, hot water and working lifts, may be better places to live than the leaking, rat-infested terraces, with outside toilets and small gas fires that they replaced. We can add to the small credit side that had Birmingham, Glasgow, Manchester and London not built high then much less of the countryside within fifty miles of these cities, and others, would exist today. The new homes had to go somewhere. Tower blocks were said to be good because they prevented 'sprawl' – the very shabby-Tudor ugliness deplored in the thirties. And some sprawl certainly was stopped. Today, it seems, we are wiser. Architects are as keen on high density as ever but now want to devise street patterns, squares and low-rise homes on a human scale. By the early eighties Britain's housing shortage was, in general terms, solved by the concrete boom: some 440,000 homes were created in tower blocks alone. But migration and the break-up of families since then have created a new housing crisis and once again skyscrapers are coming back in fashion. They are different now. From Manchester's new forty-seven-storey Beetham Tower, with its queasy-making over-hang, to plans for a 66-storey shard-shaped London Bridge Tower, these are chic palaces for the urban rich, not upended slums. They are as close to Harry Watton's off-the-peg blocks as the drug habits of supermodels are to the ravages of heroin in prison. Architecture matters; but it does not matter as much as class.

Rebellion: No to Snoek!

Back in the forties, Labour's idea of Britain was beginning to take shape. This would be a well-disciplined, austere country, organized from London by dedicated public servants, who in turn directed a citizenry which was dignified and restrained. Sanitation, reason, officialdom and fairness; it was a Roundhead vision, without the compulsory psalms and military dictatorship. Unfortunately for Labour, the real country was nothing like this. It was (and is) a more disordered, self-pleasuring, individualistic place. Labour's ethic was about restraint and fair shares. Ministers viewed consumerism with disdain, a personality defect of Americans. Yet consumerism would soon erupt with a strength never known before. People were pleased with the free spectacles and the more generous insurance arrangements, and they took to the prefabricated houses, and accepted Indian and Pakistani independence without much problem. It was just that they loathed the restrictions, the queues and the shortages, and disliked being lectured about Dunkirk seven or eight years later. And so the British did what they always do, in their way. They rebelled. They did this not in the French fashion, violently, with flying cobblestones and wild manifestos, but quietly and stubbornly. As we have seen, they rebelled over housing shortages. They refused to wear the clothes they were told they should. And they would not eat what was put in front of them, either.

Diaries and letters of the time show a country utterly obsessed by food. There had been a general assumption that as soon as the war was over pre-war variety and spice would return to the shops. Instead rations were cut and the disappointment was bitter. One response was the rise in popularity of that wartime character, the spiv. The later BBC television comedy *Dad's Army* featured in the fictitious platoon, one Joe Walker, played by James Beck (who was even wilder than his character, and died at forty-four from alcohol poisoning). Walker is a double-breasted-suit-wearing, pencil-moustached, perky villain with a heart of gold, forever upending the moral pretensions of his betters by slipping them an illicit bottle of whisky, a carton of cigarettes or a pair of stockings for the missus. Walker is the service economy in guerrilla form. He is a criminal but one whom everyone relies on. After the war the real-life spivs, the traders and dealers on street corners or in cafes, came out of the shadows and became a recognized part of life under Labour.

Moral confusion about people taking the law into their own hands features in two of the hugely popular Ealing comedies, both first shown in 1949. In *Passport to Pimlico*, the citizens of an area around a bombsite find out they legally belong not to the United Kingdom but to the Duchy of Burgundy. As Burgundians, they are free from the rationing and petty restrictions hemming in other Londoners. Almost as soon as they have finished celebrating their freedom, they are swamped by a plague of spivs, jostling, threatening and causing a breakdown of law and order. They represent the suppressed greed and wild consumerism that socialists feared was always present under the surface – as indeed it was. When the British State responds by cutting off Pimlico with barbed wire, the Burgundians hold out, in a comic mimicry of the country's stand in 1940. The people of London take their side and throw them food to keep the 'Burgundians' from having to surrender. It seems clear that this was directly copied from scenes in the real-life squatting revolt eighteen months earlier. In a comic conclusion the tensions are resolved, just as in a Shakespeare comedy. The rebels reach an amicable agreement with the authorities and return to the ration-card Britain where everything is fair and ordered, if somewhat frustrating.

Whisky Galore!, shown a few months after *Passport to Pimlico*, comes down on the other side of the argument. It relates what happens when a cargo ship full of whisky, tellingly called the SS *Politician*, runs aground off the Hebridean island of Todday. The story is fictional, taken from a comic novel, but was based on real wartime events; the actual ship was called the SS *Cabinet Minister*. The islanders, like the rest of Britain, are whisky-starved and opportunistic. The film tells the story of how the island community steals and hides huge quantities of whisky which had been intended for North America, foiling the authorities in the shape of the English Home Guard commander Captain Waggett (played by Basil Radford; a precursor to Arthur Lowe in *Dad's Army*). In the film, the puritanical British State is subverted by a tightly knit and determined island community who end with a great dance of celebration and liberation. In Todday, unlike Pimlico, the people's yearning for good things triumphs. In real life, the rather heroic struggle of a lone exciseman to recover the whisky divided the islanders, led to convictions for theft and produced a poisoned atmosphere between families which lasted for many years. The fantasy, however, is remembered and the truth forgotten.

One can see the tension between the Burgundians returning to ration books, and the islanders of Todday beating the authorities to keep the stolen whisky, as a filmic version of the political tension between wartime-style controls championed by the Labour government; and the frustrated hostility exemplified by pro-free market Tories. Eventually the controls would be partly dismantled, rationing would end and the first great consumer boom would begin, more or less in parallel with Labour's loss of power in 1950–1. In the meantime, however, a surprising degree of petty criminality was tolerated in an otherwise law-abiding country, not just on the part of spivs but the shopkeepers bending rules to help old customers, or the people who filched a little from work, or the ordinary men in pubs who would buy an extra pair of stockings for their wives. This criminality, however, would not have existed without the privations of the time, and the impertinence of officialdom. A novelist looking back a decade later caught the mood:

> Ludicrous penalties were imposed on farmers who had not kept strictly to the letter of licences to slaughter pigs; in one case, the permitted building was used, the authorised butcher was employed, but the job had to be done the day before it was permitted; in another case, the butcher and the timing coincided, but the pig met its end in the wrong building. Never had a bureaucracy so flaunted its total failure to comprehend the spirit of the times, which was low and resentful . . . So really, almost everyone participated; it was a sort of pale, hangdog spivery in back kitchens and the rear of shops.[54]

There were other ways of rebelling. The British Housewives' League, formed in 1945 by a clergyman's wife to campaign against rude shopkeepers and the amount of time spent queuing, helped remove the hapless food minister Ben Smith over the withdrawal of powdered egg. Other foods brought into the country and foisted on consumers were regarded as disgusting. Horses were butchered and sold, sometimes merely as 'steak'. Whalemeat was bought from South

Africa, both in huge slabs and in tins, described as 'rich and tasty, just like beefsteak'. It was relatively popular for a short while, but not long. Magnus Pyke, later a popular television scientist, explained that though it tasted fine to the first bite of a drooling mouth, 'as you went on biting, the taste of steak was quickly overcome by a strong flavour of – cod-liver oil'.[55] Then there was snoek, a ferocious tropical fish supposed to be able to hiss like a snake and bark like a dog.

One of the odder vignettes of wartime Britain has the young Barbara Castle, then Betts, working for the fish division of the Ministry of Food.[56] She was quartered in a grand London hotel, the Carlton, which boasted large bathrooms and generously sized baths. These were filled with fish, to be observed for experimental purposes. Barbara Castle, in short, lived with a snoek. Her report on its behaviour must have been favourable because in October 1947 the government began to buy millions of tins of snoek from South Africa. Protein was in short supply. South Africa would take pounds, not the scarce dollars. So ministers tried to persuade the British that, in salads, pasties, sandwiches, or even as 'snoek piquante' with spring onions, vinegar and syrup, the powdery, bland fish was really quite tasty. The country begged to differ and mocked it mercilessly, buying very little. Snoek became a great joke in the newspapers and in Parliament. Eventually it was withdrawn and sold off for almost nothing as catfood.[57]

The Conservatives would later put out pamphlets showing pictures of a horse, a whale and a reindeer to show 'the wide choice of food you have under the Socialists'. Labour tried hard to keep the country decently fed during a grim few years, when much of the world was at least as hungry. But between the black market organized by the spivs, which spread very widely across Britain in the forties; the British Housewives' League, whose rhetoric would be remembered by a young Conservative student called Margaret Thatcher; and the spontaneous boycott of snoek, the public showed that it was fed up to the back teeth with rationing. Fair or not, as soon as they could, Labour from 1948 and then Tory ministers began to remove the restrictions and restore something like a market in food. American aid began to flow again and spiritually the mildly anarchic island of Todday trumped goody Pimlico.

Rebellion: a Bit of Skirt

It took a long time for British clothes to brighten up. Well into the sixties, children were still wearing the baggy grey shorts and unravelling home-made jumpers of the forties, men were still dressing in heavily built grey suits for social occasions, wearing macs and hats on their days out, and women were in housecoats and hairnets. But the forties did see one celebrated revolution, which showed just how frustrated women had become at the dowdy, dreary life they had suffered. It began in Paris, with the arrival of a new fashion house, created by a young designer who was in love with the *belle époque* France of his childhood, the pre-First World War country of swirling skirts, elegance and luxury. His name was Christian Dior and his revolution was christened the New Look. One of the British women who attended the unveiling in 1947 said she heard for the first time in her life 'the sound of a petticoat' and realized that at long last the war was really over.[58]

Dior's revolution was a return to billowing, deliberately unpractical skirts and dresses, what the magazine *Harper's Bazaar* described as 'a slight, slender bodice narrowing into a tiny wasp waist, below which the skirt bursts into fullness like a flower. Every line is rounded . . .' The long skirts and padded bosoms, the pleats and extravagance, burst like a firework display over a British womanhood described later as in a 'grey state . . . weary, dispirited, cramped and cross'. It was a direct challenge to the austerity culture of the government and quickly caused a genuine political battle. The British Guild of Creative Designers complained that they did not have the materials and could not give way to French irresponsibility. Labour MPs busily threw themselves into the fight against frippery. The beefy and redoubtable Mrs Bessie Braddock denounced the New Look as the 'ridiculous whim of idle people'. Mabel Ridealgh MP said it was being foisted on women and promised that housewives would not buy it. All this padding and artificiality was bad because it made for 'over-sexiness', she added; the New Look was turning women into caged birds and removing their new freedom.

Yet from the young princesses of the Royal Family downwards, women were ignoring the political orders and doing everything they could to alter, buy or borrow for the Dior look. Ruth Adam, who worked in the Ministry of Information during the war and later became a novelist, argued that a generation of girls who had been ordered to work in factories, on pain of prison if they refused, did not see it as a liberation:

> To them, Labour MPs who lectured them about wearing 'sensible' clothing, suitable for productive work, were the same breed as the women officers who had routed them out of doorways where they were having a goodnight kiss, and sent them back to camp; and as the forewoman who had shouted at them for spending too long in the Ladies while Russia was waiting for aeroplane-parts. Now they did not have to listen to lectures about hard work and freedom any more, but could think about being feminine and glamorous.[59]

There was a pent-up yearning for the better, more colourful life that middle-class people, at least, could remember from before the war – everyone from their twenties onwards would have had a reasonably vivid recollection of mid-thirties consumerism. In a world in which men and women were still wearing roughly fitted and standardized demob suits, handed out with hats, ties and shoes as you left the forces, clothing was a powerful symbol of prosperity postponed.

Knobbly Knees and Other Fun

In and out of their homes, what were the British of the forties doing for fun? They were certainly not watching television, something owned by less than 0.2 per cent of the adult population in 1947 and by only 4 per cent in 1950. They were not travelling abroad for their holidays. For one thing, people had less time on holiday, and less money to spend too. The Holidays with Pay Act, passed shortly before the war, had hugely expanded the number of people with guaranteed paid holidays but a fortnight was more common than a month. In 1947, in the days before jet travel and with the amount of money one could take severely restricted, just over 3 per cent of people holidayed abroad, the vast majority being wealthy and going no further afield than the Mediterranean or northern France. They did not drive around the British countryside, either, or 'go motoring' in the pre-war phrase; petrol rationing had seen to that. But in that same year, slightly over half the British did take some kind of holiday. Many took the train to one of the traditional Victorian-era seaside resorts, which were soon bursting with customers. Others went for cycling and camping holidays – the roads were by modern standards almost empty of traffic. Yet more would take the charabanc or train to one of the new holiday camps, run by such early entrepreneurs of leisure as Billy Butlin.

The South African-born Butlin had come from a broken family and, on his mother's side, fairground barkers. She gave him his first taste of the showman's life with her gingerbread stall which she took around West Country market towns. After a much-interrupted education and a short spell as a commercial artist in Canada, followed by service in the war, Billy Butlin began a hoopla stall in the twenties. Year by year, he slowly built up a business in amusement parks – with haunted houses, helter-skelters, hoopla and merry-go-rounds. His big breakthrough was getting the European licence for selling the new Dodgem cars. Then, having spotted the miserable time spent by many families in seaside landladies' accommodation, he opened his first camp at Skegness in Lincolnshire in 1936.

Holiday camps of different kinds, often run for employees of a particular company, had existed before. But Butlin's Skegness was a hugely ambitious undertaking, with a swimming pool, theatre, cinema, many amusements and – crucially – creche facilities so that parents could spend time together without their children. A second camp followed at Clacton two years later and after handing over facilities to the armed forces, he ended the war with five large holiday camps just at the opportune moment. A tough little man, who had carried a cut-throat razor in his top pocket while building his fairground and exhibition business before the war, and who boasted to friends that his aims were 'money, power and women', Butlin had a shrewd understanding of what war-weary people wanted. He offered colour, fun, warm cabins, surprisingly good food and almost constant activities, from dancing to the famous 'knobbly knees' and 'glamorous granny' competitions.

Butlin, who was a millionaire within two years of the war ending and who, after various financial crises, would be knighted and receive the Queen at one of his camps, was targeting the middle classes as much as the better-off workers. Italian opera, Shakespearean productions, radio stars, politicians, the odd archbishop and sporting heroes were all invited to the camps – and came. There was nothing 'naff' about the camps, certainly in the forties and fifties, their heyday; indeed, for a lot of people they were pricey. After the wartime experiences of everyone mucking in together, the morning-to-bedtime activities provided by the Redcoats, with their relentless jollity, seems to have been welcomed. Butlin had his fingers burned with an ill-timed attempt to expand into the American market with a Caribbean camp in 1948, and the mass overseas tourism which began in the sixties would end the glory days of his camps, and their rivals. But for millions of British people they would remain a synonym for summer holiday well into the age of Benidorm. And, if cheap air travel falls victim to oil price rises or worries about global warming, the age of the domestic holiday camp may yet return.

Outside the annual holiday, the traditional spectator sports made a swift post-war return. Football had been badly hit during the war years, not just because so many players were away in the forces, leaving veterans the field to themselves, but because the English Football League had been suspended, and the country simply divided into north and south. New rules meant that League players had numbered shirts, could earn up to £12 a week, and that games could be played until they produced a result (though in 1946 this meant Doncaster Rovers and Stockport County playing into the darkness after 203 minutes without a goal, there being no floodlighting then). The great soccer teams were soon back in action, to capacity crowds.

Stanley Matthews, the Stoke barber's son who was a pre-war legend, was back amazing crowds for Blackpool after the war. In 1953, when Matthews was the ripe old age of thirty-eight, some 10 million people watched him in the first televised Cup Final. By 1948–9 there were more than 40 million attendances at football matches and a general assumption that British football was the finest there was, something seemingly confirmed the previous May when Britain had played a team grandly if inaccurately named the Rest of the World (they comprised Danes, Swedes, a Frenchman, Italian, Swiss, Czech, Belgian, Dutchman and Irishman) and thrashed them 6-1. That illusion would be dispelled before long, but in other ways too this was a golden age of football. The stands were open and smelly, the crowds unprotected and the greatest stars of the post-war era still to come. But football was relatively uncorrupt, was still essentially about local teams supported in their immediate area, and was not dirty on the pitch: throughout his long career Matthews, for instance, was never cautioned, never booked.

Another famous footballer of the time was Arsenal's Denis Compton. It is just that he was still more famous for cricket, which became massively popular again after the war. Some three million people watched the Tests against South Africa in 1947 and Compton's performance then and in the following years produced a rush of English pride and mass enthusiasm. The cricket writer Neville Cardus found him the image of sanity and health after the war: 'There was no rationing in an innings by Compton.'[60] In cricket as in football, many of the players were the stars of pre-war days who had served as PT instructors or otherwise kept their hand in during hostilities; but with the Yorkshire batsman Len Hutton also back in legendary form at the Oval, cricket achieved a level of national symbolism that it has never reached since, not even in the heyday of Botham or the summer of 2005. Again, as with football, the stars of post-war cricket could not expect to become rich on the proceeds. Hutton, a builder's son who first made his name beating teams of public schoolboys on behalf of London council schools, became England's first professional captain of the century in 1952 and the dishevelled Compton, whose father had worked in a chemist's shop, first came into decent money as the face of Brylcreem adverts.

Greyhound racing, using electric hares developed before the war, was a prime working-class focus for betting. The sport had begun in Britain in 1926 at Manchester's Belle Vue stadium and spread quickly across the country; unlike horse-racing, it was something that millions of people in the industrial towns could go and watch near home, and many of the most famous dogs were bred and trained by people using a narrow back garden or local parks. The greyhound tracks were also used for Speedway – the 500cc brakeless motorcycle racing which had arrived from Australia in the twenties and which went through a big expansion after the war. So too, more bizarrely, did bicycle speedway, with men and boys pedalling furiously around bombsites throughout Britain, the courses marked out with painted lines on grass or house-bricks. Cities such as Coventry, Birmingham and London played 'Test matches' against each other and there was even an international, England against Holland, in 1950. Eventually, rebuilding removed the courses and the craze gently subsided.

But the main leisure activities of the time were more traditional. Britain was, then as now, gardening-obsessed. Pottering around in a shed was how many a British male liked to spend any spare time, not in the pub. There was a post-war boom in attending football and cricket matches. Cinema, though, was for everyone, and to give some idea of its popularity, it is worth recording that in 1947, there were around ten times as many visits to a film as there are today, with a much smaller population. At the post-war peak, there were 4,600 cinemas in the country, each showing news films alongside the main and second features. The British film industry, which extended far further than Ealing, was turning out a steady flow of wartime adventures, history films, adaptations of Dickens and romances, but was not then or ever really able to stave off the power and glamour of Hollywood.

Did It Matter, Darling? Theatre After the War

After the war, you would not have bet on British theatre, an old national glory, surviving as something that mattered. Though television had been suspended during hostilities, cutting out dramatically during a Walt Disney cartoon, and was only reintroduced in 1946 to a small audience around London, it was clearly going to present a challenge. In 1950 there were still only 350,000 television licences but the technology and appetite were clearly apparent. The first television sit-com, *Pinwright's Progress*, had begun as early as November 1946. The first BBC attempts to produce television plays were stilted and badly lit but had already proved popular. As we have seen, cinema audiences had shot up during the war years and there was, however briefly, a thriving British film industry. For the big stars, the money was in film and if at all possible, in Hollywood. Worse, British theatre before and during the war had produced little new writing of major significance; it had become an embattled heritage theatre, with astounding Shakespearean performances, plus musical reviews and other light fare to keep people's spirits up. There had been nothing like the energy and ingenuity of the film-makers as they responded to big social and moral questions thrown up by the war and its aftermath. For these failures, history has alighted on a single scapegoat. His name was Hugh Beaumont, but his friends and his many enemies called him Binkie.

His company, H. M. Tennant Ltd, was responsible for a seemingly endless run of musical and popular hits. Later on, after the theatrical revolution of the late fifties and sixties, Beaumont, who had been born in Cardiff in 1908, would be reviled as everything that was worst about the old ways, a conventional queenie Tsar of the West End, relying on drawing-room comedies, lavish sets and star names to keep the audiences happy. He would be regularly accused of running a gay mafia for friends such as John Gielgud. Much of this is unfair. Beaumont was not so timid. He was ready sometimes to take risks, such as with the controversial 1949 production of Tennessee Williams's powerful *A Streetcar Named Desire*, starring Vivien Leigh. It was denounced by the Public Morality Council as 'thoroughly indecent . . . we should be ashamed that children and servants are allowed to sit in the theatre and see it'; the Arts Council suddenly withdrew its support, and planned Royal visits were cancelled after an outcry about American 'sewage' and sex-obsession. In beautifully produced, no-expense-spared productions such as *Oklahoma!*, *West Side Story* and *My Fair Lady*, and gripping dramas such as Rattigan's *The Winslow Boy*, Beaumont offered the middle classes of London and the Home Counties an escape from daily life and dreary politics. He made a great deal of money for his theatres and backers, and would carry on doing so for many years to come. He was the nearest equivalent to the huge popular successes of Andrew Lloyd Webber's musicals in the final decades of the century, offensive to the intellectual elite, perhaps, but keeping the West End solvent and busy. Nor was he any kind of philistine; perhaps his closest acting collaborator was the great John Gielgud, and he was responsible for some still-famous productions of Shakespeare.

Beaumont stood in the middle of a glossy circle of talent, much of it gay, which celebrated luxury and wit at a time when the country seemed short of both. The most successful of his playwright collabor-ators was Terence Rattigan, born in 1911 to a diplomat father who was sacked from the Foreign Office after an affair with a Romanian princess. Rattigan had made his name before the war with *French*

Without Tears but his most famous and well-made plays came in the forties and fifties – sharp, poignant studies of upper middle-class life such as *The Browning Version, The Deep Blue Sea* and *Separate Tables.* Homosexuality is a hidden theme, necessarily so at the time, but the veneer of clipped, upper-crust politeness made Rattigan an easy target when the national mood turned. In a notorious preface in 1953, he seemed to confirm all his critics' case by explaining the importance to him of 'Aunt Edna', the audience member always inside his brain when writing, a 'nice, respectable, middle class, middle aged, maiden lady with time on her hands and the money to help her pass it'. Rattigan, like Beaumont, would fall suddenly and dramatically out of fashion – the days would soon pass when entertaining Aunt Edna, rather than heaving verbal bricks at her, was what ambitious play-wrights wanted to do.

Among Beaumont's other key collaborators was Cecil Beaton, the photographer and designer. Born in 1904, Beaton first made his name by photographing the 'bright young things' of the twenties. He would survive to take pictures of the rock stars of the sixties and even punks of the seventies, having a long career as a Royal portrait photographer in between. His stage work exemplified the 'ooh, aah' effect that Beaumont loved, exotic and witty designs for the pinched post-war public; his film designs would later win him a pair of Oscars. An older star in the same firmament was Ivor Novello, born in 1893 who would die six years after the war's end of a heart-attack, and who had been badly shaken by a short prison sentence in Wormwood Scrubs for a wartime motoring offence. Novello's career had included composing, notably the patriotic First World War song, 'Keep the Home Fires Burning' and a stream of musicals, ending with *King's Rhapsody* in 1949 and *Guy's the Word* in 1951. Strikingly good-looking, Novello's homo-sexuality was carefully hidden from his legion of female fans; at his funeral women outnumbered men mourners by around fifty to one.

But the best-known of this group of gay stars was Noël Coward, who was forty-six by the time the war ended. By now he was acknowledged as 'the Master' after a stream of hits, such as *Cavalcade* and *Private Lives* made him one of the world's highest-paid writers. Though he had self-consciously posed as a decadent drug-taking dandy in the twenties, virtually inventing high English camp, and was briefly taken up by the intelligentsia, Coward became increasingly mainstream. His patriotism was not ironic and he bitterly regretted the passing of British imperial status; his wartime films were morale-boosters. *In Which We Serve*, the 1942 film about Lord Louis Mountbatten's destroyer HMS *Kelly*, and *This Happy Breed* helped consolidate his status as Greatest Living Englishman and although the immediate post-war years were a time of relative failure, his plays and influence would continue through the fifties and sixties. Coward showed that the British could be light, witty, amoral and yet also patriotic; he expanded the limits of the accepted national character. For this, and his devastating wit, he survived even when the kitchen-sink realism, which he loathed, took over the stage.

Though the forties and fifties saw the beginning of a new theatre, it is salutary to remember that these decades were just as coloured by people who had been born in Victorian or Edwardian times, and carried a whiff of Oscar Wilde's London around with them. Novello, Beaumont, Coward, Beaton and Rattigan were all gay, mainstream middle-class entertainers of one kind or another, highly talented and overtly patriotic. Just because they would then be pushed aside by a new generation, the self-publicizing Angry Young Men and the producers who brought talents like Samuel Beckett and Bertolt Brecht to the British stage, does not mean their years in the sun never happened. The wit and wistfulness of the Binkie Beaumont era was another British way of facing a future of grim and guttural questions. Beyond the theatre proper, it was a tone repeated in the hugely popular novels of Nancy Mitford, and the arch television performances of Joyce Grenfell.

The other dominant figure on the British post-war stage was William Shakespeare. Rarely since the days of the earlier Elizabeth had so much Shakespeare been performed to such excited adulation. Contemporary audiences thought Laurence Olivier, Ralph Richardson and John Gielgud were the equal of any Shakespearean actors, ever. They may well have been right. The Old Vic theatre at London's South Bank, seen as an embryo National Theatre, was turning out a stream of Shakespeare; the young Peter Hall, looking back at the early fifties, reflected that 'by the time I was twenty-one, I had seen the entire canon, some of it many times, and you could not do that now.'[61] There was talk of a 'bardic traffic jam' in the West End. After the wartime patriotism of Olivier's film version of *Henry V* and with a dearth of strong new writing, it was perhaps inevitable that so many directors and actors would turn to England's greatest writer, as well as to other established classics. For a literate, culture-starved public, there was nothing to complain about in that. Shakespeare probes as deeply into the human state as anyone, before or since. Audiences would reel from the latest Olivier performance as emptied and wrung-out as it is possible to be. The same goes for the few other great dramatists regularly performed at the time – Chekhov and the Greek tragedians.

Yet the question would not go away: was there nothing more contemporary, nothing more political, to be said on the stage? To ask whether the theatre matters is, in one sense, a meaningless question. If it gives people a unique insight into their situation; even if it only entertains them, then surely that is enough. Yet in other times and places the theatre has aspired to do more, to function as a social and political force. Despite censorship, it had shaken up pre-Revolutionary Russia. It had mattered in Weimar Germany, post-war Paris, and would again in the United States as the Americans experienced anti-communist hysteria and the moral impact of the world's first mass consumer society. So why not Britain? One historian of the theatre, reflecting on the early fifties, found the London stage 'completely indifferent . . . to contemporary events. The heavy costs of a rearmament programme necessitated by the Korean war; the inflationary pressures that this produced in a still war-weakened country; the continued shortages caused by rationing; the dramatic impact of the welfare state . . . the manufacture of the first British nuclear bomb: all failed to impinge upon the West End stage.'[62] Anyone who cares about live theatre hopes that the unique coming-together of certain actors, words and audiences, will produce a transformation of some kind. This was still, just, the pre-television age. The possibility of British theatre meaning more than a pleasant, or stirring, night out, was still open.

By far the most dogged and courageous attempt to make theatre matter was led by one of the true cultural heroes of the time, a Cockney-born outsider who fled RADA for a career of provincial poverty. Joan Littlewood had been heavily influenced by a communist-inclined Salford actor, Jimmie Miller, who would later change his name to Ewan MacColl and lead the folk-song revival. In the thirties, they had produced German-influenced left-wing or agitprop plays with their touring Theatre of Action, had been offered work in Moscow, and been blacked by the BBC. Reforming after the war, they hit upon the name Theatre Workshop ('workshop' would eventually be appended to every banal meeting in schools, businesses and colleges, but was then, used in this sense, a new coining). Touring through Kendal, Wigan, Blackpool and Newcastle, they would be the very first act to exploit the new Edinburgh International Festival as 'fringe' performers and could hardly have been a starker contrast to the metropolitan flash of Binkie Beaumont. Their first major play, created by Miller, was *Uranium 235*, an impassioned and funny account of the road to the nuclear bomb, with a strongly anti-nuclear message at a time when, as we have seen, the pro-Bomb Labour government was widely supported.

Theatre Workshop mixed its political fare which eventually culminated in *Oh, What a Lovely War!* in 1963, with half-forgotten Elizabethan and Jacobean classics. There were also new plays, including by the Irish republican and drunk, Brendan Behan, whose beer-sodden and misspelled manuscripts were first recognized by Littlewood as works of genius. In every case, her shows cast aside the overwrought, self-conscious style of West End acting and direction. The cast and the production staff lived almost on the breadline, making their own sets and costumes, even after finding a semi-permanent home in the rundown old Theatre Royal at Stratford, in London's East End. Critics began to come to the performances, and they would win rave reviews travelling to Paris and Eastern Europe; among the actors who worked with Littlewood would be Richard Harris, Roy Kinnear and Barbara Windsor. Yet the conservative-minded Arts Council kept them starved of funds, and political censorship plagued the group's history. When they had popular hits, such as Shelagh Delaney's 1958 *A Taste of Honey*, a shocking story about a dysfunctional family, written by a nineteen-year-old from Salford, or Lionel Bart's *Fings Ain't Wot They Used T' Be*, a Cockney musical a year later, these transferred to the West End and made a mint. Back in Stratford, Littlewood, with her long-time lover Gerry Raffles, struggled to pay the bills and turn good publicity into a secure future. On one famous occasion when Behan was being interviewed while almost incoherently drunk by Malcolm Muggeridge on BBC Television, Littlewood was reduced to crouching on the floor, holding onto his legs so he would not fall. She harassed and harangued, campaigned and cajoled. Eventually the temptations of proper wages, and the pressures of underfunded theatre on the fringe of London, lured too many people away and destroyed Theatre Workshop.

Yet the Littlewood story deserves to come ahead of the far more famous theatrical rebellion of the 'Angry Young Men', which began with John Osborne's play *Look Back in Anger* in 1956. The 'Angries' were partly a good PR stunt by the press officer of the Royal Court Theatre. They barely existed as a group, certainly not of the theatre. Newspaper hype, picked up by historians, implied that before them there had been no fresh drama in post-war Britain beyond the odd limp verse play by Christopher Fry or a middle-class romp produced by Binkie and acted by a clique of waspish homosexuals. Though Osborne himself contributed to the legend, in bitterly homophobic tirades later in his life, it is entirely untrue. The two great critics whose energy helped drive British theatre into a new age, Harold Hobson of the *Sunday Times* and Kenneth Tynan of the *Observer*, were intensely interested in Theatre Workshop and gave some of its plays rave reviews well before Osborne came along. Littlewood's problem was that her group were too obviously left-wing at a time when the Establishment was still staunchly conservative and Cold War fever was raging. The Angry Young Men's anger was less clearly directed. Comfortingly, it had no programme, no overseas admirers, no ideology. Had Theatre Workshop emerged a decade later, in the mid sixties, it might have found stronger financial support from an Arts Council and BBC by then leaning to the liberal left. But of course, in that case, it would have pioneered nothing.

Most of us think of the story of theatre as the story of actors, whose familiar faces and fruity memoirs entertain more mundane lives. Others, particularly in universities, think of a theatre as being succession of writers and playscripts – Rattigan, Wesker, Stoppard, Hare, Brenton – as if drama was fundamentally something written down, a wayward branch of solid prose literature. And of course, this is true: no great acting, no good words, no theatre. Yet the real driving force in a nation's theatre is often provided by the producers and entrepreneurs, the people who shape the institutions, discover the plays, coax the companies. So, if Joan Littlewood found Behan and sustained Theatre Workshop, another contemporary hero is George Devine, the man who found Osborne and created Royal Court's English Stage Company. An actor who had become increasingly enthralled by new

French techniques of experimental theatre before the war, which he spent fighting in the Far East, by the fifties Devine was an experienced director. At the Old Vic Centre he had overseen a radical programme of training and production, working on Shakespeare, opera and new work too. But he felt there was something lacking, a dearth of modern plays at a time when 'there had been drastic political and social changes all around us'. He was unlike Littlewood in being already a cultural insider and certainly not communistically inclined (though he admired the German Marxist playwright Bertolt Brecht). Devine drew around him some of the best young actors in London, people like Joan Plowright and Alan Bates. One of his closest friends was Samuel Beckett. But his great coup was picking up a manuscript by a younger actor, a rather less successful one.

On the hot afternoon of 12 August 1955 John Osborne was lounging on an old Rhine barge tied up near Hammersmith on the Thames, the cheap houseboat where he was living. He had written *Look Back in Anger* over nineteen days, consumed with revulsion about the state of the country, and sent his wispy typescript to as many agents and theatre managers he could find an address for. Every one had briskly refused it. Osborne was in a hole. He had acted his way round the more obscure theatres of provincial England and was flat broke. A vegetarian, he and his house(boat)-mate had been reduced to gathering nettles from the riverbank to boil and eat. The creak of rowlocks signalled the arrival of Devine, a fat man sweating in a small boat, before he was hauled up on deck by Osborne. Devine had loved the play, and now cross-questioned Osborne; he had a prejudice against homosexuals and in favour of working-class actors and Osborne satisfied him on both counts. *Look Back in Anger* is now almost universally regarded as a classic, perhaps the single most important English play of the second half of the twentieth century. The story barely matters here. What did matter was the stream of bright, sarky bitterness that flowed from the main character, Jimmy Porter, as he bickered and ranted in the company of his wife and best friend. It was a resentful, disillusioned young voice, frustrated with what had happened to Britain. Later it would be echoed in a hundred bitter rock songs and in countless novels of youthful angst, and in films. But it had not been heard on a stage before. When the play was finally produced by the Royal Court, the third in its season, immediate reactions were unpromising. The critics were hostile. Binkie Beaumont had come, but then walked out at the interval. Early audiences seemed unenthusiastic. Osborne's mother was told by the theatre barmaid: 'They don't like this one, do they dear? They don't like it at all. Never mind, it won't be much longer. We're having Peggy Ashcroft soon. They'll like that. But they don't like *this* one. Not a bit of it.'[63]

The history of theatre is the history of legends. No newspaper review of a British stage play has been remembered quite like Tynan's review of *Look Back in Anger* in the *Observer*, published on 13 May 1956. It is widely thought to have single-handedly saved the play from being taken off. It was certainly a rave review, describing Osborne's work as a minor miracle showing qualities Tynan had despaired of seeing on stage. He thought it would be a minority taste, but continued: 'What matters, however, is the size of the minority. I estimate it at roughly 6,733,000, which is the number of people in this country between the ages of twenty and thirty. And this figure will doubtless be swelled by refugees from other age-groups . . . I doubt if I could love anyone who did not wish to see *Look Back in Anger*.' The heart-on-sleeve emotion and directness of the review made waves. Yet other newspapers had spotted it too; the *Financial Times* found it 'arresting, painful and sometimes astonishing . . . a play of extraordinary importance' and the *Daily Express* felt it was 'intense, angry, feverish, undisciplined. It is even crazy. But it is young, young, young . . .' Furthermore, it was not until the play was shown on television, in extract by the BBC in October and then in full by the new ITV in November, that it really became a success.

Meanwhile, if the meeting between Devine and Osborne on the houseboat provided the first act of this story, there was a much more remarkable one to come. Though the accounts differ in detail, the substance is clear. Laurence Olivier had been to see *Look Back in Anger* and, like so many, took against it as 'a lot of bitter rattling on'. But the American playwright Arthur Miller was in London because his girl-friend Marilyn Monroe was making a bad film with Olivier. Miller was intrigued by the title of Osborne's play. He persuaded Olivier to take him to see it and found it wonderful. Afterwards, Devine came over and asked whether they would meet the young author. They went to the bar. Though Osborne says the remark came later, and to Devine, Arthur Miller tells the story thus: 'a few inches to my right I overheard with some incredulity, Olivier asking the pallid Osborne – then a young guy with a shock of uncombed hair and a look in his face of having awakened twenty minutes earlier – "Do you suppose you could write something for me?" in his most smiling tones, which would have convinced you to buy a car with no wheels for twenty thousand dollars.'[64] The part would become that of Archie Rice, a fading and seedy music-hall entertainer in Osborne's savage demolition job on Harold Macmillan's delusional Britain. Osborne was quick to point out that he had been researching the declining music hall world well before Olivier asked for a part in *The Entertainer*. But it was an astonishing request. Olivier was then the sun-king of British acting. Though his marriage was collapsing in private, he and Vivien Leigh were the royal couple of the stage and screen, courted around the world, offered the greatest parts, apparently wealthy beyond the dreams of avarice. For him to ask a young playwright at a fringe theatre for a role seemed like Lord Mountbatten of Burma rolling up and asking for a job as deckhand on a battered Hull trawler.

Yet it was one of Olivier's shrewdest career moves. This was the moment when the old theatre world, of magnificent Shakespearaan film productions, Royal Command performances and West End grandness bowed and gave way to a new, rougher Britain. It was a symbolic removing of swords, buckles and plumes in favour of loose civilian clothes and satire. Olivier was incomparably the most important figure in the story of post-war British theatre. In the thirties he had swashbuckled and starred alongside many of the great Hollywood divas. His wartime stage roles had brought him huge personal success – the scent of success, he reported back, was 'like seaweed, or like oysters' – and his knighthood and films, as well as his marriage to Leigh, made him a global star. Some idea of this is given by the guest list at a Hollywood party thrown to greet him in the late forties – Groucho Marx, Errol Flynn, Ginger Rogers, Ronald Coleman, Louis B. Mayer, Humphrey Bogart, Marilyn Monroe and Lauren Bacall turned up to pay court. Later, he would be the driving force behind Britain's National Theatre; today one of its most important venues, as well as the annual awards for acting, are named after him. Actually, to compare him to a modern monarch is slightly to undersell Olivier at his zenith. Why then did he decide to ask Osborne for a part he must have known would be shockingly different to the romantic leads and tortured princes his public expected of him? Partly, it was boredom and the crushing effect of his marriage to the increasingly mad Vivien Leigh, which he was determined to leave. After various love affairs he would eventually marry Joan Plowright, one of Devine's Royal Court regulars. He would not actually give up the great Shakespearean parts – a magnificent Othello was still to come – nor would he quite turn his back on Hollywood. But *The Entertainer* and his relationship with Plowright set him on a new direction. The answer was that Olivier was able to reinvent himself as a man of the modern world, no longer the codpiece and tights-wearing hero of mid-century.

British theatre did something similar. It found a way of mattering despite the arrival of television and the continuing huge power of cinema. It is not coincidental that, while Britain was still bleakly under provided-for in the aftermath of war, British theatre in the Binkie years was extravagant, colourful and generally shallow, while when Britain set out on a mass consumer boom, British theatre turned darker and edgier. In each case, the stage offered a contrast to what was around it. Osborne's Jimmy Porter bemoaned the lack of 'good brave causes' left in 1956; in 1946, as the Cold War began and with people still demobilizing from the army, such a sentiment would have seemed ludicrous. Similarly, the naive celebration of life which warmed London when *Oklahoma!* arrived after the war would not have made nearly such an impression on the richer city of a decade later. Live theatre would have to compete for writers and actors who found they could reach far bigger audiences and make better money elsewhere. *Look Back in Anger*, *A Taste of Honey*, *The Entertainer* and *Oh, What a Lovely War!* would all be filmed. Many of the key talents, the best actors and directors and producers, would head for the new virtual theatres at Lime Grove, Ealing and Teddington, the hangar like television studios with no seats for an audience and a forest canopy of lights and microphones.

The West End, and the big provincial theatres, would continue to provide entertainment to the middle classes who wanted to see famous actors in the flesh, and who were prepared to try out new playwrights. Of those, Harold Pinter, whose *The Birthday Party* opened to bafflement in 1958 until it was rescued from likely oblivion by a single rave review, is widely acknowledged as the greatest. His famous pauses, mundane settings, intricate use of ordinary language and background political agenda provided a way of seeing and hearing modern Britain unlike any other. He followed earlier so-called absurdist dramatists, above all Samuel Beckett, who had been given his English premier of *Waiting for Godot* by the young Peter Hall in 1955 at the Arts Theatre Club, but Pinter was as English as Beckett was French-Irish. Yet the talent pouring out of British theatre through the sixties and seventies, from the satirists like Orton, the magicians like Stoppard, the sheer entertainers like Ayckbourn, through to the great political dramatists – Wesker, Arden, Bond, Hare – showed that television had failed to kill off live drama. Londoners, indeed any British people near a major playhouse, had the opportunity to be amused, provoked, obliged to think about the world around them, with as much live wit and anger on offer to them as in any modern nation. In the twenty-first century, as Hollywood stars make a regular pilgrimage to play or direct in London theatre-land, and with the flow of good contemporary work unceasing, theatre remains, against the odds, one of the little glories of British life.

Korea: Mao, Bugles, Tins of Cheese

In March 1946, exiled from power, Churchill had made his famous 'iron curtain' speech at Fulton, Missouri. Across Central and Eastern Europe, behind that iron curtain, client Communist parties and Russian stooges had engaged in murder, vote-rigging, threats and eventually outright putsches – notably in Prague – to put themselves in power. Crisis followed crisis. Stalin had tried to throttle West Berlin, a crowded democratic atoll inside Soviet-controlled East Germany. He had hoped to persuade the West not to form an independent West German state with its own currency, but he failed. Much encouraged by Attlee and Bevin, the Americans led a massive airlift to keep the besieged city supplied. By the time the blockade ended more than 270,000 flights into Berlin had been made, carrying in fuel, food and clothing. It was an extraordinary act of succour and a dangerous one, which was wholly successful. Meanwhile there was a strong possibility of war between the Russians and the rebel communists of Tito's Yugoslavia – Stalin had planned to assassinate Tito for insubordination. With American nuclear bombers in East Anglia, and the Russians also now possessors of the Bomb, the danger seemed all-consuming and the threat relentless. And in 1950 Britain was at war again, this time alongside the Americans and a wide alliance of other countries.

Aside from military historians, Korea has become the forgotten war. Yet it was a genuinely dangerous global confrontation in which Britain played an important if subsidiary role. It was the first and only time when British troops have directly fought a major Communist army, Mao's Chinese People's Liberation Army; and it was a long and bloody conflict. Britain and her Commonwealth allies, fighting with a mixture of professional soldiers and young National Service conscripts, lost more than a thousand dead and nearly three times as many wounded. The overall UN casualties were around 142,000. All that was terrible enough, but it could have been much worse. The American commander, General of the Army Douglas MacArthur, fresh from his role as effective dictator of post-war Japan, and considered by his President to be unhinged, was keen to open full-scale operations against Communist China itself. As they struggled against a peasant army across icy, rocky hills and through paddy-fields the US military contemplated using their new atomic bombs to lay down an irradiated dead zone between Korea and China. President Truman had no intention of allowing MacArthur to start loosing off nuclear bombs but a little later, in 1953, his successor, President Eisenhower, did raise the possibility of using nuclear strikes directly against China.

In a memorandum to Attlee's government, the British chiefs of staff wrote with elegant understatement that 'from the military point of view . . . the dropping of an atomic bomb in North Korea would be unsound. The effects of such action would be world-wide, and might well be very damaging. Moreover, it would probably provoke a global war.'[65] Labour MPs wanted the nuclear bomb to be limited to use by the UN, a somewhat strange notion, and Attlee went to Washington to check that Truman was not about to engulf the world in atomic conflict. What no one in Whitehall or Washington knew then, though they might have guessed it, was that Mao had decided to use unfortunate Korea as a 'meat-grinder' war, in which the huge numbers of Western deaths would break the morale of the capitalist West and gain him vital credit with Stalin, so persuading Moscow to share nuclear secrets with Beijing. In March 1951, Mao told the Soviet dictator that his plan was 'to spend several years consuming several hundred thousand American lives'.[66] Had he been more militarily successful, the temptation to go nuclear would have been great. Though the Cuban missile crisis of 1962 is remembered, rightly, as the moment when the world came nearest to nuclear war, there was a serious possibility of it happening earlier, in Korea and China.

The scale of the challenge in Korea after the Communist north invaded on 25 June 1950 quickly persuaded the British government that troops and ships should be sent to help the Americans and the flailing southern regime of Syngman Rhee. There was little disagreement, either in the government or the Commons. Compared to Vietnam, this was a consensual war, carried out under the freshly designed blue and white flag of the United Nations. On the North Korean and Chinese side, half a million men were engaged and, by the time the war ended, three million Chinese had fought in Korea. The Chinese later told their allies that they lost 400,000 men, many of them former anti-Communist soldiers of Chiang Kai-shek's army cynically sent as useful fodder. Among UN forces there would be Australians and Canadians, Belgians, French, Dutch, Thais, Ethiopians, Greeks, Turks, Colombians and others. Wherever they came from most of those who found themselves in Korea hated the country. In winter, the front line was bitterly cold, at other times it was overrun with vermin. Human excrement was used to fertilize the fields which while hardly unknown in rural economies provided a pungent scent which remained in many veterans' minds ever afterwards.

British forces performed bravely in important battles but found the cultural divide with the Americans had grown even wider in the past five years. The most famous example was the heroic stand of the 'the Glorious Glosters' above the Imjin river in April 1951 when with other troops including Ulstermen, Canadians and Belgians, the first battalion of the Gloucestershire Regiment found itself suddenly facing the full force of the fifth major Chinese offensive of the war. Hugely outnumbered, lacking heavy artillery or aircraft support and soon cut off by the advancing tides of communist troops, Brigadier Tom Brodie called for help from the Americans, explaining that the British position was 'a bit sticky'. Not realizing that this was stiff-upper-lip for 'catastrophic', the American commander told him cheerfully just to sit tight. After the battle which followed, just 169 of the 850 Glosters were left for roll-call. Sixty-three had been killed, around 200 badly injured and the rest captured by the Chinese, who had themselves lost an astonishing 10,000 men in the attack. After four desperate days, the Glosters had been able to hold on no longer. At one point, responding to the bugles and trumpets used by the Chinese commanders to signal yet another charge, the Glosters' drum-major was told to respond with every bugle-call he could remember; so the men fought under the strains not just of 'reveille' but 'defaulters' and 'officers dress for dinner'. In another position, when the ammunition finally ran out, the Glosters were reduced to throwing tins of processed cheese at the Chinese in the (vain) hope they would be mistaken for grenades. Yet the action, for all its hopelessness and poignant comedy, did check the advance of the People's Liberation Army at a vital moment. One historian of the war concluded that at Imjin, 'the most political army in the world encountered the least political – and was savagely mauled to gain its few sterile miles of rock and paddy . . . Across the breadth of the Korean front, Peking's spring offensive had failed. Never again in the war did the communists mount an all-out assault which appeared to have the slightest prospect of strategic success.'[37]

There were further brave British actions by the Black Watch and, two years after Imjin, by the Duke of Wellington's Regiment. Three-quarters composed of young National Service conscripts earning just £1.62 a week, they held back the Chinese on a ridge nicknamed the Hook. Though eighteen-year-olds were banned from Korea many lied to see some action. British troops said the two worst-paid armies serving there were themselves and the Chinese. Throughout the war, of course, it was American commanders and politicians who directed strategy, perhaps the single most important and far-sighted action coming from the top when President Truman finally sacked Mac-Arthur. By the time of the eventual armistice in July 1953 returning British troops, including prisoners who had endured appalling torture and malnutrition, found the public largely uninterested in them. There had been a major drive by the Chinese to indoctrinate British conscripts but with the exception of a spy who was later unmasked and a single Scottish soldier who, perhaps recalling the social cheer to be enjoyed in Scotland in the early fifties, opted to remain in Red China, it was ineffective. Though the Chinese political officers included some with fluent English, there was little communication: it seems that rich Geordie, Scottish and West Country accents completely defeated them.

In some ways, Korea can be compared to the Iraq wars, the first of which had UN backing, and both of which were American wars in which Britain played a secondary role. As with Iraq, at the time of Korea half a century earlier, British public opinion found the country's regional allies unattractive and undemocratic. The Syngman Rhee regime in the south was as despotic as Pakistan or Saudi Arabia but more ruthless and vicious, as well as being spectacularly ungrateful. As with Iraq, British journalists did much to spread disenchantment about the war. James Cameron, a brilliantly talented left-wing reporter with a huge reputation, lost his job with the then-popular magazine *Picture Post* after revealing the condition of political prisoners held by the south. 'They were skeletons,' he later wrote, 'they were puppets of skin with sinews for strings – their faces were a terrible, translucent grey and they cringed like dogs.'[68] As with Iraq, Britain struggled to use what leverage she had. Attlee flew to Washington to try to persuade Truman not to use atomic weapons, as Tony Blair flew there to persuade George W. Bush to try harder for UN support. As with Iraq, British troops behaved bravely under difficult conditions and returned home to find a country that did not want to know.

East Germany's Communist leader bragged that after Korea, West Germany would be next for liberation with tanks. Stalin had indeed considered trying to grab the rest of Germany, as well as Spain and Italy, and had discussed with his advisers an attack on the American Pacific fleet. In October 1950 he told Mao that a Third World War should not necessarily be avoided: 'If a war is inevitable, then let it be waged now, and not in a few years' time.'[69] In West Germany, comfortably based in former SS and Luftwaffe barracks (the Germans had provided double-glazing, central heating, sports facilities and cinemas for the fighting men of the Third Reich), some 80,000 British soldiers were waiting for the Red Army to make a surprise attack.[70] As in Korea many were National Service conscripts. Many of the British tanks were hopelessly out of date, 1939 Valentines and clapped-out Churchills. As Soviet aircraft buzzed Western defences to test them out, there was an assumption in Whitehall that when the attack came Nato would be able to hold out with conventional forces for only a few days. It would have been 1940 all over again with one stark difference. To protect itself against the Soviet blitzkrieg the West would have had to go nuclear at an early stage. Politicians and commentators would become obsessed by the technical detail of the arms race as it lurched forward.

The huge rearmament that followed, with the Americans leading the way, Britain and France following, had grave consequences for Britain. Having been a founding member of the UN and Nato, Britain felt confirmed as a global player, with global responsibilities. The cost was crippling. Korea itself was not the cause of the financial squeeze – the official historian of that war pointed out that 'the sum was a mite compared to the volume of British rearmament for Nato during the same period'.[71] It was, however, part of the shift of resources back to khaki and jets which meant Labour hurriedly diverting money from the new National Health Service. Some 300,000 men a year were taken out of the job market at a time of serious labour shortages. Another unplanned consequence was that West Germany was quickly back on her feet again since her new machine tool factories were desperately needed to re-equip Britain. Soon these same factories would be exposing archaic, ill-managed British industry to serious competition in other areas. But perhaps the most serious domestic consequence of rearmament was on morale or the spirit of the times. The Cold War shaped post-war Europe. In Britain it helped quickly blight the sunny optimism about a better future that so briefly bloomed in the years after the war.

Jerusalem Falls

In the 1950 general election, Labour won 13.3 million votes, not so many fewer than it did in 1997, when the electorate was far bigger. Its majority then however was slashed to just five. Herbert Morrison mordantly reflected that the British people hadn't wanted to kick out Labour, just to give it a kick in the pants; 'but I think they've overdone it a bit'. The impression of fading strength was manifested in the bad health of Labour's relatively elderly leaders. Morrison had nearly been killed by a thrombosis during the crisis of 1947; new drugs given to him caused his kidneys to pour with blood. While he was still in hospital, Ellen Wilkinson, the education minister who adored Morrison and may have been his mistress, died from an overdose of barbiturates. Though Labour succeeded in raising the school leaving age to fifteen, and embarked on an ambitious school-building programme, education had been a relative failure for the Attlee government. There was too much hunger for manpower, too few qualified teachers, shortages of everything from school furniture to modern textbooks and, in the end, too little cash. Wilkinson, a small flame-haired woman who had been on the pre-war Jarrow Crusade and was much loved in the party, became increasingly depressed at the slow pace of change. On 25 January 1947, in the middle of that icy winter described earlier, she insisted on opening a theatre school in a blitzed, open-to-the-sky building in south London. Ellen became ill and seems to have muddled her medicines, though others believe she killed herself, out of a mix of love and disappointment; the coroner recorded 'heart failure following emphysema, with acute bronchitis and barbituric poisoning'.[72]

Wilkinson was an early casualty of the brutal lives lived by ministers then but far from the only one. Attlee had to be suddenly hospitalized at a key moment in the Korean crisis, with a bleeding ulcer. Bevin, utterly broken by overwork and over-indulgence, died that April. Cripps had been extremely unwell since 1949, suffering from devastating pain caused by a tubercular abscess in the spine, which eventually killed him during one of his regular Swiss hospital visits, in 1952. By the late forties, according to one account, 'the ministers began to gossip about one another's health rather like old village women. Attlee confided to Dalton his deep concern about the frailty of both Bevin and Morrison. Bevin, himself apparently on his last legs, was in turn "alarmist about Attlee". He remarked that "his mind's gone . . ." And so on, through the cabinet.'[73] By modern standards the Labour cabinet was not very old, the important players being in their early sixties or late fifties, but this was a hard-drinking, heavy-smoking and pressured time to be a politician. Most of these ministers worked late into the night, every night, and spent hours in the Commons arguing with more junior MPs. When they travelled, it was still in unpressurised, slow aircraft. Their holidays, taken mostly at home near at hand, were regularly interrupted for yet more crisis cabinet meetings. Ill-health and botched operations would dog not only Labour but the Tories too through the post-war years, with Hugh Gaitskell, Eden and Macmillan succumbing to health crises. (Only Churchill, with his cigars, brandy and strange hours of work, continued into late old age. International fame, and the habit of being listened to attentively even when you are being boring, proves a great boost to longevity.)

Apart from being ill and in some cases disillusioned, the Labour leadership had begun to fracture. The row that propelled Nye Bevan and his then acolyte Harold Wilson, 'Nye's little dog', out of government was with hindsight a silly one. The economy had been doing rather better than during the dark year of 1947. Though the country was short of dollars, the generosity of Marshall Plan aid the following year had removed the immediate sense of crisis. By 1949, it was estimated to have raised the country's national income by a tenth. Responding to the national mood of revolt over restrictions and shortages, Wilson had announced a 'bonfire of controls' in 1948 and there seemed some chance that Labour ministers would follow the change in national mood and accept that the British wanted to spend, not only to queue. Labour was always divided between ideological socialists and more pragmatic people, but there was no obvious necessity for the party to have a row with itself towards the end of its first majority government, with so many whirlpools navigated, and so many rocks narrowly avoided.

The problem was the familiar one. Should money be concentrated first on Britain's overseas commitment, symbolized by her involvement in founding Nato, and her large army facing the Russians across the Germany border; or on protecting the social advances at home? The new Chancellor, Hugh Gaitskell, had proposed charges for dental and eye treatment to help fund the massive cost of rearmament demanded by the Americans and accepted by London as the price for remaining a great power. Spending on defence would rise from 7 per cent of Britain's income in 1948 to 10.5 per cent four years later, an astonishing proportion for an economically weak country. In money terms the proposed charges hardly signified in the bill for tanks and planes, and were small too as a proportion of the new NHS budget. But hot blood and simmering rivalries turned this into a great struggle of socialist principle. Gaitskell wanted to establish his authority as chancellor. Bevan wanted to protect his ground-breaking achievement, the NHS. Neither position looks wise half a century later. Britain could not afford to be a great power in the old way, but nor could she afford to spend the Marshall Plan aid windfall mainly on better welfare, while other countries were using it to rebuild their industrial power. At

Westminster the words grew hotter. Attlee had lost his old power to hold the ring. When Bevan and his friends resigned, a wound opened in the party which would never fully heal. Bevanites began meeting in livid little cabals. Their enemies denounced them in ever nastier terms.

And so the party, which had won by such an overwhelming landslide six years earlier, seemed to have lost the will to keep going. One journalist at the time described it as like 'an old, wounded animal, biting at its own injuries' and another thought the debates in the Commons showed 'a Government suffering severe internal haemorrhage and likely to bleed to death at any moment'.[74] With hindsight, the post-war Labour years were a time almost cut off from what followed. So much of the country's energy had been sapped by war; what was left was focused on the struggle for survival. With Britain industrially clapped-out, mortgaged to the United States and increasingly bitter about the lack of any cheerful post-war dividend, it was perhaps not the best time to set about building a new socialist Jerusalem. Most attempts at forced modernization quickly collapsed. The direction of factories to depressed areas produced little long-term benefit. Companies encouraged to export at all costs were unable to re-equip and prepare themselves for tougher markets. Inflation, which would be a major part of the post-war story, appeared, rising from 3 per cent in 1949–50 to 9 per cent by 1951–2.

Again and again, Britain's deep dependency on the United States was simply underestimated by the politicians. Harold Wilson, for instance, slapped import duty on Hollywood films in 1947, when the sterling crisis made saving dollars such a priority. The Americans simply boycotted Britain, a devastating thing for a country then so film-besotted. Labour tried to encourage home-made, patriotic films to fill the gap and there were wonderful British films, and directors, but already glamour was something that came from the Pacific coast. When the tariffs and boycott were lifted, the wave of American releases swamped British studios. So the tariffs were taken off again. Then there was the dream of a 'British empire of the air', fleets of giant new commercial airliners criss-crossing the oceans in patriotic livery. Again, it was an expensive lesson in hubris. Vast aircraft like the Brabazon I and the Tudor IV proved no match for America's Lockhead planes. The best of the British jets, the Comet, was to suffer lethal commercial delays after crashes in the early fifties. Britain seemed to succeed best in international competition with a plucky, wire coat-hanger and empty squeezy-bottle approach.

But nothing sums up the paradoxes, the hope and chaos, the old State-direction and the coming consumer society, better than the famous Festival of Britain of 1951. Even now its defining images can be recalled by millions of people – the great modernistic Dome of Discovery, like a friendly flying saucer just alighted on the south bank of the Thames opposite Parliament, and the Skylon, a great aluminium spear, an anorexic rocket, seemingly suspended in mid-air – rather like, people said, the British economy. The Festival had been talked about during the war, but it was the editor of a liberal-minded, leftish newspaper, the *News Chronicle*, who championed it. Gerald Barry was in many ways like the Labour ministers he appealed to – high-minded, the son of a clergyman, radical, but also upper-crust by education. He wanted the festival to be not merely for people to enjoy but 'an expression of a way of life in which we believe'. The government liked the notion and set up an equally high-minded committee to take the project forward, including senior civil servants, an architect, a palaeontologist and a theatre manager.

In a famous essay about the Festival, Michael Frayn later said it had been devised by the 'herbivores', by which he meant the leftish post-war establishment people, 'the signers of petitions; the backbone of the BBC ... guiltily conscious of their advantages, though not usually ceasing to eat the grass' – what a later generation would call the chattering classes.[75] Luckily for the herbivores, political responsibility for the shindig was soon taken over by Herbert Morrison who, whatever his faults, was no snob and who had a robust understanding that people wanted fun and colour. A chance, as he put it later, for 'the people to give themselves a bit of a pat on the back'. It was a lesson forgotten when his grandson Peter Mandelson took charge of the Millennium Dome in the late nineties.

Eventually, 8.5 million people would visit the Festival on the Thames, and 8 million more went to the associated funfair in Battersea. Up and down the country innumerable others attended local events, everything from village pageants to a ship touring the seaports and a netball display at Colchester. The Festival showed what planning and risk-taking could achieve, and what it could not. While it lasted, a weed-covered, marshy, muddy, semi-derelict wasteland was turned into the scene of a great national display. The project had survived endless Whitehall wrangles on every issue from the materials its buildings were to be made from, to where in London they should be sited, to what the displays should be about – which turned out to be an immense display of the best of British design and manufacture, plus historical and scientific tableaux and some wonderful modern art. Airy pavilions surrounded piazzas; there was a whimsical model railway; the Ministry of Pensions hoped for a modest display of artificial limbs. Right-wing newspapers, led by the London *Evening Standard*, ridiculed the whole idea as a waste of time and 'Morrison's folly'. Americans wrote to oppose it, in one case on the grounds that it was essentially un-British and tourists wanted 'England to be the same, battle-scarred but beautiful'. In the final stages of construction, the rain teemed down and work was halted by strikes. As with the failing British airliners, there was clear and vivid ambition; but often, it seemed, not quite the ability to carry it through.

Yet the Festival was carried through. It was a moment of patriotic tingle. The State directed something which, though mocked by many, did catch the national imagination. Conservative MPs came round and so, grudgingly, did most of the newspapers. High culture, represented by abstract sculptors, classical music, the latest in design, did manage to hold hands, however briefly, with popular culture, as represented by the cafes selling chips and peas, the funfair rides, fireworks and Gracie Fields in cabaret. Opinion polls eventually showed a hefty majority in favour of the Festival. Herbert Morrison, whose official title was Lord President and who had come close to being ridiculed for the looming failures, was now known affectionately in the press as Lord Festival. It had been a close-run thing, fun snatched from the jaws of depression. Perhaps after all, Labour's 1945 dream of a socialist commonwealth, high minded and patriotic, standing aside from crass American consumerism, could be built on England's grey and muddy land?

The Festival turned out to be Labour's farewell to the country for a long time. Michael Frayn summed it up later as a rainbow, riding the tail of the storm and promising fairer weather: 'It marked the ending of the hungry forties, and the beginning of an altogether easier decade . . . it may perhaps be likened to a gay and enjoyable birthday party, but one at which the host presided from his death-bed.' If the host was a certain vision of British socialism then this grimly humorous image is spot on. Labour had made Britain a little more civilized and certainly fairer. But it had accomplished nothing like a revolution. By the time it returned to power in 1964, Britain had experienced something more like a Festival of America.

Part Two

THE LAND OF
LOST CONTENT

Between the fall of old Clem Attlee's Labour government and the return of Labour under cocky, wisecracking Harold Wilson, Britain went through a time which some believe a golden-tinted era of lost content. To others they were the grey, conformist, 'thirteen wasted years' of Tory misrule. Either way, this part of our past was truly a different country. Much of it has disappeared. You might climb into your Austin Sheerline for a visit to the Midland Bank, stopping off at a Lyons to read your *News Chronicle* or *Picture Post* while smoking a Capstan, looking forward to a weekend visit to the Speedway by tram. It was possible to imagine a different way of being British. To leaf through newspapers and magazines of the time is to glimpse just how very different the future might have been. There are the unfamiliar all-British cars with their bulky, rather innocent styling – Jowett Cars of Idle, Bradford, advertise their Javelins and Jupiters; or you could be 'well-off in a Wolseley'. There is no sign that, just as the great age of the car begins, Britain's sprawling independent car industry is about to be wiped out. Nor, for that matter, that the 'freedom of the road' will soon be replaced by a maze of new regulations, fines and documents; there are no motorways, no out of town speed limits. There are drawings of the coming passenger heliports.

People still look different. Few schoolboys are without a cap and shorts. Caught breaking windows or lying, they might be solemnly caned by their fathers. Young girls have home-made smocks and, it is earnestly hoped, have never heard of sexual intercourse. Every woman seems to be a housewife; corsets and hats are worn and trousers, hardly ever. Among men, a silky moustache is regarded as extremely exciting to women, collars are bought separately from shirts and the smell of pipe-tobacco lingers on flannel.

Above all Britain is still a military nation, imaginatively gripped by the Second World War, whose generals are famous public figures and whose new jet-bombers provoke gasps of pride. Military uniforms, which would be worn ironically by sixties hippies, were much more common on the streets. National Service had been introduced in 1947 to replace wartime conscription and began properly two years later. It would last until 1963. More than two million young British men entered the forces, most of them the Army. It brought all classes together at a young and vulnerable age, subjecting them to strict discipline, a certain amount of practical education, often to privation, and sometimes to real danger. Teenagers were introduced to drill, cropped haircuts, heavy boots and endless polishing, creasing and blancoing of their kit. In due course some would fight for Britain in the Far East, in Palestine or Egypt, and in Africa. Most would spend a year or two in huge military camps in Britain or Germany, going quietly mad with boredom. Some died. An estimated 395 conscripts were killed in action in the fifty-plus engagements overseas during National Service, while a couple of dozen are said to have been killed in secret experiments using chemical weapons at Porton Down in Wiltshire. Others were used as human guinea pigs in British atomic bomb tests and some killed themselves, as they might have done anyway. National Service mingled and disciplined much of a generation of post-war British manhood and helped therefore to set the tone of the times. Some of the anti-authority anger and sarcasm in the culture of the time derived directly or indirectly from National Service but so did the civilian habits of polishing, dressing smartly and conforming to authority in millions of homes. In general, it probably kept some of the atmosphere of the forties alive for a decade longer than might have been expected.

In other countries – Germany, France, Russia or Japan – the trauma and devastation of the Forties was still plain everywhere. In Britain, the last prisoners of war were being sent home. Bomb-sites were being filled in and functional, unromantic buildings were taking their place, but the lessons of the war were still being unpicked. People today who were children then recall, inevitably, the fifties as the normal time – the way we were and by implication always had been. Yet the urge for domestic tranquillity, with women at home, making jam and knitting, while men worked orderly and limited hours, was a conscious response to the pain and uncertainty of 1939–45 and the continued fears of nuclear war. Then, it felt new; to be at home and quiet was a kind of liberation. For the middle classes, there was also the memory of the pre-war years as a time of order. The return of Winston Churchill in 1951 added to the impression Britain really could return to hierarchies vaguely recalled from before the war. By the end of this period, in 1963, there were still nearly a quarter of a million people in 'domestic service' – maids, housekeepers, valets – and more than six hundred full-time butlers. Britain was still graced with thirty-one Dukes, thirty-eight Marquesses and a mere 204 Earls.[1] Many private companies had an almost military feel at the top, with an officer class of gents and middle-ranking NCO types below them. Outside work the public was monitored by a self-confident officialdom, hospital consultants and terrifying matrons, bishops and park keepers, bus conductors and bicycling police officers whose authority was unconstrained by modern standards. Hanging, the physical punishment of young offenders, strong laws against abortion and homosexual behaviour by men – all these framed a system of control that was muttered against and often subverted, but through the early fifties little challenged. The country was mostly orderly. People were more or less obedient citizens and subjects, not picky consumers. Patriotism was proclaimed publicly, loudly and unselfconsciously, in a way that would quickly become hard to imagine.

In the mid-fifties, Britain is a worldwide player, connected and modern. Her major companies are global leaders in oil, tobacco, shipping and finance. The Empire is not yet quite gone, even if the new name of Commonwealth is around. Royal visits abroad, and delegations of exotic natives, feature heavily in news broadcasts and weekly magazines. Australia, New Zealand and South Africa are promoted as places for holiday cruises or emigration – sunlit, rich and empty. Collectively, they are a British California, a new frontier. Commercial liners, their flags fluttering, are waiting at Southampton. This is not a country which is closed to foreign influence, far from it. But the influences seem as strong from Italy or Scandinavia as from America – coffee-bars, Danish design, scooters and something promoted as 'Italian Welsh rarebit' (later known as pizza) are all in evidence. The awesome power of American culture is growing all the time over the horizon. But for a few years the idea of a powerful, self-confident Britain independent of American culture seemed not only possible but likely. Per capita, after all, Britain was still the second-richest major country in the world.

In public a front of national confidence was kept up. After the 1953 Coronation of the new Queen, there was much talk, albeit slightly self-conscious, of the New Elizabethan Age, a reborn nation served by great composers, artists and scientists. Not all of this was false, even in retrospect. In Ralph Vaughan Williams, Benjamin Britten and Michael Tippett, Britain did have some world-class musical talents. W. H. Auden and T. S. Eliot were among the great poets of the age. Then, at least, it looked to many as if the sculptor Henry Moore and the painter Graham Sutherland were world-class figures. Churchill may have been really too old to be Prime Minister during the first few years of the fifties, but he was undoubtedly one of the few great figures of the time, an ageing colossus whose books were pouring from the presses, stamping his version of history on the public mind. Along with another star author of the fifties, William Golding, he would be a Nobel Prize-winner. In popular culture, the steady rise of television brought, at first, a traditionalist English upper-crust view of the world to millions of homes. This was the age of 'Andy Pandy' and gardening tips, of Joyce Grenfell and Noël Coward. It was also the time of Roger Bannister and his four-minute mile; the conquest of Everest; triumphs in yachting and football; even in the world of adventure and sport, Britain was doing well. With Nobel Prize-winning science in physics and biology, there was no sign yet of the brain drain of scientists to the United States.

Knowing what we know now, there were signs of social change everywhere from the disaffected teenagers just beginning to be discussed, to the rise of Maltese, Italian and home-grown crime dynasties, and the first wide-eyed, optimistic Caribbean immigrants. There was also much boredom and frustration. Working-class Britain was getting richer, but still housed in dreadful old homes, excluded from higher education, unless part of a small and lucky elite, and deprived of any jobs but hard and boring ones. Eventually, the lid would blow off. Yet to be British was something to be proud of. Even the mild hooligan element was home-grown; the exotic and expensive costumes of the Teddy boys, with their velvet collars, long jackets and foppish waistcoats, were modelled on English Edwardian dress.

Balcon's Britain

Among all the people who expressed the most optimistic spirit of Britishness in this period the best example is a Jewish adventurer's son from Birmingham, brought up in radical and suffragette circles. His films have already been mentioned, for Michael Balcon was the man behind the Ealing comedies and scores of other films. He was the great interpreter of these years, second only to Churchill in crafting how the British remember themselves in the middle of the twentieth century. In a world culture dominated by the United States he was determined that Britain should be distinct and his vision of the British family blended the high-mindedness of Attlee with the impatient spirit of the coming Tory years. Had we faced nuclear annihilation then one of Balcon's Ealing comedies would probably have been the last work of art broadcast by the BBC's young television service.[2] He is worth spending a little time on because his success and failure offers a key, or guide, to the underlying uncertainties and paradoxes of the age. Balcon bottled the most pungent elements of the spirit of Britain in the late forties and early fifties, and through his films we can inhale them freshly now as if the intervening years had not passed.

The Ealing studios are still there. The white painted, functional offices and the vast hangar-like shed would be instantly recognizable to Balcon, and they are busy, being used again to make films. Even the pub across the road where Balcon's team of writers and producers drank, smoked, dreamed and fought is not much changed, though Ealing is a multi-ethnic, trendy place compared to the relentlessly suburban, indeed dull part of West London it was when the film studios were established there in 1931. They were intended to be a small British redoubt against the power of American cinema. Certainly, it is hard to imagine a more dramatic contrast to the sprawl, bright light and self-importance of Hollywood. The studios could easily be mistaken from the outside as a provincial school. In a way, they were. During the thirties Ealing had bridged the nineteenth-century culture of the music hall and the new world of cinema, making popular comedies by the Lancashire musical stars George Formby and Gracie Fields. Balcon himself had been working for a range of film-makers, including Gainsborough and Gaumont-British, struggling with the sheer gravitational force of the Hollywood system before being lured there himself. It was not a success. He fell out spectacularly with Louis B. Mayer, who once bawled that he would destroy Balcon 'if it costs me a million dollars'. Balcon is said to have replied that he would settle for less. He happily quit to rule Ealing through the heroic days of the war, the years of New Jerusalem and carry on until 1955, the year of Eden's election. He enjoyed a continuity no politican could rival and he was as passionate about national cinema as they were about the nation.

Ealing was in some ways a miniature Britain of the period. It had its autocratic, eccentric leader. It developed a robust, vaguely socialist patriotism under the conditions of the war (though Churchill was dubious about some of the war films, and half-heartedly tried to ban a couple for being defeatist). And in 1945 Balcon and his colleagues voted Labour – what Balcon described as their 'mild revolution' but they quickly became hostile to the pressing rules and regulations of post-war life. Like Britain Ealing was badly underfunded and thrived on a make do and mend approach to film-making, the cult of improvisation. It too had a rich array of political views and immi-grants, people from the colonies, White Russians, semi-communists and militant trade unionists. Yet they were all expected to show total loyalty and to work for only modest rewards. Many decisions were taken round a large table at which free and frank expression was expected – the cabinet table, as it were – and these sessions were followed by heroic drinking bouts at that local pub. If Ealing had an ideology it was a misty one, something to do with fairness, decency, the importance of the little man, and of standing up to bullies, be they Bavarian or merely bureaucratic.

In the films shopkeepers and fishermen outwit Whitehall officials and excisemen; small boys and little old ladies outwit criminal gangs. There is an unmistakeable edge: so many heroes are working class, so many villains are posh. But they are also culturally and morally conservative. In its war films, thrillers, psychological dramas and adventure movies as well as the famous comedies, Ealing almost entirely avoids sex and violence. Writing at the end of the sixties when British horror films and 'sexploitation' films were taking off, Balcon wryly reflected that 'if there has been a sex deficiency in the films for which I have been responsible over the years no great or permanent damage has been done, as current films are more than making up for lost time . . . there are many things in life other than sex and violence. There's love, for instance . . .' In Balcon's Britain, 'love' was not yet coy code for making love. As was said of a non-Ealing film, *Brief Encounter*, the post-war British ideal seemed to be 'make tea not love'. Films of understatement, films of bitten lips and dramatic silences; and, in a phrase by the novelist E. M. Forster, films about an English nervous system which 'acts promptly and feels slowly' are a good guide to how different the country was back then. It was all very non-Hollywood. It was consciously intended as an alternative way of understanding the world. Balcon had talked about the need to project 'the true Briton' to the rest of the world. He wanted a cinema that would show the Americans, the French and the Russians 'Britain as a leader in social reform in the defeat of social injustices and a champion of civil liberties . . .' It was a noble vision yet like Britain, Ealing was too weak, too underfunded and improvisatory, to live up to its ambitions. After an extraordinary flowering of creativity in the forties and early fifties, Ealing fell back into romantic, self-congratulatory guff and the rest of the world moved on.

Small Rooms: How Governments Were Run in the Fifties

Churchill was about to be seventy-seven when he returned to office, which was an older age then than it is now. When he observed to his private secretary that he had never known a prime minister so old, the well-read civil servant replied that actually Churchill had – William Ewart Gladstone. Like Gladstone, he would still be Prime Minister in his eighties. (The Grand Old Man of the nineteenth century lasted a few years longer than the Grand Old Boy of the twentieth century perhaps because Gladstone had neither led Britain through a world war nor fuelled himself the while on brandy and cigars.) The Conservatives had radically overhauled their organization and policies during the Attlee years, in a way the party was unable or unwilling to do after later defeats. They had moved decisively towards the consensus for a Welfare State, a more centrist position than ever before, and they had very effectively played on the grimness and occasional absurdities of the rationing years. Having promised the unexciting agenda of 'several years of solid, stable administration', Churchill formed a government of cronies and old muckers, reluctant generals and businessmen. The best people were his wartime allies Eden, Macmillan and the education reformer, 'Rab' Butler.

Politics in the fifties, at least on the Tory side, was unimaginably different from politics today. There were the same rackety campaigning offices, the same ambitious young researchers dreaming of becoming ministers themselves and the same underlying ruthless struggle for personal power. But many more people were party members, the backbench MPs were more independent-minded, with more status in the country, yet far lazier, too; and above all, the top of government was small social circle which operated well out of the way of lenses, microphones or diarists. Churchill himself spent an alarming amount of his time playing the card game bezique and travelling, often slowly on ocean liners and, as would Eden and Macmillan, put great strain on the notion of genuine cabinet discussion, provoking ferocious rows, walk-outs and threatened resignations. When Churchill and his Chancellor, Rab Butler, hatched a complicated plot to save the pound, ministers were presented with a take-it-or-leave-it ultimatum and furiously protested. When Churchill fired off an invitation to a summit with the Soviets after Stalin's death, sending it while sailing in mid-Atlantic, his cabinet was equally outraged and eventually forced a climbdown. When Eden bitterly protested in cabinet that Churchill was breaking yet another promise about his retirement, other ministers complained that here was an important story about which they had been told nothing. Yet Eden's Suez plot was hatched without important ministers having any clear idea of what was really happening. And Macmillan governed by playing ministers off against one another, expertly avoiding full and frank discussions in cabinet.

Most of the key political moments of these years take place like scenes on a small stage, in rooms containing a handful of people who know one another too well. As in Shakespeare, there are crowd scenes too – the rallies against Eden; the first Aldermaston marches; race riots and trade union mass meetings for yet another strike. But in terms of day-to-day power, they are noises off. Instead we have Macmillan visiting Churchill in the latter stages of his prime ministership, to find the old man in characteristic Number Ten pose, sitting in bed with a green budgerigar on his head: 'He had the cage on his bed (from which the bird had come out) and a cigar in his hand. A whisky and soda was by his side – of this the little bird took sips later on. Miss Portal sat by the bed – he was dictating.'[3]

Eighteen months later, there will be the cosy private dinner in Number Ten, interrupted when Eden gets his first message about the nationalization of the Suez Canal, and is told he must hit Nasser quickly and hard, by one of his guests, the regent of Iraq, Nuri El Said. This guest will later be a victim of Eden's failure, having his guts ripped out by the Baghdad mob and dragged, still living, through the streets attached to the back bumper of his car. Later still, there will be the famous procession of ministers being asked privately, one by one, who should succeed Eden by the drawling aristocratic kingmaker, Salisbury, 'Wab or Hawold?' They choose Macmillan. Edward Heath, the chief whip, has to go and break the news to Rab Butler that, though almost every newspaper says he will be the new Prime Minister, they are all wrong and he has lost out. Again, two men in a dramatically lit room overlooking Horse Guards Parade: 'As I entered, his face lit up with its familiar, charming smile . . . there was nothing I could do to soften the blow. "I'm sorry, Rab," I said, "It's Harold." He looked utterly dumbfounded.'[1] After that, Macmillan's first move is to summon Heath to dinner, to reshape the government. They have to barge through a crowd of journalists – Downing Street in those days being completely open to the public – and Heath is tripped up by one, tumbling into the car which races up Whitehall to Macmillan's haunt, the Turf Club. There another member of the club, sitting at the bar with the evening newspaper announcing the identity of the new Prime Minister, looks up, sees him and politely asks whether he had had any good shooting lately. No, laments Macmillan. Pity says the clubman. As he and Heath turn towards the dining room for oysters and steak, the man politely drawls, 'Oh, by the way – congratulations.'[5]

Much later Macmillan finally decides he too must retire. He has had great pain and difficulty pissing and wrongly thinks it might be cancer. Another small room: sitting in his hospital bed wearing pale blue pyjamas, with a silk shirt and cardigan (but without a bird on his head) he tells the Queen. Later, he suggests she should summon Alec Douglas-Home to replace him. There are literally dozens of similar examples of how political life was carried on among the top Tories during this period. Of course, there have been many Labour cabals, from the paranoid huddles in Harold Wilson's Downing Street to the notorious Blair and Brown deal at Granita restaurant in Islington in 1994. But nothing quite matched the tight little world of the Churchill and Macmillan era. If they were not dining in the Commons or a handful of gentlemen's clubs in St James's – Macmillan belonged to five clubs – they were shooting grouse together or meeting in villas in the south of France. It is sometimes said that Churchill's government, stuffed with old friends and relatives, was unusual. But of Macmillan's all-male cabinet, a mere two out of sixteen had not been to a grand public school, with Eton the most heavily represented. Astonishingly, within months of his becoming Prime Minister, Macmillan was leading a government in which thirty-five ministers out of eighty-five, including seven in the cabinet, were related to him by marriage.[6]

There were outsiders too, including Powell, Heath and later Margaret Thatcher. Ernie Marples, a former sergeant-major and building contractor who would help create Britain's first motorways, was another self-made man in the government; so was Reggie Bevins of Liverpool. Most of them felt awkward and ill-at-ease, not quite officer class in the Conservative hierarchy of the fifties. The social make-up of the Tory administrations contributed to their weakness and eventually the collapse of their authority. The charmed circle of intermarried grandees were so much the country's traditional ruling order that their natural instinct was to play down crisis. Not in front of the servants, children or voters seemed to be their private motto. Because all was not well, this would fatally destroy their authority. In the 'satire boom', rule by toffs would be discredited. Their silent struggles for power would eventually spill into the public domain, giving us political catchphrases like 'Establishment' and 'magic circle'. Sex scandals and spying scandals would persuade people that there really was something rotten in the old order. Rather as New Labour connived with the press in the 1990s to mock John Major's administration to death, so Harold Wilson and old Labour would join hands with *Private Eye* and playwrights to despatch the last government of grandees.

Churchill in Old Age

When Churchill returned to power in 1951, all this was still far ahead. The old order seemed to have re-established itself far more quickly than the smashing defeat of six years earlier implied. And it was an old order. Churchill was undisputedly the greatest Englishman alive. Yet he was now fighting time. Two years into his last premiership, just after giving a speech to visiting Italians in Downing Street – always history-obsessed, he had been lecturing them on the Roman legions in England – he slumped down with a major stroke. Hurried to bed, he nevertheless recovered enough to hold a cabinet meeting the following day, though saying little. But he then deteriorated so fast his doctor thought he would die. He lost the use of his left arm, spoke only in a slurred mumble, and was unable to stand. He was hurried to his home at Chartwell. There, over two months, he recovered. It is an astonishing story in several ways. First there is the spectacle of Churchill's amazing willpower and stamina, bringing him from near death to a position where he could make a major speech to the Tory conference and then engage in full Commons exchanges within a few months. Even more astonishing, the country did not know at the time what had happened. There were vague rumours but the Prime Minister's grave illness was kept secret to all outside a very close circle. In the end he broke the secret himself, mentioning it a couple of years later in Parliament, by which time it no longer mattered much.

Before this stroke, and indeed after it, other ministers found the old lion entirely exasperating. He had brilliant moments, both in set-piece speeches and in conversation. But he was a speaking memorial to his own greatness and therefore naturally inclined to ramble on. He was described as 'senile', 'past it' and 'gaga' in the memoirs of other members of the cabinet. They wrote of their hatred for him as well as their love. Sometimes he let his private secretary write a speech for him. Sometimes he forgot what he was going to say half-way through a sentence. Sometimes even foreign leaders such as the US President, Harry Truman, expressed boredom at his long-windedness. But the person most angered, hurt and frustrated was Anthony Eden who felt that after ten years of waiting, and half a lifetime at the top of the Tory tree, it was his turn to govern. Prime ministers always find it hard to give up. Churchill resisted Eden by frequent promises that he was likely to go at some time in the future, always then putting it off. He would reshuffle his ministers, offer Eden unsuitable alternative jobs, row with him, then raise his hopes only to dash them again.

Had the pair of them not been the most powerful men in Britain, and had it not been rather cruel, it would have been almost funny. Churchill had become increasingly doubtful as to whether Eden would be any good as Prime Minister, lecturing him about the importance of keeping in with the Americans, snapping at his suggestions and complaining to friends that he didn't think 'Anthony can do it'. If all else failed Churchill, as ever, used jokes. When the death was announced of a minister's father, Churchill greeted yet another delegation sent to urge his retirement with a mournful reference to the deceased, 'Quite young, too. Only 90.'[7] Age and illness would be a big theme of the Tory years, as they had been in the latter stage of Attlee's government. Eden was frequently ill with a biliary duct problem made worse by botched surgery. By the time he finally got the top job halfway through the decade, he was physically depleted. Macmillan later said of him that he was like a racehorse who had been trained to win the Derby in 1938 but was not let out of the starting stalls until 1955. So why did Churchill carry on for so long? Undoubtedly, part of the reason was that he simply could not bear to let go. But there was a nobler reason. The old man did have a cause.

Churchill's life had been dominated by war. He came from a grand military family, brought up surrounded by the stories and mementoes of battles won. He went to fight for the Empire in the Sudan then saw the Boer War at first hand as a war correspondent who was captured and escaped. In the First World War he was a highly controversial First Lord of the Admiralty, then a colonel in France. After it, as War Secretary, he tried to strangle the Bolshevik revolution with an entirely unsuccessful Western war in support of the Whites against Lenin. His great years were as Britain's war leader in the world fight against Fascism. Many of his critics, from socialists who remembered him sending tanks against trade union strikers to Little Englanders, reviled him as a natural warmonger. So it is interesting that his last great crusade was an attempt to stop a war, this time a nuclear one. Whether it was the wisdom of age or vanity about his unique role as global statesman, Winston Spencer Churchill became the world's leading peacenik. His speeches resounded with dark warnings of the catastrophe just ahead. As early as the 1950 election campaign, speaking in Edinburgh, he had coined the modern use of 'summit' when calling for a leaders' parley with the Russians. The arrival of the hydrogen bomb increased the sense of world panic and Churchill worried in particular about an American atom bomb strike against the Chinese in North Korea (as indeed did the Chinese).

He was struggling with a new world, understanding the nuclear threat but also thinking in a highly traditional way. As soon as he returned to power in 1951 Churchill had fired off worried requests for information about the ease with which Russian paratroopers could seize strategic locations in London, and the carnage that would be caused by different kinds of surprise nuclear attack. Above all, he thought that if the atom bomb menace existed, Britain had better be as menacing as she could manage. In December 1951 he had authorized Britain's first nuclear test and at the Monte Bello islands off Australia, HMS *Plym*, one of the war-surplus frigates which had escaped being broken up or mothballed, was instead vaporized by Britain's first nuclear bomb. Then in 1954 he gave the go-ahead, with weary resignation, for work on a British hydrogen bomb as 'the price we pay to sit at the top table'. He told his cabinet, 'If the United States were tempted to undertake a forestalling war, we could not hope to remain neutral . . . We must avoid any action which would weaken our power to influence United States policy.'[8] Britain would only have a voice in restraining America if it was itself a player: 'the fact must be faced that, unless we possessed thermo-nuclear weapons, we should lose our influence and standing in world affairs.' But for Churchill it was precautionary despair; his real campaign was for a new settlement between capitalist West and Marxist East.

London and Washington did not see eye to eye on nuclear matters, as we have seen. Britain had been abruptly cut off from American nuclear secrets and in the early fifties Britain was more immediately threatened. Russian bombers could not yet reach the United States so American bases in Britain, and RAF ones, would make this country the first Soviet nuclear target. Dreadful estimates of the carnage were circulated through Whitehall. Yet for the Americans, nuclear war was still something that happened abroad. Churchill saw the death of Stalin as a heaven-sent opportunity to reopen friendlier relations with

Moscow. Though as passionately anti-Communist as ever he was worried that the US President, his wartime comrade Dwight Eisenhower, was too rigidly anti-Russian. Churchill frankly thought 'Ike' stupid and unable to comprehend that nuclear weapons were far more than the latest military technology. This reflected an accurate gulf of perception. Eisenhower believed nuclear weapons were a mere extension of ordinary weaponry and would soon be regarded as conventional. Eisenhower and his Secretary of State Dulles in turn feared that in his dotage Churchill had become an appeaser; though Churchill always used the term 'easement' or 'settlement' of East–West relations as his preferred description. Again and again he tried to persuade Eisenhower of the virtues of a superpower summit, and offered to go to Moscow himself alone – at a time when the Americans would not dream of setting foot on Soviet territory – to clear the way. Dulles was strongly hostile. Churchill bitterly called him 'that bastard'. At last, having got an insincere half-promise from Eisenhower that he could at least contact the Soviets about some meeting on neutral ground, he fired off the invitation too early, became embroiled in a white-hot cabinet row, and had to watch his vision crumble. At the top of the rival powers, no one but him really wanted to make peace just then. Everybody was too busy preparing the next generation of nuclear devices, thinking more like generals, less like statesmen. Churchill was arguing for détente twenty years before it happened. Perhaps he had been doing it with a selfish tremor, hoping for a final triumph, but as visions go it was quite something for an eighty-year-old.

Churchill's other overseas initiatives were less impressive. He was losing the battle about the Empire and knew it, even as he wrapped himself in mystical prose about the new young Queen and the coming Elizabethan age. If the real conflict was with the Soviet Union and her allies, what price Britain's other post-imperial commitments? What price trying to hang onto control in Palestine, where desperate refugees were determined to settle, and where Jewish terrorists were killing British soldiers? What price Britain's piggy-in-the-middle role in Greece, trying to protect an unpopular monarchy against a communist insurgency? A little later on, trying to hold on in Egypt, or Iran, would prompt the same question. The private thinking of Whitehall was laid out in a fascinating memo from top officials to a cabinet committee shortly after the Americans had upped the ante in the nuclear race by exploding their first H-bombs. The British cabinet paper was frank about the overall position: 'It is clear that ever since the end of the war we have tried to do too much – with the result that we have only rarely been free from the danger of economic crisis.'

About Europe, Churchill had long been inclined to make dramatic sounding suggestions. He had offered to merge British and French citizenship during the darkest days of 1940. After the war he was not averse to a fully politically united Western Europe, though he assumed the British Empire could not be a full member. When he came back to power one of the most immediate issues was whether Britain would join early moves towards that united Western Europe. In 1950, the ailing Labour government had decided against, though after very little thought. When the French Foreign Minister, Robert Schuman, announced that his country intended to share sovereignty over iron and coal with West Germany, so binding the two old enemies tightly together in their industrial effort, he gave the British government an ultimatum. Attlee was out of the country and Ernie Bevin was already very ill, describing himself with no exaggeration as 'half-dead'. It was left to Herbert Morrison to give a hurried response. He had been at the theatre and was found by officials at the Ivy restaurant in London's Covent Garden. The plan which would one day lead to the European Union was explained to Morrison in a back room, piled with chairs.[9] He thought for a moment and shook his head. 'It's no good. We can't do it. The Durham miners won't wear it.' For many Tories, watching from the sidelines, this was a disastrous mistake. Macmillan, who had been observing things from Strasbourg, where he was in Bevin's vacated hotel room, thought the decision catastrophic, later telling his constituents it was 'a black week for Britain' and the country might pay a 'catastrophic price' for isolating itself under the socialists from Europe.[10] So there was general expectation that Tory Britain would change tack.

There was already a strong case for doing so. The Empire was falling away. Relations with the Americans had already been damaged over the atom bomb, as well as disputes about Palestine and Greece. Here was a moment for the Tories to decide to ride another horse too, and join the young European club. Churchill declined to do so. Offered the chance to take up common European defence, he ridiculed the notion, to the despair of Macmillan and some of the younger

Conservatives. He showed no interest in deeper involvement. He was the last imperialist whose rhetoric about the 'English-speaking peoples' was more heartfelt than his suggestions of anti-Communist alliances between Italians, Belgians and the French. Washington was pivotal to his world as Paris never could be, still less Brussels. He wanted summits on the H-bomb and a place on the world stage, not local deals with provincial nations half-desolated by war and invasion. The Foreign Office, where Eden was esconced, was also hostile to entanglements with the Europeans – not surprising, either, perhaps, since its grand embassies and worldwide reach made iron and steel deals near at hand seem parochial. The manner of Churchill's decision-making on Europe, though, was worrying to his contemporaries. It was never properly discussed in cabinet. It was as much a shrug as a decision. It was never announced. It was never thrashed through. It might as well have been taken in the Ivy. Perhaps, as with nuclear peace-making, it was just too early for the decisive move. Yet there is an unmistakeable sense of anti-climax about Churchill's last government. Outside the world was changing. New leaders were coming to prominence. Here, it seemed, Britain was being distracted by one moving curtain-call too many.

Strikes and Money: Jack Is All Right . . .

Conservatives of the fifties have had a particularly bad press for their willingness to stick with the Attlee consensus, allowing the country's underlying economic weakness to worsen. There is much in this. Churchill had fought the 1951 election promising to defend the new Welfare State and was inclined to speak wistfully of the case for coalition government in peace as in war, a theme first heard in 1945. He felt warmly towards the small Liberal Party and had half promised to help them by introducing some kind of proportional voting, though this was quickly scuppered by the Conservative hierarchy. He railed against class war and deliberately appointed the moderate, appeasing lawyer Walter Monckton to deal with trade union and labour matters. Yet there was one moment when Britain might have experienced a Thatcher-sized jolt, a British revolution thirty years early. It came on

Churchill's watch in 1952 when his young Chancellor, Rab Butler, proposed cutting the pound free from the system of fixed exchange rates agreed after the war at Bretton Woods. The scheme was called ROBOT. In detail it was fiendishly complicated, because of Britain's network of obligations to so many other countries using sterling as their reserve. In essence, though, it was very simple. The pound would float partly free, or rather fall dramatically against the dollar, thus giving Britain's struggling exporters a huge one-off boost. The government would be unable to fund its old obligations, the huge overseas defence establishment, and much of the new Welfare State. Grand housebuilding projects would be put on hold and unemployment would initially rise. But on the other hand, the bleeding of reserves and the periodic balance-of-payments crises would be a thing of the past. Britain would get the chance of a fresh start, not unlike post-war West Germany. Imports would be cut, exports would rise, sterling's freedom in the world would be re-established and the alternative future of a genteel, endless decline might be averted. It was nothing less than a free market national coup which would, among other things, infuriate the Americans. The historian Peter Hennessy has compared it to the desperation of the Suez war: 'ROBOT was the desperate and risky response of frazzled yet clever men who had run out of both caution and alternative ideas.'[11]

ROBOT, which was never revealed at the time, caused a rare row over matters of high principle inside the government and was eventually scuppered by the Foreign Secretary, Anthony Eden, and by Churchill's own growing unease about its domestic implications. It was the kind of scheme which might have been pushed through by a determined, vigorous Prime Minister armed with a mandate for change but was too much for an old man elected on a blandly consensual ticket. And it was the only example of such radical thinking for years to come, at least at this level of government. For the most part, this was a government which ran on domestic autopilot. Above all, in the eyes of later critics, it failed to take on rising trade union power. The unions had swollen in numbers to record levels of membership. Their leaders tended to be working-class men who had left school in their teens to cut coal, drive lorries or load ships before becoming full-time organizers. In the fifties, they still had personal memories of the

General Strike of 1926. Bitterness about the Depression had been partly assuaged after Labour repealed anti-union legislation, giving them powerful immunities in the case of strike action.

These national leaders, men such as Arthur Deakin, Sam Watson and Bill Carron, tended to be patriotic and socially conservative, ready to back the Bomb and Nato, and aligned against the left in Labour Party confrontations. They were well able to do deals with middle-of-the-road Tory ministers. More were Catholics than were Communists. But their greatest card was the economy. Very high rates of employment, high demand from customers starved of goods, and relatively high corporate profits meant that there was an insatiable demand for skilled labour. It was easy for firms to pass on higher costs caused by generous wage settlements. And in terms of days lost to strikes, Britain's record was not bad in the fifties, better than many economies which were growing faster. Butler at the Treasury confessed that he had no wages policy, only 'Walter's friendship with trade union leaders' and when Monckton and Churchill did a deal to stop a bus-drivers' Christmas strike because it was too 'disturbing', the Prime Minister phoned Butler late at night to tell him the good news. On what terms had he settled, the Chancellor nervously asked. Churchill replied, 'Theirs, old cock! We did not like to keep you up.'[12]

Why fight the unions? It was a horribly difficult task, anyway. In a statist economy, ministers were abnormally close to the power of the public sector unions. By later standards, an astonishing number of industrial workers were employed by the State – some 1.7 million people in transport, the mines and the power industry alone. Again and again, from the railways to the power stations, from bus workers to coalminers, to engineering, Monckton and his successors bought them off. Ministers knew perfectly well what they were doing. In his diary for June 1955, for instance, Macmillan, when Chancellor, reflected on the settlement of a railway strike which had done 'much harm' to the economy. He comforted himself with the thought that the men got little more than they could have had earlier which 'may have a deflationary effect and do something to stop the see-saw of wages and prices which has begun to show itself in the last year or two'. By 1958, as Prime Minister, he steeled himself to hold out against just the kind of transport strike that Churchill would have settled with a phone call. Yet Macmillan too never quite took it seriously and anyway by then the unions were changing in ways that made it harder to cope with them, not easier.

Built up over decades by amalgamations and local deals, they were sprawling baggy monsters which bore little relation to organization by plant or industry. A single factory might have a maze of competing and mutually suspicious unions operating inside it. This led to the growth in power of the shop stewards, often younger and more militant people who had filled the power gap during the war years when their elders were away. They could get deals for the people around them which were better than national agreements. By the mid-fifties there were scores of thousands of them. It was ruefully noted that Britain now had more shop stewards than soldiers. Wildcat strikes were more common than full-scale national disputes and they caused more disruption and uncertainty. Meanwhile as the old guard died off more left-wing leaders were quietly moving up the union hierarchy. A good example was Frank Cousins, a former miner and truck-driver from Nottinghamshire who was running the road hauliers in Churchill's day and who became leader of the Transport & General Workers' Union in the year of Suez when more than half a million T&G men voted for him. He was Macmillan's antagonist in 1958 and became a major headache for successive Conservative governments, leading strikes in the car industry, among busmen and elsewhere before being brought into the 1964 Labour cabinet by Harold Wilson. For a time he was the most famous, or infamous of the Brothers; but there were plenty of Cousins.

If strikes were one small cloud on the edge of the sunny skies of the Tory years, inflation was another. It was always there in the fifties, getting worse as the decade continued, but not yet quite a crisis, although with so many older people living off annuities and savings, it began eating into the lives of many middle-class families. The problem was simple to describe, hard to sort, particularly after the rejection of radical measures such as ROBOT. The country was exporting all it could but its appetite for manufactured imports was insatiable. Britain no longer had enough overseas investments and was not earning enough through producing well-made, competitively priced goods, in order to earn the living its people now thought they deserved. In other times the gap had been easily closed by 'invisibles' – earnings from banking, insurance and shipping, where Britain remained a world leader. It might have done so in the fifties and sixties too, except that Britain was spending such an historically vast amount of money on defence in peacetime, and spending that money abroad. In effect, the weaker British economy was subsidizing the fast-growing West German one because of the huge expenditure on the British Army of the Rhine.

The entirely predictable result of the balance of payments gap was that the pound was under constant pressure. There were periodic devaluations which damaged the reputation of the politicians in charge at the time – though the 1949 Labour devaluation is widely credited with kick-starting the Tory good times which followed. Trying to maintain British power through the sterling area (not just most of the Old Commonwealth, except Canada, but other countries including most of Scandinavia and traditional trading partners such as Portugal) meant that defending the value of the pound was an issue inflamed by pride and political sensitivity. In the Tory years it was another problem postponed. Defend the pound and Britain's global self-image or let it fall and help Britain's exporters? 'Stop-go' saw sudden tightenings of fiscal policy, then a stab on the accelerator, as government tried to break into a new era of growth, before slamming on the brakes to deal with the resulting surge in inflation. Until the post-war Bretton Woods system broke down in 1971 there would be regular arguments about devaluation. For politicians at the time, it was like trying to solve a puzzle with one too many parts.

The Purge

It is 24 March 1954, late in the afternoon outside Winchester Castle. The great hall of the medieval building, with its famous fake of Arthur's Round Table – created in the 1300s and painted for Henry VIII – is now empty. It has served duty all day as a courtroom. Now guilty verdicts have been passed and long since, the prison sentences meted out. But still the prisoners have been kept in the small whitewashed cells under the castle, an elderly Rolls-Royce waiting to take them to jail. The trial that had just finished made front-page headlines for days across Britain, and there were fears of a minor riot when the guilty men were led outside. They included a young peer of the realm, Edward John Barrington Douglas-Scott-Montagu, known as Lord Montagu of Beaulieu; a *Daily Mail* journalist called Peter Wildeblood; and a gentleman farmer, Major Michael Pitt-Rivers. Montagu had just been sentenced to twelve months in prison and the other two, eighteen months. Their crime had been conspiring to induce two RAF men to commit indecent acts – in other words, they were homosexuals.

There was a great purge of homosexuals going on in the Britain of the fifties, whipped up by the newspapers and by a clique of politicians and officials. The press had been full of salacious if untrue stories of wild orgies fuelled by champagne, the corruption of boy scouts and, perhaps worse than all this, of men who had associated with their social inferiors. So there was, perhaps, some reason to worry that when the three men were led away there would be angry attacks by the good burghers and women of Winchester. And indeed there were such scenes. But the attacks, the hammering of umbrellas, yelling, hissing and shaking of fists, was directed at the car taking away the prosecution witnesses. When eventually Montagu, Wildeblood and Pitt-Rivers were seen by the women who had waited so long, the mood was rather different. As Wildeblood himself wrote later: 'It was some moments before I realised they were not shouting insults, but words of encouragement. They tried to pat us on the back and told us to "keep smiling", and when the doors were shut they went on talking through the windows and gave the thumbs-up sign and clapped their hands.'[13] Much later, when Wildeblood was finally released from prison, he found his neighbours and colleagues just as supportive. The English are often unexpected.

Homosexual acts between men had long been illegal, but so long as they happened discreetly and in private, and did not involve minors, they had been relatively rarely prosecuted. The war, as we have seen, saw an increase in homosexual activity. After it, however, the official mood changed dramatically. In the last full year before the war there had been 320 prosecutions for 'gross indecency', a common way of describing homosexual behaviour. By 1952 the number had risen to 1,626. The prosecutions for attempted sodomy or indecent assault were up from 822 to over 3,000. If these still seem relatively small numbers, the ripples of fear and intimidation spread far further, and in general the number of homosexual offences known to the police had risen from 1938 to 1955 by 850 per cent. A small number of men were responsible. The crackdown had started under Herbert Morrison. But the toughest years were under the Conservative politicians of the fifties. The purge was led by the former Nuremberg interrogator of Nazi leaders, Churchill's Home Secretary, Sir David Maxwell Fyfe. With him was the Director of Public prosecutions, Theobald Mathew, who would often attend court to watch the 'buggers' be sentenced, as well as Sir John Nott-Bower, a Commissioner of the Metropolitan Police determined to rip the cover off London's 'filth spots'. They were supported by a press which ran articles on the secret world of mincing pansies, or explained to stout-hearted readers 'how to spot a homo'. There were special drives to root out buggery in the Army and worried Whitehall inquiries into alleged lesbian conspiracies in the RAF. Lesbianism was not, in itself, a crime, allegedly because Queen Victoria had refused to believe it existed, but was an offence in the armed services.

Attacking homosexuals helped sell papers and certainly played to the prejudices of many politicians and clergymen but there was more to it than that. The early fifties was also the time of maximum fear about Communism, subversion and spying. Not without reason. The atom bomb spy Klaus Fuchs had caused appalling damage to British intelligence by the time he was exposed in 1950. In 1951 two of the famous KGB spies, Guy Burgess and Donald Maclean, had defected to the Soviet Union. Though a proper version of their story would not break publicly until 1955, the British government was under American pressure to show that it was tough on subversive networks. This was not formally discussed at home but friendly overseas journalists were briefed. In October 1953, the *Sydney Daily Telegraph* reported that Cmdr E. A. Cole of Scotland Yard had spent three months in Washington consulting with the FBI after 'strong United States advice to Britain to weed out homosexuals as hopeless security risks, from important government jobs'. With the arrival of Nott-Bower as the new Commissioner of Police 'the plan was extended as a war on all vice . . .' So moralism and national security worries intertwined. The homosexual, so the thinking went, had to live a double life. He was open to blackmail. He moved in mysterious circles. He was morally weak. The homosexual was therefore by definition a security risk. Burgess and Blunt had indeed lived secret sexual lives and the habits of essential deception, the feeling of belonging to a hidden and important circle, connected seamlessly to their lives as spies. Nor was the blackmail argument ridiculous. A few years after the Montagu case, John Vassall, a homosexual clerk who worked at the Admiralty and had been photographed in Moscow by the KGB at a gay sex party, was uncovered as a spy. Vassall was a conspicuous consumer, living far beyond his means, yet no one had asked the obvious questions about where his money was coming from. Again, there was much speculation about a wider homosexual and traitorous network, this time involving ministers too.

The gap in official logic was that homosexual men were open to blackmail and had to live a secret life precisely because of the law that was now being so vigorously and aggressively enforced. Some men were self-confident enough to survive, the Labour MP Tom Driberg for one, who used the Commons toilets to proposition an impressive array of fellow politicians as well as parliamentary staff, and Macmillan's colleague, the lover of his wife, Lord Boothby. But others, including the Conservative MP Ian Harvey, convicted of an offence with a soldier in Hyde Park, and the actor John Gielgud, arrested in Chelsea in 1953, were not so lucky. There was a very extensive and semi-open gay world in theatrical circles – Alec Guinness had been fined for importuning in 1946, for instance, but had escaped press attention by giving the false name Herbert Pocket. Other celebrities of the time such as Noël Coward and the impresario Binkie Beaumont hardly bothered to hide their sexuality. But the wave of prosecutions caused terror among those living outside the charmed circle of theatrical and political power.

Montagu had fallen into the middle of the police operation first suggested by Washington. A premier peer of the realm, he was about as well connected as it was possible to be. In his time with the Grenadier Guards, he had served in Palestine during the worst of the Jewish terrorist attacks, and had an informal supper with the King, Queen and future Queen Elizabeth. In the advertising world, he had helped launch the patriotic new comic, *The Eagle* – the idea of a north country vicar called Marcus Morris who himself, said Montagu later, had 'a distinctly unclerical sexual appetite, as he adored showgirls'. The peer would go on to become famous for his national motor museum at Beaulieu, help found English Heritage and marry twice. But he was bisexual, something he had suspected at Eton and was confirmed in the Guards. At one party in London, the aristocratic officers were entertained by a young naval rating doing a striptease who would later become a national treasure as the jazz musician George Melly. Yet Montagu always insisted that he had made no improper advances to two boy scouts, the reason for his arrest. Having been acquitted then, he was drawn into the later Wildeblood case. The prosecution stooped to forging an entry in his passport to try to discredit an alibi, used illegal tapping of phones, entered and searched private houses without warrants, and put appalling pressure on two RAF men to inform against their 'social superiors', in order to avoid many years of imprisonment for themselves. The witnesses, as they later admitted, had been carefully coached in their stories.

Peter Wildeblood's unusual response to the prosecution was to declare openly and unashamedly that he was a homosexual or, in the language of the day, an 'invert'; and had a right to be treated with respect. He declined to apologize. His language was very far from the gay liberation rhetoric of modern times but it was clear and dignified: 'I am no more proud of my condition than I would be of having a glass eye or a hare-lip. On the other hand, I am no more ashamed of it than I would be of being colour-blind or of writing with my left hand.' He pointed out that Lord Montagu had done patriotic service in the Grenadier Guards and that Montagu's co-accused cousin, Pitt-Rivers, had served bravely in the war, while Wildeblood himself, though he turned out to be a terrible pilot, had served with the RAF as a meteorologist in Africa. These were all, apart from their sexuality, entirely normal members of the patriotic, upper-middle-class Establishment, about as different from the Cambridge spies in their views as it would be possible to be. And, of course, since homosexuality is spread throughout society, some of the Establishment was gay, too. Lord Wolfenden's famous committee, formed in 1954 to consider the law on homosexuality, was headed by a former public school headmaster and university vice-chancellor, and included Tory politicians, a senior official in the Girl Guides, a judge, and so on. When Wolfenden later discovered that his own son was gay he wrote asking him to keep out of his way and 'to wear rather less make-up'. The committee, however, took evidence from Wildeblood among many others and after three years of private hearings in the Home Office, duly recommended in

1957 a change in the law, legalizing private homosexual activity between consenting adults aged over twenty-one.

By then the country's mood seemed to have changed. There was a feeling that the tactics used against Montagu and the others were unfair and underhand. The hostility to government interference and meddling, which had contributed to the fall of Attlee's Labour administration, was beginning to stretch to private matters. When Wildeblood was released from prison, he found his working-class neighbours in Islington to be cheerily friendly. When Montagu was released from Wakefield prison, where his fellow inmates had included Fuchs, he got a similar reception, though it was not universal. At lunch, in the fashionable Mirabelle restaurant in London's West End, he recalled 'one or two of the neighbouring tables disapproved. The atmosphere became unpleasant and remarks were made which were obviously meant to be overheard with intent to wound.' At this point, however, the then Leader of the Opposition, Hugh Gaitskell, who was also lunching there, intervened. 'He could see perfectly well what was going on. After a while, he laid down his napkin and crossed the room to our table. "How nice to see you back," he said, holding out his hand, which I shook with surprise and gratitude. The action silenced the surrounding hostility.'[14] There was continued hostility to homosexuals then and there is today, but the so-called permissive society of the sixties was already being forged by public reaction in the second half of the Tory fifties to cases such as these. For now, Parliament disagreed. In the first parliamentary debates on homosexual law reform, the Home Secretary, Maxwell-Fyfe, said he did not think the country would wear such a change. Had he been present in the Mirabelle restaurant, or had he stood a few years earlier outside Winchester Castle he might have realized he was already out of date.

The Spies: Tom and Guy in Moscow

Britain's spy networks were far more effectively hidden by upper-class connections than by the homosexual inclinations of a few of Moscow's men. The full story of the Cambridge spies does not belong here but to the thirties and the divided loyalties of the anti-fascists. The tale of how a cluster of rebellious former public schoolboys came to believe that the fight against poverty and Hitler required their allegiance to the bloodthirsty regime of Stalinist Russia, and then how they infiltrated the British intelligence and diplomatic services before and during the Second World War, is well known. The sons of a diplomat, a naval officer, an Anglican clergyman and a cabinet minister, they were about as traditionalist and patriotic in their upbringing as it was possible to be. They remained quintessentially English afterwards too. The Labour MP and journalist Tom Driberg visited one of them, Guy Burgess, a few years after he had dramatically defected with Donald Maclean. (And it was dramatic: Maclean's pregnant wife had just cooked a special ham for dinner at their home near Churchill's country house, when Burgess arrived and raced him off to Southampton for the overnight ferry to St Malo.) In Moscow, Driberg found Burgess outside a hotel, 'his bird-bright ragamuffin face . . . tanned by the Caucasian sun'. Burgess explained his job involved trying to get the Russians to translate and publish the novels of E. M. Forster. In his flat Burgess strummed the Eton boating song on his piano and proudly showed that his suit still had a stitched badge reading 'Messrs Tom Brown of Eton, High Street, Tailors'.[15] The Moscow defectors would die there, mildly regretful but entirely unrepentant, while two further traitors, Sir Antony Blunt, who became Surveyor of the Queen's Pictures, and the economist John Cairncross, privately confessed and were left unexposed and unpunished for much of their lives.

Did they matter, really? They did. Between them British traitors helped the Soviet Union acquire nuclear weapons earlier than would otherwise have happened, passed huge amounts of information to Stalin's secret police, were directly responsible for the deaths of scores of British and other Western agents at the hands of the KGB and, in Philby's case, managed to stymie an American attempt to create an uprising in Albania, so keeping that wretched country under the heel of one of the most primitive tyrannies of modern times. Their story has been made 'glamorous' by the gilded associations of pre-war Cambridge, and the idealism of being anti-Nazi when part of the British Establishment were not. Films and countless books, some by the spies themselves, have romanticized them. Yet the consequences of their spying were squalid and dangerous. Nor were they actually the most successful spies – less 'glamorous' characters such as Alan Nunn May, a scientist, and Fuchs, were more important. It was the

Dutch-born George Blake, who escaped from occupied Holland at the age of twenty, joined the Royal Navy, was recruited by MI6 and captured by the Communists in Korea, who probably caused most damage. He had been shocked, he later said, by the effects of American bombing of Korean villages and passed the names of 400 British-controlled agents in Germany to the Russians, with predictable consequences for many of them. Some think he was brainwashed. Blake was caught and in 1961 was given a prison sentence of forty-two years, which remains the longest sentence ever imposed by a British court. He, of course, was not a dapper and well-connected Old Etonian with friends to tip him off.

What is it about the British and spying? Other Western nations had their post-war spying scandals, particularly the Americans and the West Germans. But nowhere was quite so gripped as Britain by the actions of Soviet agents. Class and sex are undeniably part of the answer. But there is another half-buried theme – British anti-Americanism. Philby claimed all his life that he was a British patriot who felt that the country was simply allied with the wrong side. Another student in the same Cambridge college as Philby at the same time (though they never knew one another) was Enoch Powell who came to much the same conclusion a few years later. This anti-Americanism was something which could bring together patriotic right wingers and left-wingers in a common cause. Washington was constantly warning London about intelligence lapses and the possibility of traitors. But even when Russian defectors brought descriptions of Maclean and Philby to MI5, they were languidly dismissed; unless there were even more traitors, even higher in the system (and Philby was close to the top) then disdain and smugness must have been to blame for the grotesque failures of security.

Once traitors were discovered there was then a national case for not making too much of it because of the angry reaction from the American intelligence services, on whom Britain relied very heavily. Politicians were obliged to explain or failed to explain, the defections and the rising suspicions of third and fourth and then fifth men still uncovered. Macmillan, as Foreign Secretary in 1955, was obliged to knock down the idea that Philby might be a Russian spy who had tipped off Burgess and Maclean four years earlier (he was, of course, and had). Later, after yet more spies had been uncovered, Macmillan was told by an excited Sir Roger Hollis of MI5 that the organization had arrested Vassall. Macmillan seemed dejected at the news and when Hollis said he didn't seem very pleased, replied: 'No, I'm not pleased at all. When my gamekeeper shoots a fox, he doesn't go and hang it up outside the Master of Foxhounds' drawing room; he buries it out of sight.' Macmillan, by now Prime Minister, lamented that there would be a great public trial, the security services would be blamed, and 'there will be a debate in the House of Commons and the Government will probably fall. Why the devil did you "catch" him?' More concerned about harassing the press, Macmillan got two scalps when journalists refused to give their sources for allegations concerning Vassall and were briefly imprisoned. It was not surprising that people suspected an Establishment cover-up by chaps who belonged to the same clubs and did not like their dirty washing flapping in public.

Public Laughter

Had anyone been asked to define British humour in the aftermath of the war, they would probably have come up with the genteel, meticulous cartoonists of *Punch* whose neatly cross-hatched ink world stretched from Westminster and the Home Counties to the more remote areas of the Scottish Highlands but included little in between. They might have mentioned the rude postcards of the seaside tradition, fat overhanging bosoms and little Willies. There were some rather lame newspaper comic-strips; the radio surrealism of *It's That Man Again*; the exuberance of Flanders and Swann; and on film, the warm, ultimately optimistic humour of George Formby and the Ealing comedies. From the late thirties to the mid-forties the world had been harsh enough perhaps, without harsh laughter too.

What Britain had had, above all, was music hall. Even in the fifties musical reviews were still being widely performed, weaving a little light innuendo among the songs. Few of the hundreds of once-famous double acts, singers, comedians, slapstick artists, clowns and acrobats from the Victorian and Edwardian heyday of music hall had been recorded, though they provided the main form of mass entertainment for half a century. This was a powerful culture which required skilled, physically tough and consistent artistes who could sing, dance and tell jokes, the original 'variety acts'. Some of the fun can still be glimpsed in modern Christmas pantos and seaside summer shows, though these must be a pale shadow of that lost, garish gaiety. After the war there was a surge of one-way traffic as music hall acts were taken up by the BBC Light Programme and when, in the fifties, television began to take off a final generation of people who had learned their trade in small seaside and provincial theatres, would arrive to hoof it, clown and sing for the cameras. Bruce Forsyth, Jimmy Tarbuck, Ken Dodd, Eric Morecambe, Ernie Wise and their rivals were the last products of the old musical theatre and its relentless demand for all-singing, all-dancing comic talent. In its way, music hall is as important to the smell and colour of twentieth-century Britishness as rock music. It has just had less effective PR.

Below the surface, new kinds of comedy were slouching unsteadily towards those microphones, cameras and footlights. One could write a useful contemporary history by simply asking of any particular time: what made people laugh? To be British now became bound up with a string of radio and television shows, their catchphrases, lateral logic and increasingly rude jokes. The harder tone of new British comedy came most obviously from two sources. One was the absurdity of many people's army experiences during and after the war. The other, with the later satire boom, was the absurdities of private boarding schools. No democracy had mobilized a greater proportion of its people in the world war. No country sent more of the children of its elite to boarding schools with strange rules. What followed from these two incontrovertible facts was very funny indeed. It meant elongated, grotesque faces; weird nasal voices; nonsense words that could send apparently normal people into hysterics – a private British world created some of the most chippy, eloquent people on the planet in the sixth decade of the twentieth century. One of the most idiosyncratic and energetic aspects of British culture could be called popular surrealism. It was not the surrealism of experimental film-makers or painters, but of Max Wall, Goons and eventually Pythons as well.

The name 'Goon', picked up from Popeye cartoons, seems to have begun with Spike Milligan. In the opening stages of the war, Milligan had played childish boredom-repelling games with fellow gunners around their battery in Bexhill. Milligan was a working-class child of the British Empire. His father was Irish, and had performed in music halls as a youth, alongside another boy called Charlie Chaplin who then disappeared off abroad. He had then joined the British Army, like his father before him, so that Spike was born in India and brought up there and in Burma. It seems to have been a golden time before his father lost his army job in pre-war defence cuts and the family had to return, settling in Catford, south London. Poorly educated, Spike got a job as a clerk until he was sacked for stealing cigarettes. He taught himself to play the trumpet and dabbled in politics – joining the Young Communists and according to one report, flirting with Oswald Mosley's blackshirts too. Then in 1939, as he recalled later, an envelope arrived containing 'a cunningly worded invitation to participate in World War II'.[16] Army service bored and frightened Milligan but it was the making of him.

Tens of thousands of soldiers found that the fear of death, nutty regulations, stupid officers and the incompetence of the war machine, required a more raucous, sardonic humour than they had been used to at home. Spike was sent as a signaller to North Africa, where he was duly shelled, lost friends and was injured, always playing jokes and making up games to pass the boring times. As the fighting moved north through Italy, he saw another gunner take part in one of the Army variety shows put on to amuse the troops. This was Harry Secombe, a commercial traveller's son from Swansea, who, like Spike, had been a clerk before the war. The two were soon working together, part of a loose association of military comedians and musicians who would eventually tickle the nation when they returned (Dick Emery, Benny Hill, Frankie Howerd and Tommy Cooper among them). Meanwhile in India, Peter Sellers, a young half-Jewish impressionist was busy impersonating Sikh officers and RAF commanders. Michael Bentine, an Old Etonian intelligence officer and actor, would later complete the quartet, the most influential act of British comedy surrealism in the fifties, and one of the most important ever. Almost all of them had some music-hall connections – Sellers's mother and grandmother had been singers and dancers, and Secombe's family was saturated in music-hall culture. But they had all added a new twist, the result of those transforming army years.

The Goon Show was subversive without being party political, or even conventionally political at all. Spike Milligan described it as 'against bureaucracy . . . its starting-point is one man shouting gibberish in the face of authority.'[17] Of one of the Goons' classic villains, Milligan said that it was 'a chance to knock people who my father, and I as a boy, had to call "sir". Colonels, chaps like Grytpype-Thynne with educated voices, who were really bloody scoundrels. They'd con and marry old ladies; they were cowards charging around with guns.' And one of his producers, Peter Eton, said later: 'We were trying to undermine the standing order. We were anti-Commonwealth, anti-Empire, anti-bureaucrat, anti-armed forces.' Milligan, Secombe, Bentine and Sellers were demobilized into the rationed, bureaucrat-dominated Britain of the forties so it is hardly surprising that their humour was aimed at unthinking patriotism and official bungling. It was exactly what people wanted and needed, however nervous the BBC felt when the show began broadcasting in 1951. Older listeners found it alarming and baffling, but millions were quickly mimicking the silly voices, appalling puns and nonsense words of Goonery. Milligan remained prickly about being working class, and was political enough to support the Campaign for Nuclear Disarmament away from the microphones. His comedy was meant to sting. Yet there was a warmth about the Goons that drew some of that sting: had it been otherwise it is unlikely that the Duke of Edinburgh and the Prince of Wales would have been quite such enthusiastic fans.

All Fall Down: Suez

Some sense of the popularity of the Tories' crown prince throughout Churchill's sluggish and frustrating last government, Anthony Eden, can be gauged from his reception in the 1955 election when Churchill had at last retired. Most of the time he travelled in his own car, declaring that 'if I cannot travel in my own country without an armed guard, I would rather retire from politics.' But when he went by train, women arrived at the windows at each stop with huge bouquets of flowers. Here was the man who had stood up to Hitler, decently waited for Churchill to retire and was now a great architect of post-war global peace. Shortly after the election, Eden invited the new Soviet leader Khrushchev to London. (Despite a completely drunk translator, the visit had gone well, though at one point Khrushchev was introduced to the huntin'-and-shootin' Tory politician, Lord Lambton, as 'a shooting peer'. The Soviet leader solemnly and sympathetically shook hands with Lambton, assuming that this meant he was under sentence of death and shortly to be shot.) Eden was at root an intensely patriotic man, who thought Britain's Commonwealth links far more important than deeper entanglements with Europe. Among his weaknesses were his inherited foul temper and a racist disdain for Arabs. But for most people in 1956 Eden seemed an almost beau ideal, the man for the moment.

Suez is often seen as a very short era of bad judgement, a crisis whose origins are obscure and whose consequences are hard to discern. This sells it short. Suez was about Britain's colonial history. It had begun as something very personal, a duel between an English politician of the old school and an Arab nationalist leader of the new post-war world. Anthony Eden and what he represented for the Britain of the mid-fifties are worth dwelling on. Through most of Eden's life he had been a glittering and glamorous figure, hugely admired across the political spectrum, a global peacemaker and statesman. Remembered by one colleague as 'half mad baronet, half beautiful woman', Eden had come from a landed, if sometimes eccentric family. During the Suez crisis he was seen in Washington as the epitome of alien English snobbishness. In fact one of his forebears, a baronet of Maryland, had been a great friend of George Washington and supporter of the American Declaration of Independence. Another had written a pioneering study of the poor, warmly praised by Karl Marx. Eden was never absolutely sure of his paternity – his mother was vivacious – but it was probably the wild, spendthrift, artistic Sir William Eden. He was a baronet out of the pages of a satirical novel, much given to hurling joints of roast lamb out of windows and, when riding to hounds, jumping closed level-crossing gates without waiting for oncoming trains. He had a terrible temper and used language so bad that, when he was presiding over local police courts, Durham miners would come simply for the pleasure of hearing him swear.[18]

The boy Eden, a beautiful casket seething with unstable genes, went on to Eton. He fought bravely in the First World War, during which his oldest brother was killed in the trenches and his much-loved younger brother was killed at sea, days after his sixteenth birthday. A liberal-minded Tory MP from 1923 onwards, Eden rose to become the Foreign Office minister who had face-to-face negotiations in the thirties with Mussolini, Hitler – the two men discovered they had fought opposite one another in the trenches, and drew maps of their respective positions – and Stalin, whom Eden thought was a kind of oriental despot. After becoming Foreign Secretary and helping form the pre-war system of alliances and League of Nations agreements, he dramatically resigned in 1938 in protest at the appeasement of Nazi Germany, finally returning to serve Churchill, again as Foreign Secretary, from 1940 to 1945. A brilliant linguist, highly cultured and with a deep love of modern art, a lover of many women, a genuine diplomatist, he was familiar by the mid-fifties with most of the world's leaders. In 1954 at Geneva he had arranged a key conference to try to keep peace in the new Cold War world, a summit seen then as a last throw to prevent the Third World War.

So what of Nasser? If Eden was the model of a kind of Englishness, Colonel Gamel Abdel Nasser was the original of the anti-colonialist autocrat who would become familiar over the decades to come – charismatic, patriotic, ruthless, opportunistic. Driving the British from Egypt was the cause that burned in him from his teenage years, and not surprisingly. Egypt, though nominally independent under its own king, had been regarded as virtually British until the end of the Second World War. It had been the centre of the fight against Rommel's Afrika Corps, and the pivot around which Britain's domination of the Middle East revolved. The oil fields of Iran and Iraq which kept Britain working, the Suez Canal through which a quarter of British imports and two-thirds of Europe's oil arrived, the airfields which refuelled planes bound for India and Australia – all this made Egypt a hub; a pivot; Britain's Mediterranean naval. Most British families contained someone who had served in Egypt at some time. What was less special was the casual contempt British people tended to reserve for the Egyptians themselves, or 'wogs' as they were more commonly known. Churchill had reacted to one moment of earlier Egyptian insubordination by shouting that if they didn't look out 'we will set the Jews on them and drive them into the gutter'.

Before the Second World War Egypt had been forced to sign a treaty making it clear that the country was under Britain's thumb. Eden's head was even placed on Egyptian postage stamps to mark this humiliation. One wartime episode makes the relationship clear. In 1942, as Rommel's tanks drew nearer, and Churchill was fulminating about Cairo being a nest of 'Hun spies', the British ambassador told Egypt's King Farouk that his prime minister was not considered sufficiently anti-German and would have to be replaced. The King summoned his limited reserves of pride and refused. It was, he insisted, a step too far, a breach of the 1937 treaty. Britain's ambassador simply called up armoured cars, a couple of tanks and some soldiers and surrounded King Farouk in his palace. The ambassador walked in and ordered the monarch to sign a grovelling letter of abdication, renouncing and abandoning 'for ourselves and the heirs of our body the throne of Egypt'. At this royal determination crumbled. The king asked pathetically if, perhaps, he could have one last chance? He was graciously granted it and sacked his prime minister. Life went on, the war went on. But Egyptians took note. Down in the Sudan a young Egyptian army officer, Lieutenant Nasser, seething with indignation, complained in letters to friends about the surrender and servility shown to the British. Colonialism, he said, 'if it felt that some Egyptians intended to sacrifice their lives and face force with force, would retreat like a prostitute'.

The son of a postal worker, Nasser was soon at the centre of a group of radical army officers, Egypt's Free Officers Movement, discussing how to get the British out and how to build a new Arab state, socialist rather than essentially Islamic. At this time, and later under Nasser, the Muslim extremists, whose thinking would one day influence al Qaeda, were being persecuted and even executed. Nasser was a ruthless, quietly determined man who naturally attracted followers; when King Farouk was eventually ousted by the Free Officers in July 1952 it took just two years for the young Nasser to oust the interim leader and seize control of the country himself. For him, this was good timing. After the war Arab nationalism had made things much tougher for Britain. Its oil interests began to be challenged. Visiting British ministers found themselves stoned by Arab crowds. To Churchill's fury, Iran's prime minister, the popular and independent-minded Mohammed Mossadeq, had nationalized the Anglo-Iranian Oil Company in 1951. Though he was overthrown in a CIA-organized coup two years later (organized by a president's grandson, the gloriously named Kermit Roosevelt), Mossadeq's action was a curtain-raiser for what Nasser would do in Egypt. In Iraq, a British-sponsored king and prime minister were holding on by their fingertips and would later both be murdered by mobs. In Jordan, the British soldier who had commanded an Arab Legion there since 1939, Sir John Glubb, known as Glubb Pasha, was sacked by the young King Hussein in March 1956; an Arab now wanted an Arab in charge of his army. Though it seems a small matter now, at the time it was seen as a slap across the face for London, provoked by the uppity Arabism sweeping the region. Eden blamed Nasser for this, and told a junior minister: 'What's all this poppycock . . . about isolating and quarantining Nasser? Can't you understand that I want Nasser murdered?'[19]

Egypt was where the confrontation between old colonial power and the new Arab nationalism was always going to take place. Britain's military base at Suez, guarding its interest in the canal, was more like a small country than a barracks. It was about the same size as Wales, with a vast border which was expensive and difficult to defend, so much so that Attlee had considered closing it and pulling out shortly after the war. The base depended for survival on supplies and trade with the surrounding Egyptian towns and villages. But in the latter days of Farouk's reign, it was already being boycotted by nationalist Egyptians. One incident produced another. The tension rose. Off-duty British servicemen were shot. After one act of bloody retaliation involving the slaughter of poorly armed Arab policemen holed up in a building by British soldiers, the Cairo crowds turned on foreign-owned clubs, hotels, shops and bars and set them alight. Britain found herself facing a guerrilla war.

Eventually, following yet another coup, London began to negotiate a British withdrawal – there were, after all, other bases nearby, notably in Cyprus, where however another nationalist guerrilla war was going on, and in Jordan. Eden, then Foreign Secretary, came to think that withdrawal was inevitable and pointed out to his colleagues that 'we are ourselves in serious breach' of the treaty, having eight times as many troops in the country as stipulated. To start with, all was civilized enough. Nasser even briefly met Eden, though he didn't much enjoy being lectured by the British leader in fluent Arabic. He complained later that Eden in the grandiose surroundings of the British Embassy, which made the British 'look like princes and the Egyptians like beggars', treated him like a rather dim junior official. The agreement stipulated that Britain would keep her rights over the canal, a deal soon broken by Nasser.

At this stage, how great a threat was Nasser? His ability to rouse Arab opinion was impressive, and he wanted to make himself a spokesman for the non-aligned world generally. His Cairo Radio, broadcasting across the Middle East, was the al Jazeera of its day, though considerably less independent. At different times in the coming crisis Nasser would be compared by British politicians and newspapers to Mussolini and Hitler, presented as a stooge of the Soviet Union, and then as a regional Arabist menace. He was a dictator, certainly. He was also a socialist of a kind, with great plans for a healthier, stronger, better-educated country. He wanted to spread his power throughout the Arab world, beginning with the Yemen, Syria, Sudan and Jordan. Like Saddam Hussein, he had used poison gas against enemies and, like him, was regarded with alarm by other Arab rulers. Like Saddam, Nasser believed in the destruction of the then new State of Israel.

Yet he would have remained a local irritant had it not been for a catastrophic blunder by Washington. Nasser's great ambition was the creation of the so-called High Dam at Aswan, a gargantuan project which had been dreamed about since the mid-forties and which might transform Egypt's economy. Three miles wide, it would create a 300-mile-long lake which would give the Egyptians eight times as much electric power as they then had and increase the country's fertile land by a third. It was much more than just another civil engineering project. Nasser talked of it being 'seventeen times larger than the greatest pyramid'. With Aswan, here was a new Pharoah bringing a new age to Egypt after centuries of colonial humiliation. The problem was that such a dam was also far beyond the resources of Nasser's Egypt. Loans had been discussed for years and in 1956 Nasser had every reason to think that the Americans, followed by the British, were about to sign the cheques. Partly out of pique when he thought he was being given an ultimatum, Nasser's ambassador implied they could get help from the Russians and Chinese if the American terms were not good. The US Secretary of State, John Foster Dulles, abruptly cancelled the offer. Nasser was livid. To show his anger and to find a new and secure source of revenue, he abruptly retaliated by seizing control of the Suez canal, triggering the coup with code-words given to a mass public rally.

If the dam was not just a dam, the canal was not merely a canal. It was the ultimate liquid motorway, a vital artery of world trade, connecting Europe through the Mediterranean, with India, Australia, New Zealand and the Far East. In the days before mass air freight the only other way was round the Cape, infinitely further, slower and more expensive. Years before Eden had called it the jugular vein of the British Empire, and in the mid-fifties a quarter of all British exports and imports came through it. It wasn't only Britain. Three-quarters of Europe's oil came from the region, half of it through the canal. Indeed, a sixth of the whole world's cargoes went through it, some fifty ships every day, all of them paying tolls. Because of its international importance and the fact that it had been built by a French engineer, using French and British money, it had since 1888 been administered as an international facility, not an Egyptian one. It was run by a company, 44 per cent of which was in turn owned by the British government, thanks to an inspired piece of High Victorian entrepreneurship by Disraeli. It was not hard to see how this streak of colonial-owned internationalism running through Egypt felt like a violation. Nasser's plan, having seized it by military force just days after Dulles turned down his loan request, was to use payments from canal traffic to finance the next phase of his dam. The legality of the seizure was much debated around the world but to the British government Nasser's action was simple theft and a clear breach of international treaties. Worse, you couldn't leave Egyptians running something as sophisticated as a canal. Worse still, if it was allowed to stand, this act of impudence or bravado would inspire other Arab radicals and threaten the whole region.

Since Nasser's act had been provoked by Washington, and since his revenge hurt Britain and France, Washington's allies, it might have been expected that President Eisenhower would staunchly back action against Nasser. The situation turned out to be rather more complicated. For one thing Washington was pursuing a vigorous policy of trying to turf out the old colonial powers from the Middle East in favour of America herself. The US had oil of her own but was always worried about the future and acutely aware that two-thirds of the then known world reserves were in the region. Special deals had been made with the Saudis and Iranians. This economic interest was augmented by loud and pious anti-colonialism, particularly from the Secretary of State, Dulles, a devious and sanctimonious character who hated British imperialism with a Founding Fathers fervour. He also loathed Eden, who cordially returned the feeling. Next, there was the intense worry in Washington about the Russians, who were making menacing noises about the liberal regime emerging in Hungary. Next, there was the ticklish question of the Panama Canal which was controlled by the United States in a similar way to Anglo-French control in Suez. Ike and Dulles wanted no agreement emerging from the Middle East about international control of waterways which might affect Panama. Finally, by 1956 President Eisenhower was in the throes of trying to be re-elected on a peace and prosperity ticket and was outraged by his allies' untimely sabre-rattling. For all these reasons, America would prove to be Britain's enemy in her confrontation with Nasser, not her friend.

Little of this was understood in London, where Eden's tough line with Nasser was hugely popular. The Conservative Party was roaring its support. The Labour Opposition under Hugh Gaitskell sounded if anything even more bellicose (as it would later in the opening phases of the Falklands War, under Michael Foot). With a couple of exceptions – the *Manchester Guardian* and the *Observer* – the press, commentators and cartoonists were all on-side, and demanding punishment. The new science of opinion polling, and individual messages of support pouring into Downing Street, showed that public opinion agreed. Nasser must be sorted out. But timing in politics is everything. Under American pressure, there followed months of diplomatic manoeuvring during which Eden and his passionately anti-Nasser Chancellor, Harold Macmillan, began to lose the initiative. There were international conferences, proposed compromise deals under which the countries dependent on the canal would have a new role in administering what would formally be Egyptian property, and intensive negotiations at the United Nations. Britain kept hinting that it might yet come to war. Eisenhower and Dulles insisted that a peaceful solution should be found. By saying that America would have no part in trying to 'shoot our way through' to the canal and by referring to the problem of colonialism, they encouraged Nasser, who brusquely rejected all outside initiatives. America's attitude also encouraged Moscow, which led the diplomatic charge against Britain and France. Throughout this episode and despite the crisis caused by Russia's crushing of the Hungarians, the US and the USSR stood shoulder to shoulder against London.

This all felt increasingly ominous. And then a possible shortcut presented itself through the unlikely agency of Israel. It depended on America in the mid-fifties almost as much as it does half a century later, but the Israeli government believed Nasser and his pan-Arabism was a threat to their existence not properly appreciated in Washington. Egypt had taken delivery of large quantities of Soviet bloc armaments, including the latest jet fighters and bombers; Nasser's anti-Israeli rhetoric was bloodcurdling and he was increasingly closely echoed by the Syrians and Jordanians. The Suez crisis gave the Israeli government a one-off opportunity to strike their most serious enemy, and even enjoy Western air support while they did it. Thus came about the plot finally hatched by Britain, France and Israel to finish off Nasser. Harold Macmillan, the Chancellor, had originally suggested that Israel be used to attack Egypt from one flank, and the idea was enthusiastically taken up by Churchill in retirement. When first mentioned to Eden he thought it eccentric and dismissed it. But as the international talks dragged on and the government began to lose support and momentum at home, the idea of a plot resurfaced.

We do not know all the details for the very good reason that Eden insisted no notes were taken at the key cabinet committee discussions. He even insisted that private diaries of the time, including Macmillan's, be torn up or burned. But the Israelis approached the French who revived the idea. Israel was being harassed on her borders by guerrillas. The French, fighting a vicious colonial war in Algeria, thought Nasser was a menace to their interests there as well as in the canal. The specific plot, for an Israeli attack to be followed by an Anglo-French demand for a ceasefire, which would be refused and then followed by a 'police-action' intervention, was dreamed up by the French war hero, General Maurice Challe. So cloak-and-dagger discussions began. The place at which the details were hammered out was a modest borrowed villa at Sèvres outside Paris, a house that had once been a French resistance hideout. Eden's Foreign Secretary, Selwyn Lloyd, attended, reluctantly, having tried to disguise himself by wearing a battered old raincoat as he left London. (It did not work.)

There he met his French opposite number, the Israeli prime minister David Ben-Gurion, the country's chief of staff, Moshe Dayan, and Shimon Peres from the Israeli defence ministry. It was not an easy meeting. Britain had a close defence agreement with Jordan, another enemy of Israel at the time, and it was not so long since Israeli terrorists had been killing British soldiers. For their part, the Israelis deeply mistrusted the British. The French were also suspicious after Britain's decision a year earlier to shun the new Common Market. Finally, the deep secrecy of the meetings created its own layer of mistrust, particularly since Eden was obsessive about nothing being written down. (Eventually the outline agreement was written down, at the Israelis' insistence, and initialled by a British negotiator.) At the Sèvres house, with the help of local fish and wine, a deal was finally done. Those present solemnly swore not to reveal the details during their lifetimes, and for good reason. The agreement to ensure that French paratroops from Algeria and a British invasion force from Malta and Cyprus could attack, theoretically to separate the two sides, but in fact to grab back control of the canal, was wholly illegal. It required that ambassadors, other ministers, the head of MI6 and the Commons as well as the White House, must all be kept in ignorance. That, at least, was done highly successfully. Despite leaks from Paris to the CIA, President Eisenhower never guessed what was happening until it was too late.

Meanwhile the mood in Britain had changed. Anti-colonialism, the international rule of law and the rights of young countries were all issues which enthused Labour and the left generally. The United Nations, Nato and the European Convention on Human Rights, still smelled of fresh paint. As American hostility to military action became clearer, some MPs and commentators began to have second thoughts. Eden, rather like Thatcher and Blair later, complained that left-wing intellectuals were stirring things up against him, while 'The BBC is exasperating me by leaning over backwards to be what they call neutral and to present both sides of the case.' There was nothing quite like the drama of the Hutton Inquiry and the resignation of the BBC's Chairman and Director General in 2004, yet at a fundamental level the earlier clash went further: Eden made menacing noises about taking the BBC under direct government control. According to BBC lore, troops were placed in a building on the Strand, awaiting orders to take over the BBC's external services in Bush House: meanwhile the Corporation's engineers there had been issued with sledgehammers and told to destroy their own equipment rather than let it fall into the hands of Eden and the government. Inside the government, some ministers became uneasy about the whole escapade. Sir Anthony Nutting, a Foreign Office minister, would resign in protest, though without the public drama achieved by Robin Cook before the Iraq War. And as with the Iraq War nearly half a century later, late in the day when the opposition really organized itself, crowds turned out to protest and private unease spilled into public anger.

For the first time in modern British history, large numbers of people came onto the streets of London to challenge a government going to war. The Suez demonstrations would be followed by the great anti-Vietnam clashes of the sixties and the marches against Tony Blair's Iraq War, but in the fifties nothing like this had happened before. Suez split Britain down the middle, dividing families and friends. It brought the Prime Minister into angry conflict with Establishment institutions and Establishment grandees. Lord Mountbatten is said to have warned the young Queen that her government were 'behaving like lunatics' and a former Royal aide believed she thought her premier was mad.[20] Because of Suez a generation of politically aware younger people grew up rather more contemptuous of politicians generally, readier to mock them, keener to dismiss and laugh at them. The decline of respect for the craft of politics would probably have happened anyway in modern Britain. But the events of the winter of 1956 hastened that decline.

Even the military was affected. The call-up for Suez provoked widescale desertions and minor mutinies across Britain. Some 20,000 reservists were called back and many declined to come, some scrawling 'bollocks' across their papers. In Southampton, Royal Engineers pelted a general with stones. In Kent, there were similar scenes among reservists: 'More or less to a man they refused to polish boots or press uniforms or even do guard duty. They spent most of the time abusing the career soldiers for being idiots. The army could do nothing . . .'[21] It went further than Kent. In Malta, in the unpleasant surroundings of the Qrendi airstrip, Grenadier Guards 'fuelled by NAAFI tea, marched through the camp . . . down to the building where the officers were housed.' They were angry about conditions as much as politics but earned a stiff lecture from their commanding officer on the dire consequences of mutiny. Shortly afterwards, though, the Reservists of the 37th Heavy Anti-Aircraft Regiment of the Royal Artillery were at it again, marching through the Maltese camp to protest and shouting down their regimental sergeant-major.[22] These were minor incidents, undoubtedly, and had much to do with boredom and irritation among reservists brought suddenly to dusty, unpleasant camps, yet headlines in the press about army mutinies and protest marches sent shockwaves through the forces.

The biggest single difference between the Suez and Iraq crises was, of course, that the Americans did not want war in 1956 and were determined for it in 2003. Anguished letters and telephone transcripts tell the story of mutual misunderstanding. From Eden's point of view, the US was preventing any real pressure against Nasser while talking grandly about international law. He gave enough broad hints, he thought, for the White House to realize that he and the French prime minister were ready to use force. At different times Eisenhower's team had given the impression that they accepted force might be necessary. Dulles had talked of making Nasser 'disgorge' his prize. So while Britain could not tip off the Americans about the dangerous and illegal agreement with Israel, or give military details, there was a general belief that the Americans would understand. This was an error. From Eisenhower's viewpoint, his old allies had dropped him in the dirt at the worst possible time, during an election and when the Russians were brutally crushing the Hungarian uprising with 4,000 tanks and terrible bloodshed. Eisenhower and Dulles had failed to pick up persistent hints and worried reports from CIA agents in Paris and London, just as they had failed to understand the consequences of cancelling their help for the Aswan dam. America in the mid-fifties was a young superpower, still flat-footed. This time, it had been fooled by both sides.

So, on the early morning of 5 November 1956, British and French paratroopers began dropping from the air above Port Said. A huge British convoy which had been steaming for nine days from Malta arrived with tanks and artillery and the drive south to secure the Suez Canal began. So far, only thirty-two British and French commandos had been killed, against 2,000 Egyptian dead. In a military sense, things had gone smoothly. The politics was another matter. When the invasion happened, Eisenhower and Dulles exploded with anger. According to American White House correspondents, the air at the Oval Office turned blue in a way that had not happened for a century. Dulles seriously compared the Anglo-French action to that of the

Soviets in Budapest. Unfortunately, at much the same time as Eisenhower was hitting the roof of his office, Nasser was hitting the floor of the canal – with no fewer than forty-seven ships filled with concrete. He had done the very thing Eden's plan was supposed to prevent. He had blocked the canal. For the first and last time, the United States made common cause with the Soviet Union at the UN to demand a stop to the invasion. The motion for a ceasefire was passed by a crushing sixty-four votes to five. World opinion was aflame. India, eight years independent, sided with the Soviet Union, which was threatening to send 50,000 Russian 'volunteers' to the Middle East. In the event, as the British troops were moving south, having taken Port Said and with the road to Cairo open to them, they were suddenly ordered to stop. An immediate ceasefire and swift pull-out was being ordered by London, not because of the views of irate squaddies in the Home Counties or the private views of the Queen, or fulminations in Moscow. Britain was being humiliated by the United States in a way that had not happened since the War of Independence.

On the ground, clear-sighted about their national interest, and uninterested in American anger, the French were prepared to keep going. Britain was in a different situation. It came down to money, oil and nerves. The pound was again being sold around the world, with the US Treasury piling in to viciously turn the screw. Fuel was soon running short and, in what seemed like a return to wartime conditions, British petrol stations briefly required motorists to hand over brown-coloured ration coupons. Britain needed emergency oil supplies from the Americans which would have to be paid for in dollars. Britain didn't have enough dollars. Another loan was needed. Harold Macmillan turned to Washington and the International Monetary Fund to ask for help. The US Treasury Secretary, George Humphrey, told him, via Britain's new Washington ambassador Sir Harold Caccia: 'You'll not get a dime from the US government if I can stop it, until you've gotten out of Suez. You are like burglars who have broken into somebody else's house. So get out! When you do, and not until then, you'll get help!'

By now, the Egyptian air force had been destroyed and 13,500 British troops, with 8,500 French troops, had landed at Port Said and were making their way south towards the canal. Rather embarrassingly the Israelis, led by Ariel Sharon, later to be a controversial prime minister, had long ago reached their destination and stopped, so there was no real need to 'separate' anyone. But the game was up by then. With the country split from Buckingham Palace to the barrack room, Eden's health and nerves gave way. To many it seemed as if Nato itself was on the verge of breaking apart. After a brutally direct phone call from Eisenhower, ordering him to announce a ceasefire, Eden called his French opposite number Guy Mollet, who was begging him to hang on. According to French sources he told him: 'I am cornered. I can't hang on. I'm being deserted by everybody. My loyal associate Nutting has resigned as minister of state. I can't even rely on unanimity among the Conservatives. The Archbishop of Canterbury, the Church, the oil businessmen, everybody is against me! The Commonwealth threatens to break up . . . I cannot be the grave-digger of the Crown. And then I want you to understand, really understand, Eisenhower phoned me. I can't go it alone without the United States. It would be the first time in the history of England . . . No, it is not possible.'[23]

The ceasefire and the withdrawal that followed were a disaster for Britain, which left Nasser stronger than ever. It finished Eden, though not before he had lied to the Commons about the Anglo-French-Israeli plot at Sèvres. He said: 'I want to say this on the question of foreknowledge, and to say it quite bluntly to the House, that there was not foreknowledge that Israel would attack Egypt – there was not.' This can be compared to the French copy of the protocol of Sèvres agreed six weeks earlier which begins by stating quite bluntly: 'Les Forces Israeliennes lancent le 23 Oct 1956 dans la soirée une operation d'envergure contre les Forces Egyptiennes . . .' The canal was eventually reopened and reparations agreed, though the issue of oil security then assumed a new importance. Britain was left chastened and stripped of moral authority, Washington's rebuked lieutenant.

The effect on the US is also worth recalling. Eisenhower and Dulles had been driven by pique masquerading as high Christian principle, and their handling of the crisis encouraged the Arab nationalism which would return to haunt America in later decades. Eisenhower misled the American people about his true state of knowledge of Britain's readiness to use force. His public statement that he abhorred the invasion because the US did not approve of force to settle international disputes sat oddly with his earlier interest in using nuclear weapons in

Korea. The Russians took note and were almost certainly more belligerent afterwards. As a result of Suez, the French distanced themselves from America. It led to the Franco–German axis which endures to this day. The politics of the Middle East changed radically. Britain would not again possess independent power or influence in the region. The age of American power there, based on support for Israel and the oil alliance with the Saudi Royal Family, leading to so much later controversy, properly began after Suez. Much later, according to the then Vice President, Richard Nixon, Eisenhower had second thoughts about Suez, calling his decision to crush Britain his greatest foreign policy mistake. Dulles, who was desperately ill with cancer, told the head of the hospital where he died in 1959 that he reckoned he had been wrong over Suez too.

Other consequences of Suez were less predictable. It provoked the arrival of the Mini car, designed in the wake of the petrol price shock caused by the seizure of the canal. It even affected the fast rate of decline of the shipyards of Clydeside and Tyneside, whose small oil tankers were soon replaced by supertankers built at larger yards overseas. These, it was discovered, could sail round the Cape and deliver their cargo just as cheaply as smaller ships using the canal. Had this been realized a few years earlier, Eden might never have gone to war, and might be remembered now as one of our finer prime ministers. But it wasn't and 'Suez' became four-letter shorthand for the moment when Britain realized her new place in the world.

Muddle or Logic? Two Soldiers

Harold Macmillan's arrival as Prime Minister meant a swift acceptance of American power. Was there another way? The man who was so like him and yet so unlike him, Enoch Powell, certainly thought there was. But Macmillan, devious and wily, was the better politician. 'First in, first out' was the brutal, accurate jibe about him. Having been even more gung-ho about Nasser than Eden himself, it was he as Chancellor who felt the full impact of the run on the pound and led the political retreat. Unsettlingly, Macmillan was also having a series of private meetings with the American ambassador in London during the height of the crisis, advertising himself as Eden's deputy and suggesting ways in which the ceasefire and withdrawal could be sold to Tory backbenchers.

Macmillan and Eisenhower knew each other from the war and while it cannot be said that the Americans actually replaced Eden with a complaisant Atlanticist – the switch-over was done in the old Tory way, by a cabal agreement inside the cabinet – they certainly got the man they wanted. Macmillan swiftly tried to put Suez behind him and, greatly to France's disgust, was soon pleading with Washington for help in nuclear weapons. For a brief period Bevin's belief in the possibility of a genuinely independent British bomb had been vindicated. But this period lasts no longer than five or six years, the gap between the time it took for the new British bomb, to be dropped by long-range jet bomber, to be made militarily usable, and the moment in 1958 when Macmillan realized that British bombing and missile technology was already out of date and insufficiently threatening to deter a Russian attack.

Remaining in the tiny nuclear club wasn't the only route that Macmillan could have taken but nuclear weapons seemed a relatively cheap shortcut to retaining the full fig of global swagger. Macmillan bluffed when he could, authorizing the first British H-bomb explosion, at Christmas Island, in May 1957. It was partly a fake, a hybrid bomb intended to fool the US into thinking its ally was further ahead than we really were. The next year at a crucial showdown between British and American scientists in Washington, the British Aldermaston team persuaded Edward Teller's men from Los Alamos that Britain was just as far advanced in the theory of nuclear weaponry. Teller conceded that the laws of physics seemed to apply on both sides of the Atlantic and for a brief time the cooperation of 1940–5 was resumed although, after Suez, any illusion of equal partners working together was an obvious sham. Perhaps Britain, like France, could have broken away from the American-run military command of Nato and returned to developing her own nuclear weapons and strategy, joining full-heartedly with the new Europe. It would have been expensive and altered the shape of the post-war world but an entirely different path was available to Britain after Suez, even if it seemed a stony and unattractive one. Macmillan never considered it.

The stony path was the terrain of a politician to whom Macmillan

Right. New Dawn: Denis Healey and Roy Jenkins in uniform at Labour's 1945 party conference.

Below. Clement Attlee, driven by his wife Violet, was advised to jump in his car and head for Buckingham Palace to be made prime minister before plotters could put in Herbert Morrison instead.

UNOFFICIAL ECONOMIC ADVISER TO GREAT BRITAIN : John Maynard Keynes in His Study in Bloomsbury
It was he who foresaw the evil results of Versailles while that treaty was still under construction—and resigned an important job to make them known. To-day, at the age of 56, he has produced a plan for financing the war and avoiding its most disastrous economic consequences.

MR. KEYNES
HAS A PLAN

To carry on a war successfully we must spend over £2,000 millions a year. How are we to pay? How are we to avoid inflation? In this article Kingsley Martin, Editor of "The New Statesman and Nation," writes of the man who has given an answer to those questions, describes the answer which he gives.

WHEN "The Economic Consequences of the Peace," by John Maynard Keynes, was published in 1919 it caused a profound sensation. Here was an important member of the British delegation at Versailles, who had resigned his post in order to tell the truth about the Treaty. The sensation was due at least as much to the book's literary quality as to its exposure...

John Maynard Keynes, possibly the cleverest man in Britain, died after struggling desperately to save his country from bankruptcy. But he could not do a deal with the Americans good enough to avoid the grim austerity of the post-war years, including bread rationing, the subject of the 1946 demonstration in Trafalgar Square shown below.

Right. British women were hectored constantly about their clothes, and would soon revolt.

Below. Temporary pre-fab homes, often built using German and Italian prisoners of war, were one answer to the huge housing shortage. Some were still being used in the seventies.

Go through your wardrobe

Make-do and Mend

Despite Labour's triumph, and fearing socialism, the old order quickly reasserted itself: Cecil Beaton poses on the set of *Lady Windermere's Fan* in 1946.

Hero of the working classes: Joan Littlewood (*right*) was one of the most radical voices in British theatre. But her influence in conveying the spirit and dilemmas of a new Jerusalem was far less than that of Ealing Studios, with films such as *Passport to Pimlico* (*below*).

Bitterly disappointed by his 1945 rejection, Churchill endured his exile writing, speaking, painting – and hunting, here, four days before his seventy-fourth birthday. He would be back in 1951 (*below*), proclaiming a new Elizabethan age.

Old Labour's greatest prophet? Nye Bevan in full Welsh flow, presumably unaware that he's being mimicked by a small boy.

The comprehensive vision, pushed by Tories too: a new school in Anglesey, 1954.

The Skylon at the 1951
Festival of Britain: people
said that it, like the country,
was suspended without
visible means of support.

Simpler pleasures:
a honeymoon couple
at Billy Butlin's hotel
near Brighton, 1957.

was almost allergic. One morning in 1962, the Foreign Secretary, Lord Home, walked into the cabinet room in Number Ten to find the Prime Minister quietly shuffling the place-names around the table. He asked the cabinet secretary what has going on. Had someone died? No, came the reply, it was all to do with Enoch Powell: ' "The PM can't have Enoch's accusing eye looking at him straight across the table any more." And poor Enoch was put way down the left where Harold couldn't see him.'[24] It is not a bad symbol for the age. Avoiding eye contact with unpleasant choices was part of the art of governing and for much of this time governments got away with it rather successfully. Powell, a brilliant romantic driven by a cold, intense logic, was tormented by the choices ahead, from the economic effect of an ever-growing state, to the consequences of the loss of Empire and the effect of immigration on traditional Englishness. His answers to these questions would change over time and some would destroy his political career, but he never stopped following his agonized conscience. Macmillan, by contrast, was perfectly well aware of hard choices ahead. His diaries are full of foreboding and he could write crisp, clear-sighted private papers. He pushed decolonization hard and struggled to get Britain into the European Economic Community. But confronted by the most dangerous questions, such as whether union power and state spending needed to be reversed, he seemed rather more interested in staying in office and reassuring the people that all would be well. He was a great actor, a wonderful showman. And he put Powell so far out of eyeline that he couldn't see him.

Much though they disliked one another, Macmillan and Powell had several important things in common. They had both been soldiers and both carried a certain guilt that they had not been killed fighting Germans. Harold Macmillan had fought exceedingly bravely in the First World War. He was wounded repeatedly. He survived without ever forgetting how many of his friends and the soldiers serving under him had not. He had a shuffling walk, much mocked when he became Prime Minister as some kind of aristocratic affectation. It was, in fact, caused by shrapnel from a German shell. Powell, a much younger man, had been an intelligence officer with the Eighth Army in the Second World War and said much later, with a touch of the characteristic Powellite emphasis: 'I should like to have been killed in the war.' Both men were haunted. Both also came from humbler families than

Macmillan's marriage and pheasant-shooting, or Powell's perfect dic-
tion and fox-hunting, might have suggested. Macmillan's family had
been Scottish crofters before going into the book trade, which bought
him his privileged upbringing. Powell was the son of a Birmingham
schoolmaster who rose through mental power and ferocious hard
work. Both men were well read, particularly in the classics, and gifted
at languages, though Macmillan lacked Powell's brilliance and preferred
English novelists and political biographies. They shared a belief in
Britain's unique destiny. The differences between them were chemical
– and generational.

Harold Macmillan was a high-minded Victorian reformer, who
grew up to the sound of horse-drawn carriages and the spectacle of
the old Queen's Diamond Jubilee. A young Tory, his conscience was
stirred by the awful poverty of the Depression, notably in his Stockton
constituency. His politics in the thirties became radical to the point of
extremism. He hired the former secretary of Oswald Mosley's New
Party, a former Marxist. He called for widespread planning of the
economy, including the abolition of the Stock Exchange and the
bringing of the trade unions into the heart of economic decision-
making. He was remarkably close to the politics of Tony Benn fifty
years later. He might well not have stayed with the Tories had the
war not intervened. After it, he was still a stirrer, suggesting renaming
the Conservatives the New Democratic Party. By the time he returned
to government in 1951, his ideological wildness had matured into a
paternalistic mildness, a horror of right-wingers and left-wingers both.
Like Winston Churchill the son of an American mother, he hoped to
show that in an American world, Britain could still play the role of a
wise if wobbly parent, 'Greece to America's Rome.'

Enoch Powell, eighteen years younger, was no less romantic. But
he was formed by the university study, the Indian army and the last
days of the British Empire. Unlike Churchill or Macmillan he loathed
the Americans to the point where he seriously believed, during 1944–5,
that the next war would pit Europe and Russia on the one hand
against the anti-imperialist United States on the other. Greece to their
Rome? Had Powell not been a distinguished Latinist he would probably
have preferred to torch Rome. Where Macmillan was vague and
paternalistic in his thinking, Powell had a disconcerting habit of
beginning with first principles and then following his logic wherever it

led, which was often to uncomfortable places. Sovereignty, independence and race were not woolly abstractions for him. He distrusted wit and showmanship – though like his Labour doppelgänger and friend Michael Foot, he was always more of a showman and a personality politician than he admitted. Enoch Powell came relatively late to hunting. But compared to Macmillan, he was the wilder horseman, notorious among friends for throwing himself off while leaping unwisely over high fences with unknown drops. Macmillan was the ultimate master of staying in the saddle and would rule for years. Powell never would, but his anger matters as much for the British story as Macmillan's affectation that things were under control. Together, these two men make up the inner argument that animates the thirteen Tory years, even when looking the other way. Macmillan had the power but not the ideas. Powell lacked the power, most of the time. But he would find the ideas.

The Revolt of the Chicken Farmer

Ideas matter. And because ideas matter, so too does the story of an Old Etonian Christian Scientist, former RAF fighter pilot, chicken farmer and unsuccessful turtle rancher called Antony Fisher. In the high years of socialism and planning, from 1945 onwards, Fisher stood out as an utterly self-certain individualist and anti-socialist. 'Communism is the poison offered to the people; socialism is the cup in which it is given; and the welfare state is the tempting label on the bottle,' he liked to say. In the Britain of the forties and fifties these views made him an eccentric. Once this country had been the world centre for liberal economics, famous for its people's distrust of big government – a land without identity cards or intrusive central government. Now even its Liberal Party was a keen supporter of the post-war consensus (the party, after all, of Beveridge and Keynes). There were some standing out against it. Not many, but some. Their unlikely spiritual teacher was Friedrich von Hayek, an exiled Viennese economist, who came from the very heart of cosmopolitan intellectualism where socialism, communism, Freudianism and fascism contended. A cousin of the daunting philosopher Wittgenstein, he would help reconvert the British to their old doctrines of economic liberalism.

Hayek had arrived in London to teach economics in 1931 and developed a close rapport with another economist Lionel Robbins, the son of a London market gardener who had been taken up by that creator of the Welfare State, William Beveridge. Hayek and Robbins formed a crucial partnership at the London School of Economics, a subversive friendship which would help, eventually, to change the intellectual climate of Britain. Hayek's *The Road to Serfdom*, published in 1944, was one of the most influential books of the age, a full-throated attack on socialism which was received with contempt by many but admired – with reservations – by both George Orwell and Keynes himself. But a book is not a movement. Liberal economists did begin to meet regularly in Switzerland from 1947 but for Britain the key moment came with the arrival on the scene of Fisher, now an almost entirely forgotten man. He had been traumatized by watching the death of his brother during the Battle of Britain and rebuilt his life as a Sussex farmer. A staunch individualist, he had been entranced by Hayek's book and managed to meet his hero after the war. Hayek told Fisher not to try to become a politician but instead to try to win the battle of ideas by forming some kind of institute or organization to fight the rotting influence of the State. It was a message Fisher never forgot. Luckily for him, the State stepped in to help him spread it. In 1952 his herd of cattle contracted foot and mouth disease and had to be destroyed. Fisher used his compensation money to visit the United States.[25]

There he not only picked up the latest free-market thinking but visited a huge experimental 'broiler chicken' farm at Cornell University, where 15,000 birds were being raised under one roof. This, thought Fisher, was exactly what the meat-starved British needed. It was illegal to import the chunky American poultry central to the new factory farming, so the (anti-regulations) Fisher was reduced to covering two dozen fertilized White Rock eggs with silver foil and bringing them through in his hand luggage as 'Easter Eggs'. Back in Sussex he built sheds with gas heating systems and an overhead rail system to bring in food. Soon twenty-four chickens became 2,400 and then 24,000. Within a few years, his family were raising 1.25 million birds, Buxted Chickens had been formed, and Fisher was a very rich man, the most successful poultry farmer in Europe. Across Britain, affordable roast chicken became a staple of the Sunday lunch table, thanks to Fisher.

And with the money they made him, he was able to fund the Institute for Economic Affairs, undoubtedly the most influential think tank in modern British history. Set up by Fisher and the eccentric ex-paratrooper and Liberal, Oliver Smedley, the IEA was intended to combat the socialist influence of the Fabians.[26] Soon they would be joined by others, Ralph Harris and Arthur Seldon. Hayek would be proved right. It was the seeding of ideas that mattered most, not conventional political careers.

The IEA first touched British politics during the winter of 1957–8 when inflation was rising above 4 per cent and wage settlements were in double figures. Like so many political crises of the time this one occurred in deepest private. The question was whether government spending should be cut back as part of a wider drive to curb the amount of money in the economy. Banks were also to be instructed to cut back credit. Macmillan was far more worried about confrontation and unemployment than he was about rising prices. His Chancellor, Peter Thorneycroft, disagreed. He was insistent that savings had to be made to squeeze inflation and save the pound. His enemies thought Macmillan an unprincipled coward. He was certainly driven by a ruthless enthusiasm for staying in office. But there was another side to the Prime Minister. Brought up in the intellectual shadow of Keynes, he thought that seriously painful cuts were perhaps not necessary and that the economy was already slowing. Though Macmillan was inclined to dither, haggle and to split the difference, this was a shrewd call. And around him he had many spending ministers, looking after the armed forces, the hospitals and welfare, who were bitterly against cutting back. He feared some of them might resign.

On the other side of the argument, as it turned out, were the real resigners, Thorneycroft and his two junior Treasury ministers – the wealthy, sarcastic, ruthlessly logical and nearly blind Nigel Birch, and Enoch Powell. Their insistence that it was vital to control the money supply was not just a technical position, but was intertwined with a personal suspicion of corporatism and the big state that was close to the more intellectual economic case now being pushed by the newly formed IEA. Lionel Robbins had been advising the three ministers, despite much sucking of teeth by more consensus-minded officials, and Fisher's men would come to see Thorneycroft and his fellow rebels at Macmillan's Treasury as heroes. They provided the intellectual ammunition and connected through Powell to younger Tories, and gained them as converts. Powell had already been introduced to Hayek's thinking. In the months before the three Treasury ministers resigned, they had been dropping in on one another for a rolling conversation which showed they had all concluded the same thing – that government spending was too high and had to be severely reined back. Against the instincts of their own officials as well as their colleagues, they put together a planned series of cuts, including a 50 per cent increase in the cost of school meals, freezes on pay rises and the removal of family allowances for the second child. It would have hit five million families, including millions of the very middle-class mothers whose support the Tories most needed.

It was a deliberately tough and provocative package, and battle was duly joined in the cabinet. If there was ever a moment before the great political smash-ups of the seventies when ministers could have gripped the issue of inflation and asserted themselves against the consensus of Whitehall and the unions, this was it. Day after day, the arguments raged back and forward. Compromises were offered, partially accepted, and then rejected again. Tempers grew shorter. The Treasury team trooped in and out of Number Ten. A special cabinet was held on Friday, then again on the Sunday. But Thorneycroft, despite being accused of 'Hitler tactics' by irate colleagues, would not budge. Macmillan, anxious to get away for a tour of the Commonwealth, would not concede the cuts. All three ministers then resigned. Thorneycroft would later become chairman of the Tories under Margaret Thatcher. Birch would struggle with his growing blindness and never return. Powell's stormy career had many more crises in it yet. In apparently throw-away but actually carefully considered words, Macmillan dismissed the whole matter as 'a little local difficulty', appointed a new team, and swanned off abroad exactly on schedule. It seemed stylish, insouciant, masterly. From it, immediately, nothing flowed. Some cuts were made by the new Chancellor. The economy was in fact turning down, which suggests Thorneycroft's medicine would have been grim indeed.

Yet this was a turning point – away from the ideas of free marketeers and towards the last phase of the planning economy which would end in disaster. That, in turn, would eventually produce Thatcherism, the IEA's final triumph and the time when Antony

Fisher's eggs came home to roost. Before that could happen, another pre-election boom was engineered in 1959 and a new idea for improving British economic performance began to take hold, the central plan used by the French. By 1961 there was a 'pay pause' to try to hold down inflation, and then the establishment of a grand chat-in, the National Economic Development Council, or Neddy, which brought industrialists, civil servants and trade unionists around a table to discuss how to produce more. Reggie Maudling virtually ordered the car-makers to build new factories in Scotland, Merseyside and Wales in order to combat rising unemployment. The following year saw a 4 per cent growth target. The run-up to the 1964 election under a new Prime Minister featured a giveaway budget by Maudling, by now Chancellor, which would later be blamed by Labour for leaving an atrocious economic crisis. Almost all the weapons used by Labour to try and plan their way out of economic decline, from pay and incomes targets to national plans and regional directives, were already in place under Macmillan and his successor Alec Douglas-Home. All would fail. Antony Fisher knew why.

Things that Fall on your Feet

The best answer was clearly for British industry to produce more that the rest of the world wanted to buy, reliably and at the right price. Was that impossible? In the fifties there were plenty of successful British corporations. There were the oil giants such as Royal Dutch-Shell, product of a merger in 1906 and by then a vast international business, headquartered in London. There were the consumer combines, notably Unilever, another Dutch and British joint venture dating from 1928 which squatted across everything from soap powder to sausages, toothpaste to frozen food, and which was run on the latest principles of market research, ruthlessly targeted advertising and properly trained managers. There was the privatized-again steel industry. The Steel Company of Wales whose vast Port Talbot works in South Wales ('the city of steel which never sleeps') employed 20,000 people and could boast one of the most modern mill systems in the world. Other private steel firms, at Consett for instance, were also working at full pelt and seemed competitive with their European rivals. There was ICI, the chemical combine created in the twenties, which enjoyed a near-monopoly in many products, which employed 6,000 research workers and by the end of the fifties was spending more on R&D than all Britain's universities combined. There were electronic companies like Ferranti's and the sprawling engine-making, light bulb, fridge and washing machine group AEI; the still-successful engineers such as Rolls-Royce and Vickers and tightly run metal-bashers like Guest, Keen and Nettlefolds.

These and other groups were not allowed to sit pretty, or lack for competition. The fifties had seen the start of ruthless 'corporate raiding' by tycoons who took over, broke up and reorganized flaccid and poorly managed firms. There was much talk of learning the latest American management techniques; the big US advertising companies were already growing in London and influencing British thinking; better design was being eagerly sought out from Italy, Denmark and France. In his *Anatomy of Britain* (1962) the journalist Anthony Sampson paints a vivid picture of one of the new property tycoons who was making a fortune by breaking up the inner city portfolios of great old companies and putting up new developments – what he called his 'Canalettos', the new skylines of booming Britain.

Jack Cotton, a Birmingham boy made good, was living in a suite in the Dorchester Hotel, surrounded by surveyors, maps and paintings by Renoir, a jaunty business impresario – 'short, red-faced, fifty-nine, with smooth black hair, shrewd eyes, a pointed handkerchief in his pocket with a bow tie to match . . . His cars are called JC1 and JC2.' Then there was Hugh Fraser, the Glasgow draper's son who was building a huge network of stores and other businesses across the country. In 1948 he floated House of Fraser and created a private company Scottish and Universal Investment Trusts (SUITS) which became a mighty force in the fifties; by 1957 he had bought London's John Barker group, and two years later, Harrods. Then, another outsider, the Italian-born Charles Forte who had emigrated to Alloa in Scotland was quietly building a modest chain of roadside cafes into a huge hotel and catering business. He opened some of the first motorway cafés. From 1971 he added the Little Chef chain to his group and from 1978 he had control of the Happy Eater restaurants too, which while not necessarily the finest examples of cuisine, kept generations of travelling Britons fuelled. These men are also part of the story of the fifties, alongside the more familiar images of tweed-suited Old Etonians ambling around grouse-moors. Even in government the rumbles of modernization could be heard. The hyperactive Tory minister Ernie Marples, a self-made businessman and rare working-class *arriviste* in Macmillan's cabinet, a fireball of energy in the Jack Cotton mould, was busy recasting Britain's ancient transport system; the first parking meters, for instance, went up in London in 1958 in Grosvenor Square. Under his appointee and friend Dr Beeching, brutal cuts in the rail network would soon follow. Investment went instead to new roads and traffic management systems. During those thirteen Tory years, car ownership quadrupled to eight million and huge amounts of commerce was diverted from rail to lorries.

Britain's car industry, which would later become the ultimate symbol of industrial failure, was looking strong. The tangle of small competing companies that had marked the pre-war industry had been radically pruned. In 1952 the two great rivals, Austin and Morris, came together to form the British Motor Company. Herbert Austin's company at Longbridge, Birmingham, which traced its history to 1906, had dominated the inter-war years with its Austin Seven. This was the first British car which could be bought in large numbers by the less wealthy: good enough to be built under licence by BMW and copied by Nissan, it had sold nearly 300,000 by the outbreak of war. By 1948 a new range of Austins, the Princess and Sheerline, were spattered across magazine and newspaper adverts, and the A40 Somersets and Devons were arriving. Lord Nuffield, over at Oxford, had been one of the great industrial pioneers of modern Britain, building his first car just before the First World War, and still going strong enough at the time of the merger to become president of the new BMC. His Morris Eight and Morris Ten had won pre-war devotees. After the war, it was the Oxford company which produced the first great British car of the age of mass motoring, Alec Issigonis's revolutionary Morris Minor of 1948. This would become the first British model to sell over a million, and would still be in production as late as 1971. Lord Nuffield had not been an immediate fan, describing the car as 'that damned poached egg designed by that damned foreigner'.

The Great Arragonis

Alec Issigonis deserves a short aside in the narrative, a space for himself. He not only designed the Morris Minor but in 1959, the year Macmillan, at the height of his reputation, called a particularly success-ful election, he produced the Mini too. This was the nearest thing to chic Macmillan's age produced, though of course Macmillan himself would never have bought anything so small and vulgar. Issigonis can lay claim to being one of the more influential figures in the history of the car in Britain as well as being about the only industrial designer anyone has heard of. The son of a Greek engineer living in Turkey who had taken British citizenship, and a German brewer's daughter, his early years had been lived on the site of his father's marine engineering business, watching the drawings transform themselves into engines.

He is as good an example as any of the benefit that immigration brought to the country. He was a war refugee: the First World War peace treaties had carved up the Ottoman empire and given Smyrna, the port where Issigonis lived, to Greece. The Turks won it back and many foreigners fled. Issigonis's father died on the way and he arrived with his mother in London in 1922, virtually penniless. He learned engineering and industrial drawing in London before getting work first for Humber, then Morris. An unconventional designer, he loathed teamwork and mathematics, describing the latter as the enemy of every truly creative man. He learned in part by hand-making his own racing car, which he raced himself before the war; later he would ridicule such innovations as car radios, seatbelts and comfortable seats.

Issigonis's Morris Minor had been radical in design and structure; it was the nearest of any British car to the Hitler-era Volkswagen Beetle. His Mini-Minor was commissioned in the immediate aftermath of the Suez crisis when petrol shortages had focused attention on the case for cheap, economical cars. The country was already latching on to the cheap bubble cars being imported from Italy and Germany, and soon being made in Britain too, at a Brighton factory. Issigonis's brief was to produce something for the British Motor Corporation that could take them on, but was also a proper car, not a motorbike with pretensions. He not only made it look good, but by turning round the engine and placing it over the wheels, he found a way of packing far more space for passengers into a smaller area than any previous car. His design was so radical it needed a complete set of new machine tools to produce; Issigonis designed them, too. The Mini would become an icon of British cool, a chirpy, cheeky little car we liked to think represented the national character at its classless best. Yet the true story of the Mini is not quite as flattering to British industry. The early Minis were shoddily built, with a series of mechanical problems and poor trim; more importantly they leaked so badly people joked that every car should be sold with a free pair of Wellington boots and one journalist said he was keeping goldfish in the door pockets. Issigonis was short-tempered and intolerant with more junior design and production colleagues, who called him Arragonis and Issigonyet? He had spoken before about building a 'charwoman's car' but the lower-income families the Mini was aimed at initially took against its unfamiliar shape, small size and austere lack of trim.

In fact, for a while, the car looked as if it would be a thundering disaster. The economics behind it were also, to say the least, obscure. The basic model sold at £350, much cheaper than rival small cars such as the Triumph Herald (£495) and the Ford Anglia (£380) and indeed BMC's own old Morris Minor (£416). Yet it had been very expensive to develop and required its own machine tooling to make. How was this possible? Ford tore one apart to cost it and decided it would cost them more to build than BMC were selling it for.[27] It seems unlikely there was any profit: in their urge to undercut its competitors, the makers of the Mini were ignoring the development costs and selling the car at a loss. (Company people say they continued to sell it at a loss for years.) BMC would eventually sell more than five million Minis but its success only came about thanks to what we would now call celebrity endorsement, and even spin. Issigonis happened to know Princess Margaret's new husband, the photographer Lord Snowdon, and presented the glamorous couple with one as a birthday present. They were duly photographed whizzing round London in it. The Queen tried one out, and soon Steve McQueen, Twiggy, the Beatles and Marianne Faithfull, Mick Jagger's girlfriend, were seen in them too. This was completely the opposite image to BMC's and Issigonis's original idea of a cheap, no-frills car for the working classes; conservative-minded people found their car taken up as a chic emblem of youthful impertinence. In the end, of course, whatever works, works. Yet the mechanical problems, lack of good teamwork and unbusinesslike pricing strategy show that there was a darker side to the Mini story from the first. Issigonis's biographer concluded that 'far from being a business triumph for the shaky British Motor Corporation, the Mini was the first nail in their coffin.'

Issigonis was a naif in the world of business but he was prescient in one respect. He hated mergers. The Austin-Morris one produced huge internal pain with two mutually hostile company bureaucracies locking horns. The results were not immediately obvious. Through the fifties BMC rationalized its cars and cut the number of engines used, while keeping its old Austin and Morris dealers happy. With fast economic growth and an insatiable appetite for affordable cars, the domestic industry did well. There was American competition but then, there always had been – General Motors had been a big player in the UK since it took over Vauxhall in 1928, and Ford had chosen Britain as its European base even earlier. By the sixties, German and French imports were also frequent sights on British roads.

Still, there were few signs of a domestic car industry in crisis. Other producers were marketing long-lived and successful models, from the sleek Jaguars to the stolid and stately Rover Eights and Rover 50s. Issigonis was not the only free spirit of the times – Rover went far down the road (at 152mph) towards a commercial jet-powered car. Yet industrial action was growing, despite managers who bought off the unions with generous settlements in an era when they could easily sell every car they made. There was a particularly bad strike at BMC in 1958. There were some strange management decisions, egged on by politicians. Ministers trying to bring employment to run-down parts of Scotland and the North of England persuaded BMC to create a cumbersome and expensive empire of new factories which it did not have the expertise to manage properly. Little of this was apparent to the ordinary observer then, the first years of popular motoring mania.

The Growth of Car Mania

Britain was slow to catch the motorway addiction. There had been a spate of road-building in the thirties but it was not until 1936 that the government took national responsibility for a network of major roads. All building then stopped when war began three years later. But America's vast highways were an inspiration to British engineers; and Hitler's Germany had been known for its gleaming new autobahns. With Britain's cramped, slow, badly congested roads full of military vehicles, in 1941 a cabinet committee was being urged to consider 'motorways' as a vital part of post-war construction. The man responsible was Frederick Cook, a gifted and pushy highways engineer, though his committee included Attlee, Ernie Bevin and the founding Director General of the BBC, Lord Reith. Lord Leathers, the wartime transport minister, duly announced that Britain had been converted to the idea of 'motorways to be reserved exclusively for fast-moving traffic' while warning that they must not be developed on too grand a scale as advocated 'by some enthusiasts who are perhaps unduly influenced by continental analogies'. No Nazi speed mania here, in other words. The result was a Special Roads Act in 1949 which led eventually, when money allowed, to the motorways which began to carve up and transform the country.

In theory, motorway Britain had been only one of two possible options. The world's first industrialized nation was still wired tightly together with a massive railway network. By the end of the fifties, British Rail controlled 17,800 miles of track linking most small towns and every city. It ran more than 7,000 stations and a million freight wagons, all of it worked by a massive staff – 475,000 people in 1961. But the system was making an equally massive loss and needed major investment. With cars becoming the dream of middle-class families, perhaps the railways at that scale needed some pruning. Instead an affable, moustachioed former ICI manager called Dr Richard Beeching came along and cut them to ribbons. Beeching was greatly admired at the time as a living symbol of thrusting new Britain. In the early sixties to 'do a Beeching' became flattering shorthand for ruthless management efficiency. Hired as the chairman of the railways, he conducted a 'reshaping plan' which proposed the closure of 2,361 stations and 5,000 miles of track – and that was just for starters. It was one of the most extreme liquidations in the history of British commerce, on a par with the collapse of the car industry a decade later, or the end of shipbuilding on the Clyde.

Suspicions have been heard ever since that the Beeching cuts were politically motivated. They had been prepared for by a secret committee on which sat industrialists but no railway people. They came a few years after a savagely effective strike by two railway unions which had reminded Conservative ministers that while a country could be closed down if it was linked by trains, this was very much harder if it was a lorry and car economy. The Tories had already denationalized road transport, putting 24,000 lorries back into the hands of private hauliers; everything from fish to potatoes, newspapers to engine parts, seemed to be transferring from rail. This was what 'modern' meant. And to cap it all, the minister in charge who had given Beeching his mandate to cut the railways until they made a profit, without taking social or wider economic interests into account, was hardly neutral on the issue.

Ernest Marples was a bouncy, chirpy Manchester engineering worker's son who had won a grammar school scholarship and gone on to work as a miner, a postman, an accountant and a chef before his war service. A Labour activist in his youth, he was demobbed as a keen Tory and after becoming an MP, served as one of the few real modernizers in the 1951–64 governments. He brought in 'trunk' or automatic dialling, designed to make telephones more popular – until the late fifties, everyone had to call up a telephone exchange, give the number and wait to be put through by an operator. He had launched Britain's Premium Bonds too, denounced by Harold Wilson as a 'squalid raffle' but instantly popular. Marples's enthusiasm for the new extended most dramatically, however, to roads. He charged around the world looking for examples of the traffic systems of the future, and brought in the first yellow lines, the first parking meters, the first major roundabouts. He had formed his own civil engineering company, which would soon be responsible for West London's Hammersmith flyover, and much else. Marples was not keen on railways, though. When challenged about the conflict of interest in having his motorway construction company, he simply passed the shares to his wife. Under him, Britain finally embarked on its motorway age.

Those were the days. The first was opened on 5 December 1958, an eight-mile bypass of Preston. No major road had been built for twenty years. British engineers had learned something about pre-stressed concrete from the French, but still had a lot to discover about motorway design from colleagues in the United States. It was all something of an experiment for the man in charge, John Cox of Tarmac, who had made his name building instant airstrips during the war. The Preston bypass had to be closed forty-six days later because of frost damage. Though the central reservation later allowed it to be widened for levels of traffic undreamed-of in the late fifties, it was still too narrow and its rather beautiful bridges, which had been designed to last for 120 years, were knocked down and replaced after thirty. Still, it worked and the experience was vital for the first long stretch of British motorway, a 67-mile stretch of the M1 linking London and Yorkshire, opened the following year. Built in only nineteen months, it had three lanes in either direction and that now humdrum novelty, the first motorway service stations. Marples opened the Watford Gap service station, run by Blue Boar, on 2 November 1959. Newport Pagnell opened six months later.

Britain has never been the same since. From then on, motorway building spread at a brisk pace. Stretches of the M60 and M6 appeared during 1960–3; the first section of the A1(M) was completed in 1961 and the M5 the following year. Scotland's first motorway building, the M8 outside Glasgow, came in 1967. The early seventies saw a dramatic expansion, with the M4 linking London and Bristol, the M40 reaching towards Oxford and Birmingham and the cities of Liverpool, Leeds, Manchester and Sheffield all being interconnected. The first five-lane dual carriageway arrived outside Belfast in 1973 and it was only after the completion of the M25 round London in 1985 that the pace of building faltered. In the early years of the new century it virtually stopped. By then the network had grown from eight miles to 2,200 miles – and the A-roads servicing it greater still.

The creation of the motorway network has been called the first centrally planned roads system in Britain since the Romans left. It makes a pattern the Romans would have recognized, with London the hub, radial routes spinning out from it, and only the further West Country, rural Wales and northern Scotland ignored. The Romans might have been surprised at the absence of motorways across East Anglia, and the quantity of civil engineering lavished on the north and Midlands of England; but that is a consequence of the industrial revolution. Today's motorways are more curved than the legions would have found acceptable, avoiding hills and towns – though the straightest stretch of all, part of the A1(M) near Stilton, is so because it follows the old Roman street for seven miles. The system is rational and heavily used, heavily policed, heavily taxed and has engorged a swathe of rural England. Even as late as 1985–2001, transport projects (mainly roads) took up a further tract of sparse land equal to three times the area of Nottingham. If usage equals success, then few acts of post-war political decision making have been as popular as the designing and building of what Margaret Thatcher called 'the great car economy'. For every car or van on the roads of Britain in 1950 – 2.3 million of them – there were twice as many by the end of the decade and more than three times as many by the early sixties. By 1970 there were 12 million and by the end of the century, more than 24 million, ten times as many in half a century. This only gives part of the picture, because these cars are also used much more, going further and for longer. In the last fifteen yeas of the century, car journeys increased by nearly 30 per cent. Year by year, despite propaganda for a healthier lifestyle, high fuel taxes, congestion charging and widespread worry about global warming, the British drive more and walk, cycle or use buses less.

In the days of Marples it was believed that such an increase would also mean vastly more Britons being killed and maimed on the roads. This is one gloomy prediction that has been robustly disproved. Safety campaigns from the Tufty Club of the fifties to the Green Cross Code have had their effect but the real reason is that the British, who think of themselves as lovers of liberty, have allowed their freedom to be drastically curtailed on the roads. From the first general speed limits in the thirties to today's ubiquitous metal snoop-force of remote cameras, Britain has developed a driving culture which kills proportionately far fewer people than most comparable countries. If there is a single heroine of that part of our motoring history it is Barbara Castle. A non-driving minister in her rather glamorous mid-fifties, Castle had been disappointed to be offered Transport by Harold Wilson in 1965. She had hoped to be Home Secretary. But she was formidably ambitious and media-savvy and quickly turned the job into a great personal success. When she arrived some 8,000 people a year were dying on Britain's roads. Figures produced at the time suggested there would be half a million such deaths by the year 2000.

Castle's Road Safety Act brought in the breathalyser to combat drunk driving, extended the trial 70mph speed limit and made it compulsory for all new cars to have seat belts. There was already a bill prepared but she toughened it up, rejecting random breath tests but making the penalty a year's automatic disqualification. Castle revved up a storm. The Formula One racing driver Stirling Moss attacked 'socialist hypocrisy'. Letters came in reading 'You've ballsed our darts matches up, so get out you wicked old B' or wishing her 'evil Christmas and a whole year of unhappy days. These are the views of the public, you bitchy old cow.'[28] Her long-suffering husband Ted, who did drive, was pursued by journalists eager to catch him over the limit, and had to confine himself to tonic water at public events. But in the test's first year road deaths fell by 1,200. As Castle wrote in her autobiography, she was soon afterwards introduced to a London ambulance driver who told her that before the breathalyser, 'their night's work had followed a regular pattern. As soon as the pubs closed the accident figures shot up and they were operating at full stretch. Now, he said, they spent the night playing cards.' Seatbelts, which saved the looks of thousands of people, and the lives of others, were equally vigorously opposed as an infringement on liberty and a diabolical liberty for women with large bosoms. But they helped stem the deaths. By the end of the century, with nearly three times as many cars on the road as when Mrs Castle took office, the numbers killed each year were less than half the toll in 1965. Compared to most similar countries, Britain's roads are congested, but safe.

Slipping Through Our Fingers

To the ordinary observer, there was plenty to be cheerful about throughout British industrial life. The coal industry, though national-ized, was nevertheless at last rationalized and modernized. In these years, some 200,000 miners' jobs went and super-pits were developed using newer and safer technology, while on the other hand, around Britain the first nuclear power stations came on stream. When Calder Hall was connected to the national grid in 1956 it was the world's first nuclear power station providing energy commercially, and its Magnox gas-cooled reactor incorporated British technology. A further ten similar nuclear power stations followed. Here, as in the car industry – and lesser-known examples, such as industrial glass, chemicals and jet engines, not to mention the beginnings of the offshore gas industry –

British technology was as good as any in the world. In an entirely different area, P&O was then the largest shipping line in the world with 366 vessels, seemingly dominating commercial traffic across the oceans. This was not, in short, the basket-case industrial economy that is sometimes misremembered. But during the fifties overseas competition was quietly surveying the British market and its complacent industrial giants, planning to attack.

The story of motorbike manufacturing can stand for other industries, too. In the early years of the decade, Harley-Davidson in the United States were complaining (unsuccessfully) to Washington about the unfair competition from the better, cheaper, British-made Triumph motorbikes – one of which starred in *The Wild One*, featuring Marlon Brando, in 1954. Another American manufacturer, Indian, gave up and began importing Royal Enfield bikes; rock stars and Hollywood actors were seen on British machines; there were more than 300 Triumph and BSA dealers in the United States. Yet in 1955 Yamaha began producing their first motorbikes, followed by Suzuki, using wartime aircraft manufacturing kit. At the end of the decade, when British motorcycle sales were at their all-time peak, Honda entered its first bike in the TT race. British executives toured Japan in 1960 and were horrified by the scale of production by the three rival companies: Japan was making more than 500,000 motorcycles a year, compared to a maximum UK output of just 140,000. Two years later these Japanese bikes were winning key races in Europe and a new manufacturer, Kawasaki, appeared on the scene. It was a story that would be repeated in electronics and cameras. In this period, West Germany's share of world trade grew nearly four times as fast as Britain's, while the Japanese were already in another league for growth. The Americans were racing ahead in starved, post-war markets all round the world.

It was the structure of Britain's working world that was the problem, not the lack of hardworking people or enterprising companies – not even, at this stage, inflation or industrial militancy. On one side, the industrial companies were dwarfed by the vast nationalized corporations, sucking capital and talent away from the consumer industries that were becoming so central to people's lives. ICI was vast, as has been described; but every three years, the Electricity Board spent enough capital to create a new ICI.[29] On the other side, there were simply too many tiny companies, inefficiently and traditionally run without any knowledge of new management styles, product designs or marketing. By the middle of the fifties, of the nearly 300,000 British companies that existed, only around one in a hundred was actually listed on the Stock Market; the vast majority were under-capitalized traditional private businesses. The economic historian Keith Middlemass describes a business ecology dominated by 'the continued survival of a mass of small firms, reliant on sheltered domestic markets, which were unable or unwilling to reform their practices or their low productivity'.[30]

Was there any direct connection between this national failure and the kind of people running the country? Industrialists and entrepreneurs were not part of the Tory magic circle and were not socially much regarded. Macmillan and Eden both suffered from a pseudo-aristocratic and sentimental attitude to class. With their First World War service and their inter-war worries about the effect of unemployment, they were inclined to admire the working classes from a decent distance and to disdain the 'common' speech and attitudes of upwardly mobile entrepreneurs such as Sir Bernard Docker. They lived privileged and upper-crust lives themselves, set in landed homes and surrounded by literature and art. It was a way of life to which the self-made would aspire too: Michael Heseltine would begin by mixing margarine and butter as he built his low-rent property business, and end with a grand country home and an arboretum. For the ruling class of the fifties, the businessmen, the engineers, the factory organizers were vulgar, vulgar, vulgar. Diplomacy; country sports and farming; the arts; high politics; even journalism were all interesting, but industry was a bore. As we have seen this did not stop large companies thriving or hold back individual entrepreneurs, very often immigrants unintimidated by class barriers. But it was hardly surprising that fewer bright British students went to work for the British motor industry or the chemical giants, compared to the best of the Germans and Americans going into their equivalents. In the fifties, foreigners were not yet talking pityingly of 'the British disease' but there was talk of the 'stagnant society'. No one grasped the nettle.

The Egg-heads and Duffel-coat Rebels

One group of society was equally opposed to the Tory magic circle and the industrial entrepreneur. Its supporters wore heavy blue or beige duffel coats – the coarse, toggle-fastened woollen coats designed in Victorian Britain but which became truly popular on the Atlantic and Arctic convoys of the Second World War – and roll-necked pullovers, baggy tweed jackets, stout shoes. The men would be vigorously bearded. Their look proclaimed the opposite of stylishness or American influence. Their chosen music, too, was very different from the skiffle bands and the rock and roll beginning to infiltrate teenagers' lives. For most politically minded left-wingers folk music was the sound of the times, heard in smoke-filled and beery clubs across the nation.

Folk music became popular throughout the UK in the fifties, though it has been swamped in memory by the eruption of pop soon afterwards. It was particularly strong in Scotland where singing traditions among farm-workers and miners, and the vast popularity of Robert Burns, underpinned an audience for 'the people's music'. Edinburgh had been chosen at the end of the forties as the site of a new annual international festival of the arts (selected just ahead of Bath because it had rather less bomb damage) focusing on the traditional elite arts – opera, classical drama, ballet and fine arts. By 1950 there was growing irritation among the poets and singers at the centre of the Scottish literary revival at the way Scotland was being excluded and, by 1951, an alternative people's festival was established. Trade unions, the Communist Party, left-wing councillors and others backed the project, which in turn kicked off the post-war folk scene in Scotland. There were lectures about the danger of American culture swamping British culture, concerts and get-togethers with Gaelic musicians, films, choirs and specially written plays – but, within three years, at the height of the Cold War, the Edinburgh people's festival was closed down by the trade union movements on the grounds that it was a Communist plot. (It was Communist-tinged but it was hardly a plot.)

Outside Scotland the folk movement was strongest in the Northern and Midland regions of England and the West Country, though folk clubs spread everywhere and by 1957 there were supposed to be some 1,500 of them in Britain. There was something over-defensive about their self-proclaimed independence from American music, since the United States was undergoing its own folk revival at the same time, also strongly linked to left-wing politics and also defiantly 'authentic' in the face of the rising power of commercial music. Jimmie Miller, the best-known leader of the movement, had been born in Salford into a Scottish socialist family of militants and musicians and had had dozens of jobs in the 1930s before marrying the left-wing actress Joan Littlewood, and setting up experimental radical theatre projects with her. Later they split up and Miller wrote his best-known song 'The First Time Ever I Saw Your Face' for an American folk musician, Peggy Seeger, when they fell in love. A committed Marxist, he changed his name to Ewan MacColl as he became central to the folk revival. Among his songs was 'Dirty Old Town', later made famous by the London-Irish band the Pogues. Other key figures were the former soldier and poet Hamish Henderson, who first began collecting traditional songs and stories from across the Western Highlands and Islands; and Norman Buchan, the Labour MP. There was great talent, great energy and great optimism. For a time it seemed that Britain might produce a music radically different from the raucous new noises of North America.

Folk continued to be much enjoyed by a minority. Stars like Billy Connolly cut their teeth on folk. But outside the Celtic nations, the revival was pretty much doomed from the beginning. Any movement so suffused with nostalgia and gentle humour, played on instruments with minimal amplification, is unlikely to cut the mustard in an age of urban consumerism, when the commercial drive is to record and sell short, fast songs for a young and fickle audience no longer interested in the struggles of their grandparents. Any movement so resolutely unfashionable, so tousled, hairy and serious, was unlikely to defeat styles and songs efficiently marketed for the new teenage market. The parallel enthusiasm for modern jazz, which excited the English middle-class youth at the same time, and which seemed so rebellious in a land still contemptuous of 'negro' culture, fizzled away for similar reasons. Live performance in small clubs and songs that went on for too long, and were simply too complicated for everyone to enjoy, surrendered to quick, easy music. In a battle between the 'authentic' and the cool, when the fight is pitched for young urban consumers, it is easy to see what will happen. In the end, for all its beauty and vigour, Britain's folk music revival of the fifties was another exhibition of impotent local revolt against the coming age of America.

So was the political cause which so many of the folk and jazz enthusiasts cherished, the Campaign for Nuclear Disarmament. One of its leading figures, the popular historian A. J. P. Taylor, later reflected that CND, like the Establishment politicians it opposed, simply over-rated Britain's position in the world: 'We thought that Great Britain was still a great power whose example would affect the rest of the world. Ironically, we were the last imperialists.'[31] For a while, the campaign sent a jolt through politics and seemed to all those contemplating the swift extinction of life on the planet far more a moral act than politics as usual. It had begun with a campaign to end the radiation-spreading testing of nuclear weapons, which was causing great alarm. Popular writers, notably J. B. Priestley, and the elderly mathematician and philosopher Bertrand Russell, wrote influential articles proclaiming the moral necessity of renouncing such world-destroying weaponry entirely. The *New Statesman* appealed to Khrushchev to disarm and to its surprise got a reply back from Moscow, albeit an unhelpful one. The Labour left were almost all committed ban-the-bombers as of course was the Moscow-funded Communist Party of Great Britain. These strands, along with Quakers, pacifists and certain journalists, eventually found themselves sitting together in the appropriately named Amen Court, home of Canon John Collins of St Paul's Cathedral, where on 15 January 1958 the new organization was created. A month later, more than five thousand people turned up for the inaugural meeting at Westminster; some were arrested when they went on to protest at Downing Street.

Though CND would fail to persuade any major British party to renounce nuclear weapons throughout the Cold War and failed as well to halt, never mind reverse, the build-up of American nuclear weaponry on British soil, it did succeed in dividing the Labour Party and seizing the imagination of millions of people. For a ramshackle left-wing organization, it behaved in a thoroughly modern and media-savvy way. Its symbol, designed by a professional artist, Gerald Holtham, in 1958, and based on semaphore, became an international brand almost as recognizable as Coca-Cola: suddenly, all those duffel coats and black jumpers had some decoration. The Aldermaston marches, first from Trafalgar Square towards the base and later in the opposite direction, were never enormous but they did attract massive press coverage. Its more militant wing, the Committee of 100, using direct non-violent action, managed to get the 89-year-old Lord Russell arrested by police, a considerable act of public relations. Yet it was as Taylor described it, a movement of egg-heads for egg-heads. Another historian reflected that it was a classic 'anti-political movement of the educated, the affluent and the disaffected, a movement rooted in the leafy suburbs of the middle classes, not the slums or council estates'.[32] Its members tended to be liberal on other issues too, and to be contemptuous of the organized and stodgy routines of politics, Labour politics in particular. By the end of the fifties, radicals found Labour entirely unappetizing. Now, why was that?

Labour Destroys its Future

When the Conservatives have been out of power, they have tended to think and work hard to change themselves and win it back, the six or seven years after 1997 being an exception. When Labour has lost power it has tended, after due thought and consideration, to tear itself into small pieces. This was the case in the fifties, in the seventies and again most spectacularly in the eighties. In each case it was essentially a fight between the Labour left and right but as befits a party of altruists it was often also highly personal and vicious. Labour has not had grand family, old school tie or clubland cliques as the Tories have. It has had gangs instead. Through most of his time, Attlee had kept the socialist gangs apart and quiet, though he began to lose control when Britain rearmed at the time of the Korean War. From then on, it was mostly gang war. On one side, there were always left-wing true believers who believed the country could be dragged to a pure version of socialism – romantics, generally in love with English and Scottish revolutionary socialism, or with Marxism, or both. They were the 'if only' faction. If only the trade unions could be won by the left, then true socialist policies could be imposed on the party. If only the gang at the top could be kicked out. If only we could force Labour MPs to do what their constituency parties told them to. If only we could

capture the national executive committee, or the conference arrangements committee, or some committee or other. If only we could get
in, we could nationalize the top 200 companies and then everything
would change for ever.

Few of them, unfortunately for their cause, were working class.
Michael Foot was educated at fee-paying boarding schools and came
from a family of Cornish puritans and nonconformists, drunk on
books – his father, a solicitor and a Liberal MP, left a collection of
52,000 books, including 240 bibles, which gives some indication of the
family tone. Dick Crossman, whose diaries would later lift the lid on
the Wilson years, was a wealthy lawyer's son and Oxford academic.
Barbara Castle was from lower down the social tree, a tax-surveyor's
daughter who nevertheless went to Bradford Grammar School and
Oxford. Ian Mikardo was unusual in being the child of poor Polish
immigrants – his father's command of English was so poor he is said
to have thought for a while he was living in New York, not London –
who trained as a rabbi. The great exception was certainly working
class. The first leader of the If Onlies was Nye Bevan, the former
miner and the minister who had created the National Health Service,
before his 'health before guns' resignation. By the mid-fifties his great
years were behind him. Though he made some wonderful speeches in
Opposition and was tough enough to break with his closest supporters
over the issue of nuclear weapons, much of his behaviour seemed
petulant and self-regarding. Of his great enemy Hugh Gaitskell, he
would spit that the man was 'nothing – nothing – *nothing*' or assert,
'He's an intellectual, I'm a miner.' Barbara Castle, who never had an
entirely easy relationship with Bevan, noted when she was sitting
beside him on a conference platform: 'I have made a perturbing
discovery about him. His favourite doodle is writing his own name.'[33]
Like a political Dylan Thomas, his lavish talents were only matched by
his skill in lavishly squandering them. As we have seen, in office he
had been a great reforming minister. The bigger the job, the bigger
the man he became. In Opposition, his charisma was less well
employed and his vanity was more damaging. He became smaller.

He seemed to carry round with him a kind of portable audience,
essential to his well-being, foils to his wit, witty though many were
themselves. Yet Bevan had a bewitching charisma that made him the
focus for the left, whose positions included an increasingly reflexive

anti-Americanism and a doctrinaire insistence on nationalization and central planning. Bevan was as distrustful of the Soviet Union as the rest of the Labour leadership. There were no illusions about Moscow, particularly after an angry dinner in the Commons at which Khrushchev warned Labour that they must ally with Russia 'because if not, they would swat us off the face of the earth like a dirty old black beetle'.[34] Though he was easily beaten by Gaitskell in the leadership battle in 1955, Bevan's supporters were a formidable crowd in the party throughout this period. In 1952, fifty-seven Labour MPs abstained in a motion on Tory defence spending, which was a measure of their size. The 'Keep Left' group had become the 'Bevanites', votaries even as they protested their sturdy independence. They were a clique, with their own newspaper, *Tribune*, and their own social gatherings in the Commons, at Crossman's London house, at a country house, Buscot Park in Oxfordshire, and in Soho restaurants. They saw themselves as the romantic, rackety and principled opponents of the upper-class traitors who were taking over Labour. Soon, inevitably, they were being called a party within a party.

As suspicions grew, Bevan attacked Gaitskell personally and in public. With support from such unlikely and untrustworthy sources as the right-wing press magnate Lord Beaverbrook, Bevan and his gang started to seriously scare other Labour leaders. Gaitskell told a particularly bitter conference that it was time to stop attempted 'mob rule by a group of frustrated journalists'. A half-hearted attempt to expel Bevan from the Labour Party was matched by a half-hearted discussion among his followers about setting up a new socialist party of their own. Eventually Bevan returned to the front line as shadow foreign secretary and later deputy leader before dying of throat cancer in 1960. He did not read the new Britain well. His last party speech in 1959 predicted that when the British 'have got over the delirium of television', realized they were mortgaged to the hilt, and understood that consumerism had produced 'a vulgar society', they would turn to true socialism and 'we shall lead our people where they deserve to be led'.[35]

On the other side of the divide were Gaitskell and his gang, variously described as the Frognal Set or the Hampstead Set, after the suburban north London house where the Labour leader entertained and, the Bevanites believed, plotted to abolish socialism and lead the people to a hell of television sets and home ownership. Gaitskell was another public schoolboy, who had been radicalized by the General Strike of 1926 and the Nazi thugs on the streets of Vienna in the late thirties. Like Harold Wilson he was an economist, who had served in government during the war. As Attlee's Chancellor of the Exchequer, he had proved tough. It was his decision to fund rearmament partly by making savings by introducing NHS charges that provoked Bevan's resignation from the cabinet and began that feud. (Gaitskell was probably wrong on the numbers, and Bevan right.) In public Gaitskell could come over as a prig, with little of Bevan's champagne fizz. All his life he had been keen on uncomfortable truths. When a small child he had apparently once startled a passing woman who looked down at him by singing from his pram, 'Soon shall you and I be lying / Each within our narrow tomb'. In later life he did not lose the disconcerting style. To become Labour leader after only nine years as an MP, replacing the venerable Attlee, without a strong base in the trade unions or on the left of the party, was nevertheless a remarkable achievement. Gaitskell's mettle was soon tested over the Suez crisis when his party political point-scoring after earlier supportive noises made him hated on the Tory benches. For those who think the Commons has become too much of a bear-pit in recent decades, it is worth recording that Gaitskell contemplated giving up within a couple of years because the booing and shouting from the Conservative side was such that he felt he could not get a hearing in Parliament.

Gaitskell has been fondly remembered by historians partly because of the vivid enthusiasm of his young supporters who later rose to prominence themselves, Roy Jenkins and Tony Crosland in particular, and partly because he died suddenly at fifty-six. He had many admirable qualities, including infectious enthusiasm for literature, music, dancing and life in general. He was stubborn, brave and loyal but his record as a party leader was not unspotted. He seriously contemplated loosening the party's links with the unions, dropping nationalization and changing its name. This was bold but Gaitskell's tactics were nearly disastrous. Against the advice of the young bloods, he attempted to remove the pro-nationalization clause four from the party's rulebook as Tony Blair would do much later. In the more socialist fifties it was a fight too far over a matter of symbolism. Gaitskell retired hurt, in confusion. Beaten, at the high point of CND's first crusades, on the issue of whether Britain should have her own nuclear weapons, he famously promised to fight, fight and fight again to save the party he loved, turning the defeat into a personal public relations triumph. But having rallied the right of the party, he then confounded them by his equally passionate hostility to British membership of the European Common Market. And he had a tendency to flirt with Tory England which did not endear him to the party faithful.

Yet what made Gaitskell truly interesting as a politician of this era was that he accepted and even revelled in the new consumerism. Bevan and his friends deplored the 'affluent society' and the 'crass commercialism' of the time and claimed to feel nostalgic for the colder if nobler vision of the forties. Gaitskell danced, and listened avidly to jazz records, and liked good food and clothes. He had few hang-ups, ideological or otherwise. Gaitskell and those in his set believed you could have a more equal society without it being cheerless or lacking in fun. The essence of this was set out in a hugely influential book *The Future of Socialism,* published in 1956. Its author, Tony Crosland, was one of the wilder spirits of Frognal who had fought in the war as a paratrooper and was busy rebelling against the harshly puritanical standards set by his well-off parents, who belonged to the Plymouth Brethren sect. Crosland argued that increasing individual rights should be as great an aim for reformers as abolishing capitalism, which was already mostly tamed. Education, not nationalization, was the key to changing society. Socialists must turn to issues such as the plight of the mentally handicapped and neglected children, to the divorce and abortion laws, and women's rights in general, to homosexual law reform and the end of censorship of plays and books. Many of these things would dominate the Home Secretaryship of his friend Jenkins. He was against 'hygienic, respectable, virtuous things and people, lacking only in grace and gaiety'. He concluded with a famous swipe at the puritanical Webbs, those Edwardian saints of Labourism: 'Total abstinence and a good filing-system are not now the right sign-posts to the socialist's Utopia; or at least, if they are, some of us will fall by the wayside.'[36] This was a message that would prove popular with the new middle-class voters Labour needed, if not with the intellectuals and journalists around the party's fringes. It was the moment, really, when for Labour the forties ended and, with no intermission, the sixties began.

Gaitskell himself was forgiven by the party for losing the 1959 election. Had he survived to lead Labour into battle in 1964 he would surely have won then and the story of Labour politics would have been strikingly different. By 1962 he was utterly dominant inside his party and increasingly seen outside it as a fresh start – letter-writers and newspaper journalists used language about him which anticipated what was said about Tony Blair before the 1997 election. Like Blair, he managed to come across as less of a party man, and more 'normal' than his great rival, a truly interesting Prime Minister in waiting. None of this was to be. In January 1963 after years of grossly overworking, suffering from a rare and little-understood disease of the immune system, he suddenly died. Though there were rumours afterwards that he had been killed by the KGB as part of a plot to put in Harold Wilson, whom the conspiracists believed was a Soviet agent, it seems more likely that this was mere biology interfering with politics, as it does. With a little more medical and other good-fortune, the prime ministers of post-war Britain could well have included Herbert Morri-son, Rab Butler, Hugh Gaitskell and Iain Macleod, rather than Attlee, Macmillan, Douglas-Home and Harold Wilson. But Wilson it would be. The long-lasting significance of the struggle between the Bevanites and the Gaitskellites was that when he became Prime Minister, he was so crippled by trying to placate the various gangs that he could offer no clear direction for the country.

Leaving Mayhem: the British in Africa

A year after Macmillan's triumphant re-election, he made a speech unlikely to be forgotten. One of the bitterer ironies of Suez had been that London, accused by both the Americans and Russians of being a nest of reactionary imperialism, was actually in the middle of frantically trying to get rid of the Empire. Indian independence was followed by swift dismantling in two other places, Africa and the Middle East. The Sudan, scene of British cavalry charges in an early war against militant Islamists, had become independent in 1956. The Gold Coast, one of the most prosperous African colonies, followed a year later as Ghana and they were followed in turn by a bewildering stream of former

African possessions during the sixties – Somaliland (Somalia), Sierra Leone, the Gambia, Nigeria, Kenya, Tanganyika (Tanzania), Zanzibar, Northern Rhodesia (Zambia), Uganda, Nyasaland (Malawi), Swaziland and Basutoland, as well as the islands of Mauritius and the Maldives. Some of these countries had been British only for a short time, others had had large white settler populations who either returned home or tried, uneasily, to accommodate themselves to the new governments, but the scale and speed of the British scuttle produced remarkably little debate at home. On the far right of British politics, the League of Empire Loyalists protested but most of the country regarded it all with boredom or amusement.

In the late forties it had been felt both that Africa might become the core of Britain's new world position and that her countries were far from ready for independence. Within ten years all this was forgotten. There was a rush to independence, urged on from London. No single speech made more of an impact in seeming to settle the argument than the one Harold Macmillan made in Cape Town in 1960, known for ever as his 'wind of change' speech. It was brave not because of what he said, but because the British Prime Minister chose to make it in the white supremacist South African parliament, in front of men who would be architects of apartheid, horrifying them and appalling a large swathe of Tory opinion back in England, where the right-wing Monday Club was formed in protest. Macmillan announced that there was an awakening national consciousness sweeping through Africa. He told his startled audience; 'the wind of change is blowing through this continent' and like it or not, this was simply a fact. Hendrik Verwoerd, the South African Prime Minister retorted that the Englishman was appeasing the black man, adding that they had enough problems in Africa without his coming to add to them.

Why had London lost its nerve? Partly, it was the mere experience of looking about. The French were getting out of Africa. So too were the Belgians, leaving behind an appalling and very bloody civil war in the Congo. Private correspondence of Macmillan's suggests that he also thought the two world wars had made a fundamental change in the position of the whites around the world: 'What we have really seen since the war is the revolt of the yellows and blacks from the automatic leadership and control of the whites.'[37] It need not, however, be a bloody revolt. The experience of the Gold Coast, which became independent under Dr Kwame Nkrumah in 1957 with relative ease, suggested to London there was a gentler way of quitting.

On the other side the vicious war of terrorism against white settlers and blacks who supported them in Kenya, a revolt by the mysterious organization Mau Mau, showed the dangers of hanging on. The Mau Mau rebellion was not an attractive liberation war. It lasted for years, and involved gruesome mutilation, dismemberments, rape and bizarre oaths, claimed to be linked to black magic. Very few whites were killed, but there was a terrible black toll. It did not help that the more experienced leaders such as Jomo Kenyatta, whom we will meet later in a less heroic role, was then locked up, leaving Mau Mau to be run by the young and the angry. The white settlers of the area, who had been among the richest and most self-confident colonials in Africa, responded with vicious militia tactics, taking cash bets for the number of Africans shot or 'bagged', and keeping scorecards, as if they were grouse. The security forces came between the two and suppressed the revolt with classic anti-subversion tactics, though its general found the settlers shady people: 'I hate the guts of them all; they are middle-class sluts,' he told his wife. By the end of the fifties, government forces had killed around 10,000 Kikuyu tribesmen and hanged another thousand. Some 80,000 had been put into grim so-called rehabilitation camps. Eventually only a hard core of Mau Mau were left and at one camp, Hola, eleven were murdered by the guards. The story went round the world and caused extreme embarrassment to the government; Enoch Powell made what some thought the greatest parliamentary speech of the century denouncing British behaviour. Meanwhile in Nyasaland, another bout of violent repression was going on, with fifty-one black protesters killed. So by the time Macmillan made his speech, it seemed that trying to hold on, to protect white settlers he anyway despised, was even more dangerous than getting out.

Macmillan and his liberal Colonial Secretary Iain Macleod, have had a good press ever since. They have been seen as liberal, fair-minded and realistic politicians, who realized that the time had come to push ahead even faster with decolonization, to hit the accelerator and forget the brake. They were undoubtedly influenced by the humiliation of Suez. It was the way the world was going. Yet the story of modern Africa should make anyone look harder at the timing and methods of British decolonization. This is the failed continent. Lines drawn on the map by British imperial administrators were left to help provoke appalling civil and tribal wars. Men trained at Sandhurst, brought up inside the British Empire, turned into corrupt dictators and in the worst case, that of Uganda's Idi Amin, a monster. Few of those liberal, highly intelligent liberation leaders feted in London by the left during the fifties and sixties turned into great progressive figures back home in Africa – perhaps the only great exception being Nelson Mandela himself. Military coups, the imprisonment of opposition leaders, tribal feuds and famines followed and for all this, the former British rulers must take some responsibility. Did the British scuttle from Africa happen too fast, in a mood of political hysteria and without proper thought for what would follow? The sheer speed may not be as admirable as we have been taught to think.

Was there no example of successful British action in withdrawing from old commitments? Luckily for national pride, there is another story. It is not simply the tale of the other former colonies, from Singapore to the Caribbean, which thrived, or the prosperity of the so-called White Commonwealth nations. Not all wars were lost; in Korea, for instance, though Kim Il Sung survived to create a bleak and murderous dictatorship behind the armistice line, Mao was frustrated. But the best example of a war eventually won through intelligence, in every sense, is the one known simply as the 'emergency'. It ran from 1948 to 1960 – which must make it the longest emergency ever.

Malaya had become a crucial part of the world's industrial system thanks to seeds from a single tree, brought from Brazil to Kew Gardens in London and grown in a tropical plant house. From there, the rubber plants were taken to Malaya in the 1870s, and grew very nicely. By the post-war years, Malaya was producing a third of the world's supply of rubber. With tin, this made it Britain's most profitable colony, a rare exception to the rule. But by the late forties there was, almost inevitably, a Communist and nationalist insurgency against British rule. It went on for a dozen years and was, to all intents and purposes, a war. It has not been remembered as the Malayan War for a curious reason. The insurance policies of local businesses had clauses in them suspending cover in time of war; hence 'emergency'.

After a bad start during which the Communists tied down a huge British force, murdered many rubber planters and their workers, and when atrocities were committed on the other side including by the Scots Guards against Chinese villagers, a new strategy was developed. It was the achievement of one of the British Empire's last and least-known heroes, a clipped and driven soldier called General Sir Gerald Templer. He used helicopters as they had not been used before in warfare. He also moved entire villages away from the jungle to keep them from supporting insurgents and imposed curfews. But beside the unpopular measures Templer introduced a new 'hearts and minds' approach to win over Malaya's Chinese villagers. Roads, clean water, schools, medical centres, elected village councils and relatively restrained policing did more to confound a Communist insurgency than the machine guns and helicopters. Eventually after the Communists were defeated, Malaya became independent under a friendly government. As Malaysia it has thrived. It showed what could be done by a thoughtful and intelligent departing imperial power. After Malaya, no Communist insurgency succeeded against British forces in Africa or Asia again. Had the Americans studied Malaya a little more closely, who knows what might have followed in Vietnam.

Notting Hill

From 1948 until 1962, roughly the period of the Malayan emergency, there had been virtually an open door for immigrants coming into Britain from the Commonwealth or colonies. The British debate over immigration had been hobbled by contradiction. On the one hand, overt racialism had been discredited by the Nazi enemy. Britain's very sense of herself was tied up in the vanquishing of a political culture founded on racial difference. This meant that the few unapologetic racialists, the anti-Semitic fringe or the pro-apartheid colonialists, became outcast. Official documents would refer to the handful of MPs who were outspokenly racialist as 'nutters'. So unthreatening were they thought to be that Oswald Mosley, who had been funded by Mussolini before the war and would have been a likely puppet-leader had Germany invaded Britain, was promptly allowed out of prison after the war, to strut on the back of lorries and yell at his small number of unrepentant fascist supporters. Ignoring him, the public propaganda of Empire made much of a family of races under the British flag all cooperating, loyally together.

In Whitehall, the Colonial Office strongly supported the right of black Caribbean people to migrate to the Mother Country, fending off the worries of the Ministry of Labour about the effects on unemployment during downturns. When some 500 Caribbean immigrants arrived in 1948 on the converted German troopship SS *Windrush*, the Home Secretary declared that though 'some people feel it would be a bad thing to give the coloured races of the Empire the idea that, in some way or the other, they are the equals of people in this country,' the government disagreed: 'we recognise the right of the colonial peoples to be treated as men and brothers with the people of this country.'[38] Britain, in short, believed herself to be the logical opposite of Nazi Germany, a benign and unprejudiced world-connected island. The Jewish migration of the thirties had brought one of the greatest top-ups of skill and energy that any modern European state had ever seen. The country in fact already had a population of about 75,000 black and Asian people and labour shortages suggested it needed many more. The segregation of the American Deep South, and the arrival of the ideology of apartheid in South Africa were treated alike with high-minded contempt.

And yet everyone knew this was not really the whole story. Pre-war British society had never been as brutal about race as France or Spain, never mind Germany, but it was riddled with racialism nevertheless. Anti-Semitism had been common in popular novels and obscure modernist poetry alike. The actual practice of the British upper and middle classes had been close to the colour bar practised by Americans. Africans were tolerated as servants and musicians while in Britain, little more. White working-class people hardly ever came across someone of another colour: during the war, black GIs, though welcomed, had been followed around by awestruck locals simply wanting to touch them or hear them speak. Almost as soon as the first post-war migrants arrived from Jamaica and other islands of the West Indies, popular papers were reporting worries about their cleanliness, sexual habits and criminality: 'No dogs, No blacks, No Irish' was not a myth, but a perfectly common sign on boarding houses. The hostility and coldness of native British people was quickly reported back by the early migrants. And Hugh Dalton, a cabinet colleague of the high-minded minister quoted earlier, was also able to talk of the 'pullulating poverty stricken diseased nigger communities' of the African colonies.

For most people, questions of race were obscure and academic. The country remained overwhelmingly white and only tiny pockets of colour could be found until the sixties, most of them in the poorest inner-city areas. A quarter of the world was in theory welcome to come and stay. There were debates in the Tory cabinets of the Churchill, Eden and Macmillan years but for most of the time they never got anywhere. Any legislation to limit migration would have kept out white people of the old Commonwealth too; and any legislation which discriminated would be unacceptably racialist. Conservatives as well as socialists regarded themselves as civilized and liberal on race. By this they meant pick-and-choosy. For instance in the fifties, the Colonial Office specifically championed 'the skilled character and proved industry of the West Indians' against 'the unskilled and largely lazy Asians'.[39] Immigration from the Indian subcontinent had begun almost immediately after independence and partition, as a result of the displacement of Hindus and Muslims, but it had been very small. Sikhs had arrived, looking for work particularly in the industrial Midlands, and in the west London borough of Southall, which quickly became an Asian hub. Indian migrants created networks to buy and supply the corner shops which required punishingly long hours, and the restaurants which would almost instantly become part of the 'British' way of life – there were more than 2,000 Indian restaurants by 1970 and curry would become the single most popular dish within another generation. Other migrants went into the rag trade and grew rich.

So immigration continued through a decade without any great national debate. Much of it was not black but European, mostly migrant workers from Poland, Italy, France and other countries who were positively welcomed in the years of skill and manpower shortages. There was a particularly hefty Italian migration producing a first-generation Italian community of around 100,000 by 1971 to add to the earlier migrations which went back to the 1870s. There was constant and heavy migration from Ireland, mainly into the construction industry, three-quarters of a million in the early fifties and two million by the early seventies, producing little political response except in the immediate aftermath of IRA bombings. There was substantial Maltese immigration which did catch the public attention because of violent gang wars in London between rival Maltese families in the extortion and prostitution business (though to be fair to Malta, many of these people had arrived there from Sicily first). There was a major Cypriot immigration, both of Greek Cypriots and Turkish Cypriots, as the divided island became more politically violent. Again, apart from the enthusiastic adoption of plate-smashing and moussaka in 'Greek' restaurants in British cities, there was no discernable public fuss. Chinese migration, mainly from the impoverished agricultural hinterland of Hong Kong, can be measured by the vast rise in Chinese fish-and-chip shops and restaurants, up from a few hundred in the mid fifties to more than 4,000 by the beginning of the seventies.[40] The Poles, carefully resettled after the war, were joined by other refugees from Stalinism, Hungarians and Czechs, again without any national response other than warm enthusiasm.

Thus, if there were clear rules about how to migrate quietly to Britain, they would have started first, be white, and second, if you cannot be white, be small in number, and third, if all else fails, feed the brutes. The West Indian migration failed each rule. It was mainly male, young and coming not to open restaurants but to work for wages which could, in part, be sent back home. Some official organizations, from the National Health Service to London Transport, went on specific recruiting drives for workers, nurses or bus-drivers or cleaners, with cheery advertisements in Jamaica for ticket-clippers on London buses. Most of the population shift, however, was driven by migrants themselves desperate for a better life, particularly once the popular alternative of migration to the United States was closed down in 1952. The islands of the Caribbean, dependent on sugar or tobacco for most employment, were going through hard times. As word was passed back about job opportunities, albeit in difficult surroundings, immigration grew fast to about 36,000 people a year by the late fifties. One historian notes the scale of the change: every two years 'a number equivalent to the total non-white national population in 1951 was arriving in Britain'.[41] The black and Asian population had risen to 337,000 by 1961. And it was concentrated, rather than widely dispersed. Different West Indian groups clustered in different parts of London and the English provincial cities – Jamaicans in the south London areas of Brixton and Clapham, people from Trinidad in west London's Notting Hill, islanders from Nevis in Leicester, people from St Vincent in High Wycombe, and so on.

The way these people migrated and made their way had a huge impact on the later condition of post-war Britain and deserves analysis. The fact that so many of the first migrants were young men who found themselves living without wives, mothers or children inevitably created a wilder atmosphere than they were accustomed to in their island homes. They were short of entertainment and short of the social control of ordinary family living. A chain of generational influence was broken and a male strut liberated. Drinking dens, the use of marijuana, ska and blues clubs, and gambling were the inevitable result. A white equivalent might be the atmosphere of the Klondike gold-rush communities, not in general notable for their sobriety and respect for law. Early black communities in Britain tended to cluster where the first arrivals were, which meant in the blighted inner cities. There, as discussed earlier, street prostitution was more open and rampant in the fifties than it would later become; it is hardly surprising that young black men away from home often formed relationships with white prostitutes, and that some then went into pimping. This would feed the press and white gang hysteria about blacks (unsportingly well-endowed, it was thought) stealing 'our women'. The combination of fast, unfamiliar music, the illegal drinking and drugs and the sexual needs of the young migrants combined to paint a lurid picture of a new underworld. It was no coincidence that the Profumo affair had involved a West Indian drug dealer alongside its cast of aristocrats, politicians, good-time girls and spies.

More important for the longer term, a rebelliousness was sown in black families which would be partly tamed only when children and spouses began arriving in large numbers in the sixties, and the Pentecostal churches reclaimed at least some of their own. Housing was another crucial part of the story. For the immigrants of the fifties, accommodation was necessarily privately rented since access to council homes was based on a strict list, dependent on how long you had been living in the area. We have already seen how the early squatting revolt was ended by the threat of participants being moved to the back of the council housing queue. So the early immigrants were cooped up in crowded and often condemned old properties – the gaunt Victorian

speculative terraces of west London, or the grimy brick terraces of
central Leeds. Landlords and landladies were often reluctant to rent to
blacks. Once a few houses had immigrants in them, a domino effect
would clear streets as white residents sold up and moved. The 1957
Rent Act, initiated by Enoch Powell in his free-market crusade,
perversely made the situation worse since it allowed rents to rise
sharply, but only when tenants of unfurnished rooms were removed
to allow furnished lettings. Powell meant this to allow a cushion of
time before rents rose. Its unintended consequence was that unscrupulous landlords such as the notorious Peter Rachman (an immigrant
himself) could buy up low-value rented properties, usually with poorer
white tenants in them and then – if only he could oust the tenants –
pack in new tenants at far higher rents. Thuggery and threats generally
got rid of the old. New black tenants, desperate for somewhere to live
and charged much higher rents, were then imported. The result was
the creation of instant ghettos, in which three generations of black
British would live. The Brixton, Tottenham and Toxteth riots of the
eighties can be traced back, in part, to the moral effects of early young-
male migration and the housing practices of the fifties.

The other side to the story is the reaction of white Britain. As one
Caribbean writer ironically put it, he never met a single English person
with colour prejudice.[42] Once he had walked down a whole street,
'and everyone told me that he or she 'ad no prejudice against coloured
people. It was the neighbour who was stupid. If only we could find
the "neighbour" we could solve the whole problem. But to find 'im is
the trouble! Neighbours are the worst people to live beside in this
country.' Numerous testimonies by immigrants and in surveys of the
time show how hostile local people were to the idea of having black
or Asian neighbours. The trade unions bristled against blacks coming
in to take jobs, possibly at lower rates of pay, just as they had
campaigned against Irish migrants a generation earlier. Union leaders
regarded as impeccably left-wing lobbied governments to keep out
black workers. They were successful enough for a while to create
employment ghettos as well as housing ones, though in the West
Midlands in particular black migrants gained a toehold in the car-
making factories and other manufacturing. Only a handful of MPs
campaigned openly against immigration. Powell raised the issue in
private meetings though as a health minister he had been keen enough

to use migrant labour. But anti-immigrant feeling was regarded as not respectable and not to be talked about. The elite turned its eyes away from the door-slamming and shunning, and escaped into well-meant if windy generalities about the brotherhood of man and fellow subjects of the Crown. Most of the hostility was at the level of street and popular culture, sometimes the shame-faced 'sorry, the room is taken already' variety and sometimes violent. The white gangs of the Teddy boy age went 'nigger-hunting' or 'black-burying' and chalked the 'Keep Britain White' signs on walls. They may have been influenced by the small groups of right-wing extremists, such as the Union for British Freedom, or Mosley's remaining fascist supporters, but the main motivation seems to have been young male competition and territory-marking. These were, after all, the poor white inhabitants of the very same areas being moved into by the migrants.

All this came to a head in the Notting Hill riots of 1958. Rather like Suez a couple of years earlier, Notting Hill was more a symbol of change than a bloody slaughter. In fact, nobody was killed in the rampaging and by the standards of later riots, there was little physical damage. Furthermore, the trouble actually started far away from London, in the poor St Ann's district of central Nottingham and only spread to Notting Hill a day later. Yet it was a large and deeply unpleasant outbreak of anti-immigrant violence which ran for a total of six days, across two late summer weekends. It was no coincidence that Notting Hill was the area where the rioting happened as distinct from, say, Brixton, which also had a very large and visible black population by the mid-fifties. It had the most open, well-known street culture for black people, near enough to Soho at one side, and the new BBC headquarters on the other, to be advertised and even celebrated by hacks, broadcasters and novelists. It was known for its gambling dens and drinking clubs. It had a resentful and impoverished white population but also, as two historians of British immigration put it, 'It had multi-occupied houses with families of different races on each floor. It had a large population of internal migrants, gypsies and Irish, many of them transient single men, packed into a honeycomb of rooms with communal kitchens, toilets and no bathrooms.'[43]

Into this honeycomb poured a crowd first of tens, and then of hundreds of white men, armed first with sticks, knives, iron railings and bicycle chains, and soon with petrol-bombs too. They were overwhelmingly young, mostly from nearby areas of London, and looking for trouble. They began by picking on small groups of blacks caught out on the streets, beating them and chasing them. They then moved to black-occupied houses and began smashing windows. The crowds swelled until they were estimated at more than 700 strong, whipped up by the occasional fascist agitator, but much more directed by local whites. Racist songs and chants of 'Niggers Out', the smash of windows – though some local whites protected and even fought for their black neighbours, this was mob violence of a kind Britain thought it had long left behind. It shrunk away again partly as a result of black men making a stand, and fighting back with petrol bombs. There were 140 arrests, mainly of white youths, and though far-right parties continued to organize in the area, there was no discernible electoral impact, or indeed any more serious trouble. The huge press coverage ensured, however, that Britain went through its first orgy of national introspection about its liberalism and its immigration policy, while overseas racist regimes such as those of South Africa and Rhodesia mocked the hand-wringing British.

After the riots, many black people did 'go home'. Returns to the Caribbean soared to more than 4,000. There, West Indian governments expressed outrage at the riot and made it clear that there would be no action by them to restrict migration in order to appease lawless white thugs. Indeed the Commonwealth, whose usefulness has been questioned elsewhere in this history, clearly functioned as a kind of doorstop to maintain immigration. It retained a loose association between Crown, obligation and common citizenship which felt real to politicians of both parties. Pressure to close the open border for Commonwealth citizens hardly increased in the Tory Party after the Notting Hill riots, though extra-parliamentary campaigns, such as the Birmingham Immigration Control Association, did spring up. Of course, given that the violence was directed against immigrants by whites, it would have been grotesquely unfair had the first reaction been to send people home. Labour was wholly against restricting immigration, arguing that it would be 'disastrous to our status in the Commonweath'. The Notting Hill Carnival, begun the following year, was an alternative response, celebrating black culture openly. For many black migrants, the riots marked the beginning of assertion and organization. They were looked back on as a racial Dunkirk, the darkest moment after which the real fightback would start.

Only after Macmillan's stunning 1959 general election victory did pressure really begin to build up for some kind of restriction on immigration to Britain. Opinion polls were now showing strong hostility to the open-door policy. Perhaps as important in Whitehall, both the Ministry of Labour and the Home Office wanted a change to help deal with the new threat of unemployment. This was a case of the political class being pushed reluctantly into something which offended their notion of their place in the world, the father-figures of a global Commonwealth. One study of immigration points out that what was truly remarkable was the passive acceptance by politicians and bureaucrats of Britain's transformation into a multicultural society: 'Immigration was restricted a full four years after all measures of the public mood indicated clear hostility to a black presence in Britain, and even then it was only done with hesitation.'[44] And when the 1962 Commonwealth Immigrants Act finally passed into law, it was notably liberal, at least by later standards, assuming the arrival of up to 40,000 legal immigrants a year with complete right of entry for their dependants. Even so, it had only gone through after a ferocious parliamentary battle, with the Labour leader Hugh Gaitskell making emotional and passionate attacks on a measure which was still privately opposed by some of the Tory ministers involved. One particularly contentious issue was that the Republic of Ireland was allowed a completely open border with Britain. This may have seemed only practical politics given the huge number of Irish people living and working there already but it offended in two ways. By discriminating in favour of a country which had been neutral in the war with Hitler and declared itself a republic, but against Commonwealth countries which had stood with Britain, it infuriated many British patriots. Second, by giving Irish people a better deal than Indians or West Indians it seemed frankly racialist.

The new law created a quota system which gave preference to skilled workers and those with firm promises of employment. In order to beat it, a huge new influx of people set out in 1961 for Britain, the biggest group from the Caribbean but also nearly 50,000 from India and Pakistan and 20,000 Hong Kong Chinese. This 'beat the ban' phenomenon would be repeated later when new restrictions were introduced in the seventies. One historian of immigration puts the paradox well: in the three-year period from 1960 to 1963, despite the intense hostility to immigration, 'more migrants had arrived in Britain than had disembarked in the whole of the twentieth century up to that point. The country would never be the same again.'[45]

Incident at Birch Grove

Yet it was Britain's post-war relationship with Europe, not the fate of the Empire, immigration or the Cold War, which produced some of the deepest cracks in British public life. Why should that be? This was not of prime importance to the people of the country, certainly no more so than the cost of living or the building of a multiculture. What gave it added importance in the corridors and lobbies of the Palace of Westminster was that 'Europe' was about them – the import- ance of MPs and ministers, of mandarins and ambassadors. Britain was fading as head of the Commonwealth and had little leverage with the Washington of Eisenhower and Kennedy. Joining the European Econ- omic Community would either (depending on your point of view) give Britains elite a new, well-appointed and large theatre to try to dominate; or it might push them aside in a Babel of competing and alien politicians. By the late fifties, this choice was becoming urgent. The distant echoes ignored by Attlee and Churchill had become a deafening proposition. Across the channel, they had had the builders in.

After the iron and coal community, which the Durham miners were supposed to have been so against, the six founding EU nations – France, West Germany, Italy, Luxembourg, Belgium and the Neth- erlands – had kept designing and laying out bigger structures. The European Defence Community had foundered. But in 1955 a break- through had happened in the unlikely setting of a small and undistin- guished coastal town in Sicily called Messina. Here the foreign ministers of 'the Six' had agreed to move towards a customs union, and combine in transport, atomic know-how and energy policy. The driving force behind this was a squat, pro-British Belgian now formally revered as a European founding father, called Paul-Henri Spaak. Later, he stolidly recalled how the ministers had worked through the night to complete the proposal: 'The sun was rising over Mount Etna as we returned to our rooms, tired but happy. Far-reaching decisions had been taken.'[46] The first view from London was that, at any rate, Etna had not erupted. As the negotiations continued in Brussels about what would eventually become the EU, Britain refused to send a minister to take part, choosing instead a formidably bright but middle-ranking civil servant, a trade economist called Russell Bretherton.

This fox-like little man with a clipped moustache soon realized two things: he was being treated like a very important person by the Europeans and, second, they were deadly serious about trying to build a new political system. Bretherton was regarded by the French, Belgians and Germans as national negotiator when in truth he was a mere observer with written notes about what he could and could not say. In the mythology of the European Union, there is a wonderful story about Bretherton. It tells us that at the end of the negotiations this starchy representative of Her Britannic Majesty stood up and informed the room: 'Gentlemen, you are trying to negotiate something you will never be able to negotiate. But if negotiated, it will not be ratified. And if ratified, it will not work.' He is then supposed to have walked out, no doubt clutching his rolled umbrella. Sadly, it seems unlikely that this ever happened as reported, though it has poetic truth. The continental negotiators were disappointed and shocked by Britain's lack of serious interest and Bretherton had been given a loftily dismissive brief by his political masters; it was simply less crisp than myth tells us. At any rate the Six shrugged off Britain's attitude. They were still rebuilding shattered cities and healing torn economies, and for them the coming Union was manifest destiny. The Treaty of Rome duly followed in 1957. Coming so soon after the humiliation of Suez it was greeted by increasingly agitated head-scratching in Whitehall.

And for Britain, the world was differently shaped. The Commonwealth then meant more than a worthy outreach programme for the Royal Family. Its food and raw materials poured into Britain and there was an illusion that Britain's manufacturing future would be secured by selling industrial goods to kith and kin in Durban, Dunedin, Canberra and Calgary. In came butter, oil, meat, aluminium, rubber, tobacco and woodpulp. Out would flow engines, cars, clothing, aircraft and electronics. The poorer members of the sterling club kept their reserves in London, so Britain was banker as well as manufacturer for much of Africa and parts of Asia too. Most people believed that to cut adrift the Commonwealth and join a new club would be economically ruinous as well as immoral. For Labour, Wilson told the Commons that 'If there has to be a choice, we are not entitled to sell our friends and kinsmen down the river for a problematical and marginal advantage in selling washing machines in Dusseldorf.' Later Hugh Gaitskell told the Labour conference that membership of the European Economic Community would mean the end of a thousand years of history: 'How can one seriously suppose that if the mother country, the centre of the Commonwealth, is a province of Europe . . . it could continue to exist as the mother country of a series of independent nations?' Yet at just this time the European market, thirsting for new consumer goods, was growing spectacularly fast, while the Commonwealth trading group was by comparison falling behind. As we have seen, most of the poorer countries did not want Britain anyway. The richer nations of the old Commonwealth – Australia, New Zealand, Canada and even semi-detached South Africa – would soon turn to the United States for their consumer goods. Rileys would not long compete with Cadillacs.

Yet membership of the EEC would subordinate Britain in important ways to foreigners. This was recognized from the first. There was no illusion. Independence would be lost. Other forms of subordination and loss of independence had already happened. The foundation of the United Nations, the post-war economic system and the establishment of Nato involved relinquishing traditional freedoms of action. Those could be painful, as Suez and the various financial crises had been. Yet there seemed to be good military and security reasons there. Europe was something different. Those who had looked clearly at the Treaty of Rome were struck by its overwhelming ambition. Lord Kilmuir, Harold Macmillan's Lord Chancellor, told him that Parliament would lose powers to the Council of Ministers whose majority vote could change British law; that the Crown's power over treaties would partly shift to Brussels and that British courts would find themselves in part subordinate to the European Court of Justice.[47] He made it all clear in later parliamentary debates though this truth was hardly rammed home to the millions outside the world of high politics. Macmillan himself tended to obscure it in windily reassuring words, the old actor-manager trying to keep the whole theatre happy; but Kilmuir spoke out and so did Lord Home, the future Prime Minister.

Had Britain been involved from the start as even the French wanted, the EEC, eventually the EU, would have developed differently. There would certainly have been less emphasis on agricultural protection and more on free trade. 'Europe' might have been a little less mystical and a little more open, perhaps more democratic, though this is difficult in so many languages. At any rate, the moment passed. Even after the shock and humiliation of Suez, the Commonwealth and relations with the Americans took precedence for London. The struggle to keep in the nuclear race meant private deals with Washington which infuriated Paris. After the Treaty of Rome took effect at the beginning of 1958, French attitudes hardened. General de Gaulle, who had felt humiliated by Churchill during the war, returned as President of France, too late to stop the new European system which he had opposed on traditional nationalistic grounds, and therefore determined that it should at least be dominated by France. In the words of diplomats and journalists at the time there could not be two cocks on the dunghill.

Macmillan, always a keen Europeanist, became worried. Various British plots intended to limit the Six and hamper their project had failed. London had tried to rival the new Common Market with a grouping of the excluded countries, Britain, Austria, Denmark, Portugal, Norway, Switzerland and Sweden, calling it the European Free Trade Association (EFTA) or 'the Seven'. This was a poor arithmetical point, since the Seven had a smaller population than the Six, were geographically scattered and far less determined. EFTA was a petulant minuet of the wallflowers. Roy Jenkins, always an ardent pro-European, described it as 'a foolish attempt to organise a weak periphery against a strong core'.[48] By 1959 Macmillan was worrying that 'for the first time since the Napoleonic era, the major continental powers are united in a positive economic grouping, with considerable political aspects' which might cut Britain out of Europe's main markets and decisions. Soon in his diaries he was sounding even more alarmed, talking of 'a boastful, powerful "Empire of Charlemagne" – now under French, but bound to come under German, control'. There was much self-deception about the possible deal that could be struck. Macmillan's team, centred on Edward Heath, hoped that somehow the trading system of the Commonwealth supporting English-speaking farmers across the world could be accommodated by the protectionist system of Europe. They seem to have thought that any loss of sovereignty would be tolerable if this deal could be struck. Macmillan might have seemed as safely steeped in tradition as country houses and the novels of Trollope but he had nothing like the almost spiritual reverence for the House of Commons felt by Enoch Powell or, on the other side of politics, Gaitskell.

In the early Sixties the battle over Britain's coming loss of sovereignty was postponed because British entry was blocked – brutally, publicly and ruthlessly. Two scenes tell the story. The first occurred in November 1961 at Birch Grove, Macmillan's country house in Sussex, a substantial pile with stunning views to the South Downs. De Gaulle was due to come to Britain for talks and told the Prime Minister that, rather than visit Downing Street, he would prefer to come to his private home, two old comrades together. And they were in some ways old friends. During the war, as the leading British minister in North Africa, Macmillan had been crucial in helping de Gaulle through an immense crisis. De Gaulle, leader of the Free French, was struggling to dominate the coming government-in-exile which would take power in France after its liberation. His opponent was a right-wing general who had tolerated pro-Vichy allies but de Gaulle's arrogance and refusal to compromise with him so infuriated Roosevelt and Churchill that they wanted him kicked out of the exiled administration. Macmillan, realizing de Gaulle's huge potential, had worked frantically to soften Churchill and to shore up the general's position. De Gaulle was grateful to Macmillan personally but he left North Africa more than ever convinced of the danger to France of a coming Anglo-American alliance which would try to dominate the world.

This was the background to his arrival in Sussex, one of the oddest summits in Franco-British history. To the annoyance of local game-keepers and farmers, the woods surrounding Birch Grove had been filled with French and British police and their dogs though, to the Prime Minister's delight, one of the Alsatians did bite a *Daily Mail* reporter on the bottom. Lady Dorothy, Macmillan's wife, had been warned by the Foreign Office that she would have to find space in the fridge for the French President's blood since he travelled with a stock for transfusion in case of an attempted assassination. Mrs Bell, the family cook, then refused to have it in the kitchen fridge which was 'full of haddock and all sorts of things for tomorrow'; another fridge was set up in a squash court. When the talking finally started, the two leaders were interrupted by an angry gamekeeper, who protested that the police dogs were ruining the prospects for shooting that weekend. De Gaulle was perplexed, Macmillan hugely amused. After apologizing to the gamekeeper, they exchanged blunt views. Macmillan argued that European civilization was threatened from all sides and that if Britain was not allowed to join the Common Market, he would have to review everything, including keeping British troops in Germany. If de Gaulle wanted an 'empire of Charlemagne' it would be on its own. The French President replied that he didn't want Britain to bring in its 'great escort' of Commonwealth countries – the Canadians and Australians were no longer Europeans; Indian and African countries had no place in a European system; and he feared Europe being 'drowned in the Atlantic'. In short, he simply did not believe that Britain would ditch its old empire; and if it did, he thought it would be a Trojan horse for the Americans.

These seem formidable objections, points of principle that should have been seen as a clear warning. Yet the detailed and exhaustive talks about British entry chugged along despite them. Edward Heath clocked up sixty-three visits to Brussels, Paris and other capitals, covering 50,000 miles as he haggled and argued. But by then Macmillan was a fast-fading figure. A natural intriguer who had risen to power on the bloodied back of Eden, he was obsessed by possible political coups against himself, and increasingly (and rightly) worried about the weak state of the economy. He was failing in Europe and looked old when seen with the dapper young President Kennedy.

After an unpopular budget Macmillan drafted an alternative policy based on more planning, and decided to sack his Chancellor, a close friend, Selwyn Lloyd. The news was leaked to the papers, and over a brutal and panicky twenty-four hours in July 1962 Macmillan expanded the circle of his sackings ever more widely, removing a third of his cabinet ministers from their jobs without notice. In what became known as 'the Night of the Long Knives' Macmillan called in and dismissed a succession of bewildered, then outraged, colleagues. One protested that his cook would have been given more notice. Macmillan's official biographer described it as 'an act of carnage unprecedented in British political history'. The press portrayed him as a somewhat crazed executioner. In the Commons Jeremy Thorpe, the Liberal leader, told him, 'greater love hath no man than this, that he lays down his friends for his life.' The reaction seems odd decades on, when ruthless cabinet reshuffles have happened so often, though never again on this scale. Many of those sacked deserved to lose their jobs and Macmillan, far from relishing the butchery, found it made him vomit. But it was the final failure of sangfroid.

In November, Macmillan returned to his argument with de Gaulle, this time in the grand chateau of Rambouillet, a Renaissance confection south of Paris which has been used by French presidents for scores of summits, as well as summer holidays. The circumstances were almost as odd as at Birch Grove and again centred on the issue of pheasant shooting. Though de Gaulle did not shoot himself, he organized a fairly comprehensive welcoming slaughter, standing behind Macmillan and other guests and commenting loudly every time they missed. There was much use of trumpets and the beaters were soldiers; Macmillan shot seventy-seven birds.[49] But now, on his home turf de Gaulle's objections to British membership were even more aggressively expressed. If Britain wanted to choose Europe, she would have to cut her special ties with America. At one point, Macmillan broke down in tears of frustration at the Frenchman's intransigence, leading de Gaulle to report cruelly to his cabinet later: 'This poor man, to whom I had nothing to give, seemed so sad, so beaten that I wanted to put my hand on his shoulder and say to him, as in the Edith Piaf song, *"Ne pleurez pas, milord"*.'

Cruel or not, it was a significant moment for Macmillan, for the Tories and for Britain. The Edwardian act now seemed weak and old, not impressive. When a few months later, in early 1963, de Gaulle's 'Non' was abruptly announced in a Paris press conference, causing huge offence in Britain. A visit by Princess Margaret to Paris was cancelled. At the England–France rugby international at Twickenham a few days later, England won six-five and the captain assured Heath, the failed negotiator, that he had had a word with the team and told them 'this was an all-important game. Everyone knew what I meant and produced the necessary.'[50] Macmillan himself bitterly recorded in his diary that 'the French always betray you in the end.'

Tales of Yankee Power

In 1962 the world had come to the brink of nuclear war during the Cuban missile crisis. The people living round Scotland's Holy Loch, where Macmillan had allowed the Americans to base the first nuclear submarines, immediately realized the gravity of the Cuban crisis when they awoke in the night to the unfamiliar sound of silence. The humming of motors on the loch they had become so used to had suddenly ceased and when morning broke they saw that the US submarines had slipped away to prepare their nuclear attack on Russia. In Whitehall the historian Peter Hennessy believes that Macmillan was preparing for a cabinet meeting which would have authorized the first stage of hiding his government underground. There were no illusions about what a missile strike would mean. In 1955 secret government papers on the impact of hydrogen bombs stated that the effect 'on dense populations would remain beyond the imagination until it happened. Whether this country could withstand an all-out attack and still be in any state to carry on hostilities must be very doubtful.'[51] How many H-bombs would it take to wipe out the British military state? At an eerie encounter in 1961 between the Russian leader Nikita Khrushchev and the British ambassador Sir Frank Roberts, who found themselves together at a ballet performance in Moscow, exactly this issue came up. Khrushchev asked Roberts how many it would take and he replied, loyally hoping to limit the scale of any planned strike, that Britain would be destroyed by six H-bombs. The Soviet leader told him that 'optimists' at the Soviet forward command headquarters in East Berlin had reckoned Britain would take nine. In fact, said Khrushchev, the Soviet general staff had a higher opinion of the UK's capacity to resist and had earmarked 'several scores of bombs for use' against Britain.[52]

In the face of this horror, the British government had built huge networks of bunkers, with food and water supplies, emergency generators, communications systems, decontamination suits and the rest in order to maintain some vestigial State alive after the holocaust. Plans for regional command centres and what has been described as a form of Cromwellian military dictatorship with martial law and the shooting of civilians who resisted, were well advanced. By the early sixties, Macmillan had his post-nuclear government system ready. Whitehall had earmarked 210 people who would run the remnant of a country, from chiefs of staff and intelligence officers to typists and clerks. They would be rushed to TURNSTILE, the top secret underground bunker system with sixty miles of tunnels, built deep under the Cotswolds at Corsham. Everyone else, including the wives, husbands and children of those ordered to the bunkers, would have been left to burn, die of radiation poisoning, or otherwise expire. Sir Rodric Braithwaite, later Chairman of the Joint Intelligence Committee, said of all this planning that 'It was inescapable, it was necessary and it was lunatic.'

Something of the same mix of fatalism and fascination underpinned the determination of successive British governments to persevere with un-independent nuclear weapons, something to chuck back in the final hour. We have seen how, under Attlee and Churchill, Britain struggled to create her own nuclear deterrent, and did so hoping to maintain her independence from America. For a brief period of five or six years Bevin's belief in the possibility of a genuinely independent British bomb was vindicated but in the Macmillan years all this changed. It is striking that the original clinching argument for British nuclear weapons, which was that they would give Britain's politicians special status and leverage to influence Washington, so quickly collapsed. Leverage and dependency rarely go together. And it is even more striking that when the argument collapsed there was no radical rethinking of Britain's nuclear posture. In government nobody seemed to notice.

The RAF had been assembling a great fleet of V-bombers – Valiants, Victors and finally Vulcans – intended to fly over Russia and drop free-falling nuclear bombs. Like the bombers, the bombs had been developed independently at Aldermaston. They continued to grow in destructive power, giant squat tubes with wings and names such as Blue Danube, Yellow Sun or Red Beard. But the V-bomber fleet had been running late. So in 1958 as a stop-gap Macmillan allowed sixty huge American Thor missiles to be stationed in Britain. The UK's intercontinental ballistic missiles, Blue Streak, used liquid propellant which had to be stored separately, creating too long a preparation period in a nuclear emergency. British planners believed they would have as little as two and a half minutes' warning of a Soviet missile attack. To defend Blue Streak while the fuel was prepared would have meant building sixty vast silos deep in the ground, an epic project too expensive for Whitehall to contemplate.

Two years later in 1960 when the Soviets shot down an American U2 spy plane, flying far higher than any Victor, Vulcan or B52 could manage, the age of the bombers was over. At first that wasn't clear and Macmillan began negotiating to buy American air-launched Skybolt missiles, which it was thought could be used by the V-bomber fleet to fire at the Soviet Union from a safe distance. At Camp David, Eisenhower's Spartan retreat in Maryland outside Washington, Macmillan struck his deal. Britain could buy Skybolt and in return the United States would be allowed a deep-water base for its latest top-secret missile system, the submarine-launched Polaris, which was to be tested that year. Yet again, events overtook Macmillan. Skybolt turned out to be a dud, or at least too unreliable for the United States. The age of the nuclear submarine had arrived.

To stay in this race, Britain would need Polaris instead. Impossible to trace underwater, the submarines carrying them could cruise the oceans for months. Each submarine sailed with sixteen missiles. Each missile, once launched could not be stopped. Each carried more destructive force than all the bombs dropped in the Second World War. 'Polaris' was the ultimate doomsday fish. Thanks to Macmillan's deal at Camp David, the first American version arrived a short drive away from Glasgow. Macmillan originally talked to Eisenhower only about some base in Scottish waters, though sites in England and Wales were also considered. He had been nervous from the start, noting in his diary that 'A picture could well be drawn of some frightful accident which might devastate the whole of Scotland.'[53] The US Navy, however, searching for suitable sites, rejected the north-west Highlands as too remote. They fixed on the Holy Loch, a steep-sided inlet close to Glasgow. It had deep water, it was easy for navigation, quiet and yet submarines would quickly be able to hide themselves in the heavy marine traffic leaving and entering the Clyde. It was also close to Scotland's only international airport, Prestwick, which would be handy for American sailors. Macmillan became increasingly alarmed at the promise he had made, writing to Eisenhower that, 'It would surely be a mistake to put down what will become a major nuclear target so near to the third largest and most overcrowded city in this country. As soon as the announcement was made, Malinovsky [the Soviet defence minister] would threaten to aim his rockets at Glasgow and there would not only be the usual agitation of the defeatists and the pacifists but also genuine apprehension among ordinary folk.'

Eisenhower was blandly dismissive: they had discussed merely a Scottish base, had they not? The details would be worked out by naval people. But that was the trouble. The Royal Navy was desperate to get its hands on Polaris. Its status was crucially affected. If it became the nuclear delivery system, then after decades of air power supremacy, the navy would finally edge ahead of the RAF as the most important, as well as the senior, service. So the naval lobbyists were adamant that Macmillan must be accommodating about the Holy Loch. Macmillan was impaled. The same went for a government suggestion that the US Navy might agree to joint control over the American missiles stationed in Scotland. Again, this was vetoed. Again, the Navy was with the Americans. Macmillan buckled and allowed the deal to stand. The now inaptly named Holy Loch would welcome America's nuclear submarine fleet. When the first US nuclear supply ship arrived in the Clyde, the captain faced a tiny demonstration by Scottish CND members in canoes and kayaks which he dismissed as the protest of a few 'damn Eskimos'. Both his ship, the *Proteus*, and the first nuclear submarines into the Clyde, were targeted by protesters who managed to hold onto the bows of the supply ship, climb its side and generally win a little publicity. There was a demonstration in Glasgow and marches to the gates of the new US base but CND's plan for a blockade by dinghy and canoe was defeated by rain, choppy waters and energetic policing by local bobbies.

A few years later, Macmillan did a further deal, this time with the new US President John F. Kennedy; and the Royal Navy duly got its own Polaris fleet. Britain would build the submarines, at Barrow-in-Furness and Birkenhead, including the nuclear power systems, and would produce her own nuclear warheads. But America would supply the Polaris missiles themselves. Work started in 1963 on a new British nuclear submarine base at Faslane, just along the coast from the Holy Loch, the first new naval base since 1909. It had become perfectly obvious after the Cuban missile crisis that if Armageddon happened, it would have been triggered by some miscalculation or accident involving the US or the USSR. Every other nation, nuclear or not, would be a mere observer. And if the independent deterrence was not independent, and far from giving Britain leverage, made her a supplicant, why did Britain press on? The mixed motives of Macmillan and Alec Douglas-Home included a whiff of the old Churchillian fantasy about great power status. There was also a vague sense that the Western alliance should include more than just one nuclear power. Russia was a real threat, and if deterrence worked then Britain needed it as much as anyone. With a large British Army of the Rhine and this country the first in line for any pre-emptive Soviet missile strike, there was a remarkably wide political consensus on the need for submarines and missiles, with the Union Jack on top. Polling and voting shows that most of the time a large majority of voters agreed with this despite the campaigns of the disarmers. Labour never went anti-nuclear, even though so many of its supporters were so passionately committed to CND.

By the early sixties Britain was essentially in the same global rictus that she would adopt until the end of the Cold War. Once she had stomped the globe, imposing her will on subject peoples. Now she was stoically preparing for her own destruction, burrowing deep and buying the wherewithal for a final act of retaliation. She was sloughing off the Age of Empire, until only a few scattered dots would remain. She was America's unsinkable carrier and ally, not an independent European power. Her main commitment was to the fight against Communism and on it she was spending proportionately more money than any comparable country. This required a great rearrangement of the mental furniture, but it was rearranged by both main parties. They all struggled with it. In the Attlee years it had been the struggle for financial survival and to achieve an independent British bomb. In the sunset Churchill administration it was his forlorn attempt to make peace between the Americans and Russians. Eden suffered the disillusioning smash of Suez and Macmillan came to terms with the Americans finding that even the smallest expressions of independence, as over the Holy Loch, were brushed aside. All through these years with steadily shrinking armed forces, Britain had been fighting somebody somewhere. Any British citizen reviewing life in these islands since 1945 would conclude that they have enjoyed one of the longest periods of peace ever. Yet from outside, and in secret corners, the story had been very different. Fighters then, fighters now.

Small Worlds Collide

How might one sum up the love-hate relationship between the British Establishment and their allies in Washington, at the height of the Cold War? What metaphor might you choose? They were like competitive gamblers trying to outwit the wicked Soviets, yet constantly wary of one another. The self-assured Englishman, who moves between the world of espionage and high society, is out there taking the risks, but he simply doesn't have the cash to keep playing. The Americans, whom he treats with a mixture of condescension and admiration, are watching half-contemptuously, ready to help at the last minute. The British agent is cultured, well educated and stylish but fated to be the junior partner. He is prickly about his politics. Obsessively, he defends his country's underlying greatness despite the appearance of weakness. For one to the manner born, it is a kind of torture and he ends up naked, with his testicles hanging out of the bottom of a cane chair, having them beaten a nasty but undeniably powerful image of the humiliation of British power. All this comes, of course, from the first ever James Bond novel, *Casino Royale*, published in 1953.

Its author was in his way at least as influential a commentator on the Anglo-American relationship as most politicians. Ian Fleming is also a fine example of how British society was tightly twisted at the top. He was yet another Etonian, and yet another character who flitted between journalism, intelligence and high society. Of a Scottish banking family, he had tried Sandhurst, foreign reporting – including in Stalin's Moscow – and the City – where he was no good – before joining Naval Intelligence during the war. There his wild schemes for sabotage and dirty tricks were widely considered more fit for novels. After the war he ran a network of foreign correspondents from London and, like so many other Britons, tried to work out ways of moving out of the dreary reality of austerity London. He eventually built a house in Jamaica, then a British colony, which he called Goldeneye.

It turns out to be Ian Fleming's wife Ann, admired by her friends for her 'sharpness, determination and lack of pretence'[54] who really gives us the feel of how interconnected politics and society life were in the 1950s. Ann had originally been married to a newspaper magnate, Esmond Rothermere, owner of the *Daily Mail* and London *Evening*

Standard. She had had a high old time in the years after the war, living like an old-fashioned society hostess while making and unmaking editors and journalistic careers – it was one of her protégés who broke the story of Princess Elizabeth's engagement to Philip Mountbatten. But she had been enjoying a long affair with Fleming and eventually divorced the devastated Lord Rothermere to marry him, taking off in new directions, politically and sexually. She was a close friend of Eden's wife, Clarissa, who had in turn been loved by the novelist Evelyn Waugh, a friend of Ann's. The latter two were great letter-writers, which is how we can picture Clarissa Eden in Number Ten practising with a snorkel – for it was to Ian Fleming's Goldeneye that the Edens fled after Suez to recuperate.

Ann was dubious about the idea, writing to Waugh in November 1956 that the Prime Minister's wife 'seemed disconcerted to hear that if one wished a bath, one had to give two days' notice and that I did not know if there was a dentist on the island and that all the doctors were black. I warned her that shoes must be worn while bathing and that the reef abounded with scorpion fish, barracuda and urchins. I forgot to tell her that if [Eden] is impregnated with spines he should pee on them ... I think Torquay and a sunlamp would be more peaceful and patriotic.' The governor of Jamaica was equally concerned, but the Edens, like Noël Coward and many others, did make for the island and the Flemings' exotic home. When wounded you stick with your own, and these were tight little circles: Ian and Ann Fleming had originally heard about Burgess and Maclean's defection to Moscow, for instance, while staying with the Edens at Chequers. The memory stayed with them; defending the honour of the British secret service at a time when it was stained by treachery was one of Fleming's purposes in his novels.

It was not only the worlds of newspapers, Tory politics and writing that Ann Fleming pulled together. A few years after the Edens had visited she was describing another politician on the island, someone who had become one of her favourite dance-partners and lovers. She paints a vivid portrait of the Labour leader Hugh Gaitskell swimming, then disappearing underwater for a worryingly long time before breaking surface 'like an amiable hippo'. In her letters to friends, she was discreet about her love affair with Gaitskell, though the affectionate animal metaphors slightly give the game away – later, he is 'a very inquisitive man, he has a long inquisitive nose like the ant-eating tapir'. Gaitskell was one of the upper-crust socialists, distrusted by the Labour left. Even so, for such a Tory hostess to have an affair with him would have horrified her friends. It only matters because it shows how small and tight-woven the top of British society still was. You should have seen: everybody, darling, was there.

The history of Britain in the fifties is the history of unconscious conspiracies. The private language of upper-crust diaries and letters is mocking but nervous. The London drinking clubs remain from pre-war times but the grand houses are shutting down and the Americans are taking over. In different ways, all these people, from Noël Coward to the newspaper barons, Gaitskell to the Flemings, are struggling with timewarp lives and challenged patriotism. Morals are becoming more fluid. New kinds of pleasure are seeping in. One of his biographers wrote of the Labour leader, 'Britain was changing, growing more affluent, beginning to enjoy the peace, and Gaitskell relaxed a little alongside everyone else.'[55] Gaitskell himself, meanwhile, was able to appreciate both Flemings, writing of the Bond books in the *New Statesman* that 'I am a confirmed Fleming fan – or should it be addict? The combination of sex, violence, alcohol and – at intervals – good food and nice clothes is, to one who lives such a circumscribed life as I do, irresistible.'[56] It is hard to think of a couple of sentences which explain so well how the austerity years gave way to the Swinging Sixties. Gaitskell was one of the most intensely patriotic men in British public life, deeply wary of America, yet he was being tugged that way too.

James Bond would become one of the most successful if mildly ironic symbols of defiant British pride as the years rolled on, not least through the endless films. Gadget-packed Aston Martins; imperturbable and apparently competent Whitehall mandarins; parachutes opening to display the Union Jack; and above all Bond himself, with his self-confidence in everything from cocktails and sex to scuba-diving and skiing – this was truly a glorious fantasy for a nation in trouble. The Americans were shown as friendly and powerful but slightly slow on the uptake, while in the early novels Fleming worked to satisfy the almost pornographic lust of the British for the richer, more colourful consumer culture over the Atlantic – Gaitskell's wistful 'good food and nice clothes'. American cigarettes, nylon shirts and food are indeed lovingly described: in a characteristic passage from *Live and Let Die*, Bond leaves a 'bitter raw day ... the dreary half-light of a London fog' to go to New York, where his hotel serves him crabs and tartare sauce, 'flat beef Hamburgers, medium-rare, from the charcoal grill, french-fried potatoes, broccoli, mixed salad with thousand-island dressing, ice-cream with melted butterscotch' and Liebfraumilch wine. That a burger-and-chips with Blue Nun menu, which would soon become common in suburban lounge bars across Britain, clearly seemed so mouth-wateringly exotic in 1954 is eloquent and, in its way, touching. Though Fleming was a connected member of the elite, Bond's route to a mass audience would be through rougher trade. Fleming had pictured his agent as an Old Etonian but a working-class Scottish bodybuilder and former milkman, Sean Connery, was chosen to play the first James Bond, and he was followed by a range of shapes and accents, including an Irishman. This appeared to suggest that Bond was something of an outsider, which in turn expanded the films' appeal. In a further twist, the films were only ever made because of the financial backing of America's United Artists and the ex-Hollywood producer Albert or 'Cubby' Broccoli. He had been working in London, as had his Bond partner, a Canadian called Harry Salzman, whose earlier work included films of grittier subjects such as John Osborne's *Look Back in Anger*. James Bond would pay rather better.

Was it all a bit too much? Not really: the political scandal that happened at the fag-end of the Tory years was more highly coloured and more unlikely than much of what Ian Fleming poured into his early 'shockers'.

This tall tale began on a hot summer evening around the swimming pool of a grand house, Cliveden, in Buckinghamshire. Now a hotel for the very rich, the Italianate mansion overlooking the Thames in one of the finest locations in southern England, had once belonged to the Duke of Westminster. Its architecture has an exuberant opulence that makes you laugh out loud even now, and its original style can be summarized by the fact that it contained a dining room taken wholesale from the French palace of Madame de Pompadour. Cliveden was already notorious as a place of cliques and plotters. It had been the home of the first Lord Astor, a newspaper magnate, and his famous wife, politician and hostess, Nancy, a woman who could have given Ann Fleming a run for her money. Before the war, Nancy Astor's gatherings had been attacked by the left-wing journalist Claud Cockburn as the very epicentre of pro-appeasement thinking. At Cliveden, Cockburn insisted, Lords Halifax and Lothian and the pro-appeasement *Times* editor Geoffrey Dawson, gathered with the Astors to undermine Eden and Churchill, and plot a deal with Hitler. The evidence of actual plotting at Cliveden is scanty but the Communist Party took up the story of an upper-class conspiracy, involving highly placed Americans and members of the Royal Family ready to sell out democracy to the Nazis. Soon the 'Cliveden set' was being talked about from Berlin to Washington. Nancy Astor, then an MP, complained that she was portrayed as the centre of 'a vicious and degenerate gang' and received letters saying that she and her family 'should be taken out and shot'. When she eventually confronted Cockburn at a party she spat in his face. Remarkably, political lightning now struck the same house again. Cliveden, or rather its swimming pool, helped finish off Tory reputations a generation later.[57]

The next Lord Astor, known as Bill, was trying to live a relatively apolitical and social life. Amiable, thrice-married, he was turning Cliveden again into a party palace where well-off and eminent guests enjoyed themselves. One of his friends was a slightly sinister osteopath of extreme left-wing affectations (rather than views) called Stephen Ward. He had massaged the backs of Winston Churchill, Gaitskell, many Royals and Elizabeth Taylor. It was said of him that 'he enjoyed "handling" people's lives as he enjoyed handling their dislocated limbs or damaged muscles.' Ward, also a talented artist, kept a collection of pretty young girls whose careers he vaguely promoted in the modelling and sex business. One was called Christine Keeler. She had run away to London from her railway carriage home at the age of fifteen and lived a wild teenage youth afterwards. On the night in question, she was staying with Ward and two others at a grand, vaguely Germanic 'cottage' in the Cliveden grounds. Astor allowed Ward and his guests to use his swimming pool. On the muggy evening Keeler shed a borrowed bathing costume and was naked in the pool when Astor wandered down with one of his guests, the Secretary of State for War, John Profumo. Handsome, flirtatious, Profumo had had a good war in a cavalry regiment and was married to a then-famous actress, Valerie Hobson. The only obviously exotic thing about him was his name, which came from an aristocratic Italian grandfather. But hot summer nights are hot summer nights. The men chased Keeler around the pool and later invited her and Ward back to the main house, where Keeler and Profumo began to flirt. He contacted her later and they were soon having an affair. This would probably have remained unknown, in the discreet codes of the time, except for a rotund, cheerful Russian military attaché, and spy, called Yevgeny Ivanov. Ward knew him too (Ward knew 'everybody') because he had been introduced to Ivanov by the editor of the *Daily Telegraph* (who else?) at lunch in the exclusive Garrick Club (where else?). Ivanov also wanted to hire a cottage at Cliveden, which might have struck others as being a tad suspicious. He met Profumo at the pool too. The two men were soon engaged in a childish swimming race. A couple of years later, neatly completing the circle, Ivanov was sleeping with Keeler.

This tangled connection of minister, spy, call-girl, peer and masseur might not have hit the headlines at all, except that among Keeler's other men was a West Indian dope-dealer who was accused of firing a gun at Ward's flat. During his trial, rumours started to spread. Keeler became a minor celebrity. There was the famous photograph, attributed by many to David Bailey, of her sitting naked as she looked back from a trendy Arne Jacobsen chair. (In this story nothing should be taken at face value: the photographer was Lewis Morley, the chair was a copy and Keeler was not naked, just cleverly posed.) *Private Eye* printed a knowing cartoon and article though in fact the cartoonist and writers were largely using guesswork. Keeler had been hanging round the same crowd as the satirists and her connections were widely known in London. The *Private Eye* story so alarmed Stephen Ward, however, that he turned up at the magazine's grimy Soho offices and confirmed the lot. Political London is a village and soon the story was raised in the Commons by George Wigg, an unpleasant ex-army Labour MP and friend of Harold Wilson's, who happened to loathe Profumo. The panicking minister was hauled in and interrogated late at night by the government whips. He hotly denied that he had had sex with Keeler, a lie he then repeated to the Commons. The Prime Minister, like the rest of the Tory hierarchy, believed him.

Jack Profumo was tormented by what he had done. As the Labour opposition leader, Harold Wilson, sent Macmillan further lurid allegations that Ward had tried to get nuclear secrets from Profumo, using

Keeler and pillow-talk, the minister fled on holiday to Italy. He there admitted the truth to his wife and returned to make a public confession. He was instantly ruined, spent the rest of his life in private voluntary work in London, atoning for what he had done, and ended his life widely respected and officially honoured for his charity work. But you never escape a name that memorable. More than forty years on, newspaper billboards announced: 'Sex Scandal Minister Dies'. Back in 1963 the press was in particularly vengeful mood. During his trial for living off the earnings of prostitution, Ward killed himself with an overdose. In the most famous words uttered as the tale unfolded, Mandy Rice-Davies, Keeler's friend, was asked in court about Lord Astor's denial that he had had sex with her. She replied: 'He would say that, wouldn't he?' The frankness of her assumption that yes, of course, rich and powerful men were liars, caught the nation's mood. Most such scandals simply end. The headlines yellow, the victims limp off to try to rebuild their lives and politics thunders on as usual. The Profumo affair was different. There was a famous inquiry into it by the judge Lord Denning. His report was a bestseller when published by the government, rivalling the Beveridge Report of twenty years earlier. (The different subjects and tone tell us something about Britain's journey.) Denning cleared MI5 of failure, minimized any security aspect and concluded that Ivanov and Profumo were not sharing Keeler's bed. Yet very shortly afterwards, in a very tight race, Labour would win the 1964 general election by just four seats. It is a tiny margin. The Profumo affair caused such national interest that it might well have tipped the balance against the Tories.

If so, it was a vote against a closed world of interconnecting relationships from which too many British people felt excluded. Macmillan himself had led a blameless, indeed celibate, life in late adulthood after his wife's long affair with a fellow politician, Bob Boothby. But the tight connections between a small number of powerful political and social players were particularly intense in the fifties, before the democratizing effect of the sixties' educational and cultural revolution. The Profumo affair brought both worlds together, in collision. Astor and Profumo, the mistresses and the discreet introductions in London clubs, all came from the old world. The drug-smuggling boyfriend with a gun and the good-time girls from working class backgrounds, unshockable and impossible to intimidate, were characters from the new Britain taking shape around Macmillan. Universes collided. Energy was released. Its noise was heard as the 'satire boom'.

Beyond the Fringe

Political satire, which had been exuberantly popular in Georgian times, had become duller during the noontide of Empire, and now returned in full force, from savage cartoons in the newspapers, staged lampoons, and the fortnightly mockery of the magazine *Private Eye*. It can be tempting to treat comedy like a ball being passed down the line in a game of rugby. Among the two million regular listeners to *The Goon Show* in the mid-fifties were key members of the next generation of comics, who would sting more, men such as Jonathan Miller and Peter Cook. The Goons pass to *Beyond the Fringe*; *Beyond the Fringe* passes to *Monty Python's Flying Circus*; they pass to *Little Britain*, and so on until the touch-judge puts a flag up and stops play. Each generation does indeed catch the humour of the previous one, changes it and throws it on. Peter Cook, who is Spike Milligan's only rival as the outstanding comic genius of the age, as a schoolboy sent a script to the BBC good enough for Milligan to invite him up to London for lunch. In turn, the generation of comedians who created *Monty Python's Flying Circus* were transfixed by Cook and his friends. But the origins of the comedy keep changing. The real difference between Milligan and Secombe, and indeed many other war-trained comedians making names for themselves in post-war London, and the next lot, was public school. Had R. A. Butler acted on his original instinct and broken down the ancient class divide in British education, the country's humour would have been very different. By the 1960s, the flow of lower-middle-class and working-class children through grammar schools and into the universities was strongly affecting the atmosphere of the whole country. But in the decade after the war, the private schools still dominated things. They were often bleak institutions. The austerity years meant little heating, poor food and few modern facilities, a life decorated by brutal customs and petty hierarchies often dating back to the reign of Queen Victoria.

Peter Cook's school, Radley in Oxfordshire, deployed a private vocabulary, frequent beatings, cold showers, complicated rules about which buttons which boys were allowed to do up, compulsory star-jumps, thumpings with hockey sticks for minor transgressions, and of course a great deal of bullying, undeterred by the staff. This forced bright but vulnerable children like Cook to develop mimickry and mockery to deflect bullies – which in his case included the England cricket captain to be, Ted Dexter. Cook's biographer, Harry Thompson, himself a noted comic, quoted Cook explaining how he would make people laugh in order that they would not hit him. Thompson asked: 'How many times, over the years, has the British comedy industry had cause to be grateful to generations of public school bullies?'[58] Richard Ingrams, editor of *Private Eye*, cut his comic teeth at Shrewsbury School, sitting high above the River Severn, and at least as weird as Radley. Its new boys were called 'douls' after the Greek for slave; its day started with cold baths; it too had a byzantine dress code, involving different colours of scarf, tie and waistcoat, buttons done up or not, and the rest; when the whole school was sent on cross-country runs, the boys were chased by men with whips. Ingrams's humour was less about mimickry; instead he, Paul Foot and Willie Rushton, who would join him at *Private Eye*, turned to writing mock school magazines.

At Radley and Shrewsbury as in scores of other similar schools, such as John Cleese's Clifton College in Bristol, or indeed Prince Charles's Gordonstoun in Scotland, boys developed underground languages to cope with their aggressive and closed communities. They knew little of women, which meant the humour that emerged from this was often toe-curlingly juvenile about sex. They were rarely politically radical. They were from a privileged elite, after all. Cook's father had been a colonial civil servant in Nigeria and Gibraltar. Ingrams was the son of an eccentric banker and intelligence agent, a one-time member of the pro-Nazi Anglo-German Fellowship Society, and a Catholic mother whose father had been Queen Victoria's doctor. Both men were brought up to look down on the working classes as essentially inferior and comic, though Ingrams would have his perspective shifted as a soldier during the Korean War. Their satire would be biting, with underlying layers of anger and hurt. But it would be very public-schoolboyish too, tittering and often snobby.

The brightest then went on to Cambridge or Oxford, still then mostly male societies, and where in those days there was a direct line from the world of Oxbridge student reviews to the West End. Future satirists mingled with fellow students who would go on to become politicians and business leaders. Thompson points out that this too would affect the style of comedy soon to sweep middle-class Britain. Peter Cook's generation at Cambridge in 1957 would include the later Conservative cabinet ministers Michael Howard, Kenneth Clarke and Leon Brittan, as well as numerous actors and impresarios: 'One reason that Oxbridge has traditionally produced so many political satirists is that its undergraduates come face to face with their future political leaders at an early age, and realise then quite how many of them are social retards who join debating societies in order to find friends.' (Though in fairness it should be added that the same can apply to those joining student theatre companies and satirical magazines.) At Cambridge, Cook simply transferred his monotone sketches about the Radley school butler, to the new environment and eventually had half the undergraduates mimicking him and repeating his one-liners. Sometimes comic success is just a voice. Cook found his voice as a schoolboy and essentially never lost it; the same deadpan, bathetic philosophy swept from public school to Cambridge to Edinburgh's *Beyond the Fringe* review, to London, New York and immortality. Ingrams and Rushton, similarly, transferred their jokes and cartoon characters from a school magazine to a student one, and then, with others, to *Private Eye*. Around these people were many others from different backgrounds who would become just as important in the story of British comedy – Alan Bennett, the Yorkshire grammar school boy; Dudley Moore, the working-class boy from Dagenham; David Frost, the Methodist preacher's son from Kent. But the dominant personalities of Cook and Ingrams gave them a particular hold over the satire boom.

The day when the traditional Establishment decided it had to acknowledge its critical cousin, the comedy establishment, was 28 February 1962. The Queen visited *Beyond the Fringe* in London's Fortune Theatre to see the vicious caricature of her prime minister by Peter Cook. Cook had done his Macmillan at Cambridge and at the Edinburgh Festival Fringe already. In London he had been playing to packed houses since the previous May. There had been protests and walk-outs by people outraged at seeing the Queen's first minister lampooned in public. But the Queen herself roared with laughter.

After this Macmillan, determined to show he was a good sport and could take a joke, decided to go along too. This was a mistake. Other Tory cabinet ministers had seen it already but when the Prime Minister arrived, Cook spotted him in the audience and deviated from his script. In an Edwardian drawl, he told Macmillan: 'When I've a spare evening, there's nothing I like better than to wander over to a theatre and sit there listening to a group of sappy, urgent, vibrant young satirists, with a stupid great grin spread all over my silly old face.'

The crueller the political comedy, the greater its success. Shortly afterwards, Cook opened the briefly famous Establishment Club in Soho as the capital of the new satire movement. Every night comedy and music would be offered, along with trendy new foods and a bar. It was mobbed and its membership included much of the old Establishment. Everybody, it seemed, wanted a part of the new comedy, including some who weren't very funny themselves. A spin-off revue, where David Frost was doing his own version of Cook's Macmillan, was visited by the gangsters of the moment, the Kray twins. A few months after the Queen's visit, Cook bought the fledgling *Private Eye* too, where Richard Ingrams would soon become editor. The BBC was just holding its breath to see whether the satire boom could survive on-screen, with *That Was the Week That Was*, again compered by Frost. It ran for a short season until hurriedly taken off the air as the 1964 election approached. For a short time it seemed that a small bunch of university comics had created a republic of laughter strong enough to change the country.

This was an illusion, never shared by the key players themselves. Cook had had the idea for his club many years earlier visiting West Germany, and would refer wryly to the 'great tradition of those satirical clubs of the 1930s that had done so much to prevent the rise of Adolf Hitler'. He said different things at different times about Macmillan and the Tories. Right-wing friends tended to think he was right-wing, and socialists thought he was one of theirs, but if Peter Cook had any politics they were never consistent and always took second place to a good punchline. Richard Ingrams was certainly no socialist; his independent-minded Tory radicalism allowed him to flay party placemen from all sides and he was compared to that great nineteenth-century radical Tory William Cobbett. Harold Wilson, observing with delight the satirical onslaught on Macmillan and Alec

Douglas-Home, later tried to ingratiate himself with *Private Eye* when he became Prime Minister, inviting Ingrams to Downing Street and professing himself a great admirer of satire. His reward was to become one of the magazine's most loathed and aggressively pursued targets as the Labour years rolled on.

There were politically minded people at the edges of the satire movement of the early sixties, many of them radicalized by CND and on the left of the Labour Party. Fluck and Law, who would go on to create the latex puppetry of *Spitting Image*, were socialist friends of Peter Cook's. Richard Ingrams' closest friend was probably Paul Foot, nephew of the Labour politician Michael Foot, who became a leading light in the Socialist Workers' Party and a fine investigative journalist. But there was no organic link between the left of British politics and the wave of comedians, mimics and journalists who tore down the facade of Tory Britain fifteen years after the war. There could not have been. Too many of the satirists were public schoolboys, getting their own back on the nation's authority figures just as they tried to get their own back on schoolmasters and bullies. Macmillan was for them, in essence, just the head of a decaying prep school. Labour was full of lower-middle-class and working-class people with their funny accents and limited little lives. If there was any alliance, it was very short and entirely one of convenience.

Conclusion: A Country of Cliques is Over

The story of Britain in the years after the fall of Attlee's New Jerusalem, and before the sixties really began to swing is the story of a country still run by cliques and in-groups, rather than by visionary individuals, still less the masses. Understand the networks, the clubs and the personal associations and you understand the system. For the Tories, public school and Oxbridge links, even family ones, had provided the fusebox of power. Post-war growth had given clique politics a good run. But this Britain eventually failed. It failed over Suez, over the growing signs of economic failure, in its late attempt to copy French central planning and in its inability to grasp the new culture and society growing up all around it. The symbols of that failure were the spy scandals, the Profumo affair and the rising froth of satirical laughter. Macmillan had finished it off, bloodily, on 'the Night of the Long Knives'. Before this act of almost domestic butchery there was still a notion that the chaps at the Turf Club, the old families with their stalking and salmon rivers, that web of Old Etonian cronies, could maintain British authority and self-confidence, despite the local difficulties of a disintegrating Empire and a weak economy; that they could hang together. Patently, they could not.

The final stage in the collapse of the old authority came with Macmillan's illness and resignation, and the stitch-up which eventually put the bony, amiable, slightly bemused Lord Home of the Hirsel into Number Ten as the fourth Tory Prime Minister in a row. Much of British politics still came down to class, which threw up many ironies. In this case it was the long, ultimately successful legal fight by a Labour leftwinger, Lord Stansgate, better known as Anthony Wedg-wood Benn, better known still as Tony Benn, to disclaim or throw off his peerage. His success in court electrified the Tory struggle. There were Tories in the Commons who were popular candidates to replace Macmillan, above all Rab Butler. Yet the new ability to fling off a coronet and become a commoner and thus possibly an MP in the Commons, meant two other prominent Conservatives could now take part in the race. One was Lord Hailsham, a clever, popular but ultimately rather undignified man, favoured by Macmillan. The other was Lord Home. Macmillan was far less ill than he thought but the news that he would go turned the Tory conference of October 1963, normally a placid and deferential gathering, into wild and hysterical seaside hustings. Lord Hailsham made it clear he would renounce his peerage but then discredited himself with a display of crude and exhibitionistic self-promotion. Macmillan quickly dropped him as favourite, some suggest because he did not want a successor who would be there for long, just in case he could manage a comeback. Rab Butler made a poor speech, leading some to wonder if he really wanted to be prime minister; he was a great mind, and much admired by the brighter Tories, but he lacked the slightest evidence of killer instinct. Enoch Powell, one of his supporters, said they had put the gun in his hands, but he refused to fire it. Macmillan coldly dismissed him as lacking 'the last six inches of steel'. Up in London, Macmillan was still ill in bed and arranged for the various grandees of the party to 'take soundings' among the MPs, party workers, peers and constituency chairmen. This highly unscientific survey produced Lord Home's name and he was duly proposed by Macmillan, invited by the Queen, accepted, renounced his peerage, won a by-election in a then-tame Scottish Tory constituency and duly entered Number Ten. Fast work milord.

Widely liked but self-effacing, Lord Home, Macmillan's Foreign Secretary, had a political career which led right back to the Chamberlain government and the Munich appeasement of Hitler. This did not and should not have counted against him entirely. Butler had also been an appeaser; so had, for a while, Hailsham; indeed, so had most of the Tory Party at the time. But Home seemed utterly against the spirit of the new decade. He was the ultimate grouse-moor Tory, but without Macmillan's wily toughness. Not just a toff but worse, a nice toff. The idea outraged many Tories, notably Hailsham and the liberal Iain Macleod. Powell was equally livid and both men refused to serve under Home, who was described by press commentators at the time as 'a cretin' and 'this half-witted Earl'. In a famous article in the *Spectator*, Iain Macleod as editor attacked the choice as a stitch-up by the Conservative Party's 'magic circle'. He narrated the key soundings, involving Macmillan and functionaries such as Lords Dilhorne, Poole and St Aldwyn, pointing out in a devastating aside: 'Eight of the nine men mentioned in the last sentence went to Eton.'

As it happened, Alec Douglas-Home went on to be a tougher opponent than Harold Wilson had expected. An Etonian schoolboy contemporary, the writer Cyril Connolly, had described the new Prime Minister as 'the kind of graceful, tolerant, sleepy boy who is showered with favours and crowned with all the laurels . . . In the eighteenth century he would have become prime minister before he was thirty: as it was he appeared honourably ineligible for the struggle for life.' Home proved Connolly wrong, at least in getting to the premier position and in being ready to fight for it. Later, he would return as Heath's Foreign Secretary in 1970–4 and lived long to be a much-liked grand old man of Toryism. Yet he never overcame the handicap of being a symbol of the old ways. As Prime Minister in the early sixties he was out of time, an immaculately turned out anachronism. Macmillan unwittingly pointed this out in a draft of his resignation letter to the Queen, in which he cheerfully described Home as 'clearly a man who represents the old, governing class at its best'. By 1964, that class was bust. Wilson put it well: 'We are living in the jet age but we are governed by an Edwardian establishment mentality.'

Though in theory opposed to this fusty clique-ridden world, behind the clothing and language, Labour leaders were not quite as different as they liked to appear. That party too was a cluster of competing clubs and networks, whose own connections to business were chance friendships which would later cause much embarrassment. The trade unions were still mostly in the hands of the old right-wing leaders who manipulated and wire-pulled to stay in office; Whitehall was run by a tiny elite of clubmen, the hyper-educated classicists from Oxbridge in their striped trousers and stiff collars who knew they were cleverer than any elite, anywhere else. The Liberals, under their charismatic leader Jo Grimond, stood outside the inner clubs of fifties power which was no doubt why they began to have some spectacular by-election successes towards the end of the Tory years, particularly in Cornwall, Wales and Scotland. They were seen as somehow modern and classless, though in fact Grimond was another Old Etonian who was intertwined in the once-grand family alliances of strangely dead Liberal England. In Scotland and Wales, the Nationalist parties were just beginning to challenge the paternalists. But when Anthony Sampson published *Anatomy of Britain* he had illustrated it with a sprawling diagram of intersecting circles to show the closed and nepotistic system under which the country was organized. It was probably the most influential piece of journalism of his long career and as potent in its way as the coining of the word 'Establishment' by another journalist, Henry Fairlie, at around the same time.

Of course, all advanced societies have Establishments. France swapped her great Catholic families for the intellectual elites of the de Gaulle era; German industrialists cooperated cosily together in their assault on world markets; even the United States has its Ivy League colleges and grand families interlinked from Wall Street to Washington. But in democracies elites require prestige to survive. They need to have spread their successes widely enough to retain authority. The British elites of the early sixties failed this test. Despite the new tycoons and the cluster of truly innovative big companies, Britain's output was growing far more slowly than other comparable countries and her share of world markets was shrivelling at a terrifying speed. Despite outside shocks, from Indian independence to Suez, from the sterling crises and the failure of weapons systems, to France's rejection of her application for Common Market membership, the country had made no radical change of direction. Privately, civil servants and politicians acknowledged that there were profound problems, and agonized about what should be done. Publicly, under Macmillan and Douglas-Home, there was a complacent front of self-congratulation and business as usual.

Was this because we had been happier than other nations in our age of lost content? No revolution, invasion or wartime defeat had shaken the British as they acquired their new cars and explored their new supermarkets; British political scandals were a branch of light entertainment compared to the darker struggles convulsing Italy, France or Eastern Europe. And when Britain finally made a change, it turned out to be a surprisingly modest and ineffective one. Outside politics and the economy, a new country was breaking through – brightly coloured, fashionable, less masculine. For a brief flicker, it seemed to be matched by the arrival of a new government too. An alternative assessment came from Crossman as he contemplated the funeral gathering for Sir Winston Churchill in Westminster Hall at the end of January 1965: 'But, oh, what a faded, declining establishment surrounded me. Aged marshals, grey, dreary ladies, decadent Marlboroughs and Churchills. It was a dying congregation gathered there and I am afraid the Labour Cabinet didn't look too distinguished, either. It felt like the end of an epoch, possibly even the end of a nation.'[59]

Part Three

HAROLD, TED AND JIM:
WHEN THE MODERN FAILED

The thirteen years of Tory rule, wasted according to Harold Wilson, were followed by fifteen years when modern Britain rose and failed. 'Modern' does not simply mean the look and shape of the country formed during 1964–79, most of which is still here around us, essentially unaltered – the motorways and mass car economy, the concrete architecture, the rock music, the high street chains. It also means a belief in planning and management. This was the time of practical men, educated in grammar schools, sure of their intelligence, rolling up their sleeves and taking no nonsense. They were going to scrap the old and fusty, whether that meant the huge Victorian railway network, the grand Edwardian government palazzos in Whitehall, the historic regiments, terraced housing, hanging, theatre censorship, the prohibitions on homosexual behaviour and abortion, the ancient coinage and the quaint county names. Bigger in general would be better. Huge comprehensive schools would be more efficient than the maze of selective and rubbish-dump academies. The many hundreds of trade unions would resolve themselves into a few leviathans, known only by their initials. Small companies would wither and combine and ever-larger corporations would arise in their place, ruthless and managed on the latest scientific, American lines. Britain herself would cease to be a small independent trader and would merge into the largest corporation then available, the European Community. This was managerial self-confidence which would be smashed to pieces during the seventies and never recover.

Just seven men dominate the politics of these thirteen years. They are the three prime ministers, Harold Wilson, Edward Heath and James Callaghan; two other Labour politicians so important they stand alongside the premiers, Roy Jenkins and Denis Healey; and two men who stood increasingly outside the management consensus, leading attacks on it from right and left – Enoch Powell, and Anthony

Wedgwood Benn. All have appeared briefly in this history already but these were the years when they truly mattered. Of the five insiders none was born into remotely rich or powerful families. Four of them, Wilson, Heath, Jenkins and Healey, were grammar school boys, who had elbowed their way to an elite university education. The fifth, Jim Callaghan, had a rougher start. All of them had served in the armed forces during the war, except for Wilson who had been a civil servant. All were exceptionally clever men of wide experience brimming with the energetic certainty of those trained to hold power, not merely born to the role. Though they had many differences of outlook, in broad terms they could agree that Marxism destroyed freedom, and that the discredited liberal free market brought chaos and unfairness. For them, enlightened state management was the last big idea left standing.

So these were men more abrasive and less interested in pleasing the media than later, more nervous politicians. They were hurrying men, prepared to be rude, particularly to each other. Their language was blunt in private, sometimes in public. Heath would denounce 'the unacceptable face of capitalism' and Healey would promise to make the richest in the land 'howl with anguish'. In one important way these men did represent the Britain of their time. These were years of increased social mobility. The country was full of little Harolds and lesser Teds, bright men and women from lower-middle-class or work-ing-class families who were rising fast through business, universities and the professions, who hugely admired such leaders. When Wilson talked of the scientific revolution that would transform Britain, his audience included tens of thousands of managers and engineers, in their off-the-peg tweed jackets and flannel trousers. When Heath promised that Europe would open up great new vistas for British industry, boardrooms and offices contained impatient self-made people ready to get cracking. Callaghan's beefy working-class patriotism and conservative instincts were shared by millions of Labour voters, pro-trade union but staunchly monarchical.

But in other ways, they were already out of date. In the sixties and seventies, Britain was becoming a more feminized, sexualized, rebel-lious and consumption-addicted society. The political class was cut off from this by their age. They would rely on their children to keep them a little in touch. They might manage eventually, a brownish kipper tie or daringly wider lapels on their suits but they looked and sounded what they were, people from a more conservative and formal time.

For the vast majority the early sixties were experienced as a continuation of the fifties. Britain remained an industrial society and apparently a world power, whose future was believed to depend on factories churning out cars, engines, washing machines and electrical goods for export, and whose major cities were relics of the industrial revolution. Authority figures, police, teachers, judges and above all parents, were still clothed in the semi-military sense of order that derived from wartime experience. They were the butt of widespread mockery, in Alan Bennett's early plays, in newspaper cartoons by Giles of the Daily Express, in television sketches by John Cleese and David Frost or in film comedies about bus-drivers and diplomats. The cross-looking men with moustaches and short back and sides were losing ground. But they were visibly still in power. Little islands of change were all around. Immigration was changing small patches of the country, the textile towns of Yorkshire and parts of west London, though it had barely impinged on most people's lives. There was a growing snappiness and lightness of design, in everything from clothes to the shape of cars, an aesthetic escape from the seriousness of the immediate post-war period, which took different form year by year, but was experienced as a continuum not a revolution.

For some the country was just becoming more childish and less dignified. The refined, highbrow, purist modernism born among Europe's intellectuals before the war, had had its last throw. Benjamin Britten's musical austerities, Eliot's Anglo-Catholic seriousness and the formal stillness of the sculpture of Barbara Hepworth were falling from fashion. Classical music was receding before ear-splitting tidal advance of rock and pop, driven by radio. In poetry, politics and incantation were returning. In painting, pop art and the pleasure principle were on the attack. Though it is a huge generalization, it can fairly be argued that simpler and more digestible art forms, suitable for mass market consumption, were replacing elite art which assumed an educated and concentrated viewer, listener or reader. Throughout these years there would be self-conscious moves to create new elites, to keep the masses out. There always are. They might come from the portentous theories of modern art or the avowedly difficult atonal music arriving from France and America, but these would be eddies against the stream, tiny whirlpools in the metropolis or at universities. The general move was for easier, brighter, sweeter stuff.

The two great rebels mentioned earlier, Enoch Powell and Tony Benn, were neither easier nor sweeter. They had shared much with the five insiders and, indeed, would remain insiders through part of this era, Powell until he was finally expelled from the Tory shadow cabinet for his anti-immigration speech of 1968 and Benn until his increasing radicalism made him the silly socialist Satan of the later seventies. They both rejected the consumer society growing around them in favour of a higher vision. Powell's was a romantic dream of an older, tougher, swashbuckling England, freed of continental and imperial entanglements, populated by spiky, ingenious, hard-working (and white) people rather like himself. Benn's was of a socialist commonwealth, equal, republican, dominated by scientifically minded people thinking everything through from first principles, rather as he saw himself.

Both visions required British independence, a self-sufficient island, which ran entirely against the great forces of the time. Both were fundamentally nostalgic. If Powell harked back to the energetic Victorians, Benn dreamed of Puritan revolutionaries. Both drew sustenance from people around them who seemed to be excluded from mainstream politics. For Powell, it was the Wolverhampton constituents who had immigration imposed on them, and the small shopkeepers drowning under red tape and taxes. For Benn it was the radical shop stewards' committees on the Clyde or in Midlands factories, and his children's generation, protesting against Vietnam. In return, viewed from Fleet Street or the pulpits of broadcasting, each man was seen as an irrelevance, marching off to nowhere. Yet Powell was the prophet after whom Margaret Thatcher would stride into power while Benn represented a militant leftism which very nearly seized control of the Labour Party itself.

The Little Spherical Thing

No period of British parliamentary history has been as well and copiously described by those who were there as have the Wilson administrations of 1964–70. Two of the key ministers, Roy Jenkins and

Denis Healey, wrote autobiographies which rank as the finest such books ever. The governments contained three diarists of superb quality and rare descriptive honesty. Richard Crossman blew the lid off cabinet confidentiality. Barbara Castle was the most effective female politician in Labour history. Benn's diaries are simply unparalleled descriptions of the age. Wilson himself was no great writer. He nevertheless produced a monumental tome on the governments which sets out his side of the story, in wearisome detail. James Callaghan did the same. Two of the best biographies in modern politics, by Ben Pimlott and Philip Ziegler, were devoted to Wilson. Other very fine accounts of the time include biographies of all the key players, as well as a small bookshelf of further memoirs by aides, press officers, lawyers, newspaper-men, diplomats and backbenchers. There is also a large literature devoted to the various theories about whether Wilson was a Soviet spy and whether MI5 agents and assorted extremists really tried to remove him from office. As a result we know more about what individual ministers were thinking and doing, and more about their internal feuds with officials and each other, than is the case for any previous government. Among later ones, only the Thatcher years have been as carefully chronicled, though its diarists were never top-rankers.

Yet the figure bobbing at the centre of this oceanic ebb and flow of words remains strangely obscure. It was said of Stalin during his rise through the Soviet power game that he was a grey blur. Wilson too can seem a grey blur, moving from a stolid lower-middle-class boyhood in Huddersfield, where his main enthusiasms were school learning and the Boy Scouts, through a quiet fact-grinding career at Oxford, winning prizes but keeping well clear of the politically glamorous set, until he became an academic economist and wartime civil servant. In letters and contemporary descriptions he comes over as doughy, cautious, priggish – immensely able but not likeable. Early in his career he was used by others, from Beveridge to Cripps and Dalton, as a superior office-boy, there to gather the figures, marshal the arguments and snib the door each evening. He was old-young, growing a moustache in his twenties in order to look more mature, and living in bulging suits, with his famous pipe. Yet as we have seen he was rarely trusted. An early piece of exaggeration, when he claimed to have gone to school with children too poor to afford shoes, which was untrue and exposed as untrue, gave him a public reputation for slipperiness.

When he resigned with Bevan in 1951, many people saw this as a piece of pure opportunism – he could see Attlee was finished and thought the party would shift to the left. He was disparaged as 'Nye's little dog' but his resignation speech was shrewd enough to leave the door open to a cabinet return. Then, having infuriated the right, he infuriated the left-wing Bevanites by waltzing back into a position very quickly. Later, pressed by the left to stand against Gaitskell, he was overcome with fear. The diarist Crossman recorded: 'They all bullied Harold and threatened him and pushed at him and tugged at him and the little spherical thing kept twirling round in dismay . . .' In Labour's internal feuds he ratted, then re-ratted, then ratted again. In the early sixties he was a lonely figure at Westminster. The Labour right loathed him; the left merely despised him. Yet his sheer ability with numbers and increasingly with words kept him always in contention. When Gaitskell died suddenly, the left, without Bevan, had no other candidate than Wilson.

Sir Alec Douglas-Home became Prime Minister because Harold Macmillan was ill and conspiratorial. Harold Wilson became Labour leader because George Brown was a drunk and not nearly conspiratorial enough. Brown had assumed he would succeed, as Browns do. He was a richly talented working-class man, a lorry-driver's son from south London who rose through the trade union movement and entered Parliament in the Attlee landslide of 1945. With huge black eyebrows, a round red face, charm and a killer glare, he established himself as a forthright and at times brilliant speaker and an able young minister. He could be famously rude but also delightful and winning, and when Gaitskell died was the obvious person to take over, at least from the point of view of the right and centre of the party. The trouble, as Tony Crosland put it, was that Brown was also 'a neurotic drunk'. The party's choice, he went on, was now between 'a crook and a drunk'.[1] Brown's drinking was heavy and his personality mercurial. Later, his rants and self-pitying outbursts, his sudden disappearances, heroic sulks and astonishingly regular threats to resign from the Labour government would become legendary. A typical story about him, probably apocryphal, has him attending an official reception in Peru and, very inebriated, approaching a willowy figure in scarlet for a dance. Brown is repulsed and protests grandly that he is Her Britannic Majesty's Secretary of State for Foreign and Commonwealth Affairs;

why could he not have a nice dance? The reply comes: for three reasons, Mr Brown. First because you are disgustingly drunk, second because that music is not a dance but our national anthem, and third because I am the cardinal-archbishop of Lima. The story, at least, demonstrates why Brown's reputation would entertain, as well as appal, the Westminster village. Yet the drunk might well have beaten the crook, had not James Callaghan decided to stand as well. He had been encouraged by Wilson's team, so splitting the anti-Wilson vote and losing Brown vital momentum. In the end, Wilson won easily, by the votes of 144 Labour MPs to Brown's 103 – these were the days before trade unions or party activists were allowed a say.

Having won, Wilson's reputation soared in a way which today seems hard to explain. All his weaving, double-crossing, opportunism and deceptions were now forgiven, or at any rate forgotten. The press hailed him as a youthful master of his craft, a devastatingly witty speaker, man of the hour. Wilson's speeches had certainly improved immensely and he was an acknowledged maestro of the put-down and witty aside, essential in an age of open meetings and hecklers. He developed an acid line of attack on the easy targets of Macmillan and then Douglas-Home, and was full of vague but inspiring sounding thoughts such as 'the Labour movement is a crusade or it is nothing' and 'we need men with fire in their belly and humanity in their heart'. Yet his political thinking, as distinct from his political tactics, was stodgily conventional. He thought Britain was badly run and old-fashioned but believed more central planning, preferably by grammar school-educated technocrats like himself, would solve the problem. He was hardly young, an old-looking forty-six, whose image was comfortingly respectable. He harped on about preferring beer to champagne, tinned salmon to smoked salmon, HP sauce to any other sauce, and being a quiet, provincial sort. He seemed prudish about sex, still the Methodist Boy Scout at heart, and in many ways out of kilter with the fashionable, risk-taking, youthful Britain all around him. So why did he seem so good?

Partly it was a simple matter of class. He might send his children to private schools and live in Hampstead, but Wilson came across as a simple and ordinary man, a breath of fresh air compared to the Old Etonians whose fumbling rule was ending. He was the political equivalent to the men breaking through elsewhere in public life – the tweed-jacketed lecturers of Kingsley Amis novels or David Frost with his nasal vowels on television or Richard Hoggart, the plain-speaking lecturer called at the 'Lady Chatterley' trial. He lacked deference. His calm impertinence delighted millions. Here, in a world still run by the old lot, was a clever new man who took it for granted that he was better than the old lot. In Frost's off-the-cuff summation, it was smart Alec against dull Alec. Of course Wilson was not really any kind of outsider in politics. As an old Whitehall hand who had worked in the Cabinet Office and with Beveridge, who had visited Moscow and Washington for complex trade and business talks, he was formidably experienced by the time he took office, simply a different brand of insider. Yet he turned this to his advantage too. Britain had been going through a time of self-doubt, partly because of the seedy revelations of the Profumo affair and fears of moral decay among the old ruling class, but more importantly because of economic decline. Wilson's propaganda triumph was to bring the two themes together. The country needed to sweep away privilege and cobwebbed aristocracy, and replace it with ruthless and 'purposive' modern planning. Faced with the choice between socialists of the far left variety and the capitalist toffs, Wilson found a third way that would have appealed to Tony Blair thirty years later. It sounded unanswerable, exciting, yet vague. It was science.

In his speech to Labour's 1963 conference, the most famous he ever made, Wilson promised a scientific revolution which would require wholesale social change. 'The Britain that is going to be forged in the white heat of this revolution will be no place for restrictive practices or for outdated methods . . . those charged with the control of our affairs must be ready to think and speak in the language of our scientific age.' It was a time, after Sputnik, when the awesome power of Communist Russian science mesmerized and terrified the West. Wilson said he had studied 'the formidable Soviet challenge in the education of scientists and technologists and above all, in the ruthless application of scientific techniques in Soviet industry'. As a democrat he rejected their methods but 'we must use all the resources of democratic planning, all the latent and underdeveloped energies and skills of our people, to ensure Britain's standing in the world.' If one replaces the archaic fear of Soviet power and replaces it with the contemporary fear of the rising economies of China and India, then

Wilson's rhetoric, with its emphasis on wasted and under-educated skills, is strikingly similar to the language of New Labour in the twenty-first century.

For Wilson, the real answers were the same ones that the Attlee government had tried. State ownership and state planning would end the inefficiencies of the private system. There would be a huge expansion of university places, new state direction of R&D, even a state-sponsored chemical engineering consortium. He was offering an answer to the stop-go demand management of the Tory years. Instead, Labour would grow the economy through the supply-side reforms of better education and higher investment in science. This was the man who had been in the wartime ministry of mines, plotting the rationalization of the coal industry, who had been President of the Board of Trade in the late forties. It was the vision of an old-fashioned civil service man. But it sidestepped the weary ideological battles inside the Labour Party between right and left, and it sounded modern. From the late seventeenth century, 'science' always has done.

The problem Wilson would soon face was how to achieve a successful planned economy in a capitalist world. For all his abuse of them, the Tories had already set out on the same road. In 1962 suitably modern, scientific British businesses, such as Dunlop and Ferranti, were represented at the table alongside trade union leaders and Whitehall mandarins at the first meeting of the National Economic Development Council, or 'Neddy'. As Labour would also discover, simply talking and making optimistic forecasts was entirely useless. The Tory industrial experience of the early sixties, from the failed attempts to get voluntary agreements on prices and incomes, to the direction of entire industries in order to combat regional unemployment, were there to be learned from. But the tactical fun of teasing a Tory regime to death meant more to Wilson than carefully studying how to be a success in Downing Street.

Wilson's zigzagging through Labour factions had hardly been glorious but it had made him ruthless. He turned this ruthlessness against the Conservatives, making unfair but funny attacks on Douglas-Home's inability to understand economics except with matchsticks, and his archaic background as a Fourteenth Earl. (Though the Prime Minister famously hit back by mildly replying that he supposed – when you thought about it – he supposed Mr Wilson was the Fourteenth

Mr Wilson.) Wilson's chutzpah and increasingly self-confident style have been ascribed by many people to his political secretary Marcia Williams. Later she would become a byword for clique and scandal but she was a brilliant and loyal if unpredictable player in Wilson's inner team. She was described by another member of it, the press secretary Joe Haines, as possessing 'a brilliant political mind – probably better than any other woman of her generation'. She would rant and rail at Wilson and treated him at times like a naughty schoolboy. Many believed she had had an affair with Wilson. 'Funny fellow, Wilson,' said Macmillan. 'Keeps his mistress at Number Ten. Always kept mine in St John's Wood.' By another account, she once confronted Mary Wilson and told her she had had sex with her husband several times years before 'and it wasn't satisfactory'. She and he always denied this and would set libel lawyers (successfully) on journalists who repeated such stories. Even so, since Wilson's death some have gone much further, asserting that the Russians had blackmailed him about Marcia, persuading him to work for them. This seems highly unlikely. The Mitrokhin archive seems to clear him. What can safely be said is that she helped build up his morale, challenged his complacency and, until her apparent bullying became intolerable, probably made him a better politician than he would otherwise have been.

Some Bad News, Minister . . .

Labour came to power confronted by economic choices which would torture it in office and come close to destroying it for good when it was finally defeated at the end of the seventies. From the first weekend in October 1964 when Wilson, his Chancellor Jim Callaghan and the other senior ministers picked up their briefing papers, appalling dilemmas stared them in the face. On the face of it, the economy was not doing so badly. Inflation was still low, though rising. Unemployment was relatively low. Productivity was respectable, though falling behind Britain's competitors. Strikes were a problem. Britain's falling share of world markets was a problem. But these were all issues voters might have expected a fresh, vigorous, forward-looking new government to be able to grip. A darker story was laid bare in the official briefings. Britain under the Tories had been wildly overspending. It was living on borrowed money. Britain's balance of payments was eyed with increasing worry and suspicion by its creditors, the Americans above all. Longer term, the only solution was for the British economy to become more successful, growing faster without sucking in inflation. Labour had ideas about that – more investment, more planning, a better educated workforce. But this would take time. And there was no time.

When Callaghan arrived in Downing Street on the Friday evening after the election, his predecessor, the easy-going Tory Chancellor Reggie Maudling, is said to have passed him on the way out, stopped with his coat on his arm and apologized: 'Sorry to leave such a mess, old cock.' He wasn't talking about the furnishings. Callaghan's Treasury officials presented him with 500 typed pages, arranged into forty-nine sections. They showed that the deficit the Tories had left him was far worse than previously thought, some £800m and that he would have to begin with a programme of savage spending cuts and tax rises. Even then the pound, still a world 'reserve' currency, would be under constant pressure. This was bad enough. Labour had been elected promising a more generous welfare system, better pensions, spending on schools and much more. That was immediately in jeopardy. Prized national projects including the supersonic airliner project jointly developed with the French, Concorde, were under threat of being axed. The Governor of the Bank of England, Lord Cromer, regarded by Labour ministers as a Tory reactionary, was quickly insisting that the deflationary squeeze must be tighter still and that other pet Labour projects such as the renationalization of steel must be dropped. He only desisted when Wilson warned him that, in that case, he might have to hold an immediate election on the theme 'who governs Britain?' – familiar later on, but in the 1964 context meaning, elected politicians or bankers? It was hardly surprising that the new team felt shocked and somehow betrayed. Callaghan, who had lost his Baptist faith years before, began to pray again.[2]

Cuts and tax rises apart, there was one other obvious policy choice, which was to devalue the pound and in effect try to start again. Initially devaluation was entirely ruled out by Wilson, Callaghan and Brown who met privately on the Saturday following the 1964 election. They saw it as humiliating for Britain, cruel to poorer nations keeping their money in sterling, and possibly deadly for the Labour Party which was still saddled with the memory of devaluation in 1949. Beyond that, buffeted by the pressures on the pound and the brusque demands to cut and to tax, their only answer was – more planning. As we have seen the Conservatives had already been taken by the idea. Beeching's brutal reshaping of the railways had been an early example of the new ruthlessness. Meanwhile 'Neddy' had begun work three years before Labour came to power. Industrialists and trade unionists were sitting round large tables, creating working groups and setting plans for growth – in exports, personal consumption, government spending, capital investment. Under Maudling, the Tories had also tried voluntary restraint in prices and incomes and a National Plan.

This was all meant to be French. In the early sixties, Paris was in vogue among the politicians, just as Parisian philosophers, film-makers and singers were in vogue among the beatniks in their black turtlenecks who frequented the coffee bars a mile north of Westminster. France's system did not use production quotas or targets like the Soviet bloc. Instead 'indicative planning' meant the state directing money and materials into particular industries, regions and products, while obliging French banks to invest in new factories and techniques. This had begun in the shattered post-war nation of 1947 under the brandy merchant's son and father of the EU, Jean Monnet. Fifteen years on, France was connected by new rail and road systems, her town planning seemed radical and effective compared to the mess of British cities, and from jet fighters to cars, engineering to plastics, she appeared more technologically successful than her old adversary. But Britain did not have the crisp centralism of the French political elite, nor the self-confident young technocrats being churned out of the new system of elite education created by President de Gaulle's post-war revolution, the *enarques*. Britain had mutually suspicious captains of industry and union barons, plus a few economists and a highly independent, rather anti-manufacturing City. Under the Conservatives cheerful growth figures were duly agreed, and bore absolutely no relation to what then transpired. There were no levers.

It might have been thought that Labour, preparing for power, would have taken note. Nothing of the sort. George Brown, after swallowing his bitter disappointment at failing to become Labour leader, was soon dreaming of a dramatic new role for himself as knight commander of the British economy. The Tories' trouble, he told the

Labour conference, was that they didn't really believe in planning, which was why it was not working. Faith was needed, said Brother George. Whether or not it still moved mountains, then faith would at least move factories and output figures. It was the same vague, cheerful, fairies-in-the-garden faith in science and professionalism articulated by the wartime planner Harold Wilson. Yet professionalism, never mind science, was sadly lacking. Brown wanted to run a new ministry which would oversee everything, dominating even the Treasury. Like many Labour people he believed that the Treasury was rigidly conservative and therefore to blame for economic failure. As he later wrote, 'we were all ... expansionists at heart.' To take on the self-confident Treasury, as well as the Bank of England and by implication the City, might be regarded as rash. To succeed it would certainly need wily and careful preparation. Yet in a hurried, amateurish way the home policy committee of the Labour Party drew up its plans in 1963 to create a new department to run the economy. This would be known variously as the Ministry of Economic Expansion, the Ministry of Production, and eventually the Department of Economic Affairs, or DEA. No single document was ever produced giving details of how the DEA would work; its relationship with the Treasury; or its ultimate powers. The final agreement to go ahead with it was completed by Brown and Wilson late at night in the back of a taxi during the short journey between a London hotel and the Commons. Brown later conceded with uncharacteristic understatement: 'I think it is a pity that we didn't produce a "blueprint" setting out precisely what we wanted to achieve.'[3]

Meanwhile over at the Treasury some of the brightest minds were planning how to frustrate Brown's intended coup. In scenes which might have come from the post-1980 television satire *Yes, Minister*, a new dividing line was drawn through the building which left George Brown's DEA with a scattering of empty rooms and almost no staff. To find out about the economy Brown's newly appointed private secretary, Tom Caulcott, had virtually to steal the key economic briefing papers and smuggle them to Brown at his home. Many of the key staff Brown had hoped to use in the DEA were hurriedly switched to jobs in Downing Street or the Treasury itself before he could get his hands on them. In this stiff-collared boycott of facts, people and equipment, Caulcott even had to snatch a typewriter. Bullying and hectoring, Brown would eventually get his department up and running. In a blaze of energy he would then write another and more detailed National Plan. Yet without the oversight of taxation and spending controls operated by the Treasury machine his authority was not based on much beyond personality. Increasingly desperate, Brown went charging off round Whitehall on unexpected and often tempestuous personal visits, storming at other ministers. Breaking Whitehall protocol, he insisted on a private phone line that went directly to his desk, avoiding his private office. But the civil service is harder to beat than that. Caulcott simply arranged with the Post Office to have Brown's phone bugged. And to ensure his private office knew when he was setting off on another personal mission, they had a discreet buzzer attached to his door which would alert them as he left so he could be followed.

Unaware, Brown drew together the usual industrialists, trade union leaders and civil servants and hammered out proposals for a British economic miracle, more detailed than the Tory version, but equally lacking in levers. His first move was to create a 'Declaration of Intent' committing both sides of industry to voluntary wages and prices controls and within his first year he had a full-blown National Plan, with economic planning councils set up across Britain. One sympathetic biographer called this 'a huge personal achievement, the result of working immensely long hours, breaking every convention to get his own way and successively bullying and charming and ultimately exhausting those whose support he required'.[4] There was much shouting at officials, much searching for key documents hidden by the Treasury, which had by now taken to calling its would-be rival the Department for Extraordinary Aggression. The trouble was that by the time Brown's deal-making marathon had been completed, the economy was in such trouble voluntary controls were impossible. The Treasury had squeezed the DEA into irrelevance before it properly got going.

Crossman, the cabinet minister and diarist, was worried as early as December 1964 at the absence of economic strategy as the pound came under increasing pressure. Both Callaghan and Brown were routinely describing the situation privately as desperate; Labour's promises to its supporters, including pensioners, were already impossSible to fund. Crossman recorded: 'The pound is still being nibbled away and I feel the cabinet isn't very firm or very stable because the central leadership isn't there, the sense of priorities, the sense of grip that you need. Yes, we've got a remarkable man in Harold Wilson and a good man in George Brown ... But what we still lack is that coherent, strong control which is real policy.'[5] Roy Jenkins, later to become Chancellor himself, recorded a similar assessment. So long as the pound remained expensive compared to the dollar, 'there was hardly an event in the world which did not produce a British currency crisis. And the only way of dealing with such a crisis was a new package of hastily approved deflationary measures which seemed bereft of any strategic framework.'[6] This left the DEA a marooned and rudderless creature once the cuts had destroyed its growth targets. Brown was moved to the Foreign Office in 1966 and the department was passed around until eventually it came under the personal control of Wilson, an idea that came to him in the middle of the night after he had been woken by his adored but delinquent labrador, Paddy. That did no good, and the DEA died.

Empty Pots and Magic Boxes

In other areas, Labour was on the move. Tony Crosland, a dashing ex-paratrooper and admirer of Hugh Gaitskell, has featured earlier in this history for his rebellion against socialist puritanism and his seminal book *The Future of Socialism*, which called on the left to accept the consumer society and the mixed economy. By 1965, as MP for Grimsby, he was a rising Labour star, a glamorous, cheroot-smoking, rough-tongued man known for his ferocious attacks on the public school system. He had recently married the exceptionally beautiful divorced American journalist Susan Catling, acquired two stepdaughters and moved into a house in London's Notting Hill, no longer the scene of riots and not yet the backdrop for glossy films. Wilson had made him Education Secretary after offering the job to Crosland's friend and rival Roy Jenkins, whose children were at private schools. Crosland's next two years would make him one of the most controversial, reviled and admired ministers in the history of British schooling. His wife Susan wrote a book about him which is as tender and eloquent a portrait of a twentieth-century British politician as exists, but in it she also revealed a couple of sentences he uttered to her which have been hung around Crosland's reputation ever since. Luckily for posterity, the journalist in her trumped the pious memorialist. It was late one night in their home when he had been at a wearisome dinner with teachers' associations. Crosland's tread was ominous as he mounted the stairs.

> He stopped at our bedroom door.
> 'Good evening. You'd better come in the study.'
> I put my novel aside and got smartly out of our bed, wondering what had caused this latest vexation.
> 'If it's the last thing I do, I'm going to destroy every fucking grammar school in England,' he said. 'And Wales. And Northern Ireland.'
> 'Why not Scotland?' I asked out of pure curiosity.
> 'Because their schools come under the Secretary of State for Scotland.' He began to laugh at his inability to destroy their grammar schools.[7]

By 1965 the post-war division of children into potential intellectuals, technical workers and drones – gold, silver and lead – was thoroughly discredited. The private or 'public' schools still thrived, with around 5 per cent of the country's children creamed off through their exclusive portals. For the other 95 per cent, ever since 1944, state schooling was meant to be divided into three types of school. In practice, however, there were just two. For roughly a quarter of children there were the grammar schools, offering traditional academic teaching, including much memorizing and strict discipline. The grandest of these were the 179 direct-grant schools, effectively independent of central government and often with strong traditions of their own – schools such as Manchester Grammar, Haberdashers' Aske's, Elstree, and King Edward's in Birmingham. They tended to be long-established schools, town academies or old foundations, with uniforms, badges and school songs to match. Their brighter children would be expected to go to the expanding university sector and to become professionals. Alongside them, also traditionalist in atmosphere but with less independence and status, were some 1,500 ordinary grammar schools, maintained by the local authorities.

For the other three-quarters of state-educated children there were the secondary moderns, frankly second-rate and often in buildings which reflected their lower status. As one writer observed in 1965, 'modern' had become a curious euphemism for 'less clever'. Some of these schools were truly dreadful, sparsely staffed, crowded into ancient and unsuitable buildings and sitting almost no pupils for outside examinations before most were released to start work at fifteen. At A-level, in 1964, the secondary moderns, with around 72 per cent of Britain's children, had 318 candidates. The public schools, with 5 per cent, had 9,838. The third kind of school originally planned in 1944 was to have been the technical school, teaching specific practical skills on German lines, but these had been forgotten. In practice there was therefore a sharp, public, sheep-and-goats division of the country's children which took place at eleven years old through the 'eleven-plus' examination. It in turn was based on an IQ test supposed to scientifically measure intelligence. Among those who made it to the grammar schools, many hated being separated from their old friends – George Best and Neil Kinnock being among the innumerable examples of eleven-plus successes who then bunked off or frittered their school days in a mood of rebellion. Many of the majority who were rejected and sent to the secondary moderns never got over the sense of rejection and failure. John Prescott never forgot that his brother passed, and was given a bicycle while he failed and wasn't. Rifts opened in families. Siblings turned on each other.

Any schooling system has some problems. Most involve unfairness at one stage or another. Academic selection and examinations require children to fail, as well as to succeed. But by the late fifties, there were larger complaints. The IQ tests were shown not to be nearly as reliable as first thought. Substantial minorities, up to 60,000 children a year, were at the 'wrong' school and many were being transferred later, up or down. Different education authorities had wildly different proportions of grammar school and secondary modern places – division by geography, not examination. A big expansion of teachers and buildings was needed to deal with those post-war baby-boom children who were now reaching secondary school. Across Britain, there were rotting buildings and a shortage of around 60,000 teachers. Desperately looking for money, education authorities snatched at the savings a simpler comprehensive system might produce. Socialists who wanted more equality, among whom Crosland had long been prominent, were against the eleven-plus on ideological grounds. But many articulate middle-class parents who would never have called themselves socialist were equally against it because their children had failed to get grammar school places. With all these pressures, education authorities – that is, local councillors, not national politicians – had begun to move towards a one-school-for-all or comprehensive system during the Conservative years. Tory councils were doing this, as well as Labour ones. The Conservative Education Secretary, a man on the left of his party, Sir Edward Boyle, found that ninety of the 146 education authorities in England and Wales were making some moves towards comprehensive schooling by 1962.[8]

So when Crosland took over, the great schooling revolution, which has caused so much controversy ever since, was well under way. There were already comprehensives, on the Swedish model, and they were much admired for their huge scale, airy architecture and apparent modernity. The first had been Kidbrooke in Blackheath, south-east London, which opened for 2,200 girls in 1954. Grammar schools across the country were fighting back, particularly in cities with a strong sense of their history, such as Bristol and Nottingham, but across the country generally they were losing ground. What Crosland did was to hasten their destruction. He did this not by ordering the education authorities to go comprehensive but by requesting them to, in what has been described as the most famous circular in the history of the education department, directive 10/65. He did not say how many comprehensives must be opened nor how many grammar schools should be shut down. But by making government money for new school building conditional on going comprehensive, the change was greatly accelerated.

By 1970 when Wilson was defeated, a third of children were at comprehensives and a mere eight education authorities were holding on to the old division. The revolution simply rolled on. Edward Heath, devoted to his old grammar school, had promised to stop bullying education authorities into destroying grammar schools. Crosland's 10/65 was duly withdrawn, and Heath appointed that ultimate enthusiast for the grammar schools system, Margaret Thatcher, as Education Secretary. She duly announced a presumption against further shake-up and change. But what happened? Out of 3,612 proposals for comprehensives sent to Mrs Thatcher, she turned down just 326 and the proportion of children at comprehensives nearly doubled again, up from 32 per cent under Labour to 62 per cent under this thoroughly Conservative politician. As one of her biographers flatly pointed out, 'for all her strong prejudices against them ... Margaret Thatcher approved more schemes for comprehensive schools, and the abolition of more grammar schools, than any other Secretary of State before or since.'[9] Heath, who fought a tough campaign as Prime Minister to save his local grammar school in Bexley, blamed the desire of Tory-led authorities to save money by replacing boys-only and girls-only grammars with co-ed comprehensives. He also confessed: 'The tide was strong, but I do wish in retrospect, that the many supporters of selection had all campaigned more vigorously before it was too late.'[10]

There had always been a contradiction in the way comprehensives were sold, which was neatly summed up by Wilson when he promised that they would offer 'a grammar school education for all'. Since the essence of grammar schools was that they selected only the brightest children, this was plainly a ridiculous suggestion. Yet Wilson was reflecting back something that was deeply rooted among parents and many Labour voters, which was a simple enthusiasm for 'good' education, meaning traditional teaching in a disciplined environment, popularly associated with grammar schools. Most other countries, after all, had traditionalist, even rote-learning education in a single state system without the division of schools by academic ability. If the Germans and Americans, the French, Russians and Swedes could do it, why not the British?

It was the singular misfortune of the comprehensive experiment that it coincided with a move away from traditional education to what was called child-centred teaching. In the long run, this may well have been more important than any structural reorganization of schools. Instead of viewing the child as an empty pot, happily large or sadly small, into which a given quantity of facts and values could be poured, the new teaching regarded the child as a magic box, crammed with integrity and surprise, which should be carefully unwrapped. Perhaps a more organic metaphor is called for. The young sapling should be watered and admired, not tied to a stick, nor pruned. Here was a fundamental disagreement about the nature of humanity and social order. Philosophically it goes back to the French thinkers of the eighteenth century but it was fought out in concrete form in British classrooms throughout this period. The old rows of desks facing a blackboard began to go, and cosily intimate semicircles of chairs appeared. Children of different abilities were taught in the same room, so that they could learn from each other, causing some chaos and boredom. Topics replaced lists. Grammar retreated and creativity advanced. Teachers began to dress informally and encourage the use of an Adrian or Sara, rather than Sir or Miss. Corporal punishment went from state schools entirely and on the vast, windy sites of the seventies comprehensives, with their modernist airiness, discipline loosened. The elite remained mainly in private schools, taught much as their parents and grandparents had been. But across the country millions of parents shook their heads and wondered. Hostility to comprehensives, which would swell through the eighties and nineties, was much of the time really hostility to trendy teaching, the spirit of the sixties which was being marshalled and organized in scores of teacher training colleges.

Crosland's legacy went far beyond comprehensives. He was a high spender on education, as was Margaret Thatcher, both believing long before Tony Blair that there was no better way of investing taxes than in 'education, education, education'. In particular, he oversaw a big expansion of higher education, the creation of thirty polytechnics to supplement Britain's universities. These were to develop the technical and practical higher education enjoyed by Germans and French students but which was sadly lacking in the fustier and more academic British universities. This offended the universities, not surprisingly, who had been hoping for a major expansion in their own right. The Robbins Report had reminded the country that just 5 per cent of British youngsters went into higher education, as compared to 25 per cent of Americans or 12 per cent of French. There was a major expansion underway, from the trendiest of all, Sussex University at Brighton, to the 'redbricks' which were in fact often concrete, granite or plate glass erections, from Liverpool to Bristol, Aberdeen to Southampton. But Crosland argued the then-fashionable case that Britain needed technical and industrial colleges on the German model far more than universities. Britain had to get away from 'its snobbish, caste-ridden hierarchical obsession with university status'.[11] Later, the wheel would come full circle when the polytechnics and other colleges would simply be allowed to call themselves universities, but at the time the Crosland ideology seemed on a par with his crusade for comprehensives, a vigorous attack on the old and traditional in favour of a more efficient and egalitarian new Britain.

Perhaps the proudest educational achievement of the Wilson years was the Open University. It too was nothing if not new. First proposed in 1962 by the same Michael Young who had co-written Labour's 1945 manifesto, the Open University was hatched in government by Jennie Lee, a Scottish miner's daughter, and Nye Bevan's widow. Originally described as a 'university of the air', the OU was meant to offer higher education to millions who had not had the chance to go to a campus university. Lee was determined that it should offer serious, heavy-weight degree courses, taught by academics with a strong reputation. Attacked by the Conservatives at the time as 'blithering nonsense', it aimed to use television and the postal service to teach degree-level courses in everything from the sciences to history and law. It has been one of the most successful and liberating acts by a post-war govern-ment in education. Its critics attacked it first for being not elite enough, and later for attracting too many middle-class women but by the mid-2000s, the OU was being ranked in the top five British universities for teaching quality and had given qualifications to some 600,000 of the 2 million people who studied with it. This is often credited as Wilson's great contribution, and he was a great supporter; but Jennie Lee was the heroine of a hundred committee fights to create it.

As for Crosland he would go on to serve as the Environment Secretary who warned the high-spending local authorities in 1975 that 'the party's over' but the destruction of Labour's own high-spending instincts in the economic storm of the seventies blew away the easy optimism of his political philosophy. In 1977, still hoping to be Chancellor and after enduring a dinner sitting beside a woman whose conversation about the EEC he said was killing him, Crosland died of a stroke at the age of fifty-eight.

Roy Jenkins's Britain

The greatest changes of the Labour years were achieved by Roy Jenkins, a man Wilson had always distrusted. Back in the Tory years when he was slim and dashing, Roy Jenkins had set out his case for social reforms which would remove the State's powers over individual freedoms. He argued that the 'ghastly apparatus of the gallows' must go, as well as judicial flogging; that the persecution of homosexuals should end, as Wolfenden had suggested; that the Lord Chamberlain's powers to censor stage plays must also end; that the 'harsh and archaic' law forbidding almost all abortions should be changed; that the divorce laws, which caused unnecessary suffering, should be reformed; and that the immigration laws needed to be made more civilized. Through the mid-sixties, all these changes happened. Hanging went in 1965, before Jenkins became Home Secretary, but there was a softening on immigration in 1966, flogging went in 1967, the same year as the liberalization of abortion law, and the decriminalization of private homosexual acts between men aged over twenty-one. State censorship of plays ended in 1968, and the following year, the divorce laws were liberalized. Jenkins had also called for changes to the laws on suicide and on alcohol licensing, and those came later; but it was a formidable drum-roll of libertarian change, without precedent and never matched. Ever afterwards, Roy Jenkins has been either praised or demonized as the most liberal Home Secretary in British history, the man more responsible for the permissive society than any other. But though he himself called his first spell at the Home Office 'the liberal hour' one of the oddities of this is that Jenkins was personally responsible for few of these measures. They were private members' bills.

The abolition of hanging, on a free vote in 1965 was led by the Labour backbencher Sydney Silverman. He was building on a rising tide of disquiet about judicial death in Britain. The 8 a.m. ritual carried out from condemned cells throughout the country, often using a portable gallows transported from Pentonville Prison in London, with its pinions, white hood, last glass of brandy and unmarked grave in prison grounds, had been followed with intense interest throughout modern times. By the mid-fifties many thought the practice uncivilized. Famous writers such as Arthur Koestler, scourge of the Stalinists who had faced death himself, and famous broadcasters such as Ludovic Kennedy, were gaining a public hearing against capital punishment. That might have remained an elite interest, had it not been for some hangings that caused more general queasiness.

In 1952 two teenagers were involved in the murder of a policeman during a robbery. The one who actually fired the shot, Christopher

Craig, was sixteen at the time and therefore escaped the rope. But he was accompanied by Derek Bentley who at nineteen was old enough to be hanged. He was being held by police when the murder occurred and he had the mental age of a child, but was judged guilty. Despite a national campaign for clemency and a letter signed by more than 200 MPs, the hardline Tory Home Secretary Sir David Maxwell-Fyfe, one of the judges at Nuremberg, whom we met earlier busily persecuting homosexuals, ordered Bentley's execution to go ahead. On 13 July 1955 a young mother, Ruth Ellis, was hanged for the murder of her faithless lover, the last woman to be executed in Britain. The following year the man who had killed her, Britain's famous executioner Albert Pierrepoint, pub landlord and member of a family of public hangmen, resigned from his job. He had ended the lives of 433 men and seventeen women, ranging from frightened boys who had been in the wrong place, to some of the worst Nazi war criminals. Many believed he had retired out of a sense of disgust. This was far from the case. Pierrepoint had been having an argument about his last fee when he turned up one cold morning to find the prisoner had been granted clemency. Later he would revise his original view and support abolition.

Though there was still formidable public support for hanging, MPs were becoming increasingly unhappy about it. Silverman formed a national campaign to end the death penalty. In 1957 the Tory government radically slimmed down the offences which demanded capital punishment, to five forms of murder. The number of hangings fell from an average of fifteen a year in the first half of the fifties, to about four a year. The executions still however included some odd decisions, such as the putting to death of Hendryk Niemasz who appeared to have killed while he was sleepwalking. Against this background, the anti-hanging majority in the Commons, which had before been frustrated by the pro-hanging House of Lords, became steadily more assertive. In Silverman, a left-wing pacifist from a very poor Jewish family who had served time in Wormwood Scrubs for his views during the First World War, the anti-hanging movement had a persistent and eloquent leader, able to win over such notable non-liberals as the future Home Secretary and Prime Minister, Jim Callaghan. In two days in August 1964 three men were hanged for murder, a 21-year-old Scot who had killed a seaman, and who was executed in Aberdeen, an

Englishman in Walton Prison in Liverpool, and a Welshman in Manchester's Strangeways Prison. They were the last. Hanging was abolished for almost every offence – in practice, ended completely – in 1965. Initially the abolition was for a trial period of five years; it was then formally abolished. This did not make Britain strikingly liberal by Western standards, though executions went on in France, by guillotine, until 1977 and continue in the United States now.

The Sexual Offences Bill which ended the indictment of homo-sexuals, was led by another Labour backbencher, Leo Abse – also as it happens a Jewish left-winger, from a poor background and, like Silverman, a passionate lawyer, regarded with a mixture of admiration and suspicion by the Labour front bench. Here too, politicians were reacting to a changing mood, if not among the whole public, then at least among what would later be called with easy disparagement, the chattering classes. John Wolfenden, whose report in 1957 had called for the decriminalization of homosexual acts in private between consenting adults, was a public school headmaster. His committee included the whole card-deck of great and good professionals, from presbyterian clergy and a professor of moral theology to Tory MPs. After his conclusions were rejected by the Conservative government, the campaign spread, though it was a cliquish affair. It opened with a letter to the *Spectator* followed by another to *The Times*. Lord Attlee was a supporter, as was A. J. Ayer, the philosopher. When the Homosexual Law Reform Society was formed in May 1958, its founders included clergy, publishers, poets and MPs, few of them homosexual themselves; its first full-time worker was a married vicar, Andrew Hallidie Smith. Its first big public meeting at London's Caxton Hall attracted a thousand people.

Harold Wilson's government was privately divided about legalizing homosexuality; in general the more conventional working-class mem-bers of the cabinet were least enthusiastic and the liberal intellectuals, such as Crosland and Jenkins, were most supportive. If anything, the Conservative benches, packed with former public schoolboys, were privately more tolerant than the Labour ones. Wilson was judged to be privately hostile to reform. Yet as with hanging, the tacit support of the Home Office and its guarantee of enough parliamentary time to get the measure through, helped to win the day. And as with hanging, in Abse the measure had a hyperactive and persistent advocate. A factory worker and communist sympathiser before the war, who fought in the RAF before becoming a lawyer, Abse would go on to show time and again that backbenchers need not be lobby fodder but can affect real change. He was a curious, peacock character whose application of Freudian analysis to other politicians caused much mirth and offence later on: a whiff of his style can be had from the title of his book *Fellatio, Masochism, Politics and Love*, published in 2000. In time the Sexual Offences Act of 1967 would be criticized by gay activists for not going nearly far enough in giving equality before the law. The age of consent was higher and 'privacy' was judged very narrowly indeed, leading to a spate of indecency convictions after the law was passed. But it was a landmark nevertheless, building on the shifts in attitude that had begun in the fifties and perhaps even earlier, during the war.

If the anti-hanging movement can be traced to the executions of Bentley and Ellis, and the homosexual reform movement to revulsion against the purge of the fifties, the abortion law reform movement can be traced to two unrelated, horrible stories. The first was the rape of a fourteen-year-old girl by some guardsmen in a West London barracks shortly before the war. After one doctor refused to perform an abortion, on the grounds that since her life was not in danger he would be breaking the law, another doctor, Alick Bourne, stepped in. He performed the operation and was duly prosecuted. Bourne defended himself on the grounds that the girl's fragile mental health meant that the abortion was, in practice, essential. He won and became an instant hero to the small female campaign which had been set up to reform the abortion law in 1936. (From their point of view, this was a mistake: Bourne would later recant, declaring that mass abortions would be 'the greatest holocaust in history' and in 1945 he would become a founding member of the anti-abortion group, the Society for the Protection of the Unborn Child, or Spuc.) The second event was much more widespread. It was the Thalidomide drug disaster of 1959–62. This alleged wonder drug, which helped sleeplessness, colds, flu and morning sickness, was responsible for huge numbers of badly deformed children being born, many missing all or some of their limbs. Opinion polls at the time showed large public majorities in favour of abortions when the foetus was deformed. This was far more influential than the actions of the Abortion Law Reform Association, which had just over 1,100 members at the time.

Abortion was also clearly a class issue. In the early sixties an estimated 10,000 private abortions were taking place in Harley Street and other West End clinics, where relevant paperwork had been obtained and plenty of cash had changed hands. At the other end of the social scale, horrific back-street abortions with coat-hangers, chemicals and rubber pumps were causing injuries and some deaths. Around 35,000 women a year were being treated in National Health Service hospitals for botched abortions. Even if one takes a middle figure between the 100,000 and quarter of a million illegal abortions then taking place (vagueness about numbers is inevitable, given the hidden and private nature of the abortions) this suggests very large numbers of young women were exposing themselves to terrible risk. By the mid-sixties, botched abortions were the main cause of avoidable maternal death. It was a theme that would be crucial to the MP who took on this reform, the next in the series of backbench nation changers.

David Steel, a Scottish Liberal who had just been elected to the Commons in a by-election, was still in his twenties and just two years out of law school. 'The Boy David' would go on to lead his party and be the first Presiding Officer of the Scottish Parliament, but his dogged battle to legalize abortion was the most controversial fight of his life. He had come third in the ballot for private members' bills in 1966 and initially thought he would try to pilot through homosexual law reform, until he realized the level of hostility in Scotland (where the law would remain unchanged for years to come) meant it could only be an English and Welsh measure. A serious-minded young man, Steel had been much impressed by the Church of England's recent report on abortion, arguing the Christian case for its moderate use, and attended an abortion for himself before deciding. But essentially, he was put up to it by Roy Jenkins. Like Silverman and Abse, he had much expert opinion on his side – not a Wolfenden Report or the passionate books of philosophers, but the World Health Organization, which had declared in 1946 that health meant 'complete mental, physical and social well-being'. This implied that mental suffering to the woman could be grounds for abortion. It was written into the bill and today

In the Tory years, there were dreams of a super-technological British future: just along from Parliament, this is the planned London Heliport, complete with passenger helicopters, as pictured in 1952. Instead, 'the great car economy' was getting underway: in 1964 London's Chiswick flyover (*below*) was an early glimpse of the real future

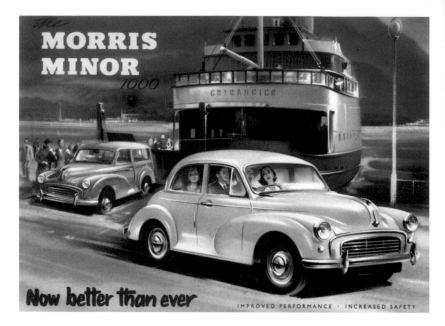

MORRIS MINOR 1000

Now better than ever

IMPROVED PERFORMANCE · INCREASED SAFETY

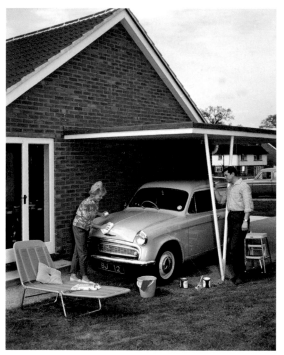

Alec Issigonis, an immigrant from Turkey, was the design genius of post-war British car-making. His first huge success, the 1948 Morris Minor, was condemned by his company boss as 'that damned poached egg designed by that damned foreigner'.

As the mass car market developed, Issigonis worked on sketches for an even more radical car (*above*), which would become the Mini. Later sketches (*below*) for 'the small car of the future' are strikingly like the rounded city runabouts of today.

Above. Cold war: RAF crews practise a scramble for their Vulcan nuclear bombers in Lincolnshire, 1960. The V-bombers were Britain's first line of attack but they were quickly made obsolete by improved Russian defences.

Below. By 1958, the anti-nuclear marches were mobilized and CND's logo was on its way to becoming one of the most recognizable symbols of all.

Opposite page. The working classes begin to be heard: Shelagh Delaney's 1958 *A Taste of Honey* was a breakthrough play set in Salford, and written when she was just nineteen.

Chaps dapper and chaps
disgraced: the well-connected
Soviet spy Kim Philby (*above, left*)
and the man who split Britain
over Suez, Anthony Eden (*above*),
knew how to put on a good front.
Stephen Ward (*left*), the man
at the centre of the greatest
scandal of the early Sixties, barely
bothered. Christine Keeler
is to his left.

Opposite page. If the reality
is disappointing, weave a
different one: Ian Fleming,
James Bond's creator, at
the card table, 1962.

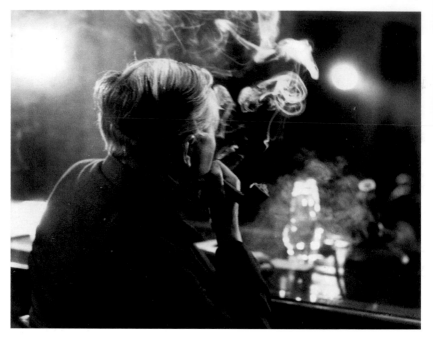

The enigma and the optimist: Harold Wilson, reflective, with pipe, in 1963, and Edward Heath, campaigning in exuberant mood, 1966.

of the 180,000 abortions taking place each year in Britain, all but 2 per cent of them are on just such grounds.

Though these were the most famous, or infamous, moments of Roy Jenkins's 'liberal hour' they were not the only ones. The old law on divorce, which generally required evidence that one party had committed adultery, and therefore the whole jig of private detectives, cameras, hotel rooms and often staged 'in flagrante' moments, would finally be ended in 1969 by the Divorce Reform Act. This was also part of the Jenkins agenda, and he had wanted to see it through two years earlier. The new law allowed divorce if a couple had lived apart for two years and both wanted it, or if they had lived apart for five years and one partner wanted divorce. This 'irretrieveable breakdown' clause, often oddly called 'no-fault divorce', was followed by a rocketing rate of divorces rising from around 7 per cent of marriages in the late fifties to close to 50 per cent now. The causes of this domestic revolution are many, and include greater publicity about sexual gratification, domestic violence and greater female financial independence. But the 1969 Act was a huge factor.

Then there was the Theatres Act of 1968, again taken through by a Labour backbencher, George Strauss, one of the founders of *Tribune*, which finally ended the Lord Chamberlain's censorship role after a particularly controversial verdict against a play at the Royal Court, *Saved* by Edward Bond. The Lord Chamberlain of the time, Kim Cobbold, was privately grateful for the end of his role. Though shows like *Hair* and *Oh, Calcutta!* quickly exploited the new freedoms of the stage to the disgust of Middle England, there was hardly a tide of filth spewing across the stage. Over the next decade or two, the plays which were genuinely controversial would be rare enough to produce media cyclones; yet hardly anyone called for the return of the Lord High Censor and his blue pencil.

Jenkins turns out to be the single most influential politician of the sixties, though never Prime Minister himself. All of these measures were given vital help by him, following a personal agenda he had set out years earlier and vigorously pursued by exercising personal decision-making and persuasive powers in the cabinet and Commons. Most private members' bills fail because they run out of time for debate (something controlled by the government). Jenkins ensured there was plenty of time. He helped pick and coach backbench leaders for reform. On numerous occasions he spoke for them. So why had he not led the charge himself? The simple answer is that Wilson's cabinet was a lot less liberal than Jenkins was, with three or four ministers utterly opposed to each of these measures. Wilson was hostile, for instance, to the ending of stage censorship, partly because he was nervous about the forthcoming stage version of *Private Eye*'s satirical 'Mrs Wilson's Diary'. The Secretary of State for Scotland, Willie Ross, was hostile to almost all the reforms. And often, backbenchers who supported one liberalization would be against another. So Jenkins proposed what he called a 'stratagem' whereby he would give back-benchers time and freedom to attack first, while allowing himself the liberty to speak in their support. This allowed his cabinet critics to vote against the changes, which were carried after very long and highly emotional late-night debates.

All transpired just as Jenkins had hoped. He felt he was at the cutting edge of a war about what it meant to be civilized. Against him and the reformers were many clergy, including the Roman Catholic Church; millions of quietly conservative-minded citizens; and much of the political Establishment. When he arrived at the old ministerial rooms of the Home Secretary (long since gone) he found an air of gloom and some very suspicious officials. There was an indicator board in one corner of his office with the names of prisoners awaiting execution. Hanging was only suspended, as it were. Originally the board had shown the names moving steadily towards the date fixed for their hanging. Jenkins had it moved out and replaced with a fridge for white wine and soda.

After supporting the abolition of hanging, and after refusing to authorize the birching of a prisoner, he became a hate-figure among many ordinary policemen as well as for the grassroots of the Tory Party, something he seemed to regard as an honour. Yet he was not liberal on everything. He believed that crime would be cut more effectively by catching more criminals and getting more guilty verdicts, than by horrific punishments. One of his most important changes was to bring in majority verdicts for English juries (Scotland had always allowed them) rather than the old rule that they must be unanimous. Many of Jenkins's critics on the right opposed this. As he noted with a certain smugness much later, seventy-four Conservatives voted against, 'including Mrs Thatcher, who went into the lobby against the change which has contributed more to the conviction of professional and dangerous criminals than any measure which was introduced by her four Home Secretaries'.[12]

The social changes were rarely argued through with clarity, or indeed honesty. Abse later described the arguments he used about homosexuality, accepting that it was a pitiable medical condition that required treatment, as 'absolute crap'. Despite endless public debate, the abortion reformers entirely played down the significance of psychological health as a reason for a termination, passionately arguing that the bill was not a charter for abortion on demand – which it certainly became. The use of separation as ground for divorce, rather than proof of adultery, was said to be a measure which would strengthen marriage; if so, it was clearly a failure. It was argued and assumed that the end of hanging would not increase the rate of murder or violent crime. Both would soon rise sharply.

All these measures had the backing of small and dedicated campaigns, generally only a few thousand strong. Each depended on celebrity intellectuals of one kind or another, to finally slaughter legislation which went back to Victorian times – and in the case of hanging, far earlier. Whether it was the philosopher Bertrand Russell inveighing against the anti-homosexual laws, or Laurence Olivier giving evidence against theatre censorship, or the British Medical Association helping turn the mood on abortions, this was a social revolution led by eggheads and experts. It showed just how influential apparently marginal people could be in the Britain of the late fifties and mid-sixties. Liberals, though unimportant politically, indeed at their low point of the century, were particularly influential – not only Steel on abortion and Ludovic Kennedy on the death penalty, but through the parliamentary enthusiasm of their leader Jo Grimond. The left-wingers and intellectuals around *Tribune*, who were being elbowed aside by Wilson, also had a real influence on these non-economic issues.

The model for egghead-led change had been the famous court case of October 1960, Regina *v.* Penguin Books Ltd at the Old Bailey, better known as the 'Lady Chatterley' trial. Again, Jenkins was there: he had been the only MP on the committee of liberalizers whose work eventually produced the Obscene Publications Act of the previous year, now about to be tested. Defending Penguin's right to publish an unexpurgated text of Lawrence's novel about the love affair between a lady and a gamekeeper, with its phallic romps through the undergrowth, its scenes of copulation and buggery and, not least, its use of the words fuck and cunt, had brought together a coalition of the permissive. From the Bishop of Woolwich to E. M. Forster, these were the people who might be expected to append their names to letters to *The Times* about the evils of colonialism, or turn up at a pro-homosexual rights meeting, or support CND – the people who would be satirized mercilessly by Michael Wharton of the *Daily Telegraph* in his Beachcomber column, and by the cartoonist Osbert Lancaster. The list of witnesses for the 'Lady Chatterley' defence included Oxbridge professors, clergymen, famous writers, a future Tory MP, and a poet laureate. It was a unique coming together of liberal and intellectual strands in British public life. Left-wing and liberal Christian thought had been in the ascendant in the Church of England during and after the war, as we have seen; the wartime Archbishop William Temple was still being quoted at the 'Lady Chatterley' trial. The big publishing houses were often in the hands of men of the high-minded liberal and centre-left, Sir Allen Lane himself or Victor Gollancz. The leftish newspapers such as the *Observer*, *Manchester Guardian* and *News Chronicle*, not to mention the resurgent *Daily Mirror*, were at the height of their influence. As with abortion or the divorce law, expert advice was used to intimidate and mock the self-appointed guardians of tradition; and to good effect.

The tactic of finding irreproachably serious and well-regarded authority figures to front radical change, so confusing the forces of tradition, was first tested over 'Lady Chatterley'. Mervyn Griffith-Jones QC, an Old Etonian, ex-Grenadier Guard, summing up for the prosecution, was explicit about the historic nature of the choice before the jury. There must be, he pleaded, 'some standards of morality, some standards of language and conversation, some standards of conduct which are essential to the well-being of our society'. Since the war the country had been suffering from increasing sex obsession, a lack of restraint and moral discipline. The jury had heard a long list of experts, Griffith-Jones concluded: 'Members of the Jury, you will not be browbeaten by evidence given by these people . . . You will judge this as ordinary men and women, with your feet, I trust, firmly planted on the ground.'

But what was ordinary now? His question as to whether male jurymen would permit their wives or servants to read such a book caused hoots of laughter round the country. Their verdict against him concluded what had been a kind of genteel liberal carnival, the opening act of the permissive society that was coming. It would mean the publication of books which, unlike Lawrence's, were mainly to be read with one hand – John Cleland's eighteenth century porn-novel, *Fanny Hill*, Pauline Reage's sado-masochistic novel *The Story of O*, and much else. In this sense the high-mindedness of the anti-censorship brigade would be quickly confounded. They had stood their ground on Lawrence, or James Joyce, elite writers. Doing so, they ushered in freedoms which would swiftly be exploited in ways they had not intended or foreseen. That, however, is the nature of freedoms.

Thus, small groups of the upper orders changed the rules of British life and found themselves unprepared for the torrent of change that followed. Some of the fastidious homosexual rights campaigners of the fifties and sixties were appalled by the shameless exuberance of the gay-lib movement. Many of the abortion rights campaigners, including David Steel himself, said later that they had not expected the sheer number of terminations that were then permitted. The argument about hanging raged more strongly, if anything, after abolition than it had before it. There were still strong conservative voices expressing unease and anger. In the Lords, the war hero Viscount Montgomery of Alamein said he favoured the age of homosexual consent being fixed at eighty. The Chief Scout protested about England going the way of ancient Greece and a bishop warned that the country was rife with 'buggers' clubs'. A world away, in a Midlands secondary school, an art teacher with strong Christian principles began planning her campaign against lewdness. Mary Whitehouse's Clean Up TV campaign would, from 1964, make her a major national figure who spoke for millions. Judges, local councils and hundreds of clergy who did not agree with the Bishop of Woolwich, would later be joined by journalists who had had second thoughts about the sixties – men such as Malcolm Muggeridge, Christopher Booker and Bernard Levin.

It is always dangerous to define an era by a few high-profile events taking place in London; yet, across Britain there is no doubt that traditional values were under attack and falling back in confusion. The reforms of the Jenkins era could all be regarded as denationalizations or 'social privatizations' in that they involved the State giving up powers that it had once had, backing away from its old authority. They can be seen as the social and moral equivalent of the industrial privatizations of the Thatcher years, when the State surrendered economic powers and ownership. The left tended to think people's private lives should be their own, even if they made choices traditional Christian society regarded as immoral; but that people's working lives, from how much they earned to where they worked, were fit for State interference. The right had a reverse view, that the State should uphold traditional moral codes with the full rigour of the law, but keep out of the economy as much as possible. The lasting changes made by each side are the ones in which politics did pull back, leaving the State smaller both morally and economically.

Did they make the country more civilized, as Jenkins and his supporters believed, or did they make it coarser and more dangerous, as right-wing commentary has alleged? Despite serious rises in violent crime, there is little campaigning for a return to hanging. Censorship too, seems something few modern Britons are keen on. Though divorce has become commonplace, causing great unhappiness as well as liberation, tougher laws to force people to remain married are on no political party's agenda. Homosexual rights have been increased; again, the movement seems all one way. Abortion, affected by changes in medical technology and by the influence of evangelical organizations, is probably the most disputed of the sixties reforms, and the one most likely to be revisited. A fair verdict is that the changes allowed the British to be more openly themselves, and that while the results are not always pretty, the apple of self-knowledge cannot be uneaten again and returned to the tree.

The Democracy of Narcissism

Much the same divided response still resonates about the whole decade. Why do the sixties seem to matter so much? Why is it that on television, in magazine articles, net debates, in books and in conversation, so much time is spent on a few events, involving a tiny number of people in a few places? There is almost autistic repetitiveness to our scratching of the images, from Minis to minis, Beatlemania to Biba, as if there are secrets still hidden there for us to uncover, some hidden pattern that gives order to history. The truth is that we have never really left the sixties. We have simply repeated them, and that goes for those who were only born later. Sixties music, shopping and celebrity culture have been spread far beyond their first makers and participants, to almost everybody in the land.

The essence of British culture in the early twenty-first century, from drug abuse to the background soundtracks of our lives, the 'celeb'-obsessed media to swift changes in fashion, the pretence of classlessness, the car dependency, was all set down first between around 1958 and 1968. We are still living then, or at least in a slightly tired copy of how the sixties were for the elite. There was a brief political interruption in the mid-seventies when Britain was said to be ungovernable and punk pogo'd past, but it was only a pause. As the eighties' economy revived, the sixties' basic preoccupations – escapism, personal fulfilment, and shopping – returned with full force. This was a time when the mass consumer culture first arrived, our democracy of narcissism. First time round, of course, it was fresher. Pioneers have an innocence their imitators lack. Sixties culture was made by people who had no idea they were setting patterns for the future.

The pop songs of the early Beatles or the Kinks were not foremost neatly packaged commodities as all pop songs later became. When Mary Quant set up her shop she was a rotten businesswoman. The fun was in the clothes. No business with so little grip on cash could be cynical. When the protest poets first howled, or artists staged happenings, there was just a fragment of a flicker of a hope that it might change something. This innocence extends even to the mistakes – the belief that drugs can make urban life more benign, rather than dirtier and more dangerous; or that tower-blocks would bring a bright, airy future to the urban working classes. And it extends to that desperate search for alternatives, other ways of living. These included anarchist utopias, Jungian analysis, Eastern religion, radical feminism, all tumbling one after another with the speed of changes in musical fashion. This 'counter-culture' was discredited and left behind. It survives as fragmented sub-cultures only. But the push back against the great force of the shopping age was, like so much else in these years, vigorous and gripping. No new ideas have come since.

At the time, of course, the sixties were a minority sport. The King's

Road and the Royal Court were as foreign to most Britons in 1965 as the King and Royal Court had been in 1765. The majority who lived through the decade have personal memories of rather conventional suburban and provincial lives. Though city centres were being torn up and new housing replacing old, from Manchester's dreadful Hulme estate to the government-award-winning Broadwater Farm in Tottenham, most working-class people were living in old-fashioned housing, brick terraced houses in the English industrial cities, tenements in Glasgow or Dundee. There were brighter coloured new cars on the roads, but much of the traffic was still the boxy black, cream or toffee-coloured traffic of the fifties. People did have money in their pockets but it was still being spent on holidays at Butlin's and the seaside rather than on decadent parties. The great working-class prosperity of the Midlands, based on the last fat years of manufacturing industry, was only just paying dividends in holidays in Spain. Wilson might be promising the white-hot heat of technological revolution, but British factories were the sprawling, dirty, assembly-line centres of class conflict they had been for decades. For children the authority figures of the wartime era, the formally dressed fathers, teachers with short haircuts and shorter tempers, remained all too visible. Schools still used corporal punishment. Mothers tended to cook and clean at home. The Britain which proudly displayed volumes of Churchill's war memoirs on bookshelves, and stood up in cinemas for the national anthem, did not disappear when Ringo Starr grew his first luxuriant moustache.

So in one way the story of 'the sixties', in inverted commas, is elitist. A relatively small number of musicians, entrepreneurs, writers, designers and others created what the rest now study and talk about. If you weren't listening in the Cavern Club in the early days, or at the Isle of Wight when Dylan went electric, if you never dodged the police horses at Grosvenor Square, or heard Adrian Mitchell and Allen Ginsberg in the Albert Hall, or sashayed out of Bazaar with a bright bag of swirly-patterned clothes . . . then sorry, Babe, you missed it, and you missed it for ever. Most of us did miss it – too young, too old, too living-in-the-wrong place. But then most people missed the Wild West and the French Revolution, and the rest of the events that come with capital letters.

Yet apart from its small number of players the new culture was far from elitist: it was shaped by working-class and lower-middle-class people who had never enjoyed this level of cultural power before. The northern cities of England, Liverpool above all but also Newcastle and Manchester, were sending their sons and daughters south to conquer, even if it was only on radio and television shows. It is hard to recall now, but the Beatles' voices, and the Geordie accents of the Animals, sounded almost shocking to the metropolitan and Home Counties listeners of the mid-sixties. The children of lorry drivers and dock workers, cleaners and shop assistants, found themselves being lionized in expensive new nightclubs and standing in line to be introduced to the Queen.

This combination of racing consumerism and pop democracy matters as much as the old debate about the sixties – whether this was a time of liberation and hope, or the devil's decade when respect for authority collapsed. The consumer market as we live it now requires constant surface change, throwing out the almost-new in favour of the newer still. At a deep level, it needs to be shallow. It also requires almost everyone to be part of it. It both trivializes and democratizes, look around. Compared to that the political significance of pop and the youth rebellion of the sixties was insignificant. The years of insolence destroyed much about traditional Britain but not in order to usher in some kind of anarcho socialist paradise full of hairy people in boiler suits dropping acid, indulging in free love and cultivating allotments. No, that older Britain with its military traditions, its thousands of slow industrial and village backwaters, its racism, its clear divisions of class and geography, was being pushed aside so that our current democracy of shopping and celebrity could nose its way smoothly in. The people would not liberate themselves with class war, but with price war, not hippy communes but Happy Eaters. Even the old fixed patterns of male and femaleness could get in the way of a self-pleasuring economy. Androgynous fashion, long hair, the Pill, a new interest in the inner psychological life – an unabashed soppiness, if you will – really marks the sixties. It was when Britain went girlie. And what do girls do? Girls shop.

Equal rights and feminism were only touching the surface. There was still a long road to travel. Too many wry memoirs recount the gross sexism of the new rock stars, the innocence of their 'chicks' and the hypocrisy of male student revolutionaries. The Pill might be on the way, and the Abortion Act would become law in 1967 but this is still a time of pregnant girls and knitting needles, the public shame of unmarried mothers, and gross domestic violence administered by drunken men. Equal pay was a long way away; many workplaces, from newspaper offices to engineering works, solicitors' practices to bus depots, were utterly unwelcoming to women wanting work. From the early to middle sixties, egalitarianism was not a real social change but – as often happens at times of change – a philosophical one first. The shift was in what it might mean to be properly human. The old virtues of stoicism, buttoned lips and obedience were retreating. Traditions of submission and obedience, hierarchies of class inherited from medieval landowning, industrial capital and imperial administration, began to wobble and dissolve into something very different, a society which was dilute, porous and mushily self-forgiving. This took place not because bad people corrupted good people or, if you are 'pro-sixties', because noble revolutionaries ushered in an age of personal freedom, but because it suited a new economic system.

Biba, an iconic symbol, promised liberation for women and girls, but liberation through spending. Its founder Barbara Hulanicki was a girl from an exiled Polish family, born in Warsaw before the war, brought up in British-controlled Palestine until her father, a UN negotiator, was murdered by Zionist terrorists. She too was a kind of outsider, later raised under the influence of a bohemian aunt in Brighton, before the inevitable stint at art school, then the launch of a cheap mail order clothing company with her husband. Biba, named after a younger sister, brought together the new obsessions of glamour and cheap prices. Hulanicki had been mesmerized by Audrey Hepburn ('her shape; long neck, small head, practically jointless') and her first top-selling design was a pink gingham dress like one worn by Brigitte Bardot at her wedding.

Her succession of boutiques were dark, chaotic spaces in which customers could lose themselves, pick up and try on, discard and collect, and sometimes steal, a great gush of new designs which seemed to change every week. The clothes were being run up at speed in the East End and ferried over to the boutique several times a week. Turnover was spectacular and soon the celebrities would be fighting with the off-duty typists and schoolgirls for Biba designs – Mia Farrow, Yoko Ono, Princess Anne, Raquel Welch and even Bardot herself. As one admirer of the Biba experience said, it 'was helping to create the concept of shopping as an experience, a leisure activity for the young'.[13] The trumpeter, cartoonist and writer George Melly called it a democratic version of Mary Quant and Hulanicki herself said: 'I always wanted to get prices down, down, down, to the bare minimum.' The cheapness and disposability of the clothes was shocking to an older Britain in which millions of families made their own clothes, buying patterns from Woolworths and sewing them up by hand or with a machine, and knitting sturdy school jerseys or woollen dresses.

This was the beginning of the buy-and-throw-away consumer culture applied to clothing, and though it would brim with moral dilemmas later, in the sixties it seemed simple freedom for millions of women. This was underscored by the Biba look, that Audrey Hepburn gawkiness. These were clothes for girls without much in the way of breasts, girls who were not defined by motherhood and marriage, the girls who would soon be on the Pill, career girls about town, girls who felt free in ways revolutionary French philosophers would never quite understand. Biba would be destroyed by the inflation of Edward Heath's Britain and by over-ambitious expansion into a giant department store selling everything from meals to Biba-branded baked beans – the greed and cynicism of its new owners, who thought it could be just another big shop. So, poor Biba: misunderstood by the left, as we will see, and by big business too.

A History of British Pop

By the beginning of the sixties all the essential ingredients of an urgent new market were in place. The commodity was music. Most histories of golden-age sixties rock groups follow a familiar pattern. There are the opening pages in which the kids discover Chuck Berry and Elvis thanks to the unreliable but glamorous Radio Luxembourg, the commercial station broadcasting to the UK from 7 p.m. onwards by the early fifties. (Its famous 208 signal concealed a strange history: the station had been built by French entrepreneurs, taken over as an organ of Nazi propaganda during the war, passed to the US forces and finally revived, funded by Ovaltine and football betting adverts, the only known contribution of the Grand Duchy to modern British culture.)

These early revelations of American rock and pop will quickly be followed by one or more of the future stars suggesting to a friend that they form a skiffle group. Skiffle, credited to a jazz session musician and son of a Glaswegian violinist called Lonnie Donegan, used simple chords and home-made instruments like washboards to produce a brisk, jaunty, jazz-meets-country blues sound, unaffected and often humorous. Unlike jazz you did not have to be much of a musician to play skiffle – as John Lennon and ten thousand others found. Twenty years later, punk fanzines would print the finger positions for three basic chords and urge their readers to go out and form a band. This was precisely the lesson of skiffle. Lonnie Donegan's hits would be faithfully copied in bedrooms and school halls round the country and, singing in a cod American accent, he would become the first British star to make the US hit parade.

Next in this composite history two seminal places would appear. One would be the coffee bar. Whether the El Toro in Muswell Hill or Liverpool's famous Kardomah, or a thousand in between, coffee bars had become vital hang-out places for young people. Often opened by Italian immigrants, they offered a rare space where music could be listened to, away from family-crowded homes or unwelcoming adult pubs. They hosted the first juke-boxes and sometimes live music. The second place to feature was more important still, the art college. In the fifties art schools played a much more important role than simply producing the next generation of designers or sculptors. Many of them were Victorian or Edwardian institutions connected to local technical colleges and originally meant to provide the craftsmen who would help sustain a town's clothing, ceramic, printing or other businesses. Before the arrival of mass university education, therefore, which would not really change things until the seventies, art schools were where bright and imaginative teenagers who failed to conform to the academic disciplines tended to end up.

John Lennon at Liverpool Art College, Ray Davies at Hornsey, Peter Townsend at Ealing, Ian Dury at Walthamstow, Keith Richards at Sidcup, Cat Stevens, the core of Pink Floyd and Roxy Music were just a few of thousands. The coffee bars were essential meeting places but the art schools were the true factories of popular culture. Art students had long been a recognized and much-mocked subsection of national life, in turtle-necked jumpers and CND badges. Such colleges had become vital rallying places and support systems for talented outsiders, relatively few of whom would end up as conventional artists. The great pop art pioneer Peter Blake, a Dartford electrician's son, had begun to create paintings and sculptures out of the wrestlers, popular magazines, pin-ups and music stars around him. Supplementing his income by teaching in three London art colleges, Blake had a huge influence on younger people and was in advance of American pop artists like Andy Warhol. In 1961 he encouraged the young Ian Dury to start depicting what interested him – 'tits and bums, gangsters, Teddy boys, Jayne Mansfield and Marlon Brando' – but Dury was one of many, reaching out hungrily for a brighter, younger culture. Across the country, student designers found themselves working next door to would-be painters, graphic artists and film-makers, so ideas quickly hopped across. The characteristic Bridget Riley op-art lines of sixties dresses and shop windows had been stolen by students from the artists they mingled with; the RAF-style roundels and bold black arrows which appeared on the clothes of bands such as the Who, and became part of the Mods' insignia, had been swiped from graphic designers and pop painters. The way the sixties and seventies looked came out of the fusion that happened in Britain's municipal applied design institutions, places not quite paralleled in America or continental Europe.

This hunger for novelty and readiness to mingle disciplines became a big force in British music, too. For the art schools had early on been bastions of folk and jazz. Why would they not be? Here were gathered thousands of bright middle-class and working-class teenagers looking for fun and hoping not to be sucked into factory design shops or office jobs. By the later fifties, the art students would be listening to skiffle, R&B and the first generation of safely packaged, toothsome and relatively unthreatening British Elvis copies. First there would be grinning Tommy Steele, then Harry Webb the Hertfordshire pub singer, reincarnated as the eyeliner-wearing Cliff Richard, then the former tug-boat hand Billy Fury. A few years on, and future members of the Rolling Stones, the Kinks and the Who were imbibing radical ideas and new looks, as clearly the product of art school as any watercolour or well-thrown pot. Ian Dury and his friends got into trouble for using their paint brushes as drum-sticks, sending off a rumble through the rest of the building. That works as a metaphor too. The ultimate art school bands would come later still. Roxy Music, led by Brian Eno of Winchester art college and Bryan Ferry, the coalminer's son who had been taught at Newcastle Art College by the original British pop artist Richard Hamilton, pioneered a decadent, clever-clever, intellectually sharp music loved by British audiences in the early seventies. Pink Floyd, the greatest of the concept album bands, is unimaginable without the art school background.

So, let us continue the composite pop star life story. You have been corrupted by Radio Luxembourg, learned to play in a skiffle band, hung around at coffee bars and had your imagination jemmied open in a provincial art school. What happens next? In a word, management. In the early sixties an unlikely sounding name and a pretty-boy face meant you had probably been discovered by 'flash Larry', or Larry Parnes, first of the Svengalis. The Svengalis feature early and often. Suddenly there is money to be made from tousled-headed boys.

Before pop the dominant popular musical styles produced low profits. Most public music was live – the piano and banjo players on music-hall stages, the star singers and then eventually the big bands of the dancehalls and the smoky subculture of jazz. Sheet-music made big money for talented composers like Ivor Novello and stage stars like Harry Lauder. Gramophone record sales had kicked off with recordings of early twentieth-century opera stars but the invention of the modern microphone in the twenties had then changed popular singing, allowing intimacy and variety of a new kind. So the recording industry had brought Gilbert and Sullivan, Louis Armstrong, the Ink Spots, Flanders and Swann, Vera Lynn, the crooners and many West End musicals, to millions of homes long before pop. By the end of the fifties there were four major British recording companies: EMI, Decca, Pye and Philips. Most of their profits came from classical music or comic recordings. Only since the spread of seven-inch 45s had records really been something teenagers could aspire to buying. Though first produced in the US as early as 1948, for working-class British youngsters they were still formidably expensive by the late fifties.

The other essential technological changes arrived at around the same time. First, loud electric guitars, invented by radio repair man Leo Fender in 1948, swiftly followed by his great rival Les Paul. Then transistor radios, originally invented in the mid-fifties to help Americans keep in touch after the coming nuclear war with Russia, and becoming popular for other purposes at the end of the decade. Without the mike, the electric guitar and the seven-inch record, rock and pop would not have happened. Without the radio, the vital cross-current influences would have been unheard. Everything conspired towards the moment. The post-war economic boom was putting money in the pockets of teenagers and young workers. The baby boom had increased their numbers. Better nutrition meant they tended to mature sexually earlier. And the mechanisms for the mass marketing of pop were already in place. Radio Luxembourg had broadcast its first Top of the Pops show in 1952. Within a few years television would follow – Rediffusion's *Ready, Steady, Go*, a crucial show in the story of British pop – then the BBC's *Top of the Pops*.

The earlier generation of American rock and blues pioneers had turned music into short, addictive bites lasting only a few minutes to be purchased anew every week or so. The radio, TV and magazine publicity machine was up and going. The equipment was in every second home, radios and record players turned out by England's then-booming electronics industry. And 'the workers', all those teenagers with stars in their eyes, desperately strumming away at cheap guitars and handwriting lyrics and chords from the radio, were just waiting to be picked up in every major city in the land. Thus, in this fictional sixties success story, the Svengali duly arrives at the back of the coffee bar basement or the private club with a contract, bought from W. H. Smith in one hand and a flash Parker pen in the other; and a decade of argument about who is ripping off whom, is about to begin. Like Parnes and the most famous of all, Brian Epstein, who managed the Beatles, the agents and middle-men were often edgy outsiders too – both those men were gay when homosexuality was illegal, and Jewish, when anti-Semitism was rife.

And so the typical pop band history will roll predictably on – the early dodgy names for the band; the cover songs; the year or two of bouncing around the narrow roads of pre-motorway Britain in hired coaches between gigs at Butlin's camps and provincial theatres; the first chart hit and the first invitation to Rediffusion's headquarters to be filmed for television; the first Bentley and the first joint; the growing tension between the guitar heroes and the drummer, who never really fitted in, the purchase of a grand house in the Home Counties, the tragic early death of a band member, by overdose, car crash or drowning; and then eventually the split followed by the comeback.

Though the stories of British rock and pop bands follow a predictable trajectory, the stories of the earlier bands are more interesting simply because the story had not occurred before. It was freshly extraordinary, that fairy-tale rocket whoosh from backstreet poverty to international fame and huge wealth; so too was the darker tale of abuse and betrayal which almost always followed. Though pop was a business it was also a story about class and morality: almost every band history will describe the tension between the marketing of the music and the attempt by the band to stay in some way authentic or true to themselves. Many of course never tried to be authentic in the first place but the important ones did and it wasn't always easy. The Kinks, four north London boys who affected a camp look and played rough, hard pop, were put into the most extraordinary confections of pink hunting jackets, ruffs and thigh-high suede boots to attract attention. Long before the New York Dolls or Velvet Underground, their gender-bending pose was also something the straighter American market found very hard to accept. The most famous band of all were bullied and cajoled by Epstein into ditching the rough jeans and leather Luftwaffe jackets image they had learned in Hamburg. To get their first recording contract, the Beatles were told to stop smoking on-stage, stop swearing, turning up late, and making spontaneous decisions about which songs they would play at their gigs. Oh yes, and they had to learn to bow smartly, all together, at the audience after every song.[14] They agreed. It would only be later that their success gave them the freedom to tell their managers and advisers where to go.

The degree of control needed to make a band exciting but not too exciting would become one of the most amusing dilemmas in modern management. The harnessing of youth spirit for maximum commercial return proved as tricky and unstable as the early days of harnessing nuclear fission – though it was finally achieved by the eighties, when the death of punk allowed entirely commercial and packaged pop unquestioned dominance. In the early days it was not always quite as obvious that money would always trump vitality. There were still battles to be had. The Who was a west London band which had, like so many others, emerged from skiffle and been kick-started by the success of the Beatles. They were encouraged by their manager, Peter Meadon, to dress stylishly and address themselves to the new audience of Mods. But their violence and guitar-smashing, while delighting their live audience, kept them away from mainstream venues for ages. Throughout a stellar career during which they gave the Beatles a run for their money in the concept-album stakes, the Who were never properly tamed. Nor were the Kinks, whose song-writing genius Ray Davies became involved in a punch-up with an American television union official who had called the band a 'bunch of commie wimps', and managed to get them banned from the States for four crucial years. One band's roughness and ire would provoke the next to go further.

Apart from keeping physical control of the new market, the big battle line was over the subject of the songs, which quickly moved beyond the easy boy-meets-girl and black American rip-offs of the early years. Rock was about escape, mainly from the urban and suburban Britain of its young consumers. For most, the teenage years would end in a conventional working life and marriage, which was more popular than ever in the sixties, with marriage rates peaking in 1972. But drugs, mysticism, gangs and sexual experimentation were some of the alternatives celebrated by pop culture, to the discomfiture of the record companies, the BBC, politicians and the newspapers. Some bands adopted a provocatively camp look, wore make-up and baited the short-haired traditional male. Songs such as 'Lola' and the Who's 'I'm a Boy' discussed transvestites; there was a lolling libertinism in the Rolling Stones' music which shocked watching parents.

Above all, the rate of experimentation and change in sixties pop itself was simply astonishing. A new sound, line-up of instruments, length of song and image seemed to come along every few months, and in 1966-8 every few weeks. It was a classic capitalist market-driven competition, with profits and status dependent on beating the rest, measured by sales, week after week. Among the great experimenters were Paul McCartney, who was feeding back discoveries about tape loops, modern composers and Bach into the music of the Beatles. As they became the ultimate über-group they however found the screaming at their concerts so loud that even they couldn't hear the music and retreated more and more to work in the studio, which in turn produced longer, more complicated and reflective sounds. On it would go. The Stones' blues-rock would challenge Merseybeat pop, the Mods would hit back, early versions of guitar-rock heavy metal suddenly appeared. The amphetamine-fuelled fast and short singles would give way to LSD-inspired albums with looping, hypnotic rhythms and surrealist covers. Acoustic protest songs were plugged in and went electric.

Hairstyles went from slicked to floppy to long to shaved, moustaches flowered and withered, huge mountain-man beards sprouted from the unlikeliest chins. Always the Beatles were pioneers, the first big stars to fall for Indian mysticism, sitars or the next drug craze and ultimately the first to find the pressures intolerable and to break up. The trajectory seemed impossible to beat. A band's success was based on its members' skills but also on their authentic claim to be kids from the streets whose anger, enthusiasm, boredom and wit reflected the actual Britain all round them, the lives of the people who would save up and buy their songs. Pop was music from below or it was nothing. Yet the successful musicians would be cut off from the world they came from by the money and the security needed to keep fans at bay until they were fated to sound introspective and irrelevant. Ultimately life in the bubble would prove airless and the music, or the band, would choke to death.

Flash, Snip, Smile: the Making of Celebrity

The contemporary cult of celebrity was born in the sixties too. All developed societies lavish attention on a small number of favoured people, rich, beautiful or talented. In eighteenth-century Europe it might be duchesses and court composers, in classical Rome orators and gladiators, in nineteenth-century Japan, warriors and courtesans. Details of their clothing, personal lives, foibles, family successes and disasters are gossiped about and vicariously enjoyed. They form a fantasy extended family, prettier and wickeder and more brightly coloured than the rest of us. What has changed in recent decades is the scale of celebrity devotion, this cargo cult of modern Britain. It has elbowed aside rival forms in television entertainment, invaded and occupied popular newspapers and produced racks of magazines breathlessly following the face-lifts, marital break-ups, boob jobs and births of celebs. All of this originated in the mid-sixties. The cloying, ingratiating tone of contemporary magazines such as *Hello!* and *OK!* when interviewing or describing some frozen-faced doll can be found in the write-ups of the young set in British newspapers, supplements and the arch glossies of the sixties. The origins of 'Big Brother' television exhibitionism are buried in game shows and agony aunt columns half a century old. The raising of footballers and musicians from being tradesmen-servants of the public to misbehaving gods began then too.

Celebrities are often mocked for being talentless. Some are, some are not. A tribute paid to the young and beautiful by the rest of us, the circle of celebrity is paradoxically both very small and very open. From the outside the celebrity world seems to be a closed, charmed place, a marquee guarded by men with shaved heads and sunglasses inside which rock stars and footballers, actresses and princesses, all magically turn out to know one another. Yet what the sixties discovered was that celebrity must be open too in the sense of letting in new people from the streets, or it congeals into a resented elite. Modern celebrity has no time for a Samurai class or for haughty duchesses – it must be a fantasy island we could all paddle our way to, at least in theory. Cultural democracy rules, even while parliamentary democracy struggles.

What was called Swinging London, or the Scene, was simply a small number of restaurants, shops and clubs where a small number of people were repeatedly photographed and written about. In Chelsea, Biba, Granny Takes a Trip, Bazaar and Hung on You were honeypots for the fashionable. In the evening it might be Annabel's or Showboat or Talk of the Town. When in 1969 the *Private Eye* journalist Christopher Booker published his drily hostile look back at the decade, *The Neophiliacs*, he found that by the summer of 1965 there were a mere twenty or so people who seemed to be at the heart of Swinging London. They included the Beatles and Mick Jagger (the other Stones had not yet quite cut through), the model Jean Shrimpton, the designer Mary Quant, the painter David Hockney, the actors Michael Caine and Terence Stamp, the photographers Lord Snowdon, David Bailey and Terence Donovan, the cartoonist and editor of the *Sunday Times* colour magazine Mark Boxer and the interior decorator David Hicks.

All these 'New Aristocrats', Booker pointed out, were in some way concerned with the creation of images. This list, though it would lose and gain constantly at the edges, had some validity. Bailey himself would pump the publicity machine with his 'Box of Pin Ups' designed by Boxer. Booker takes up the story:

> The list, which was virtually a Debrett guide to the New Aristocracy and their circle included: 2 actors, 8 pop singers, 1 pop artist, 1 interior decorator, 4 photographer/designers, 1 ballet dancer, 3 models, 1 film producer, 1 dress designer, 1 discotheque manager, 1 creative advertising man, 1 'pop singer's friend' and the Kray brothers from the East End who could only be described as 'connected with the underworld'.

The contours of all this had been sketchily apparent a few years earlier, in the Profumo affair. Old money, big business, the traditional arts and politics were edging out of the spotlight, now only to be seen at the side of the stage. Instead working-class upstarts were arriving and stealing the show. Among the photographers, Bailey was an East Ham tailor's son, Donovan a lorry driver's son, also from the East End of London – indeed, the East End did very well with photography because it also produced Terry O'Neill who made iconic images of Shrimpton, Stamp and the Beatles, and the key British war photographer of the sixties and seventies, Don McCullin. Michael Caine was a Billingsgate fish porter's son, Stamp the son of a tug-boat captain. The female pioneer aristocrats included that Polish asylum-seeker's child, Barbara Hulanicki; Lesley Hornby of Neasden, better known as Twiggy who was the daughter of a carpenter and a Woolworths shop assistant, and Priscilla White, better known as Cilla Black, from one of the rougher ends of Liverpool.

Few of these people would have made it in the London of the fifties, forties or thirties. The same goes for the Beatles, Kinks, and innumerable others. (Jagger would have made it anywhere, any time, as a successful businessman.) The intertwining of Booker's 'New Aristocrats' was as sticky and sinuous as the old Tory cliques of the fifties or New Labour's Whitehall in the nineties. A few were there entirely because of their looks, such as Jean Shrimpton, the supermodel waif (the word 'supermodel' was, inevitably, first used in 1968). But the important thing was the great sucking-in of working-class talent, a transfusion that the old Britain badly needed. The incomers were fascinated by images and they were colonizing the new media opportunities – music, fashion, colour magazines, hairdressing, radio, television, advertising – that were not the property of the City and old money.

There was a DIY spirit that has not been recovered since. Quant had been cutting up lengths of cloth bought over the counter and selling them at Bazaar since the mid-fifties. Her iconoclasm matched and outpaced a Pete Townshend or Keith Moon, as she drew, sliced and sewed up a uniform that mocked the pleated, padded extravagances of the Old New Look designers. Taking on the fashion industry of Paris and the West End from a bedsit and a tiny shop was at least as bold as taking on American rock from a Liverpool basement. Quant's shockingly short mini-skirts (named after the car, which she loved) were offensive enough for her window to be rapped by umbrella-toting male protesters and even the occasional brick to be lobbed. She always maintained she was trying to free women to be able to run for a bus, and to show off the beautifully fit, skinny bodies that post-war rationing had given young womanhood. But the sexual allure was what shocked. Michael Caine later recalled taking his mother down the Kings Road to see what all the fuss was about: 'I said, here's one now, and this girl walks by with a mini up to here. She goes by and my mother looked at her. So, we walk on a bit. She never said a word. So I said, what do you think, mum? She said: If it's not for sale, you shouldn't put it in the window.'[15]

Butterflies and Other Insects

If modern Britain found her soundtrack and her cargo cult in the sixties, she found her special vices too. In February 1967 Mick Jagger and Keith Richards were arrested at the latter's Sussex manor house Redlands during a raid by police which uncovered amphetamines and dope. Richards and Jagger received jail sentences and heavy fines, though ended up serving no more than two days behind bars in Brixton before their appeals. The whole thing had been orchestrated by the *News of the World* and set off a heated national debate, with *The Times* leading the way to protest about the excessive sentencing. In a famous editorial, 'Who Breaks a Butterfly Upon a Wheel?' its editor

William Rees-Mogg questioned the severity of the sentence, calling it 'as mild a drug case as can ever have been brought before the courts'. A month later, *The Times* carried a full-page advert which declared the law against marijuana 'immoral in principle and unworkable in practice'. The sixty-five signatories included medical experts, Nobel laureate scientists, some politicians, the novelist Graham Greene and the Beatles. By then the Beatles had been introduced to cannabis by Bob Dylan, and Paul McCartney was about to cause a further furore by admitting to taking LSD as well.

The purpose of the drugs had changed in the few years since the Beatles and others hit Hamburg. Once they had been used to keep performers awake, and then to calm them down after exhausting days or nights on the road. By the mid-sixties the agenda was rather more ambitious. LSD was a truth-bringer, allegedly opening minds to higher planes and brighter-coloured realities. This delusion was imported from the West Coast of America, though British writers had praised lysergic acid long before. Jeff Nuttall, a counter-culture writer of the time, declared that it was being launched as 'something other than mere pleasure, as a ready window on the Zen eternal, as a short cut back to the organic life, religion and wonderment'.

Neither the raptures of the counter-culture and the druggy atmospherics of Beatles music during the years when they reinvented pop, nor even campaigners, not much different from those who had successfully backed the Jenkins reforms, would manage to shift the State's hostility to such substances. Sex might be packaged and marketed and so might rock, but drugs were something else, the pleasure that would remain forbidden. Rock certainly helped extend the drugs culture. Heroin, the most dangerous example, spread steadily from a small and wealthy entertainment elite, through middle-class would-be rebels, until it finally emerged with gangs, dealers and all the paraphernalia of misery on council estates. In 1953 there were 290 known heroin addicts in Britain and by 1968 there were 2,780. These numbers are bound to be far below the true figure. On the same basis, the figure by the turn of the century was 25,000. Cannabis, a less dangerous and far more widely tolerated drug, was little used in the fifties outside small sub-cultures but by the mid-sixties there were between 2,000 and 3,000 arrests a year. The figure for 2000 was 97,000. Finally, while in the sixties cocaine was little used by comparison with other drugs, an academic survey suggested that by the new century, some 46,000 people in London alone were using the particularly dangerous version, crack cocaine. The sixties introduced mass drug use to Britain as the musical and hippy enthusiasts promoted it as a social and personal good. The authorities decided to destroy the drug culture as a social evil. Both were confounded. Nobody became wiser or more interesting through using heroin, LSD or dope, and the battle against drug use has been entirely lost. The victims began with a steady stream of performers and hangers-on who died from overdoses or drugs-related accidents and, more important by far, are the hundreds of thousands of poorer, less talented children who followed them after having far less fun.

Home Grown?

No sensible person would try to draw a neat line between British pop and its origins in America. For everyone except the Americans, rock is an import and a transplant. Rock and Roll was black American slang for having sex. It derives from the Deep South, via rhythm and blues and eventually mated with the country music of rural white America – which in turn had come from the folk music of Ireland, England, Scotland and France. Accelerated, amplified and sexualized, when it arrived in Britain it was immediately denounced as alien, indecent, anarchic, corrupting 'Negro' music, thoroughly un-British. This was not just the view of the occasional retired squadron leader sitting in his Kent garden. The hugely popular music magazine *Melody Maker* described rock as 'one of the most terrifying things to have happened to popular music . . . The Rock and Roll technique, instrumentally and vocally, is the antithesis of all that jazz has been striving for over the years – in other words, good taste and musical integrity.'[16]

Modern jazz fans and folk music purists would try to hold the line for years. Yet the diabolic Elvis and all his works, were too big, too mesmeric, to be resisted. Few of the first performers and bands in Britain wrote their own material. Donegan sang in an American voice; thousands of would-be pop stars did endless covers of Bo Diddley, Little Richard and Fats Domino. Again, it was the breakthrough lead given by Lennon and McCartney in singing their own material that persuaded scores of other bands to follow. Even today and after a lifetime of hits, there is little about the music of the Rolling Stones that feels particularly English; Dusty Springfield had one of the loveliest voices of the age, but if you didn't know you could have been forgiven for thinking that she was a black babe from Motown not a Catholic girl from High Wycombe.

Yet the British Isles had traditions which would feed back into the American musical revolution and change it dramatically, both in sound and content. We have discussed the art schools already. But there was also the folk tradition which was being revived even though the pop and rock stars rarely had first-hand experience of it. John O'Leannain (as his name should properly be written) and Paul McCartney both came from musical Irish families but had been cut off from their heritage. Bands such as Fairport Convention, which began in North London in 1967, taking its name from the house where they practiced, and Jethro Tull, founded by the Scottish and Blackpool flautist Ian Anderson in 1968, would incorporate some of the feel of British folk back into rock; others like the Ulsterman Van Morrison would cross the lines repeatedly.

A stronger influence still was the music hall, or variety tradition, discussed earlier and the humorous or sentimental music played on pianos in the home. These can be heard in the brassy, knees-up sound of Beatles songs like 'Strawberry Fields' or through most of the *Sergeant Pepper* album, in which the stomp of the fairground and the wheezing of the circus organ are not far away. As Lennon and McCartney, who both lost their mothers early, put it, 'Let's all get up and dance to a song, That was a hit before your Mother was born.' And beyond the Beatles, with their Liverpudlian nostalgia, a host of bands filled their lyrics with local references. To take just one example, Jethro Tull's *Aqualung* of 1971 name-checks Preston railway station, Hampstead Heath and Piccadilly Circus, while their following album, *Thick as a Brick*, which was a huge hit in the US, not only addresses the mood of post-sixties despair – 'the sandcastle virtues are all swept away in / the tidal destruction / the moral melee' – but manages to ask 'So where the hell was Biggles when you needed him last Saturday?'

The most impressive and sustained attempt to create a distinctively British pop came from the Kinks and was at the time a huge flop. Banned from the US while others were breaking into American stardom, Ray Davies, a cussed observer of modern life, turned back to local subjects. He had always written pop songs about everything from the death of the dance-halls to the joys of the English autumn, but *The Kinks Are The Village Green Preservation Society* of 1968 was on an entirely different scale. As Ray Davies put it himself: 'While everybody else thought the hip thing to do was to drop acid, take as many drugs as possible and listen to music in a coma, the Kinks were singing songs about lost friends, draught beer, motorbike riders, wicked witches and flying cats.'[17] He is not exaggerating. The title song calls for the preservation of, inter alia, Desperate Dan, strawberry jam, the George Cross, the 'Sherlock Holmes English-speaking vernacular', little shops, china cups, virginity, Tudor houses and antique tables, while attacking the new skyscrapers and office blocks. The album which sold in tiny numbers compared to the Beatles, worried and confused the critics who could not decide whether the Kinks were being serious or satirical. Today it is regarded as one of the great achievements of British pop in the sixties, a subtle mix of affection and derision, nostalgia and micky-taking, and no less essentially English for that. The Kinks were hugely influential not just on other bands of the time such as the Who, but on the later waves of 'Britpop'. They showed that it was possible to write inspiring rock music about what was around you, without posturing as a New Yorker or Alabama boy, indeed without pretending to be (just a little bit) black.

Rock was an arena for dreamers or harmless humorists, the fun factory for weekend rebels whose stars were too busy buying country estates, Rolls-Royces and drugs to worry about the condition of the country. Little of it was political. As John Lennon told *Rolling Stone* magazine in 1971 when asked to assess the impact of the Beatles: 'Nothing happened, except we all dressed up. The same bastards are in control, the same people are running everything, it's exactly the same.' That feeling was shared by the counter-culture left who had been attending seminars and protest meetings about Vietnam, marching against capitalist stooges in the Labour Party and ranting about the need for revolution. Like the world of pop, it was essentially an American import. When counter-culture poets had put on an evening of readings at the Albert Hall in 1965, alongside the British contingent which included Adrian Mitchell and Christopher Logue, there were the New York and San Francisco gurus, Allen Ginsberg, Lawrence

Ferlinghetti and Gregory Corso. The poets were the most eloquent voices.

The American influence was, not surprisingly, strongest in the anti-war movement. When the Vietnam Solidarity Committee organized three demonstrations outside the US embassy in London's Grosvenor Square, the second of them particularly violent, they were copying the cause and the tactics used to much greater effect in the United States. The student sit-ins and occupations at Hornsey and Guildford Art Colleges, and Warwick University, were pale imitations of the serious unrest on US and French campuses. There was even a (literally) pale imitation of the ultimate US underground movement, called rather pathetically the White Panthers. Their main revolutionary aim seemed to be free access to rock festivals, or what they called 'the People's music'. A two-week gathering to debate 'the dialectics of liberation' was organized at London's Round House in 1967. The star speaker was the American Black Power leader Stokely Carmichael. The event finished with a speech of abject apology from one of the British organizers on behalf of 'we deracinated white intellectuals, we who are bourgeois and colonizing in essence'. The conference's intellectual guru was a Californian exile from Germany, Herbert Marcuse, whose central message was that the affluent society was oppressive, based on the creation of 'false needs' and impossible to change by conventional political revolution.

In the same year a French revolutionary named Guy Debord came to England with a call to arms. When he arrived at a Notting Hill flat to meet the promised group of twenty hardcore revolutionaries only three had turned up, and they spent the afternoon drinking cans of McEwan's Export and watching *Match of the Day*.[18] Not surprisingly, Debord gave up on the Anglo-Saxons. British revolutionaries in modern times have been so little real threat that they were easily and cheerfully incorporated into mainstream television comedy through the character of Citizen Smith of the Tooting Popular Front. Debord's followers, however, taking the name 'Les Enragés', were heavily involved in the great Paris and Nanterre student uprisings of 1968. This was on a scale like nothing seen in Britain – nearly 600 students arrested in fights with the police on a single day and, at the high point of the revolt, 10m workers on strike across France. Hundreds of British students went over to join what they hoped would be a revolution, until de Gaulle, with the backing of an election victory, crushed it.

British alternative politics in print had no equivalents to the Beatles, the Who or the Kinks. The underground magazines such as *International Times*, *Black Dwarf* and *Oz* copied the rhetoric, art work and cartoon style of similar American publications and lacked the salty, surly working-class energy of rock. The greatest confrontation with the state focused on whether Rupert Bear, as manipulated by the pen of Vivian Berger, a fifteen-year-old schoolboy with a particularly lewd imagination, was behaving obscenely. The cartoon strip was central to the long summer trial in 1971 of the magazine *Oz*. At the Old Bailey, despite the best efforts of the publishers' barrister John Mortimer, the priapic Rupert was judged to be behaving disgracefully. Richard Neville, Felix Dennis and Jim Anderson ended up with suspended sentences. Immortally, the young Berger told the jury that though he wanted to shock 'your generation . . . also, I thought it was funny.'[19] A teddy bear with a stiffy: it rather sums up Britains answer to revolution.

The counter-culture would curdle and gurgle away for fairly obvious reasons. It had no practical agenda. It was deeply hostile to organization. It was largely middle class and had no effective links to the working-class socialists who wanted higher wages and perhaps even workers' cooperatives, but were less keen on long-haired students taking drugs, or indeed angry black people. Those parts of the new politics which would stick, would be anti racism; feminism, to the extent that it focused on practical and realistic ideas, such as equal pay and refuges for battered wives; and the gay liberation movement, which also had clear objectives, and also looked to the United States for a lead, particularly after the Stonewall riot. But the great irony is that the counter-culture, disdainful of sell-out pop music, was far less successful than pop at creating an indigenous British movement. It was dependent on passing American fads and voices as, by the mid-sixties, British pop was not.

Rhodesia: Rebellion of the Whites

While the message of the sixties still lives, other stories can dominate the newspapers for months on end, even years, and then are apparently forgotten almost immediately. Perhaps they are too painful to dwell on. The story of Rhodesia's Unilateral Declaration of Independence, or UDI, and of the short-lived Federation that preceded it, obsessed four prime ministers in a row, Macmillan, Douglas-Home, Wilson and Heath. It filled front pages, elbowing out other contemporary crises such as Vietnam that now bulk vastly bigger in world history. It caused deep divisions in both the main parties, with their leaders condemned as race traitors or betrayers of Africa, according to taste. It produced bizarre summits on Royal Navy warships, and dramatic confrontations at the United Nations. It pitched the young Queen Elizabeth into a constitutional fight over the hanging of three Africans. Its cast of characters, Garfield Todd, Roy Welensky, and Sir Humphrey Gibbs, forgotten now, as well as Ian Smith and Joshua Nkomo, were for a time household names. But little of this is recalled in the history of the sixties. It sits uneasily with the war protests and the fashion, the music and the tower blocks. And the final outcome of the Rhodesian crisis, a vicious guerrilla war followed by the rule of Robert Mugabe, one of the most incompetent megalomaniacs to hold power at the beginning of the twenty-first century, was genuinely tragic.

The tragedy can be traced back to the imperial idealism of High Victorian days. Cecil John Rhodes was a sickly clergyman's son from Hertfordshire whose head was filled with notions of British world destiny and whose bank accounts were filled with the vast profits of prospecting in the South African goldrush. Using diplomacy, threats, bribes and great cunning, Rhodes created a company to take concessions in the heartland of Africa, far north of the British Cape Province, and the Boer republic of the Transvaal. It was an area then known as Zambesia, now the nations of Zimbabwe, Zambia and Malawi. In it lived various tribes, notably the warlike Matabele. Cecil Rhodes's vision of a vast British territory running from the far south of Africa to the very north was never accomplished but the central area, soon known as Rhodesia after him, was carved into new settler states. Bizarrely, the British government never took direct control and allowed Rhodes's company effective autonomy, backed always by the threat of British force from outside. The white settlers, mainly from Britain and South Africa, would first use farming and mining concessions and then take complete political control of these vast, fertile and mineral-rich areas. In the north, a full-blown British colony,

Northern Rhodesia, would exploit the copper of the area and attempts were made to ensure decent treatment of the dispossessed local Africans. In Southern Rhodesia, however, whose capital Salisbury had been named after the then Conservative Prime Minister, the settlers established a system of relentless racial discrimination much like South Africa's, with a colour bar in employment and a ban on blacks owning land in cities or anywhere of agricultural value.

Though South Africans of British origin, and many Rhodesians, had fought in the Second World War, the overt racialism of the white elite was both a threat and an embarrassment to London. South Africa would eventually leave the Commonwealth in 1961. Malan, like many Boers, had been pro-Nazi and was an anti-British republican; he is generally credited, if that is the word, as the inventor of full-blown apartheid. The Attlee and Churchill governments feared Rhodesia would soon go the same way. To try to bind the stiff-necked settlers into a more benign system, London offered the lure of federation with Northern Rhodesia and what was then called Nyasaland. The latter two colonies were ruled from London, and had less aggressive polices towards native Africans. But Northern Rhodesia had the vast wealth of the copper mines so federation would give the whites of Salisbury access to an economic boom. In essence the deal, worked out by a brilliant Colonial Office civil servant, Andrew Cohen, was that in return for accepting a less 'South African' attitude to the black majority, the white settlers of Southern Rhodesia would be able to become far richer than they could from farming alone. In 1953, after intense haggling and bargaining about voting systems and land rights which depressed, then angered the few black representatives involved, a new country not much smaller than Canada was duly created: the Central African Federation.

To start with, things went relatively well. Embassies opened in Salisbury, tower blocks went up, international companies moved in. The government of Southern Rhodesia (later simply called Rhodesia, today Zimbabwe) fell under the control of a moderately liberal Christian mission school headteacher, Garfield Todd. For four years he nudged and tickled the white settlers towards a fairer system, enough to gain the cautious trust of the leaders of the twelve-to-one black African majority. Could it be that a liberal alternative to South Africa was being built on the continent? The leadership of the full Federation was taken by a railwayman, part-time boxer and anti-Communist union boss called Roy Welensky, the thirteenth child of a Polish Jew and a Boer mother who called himself '50 per cent Jewish, 50 per cent Polish and 100 per cent British'.[20] He was a much rougher character. The contradictions between British Colonial Office hopes for a steady transition to democracy, the profound racialism of the whites of Salisbury, and the increasing restlessness of black people who saw other parts of the continent breaking from the Empire could not be contained for ever. Eventually the well-meaning Garfield Todd was ousted for refusing to back laws banning sex between blacks and whites, and for campaigning for a wider franchise.

The spark that blew the huge Federation to pieces came in the least expected place. Nyasaland, now Malawi, was a comparatively undeveloped area, with strong connections to Scotland through missionaries, dating back to the days of David Livingstone. There were very few whites living there. What its people did have was an independence leader of rare shrewdness and international savvy. Hastings Banda was a poor village boy encouraged by missionaries, who managed to get himself educated in South Africa, then the United States, where he got a politics degree at Chicago and became a doctor of medicine in Tennessee. He then got a medical diploma at Edinburgh, became an elder of the Church of Scotland, and practised as a doctor in Liverpool and London. He moved to newly independent Ghana and then, in 1958, he returned home in triumph to Nyasaland. Banda was a Christian, pro-British, anti-communist and uninterested in military rebellion. He was, in short, a difficult man to caricature as a rebellious extremist.

Yet, in a series of brilliant speeches and deploying the menace of vast, angry crowds, he persuaded Welensky that he was enough of a threat for force to be used. South Rhodesian troops were sent to the area and though the Conservative government tried to impose a news blackout, Scottish missionaries smuggled back news to the *Scotsman* in Edinburgh, causing protests around the world. Banda was imprisoned, as he had hoped he would be, but after wild accusations that he was choreographing a huge murder-plot against whites were proved to be nonsense, he was eventually released at London's insistence. Nyasaland became independent and the Federation soon collapsed. Northern Rhodesia was helped to independence by the Conservative Colonial

Secretary Iain Macleod, a genuine liberal who did a deal behind Welensky's back with the man who would go on to lead independent Zambia, Kenneth Kaunda. Macleod was seen by many as the next Tory leader but this double-dealing, in a virtuous cause, led to him being attacked by the Tory grandee Lord Salisbury (grandson of the man after whom the country's capital was then named) as an unscrupulous bridge-playing twister, 'too clever by half'. The accusation of cleverness was of course fatal in the Conservative Party of the early sixties and Macleod's career never recovered.

This left Southern Rhodesia, with its 220,000 whites and 2.5m blacks, standing almost alone. The settlers wanted independence inside the Commonwealth, on the basis of a constitution that excluded the black African majority from any shred of power. Had this been accepted by London, the anger among other Commonwealth states would have been enough to cause mass resignations and, quite possibly, the end of the organization. It was not simply a matter of keeping the Queen happy, or of retaining the last vestige of Britain's formal imperial power-system. Public opinion by the early sixties was strongly hostile to the idea of apartheid being mimicked in a Commonwealth state. So there was an impasse. And to make it more impassive still, the laconic, difficult and wily figure of Ian Smith arrived on the scene as the new Prime Minister in Salisbury. Smith was a right-wing rancher, educated in South Africa, who had served in the RAF during the war and was idolized by his supporters. The old guard, led by Welensky, realized that simply declaring independence from Britain, and setting up a whites-only state, might be tricky. Rhodesia's judges and soldiers had sworn allegiance to the Queen; Rhodesia's finances and much of her trade flowed through the City of London.

Smith had no such qualms. He was quite prepared for UDI – a unilateral declaration of independence. This was hardly a re-run of the North American rebellion of 1776, but there were uncomfortable parallels. If, in the end, they were ready to go, what was Britain going to do about it? There was at least the option of sending an army and fighting – though in the American case, this had not worked out wholly successfully. But Rhodesia was thousands of miles beyond the reach of the Royal Navy and, in any case, this was a rebellion by whites who professed to be the front line against Marxist insurrection, many of them veterans of the British wartime forces. Would an attack on 'kith and kin' really be acceptable to British voters? Would its threat be taken seriously in Salisbury? On the other hand, would Rhodesian troops who had declared their personal loyalty to the Crown, fire back against British paratroopers if they landed?

This was the dilemma that Harold Wilson inherited when he took office in 1964. Pro-Rhodesian right-wingers had made things very difficult for Macleod and Macmillan as the Tories struggled to grapple with the break-up of the Federation. Now vehemently anti-colonialist left-wingers would make things almost as difficult for a Labour Prime Minister. Wilson began by warning Rhodesia of the serious economic consequences of UDI and by setting out conditions for British acceptance of an independent state, including unimpeded progress towards majority rule, the end of racial discrimination and no oppression of the majority by the minority – none of which was acceptable to Smith and his followers. Meetings in London did not help. Wilson then went on a disastrous trip to Salisbury. While there, he insisted on seeing the imprisoned African leaders, Nkomo and Sithole, and exploded with anger when they were ushered in to him thirsty and hungry. Only after Wilson threatened to lead his own staff into the shops to buy them something, did the Rhodesians offer water and food. Later, he endured rudeness and mockery from Smith's ministers. Fatally, however, Wilson made clear that he would not use force under any circumstances, confirming in a broadcast that if anyone was expecting 'a thunderbolt in the shape of the Royal Air Force, let me say that this thunderbolt will not be coming'. It was a mistake. Smith had been seriously worried by the prospect of Britain using force and believed Rhodesia would be unable even to try to resist. Perhaps Wilson was worried about the effect on the pound, or perhaps he was too mindful of the humiliation of Suez. At any rate, after Wilson's admission, Smith realized he had nothing to fear (sanctions never worried him) and briskly went ahead in November 1965 to declare the country independent.

From then on the policy of trying to squeeze Rhodesia into submission with oil and other sanctions was tried, even though few in Whitehall thought it had a chance of working. There were too many ways in and out of the country, and too many middlemen prepared to trade. Rhodesia developed her own consumer industries and sold her tobacco and other farm produce via South Africa. The oil came in through Portuguese Mozambique. Wilson tried two more summits with Smith, both on warships anchored in the Mediterranean so that neither man would have to step on the other's territory. Britain's conditions for accepting independence became more and more humiliatingly slim, but Smith brushed them aside, secure in his support at home and realizing that Wilson had no effective threat to hold over his head. The British Governor of Rhodesia, Sir Humphrey Gibbs, with the Chief Justice, Sir Hugh Beadle, kept a tiny oasis of loyalty to the Crown in the old Government House, dining in black tie and toasting the Queen, even though his car and telephone had been cut off by Smith's regime. But the brutal reality of UDI was underlined when three Africans sentenced to be hanged for murder were refused leave to appeal to London in 1968. The Queen, advised by Wilson, then used her prerogative of mercy and reprieved the three men. They were hanged anyway, an act described as assassination and murder in the United Nations. Smith went ahead with a new constitution regarded throughout the world as brutally unfair and racist. By the time Wilson left office in 1970 the Rhodesian dilemma was no nearer to being solved, and it would continue to hang over British politics into the Thatcher years, when the black majority finally won power.

The Smith regime, though regarded as a pariah state, would survive through an increasingly violent and complicated guerrilla war until finally giving way to one-party government by Mugabe. Zimbabwe's fate would be an awful one, ravaged by violence, famine and disease, as Marxist leaders tutored in extremism by their white enemies eventually extracted a revenge – less on the whites, many of whom eventually fled, than on their own people. Could any of this have been prevented by a liberal-minded Whitehall which had never exercised real power in Salisbury since the days of Cecil Rhodes? Only, perhaps, by being prepared to go to war in Africa, this time not to win land and treasure but undo the consequences of earlier adventures and to oust the English-speaking white elites. It would have been a huge risk. The bloody experience of other European countries in African wars and Britain's experience nearer to home in Northern Ireland, suggests that such a war might well then have run out of control and lost its original purpose. Harold Wilson, like his Tory predecessors and successors, decided that such a war was unthinkable. Had they had any inkling of the fate waiting for the people of central Africa, it is just possible that they might have thought again.

The Pound and the Viet Cong

Amid this maelstrom Britain, yet again, was close to bankruptcy. How to get a grip? Devaluing the pound might have given the Wilson government and the country the chance of a fresh start. In a world of fewer and floating currencies, the importance of devaluation is harder to understand now, but it was then the single most important issue facing Wilson. On the one hand, cutting the international value of your currency against others was an admission of failure on the world stage, a humiliation for any government. It would mean imports costing more so unless people bought fewer foreign goods it would mean more inflation. On the other hand it would make exports cheaper, giving British companies a chance to win back markets they were losing. If the government devalued and managed to keep a grip on the consequent inflation while industrial exports grew, then the country could in theory leap in one painful stride away from her economic problems. It was a little like dropping out of a race, intensively retraining, sweating out the fat, slimming down, working on the muscle tone, and then starting the next race better prepared – except that in the economy you never actually stop working. As for a racer, the embarrassment of dropping out would be pointless if there was not the sweat and retraining, the greater efficiency and improved productivity. It needed to be a shock to the system, not a rest from reality. Many people, including in the Labour government, seemed not to have realized this. They thought, when eventually they were prepared to consider it, devaluation would avoid the tough choices at home which, in fact, it absolutely required.

This was a choice which went beyond economics. Devaluation and world politics were inextricably linked. To devalue the pound in the mid-sixties meant Britain's overseas spending would have to be dramatically cut back, just as the ROBOT floating pound scheme of 1953 implied. Those smaller pounds would buy fewer gallons of oil, foreign-manufactured guns and accommodation for troops. So it probably meant a further withdrawal from Britain's world role, in particular 'East of Suez', the bases in Hong Kong, Malaya, Singapore, Aden and the Gulf. That would irritate Washington, particularly as communist advance in South East Asia was the issue of the hour. The alternative was to try to keep the global role and borrow from the United States. This was certainly on offer but at a large political price. As President Johnson's special assistant put it at the time. 'We want to make very sure that the British get into their heads that it makes no sense for us to rescue the pound in a situation in which there is no British flag in Vietnam, and a threatened British thin-out both east of Suez and in Germany . . . a British Brigade in Vietnam would be worth a billion dollars at the moment of truth for Sterling.'[21]

In the Commons and during the 1964 general election, Wilson had mocked Polaris as being neither independent nor British, and indeed unable to deter. Yet in the later sixties and early seventies, HMS *Resolution, Renown, Repulse* and *Revenge* were duly launched. Their names came from battlecruisers and battleships that had been the pride of an independent Royal Navy, but the new submarines' missiles were American by proxy and the same was true of their successors, the Trident submarines of today. Technological dependence now rendered any idea that this was a truly independent system absurd. In power, Wilson had the option of abandoning the nuclear option, since the submarines being built to take Polaris could have been adapted as conventional hunter-killer boats. He chose not to, and even in the mid-seventies to disguise the economics of the Polaris upgrade, codenamed Chevaline, from the cabinet sceptics. Crossman assessed the dilemma shrewdly, noting in January 1965 that Wilson was committing Britain to defence spending 'almost as burdensome – if not more burdensome – than that to which Ernest Bevin committed us in 1945, and for the same reason: because of our commitment to the Anglo-American special relationship and because of our belief that it is only through the existence of that relationship that we can survive outside Europe.'

For many this was a positive argument for devaluation. The pro-Europeans in the cabinet hoped devaluation would help drive the country towards its destiny as an ordinary member of the EEC, and away from global pretensions. They felt that Britain had to break with America, despite the financial guarantees Wilson had wrung from Washington earlier. She had to change direction, devalue, join Europe.

That, according to Barbara Castle, was what George Brown had decided: 'We've got to turn down their money and pull out the troops ... I want them out of East of Suez. This is the decision we have got to make: break the commitment to America ... I've been sickened by what we have had to do to defend America – what I've had to say at the despatch box.' Castle interjected: 'Vietnam?' and Brown replied: 'Yes, Vietnam too.' Belligerent, contemptuous, he feared that Wilson would simply go over to Washington and 'cook up some screwy little deal'. Brown at least had a clear strategic direction. Wilson did not. Cooking up screwy little deals was his forte. He was the master chef of screwy little deals.

By now the complex nature of the choice facing him was apparent. Devaluation and the future of socialism; Britain's relationship with America and attitude to the Vietnam War; and whether we could and should be in the European Community, were all completely interlinked. Had Britain broken with America during the most testing time in its Vietnamese agony, the story of the Atlantic alliance would have taken a very different turn. We would probably have entered the EEC much earlier and, again probably, have played a role closer to that of France in the following decades, less linked in nuclear defence or intelligence terms to Washington. What this would have meant for the British economy's failing experiment in continental corporatism, and for the stability of the anti-Communist world, is impossible to say. Further, because many Commonwealth countries held their reserves in sterling in London, devaluing the pound would have been a one-off and unilateral cut in the wealth of friendly and often poor countries. Deciding about the value of the pound was also a choice about Britain's place in the world.

Oddly, the thing that would do most to destroy Harold Wilson's reputation on the left was also the policy for which Britain has most cause to remember him gratefully. We have seen some of the pressure he was under to commit British troops to Vietnam. The Australians had committed a battalion, President Johnston constantly reminded him; perhaps the Black Watch might be sent, or at the very least a military band? American hints had been mingled with those American threats about the pound; and Britain's economic position was, as we have seen, weak enough. Whitehall mandarins and some of his own advisers thought he should have committed at least some troops, but though Wilson may have been tempted and though British special forces had been considered, he held back from doing so. He tried to buy the Americans off with words of support and stabs at a diplomatic solution, hoping to use his connections in Moscow and suggesting some intervention directly with the North Vietnamese. He managed to placate nobody. The initiatives infuriated Washington, while the anti-war marchers at home simply heard his supportive words for Johnson.

Wilson was berated in the streets as a murderer. His Secretary of State for Defence who had quickly realized the scale of risk that Vietnam posed and helped keep Britain clear, was rewarded on university campuses with cries of 'Hitler Healey'. When the trade union leader Frank Cousins, briefly in the government himself, asked Wilson why he wasn't taking a firmer stand against American war-making, Wilson furiously replied, 'Because we can't kick our creditors in the balls.' One of Wilson's later biographers made the case for the defence with steely eloquence. Losing all Washington's friendship and financial support would have been devastating: 'Few considered the implications for domestic social, housing, education, arts and science policies, including the probable effect on student grants. Few, indeed of those who attacked the prime minister and his colleagues simul-taneously for helping the Americans abroad and not doing more to help the poor at home, ever came to terms with the bleakness of the choice.' Yet, the same writer went on, it was over Vietnam that 'the party of conscience seemed to lose touch with its soul' and over Vietnam too that many who had pinned their trust in Wilson decided his principles were 'a shattered crystal, beyond hope of repair'.[22] Here, for once, he was doing the right thing, or the best thing, and it was over this that he was most denounced. Who said politics was fair?

Even Wilson's close supporters were at times disgusted by his twisting to keep the options open. Tony Benn, a few weeks before Wilson went to the country to try to increase his majority early in 1966, had recorded: 'My opinion of Harold was lower tonight than it has ever been before. He really is a manipulator who thinks that he can get out of everything by fixing somebody or something. Although his reputation is now riding high, I'm sure he will come a cropper one day when one of his fixes just doesn't come off.'[23] At almost exactly the same time, Crossman summed up Labour's wider problem: 'The main trouble is that we haven't delivered the goods; the builders are not building the houses; the cost of living is still rising; the incomes policy isn't working; we haven't held back inflation; we haven't got production moving. We are going to the country now because we are facing every kind of difficulty and we anticipate that things are bound to get worse . . .'

Wilson then had his successful re-election in March, when Labour's tiny majority of three was replaced by one of ninety-seven seats. This ought to have ushered in his golden years. His dominance of the Commons had helped finish off Alec Douglas-Home, who was replaced by Edward Heath. The age of the grammar-school boys was truly established. Wilson, whatever his failures of vision, had fought a near-faultless campaign and won a mandate which obliged the British Establishment to accept that Labour truly was entitled to rule. He had shown himself a self-confident showman abroad, in Moscow and Washington, and had pursued frantic diplomacy over the Rhodesian crisis. Now, surely, his time had arrived. Yet there was plenty in the record of that first Wilson administration to give pause for thought – the dithering and manoeuvring over devaluation; the mutual suspicions about screwy little deals already dividing the cabinet; Wilson's own habits of duplicity, notably over deflation and his attitude to British membership of the EEC.

At the centre of all the difficulties the government faced was the dilemma of devaluation. The Chancellor, Jim Callaghan, remained under almost intolerable pressure, as he had been from the day when he took office. At times he seemed close to giving way under the strain. Jenkins recalled a cabinet in July 1966 when Callaghan, later famous for being imperturbable, suddenly started talking away from the agenda about the appalling pressures on sterling. He suggested to the startled ministers around him 'both that the objective situation was desperate and that his own nerve had cracked. Wilson hushed him up and brought the meeting to an end rather like a policeman trying to get a blanket around a nude streaker.'[24] Indeed, Wilson regarded any talk of devaluation, public or private, as indecent. Once he, Brown and Callaghan had decided against it immediately after the 1964 election, it was known as 'the unmentionable'. From then on a complicated three-way dance had been going on in private. Brown turned in favour of devaluation as one way to revive his hopes for expansion and the

DEA. Callaghan dithered, but wanted any devaluation to be accompanied by the shock of deflation too. Wilson, against both devaluation and deflation, played the two of them off against each other, always worried that if Brown and Callaghan agreed, he would be scuppered. By July 1966 he was telling Barbara Castle in the Commons tea-room that Brown and Callaghan were plotting to get rid of him: 'You know what the game is – devalue and get into Europe. We've got to scotch it.'[25] This, however, was classic Wilson: Castle was an anti-European, so his words were calculated to flatter her. But at the same time the Prime Minister was telling pro-Europeans in the press that he intended to lead Britain into Europe himself. As the press magnate Cecil King related in his diary months earlier, Callaghan was confidently predicting that Britain would enter Europe: 'the pledges were only given to keep Barbara Castle and her kind quiet . . . Apparently Wilson thinks that after a successful election he will be able to eat any number of words with impunity.'[26]

Europe had sliced the party horizontally, cutting through the vertical divisions of left and right. Generally the party's activists and left-wing MPs believed that the Common Market was a 'bankers' ramp', a capitalist plot whose rules would prevent true socialism in Britain. The strongest view that Wilson himself had about it all was that he strongly didn't have a view. He had been against on the grounds that Europe would be 'anti planning', which seems a little odd. But as he moved camp, he told Barbara Castle, according to her diaries, that 'The decision is purely a marginal one. I have always said so. I have never been a fanatic for Europe.' And later, when she accused him of presiding over a messy, middle-of-the-road muddle about conditions for entry, he complacently replied: 'I'm at my best in a messy, middle-of-the-road muddle.'[27] He did not holiday abroad and had a strong sentimental attachment to the Commonwealth and the provincial reassurance of traditional British life. Unlike Jenkins or Heath he had no friends in continental politics. When the referendum finally came in 1975, both Wilson's wife and his political secretary Marcia Falkender voted against staying in, which probably hints at Wilson's private instincts.

Yet in the late sixties British business saw the European Economic Community as an essential escape-route into a more modern and efficient world, words which triggered a response in Wilson. The press was overwhelmingly in favour. Some of his most effective colleagues, notably Jenkins, were vehemently pro. Whitehall opinion, though divided, was leaning that way too. Europe offered Wilson a new theme when he needed it. In 1967 he and the strongly pro-European George Brown gently perambulated their way around Rome, Strasbourg and Paris discussing possible British membership, though de Gaulle was still chilly. Brown spent much of the time insulting and clumsily chatting up secretaries. Soon afterwards Wilson formally announced a renewed British membership bid. De Gaulle, though dismissive in public, privately told the British ambassador in Paris that he envisaged a new kind of Europe, wider but also looser, and led by the strongest military powers, France and Britain, then Italy and Germany. It would allow for more national sovereignty. He implied that this complete reshaping of Europe should be cooked up between Paris and London, then publicly proposed by Britain, after which France would come in to support it. This was not only an early sketch of the kind of Europe that Britain would yearn for but a classic Gaullist swipe at the federal Europe being built from Brussels. It seemed an act of French disloyalty to their German and other continental allies. In London, unsure whether it was a devilish trap, officials urged Wilson to leak the idea to the Germans. The leaks infuriated almost everyone, de Gaulle most of all, and the idea died. Despite all this, and despite warnings that food prices would rise by up to a quarter as a result of British membership, talks went on. Shortly before Wilson finally lost power, the six member states concluded their own pre-British-entry deal which badly tilted the budget system and agricultural support against the UK and the other would-be joiners.

Devaluation and a Coup

Events – dear boy – duly forced the devaluation option into centre stage. Decade by decade, government by government, the impact of energy policy on British politics is a constant theme. One could write a useful political history which did not move beyond the dilemmas posed by energy supply. We can follow it from the winter of 1947 when the frozen coal stocks blew Attlee off course, through the oil-related shock of Suez and the destruction of Eden, to Heath's double confrontation with the miners, ending in his defeat in 1974, the rise of Scottish nationalism fuelled by North Sea oil, and then the epic coalfield confrontation between Margaret Thatcher and Arthur Scargill taking the story up to today's arguments about global warming and gas dependency on Russia. The simple fact of a small and crowded island energy-dependent in an uncertain world has toppled prime ministers and brought violent confrontation to the streets.

It had its effect on Harold Wilson too, when the Six-Day War of June 1967 between Israel and Egypt led to an oil embargo on Britain by Iraq and Kuwait because of an alleged pro-Israel line from London. (Nasser, who made the allegation, of course recalled the Suez plot.) This, combined with war in Nigeria, hit Britain's finances, hoisted prices and produced more selling of sterling. If this was not enough, two months later there was a huge national dock strike, shutting first Liverpool and Hull and then, one by one, most of the rest of the major ports including London. The economic effect was dreadful, the trade figures a national shock. Wilson lashed out at the strikers. A year earlier he had been even more vituperative about striking seamen, suggesting they were being manipulated by communists or, as he called them 'a tightly knit group of politically motivated men' who had failed at the ballot box. Though that strike finished soon afterwards, Wilson's words, reckoned 'bonkers' by some cabinet colleagues, drove a further wedge between him and the left.

In the overheated atmosphere of July 1967 there was renewed talk of a plot to oust Wilson and replace him either with Callaghan or Brown. While the Prime Minister was away in Moscow, the pro-devaluers were talking. George Brown, characteristically, was threatening to resign and trying to persuade others to support him as leader; and characteristically failing. Others, including Benn, felt that if he did resign the whole government would fall. Equally characteristically since he had a weakness for grand hostesses, Roy Jenkins was at the home of Ann Fleming, who has featured earlier in this book. Wilson later told Barbara Castle that the plotting was directed by 'Ministers who went a-whoring after society hostesses.' Jenkins responded in his memoirs: 'There was indeed a certain allegorical quality about the behaviour of all of us that weekend . . . Wilson kept up his adrenalin by going on an unnecessary trip to Moscow. George Brown went berserk at the Durham Miners' Gala. And I went to stay with Mrs Fleming at Sevenhampton.'

Wilson was still determined to resist devaluation. When he discovered briefing papers on the pros and cons had been prepared by civil servants, he brusquely ordered them to be collected up and burned. This was now a personal fight, corrupted by the rivalries and ambitions which plagued the cabinet. The left-wing devaluers hoped to turn Labour at last into a proper socialist government. They preferred to keep Wilson as leader but would have ditched him if necessary. The pro-European devaluers would have liked to replace Wilson with Roy Jenkins. The ironies are multiple: as the arguments raged, some on the left toyed with leaving Labour and setting up a new left-wing party based on the trade unions to be called the Social Democratic Party. One of them was the young Neil Kinnock, who would later as leader unleash a ferocious war on another 'party within the party'. The title SDP would later be taken not by the left but by Jenkins and many of the pro-Europeans who followed him. Meanwhile the devaluation crisis turned into an ungainly and undignified dance as George, Harold and Jim, with Roy and the rest joined hands, lurched away from each other, formed new sets and jigged towards humiliation. At moments, Callaghan seemed to think devaluation might be such a national catastrophe that it would force Wilson out, and let him in. Brown wanted it for strategic reasons and hoped against the odds it might usher him in as leader. Jenkins may not have been actively plotting, but was much enjoying his stellar reputation in the press and as a leading pro-European. Wilson was determined to fend off devaluation to protect his own position.

Eventually, on the morning of 3 November 1967, the senior economic adviser at the Treasury, Sir Alec Cairncross, told Callaghan at a private meeting that the dance was over. Nothing more could be done, the music had stopped. No further foreign borrowing was available. He would have to devalue. Both knew that Callaghan would have to resign. Though his biographer called this 'the most shattering moment Callaghan was ever to experience in sixty years of public life' he seems to have taken it calmly and set about preparing yet another round of cuts, the deflation without which devaluation would be pointless. This caused cabinet arguments and threats of more resignations. Wilson, after yet another last-minute attempt to borrow more to see Britain through, eventually accepted that the pound was impossible to defend even with American support. In a 6 p.m. broadcast on 18 November Wilson announced that the pound was being devalued by 14 per cent and that defence cuts, restrictions on hire purchase, or credit, and higher interest rates would follow too. Callaghan, as Chancellor, felt utterly humiliated. He wanted to leave the government entirely but was persuaded to take the Home Office instead. Wilson, who had after all just torn up what he had for so long insisted was essential to his strategy, seemed curiously chirpy. Normally an astute reader of the mood, he made an awesomely bad mistake in his broadcast by perkily informing the nation that 'the pound in your pocket' had not been devalued. In terms of its immediate purchasing power in the local shop this was of course true but the suggestion that the pound's international fall in value could be safely ignored was ludicrous and instantly understood to be ludicrous. Wilson was also devalued, possibly by more than 14 per cent.

Roy Jenkins now became Chancellor in Callaghan's place. Under him the Treasury finally regained complete authority. Wilson tried to get his friend and ally Barbara Castle in to run the DEA but Jenkins was having none of that. From then on Labour would become as much a party of Treasury orthodoxy as the Conservatives. After being one of the most energetic Home Secretaries of the twentieth century, Jenkins himself spent a remarkable couple of years as one of its more successful Chancellors. Though he never made it to Number Ten, in terms of personal influence, there is almost a case for renaming the Wilson years the Jenkins years. His 1968 budget increased taxes by twice as much as any previous budget ever, including the wartime ones, and he returned to the attack later in the year, and again in 1969. The last of these, Jenkins pointed out, led to the only excess of revenue over government spending in the period between Baldwin and Thatcher, 'a massive turn-round in the balance of payments and a vast consequent replenishment of our gold and dollar reserves and overseas borrowing capacity'.[28] He was, however, lucky as well as tough, as he generously acknowledged in his memoirs. It turned out that the Inland Revenue and Customs & Excise had dramatically undercounted the value of British exports. With the draconian budgets designed to make the best use of devaluation the mood altered. At last, it seemed, that

that elusive 'grip' had been discovered. The trade figures improved. After so long, could it be that Labour had begun to discover a way to run the economy after all? As we will see, the answer was no, and Jenkins, along with Callaghan and most of the rest of the cabinet, must take the blame. For the other great issue was trade union militancy and in particular the rise in strikes. Grip regained on the nation's finances would be grip lost on its industrial climate.

Rivers of Blood

Harold Wilson was always a sincere anti-racialist. He had felt strongly enough about the racialist behaviour of the Tory campaign at Smethwick in the Midlands in 1964 to publicly denounce its victor Peter Griffiths as a 'parliamentary leper'. For Wilson, this was rare vehemence. But he did not try to repeal the 1962 Commonwealth and Immigrants Act, with its controversial quota system and in 1965, he and his Home Secretary, Frank Soskice, tightened it, cutting down the dependants allowed in, and giving the Government the power to deport illegal entrants, offering the first Race Relations Act as a sweetener. This outlawed the 'colour bar' in public places and discrimination in public services and banned incitement to race hatred. It was widely seen at the time as toothless. Yet the combination of restrictions on immigration and measures to better integrate the migrants already in Britain would form the basis for all subsequent policy. There would be a tougher anti-discrimination bill in 1968, and tougher anti-immigration measures to go with it. Never again would the idea of free access to Britain be seriously entertained by mainstream politicians.

One of the new migrations that arrived to beat the 1962 quota system just before Wilson came to power came from a rural area of Pakistan threatened with flooding by a huge dam project. The poor farming villages from the Muslim north, particularly around Kashmir, were not an entrepreneurial environment. They began sending their men to earn money in the labour-short textile mills of Bradford and surrounding towns. Unlike the West Indians, the Pakistanis and Indians were likelier to send for their families. Soon there would be large, inward-looking Muslim communities clustered in areas of Bradford, Leicester and other manufacturing towns. Unlike the Caribbean migrants, these were religiously divided from the whites around them and cut off from the main form of male white working-class entertainment, the consumption of alcohol. Muslim women were kept inside the house and the ancient habits of brides being chosen to cement family connections at home meant there was almost no sexual mixing, either. To many whites, the 'Pakis' were less threatening than the self-confident young Caribbean men, but also more alien.

Had this been all, then perhaps Enoch Powell's simmering unease would have continued to simmer and his notorious 'River of Blood' speech would never have been made in the apocalyptic terms it was. Whatever the eventual problems thrown up by this mutual sense of alienation Britain's fragile new consensus of 1962–5 was about to be broken by another form of racial discrimination, this time exercised by Africans, mainly of the Kikuyu people of Kenya. After the divisive terror and counter-terror of the Mau Mau campaign, Kenya had won independence under the leadership of Jomo Kenyatta in 1963 and initially thrived as a relatively tolerant market economy. Alongside the majority of Africans, however, and the 40,000-odd whites who stayed after independence, there were some 185,000 Asians in Kenya. They had mostly arrived during British rule and were mostly better-off than the local Kikuyu, well established as doctors, civil servants, traders, business people and police. They also had full British and colonies passports and therefore an absolute right of entry to Britain, which had been confirmed by meetings of Tory ministers before independence. These people have been called the Jews of Africa and the parallels between their position and that of European Jewry in the thirties are striking. Like the Jews they were an abnormally go-ahead, vigorous and prosperous group. Like the Jews they were the object of nationalist and racial suspicion, from black Africans rather than white Germans. They too were often accused of disloyalty. When Kenyatta gave them the choice of surrendering their British passports and taking full Kenyan nationality, or becoming in effect foreigners, dependent on work permits, most of them chose to keep their British nationality. In the unfriendly and increasingly menacing atmosphere of Kenya in the mid-sixties, it seemed sensible. Certainly there was no indication from London that their rights to entry would be taken away.

The pressure on them grew, in ways that also mimicked Nazi treatment of the Jews, at least before the industrial genocide of the

Holocaust. The Asians were deprived of their jobs in the civil service. They found they were unable to work or trade in the better-off parts of the country. They faced increasingly unpleasant propaganda. The minority who had opted for Kenyan citizenship found it mysteriously difficult to obtain. And so, inevitably, they began to make for Britain, their obvious refuge. Through 1967 they were coming in by plane at the rate of about a thousand a month. The newspapers began to put the influx onto the front pages and the now-popular television news showed great queues waiting for British passports and for flights. Enoch Powell, in an early warning shot, said that half a million East African Asians could eventually enter which was 'quite monstrous'. He called for an end to work permits and a complete ban on dependants coming to Britain. Other Tories, notably the former Colonial Secretary Iain Macleod, felt the party was entirely bound by the promises it had made when Kenya became independent; the Asians could not be left stateless. This division was echoed in the Labour government too, whose liberals, led by Roy Jenkins, believed the Asian migration could only be halted by pleading with Kenyatta for better treatment at home. The new Home Secretary Jim Callaghan, however, was determined to respond to the apparent mood of worry and anger about the migration. This would mean revoking or cancelling the right of Kenyan Asians to enter. It would be a betrayal of a promise.

Shamefully the same Conservative politician who had made the promise originally, Duncan Sandys, was now leading calls to cancel it. By the turn of the year around 2,000 Kenyan Asians a month were arriving: almost every aircraft seat from East Africa to London, direct or indirect, was booked. Callaghan decided to act. As his colleague Crossman recorded of a crucial cabinet committee meeting in February 1968, 'Jim arrived with the air of a man whose mind was made up. He wasn't going to tolerate this bloody liberalism. He was going to stop this nonsense, as the public was demanding and as the Party was demanding. He would do it come what may and anybody who opposed him was a sentimental jackass.'[29] The Commonwealth Immigrants Act, which effectively slammed the door, while leaving a catflap open for a very small annual quota, was rushed through Parliament that spring. Yet this not only broke the word of the British Government at the time of Kenyan independence, it also left 20,000 people adrift and stateless in a part of Africa that no longer wanted them. The bill has been described as 'among the most divisive and controversial decisions taken by any British government. For some the legislation was the most shameful piece of legislation ever enacted by Parliament, the ultimate appeasement of racist hysteria' while for others it was the moment when the political elite, in the shape of Jim Callaghan, finally listened to their working-class voters.[30] Polls of the public showed that 72 per cent supported the act.

This was the background to Powell's famous speech in Birmingham, at a small room in the city's Midland Hotel, on 20 April 1968, three weeks after Callaghan's bill had become law and the planes carrying would-be Kenyan Asian migrants had been turned round. Powell had argued before that the passport guarantee was never valid originally. He was contemptuous of the Commonwealth by now, seeing it as a high-minded constitutional myth, which stopped Britain from pursuing her self-interest freely. Most of his political fire was directed at the absurdities, as he saw them, of trying to control the level of the currency and direct the economy. Despite Heath's growing despair about his stiff-necked determination to challenge orthodoxy, Powell was still a member of the shadow cabinet. It had just agreed to cautious backing for Labour's tougher Race Relations Bill (the flip side of the Callaghan restrictions). Powell had gone uncharacteristically quiet. He was however quite aware of the size of the political explosion he was about to detonate, telling a local friend 'I'm going to make a speech at the weekend and it's going to go up "fizz" like a rocket; but whereas all rockets fall to earth, this one is going to stay up.'[31] The friend, Clem Jones, the editor of Powell's local newspaper, the *Wolverhampton Express and Star*, had advised him to time the speech for the early evening television bulletins, and not to distribute it generally beforehand. He would regret the advice.

Here is some of what Enoch Powell said. He quoted a Wolverhampton constituent, a middle-aged working man, who told him that if he had the money, he would leave the country because 'in fifteen or twenty years time the black man will have the whip hand over the white man'. Powell continued by asking rhetorically how he dared say such a horrible thing, stirring up trouble and inflaming feelings. 'The answer is I do not have the right not to do so. Here is a decent, ordinary fellow-Englishman, who in broad daylight in my own town says to me, his Member of Parliament, that this country will not be worth living in for his children. I simply do not have the right to shrug my shoulders and think about something else. What he is saying, thousands and hundreds of thousands are saying and thinking . . .' Those whom the Gods wish to destroy, he reminded his audience, they first make mad. 'We must be mad, literally mad, as a nation to be permitting the annual inflow of some 50,000 dependants, who are for the most part the material of the future growth of the immigrant-descended population. It is like watching a nation busily engaged in heaping its own funeral pyre.' The race relations legislation was merely throwing a match on gunpowder. Powell then quoted another con-stituent, this time an elderly woman whom he said was persecuted by 'Negroes'. She had excrement stuffed through her letter-box and was followed to the shops 'by children, charming wide-grinning piccaninnies. They cannot speak English, but one word they know. "Racialist", they chant.' He concluded with the peroration which gave the speech its slightly inaccurate popular title: 'As I look ahead, I am filled with foreboding. Like the Roman, I seem to see "the Tiber foaming with much blood".' If Britain did not begin a policy of voluntary repatriation, she would soon face the kind of race riots that were disfiguring America.

The speech was claimed by Powell to be merely a restatement of Tory policy. But its language and Powell's own careful preparation suggest it was both a call to arms by a politician who believed he was fighting for white English nationhood, and a deliberate provocation aimed at Powell's enemy Heath. At any rate, after horrified consulta-tions when he and other leading Tories had seen extracts of the speech on the television news, Heath promptly ordered Powell to phone him, and summarily sacked him. Heath announced that he found the speech 'racialist in tone and liable to exacerbate racial tensions'. As Parliament returned three days after the speech, a thousand London dockers marched to Westminster in Powell's support; by the following day he had received 20,000 letters, almost all in support of his speech, with tens of thousands more still to come. Smithfield meat porters and Heathrow airport workers also demonstrated in his support. Powell also received death threats and needed full-time police protection for a while; numerous marches were held against him and he found it difficult to make speeches at or near university campuses. Asked whether he was a racialist by the *Daily Mail*, he replied: 'We are all racialists. Do I object to one coloured person in this country? No. To 100? No. To a million? A query. To five million? Definitely.'

There can be no serious doubt that most people in 1968 agreed with him.

Plot! Lord Louis and the King Thing

Forty years on, the paranoid atmosphere after only a few years of Wilson's first administration is hard to credit, but there was a rising conviction among some in business and the media that democracy itself had failed. Cecil King, the tall and megalomaniac nephew of those original press barons, Lords Rothermere and Harmsworth, and the effective proprietor of IPC, which owned the *Daily Mirror*, was at the centre of the flapping. He had originally supported Wilson, both in Opposition and in the period immediately after the 1964 election, but was deeply offended when Wilson, who had egalitarian convictions, then offered King only the modish life peerage. King was outraged. He wanted a hereditary title, as befitted the boss of a popular socialist newspaper, preferably an Earldom. Wilson, to his credit, refused to budge. To the Prime Minister's discredit, though, he desperately flattered King, courted him and gave him a string of other baubles, including a damehood for his wife and positions for himself – director of the Bank of England, a seat on the National Coal Board and another on the National Parks Commission, plus repeated offers of junior government jobs and a life peerage. None of it made the slightest impression on the sulking press tycoon, who went round London telling anyone who would listen that Wilson was a dud, a liar and an incompetent who was ruining the country and who should be removed as soon as possible.[32]

King's theme, not uncommon in business circles, was that Britain needed professional administrators and managers in charge, not dodgy politicians. He insisted that 'We are coming near to the failure of parliamentary government.' The politicians had made 'such a hash of our affairs that people must be brought into government from outside the rank of professional politicians'. His private views came close to a call for insurrection or a coup, to be fronted by himself and other business leaders. This culminated in a clumsily attempted plot.

On 8 May 1968, according to King's brilliant editor-in-chief Hugh
Cudlipp, the two of them had a meeting with Lord Louis Mountbatten,
whom we have met in his role negotiating India's independence. As a
war hero, former Chief of the Defence Staff and close member of the
Royal Family, Mountbatten had a unique role in public life. He stood
above politics, though many believed he liked the notion of being
thought a man of destiny, and he was much discussed by those who
dreamed of an anti-Wilson putsch. He had made his worries about the
country known to Cudlipp, though denying he wanted 'to appear to
be advocating or supporting any notion of a Right Wing dictatorship –
or any nonsense of that sort.' Indeed, Mountbatten's idea of the
possible leader of some kind of emergency government supplanting
Wilson was . . . Barbara Castle.

Nevertheless, when King, Cudlipp and Mountbatten met, with
the government's chief scientific adviser Sir Solly Zuckerman, the talk
was wild. King told the Queen's uncle-in-law that in the coming crisis,
'the government would disintegrate, there would be bloodshed in the
streets, the armed forces would be involved' and asked Mountbatten
whether he would agree to be titular head of a new administration.
According to Cudlipp, Mountbatten then asked Zuckerman what he
made of it. The scientist rose, walked to the door and replied: 'This
is rank treachery. All this talk of machine guns at street corners is
appalling. I am a public servant and will have nothing to do with it.
Nor should you, Dickie.' Mountbatten agreed. Later, he recorded that
it was he who had told King the idea was 'rank treason' and booted
him out. King's account of the meeting is different, though hardly less
alarming. He claimed Mountbatten had said morale in the armed
forces was low, the Queen was worried and asked for advice. To
which the newspaperman replied: 'There might be a stage in the
future when the Crown would have to intervene: there might be a
stage when the armed forces were important. Dickie should keep
himself out of public view so as to have clean hands . . .'[33] Whichever
account is more accurate, the meeting certainly took place and
Mountbatten then seems to have reported the conversation to the
Queen. King, unabashed, unleashed a front page attack in the *Daily
Mirror* on Wilson, headlined 'Enough is Enough', and calling for a new
leader. He was himself putsched by a board which realized he had
become a serious embarrassment, shortly afterwards.

Does any of this matter? There is no evidence that the talk of a coup was truly serious, or that the security services were involved, as has been publicly asserted since. Yet the Cecil King story counts in two ways. First, it gives some indication of the fevered and at times almost hysterical mood about Wilson and the condition of the country that had built up by the late sixties – a time now more generally remembered as golden, chic and successful. A heady cocktail of rising crime, student rioting, inflation, civil rights protests in Northern Ireland and embarrassments abroad had convinced some that the country was ungovernable. Because British democracy has survived unscathed through the post-war period, to suggest it was ever threatened now seems outlandish. Perhaps it never was. There is a lurid little saloon bar of the mind where conspiracy theorists, mainly on the left, and self-important fantasists, mainly on the right, gather and talk. The rest of us should be wary of joining them for a tipple. Yet the transition from the discredited old guard of Macmillan-era Britain to the unwelcomed new cliques of Wilson-era Britain was a hard time.

Wilson was a genuine outsider so far as the old Establishment was concerned, and he ran a court of outsiders. The old Tory style of government by clique and clubmen gave way to government by faction and feud, a weakness in Labour politics throughout the party's history. Wilson had emerged by hopping from group to group, with no settled philosophical view or strong body of personal support in the party. Instead of a 'Wilson party', represented in the Commons and country, he relied on a small gang of personal supporters – Marcia Williams most famously, but also the Number Ten insiders Peter Shore, Gerald Kaufman, George Wigg and for, a while in these earlier years, Tony Benn too. Then there were the outside advisers. Some were brought in from academic life, such as the Hungarian-born economists Thomas Balogh and Nicholas Kaldor (popularly known as Buddha and Pest). Some came from business, such as the notorious Gannex raincoat manufacturer Joseph Kagan, or from the law, such as the arch-fixer of the sixties Lord Goodman. Suspicious of the Whitehall Establishment, with some justification, and cut off from both the right-wing group of former Gaitskellites, and the old Bevanites, Wilson felt forced to create his own gang. A Tory in that position might have automatically turned to old school tie connections, or family ones, as Macmillan did. Wilson turned to an eclectic group of one-offs and oddballs, producing a peculiarly neurotic little court, riven by jealousy and misunderstanding.

This anti-court gave easy material to Wilson's snobbish and suspicious enemies in the press, ranging from *Private Eye*, which constantly taunted the insiders with foreign-sounding names, to the MI5-connected 'red conspiracy' merchants, and even scions of the Fleet Street purple. Many in that old Establishment – the top brass, the City grandees, the clubmen – struggled to accept that Wilson was a legitimate leader of the United Kingdom. Wilson was paranoid but plenty of powerful people were out to get him, or at least to get him out.

In Place of Beer

Until the end of the decade the sixties had not been particularly strike-prone compared to the fifties. Strikes tended to be local, unofficial and quickly settled. Inflation was still below 4 per cent for most years and, being voluntary, incomes policies rarely caused national confrontation. But by 1968–9 inflation was rising sharply. Wilson had pioneered the matey 'beer and sandwiches' approach to dealing with union leaders (though he found on his first attempt the sandwiches were too thinly cut to satisfy union appetites). But he was becoming disillusioned. That seamen's strike of 1966 had been a particularly bruising experience. So for once it was Wilson who took a stand. He was supported by an unlikely hammer of the unions, the veteran left-winger Barbara Castle, now made Secretary for Employment. In a homage to her early hero, Nye Bevan's book *In Place of Fear*, she called her plan for industrial harmony 'In Place of Strife'. It proposed new government powers to order pre-strike ballots, and a 28-day pause before strikes took place. The government would be able in the last resort to impose settlements for wildcat strikes. There would be fines if the rules were broken. This was a package of measures which looks gentle by the standards of the laws which would come later. The leading trade unionists of the day, once famous men like Jack Jones and Hugh Scanlon, saw it as an unacceptable return to legal curbs they had fought for decades to lift.

The battle that followed nearly ended Wilson's career, and Castle's. Their defeat made the Thatcher revolution inevitable, though it would not come for a further decade. The failure of 'In Place of Strife' is one of the great lost opportunities of modern British politics. Why did it fail? The easy explanation is that the unions were too powerful and yet also still too popular, not least on the Labour backbenches. Barbara Castle was neither the most tactful negotiator nor the niftiest tactician. Her angry harangues put up the backs of male newspaper commentators and MPs, who compared her to a fishwife and a nag, just as they would Margaret Thatcher. She made silly mistakes, such as going away on holiday in the Mediterranean on the yacht owned by that arch capitalist Lord Forte during one of the most sensitive weeks, lying in the sun and talking of resignation. Later while Wilson sat up companionably with union leaders, quaffing brandies and puffing cigars, she would creep off exhausted to bed. Yet both Wilson and Castle were fully aware that this was a struggle for authority a serious government could not afford to lose.

In a famous confrontation in the summer of 1969 when union leaders were given a private dinner at Chequers, Scanlon had warned the two ministers directly again, that he would not accept any legal penalties, or even any new legislation. Wilson replied that if he as Prime Minister accepted such a position he would be running a government that was not allowed to govern. If the unions mobilized their sponsored Labour MPs to vote against him, 'it would clearly mean that the TUC, a state within a state, was putting itself above the government in deciding what a government could and could not do.' Uttered privately this was just the language which would be heard publicly from Heath and later even more starkly from Thatcher. Scanlon retorted that Wilson was becoming that arch turncoat, a Ramsay MacDonald. Wilson hotly denied it and referred to the Czech reformist leader who had been crushed by the Red Army the previous year: 'Nor do I intend to be another Dubček. Get your tanks off my lawn, Hughie!'

But the tanks stayed resolutely parked under his nose, Scanlon and Jones unblinking, their gun-barrels pointing at Labour's reputation. Wilson and Castle now contemplated a joint resignation. For the Prime Minister also had a weapon of last resort. If he walked away then the Tories would surely return, with tougher measures still. But as the stand-off continued, the unions merely suggested a series of voluntary agreements and letters of intent. They were toughing it out because they had excellent intelligence from inside the government and knew very well that Wilson and Castle were isolated. Not only were the usual forces of the left against reform of industrial relations – all those *Tribune* MPs attacking Castle for betraying her principles, the scores of pragmatic rebels on the Labour benches and the trade union sponsored MPs whose paymasters were jerking the reins – but also some key right-wing ministers too. As so often, below the great issue of the hour, personal vanity and ambition were writhing. Jim Callaghan, with his strong trade union links, was utterly against legal curbs on the unions. Now Home Secretary, a former trade union official himself, he voted against his own government's plans at a meeting of Labour's national executive. His enemies were convinced that he thought the failure of union reform would finish Wilson off. 'In Place of Strife' would become 'In Place of Harold'.

Callaghan's objections to the package went beyond pure self-interest but his own ideas about how to deal with the unions were thin to the point of absurdity. As Prime Minister much later he would be richly and fairly repaid for what he did in 1969. At the time he was reviled by the pro-reform ministers. In a bitter cabinet meeting, Callaghan retorted to Crossman's plea that they must all sink or swim together, with the words, 'sink or sink'. Crossman spat back: 'Why don't you go? Get out!' Callaghan's fellow Cardiff MP, later the Speaker, George Thomas, described him as 'our Judas Iscariot'. Other ministers had their own agendas too, of course, and began to peel away from Wilson and Castle. Tony Crosland, another key figure on the Labour right, hoped that if Callaghan succeeded Wilson, he would finally achieve his great ambition and become Chancellor. Jenkins, however, was not mainly motivated by the hope of toppling Wilson. For one thing, no one could tell whether Wilson's fall would mean his success, or Callaghan's. Furthermore, Jenkins knew that since his main criticism of the Prime Minister was lack of principle, to stab him in the back when he did make a stand would look absurd and discreditable. Yet late in the day Jenkins eventually ratted because he said he feared 'a government smash' if the plans were forced through. Tony Benn, who had been warmly backing Barbara Castle before, changed his mind too. After the crucial cabinet meeting, Wilson stormed out, saying to his staff, 'I don't mind running a green cabinet, but I'm buggered if I'm going to run a yellow one!'[34]

It is possible to argue that Castle's plans were too hardline for 1969, though late in life Callaghan eventually recanted and admitted penal sanctions had been necessary.[35] But had the Labour Government been united behind Wilson on this, then legislative reform of trade union practices might have been forced through even the Parliamentary Labour Party of the day, and much subsequent grief avoided. Wilson's reputation, Labour's reputation and the story of British politics would have been markedly different. But with the cabinet as well as the backbenches in rebellion, Wilson had no choice but to give way. His earlier threats to resign were swiftly forgotten. In a brutal aside about Castle which perhaps reflected the strain he was under, he said to an official: 'Poor Barbara. She hangs around like someone with a still-born child. She can't believe it's dead.'[36] The two of them reached a toothless 'solemn and binding' agreement under which unions said they would accept TUC advice on unofficial strikes. Solomon Binding was meant to be a face saver but instead became a national joke. Hypocritically, the cabinet applauded Wilson for his brilliant negotiating and, hypocritically, he accepted their praise – though Castle, on the edge of physical collapse, gave them a blast of honest contempt. The Tories and the press were rightly derisive. In his memoirs Jenkins admitted that Wilson, whom he generally did not admire, came out of it all with a touch of King Lear-like nobility. 'He did not hedge and he did not whine . . . It was a sad story from which he and Barbara Castle emerged with more credit than the rest of us.' The great background question about the Labour governments of the sixties is whether with a stronger leader they could have gripped the country's big problems and dealt with them. How did it happen that a cabinet of such brilliant, such clever and self-confident people achieved so little? In part, it was the effect of the whirling court politics demonstrated by 'In Place of Strife'.

Election Upset

In the end, the Wilson government was felled not by wild-eyed plotters but entirely conventionally by the electorate. When Wilson called the election in 1970 he was feeling optimistic despite the failure of 'In Place of Strife'. He knew his enemy. Heath had been the Leader of the Opposition since 1965, with Tory MPs voting in a secret ballot for the first time. Seen as a ruthless modernizer, he began to reshape the Tory front bench. Out went many of the cod-Edwardian grandees. In came people like Peter Walker, another grammar school boy who had made his money in the City, Geoffrey Rippon, the young former mayor of Surbiton, Tony Barber, the former RAF man and lawyer, and Margaret Thatcher, a grocer's daughter, none of them from rich families. Though a pre-1970 election policy conference at the Selsdon Park hotel outside London was much over-hyped as a lurch to the right (Wilson talked of 'Selsdon Man', as some kind of ape-like throwback), Heath was a staunchly pro-business politician. In the sixties and early seventies, after so many years of the more languid, aristocratic Tory Party, he seemed like a blast of fresh air.

Wilson and Heath cordially detested one another. Perhaps it was because they had so much in common. They came from traditionalist, pious, lower-middle-class, provincial families. They were born in the same year, 1916, Heath four months after Wilson. His family was poorer than Wilson's and his working-class origins stronger. Heath's father was a carpenter who worked for a building contractor and his mother was a lady's maid who later took in lodgers. Like Wilson, Heath rose through fierce academic ability and scholarships. Both seem to have been rather solitary and awkward as young men but benefited from the richness of pre-television community life, Wilson throwing himself into the world of Scouting and Methodist clubs, and Heath into music and choirs. Both arrived at Oxford at much the same time and were on the edge of the glamorous and passionate politics of the pre-war period there, though they never seem to have met. As we have seen, the two of them represented the triumph of the grammar school boy in politics, a class breakthrough comparable to what happened at the same time in business, the arts and the professions. Governing consecutively during 1964–76 they would oversee the near-total destruction of the grammar school in England and Wales. Both would represent moderation in their respective parties, harried by the hard left and the hard right, accused of weakness and appeasement. Each was essentially a believer in managerialism and compromise. Patriots and equally proud men, they would come to be reviled, identified with a time of national collapse and failure. They were certainly easy to caricature, Wilson's pudgy face and pipe, against Heath's vast manic grin and yacht-sailing.

There were good reasons for Labour to think that they would see off the Tories yet again. Jenkins seemed to have pulled the economy around and was self-confident enough not to use his last budget for pre-election bribes. It was in fact quite popular. The opinion polls were onside and the press was generally predicting an easy Labour victory. Even right-wing commentators lavished praise on Wilson's television performances and mastery of debate, though he pursued an avowedly presidential style and tried to avoid controversy.

Heath was regarded as a dull dud by comparison and harried by Powell who had returned to the attack again and again before the 1970 election, provoking Heath to denounce him as inhumane and unchristian, and to make it clear that he would never be asked to serve in a Conservative government. At the height of their battle for the soul of the party, in summer 1969, a Gallup poll suggested 54 per cent agreed with Powell on grants to repatriate what it called coloured immigrant families. By early 1970, 66 per cent of those polled said they were either more favourable to Powell or felt the same about him and only 22 per cent said their view of him was less favourable. Powell was by now attacking Heath over a broad front of policy, over the need for tax cuts, privatization and freer markets in economics; over Northern Ireland, or Ulster; and over British membership of the EEC, which Powell opposed as strongly as Heath supported it. So Powell's battle-cry for repatriation and an end to immigration was taken by the Tory leadership as part of his campaign to unseat Heath and then replace him.

There were plenty in the party and the country who yearned for just that. Apart from the dockers and other marchers, wealthy backers wanted to fund a campaign for Powell's leadership. Marcel Everton, a Worcestershire industrialist, raised money for a national federation of Powellite groups and talked of a march on Conservative headquarters to oust Heath. Wilson's call for an election, however, created an obvious trap which Powell could see very clearly even if his supporters ignored it. His best chance by far would be if Heath lost the election. Then he could attack him openly and perhaps even seize control of the party. Everton, like others, openly said that it would be better for right-wingers to vote Labour so that the Tory party would 'fall into Enoch's lap like a ripe cherry'.[37] Yet if Powell seemed to toy with this, he would be forever branded a traitor by tens of thousands of loyal Conservatives. Either Heath would win and Powell would be finished, or he would lose and Powell would be blamed by so many Tories the party might split.

The campaign was characterized by huge coverage of Powell, in the case of some newspapers, engorging half their reporting of the Tories' entire campaign. It has been described as the only general election campaign in British history in which immigration and race have played a significant part. Conservative meetings were full of home-made 'Enoch' signs. Heath and his colleagues were constantly irritated and embarrassed by being asked whether or not they supported their fallen angel in Wolverhampton. Unsurprisingly, Powell was portrayed by Labour and Liberal politicians as the right-wing ideologue behind whom Ted Heath anxiously waddled. Tony Benn went furthest in this, calling him 'the real leader of the Conservative party. He is a far stronger character than Mr Heath. He speaks his mind . . . Heath dare not attack him publicly even when he says things that disgust decent Conservatives.' Benn went on to assert that 'the flag hoisted at Wolverhampton is beginning to look like the one that fluttered over Dachau and Belsen.'

Late in the campaign Powell, who had been hounded by left-wing protesters, finally gave a clear and unequivocal endorsement to the official Tory campaign. Because there was indeed a late surge of support for Heath, it has been argued that Powell was responsible for his victory. But the evidence is thin to prove it and Powell himself fastidiously declined to claim such a thing. Just before the campaign had begun Jenkins learnt, too late, that yet more bad balance of payments figures were to be published along with bad inflation figures. This helped tip things away from Wilson. When the results were in the Tories had won an overall majority of thirty. Polls afterwards scotched the idea that Jenkins's pre-election budget had lost Labour the election. In fact it was quite popular. Powell, according to his biographer, once he realized the consequences of Heath's victory, 'sat around on his own with his head in his hands, deep in gloom. He had realised immediately that, after Wilson, he had been the great loser of the election.'[38]

And Wilson was bitterly disappointed. He was also surprised. With no home of his own on the mainland, he had to take up Heath's offer of a last weekend in Chequers while he desperately searched around for somewhere to live.

Blood and Shame: the Irish Tragedy Begins

Of the great crises that link Wilson and Heath together, that of Northern Ireland had as much effect on the tenor of mainland British life as any. It brought surprise and embarrassment to millions watching the violence on the streets of the province. It brought bombings, murder and shame. The longer origins of the conflict, from the settlement of Ulster by Scots Presbyterian farmers to the Partition of Ireland in 1921 and the civil war are outside the limits of this book. In the fifties and through most of the sixties, Northern Ireland barely appeared on the Westminster radar. There was a devolved Northern Ireland government, with its own prime minister and a distinct party system, along with the contingent of grey, reliable, conservative-minded Unionist MPs who rarely made ripples in London, never mind waves. The bigotry of the Protestant majority was the butt of jokes and official disapproval.

Yet there was limited English or Scottish sympathy for the cause of Irish unification – hostility to Catholicism and memories of the inglorious role played by the Republic during the war against Hitler remained strong. If the Belfast shipyards of Harland & Wolff were barred to Catholics, then too were some well-known concerns on the mainland. If there was unfairness in the allocation of housing in Londonderry, so there was in Leicester or Nottingham. There was, admittedly, a blatant form of anti-Catholic constituency-rigging, the gerrymandered boundaries designed to maximize Unionist representation. As early as 1964, when Wilson first met the Stormont Prime Minister Captain Terence O'Neill, who had been elected the previous year on a programme of mild reform, he was pressing him to end gerrymandering. Mostly, though, this was a time of dozy neglect which turned out from 1969 to have been a terrible failure of imagination – malign neglect, whose effects would haunt Britain for the next thirty years.

For under the surface, the unfairness and discrimination in jobs, in housing and in politics, had taken the temperature in the Catholic ghettos to simmering point. The changed international climate had something to do with this. Rebellion against injustice was in the air, or at least in the newspapers. Rising protests about apartheid in South Africa and the struggle for equal rights in the southern states of the US had focused attention on the squalid half-secret on Britain's doorstep. O'Neill's cautious moves towards reform had produced a hardline Protestant backlash, led by demagogues including a young and turbulent preacher called Ian Paisley. In 1967 a civil rights movement had been formed, using the language and tactics of the Deep South, and the following year, marches and demonstrations were being met with police violence. A largely Catholic and nationalist party, the Social Democratic and Labour Party, was formed. Bernadette Devlin of the more radical Ulster Unity Party was elected in 1969 to the Commons, the youngest ever woman MP, on a civil rights ticket. She treated MPs to what one of her listeners described as 'the authentic, bitter and resentful voice of Catholic Ulster'.[39] Wilson told O'Neill he thought he should go further and faster, both on housing and on local government boundaries. O'Neill replied that this would require an election. During it, his Unionist Party split and he received a bloody nose, handing over to another, though less effective, moderate, James Chichester-Clarke. At this stage, apart from occasional raids on arms dumps, the ageing and sparsely manned Irish Republican Army was little heard of.

Then, in the summer of 1969, the politics of Northern Ireland erupted. The Apprentice Boys of Derry, a Loyalist anti-Catholic organization, had planned their annual march at Londonderry on the same day and over the same route that a civil rights march was planned. There had been civil rights marches before, but they had been peaceful. This time, ordered not to march, they did so and were attacked by the police. Members of the so-called B-Specials, an unpaid and part-time but armed 12,000-strong wing of the Royal Ulster Constabulary, were particularly brutal. Among the seventy-five marchers injured that day were leading political figures, such as Gerry Fitt who would become an MP and a peer, and a powerful anti-IRA voice for moderation. The bloodied heads and the vengeful use of batons horrified millions watching that evening's television bulletins. In response the Stormont government promised reforms to local elections, housing lists and parliamentary boundaries. This sparked off Loyalist protests. More civil rights marches followed, and more attacks on them, until at the beginning of August, there was a serious pitched battle between Catholic residents, Loyalist extremists and police in the middle of Belfast. Hundreds of houses burned. Harold Wilson, who was on holiday on the Isles of Scilly, flew to Cornwall for a brief talk with his Home Secretary, Jim Callaghan. They agreed to send in the British Army if asked, in return for the abolition of the B-Specials and promises of further reforms. It was a momentous decision, taken without the involvement of the cabinet. As Crossman recorded in his diary: 'Harold and Jim had really committed the cabinet to putting the troops in and once they were there, they couldn't be taken out again, so we had to ratify what had been done.' Tony Benn wrote: 'It looks as though civil war in Ulster has almost begun.'

One of the myths about the moment when Britain sent in the troops to Northern Ireland was that it was done with little understanding of the dangers, no thought about alternatives and no appreciation that, arriving to protect Catholic homes, the troops might find themselves a target for Irish nationalists. This is all untrue. Wilson and Callaghan were acutely aware of the dangers and had put maximum pressure on Chichester-Clarke and the Unionists to hurry through political change, and they got some of what they wanted over the B-Specials and housing. In casting around for alternatives, Wilson even apparently toyed with the idea of a reverse 'plantation', evacuating the entire Ulster Protestant community out of Ireland and giving them new homes in England and Scotland.[40] When Wilson's press secretary, Joe Haines, suggested to him that the troops could be there for months, he grimly replied: 'They're going to be there for seven years at least.' Callaghan, whose handling of the crisis was his finest hour, was under no illusion that the troops would soon be facing both communities, and would indeed become a target. Benn, attending cabinet with a freshly grown beard which caused much amusement around the table, mused whether this was not 'the beginning of ten more years of Irish politics at Westminster which could be very unpleasant'.[41] Meanwhile over in Northern Ireland itself, the hard men were at work. Loyalist mobs reacted with fury to the proposed disbanding of the B-Specials and IRA men were digging into the various civil rights and citizens' defence organizations of Catholic

Belfast and Derry. In November, at a tense meeting in Dublin, the IRA split, and the pro-violence Provisional Army Council or 'Provos' came into existence.

Now the nature of the conflict would change. It had begun as a protest about unfairness, bigotry and political corruption. It turned into a fight to force an end to the United Kingdom and to bring about the unification of Ireland. Inspired by a heady mix of Marxism, romantic nationalism and the example of overseas guerrillas from Vietnam to Cuba, the Provos believed that so long as they had the support of most Catholics, they could end the partition of the island. Winning over much of the minority community took time. The IRA's first success was to convince many Catholics living in Belfast, where they were heavily outnumbered, that only they could protect them against the Loyalist thugs and that the British Army was bloodied hand in bloodied glove with their enemies. This was not so but rumour and stone-throwing provocation, followed by over-reaction and army bru- tality, would soon make it seem that way. In the Irish Republic, many were instinctively with the IRA. In 1970 two Dublin cabinet ministers, Charles Haughey and Neil Blaney, were sacked for being sympathizers with the Provos, though acquitted later of trying to illegally import arms into the Republic. Most of £100,000 voted by the Dail, the Irish Parliament, for the relief of Catholics in the North a year earlier had, in fact, been spent on arms and ammunition. Community defence was morphing into nationalist uprising.

This was the crisis inherited by Heath, the nearly man in Irish peace-making, in 1970. He knew little about Northern Ireland when he arrived in office, though he had once been smuggled across the border under a blanket for lunch in the Republic. In one crucial respect he advanced on the underlying assumption of the Labour ministers. It would not be enough to protect Northern Catholics. Heath thought they would have to be given a stake in the running of Northern Ireland too. Eventually, he hoped, greater prosperity in Ireland, more trade across the border and common membership of Europe would ease the two communities towards an easier relationship. This is what happened, though only after decades of murder had exhausted them, too.

The Yachtsman

Heath's reputation has sunk particularly low. Perhaps this is not surprising. He was defeated as leader in 1975 after losing two generation elections and fell out spectacularly with the new order, Thatcherism. The triumph of Margaret Thatcher's optimistic if divisive free-market politics attracted a blaze of intellectual, media and parliamentary support which saw her success as a refutation of Heath's time. The brighter she burned then, by narrative necessity, the duller he must be. Certainly, his attempts to rein in trade union power and to conquer inflation failed. The cause that excited him more than any other, Europe, also inflamed his enemies who accused him of lying to the country about the true, political nature of the coming European Union. Heath did not help his cause by the implacable sulk that followed his ousting, a huff he managed to maintain for thirty years. His own account of his government is wooden and wearisomely self-justificatory, in prose almost as bad as Harold Wilson's. Further, as a loner who could be extraordinarily rude even to his admirers, Heath never accumulated a team of public defenders. Those who worked with him and thought him a fine leader, such as Douglas Hurd, were rarely able to make themselves heard against the surging self-belief and vituperative journalism of the Thatcher years. Finally Heath had little time in office compared to Wilson's near eight, just three and a half years.

Almost friendless, Heath is a political leader whose reputation deserves to be revisited. He was the first outsider to break through the class barriers of the old Tory party and he promoted others like him to the cabinet. His European vision came first-hand. Before the war, on a student visit to Germany, he had literally rubbed shoulders with Hitler and met other Nazi leaders. Later he returned as a fighting officer to see their final defeat in 1945 and the war marked him more strongly than it marked Wilson. As Heath wrote later: 'My generation did not have the option of living in the past; we had to work for the future. We were surrounded by destruction, homelessness, hunger and despair. Only by working together right across our continent had we any hope of creating a society which would uphold the true values of European civilisation.' He was a genuinely compassionate and unusually brave politician, whose analysis of what was wrong with Britain in the seventies was far more acute than Wilson's. His struggle with trade union power, conducted at the worst possible time, was relentless but he was up against forces too big to conquer quickly. Like Margaret Thatcher, he believed Britain was in danger of becoming ungovernable. His strategic mistake was to attack union power head-on and in a single act, rather than piecemeal, as her wilier government would. Like her, he cut taxes and even began privatization. Unlike her, he was ruling at a time when public sympathy was more with unions than with government, and when huge rises in the price of oil and other commodities were knocking Western economies sideways. His 1972 U-turn on incomes policy and industrial intervention was indeed a humiliating moment for parliamentary democracy but, while stiff-necked and difficult, mostly Edward Heath was plain unlucky.

He had risen through the Tory Party in Parliament as a tough chief whip and then as an equally tough negotiator on Europe in the Macmillan years. But Heath's greatest achievement as a minister had come in 1964 when, as President of the Board of Trade, he abolished Resale Price Maintenance, or RPM. This is one of those reforms which sound dull and are now largely forgotten but which really did reshape the country. RPM allowed manufacturers to order shops to sell their products at a particular price. A shop which cut prices would be breaking the law. It therefore discriminated heavily in favour of small, relatively expensive shops rather than superstores; under RPM the supermarket revolution would have been much less dramatic and the 'Tesco-ification' of Britain impossible. Heath believed it stood in the way of proper competition and choice, and was inflationary. Yet were not small shopkeepers natural Conservatives? Many in the party and government opposed him, but he carried the day, a crucial defeat of producer interest by the new consumerism.

Ugandan Asians

Heath in power showed that he was desperately worried about the anti-immigration mood revealed in this most bitter of elections. While denouncing Powell, he moved quickly to pass a highly controversial and restrictive piece of legislation which removed any right to immigrate to Britain from anyone who did not have a parent or grandparent born in the country. Heath's manifesto had promised 'a new single system of control over all immigration from overseas'. Nobody had spelled out that this system would be designed to exclude blacks but not whites, yet the grandparent rule was transparently designed to allow Australians, Canadians, South Africans and New Zealanders of white British origins to return to the UK, while keeping out the black and coloured people of the Commonwealth and colonies. Powell himself likened the distinction to a Nazi race purity law; he wanted a new definition of British citizenship instead. The grandparent rule was defeated by the right and the left combining for opposite reasons, though restored two years later. Had this been all, then Heath would go down in history as being yet another panicked Establishment man, slamming the door to keep his party happy.

It was not all. For the Kenyan crisis was about to be replayed, at speed, in Uganda. Here the anti-British Prime Minister, Milton Obote, had just been replaced in a coup by the fat, swaggering, Sandhurst-educated Idi Amin who announced that he had been told in a dream he must expel that country's Asians, just as the Kenyans had theirs. Amin was clearly a monster, whose thugs clubbed his enemies to death with staves, who threatened to kill British journalists, who was rumoured to keep human flesh in his fridge and to feast on it, and who enthused about the way the Nazis had dealt with the Jews. Though Powell argued angrily that Britain had no obligation to allow the trapped Ugandan Asians into her cities, Heath acted decisively to bring them in. Airlifts were arranged, with a resettlement board to help them, and 28,000 people arrived within a few weeks in 1971, eventually settling in the same areas as other East Africans – even though Leicester, becoming the 'least white' city in England, had published adverts in Ugandan newspapers pleading with migrants not to come there.

Within a few years Powell would no longer be a Conservative. Heath had confronted him head-on and beaten him. Once seen as a future prime minister, or at least as a brilliant chancellor-to-be, Powell would spend the rest of his life far from even the fringes of power. His ideas, however, would continue to grow in power and influence. His hostility to European union would inspire the biggest revolt in the modern Tory Party, one which kept Britain out of the euro. His belief in rigorous free-market economics would powerfully influence Margaret Thatcher and her circle so that he would be treated as a prophet, Old Testament Enoch. On race and immigration, the picture is more mixed. His views frightened many and made him one of the most detested as well as admired politicians of post-war times. Those who knew him best insist he was not a racialist. The newspaper editor Clem Jones, who tried and failed to track down the little old lady chased by 'piccaninnies' from Powell's speech nevertheless said 'he was never a racist.' Jones thought he had been affected by the anger of white Wolverhampton people who felt they were being crowded out; even in Powell's own street 'of good, solid, Victorian houses, next door went sort of coloured and then another house, and he saw the value of his own house go down'. But, added the newspaperman, Powell would work very hard as an MP for constituents of any colour: 'We quite often used to go out for a meal, as a family, to a couple of Indian restaurants, and he was on extremely amiable terms with everybody there, 'cos having been in India and his wife brought up in India, they liked that kind of food.'[42]

On the numbers migrating to Britain, and the consequences for the population of non-whites living in the country, Powell's figures which were much ridiculed at the time were not far out. Just before his 1968 speech, he suggested that by the end of the century, the number of black and Asian immigrants and their descendants would number between five and seven million, or about a tenth of the population. According to the 2001 census, the relevant figures were 4.7 million people identifying themselves as black or Asian, or 7.9 per cent of the total population, though with large-scale illegal immigration since then, the true numbers are certainly higher. Immigrants are far more strongly represented, in percentage terms as well as raw numbers, in London and the English cities than in Scotland, Wales or Northern Ireland. It can also be argued that Powell did British democracy a kind of service by speaking out on an issue which had been up to then cloaked in elite silence and so provoking a debate which needed to happen at some time. Against that, his language still feels shockingly inflammatory and provocative nearly forty years later. He was talking just after the formation of the racist and fascist National Front in 1967 and though Powell himself was anti-Nazi and indeed had returned from Australia on the outbreak of war to fight the Germans, his words attracted the enthusiastic support of the would-be gauleiters of provincial Britain. Further, his core prediction, of civil unrest comparable to that suffered in the southern states of the United States, has not come about. Five notable outbreaks of inner city rioting since then, and a rise in street crime linked to disaffected youths from Caribbean and other immigrant communities do not add up to the conflagration he predicted.

Immigration has changed Britain more than almost any other single social event in post-1945 Britain – more than the increase in longevity, or the Pill, the collapse of deference or the spread of suburban housing. The only change which eclipses it is the triumph of the car. It was not a change that was asked for by the white population – though the terms and circumstances of 50 million people choosing suddenly to ask such a question are impossible to imagine. The majority of British people did not want the arrival of large numbers of blacks and Asians, just as they did not want an end to capital punishment, or deep British involvement in the European Union, or many of the other things the political elite has opted for. At no stage was there a measured and frank assessment of the likely scale of immigration led by party leaders, voluntarily, in front of the electorate. And while allowing this change by default, the main parties did very little to ensure that mass immigration from the Caribbean and the Indian subcontinent was successful. West Indians got none of the help and forethought lavished on the demobilized Poles, or even the less adequate help given to the Ugandan Asians. There was no attempt to create mixed communities, or avoid mini-ghettos. Race relations legislation did come, but late and only to balance new restrictions: it simply castigated racialism in the white working-class community, rather than trying to understand it.

So this is another example of Britain's history of rule by elite, of liberal politicians acting above their electorates. The real question is whether this neglect of public opinion, and then of the consequences of immigration, not least for the immigrant families, has produced a better or worse country. The scents, flavours, controversies and rawness of Britain in the twenty-first century divide the country from its former self. It is not just those who have come, but the huge numbers of white British who have left, to South Africa, Australia,

Canada and New Zealand, well over half a million in the sixties alone. Britain has become a world island, a little America, despite itself. Having once acquired an Empire in a fit of absent-mindedness, the British have become multi-coloured in much the same way. With new migrations from Eastern Europe, Iraq, Somalia and Ethiopia, it is now clear that this is a far bigger story than simply a tidying-up after Empire.

Floating

If Heath is associated with a single action, it is British entry into 'Europe' but throughout his time in office the economy, not Europe, was the biggest issue facing him. British productivity was still pitifully low compared to the United States or Europe, never mind Japan. The country was spending too much on new consumer goods and not nearly enough on modernized and more efficient factories and businesses. Prices were rising by 7 per cent and wage earnings by double that. This was still the old post-1945 world of fixed exchange rates which meant that the Heath government, just like those of Attlee and Wilson, faced a sterling crisis and perhaps another devaluation. It is hard to describe quite how heavily, how painfully, relative economic decline weighed on the necks of politicians of thirty and forty years ago. The unions, identified by Heath as his first challenge, had just seen off Wilson and Barbara Castle. Heath had decided he would need to face down at least one major public sector strike, as well as removing some of the benefits that he thought encouraged strikes. Britain not only had heavy levels of unionization through all the key industries but also, by modern standards, an incredible number of different unions – more than 600 altogether. Leaders of large unions had only a wobbly hold on what actually happened on the factory floor. It was a time of political militancy well caught by the 1973 hit from the folk-rock band the Strawbs, who reached number two with their anthem, 'Part of the Union'. Its chorus ran, 'Oh you don't get me, I'm part of the union' and different verses spelt out why: 'With a hell of a shout, It's out brothers, out . . . And I always get my way, If I strike for higher pay . . . So though I'm a working man, I can ruin the government's plan.' And so they could.

Almost immediately Heath faced a dock strike, followed by a big pay settlement for local authority dustmen, then a power workers' go-slow which led to power cuts. Then the postal workers struck. The mood of the government was less focused and less steely than it would be nine years later when Margaret Thatcher came to power. Douglas Hurd, later seen as a 'wet' in her cabinet, was Heath's political secretary at the time, and recorded in his diary his increasing frustration. 'A bad day. It is clear that all the weeks of planning in the civil service have totally failed to cope with what is happening in the electricity dispute; and all the pressures are to surrender.' Later, Hurd confronted Heath in his dressing-gown, warning him that the government machine was 'moving too slowly, far behind events'. Things were so bad in the car industry that Henry Ford III, with his right-hand man Lee Iacocca, came to warn Heath that they were thinking of pulling out of Britain entirely. Yet Heath's Industrial Relations Bill of 1971 was meant to be balanced, giving new rights to trade unionists while at the same time trying to make deals with employers legally enforceable through a new system of industrial courts. It was the Tories' first stab at the kind of package which had been offered to the unions by Wilson. There were also tax reforms, meant to increase investment, a deal with business on keeping price increases to 5 per cent, and even some limited privatization – the travel agents Thomas Cook and Lunn Poly were then state owned, and sold off, along with some breweries.

But the Tory messages were still, to put it gently, mixed. Cuts in some personal taxes encouraged spending and inflation. With European membership looming, Barber, Heath's Chancellor, was dashing for growth, which meant further tax cuts and higher government spending. Perhaps the most significant move in the long term was the removal of lending limits for the high street banks, producing a vast surge in borrowing. Lending had been growing at around 12 per cent a year already but in 1972 rose by 37 per cent and the following year by 43 per cent. This, obviously, further fuelled inflation but it also gave a fillip to the ancient British fetish for house price ownership and borrowing. The huge expansion of credit and the unbalanced amount of capital sunk in bricks and lawns in modern-day Britain can be traced back partly to this decision, then the new credit boom of the Thatcher years. It is not even mentioned in Heath's memoirs.

At the same time one of the historic constraints on British governments had gone. In the summer of 1971 President Nixon unilaterally tore up a key part of the post-war financial system by suspending the convertibility of the dollar for gold and allowing exchange rates to float. His problem was the awesome cost of the war in Vietnam (though it would cost only 60 per cent in real terms of the later post-September 11 conflicts in Afghanistan and Iraq), combined with rising commodity prices. The effect on Britain was that the government and Bank of England no longer had to be quite so obsessed by sterling reserves, though this remained a problem until 1977. But it opened up new questions, about how far down sterling could go and how industrialists could be expected to plan ahead.[43] Heath's instincts on state control were quickly tested when the most valuable parts of Rolls-Royce faced bankruptcy over the cost of developing new aircraft engines. Heath briskly nationalized the company, saving 80,000 jobs and allowed it to regroup and survive, to the relief of the defence industry. Rolls-Royce duly did revive and returned to the private sector, making this a clear case of one nationalization that with hindsight clearly 'worked'.

Into Europe, with the Peasants

We have seen how deeply the cause of Europe had marked Heath, and how hard he had struggled as a negotiator in the early sixties in the face of President de Gaulle's 'Non'. He had done the time, served in the tobacco-smoked rooms, haggled over the detail. As a keen European he knew his French partners better than any other senior British politician. Long before winning power as Prime Minister, he had identified Georges Pompidou who replaced de Gaulle as President as his likely interlocutor. At a meeting at Chequers, Heath later revealed, Pompidou had told him, in French, 'If you ever want to know what my policy is, don't bother to call me on the telephone. I do not speak English, and your French is awful. Just remember that I am a peasant, and my policy will always be to support the peasants.'[44]

This was fair warning about the vast expense of the Common Agricultural Policy but it was not a true reflection of Pompidou's wider vision. In fact, he wanted a Europe of large manufacturing companies able to take on the United States and the Far East. By 1970, after a decade during which Britain had grown much more slowly than the Six members of the Common Market, Heath was in some ways in a weaker position than Macmillan had been. On the other hand, Heath had some advantages. He was trusted as a serious negotiator. Britain's very weakness persuaded Paris that this time, 'les rosbifs' were genuinely determined to join. Pompidou also thought the time was right. A 'Oui' would get him out of the great dead general's shadow. France like the rest of the Community had for years been struggling to understand what Britain really wanted. This had been particularly difficult in the Wilson years, when the British left had been riven by the issue.

Heath had only promised to negotiate, not to join. His enthusiasm, however, was in total contrast to Wilson's wiggling. The best historian of Britain's relations with the rest of the EU described the difference between the two: 'It probably mattered quite a lot to the direction of later events that in early September 1939, as Ted Heath was making it back to Britain from Poland by the skin of his teeth before war was declared, Harold Wilson was motoring to Dundee to deliver an academic paper on exports and the trade cycle, and that later, while Heath was training to run an anti-aircraft battery, Wilson became a potato controller at the Ministry of Food.'[45] Yet opinion polls suggested that Heath's grand vision was alien to most British people and that the former potato controller's warnings about prices had much more effect.

With Heath in power, over eighteen months of haggling in London, Paris and Brussels, a deal was thrashed out. It infuriated Britain's fishermen, who would lose most of their traditional grounds to open European competition, particularly from French and Spanish trawlers. It was a second-best deal on the budget which would later be reopened by Margaret Thatcher. Above all it left intact the previous Common Market designed for the convenience of French farmers and Brussels-based bureaucrats, not for Britain. Vast slews of European law had to be swallowed whole, much of it objectionable to the British negotiators. Only at the very margins, dealing with New Zealand butter, for instance, did the Six make concessions – and the Commonwealth farmers' deal was won at the expense of a worse agreement on the budget. The truth was that the British negotiators had decided it was essential to the country's future to get in at any price. At a press conference at the Élysée Palace in Paris in 1971, Heath and Pompidou, after a long private afternoon of talks between just the two of them, language notwithstanding, revealed to general surprise that so far as France was concerned, Britain could now join the Community. Heath was particularly delighted to have triumphed over the media, who had expected another 'Non'.

Now there would have to be a national debate about the terms of entry and a vote in Parliament. But in Opposition, Wilson was playing true to form. When Heath began negotiations, as we have seen, Wilson was a publicly declared supporter of British membership. But the tactical Wilson soon displaced the statesman. As British accession loomed, he cavilled and sniped. As ever, he was looking over his shoulder. Jim Callaghan, a potential successor, was campaigning openly against Europe, partly on the grounds that a French-speaking institution threatened the language of Chaucer, Shakespeare and Dickens. The left was in full cry. A special Labour conference in July 1971 confirmed how anti-EEC the party had become, voting by a majority of five to one against. Labour MPs were also hostile by a majority of two to one. Wilson now announced that he would oppose British membership on the Heath terms. He was not against in principle, he insisted, just here-and-now. After the long and tortuous journey this disgusted the Labour pro-Europeans. It did not much enthuse the Labour anti-Marketeers, who simply did not believe Wilson's apparent change of heart and assumed he would sign up if he returned to Number Ten. So even Wilson's great cause, Labour unity, was lost.

When the Heath proposals for membership were put to the Commons sixty-nine Labour pro-Europeans defied the party and voted with the Conservatives. They were led by Roy Jenkins, though to his later embarrassment he did not continue voting against his party on every detail. The left, led by Barbara Castle, Michael Foot and Benn, were livid with the rebels. A divide which would eventually lead to the breakaway SDP was just beginning to be visible. For the Labour conference majority, staying out was a matter of principle. For the sixty-nine, going in was a matter of principle. Forms of words, pious evasions and bluster might patch over the cracks in opposition but this quite clearly had the potential to destroy Labour should it return to power. Caught between the moral self-belief of the Castles and Benns, and the steely self-certainty of Jenkins, Wilson protested to the shadow cabinet that 'I've been wading in shit for three months so others can indulge their conscience' and threatened to quit as party leader: 'They can stuff it as far as I'm concerned.' It was only a tantrum but as he struggled to hold things together, the left-wing *New Statesman* delivered a withering verdict on 'the principal apostle of cynicism, the unwitting evangelist of disillusion . . . Mr Wilson has now sunk to a position where his very presence in Labour's leadership pollutes the atmosphere of politics.'[46]

After winning his Commons vote on British membership of the Community, Heath went quietly to Downing Street to play Bach on the piano in a mood of triumph. For the Labour party it had been a dreadful night, with screaming matches in the voting lobbies and ghastly personal confrontations between the sixty-nine rebels and the rest.

The hero of the hour turned out to be Tony Benn, then haring leftwards at a keen lollop. 'Tony immatures with age,' said Wilson but on this issue he proved a lot shrewder than the Labour leader. Benn began to argue that on a decision of such importance the people should vote, in a referendum. His constituency was in Bristol, whence the great eighteenth-century MP and writer, Edmund Burke, had sent a letter to his electors explaining that he owed them his judgement, not his slavish obedience to their opinions. In a reversal of the argument, the other Bristol MP argued instead that a democracy which denied its people the right to choose a matter of such importance directly would lose all respect. To begin with Benn had almost no support for this radical thought. Labour traditionalists despised referendums as fascist devices, continental jiggery-pokery not to be thought of in a parliamentary democracy. Though at this stage Benn was ambivalent about the Common Market, pro-Europeans also feared this was the first move towards committing Labour to pulling out.

Harold Wilson had committed himself publicly and repeatedly against a referendum. Slowly and painfully, however, he came to realize that opposing Heath's deal but promising to renegotiate, while offering a referendum could be the way out. This could be sold to the anti-Marketeers as a swerve against Europe but the pro-Marketeers would realize he was not actually committed to withdraw. And the referendum promise would gain some political high-ground. He would 'trust the people' even if the people were, according to the polls, already fairly bored and hostile. When Pompidou suddenly announced that France would have a referendum, Wilson snatched at the Benn plan. It was an important moment. The referendum would make the attitude of the whole country clear, at least for the seventies. It was to be a device used again by politicians faced with particularly important or tricky constitutional choices.

A Dream Disintegrates

On the afternoon of May Day 1971 John Evans, the manager of the hugely popular Kensington boutique Biba, walked nervously downstairs into the basement. There had been a series of outlandish phone warnings about some kind of bomb, which to start with had simply been ignored by the girl on the till. Outside on the street were some 500 women and children who had by now been hurriedly evacuated. When Evans pushed open the door of the stock-room, there was an almighty bang, a flash of flame and a billow of smoke. The Angry Brigade, middle Britain's very own terror group, had struck again. In their communiqué explaining the attack, they misquoted Bob Dylan – 'if you're not busy being born, you're busy buying' – and went on: 'All the sales girls in all the flash boutiques are made to dress the same and have the same make-up ... Life is so boring there's nothing to do except spend all our wages on the latest skirt, or shirt. Brothers and Sisters, what are your real desires? Sit in the drugstore, look distant, empty, bored, drinking some tasteless coffee? ... The only thing you can do with modern slavehouses – called boutiques – is WRECK THEM.'[47] What they did not seem to realize (except for a cadet enthusiast Erin Pizzey, who broke with them over their Biba plan and later went off to found women's refuges instead) was that its customers found Biba not oppressive but liberating.

There are hundreds of dates and events you could pick to date the end of the sixties dream, but the Biba bombing has a piquancy all of its own. Two of the main forces behind the flowering of youth culture were at war. On the one side is the fantasy of revolution, anarchist or Leninist according to taste, the world of Che Guevara on the wall and obscure leftist handbooks by the bed promising a world in which Starbucks would never have got started. On the other side is the fantasy of benign, hippy business as part of the consumer culture, the world of eyeliner, cool clothes and gentle people making money. The two organizations, Biba and the Angries, sum up much of the underlying argument of sixties youth culture.

The small group of university dropouts who made up the grandly titled Angry Brigade would go to prison for ten years after 123 attacks and are little remembered now. But they were the nearest Britain came to an anarchist threat. They took their philosophy from two counter-culture theorists, the Frenchman Guy Debord and the Belgian poet and teacher, Raoul Vaneigem, who argued that capitalism and Soviet Communism were equally repressive. All organizations were eventually taken over by capitalism which turned everything into a commodity for sale. Even attacks on capitalism could be marketed and sold – witness all those commercially produced Che Guevara badges and posters of Mao. Debord in particular extended his attack from old-style Communists, Western politics, the media and other familiar targets, to the drug-taking hippy culture, modern architecture, even tourism. Once people had so many things they were bored of simply possessing, then capitalism would sell them experiences too, such as foreign travel and nostalgia.

So the 'Situationists', as they called themselves, resolved to attack targets such as shopping centres, museums, and the media, where 'scandalous activity' might provoke repression, and therefore help the scales to drop from people's eyes. They staged a little revolution at Strasbourg University, where they took control of the student union and mocked their contemporaries for merely pretending to be radical, while actually being seduced by 'clothes, discs, scooters, transistors, purple hearts', proving them to be merely conventional consumers. It was a shrewd assessment of what would happen to most radical students.

Debord himself was almost a caricature French intellectual. He was disdainful of Anglo-Saxon culture, committed to fine food, drink, free love and philosophical conversation. His work had been badly translated and spread among students in Britain. At Croydon Art School it had influenced a group calling itself King Mob (after graffiti used by the mob in a London riot in 1790). A belief in anarchy and disorder was spread by this and other groups in magazines and handbills whose scrawled writing and cut-out letters look remarkably like the punk fanzines of the seventies. This is not coincidental. Among the British admirers of the 'Situationists' was the young art student Malcolm McLaren, later the creator of the Sex Pistols. Notes for a film he wrote in 1971, insisting 'the middle classes invented the commodity. It defines our ambitious, our aspirations, our quality of life. Its effects are repression – loneliness – boredom' could have come from an Angry Brigade communiqué of the same time.[48] When McLaren and Vivienne Westwood opened their clothes-to-shock shop in Kings Road, they were producing just the rebel imagery dreamed of by political rebels a few years earlier. Punk in England in the seventies had roots in what happened in Paris in 1968.

Nothing might have followed Debord's calls to revolution in London, had it not been for another European influence, this time dating back to the Spanish Civil War. Anarchists who continued small-scale guerrilla attacks on the Franco regime had developed the key techniques which would later be copied by terrorist groups from the IRA to the Baader Meinhoff group, indeed to al Qaeda – the use of a cell structure to make the group harder to break, and public communiqués, issued to the mainstream media with code-words, to explain their actions. They were a little more serious.

From 1966 the First of May group was carrying out machine-gun attacks and small-scale bombings across Western Europe. Within a few years they were in contact with British admirers, in particular former students from Cambridge and Essex Universities. At Essex, a new and bleak place then, Anna Mendelson, from a girls' high school in Stockport, and Hilary Creek, from a private school in Bristol, had been eagerly watching the 1968 revolt. So over at Cambridge had John Barker, from the posh Haberdashers' Aske's School, a journalist's son, and Jim Greenfield, a lorry driver's son from Widnes in Cheshire, studying medicine. They had studied the 'Situationists' and joined the 'Kim Philby Dining Club' in honour of the University's most famous traitor. All of them committed radicals, they got to know each other through communes and the squatting movement in London, then threw themselves into the Claimants Union, an organization set up to try to extract maximum welfare payments for as many people as possible – and successful enough to have eighty branches across the

UK by 1971. Through a young Scottish anarchist called Stuart Christie, who had spent three years in a Spanish prison for his part in a bungled plot to blow up General Franco, the university quartet – a strikingly handsome group – made contact with the First of May group. With others, including a petty criminal and heroin addict called Jake Prescott and a Vietnam Solidarity Campaign activist called Ian Purdie, they began to make and use bombs.

As well as Biba their targets included the Miss World contest at the Albert Hall, a Spanish airline plane at Heathrow, the Commissioner of the Metropolitan Police, Sir John Waldron, the site of the new Paddington Green police station (where IRA and al Qaeda suspects would later be held), the police computer, a Territorial Army centre in Holloway, the home of the chairman of Ford in Britain, a Rolls-Royce showroom in Paris, and two Conservative cabinet ministers – the trade minister, John Davies, and the employment secretary, Robert Carr, who was struggling to get Heath's trade union legislation through Parliament, and whose white stuccoed home was hit by two bombs, one at the front door and one at the back. In all these attacks, no one was actually killed and just one person, a bystander, was hurt. The Angry Brigade issued regular communiqués under names from films such as *Butch Cassidy and the Sundance Kid* or *The Wild Bunch* and announced that their targets had been selected for execution. They would take on 'High Pigs, Judges, Embassies, Spectacles, Property' they said, and attack 'the shoddy alienating culture pushed out by TV films and magazines . . . the ugly sterility of urban life'. After nine months the Angry Brigade were picked up by the police after a trip to Paris to collect gelignite. Raiding their squats, guns and bomb-making equipment were discovered and all the key players were given long prison sentences. The judge blamed their actions on 'a warped misunderstanding of sociology' and the English revolution was again postponed for lack of interest. The violent fringe of protest would continue, but always over secondary issues, such as Scottish and Welsh nationalism and the Irish 'troubles'.

Though in many ways the Angry Brigade were a non-event they represent the only direct confrontation between revolutionary protest, supposed to be one of the key ingredients of the sixties, and the evolving economy of pleasure which was the sixties' real story. Other left-wing groups, mainly Trotskyists, would argue with each other and march, protest and publish about employment and foreign affairs. Revolutionary protest was only felt in its full force in Ireland.

Bloody Sunday

Heath had worked closely with the Taoiseach (Prime Minister of the Irish Republic), Jack Lynch, and the new Stormont leader, Brian Faulkner, who, as a middle-class businessman by origin, was more in Heath's image than the Old Etonian landowner, Chichester-Clark, had been. Eventually he had even managed to get the leaders of the Republic and Northern Ireland to sit and negotiate at the same table, something that had not happened since Partition in 1920. A measure of the intricate diplomacy required was that Heath served a bottle of Paddys whiskey, from the Republic, at Lynch's end of the table, and Bushmills, made in Ulster, at Faulkner's, with a bottle of Scotch between them, and considered it a significant sign when they both opted for Scotch. Chichester-Clark had simply demanded more and more troops, more and more repression, but Faulkner was open to a political solution. Inside Downing Street, three options were being studied. Northern Ireland could be carved into smaller, more intensely Protestant areas, with the rest surrendered to the Republic, thus effectively getting rid of many Catholics. Or it could be ruled by a power-sharing executive, giving Catholics a role in government. Or, finally, it could be governed jointly by Dublin and London, with its citizens having joint citizenship.

Though Heath rejected the first option because it would be crude and leave too many people on the wrong side of borders and the last one, because the Unionists would refuse it, his second option would be followed by the British governments that followed him. A fourth option, advocated by Enoch Powell who continued his political odyssey by becoming an Ulster Unionist MP, was that the UK should fully incorporate Northern Ireland into British structures and treat it like Kent or Lincolnshire, but this was never taken seriously by Heath. His readiness to discuss other radical solutions gives the lie to the idea that London was pig-headed or unimaginative. But before he had a chance to open serious talks, the collapsing security situation had to be dealt with.

Now politics shrivelled.

If there was one moment when the 'troubles' became unstoppable it was 30 January 1972, 'Bloody Sunday', when troops from the Parachute Regiment killed thirteen unarmed civilians in Londonderry. Ordered in from Belfast to put a stop to stone-throwing Bogside demonstrators, they erupted into the Catholic ghetto and began firing, as it turned out, at unarmed people, many of them teenagers. Some were killed with shots to the back, clearly running away. It was the climax of weeks of escalation. Reluctantly, Heath had introduced internment for suspected terrorists. Reprisals against informers and anti-British feeling meant that the normal process of law was entirely ineffective against the growing IRA threat so, despite the damage it would do to relations with other European countries and the United States, he authorized the arrest and imprisonment in Long Kesh of 337 IRA suspects. In dawn raids, 3,000 troops had found three-quarters of the people they were looking for. Many were old or inactive. Many of the real Provo leaders escaped south of the border. Protests came in from around the world. There was an immediate upsurge in violence, with twenty-one people being killed in three days. The bombings and shootings simply increased in intensity. In the first eight weeks of 1972, forty-nine people were killed and more than 250 seriously injured.

This was the background to the events of 'Bloody Sunday' which, despite endless continuing inquiries and arguments, remains disputed territory. Who shot first? How involved were the IRA in provoking the confrontation? Why did the peaceful march split and stone-throwing begin? Why did the paratroopers suddenly appear to lose control? Whatever the answers, this was an appalling day when Britain's reputation was damaged around the world. In Dublin, ministers reacted with fury and the British embassy was burned to the ground. 'Bloody Sunday' made it far easier for the IRA to raise funds abroad, particularly in the United States. The Provos hit back with a bomb attack on the Parachute Regiment's Aldershot headquarters, killing seven people there – none of them soldiers. The violence led to yet more violence and by degrees to the imposition of direct rule by London and the no-jury Diplock Courts. In July 1973, twenty bombs went off in Belfast, killing eleven people. Mainland Britain became a key Provo target. In October the following year, five people were killed and sixty injured in attacks on Guildford pubs and in December, twenty-one people were killed in pubs in Birmingham city centre.

Assassinations would follow, of Tory MPs such as Airey Neave, Mrs Thatcher's close adviser, and Ian Gow, her popular former parliamentary private secretary. Vocal opponents of the IRA such as Ross McWhirter, would be gunned down and in 1975 a couple in London's Marylebone were taken hostage by an IRA gang in the Balcombe Street Siege. Later IRA 'spectaculars' included the murder of Lord Mountbatten of Burma when boating with his family in Sligo in 1979, and culminated in the attempted assassination of Mrs Thatcher and her cabinet in Brighton in 1984. The 'troubles' in Northern Ireland itself would see endless tit-for-tat car bombings and shootings, routine murder, torture and knee-capping of suspected informers and a quiet steady migration of ambitious people from the province. The security services would break the law in their desperate search for suspected terrorists. 'Dirty protests', involving the smearing of excrement on cell walls and fatal hunger strikes, would be used by republican prisoners in their war against the British State. Within a few years, what had been essentially a policing role by the British Army, separating Prot-estant bigots from rebellious Catholics, had become a full-scale terrorist or counter-insurgency war with all the paranoia, the kidnappings, the apparatus of repression and the corruption of political life that it brings.

In his last attempt to avert what was coming, Heath believed he needed to persuade Dublin to drop its longstanding constitutional claim to the North, and to persuade mainstream Unionists to work with Catholic politicians. He failed, but not through want of trying. His first Secretary of State for Northern Ireland, a new job made necessary by direct rule, was the bluff, amiable Willie Whitelaw. He met Provisional IRA leaders, including Gerry Adams, for face-to-face talks, a desperate gamble which, however, led nowhere: there was no compromise yet available. So, ignoring the IRA, Sunningdale Agree-ment proposed a power-sharing executive, with six Unionists, four SDLP members and one from the non-sectarian Alliance Party. There would also be a Council of Ireland, bringing together politicians from Dublin and from the North, with authority over a limited range of issues, in return for Dublin renouncing authority over Northern

Ireland. It was an ingenious multi-sided deal not so different in essence from what was later proposed by John Major and Tony Blair in the nineties. But too many Unionists were implacably opposed to it, and the moderates were routed at the first 1974 election. Meanwhile, in the Republic, its leader's renunciation of the territorial claim to the North was declared unconstitutional and illegal. Heath concluded, with understandable bitterness: 'Ultimately it was the people of Northern Ireland themselves who threw away the best chance of peace in the blood-stained history of the six counties.'

Authority Undermined

Then the miners struck. At the beginning of 1972 the National Union of Mineworkers began their first national strike since the dark days of the twenties, pursuing a pay demand of 45 per cent. The government, with modest coal stocks, was quickly taken by surprise at the discipline and aggression of the strikers. A young unknown militant, a miner from Woolley colliery, organized some 15,000 of his comrades from across South Yorkshire in a mass picket of the Saltley coke depot, on which Birmingham depended for much of its fuel. Arthur Scargill, a rousing speaker, former Communist Party member and highly ambitious union activist, later described the confrontation with Midlands police at Saltley as 'the greatest day of my life'. Soon he would be catapulted up as agent, then president of the Yorkshire miners. Heath blamed the police for being too soft. Scargill's greatest day was, for the Prime Minister, 'the most vivid, direct and terrifying challenge to the rule of law that I could ever recall emerging from within our own country . . . We were facing civil disorder on a massive scale ' It was clear to Heath that the intention was to bring down the elected government but he decided he could not counter-attack immediately. Confronted with 'the prospect of the country becoming ungovernable, or having to use the armed forces to restore order, which public opinion would never have tolerated', Heath turned to a judge, Lord Wilberforce, for an independent inquiry into miners' wages. From his point of view, it was a terrible mistake. Wilberforce said they should get well over 20 per cent, nearly 50 per cent higher than the average increase. The NUM settled for that, plus extra benefits, in one of the most clear-cut and overwhelming victories over a government that any British trade union has ever enjoyed.

Heath and his ministers knew that they might have to go directly to the country with an appeal about who was in charge but before that, they tried a final round of compromise and negotiation. Triggered by the prospect of unemployment hitting one million, there now follows the famous U-turn which afterwards so scarred Heath's reputation. It went by the ungainly name of 'tripartism', a three-way national agreement on prices and wages, investment and benefits, involving the government, the TUC and the CBI. The Industry Act of 1972 gave a Tory government unprecedented powers of industrial intervention, gleefully cheered by Tony Benn as 'spadework for socialism'.[49] There was much earnest wooing of moderate trade union leaders. Money, effort and organization went into Job Centres as unemployment rose steadily towards a million. The industrialists did as much as they could, sitting on yet more committees when in truth they might have been more usefully employed trying to run their companies. The unions, however, had the bit between their teeth. By first refusing to acknowledge Heath's industrial relations court 'as really legitimately a law of the land' and then refusing to negotiate seriously until he repealed the Act, they made the breakdown of this last attempt at consensual economics inevitable. Within a year the CBI too would be calling for it to be scrapped.

By now Heath had leaned so far to try to win the unions over that he was behaving like a Wilson-era socialist. He was reinstating planning, particularly regional planning. He was bailing out failing companies such as Upper Clyde Shipbuilders, partly because of the work-in discussed elsewhere – something Heath later believed was a mistake. He was offering the unions a privileged place in the running of the nation. From his perspective this was a last attempt to run the economy as a joint enterprise of British patriots, in which individual roles – trade union leader, company director, party politician – took second place behind a general belief in the common good, the wider politics of 'Buy British'. Individuals followed the logic of their own interests instead. Trade union leaders had got their jobs by promising their members higher wages and better conditions. They could hardly be blamed for doing everything they could within the law to carry out the role they had been given. Industrialists, similarly, would live or die by profit margin and return to investors. They were not auxiliary politicians. Thatcherites later criticized Heath's government for doing things which a government ought not to do, and not doing things it ought to. Governments should not try to run businesses, or do the wage bargaining of trade union officials and companies for them. They should not tell factories where to go. They should not attempt to control prices.

All these things, said Tories of ten years later, were better left to the market. What government should do instead was set tough and clear rules by which the other forces in society had to live. Government should ensure low inflation by controlling the supply of money. It should enforce strong laws against intimidation or law-breaking at work. It should allow firms that fail to suffer the consequences. Overall, the Thatcher critique has been applauded, not simply in Britain but around the world, and Heath's tripartism, or 'corporatism' has been derided and forgotten. Yet he started with an almost identical view to her later one. He had been an enthusiast for letting the market decide prices. He promised not to let lame ducks survive. At the time, Thatcher was his fervent supporter and even her outrider Sir Keith Joseph only converted to a full free-market philosophy in the middle of the seventies, after the fall of the Heath government in which he had been a notably high-spending minister. The argument between the two sides of the Conservative Party was not one between toffs and the hard-nosed middle classes, or 'ordinary people', as many Thatcherites would later claim. Heath was no toff and his nose, though famously Concorde large, was as hard as any.

Heath was blown off course by a political version of the impossible storm that later wrecked his beloved yacht *Morning Cloud*. Much of the country was simply more left-wing than it was later. The unions, having defeated Wilson and Castle, were more self-confident than ever before or since. Many industrial workers, living in still-bleak towns far away from the glossy pop world of the big cities, did seem underpaid and left behind. After the Macmillan, Douglas-Home and Wilson experiences, politicians did not have the automatic level of respect that they had enjoyed when Heath had first entered the Commons. Heath always argued that he was forced to try consensus politics because in the seventies the alternative policy, the squeeze of mass unemployment which arrived in the Thatcher years, would simply not have been accepted by the country. And given the very rocky ride Mrs Thatcher had a full ten years later, after industrial and some social breakdown had softened the way for her radicalism, he was surely right.

What finally finished off the Heath government was the short war between Israel and Egypt in October 1973, the Yom Kippur War. Israel's swift and decisive victory was a humiliation for the Arab world and it struck back, using oil. OPEC, the organization of the oil-producing countries dominated by the Saudis, had seen the price of oil rising on world markets for some time. They decided to cut supplies to the West each month until Israel handed back its territorial gains and allowed the Palestinians their own state. There would be a total embargo on Israel's most passionate supporters, the United States and the Netherlands. And those countries which were allowed oil would pay steadily more for it. In fact, prices rose fourfold. It was a global economic shock, shovelling further inflation into the industrialized world, but in Britain it arrived with special force. The miners put in yet another huge pay claim, which would have added half as much again to many pay-packets. Despite an appeal by its leader, the moderate Joe Gormley, the NUM executive rejected a 13 per cent pay increase and voted to ballot for another national strike. These were the days, just, before North Sea oil and gas were being produced commercially. Britain could survive high oil prices, even shortages, for a while. The country could hold out against a coal strike, for a while. But both together added up to what the Chancellor, Barber, called the greatest economic crisis since the war. It certainly compared to that of 1947. Coal stocks had not been built up in preparation. Now a whole series of panic measures were introduced.

Plans were made for petrol rationing and coupons printed and distributed. The national speed limit was cut by 20 miles per hour to 50 miles per hour to save fuel. Then in January 1974 came the announcement of a three-day working week. Ministers solemnly urged citizens to share baths and brush their teeth in the dark. Television, by now the nation's sucky-sweet, was ended at 10.30 p.m. each evening. It is remembered as the darkest day (literally) in the story of mid-seventies Britain, and it was an embarrassing time in many ways. Yet it also gave millions an enjoyable frisson, the feeling of taking a holiday from everyday life. The writer Robert Elms recalls that though 'this proud nation had been reduced to a shabby shambles, somewhere between a strife-torn

South American dictatorship and a gloomy Soviet satellite, Bolivia meets Bulgaria, a banana republic with a banana shortage . . . The reality of course is that almost everybody absolutely loved it. They took to the three-day week with glee. They took terrible liberties.'⁵⁰

Heath and his ministers struggled to try to find a solution to the miners' claim, though the climate was hardly helped when Mick McGahey, the legendary Scottish Communist mineworkers' leader, asked by Heath what he really wanted, answered 'to bring down the government'. Much messing about with intermediaries and many mixed messages, not least from the government's own Pay Board, ensured that no effective compromise could be found. When the miners voted, 81 per cent were for striking, including those in some of the most traditionally moderate areas in the country. In February 1974 Heath asked the Queen to dissolve Parliament and went to the country on the election platform he had prepared two years earlier: 'Who governs?' The country's answer, perhaps taking the question more literally than Heath had hoped, was 'Not you, mate.'

Harold Wilson had expected the Tories to win again, and began the campaign in a depressed mood. A year earlier in Opposition he had prepared his own answer to inflation and the unions, the so called Social Compact, or Social Contract. Agreed jointly between the union leaders and the Labour shadow cabinet, it was essentially a return to the politics of the forties, with price controls, a complex system of food subsidies, direct redistribution of wealth, controls on housing and investment and the end of the Tory union laws. In return for this Attlee-age manifesto from the politicians, the unions gave vague promises of voluntary pay restraint. It was a one-way deal but it was in Wilson's interests to pretend that he could find practical agreements where Heath could not. It was in the unions' interests to pretend they were signing up to a new era, if that would help expel the Tories and destroy their legislation. Outside observers saw it more plainly as a recipe for inflation which also offered the TUC a privileged place in government in return for very little.

But what was the alternative? The three-day week was not, it later turned out, quite the economic disaster it seemed. Industry had maintained almost all production – which shows how inefficient five-day working must have been – and relatively few jobs had been lost. But politics is half symbol, and Heath's authority had gone. In the

election campaign a public fed up of chaos and desperately looking for
good news clutched at the Social Contract. Wilson was able to appear
as the calm bringer of reason and order. This time, he was lucky as
well. A slew of bad economic figures arrived during the campaign.
Enoch Powell, Heath's ancient nemesis, suddenly announced that he
was quitting the Conservatives over their failure to offer the public a
referendum on Europe, and called on everyone to vote Labour. A
mistake by the Pay Board suggested that the miners were in fact
relatively lower paid than had been recognized. And a surge in Liberal
support, which took them from single-figure support to the backing
of a quarter of those voting, turned out to help Labour more than
the Tories. All this helped produce a late surge in Wilson's favour.
By the end of the campaign he had recovered some his old chirpiness
and bounce. Having decided that Heath should not rule, however,
the country seemed unsure that Wilson should either. Though Labour
had won the most seats, 301 against the Conservatives' 297, no party
had an overall majority. Heath hung on, trying to do a deal with
the Liberal leader Jeremy Thorpe, who had 14 MPs, but eventually
conceded defeat. Rather fatter, greyer and more personally conservative than he had been ten years earlier, Harold Wilson was back.

So Mick McGahey and friends had brought down the Heath
government, with a little help from the oil-toting Saudi Royal Family,
the Liberals and Enoch Powell. A more bizarre coalition of interests is
hard to imagine. Edward Heath's three and three-quarter years in
Number Ten will be remembered for the three-day week, a rare
moment when politics actually shakes everyday life out of its routine;
and for taking Britain into Europe. But other important changes
happened on his watch, too. The school-leaving age was at last raised
to sixteen. To cope with international currency mayhem caused by
that Nixon decision to suspend convertibility, the old imperial sterling
area finally went in 1972. The Pill was made freely available on the
National Health Service. Local government was radically reorganized,
with no fewer than 800 English councils disappearing and huge new
authorities, much disliked, being created in their place. Heath defended
this on the basis that the old Victorian system could not cope with
'the growth of car ownership and of suburbia, which were undermining the distinction between town and country'. Many others saw it as
dreary big-is-better dogma. There was more of that when responsibility

for NHS hospitals was taken away from hundreds of local boards and passed to new regional and area health authorities, at the suggestion of a new cult then just emerging – management consultants.

Political cynicism had been provoked in the fifties and sixties by the behaviour of the cliques who ran the country. By the seventies it was driven more by a sense of alienation. To many older Britons these were years of out-of-control change. Much of the loathing of Heath on the right of politics came from British membership of the Common Market which seemed the ultimate emblem of this rage for bigger and untraditional systems. Decimalization was almost as big a change to daily life. Though the original decision had been taken in 1965 during the first Wilson government, the disappearance in 1971 of a coinage going back to Anglo-Saxon times was widely blamed on Heath. Away flew the florins and half-crowns, halfpennies, farthings and sixpences, away went all the intricate triple-column mathematics of pounds, shillings and pence; and in came an unfamiliar if more rational decimal currency. Where would this end? Negotiators in Europe specifically fought to maintain the British pint measures in beer and milk, and the mile continued to keep the kilometre at bay. But in the seventies, the familiar seemed everywhere in retreat.

Wilson

At least Wilson was familiar. His February election victory meant he was governing without a Commons majority. He was trying to do so at a time when the economy was still shaking with the effect of the oil price shock, with inflation raging, unemployment rising and the pound under almost constant pressure. Further, the fragile and implausible Social Contract now had to be tested. Almost the first thing Labour did was to settle with the miners for double what Heath had thought possible. The chances of the new government enjoying easy popularity were nil, though at least an Opposition so internally divided between bruised Conservatives, Liberals, Nationalists and Northern Irish Unionists was unlikely to combine often to defeat it.

The new Chancellor, Denis Healey, introduced an emergency Budget a few weeks after the election, followed by another in the autumn, during which he raised income tax to 83 per cent at the top rate, or 98 per cent for unearned income, a level so eyewateringly high it was used against Labour for a generation to come. In the spirit of the Social Contract Healey also increased help for the poorest, with higher pensions and housing and food subsidies. He was trying to deliver for the unions, as Wilson did in abolishing the Conservative employment legislation. For the time being Heath remained as Tory leader, despite some grumbling from the party. He was convinced that before long Wilson would have to call a second election and his chance for revenge would arrive. In October, however, the second election confirmed the earlier verdict, with Labour gaining eighteen seats and a precarious but quite workable overall majority of three.

The fetid atmosphere of Wilson's new government was like that of the mid-sixties, only more so. Marcia Williams still had him mesmerized. As one young Number Ten aide recalled, her dramatic and sometimes destructive power 'was not only exercised through her bewitching domination of the prime minister himself. Once launched against any human obstacle or perceived personal enemy, her frenzied tirades were very impressive and virtually ungovernable.'[51] It was alleged that she would swear and curse like a trooper at Wilson, storm out of dinners and meetings, and threaten him with terrible revenge if he crossed her. Some sources claimed that in Opposition, she had locked all his personal papers in a garage and refused to let him see them. Desperate to write his account of the 1964–70 governments, Wilson had been forced to team up with her brother Tony, break into her garage, and steal them back, although only the three of them would know if this were true. Now, she gave him a new problem when a press furore broke about land deals. The brother, a geologist, had bought slag heaps and quarries and then moved into land speculation, falling in with dodgy Midlands businessmen. There was a forged letter purporting to come from Wilson. There was no evidence that Marcia knew of the deal, but the close connections between Marcia and her brother, and the Prime Minister, began a media frenzy which prefigured many of those directed at the Labour ministers of the nineties and early 2000s. Wilson stood by his inner circle while the attacks rose in intensity, eventually making Williams a peeress, Lady Falkender. This was described by one of Wilson's biographers as 'a magnificently arrogant gesture, contemptuous of almost everybody'[52] and the whole experience broke for ever his once-good relations with the press. The old rumours about links with Russian intelligence and affairs resurfaced and the mood of bitterness and paranoia inside Number Ten was as grim as anything in the equally harassed administrations of John Major and Tony Blair.

In another way, however, Wilson had changed. He interfered far less and seemed less worried by the manoeuvrings of his ministers. He wasn't planning to stay long. There are many separate records of his private comments about retiring at sixty, after another two years in power. If he had not privately decided finally that he would go in 1976, he certainly acted as if he had. The question of who would succeed him, Jenkins or Callaghan, Healey or even Benn, had become one about the direction of the Labour government, rather than a personal threat to Harold Wilson, so there was less rancour around the cabinet table. Wilson was visibly older and more tired. He seems likely to have known about the early stages of Alzheimer's, which would wreak a devastating toll on him in retirement. He forgot facts, confused issues and repeated himself. For a man whose memory and wit had been so important, this must have been a grim burden. There is therefore no need to assume that dark forces, some nether world of MI5 plotters and right-wing extremists, finally removed him from power with threats of blackmail and dirty tricks.

Wilson himself was as fascinated as ever by Security Service plotting and had Marcia Williams dig out files on Jeremy Thorpe's lover, Norman Scott, to try to show that he was being framed by the South African secret service, BOSS. At other times he would suggest Israel's Mossad were after him. In a famous interview given to two BBC reporters, Barry Penrose and Roger Courtiour, after his retirement, he claimed that right-wing officers in the Security Service had been plotting against him. Wilson's state of mind is vividly evoked by his fantastical language to them: 'I see myself as the big fat spider in the corner of the room. Sometimes I speak when I'm asleep. You should both listen. Occasionally when we meet I might tell you to go to Charing Cross Road and kick a blind man standing on the corner. That blind man may tell you something, lead you somewhere.' The Cecil King plot of 1967 and later memoirs by a wild MI5 man show that Wilson's fears were not completely groundless, but this sounds like the raving of a deluded old man.

The Stairs Were on Fire

If Roy Jenkins had in many ways been the most important minister during the mid-sixties, it was Denis Healey who dominated public perceptions of Labour in the mid-seventies. As a Chancellor of the Exchequer during the worst economic storm of post-war times, through both the Wilson and Callaghan governments, he rivalled each of them as a public icon. His scarlet face, huge eyebrows and rough tongue were endlessly caricatured and mimicked, above all by the TV impressionist Mike Yarwood, who invented 'you silly billy' as Healey's catchphrase, one quickly taken up by the Chancellor himself. Healey was one of the most widely read, cultured, intelligent and self-certain politicians of modern times, whose early Communism, active war service and vast range of international contacts helped mulch and decorate his famous beyond-politics 'hinterland'. But there was little poetry, relaxation or fun about the job he took up in 1974 and would hold, through near-farcical crises and grim headlines, for the next five years. He described the economy he had inherited from Heath and Barber as 'like the Augean stables'. Much of his energy would be thrown into dealing with the newly unstable world economy, with floating currencies and inflation-shocked governments. In effect, after the great devaluation argument of the first Wilson administrations, this one was quietly devaluing all the time, as the pound sank against the dollar.

Where were the levers of control? Healey was taxing and cutting as much as he dared but his only real hope was to control inflation by controlling wages. Wilson insisted that an incomes policy must be voluntary. After the torture and defeat of Heath there must be no going back to legal restraints. The unions, under the leadership of men who had risen as shop stewards in the great revolt of the fifties and sixties, the Spanish Civil War veteran Jack Jones, the wily and cynical Hugh Scanlon, and the grammar school boy and ex-Communist Len Murray, became increasingly worried that rampant inflation might destroy Labour and bring back the Tories. So for a while the Social Contract did deliver fewer strikes. From 1974 to 1975, the number of days lost to strikes halved, and then halved again the following year. Contrary to popular myth, the seventies were not all about mass meetings and walk-outs. After Heath had been beaten, the real trouble did not start again until 1978–9. But the other half of the Social Contract was meant to deliver lower wage settlements and that was an utter failure. Despite Labour delivering on its side of the bargain, by the early months of 1975 the going rate for increases was already 30 per cent, a third higher than inflation. By June inflation was up to 23 per cent, and wage settlements even further ahead. The unions suggested a new deal of a cash limit of an extra £6 a week for most workers. The government did introduce an element of compulsion, but targeted employers who offered too much, not workers who demanded too much.

Yet persuading people not to make deals about pay is extremely difficult. It cannot last long in a free society. There will always be special cases, and one special case inspires the next. Healey reckoned two-thirds of his time was spent trying to deal with the inflationary effects of free collective bargaining and the rest with the distortions caused by his own pay policy. As he reflected later: 'Adopting a pay policy is rather like jumping out of a second floor window: no one in his senses would do it unless the stairs were on fire. But in postwar Britain the stairs have always been on fire.'[53] By refusing to allow companies to pass on inflationary wage increases as higher prices, and by endless haggling with union leaders who were themselves alarmed about the fate of the country, Healey did manage to squeeze inflation downwards. He believed that if the unions had kept their promises it would have been down to single figures by the autumn of 1975.

In all this, Healey was under constant pressure to show that he was delivering for socialism. He could not spend more. So he sent what signals he could by skewing the tax system dramatically against higher earners, concentrating any tax cuts on the worse off. Though notorious for warning that he would make the rich 'howl with anguish' and often misquoted as promising to squeeze the rich 'until the pips squeak', Healey argued that it was the only way of making the country fairer. He never accepted the Conservative argument that high taxes stopped people working harder and blamed Britain's poor industrial performance instead on low investment in industry, poor training and bad management. A villain and bogeyman for many in the middle classes, Healey did at least suffer from his own policies: 'As a result of my tax changes and my determination to prevent ministerial salaries from rising as fast as the pay norm, my own real take-home pay as Chancellor fell to only half what I had been earning as Defence Secretary, although I was working harder and longer.'

Referendum

Wilson carried out his promised renegotiation of Britain's terms of entry to the EEC and then put the result to the country in the Benn-inspired 1975 referendum. The renegotiation was largely a sham but the referendum was a rare political triumph for that bleak decade in the story of Westminster. On the continent, the reopened talks were understood to be more for Wilson's benefit than anything else. Helmut Schmidt, the new German Chancellor, who travelled to London to help win round the Labour conference, regarded it all as a successful cosmetic operation. Wilson had needed to persuade people he was putting a different deal to the country than the one Heath had won. This he was able to do, though, when the referendum actually arrived, Wilson's old evasiveness returned and he mumbled vaguely in support, rather than actively or enthusiastically making the European case.

There were plenty of others to do it for him. To preserve longer-term party unity, he had allowed anti-Brussels cabinet ministers to speak from the 'No' platform and Barbara Castle, Benn, Peter Shore and Michael Foot were among those who did so, in alliance with Enoch Powell, the Reverend Ian Paisley, the Scottish Nationalists and others. But the 'Yes' campaign could boast most of the Labour cabinet, with Roy Jenkins at the front, plus most of the Heath team, and the popular Liberal leader Jeremy Thorpe. It seemed to many people a fight between wild-eyed ranters, the outlandish and the discontented, on the one hand and sound chaps on the other hand, men and women with that curious but apparently essential British quality 'bottom'. More important, perhaps, was the bias of business and the press. A CBI survey of company chairmen found that out of 419 interviewed, just four were in favour of leaving the Community.[54] Almost all the newspapers were in favour of staying in, including the *Daily Mail*, *Daily Telegraph* and *Daily Express*. So was every Anglican bishop.

A fight between the Establishment and its critics was funded accordingly. Britain in Europe, leading the 'Yes' campaign, outspent the 'No' camp by more than ten to one. In this grossly unequal struggle, both sides used scare stories. Britain in Europe constantly warned of a huge loss of jobs if the country left the Community. The 'No' camp warned of huge rises in food prices. Yet this was also an almost carnival-like participatory argument of a kind post-war Britain has rarely known. There were meetings, several thousand strong, night after night around the country – proper meetings with hecklers and humour. Despite miserable weather, including a showering of June snow, there were stunts of all kinds and the country seemed covered with posters. The spectacle of politicians from rival parties who normally attacked one another sitting down together agreeing was a tonic to those watching.

There were good television arguments, notably between Jenkins and Benn. And on the Labour side there were awkward moments when rhetoric got too fierce, and Wilson had to intervene to rebuke warring ministers. Even Margaret Thatcher was out campaigning, for Brussels of course, in a spectacularly hideous jumper with the flags of the member states knitted across her breasts. In the end, to the simple question, 'Do you think that the United Kingdom should stay in the European Community (The Common Market)?', 68.3 per cent, or around 17 million people, said 'Yes' and 32.8 per cent, some 8.5 million, said 'No'. Only Shetland and the Western Isles of Scotland voted 'No'. Symbolically, Jenkins thought, the sun came out and there followed a baking, almost cloudless few weeks. Benn instantly conceded full defeat though privately considered the vote 'some achievement considering we had absolutely no real organisation, no newspapers, nothing'. Powell, however, warned that the decision was only 'provisional' and might be reopened in the future. As so often, his was a lone voice.

More than thirty years later, the biggest question both about Heath's triumph in engineering British membership and then about the Labour referendum, is whether the British were told the full story and truly understood the supranational organization they were signing up to. Ever since, many of those among the 8.5 million who voted against, and younger people who share their view, have suggested that Heath and Jenkins and the rest lied to the country, at least by omission. Had it been properly explained that Europe's law and institutions would sit above the ancient Westminster Parliament, it is said, they would never have agreed. What is the truth? The Britain in Europe campaigners can point to speeches and advertisements which directly mention loss of sovereignty. One of the latter read: 'Forty million people died in two European wars this century. Better lose a little national sovereignty than a son or a daughter.' Yet both in Parliament and in the referendum campaign, the full consequences for national independence were mumbled, not spoken clearly enough. Geoffrey Howe, as he then was, who drafted Heath's European Communities Bill, later admitted that it could have been more explicit about lost sovereignty. Heath talked directly about the 'ever closer union' of the peoples of Europe but was never precise about the effect on British law, as compared, say, to Lord Denning who said the European treaty could be compared to 'an incoming tide. It flows into the estuaries and rivers. It cannot be held back.' Hugo Young, the journalist and historian who studied the campaign in great detail, wrote: 'I traced no major document or speech that said in plain terms that national sovereignty would be lost, still less one that categorically promoted the European Community for its single most striking characteristic: that it was an institution positively designed to curb the full independence of the nation-state.'

There were, of course, the explicit warnings about lost sovereignty delivered by the 'No' campaigners among the more populist arguments about food prices. They came above all from Enoch Powell, Michael Foot and Tony Benn. Powell's language can be gauged from a speech he gave to political journalists in the Commons while the Bill was being debated. He lamented that the Commons was 'perishing by its own hand. Week by week, month by month, the House of Commons votes to divest itself of what it had gained through a length of time not much shorter than the history of England itself.'[55] Foot, though recovering from an operation and so partly out of action, wrote in *The Times* that the British parliamentary system had been made farcical and unworkable. Historians, he said, would be amazed 'that the British people were urged at such a time to tamper irreparably with their most precious institution; to see it circumscribed and contorted and elbowed off the centre of the stage.'[56] Benn, confiding to his diary his reaction on the possibility of a Europe-wide passport, showed how much the left's instincts could chime with those of the right-wing opponents of European change: 'That really hit me in the guts . . .

Like metrication and decimalisation, this really strikes at our national identity.' All these arguments were made in the press, despite its overall bias, and repeatedly in public meetings and broadcast debates.

So it was not as if people were not told. The truth revealed by opinion polls is that sovereignty as an issue did not concern the public nearly as much as jobs and food prices. By later standards the position of Parliament was not taken terribly seriously in public debates. It may be that sovereignty is always of absorbing interest to a minority – the more history-minded, politically aware – and of less interest to the rest, except when a loss of sovereignty directly affects daily life and produces resented laws. In the seventies, Britain's political class was not highly respected, and Europe seemed to offer a glossier, richer future. Though the pro-Community majority in business and politics did not strive to ram home the huge implications of membership, they did not deceitfully hide the political nature of what was happening, either. It was just that, when the referendum was held, people cared less. The argument would return, screaming, demanding to be heard, fifteen years later.

Power Ages

As to the rest of Wilson's short final government, much of his energy was spent on foreign affairs. Despite American disapproval the Labour government began the final withdrawal from east of Suez, giving up any pretensions of British influence in the Far East. The Empire was formally over. A scattering of individual outposts and impoverished islands too weak to enjoy independence were all that was left, a few last governors in places like Hong Kong and Bermuda. In the Middle East, British pens in British fingers had drawn many of the lines on the map – Transjordan, the new state of Israel, Iraq – and all that uncertainty went. It went after guerrilla war and partition among the lemon groves of Cyprus, after gruesome murders of British soldiers in the Holy Land, a nasty little colonial war in Aden which left behind a Marxist and Soviet satellite. It left an unstable and unpopular king in Iraq, soon overthrown by military coup, leading to the regime of Saddam Hussein. In Iran, the British-backed Shah was many years later overturned by Ayatollah Khomeni's Islamic revolution. The decades that followed have been awful ones for the region, marked by major and minor wars, the regular use of torture, assassination, repression, censorship and suicide bombings. The Middle East, rich in oil and history, has become the world's most dangerous zone; and many of the decisions that made it so dangerous originated in Europe, including London, as well as in Washington.

There remained that strange half-life empire called the British Commonwealth, an illogical world-straddling organization that embraced republics such as India, despotisms and democracies, slavish admirers of Britain and frank opponents of London, as well as all the former white dominions which retained their loyalty to the Crown. The Commonwealth was not a coherent policy-setting organization, particularly after Britain decided to join the European Economic Community. Her members often had diametrically opposed trading interests. When it came to defence, some were firmly non-aligned, even at times leaning to Moscow or Beijing, while others such as the Australians looked increasingly to the United States not Britain. Time and again, on issues such as apartheid South Africa, or Rhodesia, or the misbehaviour of newly independent rulers, or questions of migration, the Commonwealth would fracture, or embarrass London. Lacking an army, trade agreements or common views, it seemed to many a pointless organization, fit for nothing more than acrimonious summits and regular athletic Games which functioned as a low-rent version of the real ones, the Olympics. Was it kept going merely out of sentimentality or to give the Queen something to do? At least it has done no harm and kept different parts of the world in contact. Outside football, it is also the last English-speaking worldwide organization not dominated by the Americans.

Wilson spent much of his domestic energy on resisting the attempt by Tony Benn (by now his bugbear) to introduce a socialist economy via the National Enterprise Board. Benn hoped that this would be a generously funded body which would take over a large range of companies, successful and unsuccessful, bringing state ownership and direction into the heart of the economy. Wilson, by now clearly to the right of his party, was equally determined that this should not happen. He had his way. When it eventually arrived, the NEB was a weak, ill-funded repository for lost causes, British Leyland in particular. Benn's enthusiasm for workers' control continued to amuse and

British cool?
The actor David
Hemmings in
Swinging London,
1966, and the Kinks,
struggling with
trousers and ruffles.

The Liberal Hour: the flamboyant MP Leo Abse (*left*) was one of the Labour backbenchers who led reform, in his case to legalize homosexual acts between men.

Below. In 1971, the editors of the underground magazine *Oz* were prosecuted for obscenity. A libidinous cartoon Rupert Bear was at the centre of the case; the significance of the whip is unclear.

Violence becomes a theme: Catholic demonstrators (*above*) in Londonderry/Derry after the killing of thirteen civil-rights marchers on 'Bloody Sunday', 1972, and (*right*) the nearest Britain came to left-wing terrorists, the Angry Brigade, outside the Old Bailey, a few months later.

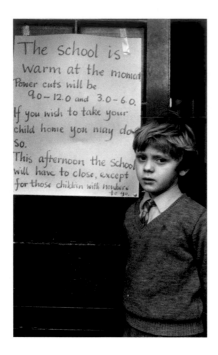

When the country failed:
a boy stands outside his school,
closed because of a lack of fuel
during the miners' strike of 1972.
The miners (*below*) were badly paid,
and went on to humiliate Heath
and the Conservatives.

Opposite page. It's the beans, stupid.
In the 1975 referendum on British
membership of the European
Common Market, both sides
campaigned more about the cost of
food than about the constitutional
implications of surrendering
sovereignty.

Two men as influential as
most prime ministers.
Enoch Powell (*left*),
opponent of immigration,
and (*below*) Denis Healey,
chancellor during Britain's
economic storm, making
a characteristic point to
his opponents.

Punk gets cheeky: Vivienne Westwood (centre), Chrissie Hynde (left) and Jordan advertise Westwood's King's Road punk shop Sex, in 1976.

But nothing was sexy about the economy: rubbish piles up in London during the 'winter of discontent', 1979

Michael Foot, the most literate and radical man to lead Labour,
points in the general direction of the political wilderness. But his harshest
critics, the SDP's Gang of Four, failed to return to power, either.
Bill Rodgers, David Owen and Roy Jenkins plot over a glass or two in 1982.
The fourth member of the gang was not, as this photograph below suggests,
surprisingly well-endowed but was Mrs Shirley Williams.

infuriate most of the other ministers and civil servants he worked with and he confided in his diary that he felt as if he was 'trying to swim up the Niagara Falls'. He was particularly keen about cooperatives and took up the cause of the Meriden motorcycle factory, struggling to survive under workers' control. He was much excited by what he took to be its Chinese Communist atmosphere: 'I described our industrial policy, and then they sang "For he's a jolly good fellow" which was very touching.'

It wasn't only Wilson who thought Benn's socialist affection for cooperatives and nationalization was out of time. Jack Jones pinned him down over lunch at the Westminster restaurant Locket's to warn: 'Nationalization is no good. People don't want it. Management in nationalized industries is very bad.' Benn explained that he wanted to take over other firms, including the *Scottish Daily News* and challenged Jones about British Leyland itself. The fiery trade unionist, to Benn's astonishment, suggested selling it off to General Motors. The final phase of nationalization produced little except heartache, though the struggling Chrysler car factory at Linwood in Scotland was kept going for a while. These were truly the last days for planning and public control, which had been so widespread immediately after the war. We should see Benn as a traditionalist in this, as much as a radical. Later Healey would brutally sum up his contribution as a minister to British industry. There were only two monuments to Benn in power, he said: a uranium mine in Namibia he had authorized as energy secretary, which helped support apartheid; and Concorde, used by rich people on expense accounts and subsidized by poorer taxpayers. The only planning agreement actually existing when he left office was the old Farm Price Review 'chaired in my time by the Duke of Northumberland'.

Monuments for this last Wilson government were few. One was the radical refashioning of the failing pensions system by Barbara Castle and her team, with the State Earnings Related Pension, or Serps, which linked pension to rises in earnings or prices, whichever was higher. It was notably generous, particularly to women whose pension rights had been whittled away by years of caring for children or elderly relatives, and in allowing people to claim a pension based on their best twenty years of earnings, not necessarily their final earnings. Castle had won a reputation as a battler for feminism much earlier, in 1968 during the celebrated women's strike at Ford's plant in Dagenham. The women were operating sewing-machines to upholster car seats but were paid only 85 per cent of men's wages for doing the same job. After Castle intervened directly, the company closed most of the gap, and other women took action round the country too. She had also intervened to stop the Commons voting male MPs better pensions than female ones. Though Castle always jibed at being called a feminist, and had underestimated the cost of Serps, so that the earnings link would eventually be broken again by the Conservatives to keep the price down, it was a rare civilizing reform which stuck, at least for a decade.

Meanwhile Wilson, quietly preparing a scandalous resignation honours list for his cronies, and muttering about moles, plots and the possible activities of South African and British agents, left future British governments with one final gift. Working as secretively as Attlee he authorized a vastly expensive modernization and replacement of Britain's nuclear deterrent Chevaline, the cost of which would rise from a planned £24m to more than £1,000m within a few years. He then retired as he had always said he would, at sixty, leaving much of his cabinet utterly astonished and London awash with rumours. Power ages, as well as corrupts and Roy Jenkins speculated that perhaps he had faked his birth certificate and had been ten years older than he admitted all along. It would certainly have explained his precocious rise and precocious retirement. But Wilson was still wily enough to give his preferred successor Callaghan ('I'm making way for an older man') a tip-off which helped him steal a march on the rest, including Healey, who only heard the news from Wilson in the gents toilet before the cabinet meeting when he formally announced it. Wilson would retire to see his reputation sink steadily downwards as his memory started to go. For such a pugnacious and fundamentally decent man, whatever his political failures, it was a sad way to subside.

Peasants Revolt: One, the Right

The underlying political story of the middle and later seventies would not, however, be played out mainly in Parliament. It is the story of how, across the quivering body of a profoundly sick country, two new rival forces emerged to fight for the future. The first came from the right.

In the middle of June 1974, something unusual had happened. A politician said sorry. He did not say sorry for something in his personal life, an error of judgement or even a failed policy. He said sorry for Everything. He said sorry for what had happened to Britain since 1945, and his party's role in that, and his role in that party. The serial apologist was a haggard, anguished-looking man. The son of a rich London businessman, he had risen to become housing and then health minister, and had been until then a conventional-looking Tory. Under Macmillan he had ordered the smashing down of old terraces for new tower blocks. Under Heath he had spent heavily on a bigger bureaucracy for the NHS and higher social security levels. Now Sir Keith Joseph was quite literally wringing his hands and rolling his eyes with mortification. There had been thirty years of interventions, good intentions and disappointments, thirty years of socialism under both Labour and the Tories: 'I must take my blame for following too many of the fashions.'

Joseph's conversion to free-market, small-state economics had the force of a religious experience. Crucial to it would be controlling the amount of money in the economy to keep out inflation, which meant squeezing how much was borrowed and spent by the State. He had joined the Tories in the early fifties but had not been a Conservative, he said: 'I had thought that I was a Conservative but now I see that I was not really one at all.' This kind of thinking would lead within five years to the Thatcher revolution, and the wholesale rejection of the Heath years, taking the economic ideas of intellectuals who featured earlier in this history right into the centre of British public life. Other fellow travellers were professors, Americans or a few Powellite Tories outside the mainstream of the party. But Joseph was different, a former cabinet minister with close and direct experience of government. With his Centre for Policy Studies, he was the rain-maker, the storm-bringer, the Old Testament prophet denouncing his tribe.

Joseph argued that Britain by the mid-seventies had a fundamental choice to make between a socialist siege economy or a breakaway into proper liberal capitalism – in effect, Benn or Joseph. He could not have formed his ideas without the libertarian and monetarist thinkers of the fifties and sixties, men we met earlier. During the Tories' years in opposition from 1964 to 1970 he had educated himself in free-market economics and was soon using as his speechwriter the violently spoken, irrepressible Alfred Sherman, an East End boy from a left-wing family who had fought as a machine-gunner in the Spanish Civil War before swinging right round later and becoming an insistent right-wing critic of the British way. It was well said of Sherman that by the fifties his enthusiasm for the free market 'put him as much on the fringes of Macmillan's Britain as Communism had put him on the edge of politics in Neville Chamberlain's Britain'.[57] But to Sherman's disappointment, when Joseph returned to office in 1970 as Secretary for Health and Social Security, his radicalism went into hiding again, he forgot his enthusiasm for introducing more private money into health, and Sherman took to describing him dismissively as 'a good man fallen among civil servants'.

But the defeat of 1974 had shaken Joseph. With other monetarists he began a thorough rethink of the Heath years, culminating in a shadow cabinet post-mortem, when they argued that the early radicalism of 1970–1 had been right, and the subsequent U-turn a disaster. Heath blankly refused to listen, or at any rate to heed, the attack. Heath's haughty assessment in his autobiography was that Joseph 'had resumed a friendship with a person called Alfred Sherman, a former communist, and undergone what he liked to call "a conversion" as a result ... [this] failed to cut any ice with the great majority of his colleagues, though we did them the courtesy of listening.' In fact, many Tories were beginning to listen. With Joseph were Geoffrey Howe and the quiet, watchful figure of Margaret Thatcher. Early on, Howe warned, 'I am not at all sure about Margaret. Many of her economic prejudices are certainly sound. But she is inclined to be rather too dogmatic for my liking on sensitive matters like education and might actually retard the case by simplification.'[58] There were other new radicals, such as the Powellite Tory MP John Biffen, the young economics writer Nigel Lawson and a crowd of journalists and academics.

Here was an intellectual analysis, hard and uncompromising, which excited a generation of new recruits to the party, while it repelled Tories of the comfortable Macmillan persuasion. Macmillan himself said of Joseph that he was 'the only boring Jew I've ever known' and later there would be much snide muttering about the men Thatcher learned from and worked with – Hayek, Sherman, Joseph, Lawson and Friedman. The truth was that Jews were prominent in intellectual thinking on the right, as on the left, bringing opposite lessons to Britain from the disasters of continental Europe. A serious commitment to ideas and old-fashioned attitudes to education gave them their unique influence in politics. Thatcher was open to the ideas, ready to listen, unprejudiced; many traditional Tories were not.

In the winter of 1974–5 after Heath had lost his second successive election, there was no such thing as 'Thatcherism'. She was expressing her public support for the policies of consensus, whatever her developing inner feelings. She backed intervention in the housing market and had queried council house sales. There was no sign that she would become leader. Heath was anyway stubbornly determined to stay on. He insisted his supporters, who included most of the well-known Tories of the day, back him. Polls suggested 70 per cent of Conservative voters wanted him to stay. Yet there was deep dissatisfaction on the Tory benches in Parliament. A City slicker, Sir Edward du Cann, who chaired the backbenchers' 1922 Committee, began to take soundings about challenging Heath. He was backed by the war hero, Tory MP and arch-intriguer, Airey Neave, but Neave soon pulled out. Joseph stepped up to the plate before making a catastrophically ill-judged and offensive speech in which he seemed to suggest that working-class women were having too many babies and should be stopped because they were degrading the gene pool. This finished the man *Private Eye* was already calling the 'mad monk'. So who could the right find as a candidate?

If Heath had realized that two successive election defeats meant he really had to go, and had he allowed other Tory moderates to prepare campaigns to replace him, Mrs Thatcher would have had no chance. Had Joseph not made a disaster of a speech, she would have been committed to backing him, and so would not have stood herself. Had du Cann stood, the brilliant campaign manager Neave would not have worked for her. Many Tory MPs were persuaded by him to vote for her because she had no chance, as a way of easing out Heath. Then more 'serious' candidates could stand. It was a brilliant ruse. On 4 February 1975, she shocked everyone by defeating Heath in the first ballot by 130 votes to 119. She then went on to beat the also-rans easily. A current of right-wing free-market thinking that had been gurgling almost unnoticed underground since the fifties would break ground in spectacular fashion, changing Britain for ever. 'Josephism' became 'Thatcherism'. Few of the Tory MPs in what was called 'the peasants' revolt' realized quite where their new leader would take them. For the next few years, supercilious smirks and patronizing remarks from Wilson and then the new Prime Minister, James Callaghan, would be her lot. And then she would show them.

Beyond Pop

The seventies was an extreme decade; the extreme left and extreme right were reflected even in its music. Drawing neat lines between popular culture and the wider world of politics and economics is a dangerous game. Any art follows its own internal logic and much of what happened to British music and fashion during the seventies was driven by the straightforward need to adopt then outpace what had happened the day before. Clipped, hard-edged styles appear on the street to mock floppy, romantic ones, and then it happens in reverse. The high-gloss extravagance of the late Teds is answered by the neat, fresh, cool look of the Mods, which will be met by the psychedelic extravagance and hairiness of the Hippies. They are answered by the super-Mod working-class cool of the first skinheads, though in due course wannabe Ziggy Stardusts will bring androgyny and excess back to the pavement and playing ground. Leather-bound punks find a new trump card to offend the older rockers; New Romantics with eyeliner and quiffs challenge Goths. Huge baggy trousers are suddenly in then disappear as quickly. Shoes, shirts, haircuts, mutate and compete. For much of the time, this game doesn't mean anything outside its own rhetoric, it simply is – and then isn't.

Exactly the same can be said about musical fads, the way Soul is picked up in Northern clubs from Wigan to Blackpool to Manchester; the struggle between the concept albums of the art-house bands and the arrival of punkier noises from New York in the mid-seventies; the dance crazes that come and go. Often the motivation for change is boredom. We have heard enough of that three-minute noise and it's time for something shorter and louder, or longer and quieter. Nothing lasts long. Like fashion, musical styles begin to break up and head in many directions in this period, coexisting as rival subcultures across the country. Rock and roll is not dead, nor is Motown, when reggae and ska arrive. The Rolling Stones and Yes carry on oblivious to the arrival of the Sex Pistols and the Clash. Every individual who drank in popular culture feels a sudden rush of remembrance of days past when a particular band, song or look is revived. But we should not fool ourselves that emotion equals meaning. The life lived and its sound-track are not quite the same.

Yet in this musical and stylistic chaos, which runs from the early seventies to modern times, there are moments and themes which stick out. Perhaps the most important statistic to hold in mind is that between the early fifties and the mid-seventies, real disposable income – what people had in their hand to spend, taking inflation into account – exactly doubled. Between Lonnie Donegan and Led Zeppelin, as it were, people became twice as well off. Yet from 1974 until the end of 1978, living standards actually went into decline.[59] The long working-class boom had ended. Broadly speaking, British pop was invented during the optimism of 1958–68, when the economy was most of the time still booming and was evolving in its fastest and most creative spirit. Then the mood turned in the later sixties and seventies towards fantasy and escapism in wider and wilder varieties, as unemployment arrived and the world seemed bleaker and more confusing. This second phase involved the sci-fi ambiguities and glamour of Bowie, the gothic, mystical hokum of the heavy bad-boy bands like Black Sabbath and Led Zeppelin, and the druggy obscurities of Yes. The second half of the seventies were the years of deep political disillusion, strains which seemed to tear at the unity of the UK: Irish terrorism on the mainland, a rise in racial tension and widespread industrial mayhem. The optimism which had helped fuel popular culture suddenly gurgled dry. So it is not perhaps a coincidence that this period is a darker time in music and fashion, a nightmare inversion of the sixties dream. After the innocent raptures of England's 1966 World Cup victory and Manchester United's European Cup triumph two years later, the mid-seventies invent the modern football hooligan and by the eighties, English clubs were being banned from European competitions because of their followers. Vivienne Westwood and Malcolm McLaren turn from creating cod-fifties drape coats and beatnik jumpers to the ripped T-shirts and bondage gear of punk; the Sex Pistols portray themselves as a kind of anti-Beatles; older musical heroes flirt with fascism.

Westwood was in many ways a perfect inheritor of Quant's role a dozen years earlier. Like Quant, she was brought up to make clothes herself and came through art college. Like Quant she had a male partner who had a touch of business genius. Like Quant she was interested in the liberating power of clothes. Like Quant she set herself up in the Kings Road in a shop which first of all had to be braved rather than simply patronized. Her clothes would shock passers-by just as Quant's had horrified Michael Caine's mother. Like Quant she was sardonic and fearless and later on, she out-Quanted Quant as the grand dame of British fashion. Westwood received a Damehood from the Queen whose face she had famously impaled with a safety-pin earlier on, and was honoured with a huge retrospective show at the Victoria and Albert Museum.

Yet this daughter of a Derbyshire mill-weaver and a shoe-making family was also startlingly different from Quant, the Welsh teachers' child. Westwood had first mixed and matched to create a style of her own at the Manchester branch of C&A and said with only a twinge of irony, 'my work is rooted in English tailoring.'[60] Her vision of fashion was anything but uncluttered. It was a magpie, rip-it-up and make-it-new assault on the history of couture, postmodern to Quant's straight-forward modern. And in the mid-seventies, working from a shop recently renamed simply Sex, Westwood's vision was a fetishistic, rubbery, vaguely sado-masochistic assault on mainstream decencies. Chains, zips in odd places, rips, obscene slogans and provocative images, referring for instance to a notorious serial rapist, all featured. She once declared that she had 'an in-built perversity, a kind of in-built clock which reacts against anything orthodox'. Her helper and model Jordan (aka Pamela Rooke) used to set off on a commuter train to the shop, wearing rubber clothes, fishnet stockings and a beehive hairdo and attracted so much attention British Rail put her in a first class compartment for her own protection. Quant's vision had been essentially optimistic – easy to wear, clean-looking clothes for free and liberated women. Westwood's vision was darker. Her clothes were to be worn like armour in the street battle with authority and repression, in the England of flashers and perverts.

Nor was her then partner Malcolm McLaren in any way like Plunkett Alexander-Greene, the aristocratic businessman husband of Quant. McLaren was also an art college product and, as we saw earlier, had been influenced by the radical anger of the 'Situationists' and the raw typography of King Mob. The son of a dysfunctional Jewish and Scottish family he had drifted through the worlds of fringe politics, music and film-making but was now remaking himself as a kind of wideboy entrepreneur of street culture, a latter-day Svengali modelled on 'Flash Larry' Parnes. He had already offered style advice to the New York Dolls and was on the lookout for his anti-Beatles, duly forming the Sex Pistols in December 1975. Steve Jones, Paul Cook, John Lydon and Glen Matlock – who much admired the Beatles – were another working-class quartet in their late teens. But they expressed the self-loathing spirit of the times as the Beatles had expressed the geeky optimism of an earlier Britain. Pock-marked, sneering, spiky-haired, exuding violence and playing with a wild and simple thrash of a sound, they dutifully performed the essential duty of shocking a still easily shocked nation. Their handful of good songs have a leaping energy which really did take the ageing, lumbering rock establishment by storm, but their juvenile side quickly became embarrassing.

Compared to the most self-important assertions of John Lennon, their notorious performance on the London television show *Thames Today* with Bill Grundy, was desperate stuff. (Grundy: 'Go on, you've got another ten seconds. Say something outrageous'. Steve: 'You dirty bastard.' Grundy: 'Go on, again.' Steve: 'You dirty fucker!' Grundy: 'What a clever boy!' Steve: 'You fucking rotter!' It leaves later satirical attempts to depict punk rockers as in the television comedy *The Young Ones* floundering.) But the tabloid papers and stupider backbench MPs duly played their allotted role and helped fan the Sex Pistols' publicity engine. McLaren thrived on outrage and played up to the role of cynical charlatan for all he was worth. The Pistols played a series of increasingly wild gigs, including in the broken-up set of the bankrupt Biba shop (everything connects) and made juvenile political attacks in songs such as 'Anarchy in the UK' and, in the year of the Silver Jubilee, 'God Save the Queen'. (Jim Callaghan can be accused of many things, but presiding over a 'fascist regime' is not one of them.) Yet punk was the first revival of fast, belligerent popular music to concern itself with the politics of the country, and this was the first time since the brief 'street fighting man' posturing of the late sixties when mainstream society needed to notice rock.

On the other side of the political divide was an eruption of racist, skinhead rock, and an interest in the far right. Among the rock stars who seemed to flirt with these ideas were Eric Clapton, who said in 1976 that 'Powell is the only bloke who's telling the truth, for the good of the country' and David Bowie, who spoke of Hitler as being the first superstar, musing that perhaps he would make a good Hitler himself. Though the Sex Pistols liked to see themselves as vaguely on the anarchist left, their enthusiasm for shocking, particularly after the nihilistic and amoral Sid Vicious joined them, at least left room for ambiguity. McLaren and Westwood had produced clothing with swastikas and other Nazi emblems, if only to outrage people (it worked) while Vicious's contribution to political thought can be summed up by his lyric 'Belsen was a gas / I read the other day / About the open graves / Where the Jews all lay . . .'

Reacting to the surrounding mood, Rock Against Racism was formed in August 1976, helping create the wider Anti-Nazi League a year later. Punk bands were at the forefront of the RAR movement, above all the Clash whose lead singer Joe Strummer became more influential and admired than Johnny Rotten or the rest of the Sex Pistols, and bands such as the Jam. Black music – reggae, ska and soul – was popular enough among white youths for it to have had a real influence in turning the fashion in street culture decisively against racism. Ska revival bands such as the Specials and the reggae-influenced Police and UB40 (the latter from the West Midlands, home of Powellism) had an effect which went beyond the odd memorable song. Hard-left politics had often been a joyless business but the seventies produced, in the middle of visions of social breakdown, a musical revival which cheered up the lost generation. The racist skinhead 'Oi' bands found themselves in a violent and uncomfortable ghetto. As one cultural critic of the time put it, 'A lifestyle – urban, mixed, music-loving, modern and creative – had survived, despite being under threat from the NF.'[61] The streets might be dirty and living standards falling, but it was not all bad news.

Sunny Jim, Stormy Winter: the Callaghan Years

Jim Callaghan has featured already, both as hero in Northern Ireland and as rather a villain when he stabbed Wilson and Castle in the front over trade union reform. In the spring of 1976 he finally entered Number Ten after a series of votes by Labour MPs shaved off his rivals – Denis Healey, Tony Crosland and Roy Jenkins on the right, and Michael Foot and Tony Benn on the left. After three ballots, he beat Foot by 176 votes to 137 and replaced Wilson as Prime Minister. For three turbulent years he would run a government with no overall majority in Parliament, kept going by deals and pacts, and in an atmosphere of repeated, though not quite constant crisis. Callaghan was by now a familiar and reassuring figure in Britain, tall, ruddy, no-nonsense, robust and, by comparison with Wilson, straightforward. He had had all the top jobs in politics, though had not distinguished himself either as Chancellor or as Home Secretary. Latterly he had been Foreign Secretary, deeply involved in the early stages of détente, bringing an end to the Cold War, and forging close personal relations with Germany's Chancellor, Helmut Schmidt, America's Henry Kissinger and the amiable but derided President Ford. At sixty-five he was one of the most experienced politicians to become Prime Minister. After Wilson and Heath he was the third and last of the centrist seekers after consensus, the wartime avoiders of national confrontation. Yet behind the genial, occasionally stubborn-looking face with its protuberant lower lip and owlish glasses there was a man who, in the growing contest between hard left and right, was a Labour leader now instinctively looking to the right.

Churchill apart, all of his post-war predecessors had been Oxbridge men. Callaghan had not been to university at all. The son of a Royal Navy chief petty officer who had died young, and a devout Baptist mother from Portsmouth, he had known real poverty and had clawed his way up as a young clerk working for the Inland Revenue, and then as a union official, before wartime naval service. One of the 1945 generation of MPs, he was a young rebel who drifted right, though always keeping his strong pro-trade union instincts. His wounding experiences as Chancellor during the dark days of 1966–7 had nearly broken him but he had found, as the best politicians do, that what did not kill him made him stronger. He was a social conservative, uneasy about divorce, homosexuality and vehemently pro-police, pro-monarchy, pro-armed forces, though he was anti-hanging and strongly anti-racialist too. As Home Secretary he had announced that the permissive society had gone too far. As Prime Minister, he would try to initiate a 'great debate' against trendy teaching in schools, calling for an inquiry into teaching methods, standards, discipline and the case for a national curriculum. On the economy, he would become steadily more impressed by the case for monetarism, then raging on the right. Famously, he told a stunned 1976 Labour conference used to the Keynesian doctrines about governments spending their way out of recession, cutting taxes and boosting investment: 'I tell you in all candour that that option no longer exists and that insofar as it ever did exist, it worked by injecting inflation into the economy . . . Higher inflation, followed by higher unemployment. That is the history of the last twenty years.'

Yet even if he could read the runes, in the national memory Callaghan is forever associated with failure. There is the humiliating, cap-in-hand begging for help from the International Monetary Fund, the soaring inflation and interest rates of the late seventies and finally the piled rubbish, vast strike meetings and unburied dead of the 1979 'winter of discontent'. There is an arc which plummets through earlier crises under Wilson and Heath, before crashing into final chaos and destruction under Callaghan. Only after the wasteland of his time in office can the bold remaking of Britain under Margaret Thatcher begin. And Callaghan himself had been part of the problem. His sentimental failure to understand the aggression of the union challenge to elected power, and his earlier lack of interest in radical economic ideas, came home to haunt him in Downing Street. But the story of the Callaghan and Healey years, for the two must be taken together, is more intriguing than its body-strewn, gore-splattered final act. It is also a story of comparative success, of wrenching inflation down again, doing the best deals with international bankers that could be done, and facing up to challenges that had been dodged for decades. It did not end well for the protagonists, but then few interesting tragedies do.

Callaghan had a brutal side to him. In remaking his cabinet, he purged much of the left, leaving Michael Foot as his loyal and invaluable leader in the Commons delivering the votes, but sacking

Barbara Castle as 'too old' and too left wing. The leader of the right, Roy Jenkins, was out too, off to take up the job of European Commissioner in Brussels. Crosland, briefly Foreign Secretary, died, so Callaghan had no serious rivals left. He responded by constructing the most right-wing Labour cabinet since the war, whose new faces included Bill Rodgers, Shirley Williams and David Owen. All would later join Jenkins in the breakaway Social Democratic Party (SDP). By the standards of New Labour after 1997 this was still a left-wing government, keen on redistribution, still describing itself as socialist, levying high rates of income tax. It believed in nationalization, adding shipbuilding, the new oil industry and the aircraft manufacture to the State's bulging holdings, and in such traditional anti-privilege issues as the abolition of pay beds in NHS hospitals. Some of its cabinet members, including Shirley Williams, joined the picket line during the violent 1977 Grunwick dispute at a film processing laboratory in London – one where Asian female workers, barred from joining the union APEX, had some moral right on their side but which became a bloody mob confrontation. It is hard to imagine New Labour ministers doing the same.

But by the standards of Labour's history, Callaghan's suspicion of liberalism, his admiration for American republicans like Kissinger and Ford, his new faith in monetarism and his increasingly aggressive attitude to high pay demands, put him to the right even of Wilson. In private he toyed with policies which would later make Mrs Thatcher famous, such as selling off council houses. His famous and much quoted remark to an aide, just as Labour was losing power in 1979, that the country was going through a once-in-thirty-years sea change suggested that he half accepted the consensus years had failed: 'There is a shift in what the public wants and what it approves of. I suspect there is now such a sea-change – and it is for Mrs Thatcher.' About this, he was right. But if as Enoch Powell said, all political careers end in failure, then what happened before Callaghan's final failure is still an extraordinary story of despair, courage, hope and bungled accounting.

Cap in Hand

Jim Callaghan's first few days as Prime Minister in April 1976 must have brought back some grim memories. A dozen years earlier, as Chancellor, he had been confronted with awful economic news which nearly crushed him and ended in the forced devaluation of the pound. Now, on the first day of his premiership, he was told the pound was falling fast (it had been 'floating' since the Heath years but this had become a euphemism). A devaluation by sterling holders was likely. The Chancellor, Denis Healey, had negotiated the £6 pay limit and this would feed through to much lower wage increases and eventually to lower inflation. Cash limits on public spending brought in under Wilson would also radically cut public expenditure. But in the spring of 1976 inflation was still rampant and unemployment was rising fast. Healey now told Callaghan that because of the billions spent by the Bank of England supporting sterling in the first few months of the year, a loan from the International Monetary Fund looked essential. In June standby credits were arranged with the IMF and countries such as the United States, Germany, Japan and Switzerland. What would follow was about as humiliating as peacetime politics gets.

Healey had imposed tough cuts in the summer but by its end, as he returned from a desperately needed break in the Scottish Highlands, the pound was under intense pressure again. On 27 September 1976 Healey was meant to fly out to a Commonwealth finance ministers' conference in Hong Kong with the Governor of the Bank of England. But so great was the crisis and so panicked were the markets that he decided he could not afford to be out of touch for seventeen hours' flying time. (This was before in-flight phones.) In full view of the television cameras, he turned round at Heathrow airport and went back to the Treasury. There he decided to apply to the IMF for a conditional loan – one which gave authority to the international banking officials above Britain's elected leaders. With exquisite timing, the Ford workers began a major strike. Healey was close to collapse, to 'demoralization', he later said, for the first and last time in his life.

Against Callaghan's initial advice, he decided to dash to the Labour conference in Blackpool and make his case to an anguished and angry party. As we have seen there was a powerful mood at the time for a siege economy, telling the IMF to get lost, cutting imports and nationalizing swathes of industry. Given just five minutes to speak from the floor because of the absurdities of Labour conference rules, the Chancellor warned his party this would mean trade war, mass unemployment and the return of a Tory government. But, he shouted against a rising hubbub, with something of the young Major Healey who had visited the 1945 conference in battledress, he was speaking to them from the battlefront. He would negotiate with the IMF which would mean 'things we do not like as well as things we do like. It means sticking to the very painful cuts in public expenditure . . . It means sticking to the pay policy.' As Healey ruefully recorded in his autobiography, he had begun with a background of modest cheers and a rumble of booing: 'When I sat down, the cheers were much louder. So were the boos.' Benn called his speech vulgar and abusive: in fact Healey's final arm-clasp of triumph was a last throw by one of politics' great showmen.

So, with the cabinet nervously watching, the negotiations with the IMF started. Callaghan and Healey naturally wanted to limit as far as they could the cuts being forced on them. The IMF, with the US Treasury standing behind them, was under pressure to squeeze ever harder. The British side was in a horribly weak position. The government was riven by argument and threats of resignation, including from Healey. There were incredibly long and difficult cabinet arguments about what levels of cuts were acceptable and whether there was any real alternative in a leftist siege economy. In deepest secret, Callaghan and the lead IMF negotiator from Washington had bitter private talks, in which the Prime Minister warned that British democracy itself would be imperilled by mass unemployment. When it came to the very end of the tense and complicated haggling, the IMF was still calling for an extra billion pounds' worth of cuts and it was only when Healey, without telling Callaghan, threatened the international bankers with yet another 'Who runs Britain?' election, that they gave way. The final package of cuts was announced in Healey's budget, severe but not as grim as some had feared, and greeted with headlines about Britain's shame.

But the truly extraordinary thing about this whole story is that it was unnecessary from the start. The cash limits Healey had already imposed on Whitehall would cut spending far more effectively than anyone realized. More startling still, the public spending statistics (on which the cuts were based) were wildly wrong. Public finances were stronger than they appeared. The Treasury estimate for public borrowing in 1974–5 had been too low by £4,000m, a mistake greater than any tax changes ever made by a British Chancellor; but the 1976 estimate was twice as high as it should have been. The IMF-directed cuts were more savage than they needed to have been. As to the bloated State, another major issue of the day, the amount of Britain's wealth spent by government was miscalculated too. A government white paper early in 1976 had put it at about 60 per cent – huge by the standards of the West. But this was, as Healey put it, 'unforgiveably misleading'. When Britain's spending was defined in the same way as other countries' and at market prices, the figure fell to 46 per cent. By the time Labour left office it was 42 per cent, about the same as West Germany's and well below that of social democratic Scandinavian countries. Britain's balance of payments came back into balance long before the IMF cuts could take effect and Healey reflected later that 'If I had been given accurate forecasts in 1976, I would never have needed to go to the IMF at all.'

In the end only half the loan was used, all of which was repaid by the time Labour left office. Only half the standby credit was used and it was untouched from August 1977 onwards. During the IMF negotiations Healey had talked about 'Sod Off Day' when he and Britain would finally be free of outside control. That came far sooner than he had expected. Of course, at the time, nobody did know that Britain's finances were so much stronger than they had seemed. Yet all the lurid drama which imprinted itself on Britain's memory – the rush back from Heathrow, the dramatic scenes at the Labour conference, the humiliating arrival of the IMF hard men, backed by Wall Street, a political thriller which destroyed Labour's self-confidence for more than a decade and which was used repeatedly in the Thatcher years as clinching evidence of its bankruptcy – all this could have been avoided. That is only the start. It was the prospect of ever greater cuts in public spending, inflation out of control, and the economy in the hands of outsiders that helped break the Labour Party into warring factions and gave the hard left its great opportunity. Had the IMF crisis not happened would the 'winter of discontent' and the Bennite uprising have followed?

Healey later said he forgave the Treasury for its mistakes in calculating public sector borrowing needs, because nobody had got their forecasts right. He and they were operating in a new economic world of floating exchange rates, huge capital flows and speculation still little understood. It made him highly critical of monetarism, however, and all academic theories which depended on accurate measurement and forecasting of the money supply. He liked to quote President Johnson, who at about this time reflected that making a speech on economics 'is a lot like pissing down your leg. It seems hot to you, but it never does to anyone else.' Healey was bitter, though, about the Treasury's mistakes over the true scale of public spending which so hobbled his hopes of being seen as a successful Chancellor. He said later he could not forgive them: 'I cannot help suspecting that Treasury officials deliberately overstated public spending in order to put pressure on governments which were reluctant to cut it. Such dishonesty for political purposes is contrary to all the proclaimed traditions of the British civil service.'[62]

The Callaghan government is remembered for the IMF crisis and for the 'winter of discontent'. His defenders point out that Callaghan actually presided over a relatively popular and successful government for more than half his time in power – some twenty months out of thirty-seven. Following the IMF affair, the pound recovered strongly, the markets recovered, inflation fell, eventually to single figures, and unemployment fell too. By the middle of 1977, the year of the Queen's Silver Jubilee, North Sea Oil was coming ashore to the tune of more than half a million barrels a day, a third of the country's needs. Britain would be self-sufficient in oil by 1980 and already was in gas. The pay restraint agreed earlier with Healey was still holding, though only just. The new American President, Jimmy Carter, visited for a much-praised summit. Callaghan, for the first time, was getting a good press while the Tory opposition under Margaret Thatcher seemed to be struggling. After having to rely on an odd mixture of nationalist MPs for its precarious Commons majority, Labour entered a deal with David Steel's Liberals from March 1977 to August of the following year, giving Callaghan a secure parliamentary position for the first time. The Lib-Lab pact gave the smaller party, which then had only thirteen MPs, rights only to be consulted, plus vague promises on possible voting system changes: it was much more helpful to Labour. Labour regained a modest majority over the Tories in the opinion polls and the prospect of Callaghan and Labour continuing to govern well into the eighties looked perfectly reasonable. This did not look like a dying government, still less the end of an era.

Peasants' Revolt: Two, the Left

We have seen the peasants' revolt of the right, but there was another too, from the left. This would be publicly associated with Tony Benn, the face of the left in Labour's highest circles. But it was a wide and a deep political force, with complicated roots. The Communist Party of Great Britain had almost collapsed, so great was the disillusion with the Soviet system to which it pledged undying and largely uncritical obedience. By the seventies it was riven by arguments of the kind that split most declining organizations. Further left were a bewildering number of Trotskyist groups, all hostile to the Soviet Union, all claiming to be the true party of Lenin, all denouncing one another over ideological and tactical detail. They tended to be dour and puritan. Only two had any real following: the Socialist Workers' Party, or SWP, and the Militant Tendency. Each had descended by political split and fusion from earlier groups which had first organized in Britain in the forties.

Militant would later cause a huge convulsion in the Labour Party. Wilson complained a lot about 'Trots' trying to take the party over but in the seventies he was largely ignored and Militant built up strong local bases, particularly in Liverpool. The SWP, outside the Labour Party, campaigned on specific issues such as strikes and racism. Their distinctive clenched fist logo and dramatic typography appears in the background of countless industrial and political marches, pickets and rallies. The SWP's single biggest influence was in combating the rise of the National Front.

The NF, under its tubby would-be führer Martin Webster and the bullet-headed John Tyndall, had been founded in 1967 after the original British National Party and the old League of Empire Loyalists joined together. Electorally it was struggling, though Webster polled 16 per cent in the West Bromwich by-election of May 1973 and in the two 1974 general elections the NF put up first fifty-four and then ninety candidates, entitling them to a television broadcast. More important to their strategy were the street confrontations, engineered by marching with Union Jacks and anti-immigrant slogans through Bangladeshi or Pakistani areas in Leeds, Birmingham and London. A more extreme offshoot of the original skinheads attached themselves to the NF's racialist politics and by the mid-seventies they too were on the march. The SWP determined to organize street politics of their own and bring things to a halt and formed the Anti-Nazi League in 1977. The League drew in tens of thousands of people who had no particular interest in the obscurities of Leninist revolutionary theory, but who saw the NF as a genuine threat to the new immigrant communities. And the young flooded to their rallies, marches and confrontations, during which there were a couple of deaths as the police weighed in to protect the National Front's right to march. Beyond Militant and the SWP, other far-left groups inside and outside the Labour Party would achieve brief notoriety because they were supported by a famous actress, such as Vanessa Redgrave, or through influence in a local party or borough. Eventually the 'loony left' would come to the boil, enjoying enough influence, particularly in London, to shred Labour's credibility. But in the seventies, this was still a slowly developing, obscure story.

Much more important then was the influence of socialists who were not working for secretive Trotskyist or communist parties, but had simply wanted to bring down Wilson and were now gunning for Callaghan and his friends. Like Thatcher and Joseph, they believed the old consensus politics was failing. Som of their thinking was also shared by the right – they were mostly hostile to the European Community, for example, opposed Scottish and Welsh nationalism, and were hostile to America. But that was where the similarities ended. The Labour left wanted to deal with world economic chaos by pulling up the drawbridge, imposing strict controls on what was imported, taking direct control of the major industries, and the City too. The left thought planning had failed because it was too weak, and should therefore be dramatically extended. Any strongly held political view which is excluded from the centre of power tends to develop a conspiracy theory. The Powellites believed Heath had lied to the British people. The Labour left believed Wilson, Callaghan and Healey had been captured by international capitalism, as had many MPs. The answer was to make them accountable to 'ordinary people', as the obsessive meeting-attenders of Labour politics innocently believed themselves to be. So the siege economy or 'Alternative Economic Strategy' and mandatory reselection of MPs became the two main planks of the left.

Tony Benn became the voice and leader of Labour's peasants' revolt. His enthusiasm for workers' cooperatives and a National Enterprise Board had already made him a figure of ridicule in Fleet Street. Later he would become a kind of revered national grandfather, a white-haired, humorous sage whose wry memories of Attlee and Wilson would transfix audiences of all ages and views. His unbending hostility to nuclear weapons, American and British war-making, and market capitalism would inspire hundreds of thousands deep into the years of New Labour. But between the eager-beaver Anthony Wedgwood Benn, champion of Concorde, and the paternal Grandpa Tony, came the turbulent years of 'Bennism', the central phase of his political life. Radicalized by his children towards the politics of feminism, anti-nuclear campaigning and much else, he became increasingly detached from his colleagues as the Wilson–Callaghan government staggered towards collapse. Benn had come close to leaving it over his opposition to Labour's deal with the Liberals, and he fell out badly with the other notably left-wing cabinet minister Michael Foot over parliamentary tactics on Europe.

His general attitude to the party is well caught by his diary entry for 15 January 1978: 'The whole Labour leadership now is totally demoralised and all the growth on the left is going to come up from the outside and underneath. This is the death of the Labour Party. It believes in nothing any more, except staying in power.' Benn was in the curious position of still being a senior member of the government when he wrote this, attending intimate gatherings at Chequers, hobnobbing with visiting Americans, hearing deep military and security secrets, while at the same growing the eyes and ears of an outsider. He was on the side of the strikers who brought much of the country to a halt and his new friend Arthur Scargill, the miners' leader, was telling Benn he could be the next Labour leader himself. Though it seemed a fantasy in 1978, within a few years Benn would come within a hair's breadth of winning the deputy leadership on a left-wing socialist ticket, during the middle of a vicious and deeply damaging Labour civil war.

Then Was the Winter of their Discontent

The 'winter of discontent', a Shakespearean phrase, was used by Callaghan himself to describe the industrial and social chaos of 1978–9. It has stuck in people's memories, as few political events do – the schools closed, the ports blockaded, the rubbish rotting in the streets, the dead unburied. Actions by individual union branches and shop stewards were reckless and heartless. Left-wing union leaders and activists whipped up the disputes for their own purposes. Right-wing newspapers, desperate to see the end of Labour, exaggerated the effects and rammed home the picture of a nation no longer governable. But much of the fault for this was Callaghan's. It was not just that he had opposed the legal restrictions on union power pleaded for by Wilson and Castle, and then fought for vainly by Heath. It was not even that he and Healey, acting in good faith, had imposed a more drastic squeeze on public spending and thus on the poorest families, than was economically necessary . . . though none of that helped. It was also that by trying to impose an unreasonably tough new pay limit on the country, and then dithering about the date of the election, he destroyed the fragile calm he had so greatly enjoyed.

Most people, including most of the cabinet, had assumed that Callaghan would call a general election in the autumn of 1978. The economic news was still good, Labour was ahead in the polls. Two dates in October had already been pencilled in, though 12 October had been ruled out because it was Margaret Thatcher's birthday. But Callaghan, musing at his Sussex farm during the summer, decided that he did not trust the polls. He would wait, soldiering on until the spring. When the Prime Minister invited half a dozen trade union leaders to his farm to discuss the election, they left still thinking he was going in the autumn. Then, at the TUC conference, with the world agog for an announcement, Callaghan sang a verse from an old music hall song, originally by Vesta Victoria:

> There was I waiting at the church, waiting at the church, waiting
> at the church
> When I found he'd left me in the lurch, Lor' how it did upset me

All at once he sent me round a note, here's the very note, this is
    what he wrote,
Can't get away to marry you today, My wife won't let me.

While a good enough song in its day, it was hardly a clear message to
Britain. Was the jilted bride Mrs Thatcher? The trade union movement? Callaghan's intention was to suggest that he was delaying the
election but many trade union leaders and newspaper correspondents
assumed just the opposite. When he finally came clean to the cabinet,
they were shocked.

This might not have mattered so much had Callaghan also not
promised a new 5 per cent pay limit to bring inflation down further.
Because of the 1974–5 cash limit on pay rises at a time of high
inflation, take-home pay for most people had been falling. Public sector
workers had had a particularly hard time. There were the inevitable
stories of fat cat directors and bosses awarding themselves high
settlements. The union leaders and many ministers thought that a
further period of pay limits would be impossible to sell, while a 5 per
cent limit, which appears to have come from Callaghan almost off the
cuff, was widely considered to be ludicrously tough.

Had Callaghan gone to the country in October then the promise
of further pay restraint might have helped boost Labour's popularity,
while the unions could have comforted themselves with the thought
that it was probably mere window-dressing. By delaying the election
until the following spring, Callaghan ensured that his 5 per cent would
be tested in Britain's increasingly impatient and dangerous industrial
relations market. First up, almost as soon as Callaghan had finished
his music-hall turn, were the 57,000 car-workers employed by Ford,
the US giant. The Transport & General Workers' Union called not for
5 per cent but for 30 per cent, on the back of high profits (and, it has
to be said, an 80 per cent pay rise just awarded to Ford's chairman).
Callaghan was badly embarrassed – his son, as it happened, worked for
the company – and when after five weeks of lost production, Ford
eventually settled for 17 per cent, he became convinced he would lose
the coming election.

There was a vale of tears to be endured first. Oil tanker drivers
also in the TGWU came out for 40 per cent, and were followed by
road haulage drivers, workers at Ford's nationalized rival British

Leyland, then water and sewerage workers. BBC electricians threatened a blackout of Christmas television. The docks were picketed and closed down. Blazing braziers, surrounded by huddled figures in woolly hats, with snow whirling round them, were shown nightly on the television news. Hull, virtually cut off, was known as the 'second Stalingrad'. The effects were felt directly by ministers along with the rest of the country. Bill Rodgers, the transport minister, whose mother was dying of cancer, found that vital chemotherapy chemicals were not being allowed out of Hull. Later, when the Health Secretary David Ennals was admitted to Westminster Hospital the local shop steward announced gleefully that he was 'a legitimate target' for action: 'He won't get the little extras our members provide patients. He won't get his locker cleaned or the area around his bed tidied up. He won't get tea or soup.'⁶³ In the middle of it all Callaghan went off for an international summit on the Caribbean island of Guadeloupe, staying on for talks and sightseeing in Barbados. Pictures of him swimming and sunning himself did not improve the national mood. When he returned to Heathrow, confronted by news reporters asking about the industrial crisis, he replied blandly: 'I don't think other people in the world will share the view that there is mounting chaos.' This was famously translated by the *Daily Mail* and then the *Sun* into, 'Crisis? What Crisis?' The nation's mood grew no sunnier.

As the railwaymen prepared to join the strikes, the worst blow for the government came from the public sector union NUPE, who called out more than a million school caretakers, cooks, ambulance men, refuse collectors on random stoppages for a £60 a week guaranteed minimum wage. Strikes by car workers were one thing. But now the public was being hit directly, and the most vulnerable were being hit the hardest. Children's hospitals, old people's homes and schools were all plunged into trouble. The single most notorious action was by the Liverpool Parks and Cemeteries Branch of the General & Municipal Workers' Union, who refused to bury dead bodies, leaving more than 300 to pile up in a cold storage depot and a disused factory, and Liverpool council to discuss emergency plans for disposing of some corpses at sea. Funeral corteges were met at the cemeteries by pickets and forced to turn back. Strikers were confronted in local pubs and thumped.

In the centre of London and other major cities, huge piles of rotting rubbish piled up, overrun with rats and a serious health hazard. Inside government, ordinary work almost ground to a halt. It must be recorded that most of those striking, the public sector workers in particular, were woefully badly paid and living in relative poverty; and that they had no history of industrial militancy. Nor was the crisis quite as dreadful as some of the papers and politicians showed it. As with Heath's three-day week, many people gleefully enjoyed the enforced holiday from their public sector jobs. Nobody was proved to have died in hospital as a result of union action, there was no shortage of food in the shops and there was no violence. Troops were never used. This was chaos, and a direct challenge to the authority of the government. It was not a revolution, or an attempt to overthrow a government.

Yet that is the effect it had. The revolution would bring in Thatcherism not socialism, and Labour would be overthrown, plunging quickly into civil war. A 'St Valentine's Day concordat' was eventually unveiled between the government and the TUC, talking of annual assessments and guidance, targeting long-term inflation, virtually admitting the 5 per cent limit had been a mistake. After all the drama, it was a fig-leaf so thin and ragged it was barely worth holding up. By March most of the action had ended and various large settlements and inquiries had been set up. But in the Commons, the government was running out of allies, spirit and hope. The failure of the referendum on Scottish devolution meant that under previously agreed rules, the act would have to be repealed. This in turn gave the Scottish Nationalists no reason to continue supporting Labour. The Liberals, facing the highly embarrassing trial of Jeremy Thorpe for conspiracy to murder (he would later be acquitted), had their own reasons for wanting an early election. In the drink-sodden, conspiracy-ridden, frenetic atmosphere of an exhausted Parliament, in which dying MPs had been carried through the lobbies to keep the government afloat, final attempts were made by Michael Foot and the Labour whips to find some kind of majority – Ulster Unionists, Irish Nationalists, renegade Scots were all approached. Callaghan, by now, was in a calmly fatalistic mood. He did not want to struggle on through another summer and autumn. Finally, on 28 March 1979, the game ended when the government was defeated by a single vote, brought down at last by a ragged coalition of Tories, Liberals, Scottish Nationalists and

Ulster Unionists. Callaghan was the first Prime Minister since 1924 to have to go to Buckingham Palace and ask for a dissolution of Parliament, because he had lost a vote in the Commons.

The five-week election campaign started after the Irish assassination of Mrs Thatcher's wily leadership campaign manager, the Tory MP Airey Neave, murdered by a car-bomb on his way into the Commons underground car-park. On the Labour side it was dominated by Callaghan, still more popular than his party, who emphasized stable prices and his deal with the unions, if such it was. On the Tory side, Thatcher showed a new media savvy, working with the television news teams and taking the advice of her advertising gurus, the Saatchis. Callaghan, who had never expected to win, was soundly beaten. The Conservatives took sixty-one seats directly from Labour, gaining nearly 43 per cent of the vote, and a substantial overall majority, with 339 seats.

What of the players in the last act of Old Labour and the Broken Consensus? Callaghan would stumble on as leader before retiring in October 1980. Healey would fight a desperate struggle against the left, as his party did its level best to commit suicide in public. Numerous moderates would form the breakaway SDP. The Scottish Nationalists, derided by Callaghan when they voted him down as 'turkeys voting for Christmas', lost eleven of their thirteen MPs. The unions would eventually lose almost half their members and any political influence they briefly enjoyed. More important than all that, mass unemployment would arrive in Britain. The one economic medicine so bitter that no minister in the seventies had thought of trying it was duly uncorked and poured into the spoon. It was time for Britain to grimace and open her mouth.

Part Four

THE BRITISH REVOLUTION

Margaret Roberts, Superstar

In politics, if your tactics work and if you are lucky – then you will be remembered for your principles. Margaret Thatcher's tactics did work; she was shrewd, manipulative and bold, verging on reckless. She was also extremely lucky. Had Labour not been busy disembowelling itself and had a corrupt, desperate dictatorship in South America not taken a nationalistic gamble with some island sheep-farmers, her government would probably have been destroyed after a single term. Had the majority in her cabinet who disagreed with her about the economy been prepared to say boo to a goose, she might have been forced out even before that. In either case her principles, 'Thatcherism', would be a half-forgotten doctrine, mumbled about by historians instead of being the single most potent medicine ever spooned down the gagging post-war British.

Looking back more than a quarter of a century later, the epic events of the early eighties seem to have a clear pattern. Powerful ideas challenge the consensus and, after a nail-biting struggle, defeat the consensus. The early reverses of the Thatcherites, the 'New Right' promising 'a New Enlightenment', are turned into massive, nation-changing victories. Freedom wins. Yet if you stand back and ask what sort of Britain Mrs Thatcher, the grocer's daughter, the devout Lincolnshire Christian, hoped to create, the story is odder. She did not believe in privatizing industries or defeating inflation for merely economic reasons. She wanted to remoralize society, creating a nation whose Victorian values were expressed through secure marriages, self-reliance and savings, restraint, good neighbourliness, hard work. Though much attacked by church leaders she talked of God and morality a lot: 'I am in politics because of the conflict between good and evil.' Yet Thatcherism heralded an age of unparalleled consumption, credit, show-off wealth, quick bucks and sexual libertinism. That is the thing about freedom. When you free people, you can never be sure what you are freeing them for.

In the index to Lady Thatcher's memoirs of her years as Prime Minister, under 'monetary policy', 115 separate page references are given. For 'unemployment' there are fifteen. This is a fair clue to the economic experiment which began immediately after she took office in 1979 and provides the first, the most important, and still the most controversial part of her story. An attentive reader of the Conservative manifesto for the 1979 election would have missed it. After four years of her leadership the Tories were still talking about a wages policy and the importance of consulting with the trade unions, perhaps on the German model. There was talk too of the need to control the money supply and offer council house tenants the right to buy their homes. But other privatization barely featured. Only the comparatively insignificant National Freight Corporation was to be sold. As to unemployment, Mrs Thatcher herself had been vigorously attacking the Labour government for its failure there. In 1977, when it stood at 1.3 million, she had told the country it was absolutely wrong to associate the Tories with people losing their jobs: 'We would have been drummed out of office if we'd had this level of unemployment.' And in case anyone had forgotten the message, the most successful Conservative campaign poster of the election, created by Charles and Maurice Saatchi, her advertising maestros, featured a long queue of gloomy-looking people (in fact Tory activists from North London) filing under a sign reading Unemployment Office, with the headline: 'Labour Isn't Working'.

If voters had studied the new Prime Minister a little more closely they would have noticed a more abrasive edge. She had been aggressive about the failure to control the trade unions – 'Never forget how near this country came to government by picket' – and had already won the insult from the leaders of the Soviet Union of 'Iron Lady' for a powerfully anti-communist speech in 1977. It was an insult that pleased her very much rather as the derisive cartoon lampooning Harold Macmillan as 'Supermac' had become a badge of honour for him and 'Tarzan' would for Michael Heseltine. Irony rarely works with politicians of the first rank. But the voter might then have looked at the people around the Iron Lady and noted just how many of them were old-style mainstream Conservatives in the Heath tradition. To the extent that she was radical, she was clearly completely surrounded and outnumbered. It was calculated that of the possible Tory cabinet members, just two (Keith Joseph and Norman St John Stevas) had actually voted for her in the leadership contest of 1975. There had even been a bizarre notion to lure the former Labour Chancellor, Roy Jenkins, back from Brussels, where he was in rather happy self-imposed exile from British politics, to take over the Treasury again as Mrs Thatcher's Tory Chancellor. The mind boggles – as it presumably did in 1977, for the offer was never made.[1] A cabinet of ruddy-faced middle-aged Tory squires and former Heath supporters hardly looked like a revolutionary economic cabal. The man who did become Chancellor, Geoffrey Howe, was eye-rubbingly reassuring, blander than warm milk. Denis Healey had memorably compared being attacked by him in the Commons to being savaged by a dead sheep. A magazine competition of the time asked readers to think of a line to use if the door rang one night and neighbours you could not stand were on the doorstep keen to join a party. The winning answer was. 'Oh, do come in. Sir Geoffrey's on sparkling form tonight.' What could possibly be threatening about this lot?

The answer was buried in the personality of the Prime Minister herself, a far more determined woman than most people realized. The single most important influence through her life seems not to have been an economic theorist or even her husband Denis, but her father. Alderman Alfred Roberts was a self-made, austere, hard-working owner of a grocer's shop strategically placed on the main road north from London, the A1, at Grantham in Lincolnshire. He did not believe in fripperies or waste – there was no inside loo or hot running water in Margaret's childhood – and was a strong Methodist. Though an independent in local politics and keen enough for municipal action when he became mayor in 1945, Roberts was of Tory instincts. He was a pillar of the local community in an age when both pillar and community meant something – not only serving as mayor but chairing local charities, the Workers' Educational Association and acting as a director of a local bank. He was a living exemplar of the kind of independent-minded local politics that would be devastated by the governments of his daughter and her successor. Meanwhile, he taught his daughter to argue. In this he was extremely successful.

Margaret Roberts was not only self-certain but clever. She won a scholarship place at the local grammar school. She went to Oxford to study chemistry, taught by among others the Nobel Prize-winning Dorothy Hodgkin, who rated her, and whose portrait hangs in Downing Street to this day. More significantly, she joined the University Conservatives, something regarded as eccentric in Attlee-era Oxford. Her early career was as an industrial chemist and she can be blamed for the waxy, air-filled texture of cheap ice creams sold from vans in summertime. She moved on to become a tax barrister, though not the kind who used the Bar as a training for politics. Tax law and chemistry meant an attention to facts and to detail. None of this was glamorous. At Oxford and in London, she was more the anonymous hard worker, like that other provincial Methodist who recoiled from public schoolboy flash, young Harold Wilson. But she was a Tory and ambitious; unlike Wilson who kept his Yorkshire accent as a badge of belonging, she lost her Lincolnshire burr as a passport in her direction of travel. In the words of her biographer Hugo Young, she 'was born a northerner but became a southerner, the quintessence of a Home Counties politician'.

Her two failed attempts to enter Parliament for Dartford in Kent brought her the other crucial figure in her life, her husband Denis. A divorced Kent businessman who had had a good war, his political views were to the right of hers. A keen rugby coach and good golfer, he would become much satirized later as bumbling and henpecked, always with a large G&T in one hand a nervous glance for She Who Must Be Obeyed. In fact Denis was a highly successful executive, rising through the sale of a family paint and chemicals company to the top of Burmah Oil, and retiring very rich in 1975. He provided her with the money and the political, moral support which allowed them to have twins while Mrs Thatcher, as she now was, devoted herself to politics. In the eighties, he managed to keep out of the limelight so that his hard-right views on South Africa, immigrants, the BBC and the feckless working classes created no scandal.

It was a loving marriage which sustained her superbly. In the fifties there was nothing distinctive about the politics of his young wife. It was enough that she was fighting to win a seat as one of the very few women in the Commons, something achieved when she was elected for the well-off middle-class seat of Finchley in 1959. Her politics were formed, nevertheless, by the experience of the post-war years. Seen from above, the socialist experiment in planning and fair shares might have looked noble, she concluded. But from below it was a maze of deprivation, shortage and envy. The Housewives' League has been mentioned earlier in this book. Far later, Thatcher looked back: 'No one who lived through austerity, who can remember snoek, Spam and utility clothing, could mistake the petty jealousies, minor tyrannies, ill-neighbourliness and sheer sourness of those years for idealism and equality.'[2]

As we have seen, Thatcher had risen quietly through the party until as Heath's Education Secretary she had presided over a joyous, reckless slaughter of grammar schools and played her part in the high-spending consensus policies she later repudiated. When Joseph had his great conversion to free-market economics and monetarism she was with him but still several paces behind. She had won the leadership from Heath to general stupefaction and had been patronized and sneered at as Opposition leader. Only a few commentators had spotted what was coming. In romantic vein the former Labour MP and now television interviewer Brian Walden was telling people that the country needed someone like Margaret Thatcher. 'In years to come great novels and poems will be written about her.'[3] But this was not the general view. During the 1979 election, using all the skills of her new image-makers and advertising agency, and with a shrewd understanding of the importance of television, she was still trailing Callaghan in the personal popularity stakes, by six points at the beginning of the campaign and a whopping nineteen points by the end. It was Labour unpopularity that cost the party power, not Mrs Thatcher's allure.

The quotation chosen for her to say as she stood for the first time as prime minister on the steps of Number Ten was popularly but wrongly attributed to St Francis of Assisi. It was in fact Victorian. It was also endlessly used to show what a hypocrite she was. Taking what she said as a whole, this is not fair. It read: 'Where there is discord, may we bring harmony. Where there is error, may we bring truth. Where there is doubt, may we bring faith. Where there is despair, may we bring hope.' The harmony, it is fair to say, she rather fell down on. As for truth, in politics it is in the eye of the observer. But for the people she had determined to govern for, the inflation-ravaged and despairing middle classes who doubted whether Britain had a future and believed the unions could never be tamed by the

State, she brought both faith and hope. And more than any Prime Minister since the war, she made the difference herself. Without her the Tory government of 1979–83 would have been entirely different. Without that confrontational self-certainty and determination not to be bested, Britain would have been back with a pay policy, Keynesian public spending policies and a business-as-usual deal with the European Community within eighteen months. Only a few had the chance to see the real Thatcher before she won power. The British ambassador in Iran was one. In 1978 he had been with her on a visit to Tehran, when she suddenly said that there were still people in the Conservative Party who believed in consensus politics. The ambassador, Sir Anthony Parsons, replied that most British people did, including him. 'I regard them as Quislings, as traitors,' she replied. Strong language? 'I know. I mean it.' The 'Assisi' quotation was pious and a hostage to events but it was not cynical. Had people been able to hear her words to Parsons at the time, they would have had the full picture.

The crucial issue was grip, which in 1979 meant gripping inflation, which to the Thatcherites meant monetarism. As we have seen, modern monetarism originated in the fifties but had only really become fashionable by the mid-seventies after Heath and Barber let the money supply out of control and huge inflation followed. Its most prominent theorist, the American economist Milton Friedman, was awarded the Nobel Prize in 1975. Denis Healey had pursued a policy of restraining public spending through cash limits and tax rises which had the effects monetarism suggested, though never believing in the numbers and targets he was obliged to publish. The basic proposition of monetarism is almost universally accepted, which is that inflation is related to the quantity of money in the economy. Where it diverges from Keynesian economics is in arguing that the sole important job of government in economic management is therefore to control the money supply and that this can be scientifically measured and calibrated. The other issues, unemployment, productivity and so on, will eventually resolve themselves. The intellectual attraction is obvious. Conventional economic management had become a horrendously difficult and uncertain business, juggling uncertain and out-of-date information about output, the balance of payments, unemployment, inflation – a game with one too many rules ever to fully grasp. Monetarism swept away all that. Only hold firm to the principle, get the money supply down, and you will succeed. In 1979 it had not been widely tested outside the military dictatorship of Chile.

In practice Thatcher and her tight circle of economic ministers and advisers, who kept the rest of the cabinet in the dark, did have other objectives. They could have restricted the money supply by raising income tax but she was a tax-cutter. Almost immediately Howe cut the basic rate of income tax from 33 per cent to 30 per cent and the top rate from 83 per cent to 60 per cent. Spending cuts were agreed too but to make up the difference a huge rise in value added tax, doubling to 15 per cent, came in. Money was being redistributed from the masses, paying more for meals, clothes and other items, to higher-rate taxpayers. One of the Tory moderates, Jim Prior, following the manifesto, unveiled a bill for trade union reform that banned the closed shop unless 80 per cent of workers wanted it, provided public money for strike and union ballots, and outlawed secondary picketing of the kind that had been so widely seen during the 'winter of discontent'. It would have been radical under another government. Thatcher expressed bitter disappointment that it did not go further and outlaw all secondary action. She castigated him as a 'false squire', one of a class of Tories who 'have all the outward show of a John Bull – ruddy face, white hair, bluff manner – but inwardly they are political calculators who see the task of Conservatives as retreating gracefully before the Left's inevitable advance.'[4] This was a mean and foolish verdict; Prior was simply a shrewd politician, taking one step at a time. In frustration Thatcher suddenly announced that strikers would now be assumed to be getting union strike pay and so would not qualify for social security. The battle lines were being clearly set.

Howe pursued his strategy through a second Budget in 1980 setting out the scientific sounding Medium Term Financial Strategy, or MTFS, with detailed predictions about the growth of the chosen measurement of money, sterling M3. But with inflation raging, a recession biting and credit restrictions loosened, it was impossible to enforce, just as Healey had predicted. The money supply was meant to be growing for 1980–1 at around 8 per cent but actually grew at nearly 19 per cent. The monetarists risked looking like fools. Strike-ravaged and low-productivity British Leyland came begging for yet more money but instead of telling the State car-maker to close, or ordering it to be sold off, Thatcher gave way, very much as Heath had when Rolls-Royce had tested his opposition to bail-outs. Rolls-Royce eventually thrived, however, while BL died. There was a steel strike and though the government talked tough and stood firm, the eventual settlement was high and the unions were certainly not humiliated. By the second half of the year unemployment was up by more than 800,000 and hundreds of manufacturing businesses were going bust, throttled by the rising exchange rate. Industrialists, who had looked to the Tories with such delight, were beginning to despair. Prices were up by 22 per cent in a year, wages by a fifth. At the Tory conference of 1980 cabinet dissidents began to make speeches subtly criticizing the whole project. These coded bat-squeaks of alarm, demonstrating early on that the Tory left had little real fight in it, were dismissed by Thatcher in a phrase found for her by the playwright Ronald Millar: 'You turn if you want to. The lady's not for turning.'

The word 'wet' was a public schoolboy term meaning soppy or weak. It was being applied by monetarist Tories to their Heathite opponents by the mid-seventies. In the great Thatcher cabinet battles of the early eighties it was appropriated to refer particularly to the senior ministers who did not agree with her – notably Prior, Francis Pym, Sir Ian Gilmour, Mark Carlisle, Norman St John Stevas, Peter Walker, Christopher Soames and (arguably) Michael Heseltine. All had subtly different analyses but all were panicking about the deflation being visited upon an already weak economy by Howe. She would punish them for their lack of faith. They were in the majority and had they revolted the history of Britain would have been very different. But 'wet' was accurate in a wider sense. They rarely tried to face her down, they did not settle on joint action to make her change course and though there were many threats to resign on points of principle, the cabinet dissidents waited till she fired or demoted them.

The great confrontation would have come in 1981. Howe believed that despite unemployment at 2.7 million and heading towards 3 million, despite the economy continuing to shrivel, with new bankruptcies being reported by the day and the biggest collapse in industrial production in a single year since 1921, and despite the lack of any clear control over the money supply, he must go further still. Swingeing cuts and rises in taxes, this time by freezing tax thresholds, would take a further £4 bn out of the economy. Thatcher told her new economic adviser Alan Walters that 'they may get rid of me for this' but that it would be worth it for doing the right thing. Outside her circle, it seemed anything but right. Famously, 364 economists wrote to the papers denouncing the policies. The Conservatives crashed to third place in the opinion polls behind the SDP and the left-wing Labour Party of Michael Foot. On the streets rioting seemed to be confirming all the worst fears of those who had predicted that monetarism would tear the country apart.

This was the moment when Thatcher's self-certainty would be tested most clearly. Any normal politician would have flinched. Churchill, Macmillan, Heath, Wilson and Callaghan would have ordered in the Chancellor and called quietly for a change in direction, blowing smoke in all directions to hide the retreat. Thatcher egged her Chancellor on. If anything, she thought he had not gone far enough. In ringing terms she told the Tory Party faithful to stay calm and strong: 'This is the road I am resolved to follow. This is the path I must go. I ask all who have spirit – the bold, the steadfast and the young at heart – to stand and join with me.' In early April 1981 riots broke out in Brixton. Shops were burned and looted, streets barricaded and more than 200 people, most of them police, were injured. Mrs Thatcher's response was to pity the shopkeepers. Lord Scarman was asked to hold a public inquiry; but in the first week of July, trouble began again, this time in the heavily Asian west London suburb of Southall, with petrol-bombs, arson attacks and widespread pelting of the police. Then Toxteth in Liverpool erupted, the worst of all, and continued for nearly two weeks. Black youths, then whites, petrol bombed the police, waved guns and burned both cars and buildings. The police responded with CS gas, the first time it had been used on the streets of mainland Britain, and with baton charges. As in London, hundreds were injured and here one man was killed. Toxteth was followed by outbreaks of looting and arson in Manchester's Moss Side.

With unemployment reaching 60 per cent among young blacks, and both Liverpool and Manchester having suffered badly from recent factory closures, many saw this as clearly linked to the Thatcher–Howe economics; what Denis Healey, from opposition, was now calling 'sado-monetarism'. (He had called it punk monetarism but his children told him this was unfair to punk rockers.) Michael Heseltine at his own insistence was despatched for a series of extraordinarily frank exchanges with young black men in Toxteth. He took up their frank allegations of racism with the local police and bullied local bankers and industrialists into coming with him to see how bad conditions were at first hand. Back in London he wrote a famous internal memorandum, 'It Took a Riot', calling for a change of industrial and social polices to help places like Toxteth – government money to bring in private investment, job creation schemes and a minister for Liverpool, for the next year at least; Heseltine argued that anything less was not compatible with the best traditions of the Tory Party. He stuck with Liverpool for well over a year, helping bring renovation projects, new money and a morale-boosting garden festival, attended by 3 million people.

Mrs Thatcher knew a rival when she saw one. There was only room in this party for one blonde. She described the Heseltine initiative merely as 'skilful public relations'. She had also visited Liverpool and drew very different conclusions:

> I had been told that some of the young people involved got into trouble through boredom and not having enough to do. But you only had to look at the grounds around these houses with the grass untended, some of it almost waist high, and the litter, to see this was a false analysis. They had plenty of constructive things to do if they wanted. Instead, I asked myself how people could live in such circumstances without trying to clear up the mess.

The problem was lack of initiative and self-reliance created by years of dependency on the State, and compounded by the media. It was nothing whatever to do, she snorted, with sterling M3*. No better expression can be found of the gap between the monetarist true believers and the old Tories.

Her views unaltered, Thatcher then went into full-scale battle with the 'wets'. The provocation on both sides was Howe's discovery that after the ferocious Budget of 1981, he would need to implement yet another tight squeeze in the coming year. Another £5 bn cut was needed for the 1982 Budget. There was something like a full-scale cabinet revolt. Heseltine, fresh from Liverpool, warned of despair and electoral meltdown. Other ministers called for a return to planning, warned wildly of what had happened in Hitler's Germany and, in the case of Gilmour, lethally quoted Churchill too: 'However beautiful the

---

* Thatcher's favoured measurement of the money in circulation, and hence short-hand for monetarism.

strategy, you should occasionally look at the results.' Even monetarist true believers seemed to be deserting. Thatcher herself called it one of the bitterest arguments in a cabinet in her time. She became extremely angry. She had once said that given six strong men, she could get through what was ahead. Now she was well short. Drawing the meeting to a close, she prepared to counter-attack. St John Stevas had already been sacked. Now Soames, Mark Carlisle and Gilmour went too, while Prior was moved away from the centre, to Northern Ireland. She had realized she could afford to take her internal critics out, department by department, clever riposte by clever riposte.

They might have guessed. It was not just on the economy that she was, by the old standards of the seventies, ferociously determined. In a series of strikes she had intervened to stop ministers settling with public sector workers, even when it would have been cheaper to do so. She had already shown her contempt for the top civil servants. She had kept the trade union leaders locked out. Len Murray, the TUC chairman who had spent half the Wilson and Callaghan years sitting round tables with the two of them, lugubriously grazing on the taxpayers' sandwiches, was allowed into Downing Street just three times in Mrs Thatcher's first five years. But the best evidence of the Thatcher style to date had been the struggle with the other European leaders to reclaim roughly £1 bn a year of net British payment to the Community – or, in Thatcherspeak, to get our money back. Doing so involved an anti-diplomatic brawl that careered from Dublin to Luxembourg and from Luxembourg to Brussels. She would not shut up and she would not back down.

The German Chancellor, Helmut Schmidt, pretended to go to sleep and the French President, Valéry Giscard d'Estaing, began to read a newspaper, then got his cars outside to rev their engines – not a subtle hint. She was entirely unfazed. In an epic four-hour meeting over dinner, she simply refused to shut up. Diplomats from all sides suggested interesting side-deals, trade-offs, honourable compromises. She brushed them all aside. Astonishingly, in the end, she got three-quarters of what she had first demanded. Astonishingly, she then said 'No'. It was only when almost her entire cabinet were in favour of settlement that she grudgingly agreed, like a bloodied prizefighter desperate for just another slug, hauled away by worried friends. She might have had the mother of all makeovers – softer voice, softer hair, better teeth – but she was a raw, double-or-quits killer when she was cornered. The press and the country were beginning to notice it. And she wanted supporters, not colleagues, alongside her. Into the ring came Nigel Lawson, Cecil Parkinson and Norman Tebbit. She would need them. For a while chaos inside the Labour Party had helped protect her from the electoral consequences of her move away from the centre-ground. The Tories might be hated but Labour were unelectable.

The Left at War With Itself

Civil wars tend to start with arguments about constitutions, which are always about raw power. Labour's was no different. In its detail it was mind-dazingly complicated. It involved a host of organizations on the left, an alphabet soup of campaigns, coordinating committees and institutes run by people most of whom then disappeared from public life. It began with arguments which seemed merely about party rules, such as whether or not MPs should be able to be sacked by their local parties, and the exact percentage of votes for a Labour leader held by the unions, the party activists and MPs. It was nasty, personal, occasionally physical, and so disgusted the outside world that Labour very nearly disappeared as an effective organization. Those who mocked the smoothness and blandness of Tony Blair's New Labour rarely remembered the voter-repelling punch-up that preceded it. This fight would be fought far from Westminster, in the bars and halls of Blackpool, Brighton and Wembley at Labour and trade union conferences. The issue was simply control – who ran the Labour Party and where was it going?

There was widespread bitterness about what was considered to be the right-wing politics of the defeated Wilson–Callaghan government, and the paltry number of conference decisions which had actually made it into Labour's election manifesto. For years lobby groups had beavered away to change the party's policy, then finally won some 'historic' conference vote, only to see the Labour leadership ignore it all, and then lose anyway. Callaghan, for instance, had simply vetoed an elaborately prepared pledge to abolish the Lords. At the angry Labour conference of 1979 the party's general secretary, no less, told him he wished 'our prime minister would sometimes act in our interests like a Tory prime minister acts in their interests'. One former Labour MP, Tom Litterick, angrily flung a pile of Labour handbooks whose pledges on Europe, housing, women's rights, the disabled and so on had been ditched by Callaghan from the manifesto: ' "Jim will fix it," they said. Aye, he fixed it. He fixed all of us. He fixed me in particular.'[5]

In this atmosphere, the left wanted to take power away from right-wing MPs and the traditional leaders and carry out a revolution from below. They believed that if they could control the party manifesto, choose the leader and bring the MPs to heel, they could turn Labour into a radical socialist party and then, when Thatcher's economics destroyed her, win a general election. Some idea of their ultimate objective is clear from the agenda voted through at Labour's October 1980 conference at Blackpool, which called for taking Britain out of the EC, unilateral nuclear disarmament, the closing of US bases in Britain, no incomes policy and State control of the whole of British industry, plus the creation of a thousand peers to abolish the House of Lords. Britain would become a North Sea Cuba. The Trotskyite Militant Tendency, which had infiltrated the Labour Party, believed in pushing socialist demands so far that the democratic system would collapse and full class revolution would be provoked. Benn, who thought that 'their arguments are sensible and they make perfectly good radical points', saw Militant as no more of a threat than the old *Tribune* group or the pre-war Independent Labour Party. Always a thoroughly decent man, Benn believed the left would end up with a thoroughly decent socialist victory. In fact thuggish intimidation in many local Labour parties by Militants was driving moderate members away in droves. In alliance with them were many mainstream trade unionists who simply felt let down by the Callaghan and Wilson governments; left-wing activists who were not Marxists, and those who were driven above all by single causes such as nuclear disarmament.

Shrewd tactics and relentless campaigning enabled a small number of people to control enough local parties and union branches to have a disproportionate effect in Labour conference votes, where the big and undemocratic union block votes no longer automatically backed the leadership. At the 1980 conference the left won almost every important vote, utterly undermining Callaghan, who quit as leader two weeks later. Because new leadership rules were not yet in place, awaiting a special conference in January, Labour MPs had one final chance to choose their new leader. Michael Foot, the old radical and intellectual who had begun his time in Opposition, characteristically, by composing a book of essays about Swift, Hazlitt, Paine, Disraeli and other literary-political heroes, was persuaded to stand. Benn would have had no chance among Labour MPs, many of whom now saw him as a menacing figure, allied with the Trotskyist sans-culottes outside who would take away their privileges. But Foot was a great parliamentarian and someone had to be found to beat Denis Healey. The former Chancellor, whose natural pugnacity and abusive wit made him plenty of enemies at party conference, had become the villain of the Labour left.

Early on Healey had pinpointed the fatal flaw in their strategy which was that if they did take over the Labour Party, the country wouldn't vote for it. Activists, he told them, were different from 'the great mass of the British people, for whom politics is something to think about once every year at most'.[6] His robust remarks about what would later be called the loony left were hardly calculated to maximize his chances, despite his popularity in the country at the time. At any rate he was eventually beaten by Foot by 139 votes to 129. There are plenty who believe that Foot, who would endure much mockery as a party leader for his shabby appearance and rambling media perform-ances, was actually the man who saved the Labour Party since he was the only leader remotely acceptable to both the old guard and the Bennite insurgents. It was a job that Foot took on entirely out of a sense of duty. With his old-style platform oratory, his intellectualism and his stick, he was always an unlikely figure to topple Margaret Thatcher. Worzel Gummidge against the Iron Lady; it was the stuff of children's pop-up books. It was also the last blast of a romantic socialist intellectualism against the free market.

The left marched on. At the special party conference Labour's rules were indeed changed to give the unions 40 per cent of the votes for future Labour leaders, the activists in the constituencies 30 per cent and the once-dominant MPs only 30 per cent. Labour's struggle now moved to its next and decisive stage, with the left in exuberant mood. It was decided that Benn must challenge Healey for the deputy leadership the following year. This would signal an irreversible move. A Foot–Benn Labour Party was a very different proposition from one in which Healey had a strong voice. Both sides saw it as the final battle. Around the country Benn went campaigning with verve and relentless energy. At public meetings, Healey was booed and heckled and spat at. The vote was clearly going to be very close though with the complicated new electoral college system, no one knew how close.

At this point, two other characters need to be reintroduced, both miners' sons, both left-wingers, both men who had made their names by attacking Heath, one on picket lines and the other on the floor of the Commons. They were Arthur Scargill, the NUM boss, and Neil Kinnock. The intimidation of anyone who would not back Benn was getting worse though Benn himself sailed imperturbably through all that, apparently not noticing what was being said and done in his name. Scargill was one of the most aggressive, enough to finally provoke Kinnock into deciding that he could not support Benn. Nor could he support Healey, a right-winger. So he would abstain. He announced his decision in the Labour newspaper *Tribune*. Kinnock had been slowly moving away from the hard left, and had taken a position as the party's education spokesman. He had run Foot's campaign. Popular in the party, he was regarded with increasing suspicion by Benn himself. But this open break with the left's champion shocked many of his friends. At the conference in Brighton, Benn was eventually beaten by Healey by a whisker, less than one per cent of the votes. Kinnock and Scargill clashed angrily on television. The seaside town was awash with ugly scenes and talk of betrayal. Kinnock was involved in several scuffles and finally, when attacked by a man in a public toilet, 'beat the shit out of him . . . apparently there was blood and vomit all over the floor'. It was the inelegant end to an inelegant revolt; after that the left would be powerful in the party but could never hope to seize it.

The Nice Gang

By then, however, many thought it was already too late. For a breakaway had begun and a new party was being formed. The idea had come first from Roy Jenkins before the Bennite revolt, as he contemplated the state of the British party system from his grand offices in Brussels, where he was President of the Commission. Offered a BBC lecture in 1979 to ruminate about the future, he argued that perhaps the two-party system established since Victorian times had come to the end of its useful life. Coalitions, he said, were not such a bad thing. It was time to strengthen 'the radical centre' and find a way through that accepted the free market economy but which also took unemployment seriously. His lecture was coded, tentative but clear enough. He was no longer a Labour politician and he was looking around. He was in touch with David Steel, the Liberal leader, but felt that although he was close to Liberal thinking, only a new party would give British politics the hard poke it needed. Always a famous host, he began holding lunches for old friends from the right of the Labour party, including Bill Rodgers, who was still in the shadow cabinet, and Shirley Williams, who had lost her seat but was still one of the best-liked politicians in the country. Then Jenkins made a second speech to journalists and their guests, Kinnock among them, in the Commons where he speculated more openly about a new party as 'an experimental plane' which might just take off. At this stage the public reaction from Labour MPs was discouraging. Williams had said that a new centre party would have 'no roots, no principles, no philosophy and no values'. David Owen, the young doctor who had been a rare glamorous star as Foreign Secretary in the Callaghan government and was now fighting against unilateral nuclear disarmament, said Labour moderates must stay in the party and fight even if it took ten or twenty years.

The Bennite revolt changed many minds. After the Wembley conference, at which Owen was booed for his views on defence, he, Jenkins, Williams and Rodgers issued the Limehouse Declaration, describing Wembley as 'calamitous' and calling for a new start in British politics. That was duly formalized as the Social Democratic Party or SDP two months later, in March 1981. In total thirteen Labour MPs defected to it and many more might have done had not Roy Hattersley and others fought very hard to persuade them not to. Within two weeks 24,000 messages of support had flooded in and a temporary headquarters, manned by volunteers, had been found. Peers, journalists, students, academics and others were keen to join. The nice people's party was on its way. Public meetings were packed from Scotland to the south coast of England. Media coverage was lavish and flattering. In September an electoral pact was agreed with the Liberal Party after delirious scenes at the party's Llandudno conference, and the Alliance was formed. Trains proved an unlikely theme of the new party, with the SDP holding (literally) rolling conferences for their first two years, journalists and politicians crammed together singing their way round provincial Britain. After giving Labour a terrible shock in the Warrington by-election, the SDP won their first seat when Shirley Williams took Crosby from the Conservatives in November, with nearly half the votes cast, followed by Jenkins winning Glasgow Hillhead from the Tories the following year. Some sense of the early excitement can be captured by the thought that had they taken their stratospheric opinion poll ratings seriously (which sensibly they did not) the SDP could have expected to win nearly 600 out of the then 635 parliamentary seats.

His victory allowed Jenkins to become the leader of the party in the Commons. But he had lost his old mastery of the place; or perhaps leading a rump group caught between Thatcher's Conservatives and the baleful Labour ex-comrades was simply impossible. In due course Jenkins would lose his seat at the general election and Owen would take over as leader. The personality problems that would later cause such mayhem were soon unavoidable. David Owen was handsome, romantic, arrogant, dogmatic, Welsh, patriotic and never a team player. He had always believed that leadership was more rightly his and feared that Jenkins was leading the SDP towards a merger with the Liberals. Owen saw himself still as a socialist although of a new kind. Jenkins, for his part, found his old protégé Owen prickly and arrogant. In short, their relationship was every bit as cordial as that between Tony Blair and Gordon Brown in later years. As with that, personal rivalry did hold the party back. The upsurge of the SDP shook even Mrs Thatcher, while it led some in the Labour Party to fear their cause was finished.

It also gave a new lease of life to the Liberals. In the early fifties, the once mighty party of Gladstone and Asquith had been a negligible force, down to half a dozen MPs and 3 per cent of the national vote. Under Jo Grimond it had enjoyed a revival as the party of genuine liberalism and in the sixties it attracted an increasingly radical wing, anti-nuclear, anti-apartheid, in favour of community politics and, in general, amiably stroppy. Liberal conferences were distinguished by stalls of organic apples, large hairy men in sandals and enthusiasts for obscure forms of land taxation, as if a medieval fair had somehow collided with a chartered surveyors' seaside outing. Yet so great was the public disenchantment with conventional politics that this unlikely caravan rumbled ahead, particularly under the flamboyant, dandyish, sharp-witted Jeremy Thorpe. Faced with allegations about a homosexual affair and a murder plot (though only a dog perished, and the prosecution failed), Thorpe resigned. By the early eighties the party was being led by Steel, 'the boy David', looking for a strategy. The SDP provided a route back to the centre ground but Owen was not alone in despising the Liberals and the eventual merger between the parties was bitter and difficult. Nevertheless, by the early spring of 1982 the SDP and Liberals could look forward with some confidence to breaking the mould of British politics. Mrs Thatcher was hugely unpopular. Labour was in uproar. What could possibly go wrong?

The Falklands: Big Hair and Bald Men

One of the many ironies of the Thatcher story is that she was rescued from the political consequences of her monetarism by the blunders of her hated Foreign Office. In the great economic storms of 1979–81, and on the European budget battle, she had simply charged ahead, ignoring all the flapping around her in pursuit of a single goal. In the South Atlantic she would do exactly the same and with her great luck she was vindicated. A pattern was being established – 'blinkered and proud of it' – and she would move in the space of a couple of months from being one of the least popular prime ministers ever to being an unassailable national heroine. It could all so easily have gone wrong. A few more fuses working on Argentine bombs, another delivery of French-made Exocet missiles, a different point chosen for the attack, and the Falklands War could have been a terrible disaster, confirming an Argentine dictatorship in power and ending Mrs Thatcher's political career. Of all the gambles in modern British public life, sending a task-force of ships from the shrunken and underfunded Royal Navy 8,000 miles away to take back some islands by force was one of the more extreme.

On both sides, the conflict derived from colonial quarrels. The Falkland Islands had been named after a Royal Navy treasurer when English sailors first landed there in 1690 and though there had been Spanish and French settlements, the scattering of islands had been declared a British colony in 1833. Argentina, formed out of old Spanish colonies, had claimed them from the start too on the basis of proximity. By the sixties, the economic future of the 1,800 islanders who depended on sheep farming and fishing looked bleak and the Foreign Office was clearly keen to somehow dispose of the problem. Labour had sent a submarine at one point to warn off an increasingly menacing Argentina. Under the Conservatives, however, a couple of serious mistakes were made. First there was a proposal to give sovereignty to the Argentines, but to lease back management of the islands for a fixed period, so that their Britishness would remain intact. Margaret Thatcher later distanced herself from the whole idea, but it was seriously entertained at the time and only withdrawn after protests from the islanders and angry backbench criticism. Then came the announced withdrawal of the only British naval vessel in the region, a patrol vessel HMS *Endurance*, while the Falkland islanders were given no special status in new legislation on British nationality. In Buenos Aires a newly installed junta under General Leopoldo Galtieri thought it understood what was going on. Galtieri was heavily dependent on the backing of the Argentine navy, itself passionately keen on taking over the islands, known to Argentina as the Malvinas. The following year would see the 150th anniversary of British ownership which the Argentines feared would somehow be used to reassert the Falklands' British future. The junta misread Whitehall's lack of policy and concluded that an invasion would be easy, popular and never reversed.

In March an Argentine ship tested the waters, or rather the land of South Georgia, a small dependency south of the Falklands, landing scrap-metal dealers there without warning. Then on 1 April the main invasion began, a landing by Argentine troops which had been carefully prepared for by local representatives of the national airline. In three hours it was all over, and the eighty British marines surrendered, having nonetheless killed five Argentine soldiers and injured seventeen with no losses of their own. In London, there was mayhem. Thatcher had had a few hours' warning of what was happening from the Defence Secretary, John Nott. Calling a hurried meeting in her

Commons office, she had to wait while the Chief of the Naval Staff, Sir John Leach, was rescued by a Tory whip after being detained by the Commons police, who had not recognized him in his civilian clothes. But Leach made the difference, giving her clarity and hope when her ministers offered confusion. He was her kind of man. He told her he could assemble a task-force of destroyers, frigates and landing craft, led by Britain's two remaining aircraft carriers, *Hermes* and *Invincible*. The task-force would be ready to sail within forty-eight hours and the islands could be retaken by force. She told him to go ahead. She would decide later whether to authorize it to actually try to re-invade the islands. Could some kind of deal be done?

A part of the Falklands story not revealed at the time was the deep involvement, and embarrassment, of the United States. Mrs Thatcher and Ronald Reagan had already begun to develop a personal special relationship. But the Argentine junta was important to the US for its anti-communist stance and as a trading partner. The United States began a desperate search for a compromise while Britain began an equally frantic search for allies at the United Nations. In the end, Britain depended on the Americans not just for the Sidewinder missiles underneath her Harrier jets, without which Thatcher herself said the Falklands could not have been retaken, but for intelligence help and – most of the time – diplomatic support too. These were the last years of the Cold War. Britain mattered more in Washington than any South American country. Still, many attempts were made by the US inter-mediary, the Secretary of State, Alexander Haig, to find a compromise. They would continue throughout the fighting. Far more of Thatcher's time was spent reading, analysing and batting off possible deals than contemplating the military plans. Among those advising a settlement was the new Foreign Secretary, Francis Pym, appointed after the thoroughly decent Lord Carrington had insisted on resigning to atone for his department's sins. Pym and the Prime Minister were at loggerheads over this and she would punish him in due course. She had furious conversations with Reagan by phone as he tried to persuade her that some outcome short of British sovereignty, probably involving the United States, was acceptable.

But as with the European budget Thatcher broke down the diplomatic deal-making into undiplomatic irreducibles. Would the islanders be allowed full self-determination? Would the Argentine aggression be rewarded? Under pulverizing pressure she refused to budge. She was confronted too by a moral question she did not duck, which was that many healthy young men were likely to die or be horribly injured, to defend a word, sovereignty. In the end, almost a thousand did die, one for every two islanders, and many others were burned, maimed and psychologically wrecked. But she argued that the whole structure of national identity and law were in play. She wrote to President Reagan, who had described the Falklands as 'that little ice-cold bunch of land down there', that if Britain gave way to the various Argentine snares, 'the fundamental principles for which the free world stands would be shattered'. Reagan kept trying. Pym pressed. The Russians harangued. Michael Foot, who had been bellicose at first, now entreated her to find an answer. Later she insisted that she was vividly aware of the blood-price that was waiting and not all consumed by lust for conflict. As it happened, the Argentine junta, divided and belligerent, ensured that a serious deal was never properly put. Their political position was even weaker than hers. Buenos Aires always insisted that the British task-force be withdrawn from the entire area, that Argentine representatives take part in any interim administration and that if talks failed Britain would lose sovereignty.

Politically, Thatcher had believed that from the start that to cave in would finish her. The press and the Conservative Party were seething about the original diplomatic blunders. Pressed to the wall, even Labour seemed to be in favour of force to recapture the islands, with Foot harking back to the appeasement of fascism in the thirties. For the SDP David Owen was as belligerent as any Tory. Thatcher established a small war cabinet, keeping her Chancellor, and hence mere money, out of it. Nor were the politicians out of touch with the mood of the country. The polls showed anger with the government for allowing the invasion to happen. So the task-force, now up to more than twenty vessels strong, was steadily reinforced. Eventually it would comprise more than a hundred ships and 25,000 men. The world was transfixed, if also bemused. The headline on a New York paper read 'The Empire Strikes Back.'

Well so it did. By the end of the month South Georgia was recaptured and a large number of Argentine prisoners taken: Thatcher urged questioning journalists simply to 'rejoice, rejoice'. Then came one of the most controversial episodes in this short war. A British submarine, the *Conqueror*, was following the ageing but heavily armed Argentine cruiser, the *Belgrano*. The British task-force was exposed and feared a pincer movement, although the *Belgrano* later turned out to be outside an exclusion zone announced in London, and steaming away from the fleet. With her military commanders at Chequers Thatcher authorized a submarine attack. The *Belgrano* was sunk, with the loss of 321 sailors. The *Sun* newspaper cheered: 'Gotcha!' The Labour MP Tam Dalyell, a rare early opponent of the war in the Commons, began a lonely campaign to show that the sinking was politically motivated and immoral, possibly connected to an attempt to scotch the latest peace move. Soon afterwards, a British destroyer, HMS *Sheffield*, was hit by an Argentine Exocet missile. Forty died and she later sank. The war had started for real.

On 18 May 1982 the war cabinet agreed that landings on the Falklands should go ahead, despite lack of full air cover and worsening weather. By landing at the unexpected bay of San Carlos in low cloud, British troops got ashore in large numbers. Heavy Argentine air attacks, however, took a serious toll. Two frigates were badly damaged, another was sunk, then another, then a destroyer, then a container ship with vital supplies. In London the success of the landing seemed on the edge. The requisitioned liner *Queen Elizabeth 2* was nearby, vulnerable and carrying 3,000 troops. Thatcher called it the worst night. And indeed, had the Argentine air force bombs been properly fused for the attacks, far more would have exploded; had their navy had more Exocets, far more would have been launched. Had British Harrier jets not been equipped with the latest US missiles and helped by the secret provision of American AWACS radar cover, the situation would have been desperate. As it was, 3,000 British troops had a secure beach-head and began to fight their way inland. Over the next few weeks they captured the settlements of Goose Green and Darwin, killing 250 Argentine soldiers and capturing 1,400 for the loss of twenty British lives. Colonel 'H' Jones became the first celebrated hero of the conflict when he died leading 2 Para against heavy Argentine fire along with Sergeant Ian McKay of 3 Para.

The battle then moved to the tiny capital, Port Stanley, or rather to the circling hills above it where the Argentine army was dug in on Mount Tumbledown, Wireless Ridge, Sapper Hill and Mount William. Before the final assault two British landing ships, the *Sir Tristram* and the *Sir Galahad*, were hit by missiles and the Welsh Guards suffered dreadful losses, many of the survivors being badly burned. Ministers talked of losing a ship a day, while at a summit in Versailles Thatcher was again swatting off attempts to halt the fighting by diplomatic means. By now she was determined that nothing short of Argentine surrender would do. The United States, on the other hand, was still desperately hoping to preserve the junta and avoid its humiliation. The scenes at the United Nations were close to farce. They ended after the final attack on the demoralized and badly led Argentine troops forced their leader, General Menendez, to surrender. The British commander arrived at the door of the West Store in Stanley, where many islanders were taking refuge, with the immortal words, 'Hullo, I'm Jeremy Moore. Sorry it's taken rather a long time to get here.'[7]

Many people thought the war mere butchery for a meaningless prize. The most famous comment came from that mordant South American writer Jorge Luis Borges who said it reminded him of two bald men fighting over a comb. Tam Dalyell hounded the Prime Minister with parliamentary questions as he sought to prove the sailors on the *Belgrano* had been killed to keep the war going, not for reasons of military necessity. He was not alone in his outrage. One of the few genuinely dramatic moments in the 1983 election campaign came when Mrs Thatcher was challenged on television about the *Belgrano* by a woman who seemed a match for her, as few men were. Among the Labour leadership, Denis Healey accused her of glorying in slaughter and the next leader, Neil Kinnock, got into trouble when, responding to a heckler who said that at least Margaret Thatcher had guts, he replied that it was a pity other people had had to leave theirs on Goose Green to prove it.

The Falklands War was both throwback and throw-forward. For millions it seemed utterly out of time, a Victorian gunboat war in a nuclear age. Yet for more millions still (it was a popular war) it was a wholly unexpected and almost mythic symbol of rebirth. Margaret Thatcher herself lost no time in telling the country what she thought the war had meant. Speaking at Cheltenham racecourse in early July, she said: 'We have ceased to be a nation in retreat. We have instead a newfound confidence, born in the economic battles at home and found true 8,000 miles away . . . Printing money is no more. Rightly this government has abjured it. Increasingly this nation won't have it . . .

That too is part of the Falklands factor.' The old country had rekindled her old spirit, she concluded: 'Britain found herself again in the South Atlantic and will not look back from the victory she has won.' The Toxteth riots may not have had anything to do with sterling M3 but apparently the activities of 2 Para did.

The Falklands War changed Margaret Thatcher's personal story and the country's politics. But it merged into a wider sense that confrontation was required in public life. There was a raw and bloody edge to the spirit of the age. In Northern Ireland, from the spring of 1981, a hideous IRA hunger-strike was going on, which would lead to the death of Bobby Sands and nine others. 'A convicted criminal,' Margaret of Lincolnshire briskly called him. 'He chose to take his own life. It was a choice that his organisation did not allow to many of its victims.' As with civil service strikers or the United Nations peace party, Thatcher was utterly determined not to flinch, as rock-hard as her ruthless Irish republican enemies. They had assassinated Lord Mountbatten in 1979 and the mainland bombing campaign went on, with attacks on the Chelsea barracks, then the Hyde Park bombings, when eight people were killed and fifty-three injured. And, indeed, none of them were offered any choice.

Overhanging the violence at home and part of the backdrop of the Falklands War, was the residual fear of global nuclear war. With hindsight the grey old Soviet Union of Brezhnev, Andropov and Chernenko may seem a rusted giant, clanking helplessly towards its collapse. This was not how it seemed in the early eighties. The various phases of strategic arms reduction treaties were under way but to well-informed and intelligent analysts the Soviet empire still seemed mighty, belligerent and unpredictable. New SS20 missiles were being deployed by the Russians, targeted on cities and military bases across Western Europe. In response, Nato was planning a new generation of American Pershing and Cruise missiles to be sited in Europe, including in Britain. In the late winter of 1979 Russian troops had begun arriving in Afghanistan. Mikhail Gorbachev was an obscure candidate member of the Politburo, twenty-eighth in the pecking order, working on agricultural planning, and *glasnost* was a word no one in the West had heard of. Poland's free trade union movement Solidarity was being crushed by a military dictator.

Western politics echoed with arguments over weapons systems, disarmament strategies and the need to stand up to the Soviet threat. Moscow had early and rightly identified Thatcher as one of its most implacable enemies in the West and when, eighteen months after her election victory, she was joined by a new US President, Ronald Reagan, she had a soul-mate in Washington. Reagan may have been many things Thatcher was not – sunny, lazy, uninterested in detail and happy to run huge deficits. But like her he saw the world in black and white terms, a great stage where good and evil, God and Satan, were pitched in endless conflict. Their shared detestation of socialism in general and the Soviet Union in particular underpinned a remarkably close personal relationship; she was his first overseas visitor after his election; for her he was always 'Ronnie'. To young politicians watching from the wings – people such as Tony Blair – lessons about the effect of a popular war and the importance of keeping close the White House were being quietly absorbed.

To the public who had barely focused on Thatcher a few years earlier, she was now becoming a vividly divisive figure. On one side were those who felt they at last had a warrior queen for hard times, a fighter whose convictions were clear and who would never quit, someone who had cut through the endless dispiriting fudging of earlier decades. On the other were those who saw her as a dangerous and bloodthirsty figure, driven by an inhumanly stark world view. To the cartoonists of the *Sun*, *Daily Mail* and other right wing papers she was a Joan of Arc, a glorious Boudicca, surrounded by cringeing wets, apelike trade unionists and spitting Irish terrorists. To the cartoonists of the *Guardian*, *Daily Mirror* and *Spitting Image* she was simply mad, with sharply curved vulture's beak nose, staring eyes and rivets in her hair. Sexual confusion was rife. She was the only real man in her cabinet, or the ultimate housewife who had seized control of the country; or she was the eerie repudiation of femininity, cold, barren and vengeful. France's President Mitterand, who in fact had quite a good relationship with her, summed up the paradox better than any British observer when, after an early meeting he told his Europe minister, 'She has the eyes of Caligula but she has the mouth of Marilyn Monroe.'

The Falklands War confirmed and underlined these opposing views of Thatcher. In a flush of over-confidence she seized her moment so hard she nearly throttled it. She encouraged the government's internal think tank, the Central Policy Review Staff, to come up with a paper about the future of public spending. They came up with a manifesto which can be summed up as Margaret Thatcher unplugged, what she would have liked to do, unconstrained. They suggested ending state funding of higher education; student loans to replace grants; no increases in welfare payments in line with inflation and the entire replacement of the National Health Service with a system of private health insurance, including charges for doctors' visits and medicines – in effect, the end of the Attlee Welfare State. Though some of these ideas would become widely discussed much later and student loans would be brought in by a Labour government, at the time the prospectus was regarded as bonkers by most of those around her. The Prime Minister battled for it but ministers who regarded it as her worst mistake since coming to power leaked the CPRS report to the press in order to kill it off. In this they were successful. The episode was an early indication, long before the poll tax, that Thatcher's charge-ahead politics could produce mistakes as well as triumphs.

The electoral consequences of the Falklands War have been argued about ever since. The government had got inflation down and the economy was at last improving but the overall Conservative record in 1983 was not impressive. The most dramatic de-industrialization of modern times, with hundreds of recently profitable businesses disappearing for ever, had been caused in part by a very high pound, boosted by Britain's new status as an oil producer. This, with the Howe squeeze, was deadly. Later Joseph admitted that 'we hadn't appreciated, any of us' that this 'would lead to such rapid and large de-manning'. Unemployment 'had not been considered a huge problem'.[8] Given the shrinking of the country's industrial base and unemployment at 3 million this was a mistake and a half. Further, this pro-tax-cutting government had seen the total tax burden rise from 34 per cent of GDP to nearly 40 per cent. Public spending, intended to be 40 per cent of GDP, was 44 per cent. The apparently crucial measurement of the money supply showed that it had grown at about double the target.

So there were plenty of large and obvious targets for competent Opposition politicians to take aim at. In an ordinary election the state of the economy would have had the governing party rocking back on their heels. But this was no ordinary election. After the war the Conservatives shot into a sudden and dramatic polls lead over the two

Opposition groups now ranged against them, finishing the equally sudden and dramatic rise of the SDP. In the 1983 general election the new party and its partners, the Liberals, took nearly a quarter of the popular vote. But the electoral system rewarded them with just twenty-three MPs, only six being from the SDP, a bitter harvest after the iridescent bubble-year of 1981–2. Labour was nearly beaten into third place in the votes cast. And the Conservatives won a huge victory, giving Mrs Thatcher a majority of 144 seats, a Tory buffer which kept them in power until 1997. Though there were other factors at play it seems perverse to deny that the Falklands conflict was crucial. It gave Thatcher a story to tell about herself and the country which was simple and vivid and made sense to millions.

The Plague

On 4 July 1982, a gay man called Terry Higgins died in St Thomas's Hospital in central London. He was thirty-seven and one of the first British victims of AIDS, acquired immune-deficiency syndrome, that weakens the body's natural defences and is passed through a virus, HIV. A group of his friends set up a small charity in a flat, the Terrence Higgins Trust, to spread the word about AIDS among gay men, encouraging the use of condoms – since it is spread by blood and body fluid contact – and offering support for others. Though the disease had undoubtedly been present in the late seventies, it was first identified in California in 1981 when gay men started to turn up in medical centres complaining of a rare lung disease and a form of skin cancer until then confined to the elderly. Within a year hundreds of cases had been found, many deaths were occuring and it was clear that the vast majority were among homosexual men – though other groups began to be affected, including some women, intravenous drug users, Haitians, and in Uganda villagers suffering from a mysterious and deadly ailment they called 'slim'. The first target in America was the gay bath houses and saunas known for promiscuous, wild and unprotected sex. These had grown up in San Francisco and Los Angeles, and in New York too, as gay men migrated across America during the sixties and seventies to find the most liberal and liberated culture available.

A similar shift had happened in Britain after the legalization of homosexual acts by men. As in America, gay liberation was confined to the most liberal areas of the largest cities only, in this case mainly London – the gay scenes of Manchester, Edinburgh and other towns followed slightly later. Gay clubs, gay discos and gay saunas, the latter really places for as much promiscuous sex as possible, flourished. Men came south and made up for lost time. Something close to a climate of sexual frenzy developed – a frenzy which would later be imitated by heterosexual youngsters on foreign holidays and resorts. After the years of rationing, the sweetie shop was open. Through the seventies, amid the political and economic grime, a street culture of excess flourished. The excess in clothing, music and football violence has already been discussed. It was accompanied for many by a breaking of sexual restraint, the arrival of the freely available pill for heterosexuals and the new climate of legality for homosexuals. If there was optimism around in these years, it was personal – new freedoms that allowed respite from the surrounding climate of national failure.

So the arrival of AIDS came at a particularly cruel time. Just when homosexuals felt the centuries of repression and shame were finally over, along came a deadly and mysterious disease to destroy their new way of life. For social conservatives, this was exactly the point. AIDS was the medical and moral consequence of promiscuous and unnatural sexual behaviour. As you sow, so shall you reap – almost literally. And thus the scene was set for a confrontation between contending moral philosophies that had been at war since the sixties. Gay culture was briefly on the retreat, clubs closed, clerics drew conclusions. Though gay men were at the cutting edge of the AIDS crisis, it had wider implications. It was not only among homosexuals that promiscuity had become more common; in many ways, gay culture had drawn straight culture along in its wake. So for traditionalists there was a message to the whole society, the possibility of a turn away from the new liberalism.

Except, in the end, it did not turn out quite as anyone expected. Gay organizations sprung up to spread the safe sex message very quickly – the Terrence Higgins Trust became a national institution and is now one of the biggest sexual health charities in Europe, with a staff of 300, plus 800 volunteers. The establishment turned out to be far more sympathetic than might have been expected, from Princess Diana opening the first AIDS-specific ward at Middlesex hospital in 1987, to

Thatcherite ministers talking about condoms. It was a cultural turning point of a kind, and certainly a national education. In the early days, the media fell prone to 'we're all doomed' panics, and the moral condemnation of homosexuals as unnatural creatures, getting what they deserved. James Anderton, the chief constable of police in greater Manchester, talked of homosexuals 'swirling about in a human cesspit of their own making'. His language was widely condemned, but many millions of Britons, mainly but not exclusively older people, are likely to have agreed with his condemnation of buggery and other 'abominable practices'. Dislike of homosexuality was, and still is, strongly rooted. Alongside this was a prudishness about sex generally, which meant early discussion of how AIDS was transmitted was so vague it simply was not understood.

Tabloid newspapers described the 'gay plague' which could, according to rumours passed on by newspapers, be variously caught from lavatory seats, kisses, handshakes, communion wine or sharing a restaurant fork with an infected person. In the early eighties, the BBC was predicting that 70,000 people in England and Wales would die within four years (nearly twenty-five years later the total death toll is 13,000) and that 'by the end of the century there won't be one family that isn't touched in some way by the disease.' The BBC science programme *Horizon* had led public awareness of AIDS in the early days, but in 1986 its film about gay men's sex lives and how the disease was actually transmitted was considered so close to the bone that it was banned, and the negatives solemnly destroyed. Yet across the media, as throughout the political world, attitudes changed rapidly. The same newspapers that spoke about buggers getting their just desserts, now enthusiastically promoted AIDS awareness. The homophobic jibes continued but with less self-confidence. Campaigns for abstinence or the reclaiming of gays back into heterosexual life, which have been common among church groups in America, barely touched more secular Britain. Gay Pride parades, which began as angry, edgy affairs in the eighties, slowly became mainstream to the point where politicians rushed to be associated with them. None of this was expected when AIDS first arrived.

In retrospect, part of the shift in attitude happened not in spite of AIDS but because of it. The public health crisis jolted the way sexuality was discussed. There needed to be a new frankness. This wounded, if not fatally, the grand British tradition of titter and snigger. As it became clear that AIDS could be caught from infected needles and blood transfusions, and occasionally through heterosexual sex, the gay stigma was diluted. Indeed, by rapidly changing sexual practices, gay men were for a time ahead of the rest of the population. Coping with AIDS was one of the most effective public information and healthcare stories of modern times. The turn came in 1986 when Norman Fowler, the health secretary, and Willie Whitelaw, Mrs Thatcher's deputy prime minister, were told to create a national public awareness campaign that would be properly effective. Two more conventional and straight men it would be hard to imagine; Fowler's main concern was family values and he was quickly lobbied by church groups, MPs and others to send out a traditionalist moral message of abstinence. He did nothing of the kind. The advertising agency TBWA was commissioned to produce a campaign, 'Don't Die of Ignorance', which would shock the country into changing sexual habits. They came up with an iceberg image, and a gravel-voiced commentary by the actor John Hurt, which began with the words, 'There is now a dreadful disease . . .' Every single household in Britain received a clear and for the time explicit leaflet.

Over the next few years £73 million was allocated to the campaign. Broadly speaking, it worked. New diagnoses of AIDS, running at more than 3,000 in 1985, fell dramatically over the next few years, staying stable until 1999, when they began to rise again, because of heterosexual cases, mostly connected to Africa, which was undergoing a much worse, indeed genuinely catastrophic pandemic. Because of the wider use of condoms, all sexually transmitted infections fell in the same period, so that cases of syphilis were just a tenth of their pre-AIDS level by the end of the decade. Fowler said later that all the research on his campaign showed that 'the public saw it, that they understood it, that they remembered the campaign, and most of all it actually did change habits'. Britain's figures on the fall of new cases were better than almost any other country's.

The Enemy Within

If the first Thatcher government had been dominated by monetarism and the Falklands War, the second would be dominated by the miners' strike. This was the longest such strike in British history, one of the most bloody and tragic industrial disputes of modern times, and resulted in the total defeat of the miners followed by the virtual end of deep coal-mining in Britain. For Thatcher the lessons were even bigger: 'What the strike's defeat established was that Britain could not be made ungovernable by the Fascist Left. Marxists wanted to defy the law of the land in order to defy the laws of economics. They failed and in doing so demonstrated just how mutually dependent the free economy and a free society really are.' It was a confrontation which was peculiarly soaked in history on all sides. For the Tories, it was essential revenge after the miners' humiliation of Heath, a score they had long been waiting to settle; Margaret Thatcher did indeed speak of 'the enemy within', as compared to Galtieri, the enemy without. For thousands of militant members of the National Union of Mineworkers it was their last chance to end decades of pit closures and save communities under mortal threat. For their leader Arthur Scargill it was an attempt to pull down the government itself and win a class war. As we shall see he was not interested in the detail of pay packets, or in a pit-by-pit discussion of which coalmines were economic. He was determined to force the government, in Thatcher's contemptuous but accurate words, to pay for mud to be mined rather than see a single job lost.

The government had prepared more carefully than Scargill. An early dispute with the NUM had been settled quickly because the battlefield was not yet ready. For two years the National Coal Board had been working with the Energy Secretary, Nigel Lawson, to pile up supplies of coal at the power stations; stocks had steadily grown, while consumption and production both fell. After the Toxteth and Brixton riots the police had been retrained and equipped with full riot gear without which, ministers later confessed, they would have been unable to beat the miners' pickets. Meanwhile, Thatcher had appointed a Scottish-born American, Ian MacGregor, to run the NCB. He had a fierce reputation as a union-buster in the United States and had been brought back to Britain to run British Steel where closures and 65,000 job cuts had won him the title 'Mac the Knife'. He was briefly idolized by the Prime Minister, rather as she admired John King, later Lord King, who had turned round British Airways in the same period, sacking 23,000 staff, about 40 per cent of the total, and turning the loss-maker into a hugely profitable business. These were her tough, no-nonsense men, a refreshing change from the cabinet, though later she would turn against MacGregor, appalled by his lack of political nous. MacGregor's plan was to cut the workforce of 202,000 by 44,000 in two years, then take another 20,000 jobs out. Twenty pits would be closed to begin with. Though elderly and rich, he was no suave PR man. When MacGregor turned up to visit mines he was pelted with flour bombs, abused and, on one occasion, knocked to the ground.

Arthur Scargill seemed to be relishing the fight as much as the Prime Minister. We last glimpsed him in the miners' confrontation with Heath, when he had led the flying pickets at Saltley coke depot, and then tangling with Kinnock during Labour's civil war. Some sense of his unique mix of revolutionary simplicity and wit comes from an exchange he had with the Welsh miners' leader Dai Francis, when he called to ask for flying pickets to come to Birmingham and help at the coke depot. Francis asked when they were needed:

'Tomorrow, Saturday.'

Dai paused: 'But Wales are playing Scotland at Cardiff Arms Park.'

There was a silence and Scargill replied, 'But Dai, the working class are playing the ruling class at Saltley.'[9]

Many found Scargill inspiring; many others found him frankly scary. He had been a Communist and retained strong Marxist views and a penchant for denouncing anyone who disagreed with him as a traitor. Some found a megalomaniac atmosphere at his Barnsley headquarters, already known as Arthur's Castle. Kim Howells, then a Communist and later a New Labour minister, visited him there and was taken aback to find him sitting at 'this Mussolini desk with a great space in front of it' and behind him a huge painting of himself on the back of a lorry, posed like Lenin, urging picketing workers in London to overthrow the ruling class. Howells thought anyone who could put up a painting like that was nuts and returned to express his fears to the Welsh miners. 'And of course the South Wales executive almost to a man agreed with me. But then they said, "He's the only one we've got, see, boy. The Left has decided." '[10]

Scargill had indeed been elected by a vast margin and had set about turning the NUM's once moderate executive into a reliably militant group. His vice-president, Mick McGahey, was a veteran Scottish Communist who, though wiser than Scargill, was no moderate; and the union's general secretary, Peter Heathfield, was well to the left in union politics. Scargill had been ramping up the rhetoric for some time. 'Sooner or later our members will have to stand and fight,' he said repeatedly – not on the traditional issue of wages, but on the very future of coalmining in Britain. He told the NUM conference in 1982, 'If we do not save our pits from closure then all our other struggles become meaningless . . . Protection of the industry is my first priority because without jobs all our other claims lack substance and become mere shadows. Without jobs, our members are nothing . . .' Given what was about to happen to his members' jobs as a result of the strike, there is a black irony in those words. By adopting a position that no pits should be closed on economic grounds, even if the coal was exhausted – more investment would always find more coal, and from his point of view the losses were irrelevant – he made sure confrontation would not be avoided. Exciting, witty Arthur Scargill brought coalmining to a close in Britain far faster than would have happened had the NUM been led by some prevaricating, dreary old-style union hack.

The NUM votes which allowed the strike to start covered both pay and closures. But from the start Scargill emphasized the closures. To strike to protect jobs, particularly other people's jobs, in other people's villages and other counties' pits, gave the confrontation an air of nobility and sacrifice which a mere wages dispute would not have enjoyed. Neil Kinnock, the new Labour leader, the son and grandson of Welsh miners, found it impossible to forthrightly condemn the aims of the dispute despite his growing detestation of Scargill. As we shall see, it cost him dear. With his air-chopping, flaming rhetoric, Scargill was a formidable organizer and a conference-hall speaker on Kinnock's level. Yet not even he would be able to persuade every part of the industry to strike. Earlier ballots had shown consistent majorities against striking. In Nottinghamshire, 72 per cent of the area's 32,000 miners voted against striking. The small coalfields of South Derbyshire and Leicestershire were against, too. Even in South Wales, half the NUM lodges failed to vote for a strike. Overall, of the 70,000 miners who were balloted in the run-up to the dispute 50,000 had voted to keep working. This is crucial to understanding what happened. Scargill felt he could not win a national ballot so he decided on a rolling series of locally called strikes, coalfield by coalfield, Yorkshire then Scotland, Derbyshire and South Wales. These strikes would merely be approved by the national union. It was a domino strategy; the regional strikes would add up to a national strike, without a national vote.

But Scargill needed to be sure the dominos would fall. He used the famous flying pickets from militant areas and pits to shut down less militant ones. Angry miners were sent in coaches and convoys of cars to close working pits and the coke depots, vital hubs of the coal economy. Without the pickets, who to begin with rarely needed to use violence to achieve their end, far fewer pits would have come out. But after scenes of physical confrontation around Britain, by April 1984 four miners in five were on strike. To Scargill's horror, however, other unions refused to come out in sympathy, robbing him of a re-run of the 1929 General Strike. It became clear that the NUM had made other historic errors. Kinnock was not the only one from a mining back-ground baffled as to why Scargill had opted to strike in the spring, when the demand for energy was relatively low. The stocks at the power stations were not running down at anything like the rate the NUM hoped, as confidential briefings from the power workers con-firmed. It seemed the government could indeed sit this one out. There were huge set-piece confrontations with riot-equipped police bussed up from London or down from Scotland, Yorkshire to Kent, Wales to Yorkshire, generally used outside their own areas to avoid mixed loyalties. It was as if the country had been taken over by historical re-enactments of civil war battles, the Sealed Knot society run rampant. Aggressive picketing was built into the fabric of the strike. Old county and regional rivalries flared up, Lancashire men against Yorkshire men, South Wales miners in Nottinghamshire.

The Nottinghamshire miners turned out to be critical. Without them the power stations, even with the mix of nuclear and oil and the careful stockpiling, might have begun to run short and the government would have been in deep trouble. Using horses, baton charges and techniques learned from the street riots of the previous few years, the police defended the working miners with a determination which delighted the government and alarmed many others. A battle at Orgreave in South Yorkshire was particularly brutal. As the strike went on, macho policing was matched by violence from striking miners. Scargill could count on almost fanatical loyalty to the union in towns and villages across the land. Miners gave up their cars, sold their furniture, saw their children suffer and indeed lost materially all they had in the cause of solidarity. Food parcels arrived from other parts of Britain, from France and even from Russia. There was a gritty courage and selflessness in mining communities most of the rest of country could barely understand. The other side of the coin was a desperation to win which turned ugly. A taxi-driver taking a working miner to work in Wales was killed when a block of concrete was dropped on his car. There were murderous threats to 'scabs' and their families. When Norman Willis, the affable general secretary of the TUC spoke at one miners' meeting, a noose was dangled above his head.

Violence relayed to the rest of the country on the nightly news, followed eventually by legal action on the part of Yorkshire miners complaining that they had been denied a ballot, put the NUM on the back foot. Scargill's decision to take money from Libya found him slithering from any moral high ground he had once occupied, though some believe this was part of a Security Service 'sting' operation to discredit the NUM leadership. As with Galtieri, Thatcher was lucky in her enemies. Slowly, month by month, the strike began to crumble and miners began to trail back to work, first in tens and scores, then in their hundreds, then in their thousands. There were many crises on the way – a possible dock strike; a vote to strike by pit safety officers and overseers, which would have shut down the working pits too and was promptly bought off, and problems with local courts too over-loaded to prosecute strikers. But by January 1985, ten months after they had first come out, strikers were returning to work at the rate of some 2,500 a week; by the end of February more than half the NUM's membership was back at work. In some cases they marched back behind pipes and drums, weeping.

Scargill's gamble had gone catastrophically wrong. He has been compared to a First World War general, a donkey leading lions to the slaughter. There is something in the comparison. The political force ranged against the miners in 1984 was entirely different from the ill-prepared, Heath administration they had defeated ten years earlier. A shrewder non-revolutionary leader would not have chosen that fight at that time or, having done so, would have found a compromise after the first months of the dispute. Today, there are a handful of thousand miners left of the 200,000 who went on strike. Scargill himself lingers on as an official of an international miners' union because he has run out of miners to lead at home. He might once have dreamed the revolution would raise a statue to him. If anyone does, it should be the green lobby, in a spirit of irony. An industry whose origins went back to the Middle Ages and which made Britain a great industrial power, but which was always dangerous, dirty and polluting, lay down and died. For Conservatives, indeed for the majority of people, Scargill and his lieutenants were fighting parliamentary democracy and were an enemy which had to be defeated. But the miners of Kent, Derbyshire, Fife and Yorkshire, Wales and Lancashire were nobody's enemy, just abnormally hard-working, traditional people worried about losing their jobs and overly loyal to their wild and incompetent leader.

Whirlybird Madness

It is a reasonably safe rule in politics that the big fights are about big issues. The great Westland Helicopter crisis that broke over the Thatcher government in the winter of 1984-5 was on the face of it a barmy thing for ministers to fight about. Should a European consortium of aerospace manufacturers or an American defence company, working with an Italian firm, be favoured to take over a struggling West Country helicopter maker? Who cared? This was a government that boasted about its refusal to micro-manage industry, yet the fight about the future of a Yeovil manufacturer cost two cabinet ministers their jobs and led at one point to Margaret Thatcher herself doubting whether she would last the day as Prime Minister. It pitted her against the only other member of her government with real glamour – and as big a shock of hair as hers – and it dominated political life for months. It produced the only walk-out resignation from a cabinet meeting in modern times, indeed since 1903, and the only spontaneous one ever. So what was it all about?

The small storm of Westland gave early notice of the weaknesses that would eventually destroy the Thatcher government, though not for another five years. One was the divide throughout the Tory Party about Britain's place in the world. Helicopters were by the mid-eighties no longer a marginal defence issue. For projecting Western power in countries as far afield as Somalia, Bosnia and Iraq, they would be crucial – the new army mule hauling cannon over mountains, the new floating gunship. Supply an army's helicopters and you have a big hold over that country. United Technologies, the American company whose Sikorsky subsidiary built the Black Hawk helicopter, wanted control over part of Britain's defence industry. Alexander Haig, the US Secretary of State who had been so helpful during the Falklands War, was now back with his old company, and 'called in his markers' for the American bid. The Prime Minister, adopting a position of outward neutrality, would probably have favoured it anyway as further strengthening of the British-American alliance. But on the other side, supporting the European consortium of companies, were those who felt that the EU had to be able to stand alone in defence technology. Michael Heseltine and his business allies thought this was vital to preserve jobs and the cutting-edge science base. The United States must not be able to dictate prices and terms to Europe. So this was about where Britain stood: first with the US, or first with the EU? It was a question which would grow steadily in importance through the eighties until, in the nineties, it tore the Conservative Party apart.

The second issue thrown up by Westland mattered almost as much. It was the Thatcher style of government, which was more presidential and disdainful of her cabinet than that of any previous Prime Minister. We have already seen how she despatched the 'wets' who challenged her on economic policy. She would rage against, mock and browbeat ministers who were on her side too. Sir Geoffrey Howe in particular had a miserable time from her tongue-lashings. The satirical television puppet show *Spitting Image* began to dress their Thatcher figurine in trousers and summed up the popular perception in a sketch showing her lunching with her ministers. She orders her beef. Asked by the waiter, 'What about the vegetables?' her puppet snarls, 'They'll have the same.' Rather more seriously in the real world, she was conducting more and more business in small committees or bilaterally, with one minister at a time, ensuring her near-absolute dominance. A small clique of advisers assumed more significance than the ministers with their grand offices and titles. Later, just before her fall, Nigel Lawson would conclude that she was taking her personal economic adviser Sir Alan Walters more seriously than she was taking him, her Chancellor of the Exchequer. Throughout it all, she was using her beloved press officer Bernard Ingham to cut down to size any ministers she had taken against, using the then-anonymous lobby system for Westminster journalists to spread the message.

In her memoirs she portrays Heseltine as a vain, ambitious and unprincipled man who flouted cabinet responsibility. The Westland crisis, in her view, was simply about his psychological flaws. Ingham, in his memoirs, angrily defends himself against improper briefing. Yet there are too many other witnesses who found the Thatcher style more like a Renaissance court than a traditional cabinet, a place which demanded absolute loyalty and was infested with favourites. It would destroy her, as it would cripple New Labour, this way of ruling. But in the mid-eighties it was a new phenomenon and to ministers on the receiving end, freshly humiliating. And if there was one minister unlikely to take such treatment for long, it was Michael Heseltine. He was the only serious rival as darling of the party and media star in the glory days of Thatcherism. Handsome, glamorous, rich and an excellent public speaker, he was popularly known as 'Tarzan'. The story was told about him by his fellow Tory MP, friend and biographer Julian Critchley, that at Oxford he had mapped out his future career on the back of an envelope, running through the need to make a fortune, marry well, enter Parliament and then, '1990s, Prime Minister'. Though Heseltine said he could not remember doing this it was in character. As a young man he had flung himself into the characteristic sixties businesses of property investment and magazine publishing, coming close to bankruptcy before handing his worldly goods to his bank manager and slowly turning his companies round. A passionate anti-socialist, he had won a reputation for hot-headedness since once picking up the Mace, symbol of parliamentary authority, and waving it at the Labour benches during a Commons row about steel nationalization. His speeches to Tory Party conferences were music-hall extravaganzas, full of blond hair-tossing, hilarious invective and fist-thwacks-palm drama. So macho that he was almost camp, he was known for the swoop on Merseyside already described and for dressing up in army gear while taking on the female CND protesters of Greenham Common. As an experienced businessman with a relish for vehement anti-Labour rhetoric he was hardly a typical 'wet', and indeed agreed with Thatcher about much. But he was a more committed anti-racialist than her and deeply in favour of the EU; she always regarded him as a serious and dangerous rival. The two biggest beasts of the Tory Party in the eighties had been eyeing each other and quietly sharpening their claws under the cabinet table well before Westland.

They went to war on behalf of the two rival bidders for Westland. She was livid that he was using his considerable leverage as Defence Secretary to warn the company's shareholders about the dangers of going with the Americans, potentially shutting out European business. She thought he was tipping the scales against Sikorsky, despite Westland's preference for them. Certainly, Heseltine repeatedly made it clear the Ministry of Defence would not be buying their Black Hawk helicopter and did much to rally the European consortium. Thatcher, meanwhile, was deploying the public line that she was only interested in what was best for the shareholders while trying to make sure the Americans were kept in the race, ahead of the Europeans. Eventually she sought advice from the government law officers about whether Heseltine had been behaving properly. A private reply, meant to weaken his case, was leaked. Furious at this wholly improper act which he suspected was the responsibility of Thatcher and Ingham, Heseltine demanded a full inquiry. During a meeting of cabinet she counter-attacked, trying to rein him in by ordering that all future statements on Westland must be cleared first by Number Ten. Hearing this attempt to gag him, Heseltine calmly got up from the cabinet table, announced that he must leave the government, walked by himself into the street and told a startled solitary reporter that he had just resigned.

The question of exactly who had leaked the Attorney General's legal advice in a misleadingly selective way to scupper Heseltine and the European bid then became critical. The leaking of the private advice broke the rules of Whitehall confidentiality, fairness and collective government. The instrument of the leak was a comparatively junior civil servant, the Trade Secretary Leon Brittan's head of communications, Colette Bowe. But who had told her to do this? Many assumed it was her boss, the Number Ten press chief Bernard Ingham. He denied it. He had known she was going to leak the advice and had not ordered her to stop, which he later said he bitterly regretted. But the initiative, he said, had not come from him or Mrs Thatcher. For her part she said she had not known and would not have approved the leaking of the letter had she been asked. None of this matters, except that it nearly finished off the Lady in her prime. After dramatic Commons exchanges during which she seemed vulnerable to the charge of lying to the House, she pulled through. It was Brittan who went for a comparatively trivial mis-statement about another confidential letter – a scapegoat, said the Opposition, which had singularly failed to get the glossy scalp they had hoped for.

After the political row there was a dirty and in some ways even more dramatic struggle for control of the company conducted in hotels and City boardrooms. Some of Thatcher's greatest business supporters such as Rupert Murdoch weighed in on the side of the American-led bid. Eventually amid accusations of arm-twisting and dirty tricks the Europeans were defeated and the company went to Sikorsky. The storm subsided. But it had revealed the costs of the new Thatcher style. Getting your way at all costs with foreign dictators and militant union leaders was one thing. Behaving similarly with senior politicians in your own party was another. Heseltine later wrote: 'I saw many good people broken by the Downing Street machine. I had observed the techniques of character assassination: the drip, drip, of carefully planted, unattributable stories that were fed into the public domain, as colleagues became marked as somehow "semi-detached" or "not one of us".' The great strength of Thatcher's way of governing was the way her self-certainty gave her administration and the country a surging sense of direction. Its weakness was it cut out so many others, ignored advice and humiliated anyone not seen as an uncritical supporter.

Very Big Bang

The City, with its huge bonuses and salaries, freshly sprouted glass towers, banks and merchants from across the world, is so familiar it can be taken for granted, as naturally British as the Jurassic coast. Yet in the fifties there would be no good reason for an observer to believe that the sleepy world of the London Stock Exchange, the venerable merchant banks and the rest would become a global success story, while British car-making, for instance, with its splendid variety of models and its famous names, would wither to nothing. The great days of the City had been a lifetime earlier in the heady financial markets before the First World War when sterling was a dominant world currency, loans and bonds sluiced freely round the world, and Britain was a great creditor nation. After the Second World War the pound was under almost constant pressure, the dollar was king, post-war exchange controls hobbled any chance of big overseas deals and Britain was a big global debtor.

The wizened traditions of Money remained – the obscure hierarchies, the bowler hats, the rigid division between brokers and jobbers, the long lunches and coal fires, and the exotic titles of firms that had risen in the days of Queen Victoria, engraved on nameplates between the bombed-out squares. But the City was no longer buccaneering. In the age of Macmillan and Wilson its grandees were forced to concentrate on humble domestic business and the modest trade of the unwinding empire, occasionally pootling along to their masters at the Bank of England to lobby for a loosening of regulations, fruitlessly. Magazines and films still exploited the image of the crisp young banker with a furled brolly and bowler hat. But, in truth, the Square Mile was becoming part of heritage Britain, its declining firms like the cashless Palladian houses of Oxfordshire, in which grumpy men with famous names stamped their feet against the cold and mentally apologized to grandpapa. Perhaps it was inevitable? Historically, financial clout had run alongside commercial and political power. A weak Britain meant a weak pound and a weak City. In the forties, fifties and sixties, the golden age of the great US dollar, it was as obvious that New York would replace the Square Mile, as it was equally obvious that the US fleet would take over from the Royal Navy.

That it did not happen was the result of paranoia and bad judgement far away from London, exploited by bright British financiers. At the height of the Cold War, Moscow and her satrapies declined to let wicked capitalist New York look after their dollars. These dollars ended up instead in (apparently less wicked) London and were used from 1957 by a few far-seeing British banks to finance overseas trade in the capital-hungry post-war world. If you are not allowed to fund the world with home-grown pounds, why not do it with other people's dollars? The boss of the Bank of London and South America, Sir George Bolton, was heard in clubs and boardrooms loudly asking why London, with her expertise, should not jump into a new age of world capitalism? London's second opening came thanks to New York itself. Since the war, American bankers had been enjoying the easy pickings from loans to other countries and overseas investors. They were lazily uninterested in the secondary market in such loans. By the early sixties, the ballooning US balance of payments deficit turned the mood in Washington against loans to overseas customers in general. In 1963 President Kennedy worsened Wall Street's position dramatically with a new tax on Americans buying foreign stocks from foreigners. With New York cut off from a surging new international business, London moved in.

The first such 'Eurodollar' loans were negotiated in 1963 between the British merchant banks Warburgs and Samuel Montagu on the one hand, and an Italian state-owned steelmaker and the Belgian government on the other. To avoid British regulations and taxes, deals were done in Holland's Schiphol airport and Luxembourg. Warburgs dodged and hopped around endless obstacles until at the end they found there was no one to print the new bonds to the high pre-war standards demanded by the London Stock Exchange. At the last moment the playing card manufacturers De La Rue found two very old Czech engravers who were brought out of retirement to do the job.[11] Dollar loans by Hambros for hydroelectric schemes in Norway and by a group of merchant banks for the Austrian government quickly followed. Then a spate of loans for the Japanese . . . and a new world suddenly opened up for the beaten-up old City of London. Pipelines across the Alps, American oil refineries and exploratory ventures, Japanese office buildings, early computer factories, all would be financed from London, just as in the days of Edwardian finance. As overseas bankers realized what was happening, they began to converge on London for some of the action. European banks were already present, but the big four finance houses in Tokyo opened London offices and so too did the big names on Wall Street. Citibank, Chase Manhattan, Merrill Lynch and Nomura were all there, taking traditional British business as well as trading in the Eurodollar markets.

The influence of the Eurodollar and Eurobond market on the culture of the City and by extension British business life generally can hardly be overstated. From the early sixties, it was internationalizing and shaking up London, introducing more aggression, fatter salaries and less of the old school tie. Harold Wilson might complain about sinister international financiers. The traditionalists of the Stock Exchange and the older banks might hint at sharp practice and unsavoury deals. But the Euro-market thrived and grew, shrugging off the crash of 1974 and the Arab boycott of Jewish businesses alike. Just a whiff of the can-do, devil-may-care Wild West spirit was suddenly felt again in the streets of old London.

Only in the side streets, however. For most investors the world of controls still applied. Sir Nicholas Goodison, later Chairman of the Stock Exchange in the Thatcher years, looked back on the mood by the late seventies: 'We still had exchange controls. We had a Labour government intent on controlling everything, and no freedom of capital movement. British people were not allowed to take capital abroad; British institutions weren't allowed to invest capital abroad except by special Treasury permissions ... we were an insulated market.'[12] It was this world which was swept away on 23 October 1979 when Geoffrey Howe, to general shock, abolished exchange controls. Despite what she later said, Thatcher was wobbly and uncertain about the gamble. Howe himself likened it to walking off a cliff to see what happened. Bankers noted there was no planning for this revolution. Tony Benn said it showed that international capitalism had finally defeated democracy. What is certainly clear is that abolishing exchange controls made it inevitable that the core of the 'old City' would be exposed to the cultural revolution that the Eurodollar market-makers had already enjoyed in the side streets. The smaller merchant banks, Antony Gibbs, Keyser Ullman and others, were already disappearing; even the biggest London merchant banks such as Kleinwort Benson had profits of little more than a tenth of Japan's Nomura and a seventh of Wall Street's Merrill Lynch. For the huddled world of the traditional City, it was suddenly a choice between looking for big protective overseas partners or struggling to survive alone.

In 1982, another slice of American business life came to London in the multi-coloured jackets and raucous bear-pit atmosphere of the new international financial futures market, or LIFFE. Here the high-risk bets were made on the future value of commodities and currencies, in one of the older buildings of the City, the Royal Exchange. Inside its elegant shell roared an atmosphere borrowed straight from Chicago, likened by startled observers at the time to an ill-bred casino. LIFFE would turn out to be very profitable for the traders, the raucous 'barrow boys' pumped up on booze, cocaine and fear of failure who became such an emblem of eighties life, many retiring exhausted and vastly rich by their early thirties. It would also be the scene of broken dreams. It was in the derivatives market that old Barings Bank, one of the grander names of the traditional City, lost its money and died. And so to the next question for the City: for how long could the traditional distinction between brokers, dealing with the public, and the jobbers or wholesalers, dealing only with stockbrokers, be maintained? It had been seen as an essential barrier to protect the public, as important for the City as the division between barrister and solicitor was in English law courts. Yet in these new markets it was barely recognized.

The new Chancellor after the 1983 election, Nigel Lawson, a former financial journalist, and the new Trade Secretary, Cecil Parkinson, decided to do a deal with the increasingly archaic looking Stock Exchange. It was struggling with a long and wearisome court case brought by the Office of Fair Trading. The ministers promised the legal action would be dropped if the Stock Exchange reformed itself. This was the final piece of action which led to the 'Big Bang' of City deregulation, something which has a claim to be the single most significant change of the whole Thatcher era, on a par with confronting the unions or privatization. The situation in 1983–4 could be compared to an old market town high street, with its long-established specialist shops, the fishmonger and the drapers, old Mr Bunn at the bakery and Miss Manila the trusted postmistress, at just the moment when a huge new retail park opens on the outskirts. The supermarkets in it are the international financial service companies and the global-trading banks offering every financial service under one roof. Chase Manhattan and Merrill Lynch here play the role of Tesco and Walmart. The high street shops are the City firms, small and specialized but without the financial clout and scale to compete. What do they do? Some doggedly hang on, hoping their name, expertise and traditional customer base will see them through. Others negotiate with the supermarkets, trying to find a space under the roof to carry on trading. Others frantically merge, creating newer, bigger high street retailers.

This is what happened in the City when it became clear that the old rules were about to be abolished. During the winter of 1983–4 jobbers, brokers and bankers began to merge in an unprecedented explosion of defensive alliances. Old merchant banks opened talks with the US mega-banks. Scores of ancient names disappeared or were compressed into new assemblages of initials. In family firms such as N. M. Rothschild and Barings, there were family fights, with sons and brothers going different ways. The streets echoed to the sound of cultures clashing. Cricket and baseball were at war on the same pitch. With a new market for shares in smaller, riskier companies (the Unlisted Securities Market) and the creation of a new joint index of the shares of the hundred biggest companies on the Stock Exchange, the FTSE 100, or 'Footsie', there was a revolutionary mood in the air, a frenzy of optimism and activity which roared through 1984. Many noted the contrast with the devastation of Britain's coal-mining industry as the strike dragged on during just the same time. Across the City big gleaming new dealing rooms were unveiled, filled with computers, edged with glass and marble. Paintings of venerable Jewish patriarchs from Edwardian days were rehung in bland new surroundings. Minimum commissions, bedrock of the old cartel, went overnight. Outsiders were at last ushered into the temple of temples, the Stock Exchange itself.

And then on 27 October 1986, this London Stock Exchange ceased to exist as the institution it had formerly been. Its makeover made it all but unrecognizable. The new screen-quoted system SEAQ finally came on stream, the moment remembered as the 'Big Bang' itself. A few months later the physical floor of the Stock Exchange, once heaving with life, was almost desolate as the deals were made by computer screen and phone. Scandals, shocks, crashes would follow but as the spring and summer of 1987 arrived, it was clear there would never be any way back to the cosy, particular, tradition-hallowed old high street of London's City a few years before. Twenty years on, share deals which had taken quarter of an hour or longer to process were completed in a few seconds. The markets were opening two and a half hours earlier each morning, and closing a couple of hours later. The volume of trading was fifteen times higher than it had been in the early eighties. A country which had exported £2 billion of financial services a year before the Big Bang was exporting twelve times that amount. With only 330,000 people working there in City jobs, it was supporting the entire country's overseas account.[13] Though the City brought a super-rich class to Britain, whose vast salaries and staggering annual bonuses made a good swathe of the middle class feel ill over their breakfast newspapers when they were reported each year, and which pushed the more beautiful, well-placed and prestigious homes out of reach of hospital consultants, criminal lawyers, head-teachers and diplomats, the truth is that without the Big Bang, Britain's books would be in much worse condition.

For millions of ordinary Britons who had only the haziest idea about the world of finance, the revolution in lending to buy their houses was as big a shock. Until the early eighties, most people's experience of getting a mortgage involved a barrage of suspicious questions from a building society manager, followed by a long wait (for the loans were rationed) and eventually followed by a mortgage whose cost was fixed by the Building Societies' Association. Generally speaking, the size of the low-cost loan, funded by deposits from building society members, would be limited to two and a half times the would-be homeowner's annual salary. But by 1983 the ordinary clearing banks were muscling in on the business and this cartel began to go too. American and other mortgage lenders offered better deals. As Nigel Lawson later wrote, this happened in the new deregulated world 'in which direct credit controls were out of the question; and the only checks on excess were the price of credit, which the Government remained able to control [it cannot do so now] and prudence, which it cannot.' Three years later he responded to the clamour of building societies who felt unfairly hampered by their old status. He freed them to raise money in the capital markets, issue chequebooks and cheque guarantee cards, make other loans and indeed behave almost like banks. He also allowed them to convert themselves into banks if they got a sufficiently large majority of their members to agree. This duly happened, beginning with the Abbey National.

The effect of this was to suddenly take the brake off mortgage lending and to upend the old power relationship. Before, would-be borrowers limped along to the local building society and patiently endured many obstacles before they were allowed a mortgage. Now the building societies and banks started to ingratiate themselves with the public, thrusting credit at them. It became a good thing, a virtuous thing, to be a big-time borrower. People found themselves harangued in advertisements and junk mail to borrow more, to defect from one bank to another, to extend the mortgage rather than paying it off. The old rules about the maximum proportion of income began to dissolve – four times income began to be acceptable in some cases. House prices began to rise accordingly. (Today the average cost of a house in Britain is rising towards five times average income.)

In many cases banks and building societies began to lend people more than the total value of the house they were buying. The extra helped fuel a more general high-street splurge. The old system of checking people's real financial status went out of the window. During 1986–8 a borrowing frenzy gripped the country, egged on by swaggering speeches about Britain's economic miracle from the Chancellor and Prime Minister. The abolition of mortgage tax relief saw a rush of borrowing to meet the deadline. Lawson, not a man to underrate his achievements, acknowledged a critic who said 'my real mistake as Chancellor was to create a climate of optimism that, in the end, encouraged borrowers to borrow more than they should and lenders to lend more than they should.' All this would end in tears with the bust that followed and would be used for many years afterwards by Labour's Gordon Brown as evidence of the Tory 'boom-and-bust' policies. But it was the consequence of a decisive break in the financial regulations governing City and everyday life, which changed Britain, probably for ever. It felt heady and exhilarating to millions. It was like getting properly drunk for the first time.

The Big Bang itself was thus only a moment in a longer process, rooted in the Eurodollar market of the sixties and given its most dramatic kick by Geoffrey Howe's abolition of exchange controls, followed by the deregulation of lending. It meant that Britain for the first time in her history, and entirely willingly, gave up control over financial dealings done from her soil except as a neutral regulator. The State lost control over credit. In return the City gained a huge quantity of international financial business, the profits dripping down from some of the biggest deals in the world which might otherwise have gone to Berlin, Tokyo or (more likely) New York. The end of the age of controls and nationalistic finance meant also that British manufacturing lost any hope of the kind of long-term banking arrangements that German and French rivals had enjoyed. The asset-stripping habit, buying companies, dismantling them into component parts and selling them on, had become a controversial part of British business life in the seventies. The eighties' financial revolution ensured it would remain so. There would be no room for old connections or long-term thinking in the new world.

For politics, the freeing of the City gave Margaret Thatcher and her ministers an entirely loyal and secure base of rich, articulate supporters who helped see her through some rough times. Rothschilds and other banks would spread the get-rich-quick prospect to millions of people in Britain through the privatization issues and the country would, for a time, come closer to the share-owning democracy Thatcher dreamed of. But all this came at a price – the crude and swaggering 'loadsamoney' years satirized by the comedian Harry Enfield and the culture of excess and conspicuous display that would percolate from the City through London, then the Home Counties, then much of southern England. For one generally sympathetic observer of the City in the mid-eighties it was worryingly infected with hype: 'Febrile, driven by greed, pushing back the boundaries of acceptable behaviour, this was a brief, intense phase that in some ways was a rerun of the late 1920s, this time with added attitude.'[14]

Sid Gets Lucky: the Privatization Years

There is a popular belief that the Thatcher governments never really intended to privatize very much, and that they stumbled upon an easy way of raising cash by selling off assets almost by accident. If so, it was one heck of a stumble. During the decade £29 bn was raised in sales of land and businesses and £18 bn from the sale to their tenants of 1.24 million council homes. The gas that cooked meals and warmed houses, oil coming ashore, aircraft taking businessmen and holiday-makers, and the airports they flew from, the phones and phone-lines used to communicate, cars, engines, steel and the water pipes and filtration systems bringing the British their baths and tea – all would be affected by the greatest shift of assets from the State to private companies and individuals in the history of this country. By the 1992 election, forty-six businesses had left the public sector, carrying with them 900,000 people. The notion that this was accidental is wrong. The Conservatives had promised to sell off council houses to their tenants from the mid-seventies. Privatization of state corporations had not featured much in the 1979 manifesto only because the party's plans were still sketchy and partly because its leader did not want to scare off the voters. But privatization had been long discussed on the right. In his first Budget speech Howe said he wanted to reduce the size of the public sector, that 'the scope for the sale of assets is substantial' and that this was 'an essential part of our long-term programme'.

So it would prove. One of the influential economic writers about the Thatcher years said that coining the word privatization was 'a master-stroke of public relations' by the government, which put it into worldwide circulation. Privatization would become the major idea exported from Britain in modern times, though as it happens the word was not one Mrs Thatcher liked or much used. ('De-nationalization' was even uglier, however, and inaccurate, since some of the corporations and assets sold had never been nationalized in the first place.) It started tentatively, with small steps in 1981–2 including shares in BP, the scientific corporation Amersham, half of Cable & Wireless and then the British National Oil Corporation, discussed elsewhere. The motives were mixed. Early on, with a horrendous public sector borrowing requirement to fund, simply raising cash was important. Yet this was neither the origin of the idea, nor its real point. Howe and Lawson were making clear from 1980 onwards that creating a large bulwark of new shareholders was essential to the Tories' political vision. Lawson would cite the fears of extending voting in the nineteenth century, allowing political power to people who had no stake in the country: 'But the remedy is not to restrict the franchise to those who own property: it is to extend the ownership of property to the largest possible majority of those who have the vote. The widespread ownership of private property is crucial to the survival of freedom and democracy.'

Another way of putting it was that this was one part of the one-way ratchet, pulling Britain away from socialism. If Labour had been accused of creating a giant state sector whose employees depended on high public spending and could therefore be expected to become loyal Labour voting-fodder, then the Tories were intent on creating a 'property-owning democracy' of voters whose interests were entirely different. The despair of Labour politicians as they watched it working was obvious. There was now to be a large and immovably pro-private sector Britain of share-owners and home-owners, probably working in private companies and increasingly un-unionized. The cost of renationalizing the industries made Labour pledges about it increasingly hollow. Twenty years later the idea of reversing privatization is something discussed only on the very margins of politics. The proportion of adults holding shares rose from 7 per cent when Labour left office, to 25 per cent when Thatcher did. Thanks to the 'right to buy' policy, more than a million families purchased their council houses, repainting and refurbishing them and watching their value shoot up, particularly since they had been sold them at a discount of between 33 and 50 per cent. The proportion of owner-occupied homes rose from 55 per cent of the total in 1979 to 67 per cent a decade later. And people did indeed become much wealthier, overall, during the Tory years. In real terms, total personal wealth rose by 80 per cent in the eighties, entirely changing the terms of trade of ordinary politics. Old Labour was killed off not in the Commons but in the shopping centre and the estate agents' office.

Yet if we look a little below the surface, the story is more blurred. Of that huge rise in wealth, relatively little was accounted for by shares. An increase in earnings and the first house-price boom were much more important. And the boom in shareholding was fuelled more by the prospect of a bargain than by any deep change in culture. Clearly, there was always a potential conflict between the government's need to raise money quickly, and its hopes of spreading share ownership – both of them intensely political, since the former affected tax levels and the latter the size of the property-holding electorate. Again and again, from the grossly undervalued Amersham sale, to the later and greater privatizations, ministers erred on the side of getting the maximum spread of ownership, rather than the maximum price. The breakthrough privatization was that of 52 per cent of British Telecom in November 1984, which raised an unheard-of £3.9 bn. It was the first to be accompanied by a ballyhoo of television and press advertising. It was easily oversubscribed.

In the event 2 million people, or 5 per cent of the adult population, bought BT shares, almost doubling the number of people who owned shares in a single day. After this came British Gas. Natural gas fields had been supplying Britain from the North Sea since the late sixties, pumping ashore at Yarmouth and Hull, and replacing the old 'town gas' system of coal-produced gas, which had long given so many neighbourhoods their distinctive architecture and smell. With its national pipe network and showrooms it had become the country's favourite source of domestic energy and was, in most respects, a straightforwardly monopolistic business. Its chairman Sir Dennis Rooke fought a riotously aggressive private campaign to avoid British Gas being broken up before the sale, and was successful. Again, the government and its advisers prepared for the sale with a TV campaign featuring an anonymous neighbour who had to be kept away from a good thing – 'Don't Tell Sid' – and then, when the issue details were finally announced, 'Tell Sid'. This raised £5.4 bn, the biggest single privatization of all.

Yet there was something about the very name that fell oddly on the ear. Does 'Sid' perhaps have a half-echo of 'spiv'? Was someone in the advertising team subconsciously sending a message? For the truth was that the huge oversubscribing of shares reflected a general and accurate belief that something was being given away for nothing, that this was a one-way bet. Sid knew which side his bread was buttered on, but this did not necessarily make him a kitchen capitalist. With the equally bargain-price shares offered to members of building socie ties, such as Abbey National, when they demutualized and turned themselves into banks, Britain developed a 'thank you very much' class of one-off shareholders. In the early years of the twenty-first century, the Office of National Statistics looked back at the privatiza- tion story and found that the proportion of stockmarket wealth held by private shareholders had fallen from 20 per cent in 1991 to 14 per cent. 'Many shareholders', they said, 'have clearly subsequently dis- posed of their holdings rather than become long-term stockmarket investors as was once hoped.' Of the 22 per cent of adults holding stocks or shares, more than half only had their old privatization or building society ones. The UK Shareholders' Association concluded that 'there are enormous number of shareholders in the UK (about 10m perhaps) but the vast majority hold only a few shares, and many of those will have come from privatisations, demutualisations or former employments. Such shares are rarely traded.'

The failure to get a shareholding democracy properly rooted, despite endless Treasury initiatives to nurture it, is a more telling criticism of privatization than the one most commonly heard at the time, which was that the assets were being sold off too cheaply. They were – to the tune in total of some £2.5 bn, according to the National Audit Office. But in part this was deliberate – 'wider share ownership was an important policy objective and we were prepared to pay a price for it,' said Lawson. Second, as the government and its advisers learned from each privatization, the pricing grew shrewder. Third, the price critics would not have sold the companies anyway. What the stultified share ownership pattern showed was that, below the level of political rhetoric, there were limits to the Thatcher revolution.

The other great question is whether privatization increased the efficiency and responsiveness of the corporations being sold. This was supposed to happen not because public sector managers were inherently lazy but because they lacked the spur and whip of a stockmarket price and the possibility of going out of business. Yet the impetus of being in the private sector would be much less if the business was still a monopoly. The most successful privatizations in that sense were the ones where the company was pushed instantly into full competition, as British Airways was, or Rolls-Royce, or British Aerospace. But the utilities – gas, electricity, water – were always different. It was hard to envisage rival North Sea natural gas companies competing in every part of the country with their own system of pipes and storage. It was hard to imagine many different energy companies with their own grids. Yet without competition, where would the efficiency gains come from? The technical and political argument behind these privatizations was how to break up the state monopolies to create competition, without infuriating and discommoding the consumer.

In the heyday of the Thatcher privatizations, it was more common for public corporations to be sold as single entities than broken up. British Telecom made the case that to compete in international markets, it must stay as a single unit, able to make the big investments needed for the telecommunications revolution. British Gas, under its pugnacious boss, managed to play the Whitehall power game sufficiently well to stay single. The water and electricity industries were split up, but to create local monopolies, with power generation being split into just two mega-companies, National Power and Powergen.

(The railway industry would prove one of the most intellectually demanding and least successful of all, though this story comes later.) In essence, what ministers did was to replace competition by regulation and the growth of new public bodies, such as the National Rivers Authority. Oftel, Ofcom, Ofgas, Ofwat were all given detailed targets and penalty systems to oversee the newly privatized utilities. Only much later would some of them, such as British Gas, be further broken up in the private sector, generally by government diktat through new competition policies, and exposed to more realistic market pressures. Soon, foreign firms would begin to move in and buy up the fragmented privatized utilities, causing remarkably little public protest, except when years of poor investment or management meant a service was patently failing, such as the leaking pipe systems of German-owned Thames Water.

Politicians learned two things. The first was that outside the Westminster village, few British people seemed to care at all who owned the companies and services they depended upon, so long as the service was acceptable. This was becoming a much less ideological country. The second thing they learned was that politics could not step back and wash its hands of what the privatized companies then did. Ministers, not simply chief executives, would still be the target of public anger and held responsible for any failings. This was becoming a more aggressively consumerist country. The result was that, while hundreds of thousands of employees left the public sector to work for newly private corporations, the State grew in other ways, through the quangos, regulatory bodies and bureaucrats now found necessary to regulate and oversee the privatized services.

Rainbows and Pots of Black Gold

Jim Callaghan was brought up piously, so when he told an audience in 1977 that God had given Britain her best opportunity for a hundred years in the shape of North Sea oil, there is a chance that he meant it. The Foreign Office, in a memo a little earlier, had called it 'a rainbow spanning the sombre horizon'. These had been terrible days for Britain, with 25 per cent inflation and the stockmarket plunging. The oil seemed like a fairytale intervention, for whichever group of politicians found themselves in power when the pot of gold could finally be yanked open. The story of what happened to the Almighty's handout, a ripple of organic residue left 9,000 feet below the seabed from dinosaur-haunted landscapes and warm seas of 200 million years earlier, is one of the most remarkable and under-discussed in modern British history. The discovery and exploitation of huge oil and gas fields far out under cold, stormy and turbulent waters – so far out that the biggest fields were roughly equidistant between Scotland and Norway – is a modern epic of technical skill, bold finance, endurance and individual courage. Hundreds would die, few fortunes would be made. By the boom year before prices suddenly fell, 1985, Britain was producing 127 million tonnes and was responsible for nearly a tenth of world exports. She had broken free from the old shackles of oil dependency, at least for a while. Official figures suggest Britain will be importing oil again by 2010 though many economists think it will be sooner. So we are talking about a span of between thirty and forty years. Was it well managed, that great gift?

This story is, to begin with, technically awe-inspiring. The oil in most of the rest of the world was ridiculously easy to win compared to the job of finding and pumping out very deep deposits a long way from dry land in very stormy seas. In civil engineering terms, from the steel and concrete jackets as tall as the Post Office Tower that had to be built in specially chosen havens and floated hundreds of miles out, to the huge undersea pipelines dropped from boats, this was a project unlike any other in peacetime since the Victorians' creation of the railways in the 1840s.[15] Its impact on the politics and public finances of Britain, first in the dying days of old Labour and then during the crucial years of the early Thatcherite experiment in monetarism, can hardly be exaggerated. It helped bankroll Thatcherism, for Britain was self-sufficient in oil by 1980. As the future Chancellor, Nigel Lawson, noted, revenues for the government 'soared from zero in 1975 to nearly £8 billion in 1982–3, at which point they accounted for almost 8.5 per cent of all tax revenues.' Some economists, though certainly not Lawson, have argued that without it the Thatcher experiment would have collapsed during 1981–2. One observer says: 'The industrial shake-out of the early eighties, of which unemployment above three million was the consequence, was indeed financed with the considerable help of the oil revenues.'[16] So there, to start with, is an irony. A great new source of national wealth helped to produce mass unemployment, or at least make it politically possible.

The possibilities of the oil boom were not underestimated at the time. Thanks to the oil price shocks of earlier years, the power and wealth of the Sheikhs, epitomized by the ebullient Saudi oil minister Yamani, was well understood. Could Britain have a little of that? In the seventies, in clubs of St James's and the City offices of the *Financial Times*, or the new little tower-block where *The Economist* was edited, they argued about whether oil would so boost the pound that manufacturing industry would be destroyed; or alternatively whether it would mean a golden age for Britain, when vast fortunes could be reinvested in wonderful schools and cutting-edge high-tech industries.

Whitehall's defence experts worried about how to defend the hundreds of miles of pipes against Irish terrorists, and the rigs against the Soviet navy. In those parts of the Commons tea-room and bars colonized by Labour MPs, there was a vigorous argument between those who wanted to see oil nationalized and kept under direct government control and those who felt this was impracticable. For by the time the big strikes had been made, the great American 'oil majors' were the people who had actually invested in the risky and technically difficult business of finding the stuff and preparing to bring it ashore. In the first few years, official Britain was hugely excited by the whole thing. When the first oil arrived ashore in November 1975 at Cruden Bay in Aberdeenshire, the Queen was present with the Prime Minister, assorted other ministers, pipers, a huge tent, red carpets and crowds with Union Jacks. (The oil workers, being in general rather hairy and impolite, were kept well out of the way.)

So it is curious that this great technical, economic and social story features so little afterwards in the memoirs and biographies of the politicians most affected by it. In her autobiography Margaret Thatcher barely touches on North Sea oil, even though her husband Denis was an oilman, involved in the near-collapse of Burmah Oil in 1975, and even though she took a close day-to-day interest in the relevant cabinet committees. About this awesome story she manages just four or five throwaway references, tacked to the end of remarks about exchange controls or tax policy. Geoffrey Howe dismisses the epic tale in a few words, far fewer than he devotes to the mildly amusing theft of his trousers from a train. Neither of them mentions the great tragedy of

Piper Alpha, when 185 men were burned or blown to death (two thirds of the British toll in the Falklands War). The great tomes on Wilson and Callaghan, Major and Blair, likewise find nothing much to say about North Sea oil. Nigel Lawson writes lucidly about it, brushing aside the arguments in favour of treating oil as a national resource to be husbanded with his customary panache. In many of the more general histories, economic and political, North Sea oil gets meagre treatment. Its cultural legacy seems slender, too: the occasional agit-prop play, a few poems, but no memorable novel, television drama or film, unless one counts *Local Hero*, which is more about a village community. Those wild years, when 80,000 hard-drinking, hard-working, brave and often dysfunctional men turned a corner of Scotland into the Wild East have left few footprints. A rare historian of the industry points out that among Scotland's hundreds of museums there is not one devoted to oil. Compared to the much-discussed miners' strikes, or the IMF crisis, or the City rude-boys of the Big Bang, North Sea oil – which continues to profitably flow – is already forgotten.

Why is this? Those parts of the national story that nobody seems keen to talk about have messages of their own. In the case of oil, embarrassment and confusion are part of the answer. For the truth is that the great adventure was lived at the edge of the British experience. It was not just that the rigs were so far from the coast, halfway to Scandinavia, and that the wild scenes were played out in the bars of Aberdeen and Shetland, both remote from the media in Glasgow, never mind London. It was also that the funding of the exploration and production was so heavily dominated by the United States and that so much of the technology was designed and built outside Britain that it is hard to tell, thirty years after it began to flow, quite what message God was really sending with the oil. The number of British refineries actually fell during the great oil decade of 1980–90, from twenty-one to thirteen, and 40 per cent of that was American-owned. Government advisers had prepared detailed plans about how to grab a great industrial bonanza on the back of the oil boom but by 1974, when the rigs were desperately needed to cope with the huge discoveries out at sea, only three rigs out of 119 were being built in Britain. The ageing, underfinanced yards of the Clyde, Tyneside and Belfast, which in the forties had still produced nearly 40 per cent of the world's ships, were now down to 4 per cent. Cheaper, better-equipped deep-water yards overseas had taken over. So when it came to the rigs, Norway, Finland even France were getting more of the business. Scotland's specialist yards for the huge 'jackets', like the Meccano sets of giants, at Nigg, Ardersier and Methil, lurched, it has been well said, 'between clamour and closure'. It was the same story with the all-important service boats bringing vital drilling supplies alongside. The technical breakthrough of positioning propellers at the bow as well as the stern, so they could keep position in heavy waters beside the platforms was made by Norwegian yards. It was their boats, not British ones, which were then sold around the world. Even when it came to oil supply services, which more or less had to come locally, British companies were slow to catch up and won little extra business overseas.[17]

Finance was a similar story. In the early days of exploration, the US giants were able to fund their work in the North Sea themselves, developing rigs from their earlier experiences in the Gulf of Mexico. The opaque nature of their internal accounting, and the much higher cost of getting any oil out, meant they were appallingly hard for British ministers and the Treasury to deal with. The government's handling of early leases for exploration, blocks of a hundred square miles each, was criticized by the Commons public accounts committee in 1972 as far too generous, 'as though Britain were a gullible Sheikhdom'. In the Middle East, they thought so too. Among the odder political vignettes of the seventies was an interview between Britain's energy minister Tony Benn and the Shah of Iran, at the latter's palace in Tehran. There, after noting the signed photographs of Brezhnev, Mao and the Queen, Benn was informed that North Sea oil could transform Britain's prospects 'if we were not imprudent'.[18] The Shah warned Benn to stand up to the American giants of the oil business. Benn went back and did his best which in the case of Amoco left him 'boiling with rage – I felt like the president of a banana republic negotiating with a multinational'. Labour's answer was to set up the British National Oil Corporation, BNOC, in 1976, which was meant to be both the government's eyes and ears in the industry, to buy 51 per cent of the oil landed, and then to sell it on. It gave the government some grip on the developing industry and built up formidable expertise at its Scottish headquarters. Yet it was essentially a bystander with modest powers, compared to the great oil companies. Its oil-producing business was in any case privatized by Nigel Lawson in 1982, the largest privatization the world had then seen; and the subsequent company Britoil was taken over by BP six years later.

British business as well as British manufacturing was slow to seize the possibilities of the oil boom, though the Scottish banks and the merchant banks clustered round Edinburgh's genteel Charlotte Square began forming oil subsidiaries and hiring expert economists by the end of the seventies. Among the partnerships was one between Thomson Scottish Petroleum, part of the group which also owned the *Scotsman* newspaper; and Armand Hammer, the one-time business ally of Lenin, with Occidental. They found the Piper field, one of the big ones following the huge Forties find by BP and Brent by Shell and Exxon. There were many smaller oil-investing companies, some of them successful. Onshore, some Aberdeenshire companies did well in building the offices and prefabricated living quarters, servicing the endless helicopter flights, developing expertise in valves and electronic equipment. Yet the grand hopes of ministers back in the mid-seventies that the oil discoveries would kick-start a great renaissance in banking, engineering, shipbuilding and new service industry, was very wide of the mark.

Why was this? It was partly that the boom came just when British industry was at its lowest ebb, strike-prone, short of money, short of good management. It was partly that the oil-boosted pound did indeed make the recession of the early eighties even worse, rising faster and further than ministers expected. The petro-currency helped squeeze the economy and improved efficiency, at the inevitable cost of widespread closures, sufficient to enrage many naturally pro-Conservative business people. Michael Edwardes, Chairman of the State-owned carmaker British Leyland, said at the time that if the government could not find a way to deal 'with North Sea oil, then I say: leave the bloody stuff in the ground'.[19]

Before 1979 Labour was struggling to rein in the American companies that had arrived early and eager. But after 1979 the Conservatives were determined to use the oil revenues quickly, to pay debt and cut taxes, rather than to invest it in some long-term plan for industry. This was the key 'rate of depletion' argument played out across Whitehall, which was really about how best Britain should use its bonus. The Norwegians, with a much smaller population and their industry run by the State, invested the proceeds in a great Nordic piggy-bank. When the Scottish Nationalists seized the oil issue in the early seventies they came up with a similar plan for a Scottish oil fund, paying out a permanent dividend to benefit the Scots henceforth. The argument between 'extract as much as possible now, and spend the proceeds' and 'extract slowly, and invest' was, however, a complicated one, since nobody knew what would happen to the oil price. With North Sea oil so expensive to produce, leaving the stuff under the seabed might mean that if the world price fell it became uneconomic.

Nor was it clear that money invested elsewhere by British ministers would turn out to be money well invested – particularly if it was also meant to kick-start industries. Under Labour, the so-called Varley assurances had been given to the oil industry, a promise that the government would not impose cutbacks beyond a certain level but allow the oil companies to take out most of what they could. According to Professor Alex Kemp of Aberdeen University, who has been writing the official history of North Sea oil, the argument in the early Tory years was between David Howell at the Department of Energy, who believed in slower extraction, and Howe at the Treasury, who needed the revenue as quickly as possible. Howe won the day, with Margaret Thatcher's consent, imposing a punitive 90 per cent marginal tax rate and treating oil taxes just like income tax or VAT even though oil revenue was finite, a one-off. Professor Kemp concludes that 'oil revenues were used as part of macro-economic management rather than energy policy, looking thirty years ahead.'

Good thing, or bad thing? This can be seen as a one-off waste, funding the squeeze of the early Thatcher years but leaving little for future generations left in the pot of gold at the end of the North Sea rainbow. Yet for those who saw that drastic economic squeeze as essential, it was money well spent. Lawson said the oil taxes gave 'a healthy kick-start' to the process of cutting the government deficit, though he always argued that the overall impact of North Sea oil was exaggerated. As to the profits from oil, they would be better invested privately. Lawson made his point by comparison: 'A peasant finds gold in his garden. Should he be allowed to mine it at his own speed and be left to allocate the proceeds between extra spending and saving for the day when the gold has been exhausted? Or should some authority force him to leave some of the gold in the ground to guard against profligacy?'[20] So in his view, the transfer of oil profits into investments overseas, as happened after the abolition of exchange controls, rather than in (say) British manufacturing, was a good bargain for the country as a whole.

British manufacturing continued to slither downhill, falling from 34 to 30 per cent of national output in 1970–7, before oil properly came on stream, and then from 30 per cent to 23 per cent in the great oil decade. (By 2006 it accounted for less than 15 per cent.) According to the government's own figures, 2 million manufacturing jobs were lost at this time. Productivity inevitably rose in consequence and the economy would recover very strongly, though this does finally answer the question about whether too much expertise and chains of supply were lost, putting Britain permanently out of markets she could otherwise have retained. Whichever view you take, this 'British revolution' could not have been sustained without the pipes and the rigs. Why did Margaret Thatcher say so little about North Sea oil? Or Geoffrey Howe? Could it be simply that in the heroic story of their remaking of the British economy, the Almighty's underwater gift was an embarrassingly vital support mechanism, for which they could take absolutely no credit? And that therefore they were as unlikely to draw attention to it, as actors apparently leaping through the air would be to the wires supporting them? Still, it was unfortunate. The rough-necks and roustabouts, the shuttle helicopter pilots landing in gale-force winds on postage-stamp-like platforms, and the divers taking horrible risks on the ocean bed, deserve a larger role in modern history. Un-unionized, risk-taking, freebooting, they were after all, model Thatcherites, every one.

Let us return to Lawson's metaphor of the peasant with gold in his garden. The question is, whose garden? Had Scotland been an independent country and had the lines of national territorial waters been drawn at an appropriate angle (the legal arguments about this were dense), then Scotland would undoubtedly have been a rich country. Like Biafra in Nigeria, it could have funded a breakaway on the basis of oil – though hopefully with less tragic effects. As we have seen, the Scottish National Party had spotted the possible consequences of oil early on. They had begun to worry Labour in the sixties with a series of stunning by-election successes. Whitehall had hit back; the Treasury produced a notional Scottish budget for 1967–8 showing

Scotland deeply in the red. Given that Scotland had a relatively poor and relatively scattered population, and a shrinking economic base, this was hardly surprising. But what difference would the oil revenues make? Suddenly, Whitehall came over all coy. Oil money was expertly mixed into national revenues. Jim Sillars, the MP who moved from Labour to the SNP via the briefly fashionable Scottish Labour Party, protested: 'The potential embarrassment of each drop of the magic oil was dealt with by the simple, crooked device of removing oil revenues from any purely Scottish statistics . . . The fish caught and landed from Scottish waters are allowed to remain in Scotland's accounts, but the oil over which those fish swim – well, that's different!'

The SNP was not waiting for official confirmation of what it suspected, however. It had strong covert support in the Edinburgh banking world and could draw on some of the brightest economists north of the border. Within months of the first big BP oil strike its chairman Billy Wolfe was declaring that oil should be a dominant part of its propaganda. In 1972 it launched its most famous slogan, 'It's Scotland's Oil' followed a year later by the still more aggressive, 'Rich Scots or Poor Britons?' Thanks to the recent release of government documents we now know just how jumpy this made Whitehall. Civil servants told Labour ministers after the second 1974 election they should delay Harold Wilson's promised Scottish assembly ('Powerhouse Scotland') to stop the British economy being destabilized. By then the SNP was claiming the support of a third of voters and had won eleven seats in the Commons. 'Progress toward devolution should be delayed for as long as possible . . .' said one mandarin: 'The longer this can be played, the better.' The problem was that the civil service thought the SNP's calculations on the huge wealth that could come Scotland's way with oil were, if anything, an underestimate. One Treasury official wrote: 'It is conceivable that income per head in Scotland could be 25 per cent or 30 per cent higher than that prevailing in England during the 1980s, given independence.' Another wrote bluntly: 'The Scots have really got us over a barrel here.'[21] But the Scots, whatever their suspicions and however vigorous the campaigning of the SNP, never knew quite how large that oily barrel was. Had they done so, it is likely that the politics of the later seventies and eighties would have been very different.

The Scots and the Welsh Leave Us Close to Tears

Scotland and Wales had very different political cultures but by the sixties they shared the sense of being parts of the UK in decline, whose old Labour elites no longer delivered the goods. Scotland's industrial heartland was dominated by coal, steel, shipbuilding and engineering. South Wales, built on coal and steel, was also culturally besieged, as people migrated to the richer new towns of southern England, and the Welsh language declined. Both these smaller countries asked themselves whether, if they cut free from the United Kingdom, they might somehow achieve a new beginning. The European Common Market showed that it was possible for small countries to thrive perfectly well. Even outside it, the Norwegians, Icelanders and Swiss seemed to be managing. No Western country seriously felt threatened by her neighbours any more. Living through the political traumas of the seventies, almost everyone in England was to an extent trapped inside the nightmare. For Scots and the Welsh there was the possibility at least of simply closing the door and walking away.

Yet in neither country did the secessionists ever have majority support. In both countries, their base tended to be among small business people, academics and public servants, the kind who in England were at the same time joining the Liberals. But the Scottish National Party and Plaid Cymru had clear objectives, effective political organizations, a certain fashionable rebel quality; and they scared the wits out of the established parties. These would be years when the breakup of Britain haunted many politicians and when nightmares of IRA-style violence being copied elsewhere fuelled best-selling books and television dramas. Once it had been easy to satirize Druidical Welshmen capering about and plunking their harps, or collections of wild-eyed, bushy-haired Scottish poets in kilts and jerseys. But by the seventies, it was not funny any longer.

The Scottish story can be traced back to the beginning of this postwar story. On 29 October 1949, a raw day in Edinburgh, a solemn faced, dark suited crowd walked into the gloomy headquarters of the Church of Scotland, a parade of landowners and miners, aristocrats and shipyard workers, fat businessmen and lean clerics. They had come to sign a Scottish Covenant, a practice last heard of in the bloody seventeenth century, when fanatic Presbyterians were taking on London and the losers had their heads lopped off in public. But this lot were hardly a revolutionary sight, and their document was full of sonorous assertions about their loyalty to the Crown. There was an impromptu prayer. The Duke of Montrose signed his name. There would be another 2 million signatures in due course, nearly half of Scotland's adult population, politely requesting a Scottish Parliament again.

Fast forward a few months, and move to Westminster Abbey at dead of night. A handful of dark-coated Scottish students were busily jemmying loose a lump of stone allegedly carried by a Greek prince and Pharaoh's daughter in the time of Moses to Scotland, via Ireland. This is the 'Stone of Destiny' on which Scotland's ancient kings sat to be crowned. It had been swiped by the wicked English and was being smuggled back to Scotland where it would be hidden as an inanimate hostage. (The Stone was eventually returned to the police, draped in Scottish flags, and was finally returned to Scotland again in the nineties by the Conservatives.) Soon afterwards brand-new postboxes with the symbol QEII for the new Queen, were being defaced or blown up across Scotland, where there had been no QEI. These are parts of the history of post-war Britain which hardly anyone in England has heard about, or understands. Yet at a time when Scotland is becoming ever more politically disassociated from London, it is a story which deserves to be remembered.

Having abolished their own parliament in the 1707 Act of Union, the Scots had become steadily keener on getting it back again, ever since Victorian times. The first National Party of Scotland was formed in 1928, merging with the Scottish Party to become the Scottish National Party or SNP in 1934. By the end of the Second World War Labour was committed to some kind of Scottish Parliament. Yet home rule disappeared as an issue again for most people during the forties and fifties, and indeed into the sixties. This was partly the binding-together effect of the war, which increased pride in being British. It was also because both Labour and the Conservatives (called Unionists in Scotland) had pursued policies of granting the Scots factories, agencies and jobs. In the age of centralism and planning, Scotland seemed to be getting quite a good deal.

During the war, Churchill had appointed a visionary socialist called

Tom Johnston, who had once been considered an excellent alternative
to Attlee as the next Labour leader, as his Secretary of State for
Scotland. Johnson was soon dubbed 'the uncrowned King of Scotland'
and set about scattering hydroelectric schemes through the Highlands,
bringing electricity and work; ordering great commercial forests to be
planted; reforming education, and generally carrying on like a progressive dictator. After the war, he continued running the hydro schemes,
forestry and Scottish tourism outside party politics, a one-man socialist
planning bureaucracy. He even tried to get fish farming started, half a
century before the technology was ready, though it would eventually
employ tens of thousands. The Tories, then quite popular in Scotland,
pursued similar policies, doling out industrial plants such as the
Ravenscraig steelworks and obliging the British Motor Corporation to
build cars in Bathgate, and the Hillman Imp to be constructed at
Linwood. During the Wilson years, Scotland was run by Willie Ross,
a Scottish Secretary as authoritarian, self-certain and skilled as Johnston
himself, a veritable second uncrowned king. His gifts included a nuclear
reactor at Dounreay, the Invergordon aluminium smelter and rescuing
a Clyde shipyard. He set up the Highlands and Islands Development
Board and the Scottish Development Agency. If planning could make
a country rich, Scotland would be paradise. In the sixties, public
spending per head there was a fifth above the English average.

Through most of this time Scottish Nationalism was a mere midge
of a movement, producing intense but very local irritation. That grand
Scottish Covenant signed in 1949 had simply been ignored. Labour
dropped its old commitment to a Scottish Parliament in 1956. Nationalism was associated with poets, dreaming students and the odd
eccentric aristocrat, a tartan irrelevance to the modern world. The
man who did most to change that is almost forgotten now, including
in his own party. He was not Billy Wolfe, the SNP's first charismatic
post-war leader, but a farmer from Ayrshire called Ian Macdonald who
left his farm to organize the 'Nats' full-time. Before 1962 when he took
over, the SNP had fewer than twenty active branches and a membership of around two thousand. Three years later under Macdonald's
organizing, there were 140 branches and six years on, in 1968, the SNP
had 484 branches across Scotland and 120,000 members. It is hard to
think of a similar rate of growth in any British political party. With the
distinctive CND logo everywhere at the time, the SNP came up with

its own modernistic thistle loop, and that was soon glinting from lapels and jerseys across Scotland.

It was at this stage a classic protest party, whose members tended to be prominent in anti-Vietnam and anti-nuclear protests. As disillusion grew, both with the post-Profumo Tories and with Harold Wilson, the SNP began to win first local council seats and then parliamentary by-elections. The first breakthrough came in Hamilton, a small industrial town outside Glasgow where one of the SNP's new generation, Winnie Ewing, won a safe Labour seat in 1967 and was driven in triumph in a scarlet Scottish-made Hillman Imp to Westminster. Though she lost the seat in the general election she was followed by Margo MacDonald, the 'blonde bombshell' of Govan on the Clyde, and by rising success in local elections. In 1970 Donald Stewart became the first SNP victor in a general election contest, winning the Western Isles. In the first 1974 election, the party won a further six Commons seats, and four more in the October election, taking its total to an all-time record of eleven, and the support of just over 30 per cent of Scottish voters. This would give them a crucial power-broking role in the politics of the late seventies which, as we shall see, they badly mishandled. Scotland's economy was doing badly in profound ways. Apart from the short-term boost of oil-related jobs, mainly in the north east, industry was old-fashioned, riven by strife, badly managed and losing ground in every direction. There was a feeling that the country could not be run worse by its own parliament; that the days of London planning and the gifts of uncrowned kings had not, in fact, produced the modern country everyone hoped for.

Labour became increasingly panicky. Harold Wilson deployed a favourite device, the setting up of a Royal Commission ('takes minutes and wastes years' in his own formulation) which duly suggested devolution for Scotland and Wales. After plots and counter-plots Wilson finally imposed this on a reluctant Scottish party. It was a form of devolution strong enough to outrage many Labour left-wingers at Westminster, including the young Neil Kinnock, yet too weak to please the out-and-out home rulers in Scotland. A handful of politicians, officials and journalists left the Labour Party in the winter of 1975 to form the breakaway Scottish Labour Party under the charismatic Jim Sillars. It briefly captured the headlines before being infiltrated by Trotskyists who, like crocheted bedspreads and lava lamps, seemed to turn up everywhere in the Seventies. The SLP duly split and then collapsed. Some of its members returned to Labour. Others, including Sillars, eventually ended up in the SNP.

Back at Westminster the new Labour leader Jim Callaghan began a long and weary battle to deliver home rule. Leading the fight was Michael Foot, a romantic enthusiast for devolution, despite the fact that his great hero Nye Bevan had been wholly opposed to such 'chauvinism'. Yet the most single-minded and influential MP in the devolution debates of the seventies was probably the anti-devolution backbencher Tam Dalyell who later led the *Belgrano* inquisition. An Old Etonian left-winger, he fuelled himself late into the night with pockets full of hard-boiled eggs prepared by his housekeeper and a head full of hard-boiled arguments about the breakup of Britain, prepared entirely by himself. His 'West Lothian question' asked how Parliament could tolerate having Scottish and Welsh members who could vote on matters affecting the English, while not having any authority over the same issues in their own constituencies (because they would be handled by a devolved parliament). It has never been satisfactorily answered. Many believe it will one day end the Union of Scotland and England. A bill for Home Rule was eventually enacted on 31 July 1978 after an exhausting parliamentary battle in which the government's fate hung in the balance night after night. But a key concession would end up scuppering the bill and Callaghan and the SNP too.

The government had accepted that the Scottish Parliament would only be set up after a referendum in Scotland in which a simple majority would not be enough; at least 40 per cent of the Scottish electorate must vote 'Yes'. Would this be so hard to achieve? When the referendum was finally held, the 'Yes' and 'No' campaigns were both rather ragged. Most of the Scottish media were in favour of devolution revolution and a 'Yes' vote was generally thought to be inevitable. The timing, however, was pitch-perfect terrible. The campaign ran in February 1979 against a backdrop of the 'winter of discontent', terrible weather and a collapse in government prestige. Voting against devolution was for some a way of registering contempt for Labour. Others simply could not be bothered. In the end, though most of Scotland voted in favour of home rule, turnout was low and only 32.9 per cent voted 'Yes', far below the 40 per cent hurdle.

Devolution was dead for twenty years to come. Callaghan, Foot and John Smith did everything they could to find some way of reviving the bill or postponing it but by now the majority of the SNP had had enough. They issued ultimatums to the government and eventually put down a motion of censure, though not all of them voted. Mrs Thatcher saw her chance. Labour lost the vote by a whisker and the general election of 1979 was duly triggered. This would bring about the election of a now implacable opponent of home rule. It would plunge Labour into chaos in Scotland as well as elsewhere. The SNP group was cut from eleven MPs to just two, and never regained the initiative. Earlier in this section we noted that Mrs Thatcher was lucky in her enemies and the Scottish Nationalists were yet another good example.

Wales's part in the story runs parallel to Scotland's in many ways. Like Scotland, Wales had become a post war Labour stronghold in her industrial heartland, with a Liberal tradition in the rural areas. Like Scotland, Wales had experienced a rise of interest in the national question between the wars. Plaid Cymru, the party of Wales, had been founded in 1925, nine years before the SNP. Like the Scottish nationalists, the Welsh nationalists were dominated in the early years by literary men, poets and lecturers, and had little working-class support. In the post-war years Wales, like Scotland, had benefited from the scattering of regional policy initiatives, above all the great steel rolling-mill at Llanwern in 1962 but also the Shotton blast furnace, the Licensing Centre at Swansea, the Passport Office at Newport, two nuclear power stations, and factories run by Rover, Ford, Hoover, Hotpoint and others – the equivalent to the car-making plants and aluminium smelters of the Scots. Just as in the Scottish Highlands, vast acreages of conifers were planted by the Forestry Commission, so too it happened across the hillsides of rural Wales. The Scots got a development agency. So did the Welsh. If the Scots popularly expressed their national pride through the up-and-down fortunes of their football team, and the occasional even dodgier pop phenomenon like the Bay City Rollers, the Welsh had rugby. At Cardiff Arms Park, renamed the Welsh National Stadium in 1970, England failed to win a single game between 1964 and 1979.

Politically, however, Wales was in a weaker position. She had been incorporated by England too early in her history to have developed separate institutions of modern statehood. Her 'Act of Union' came in 1536, not 1707, and it was a crucial difference. Wales had no single powerful national church, no parliament to look back on, no Enlightenment universities or modern legal code of her own. Indeed she had no official capital until Cardiff was recognized as such as late as 1955; no minister or administrative offices until the fifties and no Secretary of State for Wales until 1964. Welshness was celebrated more as a linguistic and religious quality, though the decline in religious attendance hit the nonconformist chapel tradition almost as hard as it hit the Church of England. Politically, the Welsh had looked to Westminster men as their heroes, David Lloyd George most obviously, but Nye Bevan too. The decline of Liberalism had left Wales dominated by Labour and with all the drawbacks of the one-party statelet – internal backbiting, political stagnation and an unbalanced attitude to London, which was simultaneously the remote and alien capital and the source of power, money and jobs. Clever Welshmen from Raymond Williams to Dylan Thomas often emigrated, becoming exiled professors and writers, endlessly harking back to the romantic day-before-yesterday.

In the Fifties Welsh nationalists began to find cultural and political issues which spurred them on. Instead of attacking post-boxes and stealing the Stone of Destiny, Welsh nationalism was inspired to fight for the survival of the Welsh language. English road-signs would be painted out, people refused to fill in forms written in English and there were successful campaigns for more Welsh broadcasting. But the biggest early spur was water. Indeed it could almost be said that water was the Welsh oil, particularly after the drowning of the Tryweryn valley in north-west Wales to create a reservoir for the people of Liverpool. This was done by Act of Parliament in 1957, despite almost all Welsh MPs voting against it. As one historian put it: 'Liverpool's ability to ignore the virtually unanimous opinion of the representatives of the Welsh people, confirmed one of the central tenets of Plaid Cymru – that the national Welsh community, under the existing order, was wholly powerless.'[22] Attacks on the Tryweryn reservoir followed and the Free Wales Army was formed in 1963. Violent Welsh nationalism was, thankfully, almost as unpopular and badly organized as violent Scottish nationalism, but there were explosions in the sixties and two men died in 1969 trying to blow up the Royal train during the Prince of Wales's Investiture. There would also be a more

Above. The Iron Lady
on manoeuvres.
Margaret Thatcher
at the peak of her power,
with tank and flag, 1986.

Right. The Tories had
another blonde who felt
the call of destiny:
Michael Heseltine,
Conservative conference
darling.

FRONT OF BRASS AND FEET OF CLAY

When Thatcher took on the moderate 'wets' in her own cabinet, she could rely on the support of much of the press. But it was the Falklands that changed everything: a soldier aboard the 1982 task force waits for the shooting to start.

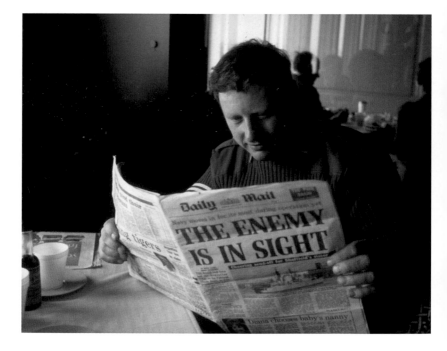

Rebel faces: picketing miners caught and handcuffed to a lamp-post by police, 1986, and the notoriously violent poll-tax riot of 1990 in Trafalgar Square.

Above. Two lost leaders: Labour's Neil Kinnock attacking left-wing Militants at the party conference in 1985 and his successor John Smith, who would probably have become prime minister in 1997, but died of a heart attack.

Left. In June 1988, 185 men died when a North Sea oil platform, Piper Alpha, blew up – yet the extraordinary story of the oil boom is little mentioned in politicians' memoirs.

Bitter-sweet: Tory chairman Chris Patten helped John Major win a triumphant electoral victory in 1992, but lost his own seat at Bath, and was sent as the last governor to Hong Kong.

The death of Diana in 1997 produced an almost Mediterranean outpouring of grief across the country. A small field of flowers lies outside Kensington Palace.

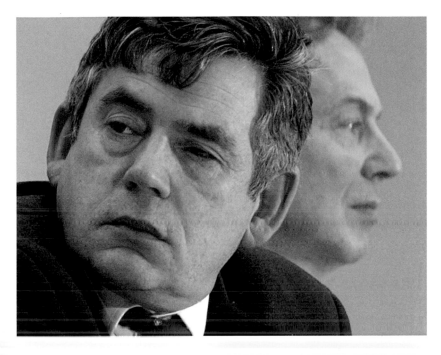

What's waiting in the wings?
Alastair Campbell guards his
master's back (*opposite, top*).
New Labour was famously
image-obsessed, but (*above*)
by 2005 neither Tony Blair nor
Gordon Brown could be bothered
to disguise their mutual enmity.

Tony Blair's legacy?
Anti-war protestors became
a familiar sight on the streets
of Britain (*opposite*), while British
troops did their utmost in the
devastated and violence-plagued
world of post-war Iraq. By 2007,
(*right*) they were still not
welcomed by many Iraqis.

More than four-million closed-circuit television cameras now watch the British: a surveillance society that echoes the wartime world of identity cards and observation with which this history began.

The biggest social change continues to be migration, latterly from eastern Europe: Polish road signs to help drivers in Cheshire, February 2007.

widespread and persistent campaign of burning out holiday homes and full-time homes owned by English incomers to Welsh-speaking areas.

Plaid Cymru's first breakthrough came at the Carmarthen by-election of 1966, a year before the SNP won Hamilton. Gwynfor Evans, a nationalist campaigner since the thirties and Plaid Cymru's leader since 1945, would lose the seat in the 1970 general election but two striking Plaid Cymru by-election performances in Rhondda West and Caerphilly in 1967 and 1968 suggested it was no flash in the pan. At last complacent Welsh Labour was being challenged. In the first 1974 election, Plaid Cymru would win two seats, and take a third in the second election of that year. Just as in Scotland, this produced a divided response among Labour in Wales. Should the nationalists be fought, as Neil Kinnock believed, or should they be paid to go away, with offers of devolution, as Michael Foot thought?

By then, like Scotland, the client economy of Wales was in very deep trouble. Yet despite the success of Plaid Cymru in local elections during the final years of 'old Labour' rule, they did not seem to pose quite the threat of the SNP. And of course, there was no oil boom in Welsh waters. So the proposed Welsh assembly was to have fewer powers than the Scottish one. It was to oversee a large chunk of public expenditure but would not be able to make laws. This was hardly likely to make anyone's blood pound. When the matter was put to a referendum the Welsh voted overwhelmingly against the planned assembly, by 956,000 votes to 243,000. Every one of the new Welsh counties voted 'No'. Plaid Cymru, unlike the SNP, did not vote for the end of the Labour government but in the Thatcher years Wales, like Scotland, was dominated by the politics of resistance to Conservatism. It would be a long wait.

The Boyo and the Bolsheviks

Michael Foot's leadership saved the Labour Party from splitting into two but was in all other respects a disaster. He was too old, too decent, too gentle, to take on the hard left or to modernize his party. Foot's politics were those of a would-be parliamentary revolutionary detained in a second-hand bookshop. When roused (which was often), his hair would flap, his face contort with passion, his hands would whip around excitedly and denunciations would pour from him with a fluency Martin Luther would envy. He was in his late sixties during his time as leader – he would be seventy just after the 1983 election – and he looked his age. Contemptuous of the shallow presentational tricks of television, he could look dishevelled and was famously denounced for wearing a 'donkey jacket' (it was actually, he insisted, rather a smart green woollen coat) at the Cenotaph. His skills were for whipping up the socialist faithful in meetings or for finger-stabbing attacks on the Tory enemy in House of Commons debates. He seemed to live in an earlier century, though it was never clear which one, communing with heroes such as Swift, Byron or Hazlitt, rather than in a political system which depended on television performance, ruthless organization and managerial discipline. He was a political poet in a prose age.

Perhaps nobody in the early eighties could have disciplined the Labour Party or reined in its wilder members. Foot did his best yet he led Labour to the party's worst defeat in modern times, on the basis of a hard-left, anti-Europe, anti-nuclear, if-it-moves-nationalize-it manifesto aptly described by Gerald Kaufman as 'the longest suicide note in history'. Kaufman had also bravely but fruitlessly urged him to stand down before the election. The campaign which followed has gone down in history as one of the least competent, most disorganized few weeks of chaos ever arranged by a modern political party. Foot impersonated a late nineteenth-century radical, touring open meetings and making long semi-literary effusions from crowded platforms to gatherings of the faithful. It was as if had not condescended to notice the radio age, never mind the television one. He appeared with the very Trotskyists he had earlier denounced and was clearly at odds with his deputy, Denis Healey, over such minor matters as the defence of the country. Labour's two former prime ministers, Wilson and Callaghan, both publicly attacked Foot's principled unilateralism. After all this, it was surprising that the party scraped into second place and held off the SDP-Liberal Alliance. It is a measure of the affection felt for Michael Foot that his swift retirement after that defeat was greeted with little recrimination.

Yet it also meant that when Neil Kinnock won the subsequent leadership election he had a mandate for change no previous Labour leader had enjoyed. 'Enjoyed' is perhaps not the word. Kinnock had won by a huge majority. He had 71 per cent of the electoral college votes, against 19 per cent for his nearest rival Roy Hattersley, while Tony Benn, the obvious left-wing challenger, was out of Parliament briefly, having lost his Bristol seat. Kinnock had been elected after a series of blistering campaign speeches, a left-winger by the standards of anyone who wasn't actually a revolutionary. He wanted the swift abandonment of all Britain's nuclear weapons. He believed in nationalization and planning. He wanted Britain to withdraw from Europe. He wanted to abolish private medicine and to repeal the Tory laws on trade union reform. And to start with, the only fights he picked with his party were over organizational matters, such as the campaign to force Labour MPs to submit to reselection, which handed a noose to militant local activists. Yet after the chaos of the 1983 campaign, he was also sure that the party needed radical reform.

Though the modern age of attempted ruthless control over the media is popularly believed to have begun with Peter Mandelson's arrival as Labour's director of communications, it actually began when Patricia Hewitt, a radical Australian known for her campaigning on civil liberties, joined Kinnock's new office. It was she who began keeping the leader away from journalists, trying to control interviews and placing him like a precious stone only in flattering settings. Kinnock, for his part, knew how unsightly old Labour looked to the rest of the country and was prepared, if not happy, to be groomed. He gathered round him a rugby scrum of tough and aggressive aides, many of whom went on to become ministers in the Blair years – Charles Clarke, the burly son of a powerful Whitehall mandarin; John Reid, a wild former Communist Labour backbencher; Hewitt; and Peter Mandelson. Kinnock was the first to flirt, indeed to enter into full physical relations, with the once-abhorred world of advertising, and to seek out the support of pro-Labour pop singers such as Tracey Ullmann and Billy Bragg, long before 'Cool Britannia' was thought of in the Blair years. He smartened up his own style, ending the informal mateyness which had made him popular among colleagues, and introduced a new code of discipline in the shadow cabinet, a code which would have had him thrown out a few years earlier.

In the Commons he tried hard to discomfit Thatcher at her awesome best, which was not easy and rarely successful. The two of them loathed each other with a chemical passion. Labour's dreadful poll ratings very slowly began to improve. There was talk of 'the Kinnock factor'. But there were awesome problems for Labour which could not be dealt with by pop stars, friends in the advertising world or well-educated Australian ladies barking at journalists. The first of these was that the party harboured a substantial and vocal minority of people who were not really parliamentary politicians at all, but revolutionaries of one kind or another. They included Arthur Scargill and his brand of insurrectionary trade unionism; the Trotskyist Militant Tendency, which had been busy infiltrating the party since the sixties; and assorted hard-left councils, determined to defy 'Thatcher' (also known as the democratically elected government) by various illegal stratagems.

Kinnock dealt with them all. Had he not done so New Labour would never have happened and Tony Blair would have enjoyed a well-remunerated and obscure career as a genial barrister specializing in employment law. Yet Kinnock himself was a passionate man whose own politics were to the left of the new mood of the country. He was beginning an agonizing journey which meant confronting and defeating people who sounded not so different from his younger self; while moving steadily, but never quite far enough, towards the centre. On this journey much of his natural wit, his balls-of-the-feet, exuberant, extempore rhetoric and convivial bounce would be silenced, sellotaped and sedated (as he might well have alliterated). He had come into politics as if it was rugby, us against them, a violent contact sport much enjoyed by all participants. He found that in leadership it was more serious, drearier and nastier than rugby. The game was changing. Week after week, he was confronting in Thatcher someone whose principles had set firm long before and whose politics, love them or hate them, seemed to express those principles. Yet he was by necessity changing, a man on the move, who could not renounce his former beliefs nor yet quite stand by them. He was always having to shade, to hedge and to qualify, to dodge the ball, not kick it. The press soon dubbed him 'the Welsh windbag'.

The first and hardest example of what he was up against came with the miners' strike. As we have seen, Kinnock and Scargill loathed each other – indeed, the NUM president may have been the only human being on the planet that Kinnock disliked more than Margaret Thatcher. He distrusted Scargill's aims, despised his tactics and realized early on that he was certain to fail. As the spawn of socialist Welsh miners, Kinnock could not demonize the strike without demonizing his own upbringing and origins, yet he knew it was a disaster. As the violence spread, the Conservatives and the press were waiting for him to denounce the pickets and to praise the police. He simply could not. Too many of his own side thought the violence was the fault of the police. As the strike hardened, one obvious tactic was to attack Scargill's failure to hold a national ballot. Yet acutely conscious of the feelings of striking miners, he could not bring himself to attack the embattled trade union. So he was caught, volubly, even eloquently inarticulate, between the rock of Thatcher and the hard place of Scargill. In the Commons, white-faced, week by week, he was taunted by the Tories for his weakness. In the coalfields he was denounced as the miner's son too frightened to come to the support of the miners. So he made lengthy arguments about the case for coal and the harshness of the Tories which were, as he knew full well, only adjacent to the row consuming the nation. These were impossible circum-stances. In them, Kinnock at least managed to avoid fusing Labour and the NUM in the mind of floating voters, ensuring that Scargill's utter political defeat was his alone. But this lost year destroyed his early momentum and damped down his old blazing certainty. It stole his hwyl – and a Welsh politician without hwyl is like a Jewish agent without chutzpah.

It is said that the difference between being an Opposition politician and a Government one is that in Government you get up each morning and decide what to do while in Opposition you get up and decide what you are going to say. It is hardly Kinnock's fault that in British politics he is remembered for talking. His critics recall his imprecise long-windedness, the product of self-critical and painful political readjustment. His admirers recall his great platform speeches, the saw-edged wit and air-punching passion. There was one time, however, lasting for just a few minutes, when Kinnock spoke so well he united most of the political world in admiration

This happened on 1 October 1985 at the main auditorium in Bournemouth, the well-off Dorset coastal resort where Labour confer-ences never seem entirely at home. A few days earlier Liverpool City Council, formally Labour-run but in fact controlled by the Revolution-ary Socialist League, had sent out redundancy notices to its 31,000 staff. The revolutionaries, known by the name of their newspaper *Militant*, were a party-within-a-party, a parasitic body nuzzled inside Labour and chewing its guts. They had some five thousand members who paid a proportion of their incomes to the RSL, so that the Militant Tendency had 140 full-time workers, more than the staff of the Social Democrats and Liberals combined.[23] They were present all round the country but Liverpool was their great stronghold. There they practised Trotsky's politics of 'the transitional demand' – the habit of making impractical demands for more spending, higher wages and so on, so that when the capitalist lackeys refuse them, you can push on to the next stage, leading to collapse and then revolution. In Liverpool where they were building thousands of new council houses, this meant setting an illegal council budget and cheerfully bankrupting the city. Sending out the redundancy notices to the council's entire staff was supposed to show Thatcher they would not back down, or shrink from the chaos ahead. Like Scargill, Militant's leaders thought they could destroy the Tories on the streets.

Kinnock had thought of taking them on a year earlier but had decided the miners' strike made that politically impossible. The Liverpool mayhem gave him his chance. So in the middle of his speech at Bournemouth, up to then a fairly conventional Labour leader's address, attacking the other parties and cheering up the hall, Kinnock struck. It was time, he suddenly said, for Labour to show the public that it was serious. Implausible promises would not win political victory.

> I'll tell you what happens with impossible promises. You start with far-fetched resolutions. They are then pickled into a rigid dogma, a code, and you go through the years sticking to that, outdated, misplaced, irrelevant to the real needs, and you end in the grotesque chaos of a Labour council – a *Labour* council – hiring taxis to scuttle round a city handing out redundancy notices to its own workers.

By now he had whipped himself into real anger, shouting yet also – just – in control. The best speeches are made on the lip of the curve of the track, an inch away from crashing into incoherence. Kinnock's enemies were in front of him. All the pent-up frustrations of the past year were being released. The hall came alive. Militant leaders like Derek Hatton, a man with the looks of a recently retired footballer, stood up and yelled back. Boos came from left-wingers. Uncertain applause came from the loyalists. The pompous left-wing MP Eric Heffer (who had once begun a speech in the Commons with the immortal words, 'I, like Jesus Christ, am the son of a carpenter') stood up and stomped from the hall, followed by camera crews and journalists. This was drama of a kind even Labour conferences were unused to. Kinnock went on:

'I'm telling you, and you'll listen, you can't play politics with people's jobs and with people's services, or with their homes.'

There was another huge outburst, now both of cheers and of boos. Kinnock insisted that the voice of people with real needs was louder than all the booing that could be assembled: 'The people will not, cannot, abide posturing. They cannot respect the gesture-generals or the tendency tacticians.'

Alliteration, then eruption. Most of those interviewed said it was one of the most important and courageous speeches they had ever heard, though the hard left was venomously hostile. The newspapers, used to kicking Kinnock, were almost delirious with praise. David Blunkett, the blind socialist leader of Sheffield city council, who would later serve in the Blair cabinets, organized a climb-down on a Militant-sponsored motion, much to Kinnock's annoyance. But the speech was a genuine turning point. By the end of the following month Liverpool District Labour Party, from which Militant drew its power, was suspended and an inquiry had been set up. By the spring of 1986 leaders of Militant had been identified and charged with behaving in a way incompatible with Labour membership. The process of expelling them was noisy, legally fraught and time-consuming, though more than a hundred were eventually expelled. As important, there was a strong tide towards Kinnock across the rest of the party, with many left-wingers cutting their ties to the revolutionaries. There were many battles with the hard left to come, and several pro-Militant MPs were elected to the Commons. Newspaper stories about 'loony left' councils allegedly banning black bin bags on the grounds of racism and ordering teachers to stop using nursery rhymes for the same reason, would continue to be used to taunt Labour. Yet by standing up openly to the Trotskyist menace, as Wilson, Callaghan and Foot had not, Kinnock gave his party a new start. It began to draw away from the SDP-Liberal Alliance in the polls and do much better in local elections too. It was the moment when New Labour became possible.

Yet neither this, nor the new fashion for better-controlled, slicker and sharper management that Kinnock brought it, would do the party much good against Thatcher in the election that followed. Whatever glossy pamphlets, well-made adulatory films and carefully planned photo-opportunities could do, was done. Mandelson, a former student leader and television producer whose grandfather had been Herbert Morrison, became the best-known of the modernizers. Prince Charles greeted him as 'the red rose man' for his role in ditching the old red banner as Labour's symbol and substituting a long-stemmed rose. Mandelson was certainly a single-minded and devoted reformer, cajoling and bullying a generally anti-Labour press. But he was not the only one. The red rose had been suggested by others, a copy of European socialist party imagery. Yet symbolism could not mask the fact that in its policies, Labour was still behind the public mood. Despite mass unemployment Thatcher's market optimism was filtering through. Labour might have ditched the red flag but it was still committed to renationalization, planning, a National Investment Bank and unilateral nuclear disarmament, a personal cause for both Kinnock and his wife Glenys over the previous twenty years.

The mid-eighties were a time when, after ferocious arguments about disarmament and the Russian invasion of Afghanistan, then a spate of espionage cases, the Cold War was finally thawing. In the White House President Reagan, scourge of the 'evil empire', was set on creating 'Star Wars', the orbiting satellite and anti-missile system intended to make the United States invulnerable to Russian attack. Yet he was ready to talk too, as the famous summit with Gorbachev at Reykjavik showed. There the Russians agreed to big missile reductions and the Americans declined to scrap 'Star Wars'. It was not a time for the old certainties. Yet for Kinnock, support for unilateral nuclear disarmament was fundamental to his political personality. It was the reflex response to those who accused him of selling out his socialism. It was a source of some of his best rhetoric. He therefore stuck with the policy, even as he came to realize just how damaging it was to Labour's image among swing voters.

He was clear about it. Under Labour all the British and American nuclear bases would be closed, the Trident nuclear submarine force cancelled, all existing missiles scrapped and Britain would no longer expect any nuclear protection from the United States in time of war. Instead more money would be spent on tanks and conventional warships. Kinnock was forceful and detailed about all this, and the more he spoke, the more Labour's ratings went down. He set off gamely trying to sell the CND line as no kind of surrender when in Russia; and something wholly compatible with Nato membership while in Washington, where on his third visit Reagan's team humiliated him with a twenty-minute meeting, followed by a coldly hostile briefing. All of this did him a lot of good among many traditional Labour supporters; Glenys turned up at the women's protest camp at Greenham Common. But it was derided in the press, helped the SDP and was unpopular with just the floating-voter, middle England people Labour desperately needed to win back. In the 1987 general election campaign Kinnock's explanation about why Britain would not simply have to surrender if threatened by a Soviet nuclear attack sounded as if he was advocating some kind of *Dad's Army* guerrilla campaign once the Russians had got here. With policies like these, he was not putting Thatcher under the kind of pressure which, perhaps, she needed.

A Revolution's Mid-Life Crisis

There had been some bad moments for the second Thatcher government. Most obviously, she had nearly been assassinated. The IRA bomb which demolished a chunk of the Grand Hotel at Brighton during the 1984 Conservative conference was intended as a response to Mrs Thatcher's hard line at the time of the 1981 hunger strike. The plot had been to murder the British cabinet and Prime Minister and plunge the country into political chaos, resulting in withdrawal from all Ireland. As for her, when it went off at 2.50 she was still working on an official paper about Liverpool's garden festival, having finished writing her speech ten minutes earlier so she was not even woken up. The blast scattered broken glass on her bedroom carpet and filled her mouth with dust. She then decamped to lie fully clothed in the bedroom of a nearby police college, pausing only to kneel and pray with her personal assistant Cynthia Crawford, or 'Crawfie', when they heard that the bomb had killed the wife of the cabinet minister John

Wakeham and nearly killed him; killed the Tory MP Anthony Berry; had badly injured Norman Tebbit, and paralysed his wife.

After less than an hour's fitful sleep and with her cabinet hurriedly dressed in clothes from a nearby branch of Marks & Spencer, their dresses and suits still being in the half-wrecked hotel, she rewrote her speech and told the still stunned conference that they had witnessed an attempt to cripple the government. 'And the fact that we are gathered here now, shocked but composed and determined, is a sign not only that this attack has failed, but that all attempts to destroy democracy by terrorism will fail.' The final death toll from Brighton was five dead and several more seriously injured but its consequences for British politics, which could have been momentous, turned out to be minimal.

If the IRA could not shake her, could anything else? There had been internal rows, not only over Westland but more ominously for the future, about economic policy. Her Chancellor, Nigel Lawson, had wanted to replace the old and rather wobbly system of controlling the money supply through targets, the Medium Term Financial Strategy, with a new stratagem – tying the pound to the German mark in the European Exchange Rate system, or ERM. This was an admission of failure; the older system of measuring money was useless in the world of global fast money described earlier. Using Germanic bondage was an alternative. In effect, Britain would have subcontracted her anti-inflationary policy to the more successful and harder-faced disciplinarians of the West German Central Bank. Lawson was keen. She was not; if anyone was to play dominatrix round here, it would be her. At the time, little of this debate bubbled from the specialist financial world into general political life.

Other rows did. There was the Westland affair itself but also a botched sale of British Leyland and the highly unpopular use of British airbases for President Reagan's attack on Libya in 1986. After her hugely successful fight to claw back some of Britain's overpayment to the European Community budget in her first term, these were years of Thatcherite drift over Europe, which would so fatally damage her at the end. Jacques Delors, later her great enemy, had been appointed President of the European Commission and begun his grand plan for the next stages of union. The Single European Act, which smashed down thousands of national laws preventing free trade inside the EC, promising free movement of goods, capital, services and people, and presaging the single currency, was passed with her urgent approval. She pooh-poohed the idea that when the continentals talked of economic and political union, they really meant it. She would regret all this later.

At home a wider dilemma was emerging right across domestic policy, from the inner cities to hospitals, schools to police forces. It was one which would puzzle both her successor governments, John Major's and Tony Blair's. It was simply this: how does a modern government get things done? In the economy, she had an answer. Government sets the rules, delivers sound money and then stands back letting other people get on with it. In practice she often behaved differently, always more pragmatic and interventionist than her image suggested. At least, however, the principle was clear. But when it came to the public services there was no similar principle. Where were the staunch, independent-spirited movers and shakers in the hospitals, town halls or the school system, the equivalent for public life of the entrepreneurs and risk takers she admired in business? If government stood back and just let go of schools, hospitals, inner cities, who would be waiting to catch them?

Before the Thatcher revolution the Conservatives had been seen as, on balance, defenders of local democracy. They were very strongly represented in councils across the country and had been on the receiving end of some of the most thuggish threats from Labour governments intent, for instance, on abolishing grammar schools. Conservatives had seen local representatives on hospital boards and education authorities as bulwarks against socialist Whitehall. Margaret Thatcher herself had good reason to recall the days of sturdy local independents, doing the public's work on unpaid committees for her father, Alderman Roberts, had been one of them. In the seventies, Tory think tanks regularly produced reports calling for stronger localism, the building of a rich 'civil society' in which independent institutions – churches, schools, charities, clubs and the rest – would spread autonomy and freedom. It was the theme of the most influential conservative philosopher of post-war Britain, Michael Oakeshott. The Tory vision emphatically included elected local government. In 1978, two right-wing Conservative politicians, for instance, wrote a passionate pamphlet complaining that 'local government is being deprived of more and more of the functions it used to be thought capable of fulfilling.'[24]

Yet in power, Thatcher and her ministers could not trust local government, or any elected and therefore independent bodies at all. Between 1979 and 1994, an astonishing 150 Acts of Parliament were passed removing powers from local authorities, and £24 billion a year, at 1994 prices, had been switched from them to unelected and mostly secretive gatherings. The first two Thatcher governments transferred power and discretion away from people who had stood openly for election, and towards the subservient agents of Whitehall, often paid-up party members and well-meaning stooges. Ministers, whether 'wet' or 'dry', competed to show her their zeal by taking the initiative away from organizations on the ground. Michael Heseltine attacked local government with new auditing arrangements, curbs on how much tax they could raise, and then spending caps as well. Nicholas Ridley, an Environment Secretary, forced them to put out a wide range of services to tender for private companies, telling local councils in the harshest terms that no dissent was permissable: 'we might have to force them to expose their activities to competition if they did not choose to do that themselves.'[25]

So there was no public service equivalent of privatization. In hospitals and schools Thatcher had eventually rejected the radical alternatives of fees, private management, selection and independence when offered them by the CPRS (Central Policy Review Staff). Stirred by the idea, she was too cautious to follow where it led. If neither new private nor old public, then what? The answer turned out to be expensive bureaucratic central activity which made ministers feel important. In the health service, early attempts to decentralize were rapidly reversed and a vast top-down system of targets and measurements was put in place, driven by a new planning organization. It cost more and the service seemed to get worse. Similar centralist power-grabs took place in urban regeneration, one of the most visible and immediate areas of government action, where unelected corporations, UDCs, rather than elected councils, got the money to pour into rundown cities. The biggest city councils, notably the Greater London Council, were simply abolished. Its powers were distributed, including to an unelected organization controlled by Whitehall. As one critic, Simon Jenkins, pointed out, by 1990 'there were some 12,000 laymen and women running London on an appointed basis against just 1,900 elected borough councillors.' Even in housing, the gap left by the sale of council homes was met by the rise of the Housing Corporation, disbursing 90 per cent of the money used by housing associations to build new cheap homes. In the Thatcher years its staff grew sevenfold and its budget, twentyfold.

Back in the mid-eighties she did, to be fair, have other things on her mind. Personal relationships matter as much in modern diplomacy as they did in the Renaissance, and the Thatcher–Gorbachev courtship engaged her imagination and human interest. She was becoming the closest ally Ronald Reagan had, in another international relationship which was of huge emotional and political significance to her. In these years she had become an international diva of conservative politics, feted by crowds from Russia and China to New York. Her wardrobe, coded depending on where an outfit had first been worn, told its own story: 'Paris Opera, Washington Pink, Reagan Navy, Toronto Turquoise, Tokyo Blue, Kremlin Silver, Peking Black'.[26] Meanwhile she was negotiating the hard detail of Hong Kong's transitional status before it was handed over to Communist China in 1997. She got a torrid time at Commonwealth conferences for her opposition to sanctions against the apartheid regime in South Africa – and where she gave as good as she got. At home, the problem of persistently high unemployment was nagging away, though it started to fall from the summer of 1986, while Tory strategists still seemed to lack a clear idea about how to deal with the unfamiliar threat of the 'two Davids' and the Liberal-SDP Alliance. And electorally, the multiple failures and political threats turned out to matter not at all.

1987: The Revolution Confirmed

When the 1987 election campaign began, Thatcher had a clear idea about what her third administration would do. Just like Tony Blair later, she wanted more choice for the users of state services. There would be independent state schools outside the control of local councillors, called grant-maintained schools. In the health service, though it was barely mentioned in the manifesto, she wanted money to follow the patient. Tenants would be given more rights. The basic rate of income tax would be cut. She would finally sort out local government, ending the rates and bringing in a tax with bite. On paper the programme seemed coherent, which was more than could be said for the management of the Tory campaign itself. Just as Kinnock's Labour team had achieved a rare harmony and discipline, Conservative Central Office was racked by hissy fits and screaming cat-fights between politicians and ad-men. The Leaderene began to snap at her former favourite, the carnivorous 'Chingford Skinhead', Norman Tebbit, now party chairman.

At one point in the campaign when the Labour leader seemed to have closed the gap to just four points and when Mrs Thatcher herself was performing badly, hit by agonizing toothache, the Tories had a real panic, 'Wobbly Thursday'. That dreadful Kinnock, it seemed, was having a better campaign than she was. He sailed around, surrounded by admiring crowds, young people, nurses, waving and smiling and little worried by the press while she was having a horrid time. What was going on? In the event, the Conservatives need not have worried at all. Despite a last-minute BBC prediction of a hung Parliament, and a late surge of Labour self-belief, they romped home. The Tories had an overall majority of 101 seats, almost exactly the share of the vote (42 per cent) they had enjoyed after the Labour catastrophe of 1983. Labour had made just twenty net gains. At home in his Welsh constituency, despairing, Kinnock punched the wall. His police protection officer, who had been much moved by some of the great Kinnock speeches he had witnessed in the past three weeks, offered words of comfort. 'Don't worry, sir, it could have been worse.' Kinnock is said to have swivelled round towards him, eyes narrowed, looking suddenly dangerous. 'Worse? Could have been worse? Just tell me, how could it have been worse?' The police officer blandly replied: 'Well sir, in the old days, they'd have chopped your head off.'

Afterwards, surveying the wreckage of their hopes, Kinnock and his team won plaudits from the press for the brilliance, verve and professionalism of their campaign. It had been transformed from the shambles of only four years earlier. At the same time the Conservatives had been flat-footed and unsure of themselves compared to their previous two elections, which only goes to show that the detail of electioneering, which obsesses Westminster politicians, is perhaps less important than they think. And what of the SDP-Liberal Alliance, the big new idea of eighties politics? They were out of puff. They had been floundering in the polls for some time, caught between Kinnock's modest Labour revival and Thatcher's continuing popularity with a large and solid minority of voters. Their gamble was that Labour was dying, and it had failed. The public had enjoyed robust media mockery of the competing David Steel/David Owen dual leadership as much as the leadership itself. Though Owen was popularly seen as the dominant partner his Social Democrats had a woeful election, seeing their eight MPs reduced to five and losing Roy Jenkins in the process, a tribulation Owen bore with fortitude. The SDP would soon begin to fall apart, though an Owenite rump party limped on for a while after the rest merged with the Liberals. Good PR, good labelling, goodwill; none of it had been good enough. In 1987 Thatcher had not created the country she dreamed of, but she could argue that she had won a third consecutive victory on the back of ideas, not on the back of envelopes.

The Year of Hubris, 1988 – and Why We Still Live There

For true believers the story of Margaret Thatcher's third and last administration can be summed up in the single word, betrayal. Her hopes of a free-market Europe were betrayed by the continentals, abetted by her own treacherous Foreign Office. Her achievements in bringing down inflation were betrayed by her Chancellor, Nigel Lawson. Finally she was betrayed directly – 'treachery with a smile on its face' – when her cabinet ministers turned on her and forced her to resign on 20 November 1990. The British revolution was sold out by faint-hearts, its great leader exiled to an executive home in south London, and glory departed from the earth. But there is another word that sums up the story better – not betrayal, but hubris. In the late eighties the Thatcher revolution overreached itself. The inflationary boom happened because of the expansion of credit and a belief among ministers that, somehow, the old laws of economics had been abolished; Britain was now in a virtuous, endless upward spiral of increasing prosperity. Across the Welfare State swaggering, high-handed centralism continued on steroids, ever grander. Near the end, Thatcher's fall was triggered by a disastrous policy for local taxation whose blatant unfairness was never properly considered by ministers, as if it did not really matter. And by the end, her own brutal rudeness to those around her left her almost friendless. She had been in power too long.

The year after the election, 1988, was the real year of hubris. The Thatcher government began laying about it with a frenzy unmatched before or since, flaying independent institutions and bullying the professions as if it was a short-tempered teacher and they were uppity children. England's senior judges came under tighter new political control. They would hit back. University lecturers lost the academic tenure they had enjoyed since the days when students arrived by ox-cart, making jokes in Latin. In Kenneth Baker's Great Education Reform Bill, or 'Gerbil' of that year, Whitehall grabbed direct control over the running of school curriculums, creating a vast new state bureaucracy to dictate what should be taught, when and how, and then to monitor the results. Teachers could do nothing. The cabinet debated the detail of maths courses; Mrs Thatcher spent much of her own time worrying about the teaching of history. It happened at a time when education ministers were complaining bitterly in private about the appalling quality of talent, not among teachers, but civil servants, the very people they were handing more power to.

A former and penitent Education Secretary from the age of comprehensives, Thatcher believed schooling was now a national disgrace. She wanted to scupper trendy-lefty teachers by giving parents, generally traditionalist, more choice about which school to choose. That meant establishing Whitehall-controlled independent state schools specializing in technical subjects, City Technology Colleges. It also meant persuading other schools to opt out of local authority control to become grant-maintained, rewarded with a small bribe. Neither idea worked. Only a small number of highly costly CTCs ever opened and the few schools who opted out found they had opted in – to tight Treasury and Department of Education control. Later under John Major's government, the inevitable extension of central financial control would produce yet another Whitehall-style organization (though, in fact, based in York), the Funding Agency for Schools. It was meant to be able to close schools, open schools, expand them, change their character and cut their scale, all without reference to local wishes. It was described by a right-wing think tank as having 'an extraordinary range of dictatorial powers' giving the Education Secretary 'authority similar to Henry VIII's dissolution commissioners'.[27]

It was the same pattern in health. In 1988 too, the new Health Secretary, Kenneth Clarke, pressed ahead with the system of 'money following the patient', a Monopoly-board version of the market in which hospitals 'sold' their services, and local doctors, on behalf of the ill, 'bought' them. The market was not real, of course, because the hospitals could not go out of business and the doctors, with a limited range of hospitals to choose from, could hardly withhold their money and refuse to buy their patients a heart bypass or hip replacement. The initial theory was perfectly intelligent. It was an attempt to bring private sector-like behaviour into the health service, a new regime of efficiency and tight budgeting. It looked enough like a real market to cause a huge and lengthy revolt by doctors and patients' groups. They were worrying about the wrong problem.

Because the government did not really trust local people to work together to improve the health service, the Treasury seized control of budgets and contracts. And to administer the system nearly 500 National Health Service trusts were formed, apparently autonomous but staffed by failed party candidates, ex-councillors and party donors. Any involvement by elected local representatives was brutally terminated. Mrs Thatcher later wrote: 'As with our education reforms, we wanted all hospitals to have greater responsibility for their affairs . . . [and] the self-governing hospitals to be virtually independent.' But as with her education reforms, the real effect was to create a new bureaucracy overseeing a regiment of quangos. Every detail of the 'internal market' contracts was set down from the centre, from pay to borrowing to staffing. The rhetoric of choice in practice, meant an incompetent dictatorship of bills, contracts and instructions. Those who could voted with their chequebooks. Between 1980 and 1990, the number of people covered by the private health insurance company Bupa nearly doubled, from 3.5 million to a little under 7 million. It wasn't only salaried, professional people with health insurance written into their contracts who paid for private medicine: by the late eighties private hospitals had queues of tattooed men in jeans waiting to be seen, cash in hand.

Hubris about what the State can and cannot do was found

everywhere. Training may be unglamorous but it is crucial to any modern economy. Here too a web of unelected bodies was spun, disbursing Treasury money according to Whitehall rules. The same happened in housing, which Thatcher said was more serious a matter even than health and education at the time, and which in 1988 saw the establishment of unelected Housing Action Trusts to take over the old responsibility of local authorities for providing cheap homes. Nearly twenty years after most of these bodies began work, there is still a puzzle here.

Mrs Thatcher said she was trying to pull the State off people's backs. In the end, that was the point of her. She thought so, too. In her memoirs she wrote of her third government, 'the root cause of our contemporary social problems . . . was that the state had been doing too much.' So why did she let it bustle around doing more and more? Simon Jenkins concluded that 'Her most potent legacy was potency itself.'[28] The more a leader is self-certain, the more there is in the world around her that she wants to change and the fewer other people she can trust. That means taking more powers. Letting other institutions and smaller-scale leaders find their own way through a busy world goes for a Burton. The institutions most hurt were local councils. Under our constitution, local government is defenceless against a Prime Minister with a secure parliamentary majority and a loyal cabinet. So it has been hacked away. It is time to address the moment when this programme of crushing alternative centres of power came so badly unstuck it destroyed the Lady Lenin of the free market herself.

Enter the Peasants, with Billhooks

Margaret Thatcher would say the poll tax was actually an attempt to save local government. Like schools, hospitals and housing, councils had been subject to a grisly torture chamberful of pincers, bits, whips and flails as ministers tried to stop them spending money, or raising it, except as Whitehall wished. Since the war local government had been spending more but the amount of money it raised independently came from a relatively narrow base of people, some 14 million property-owners. Thatcher had been prodded by Edward Heath into promising to replace this tax, the 'rates', as early as 1974 but nobody had come up with a plausible and popular-sounding alternative. She intensely disliked rates, regarding them as a tax on self-improvement and inherently un-Conservative. Yet in government, the problem nagged away at her.

There was a malign dynamic at work. The more powers government took away from local councils, the less councils mattered and the more local elections were used merely as giant referendums on central government, a cost-free protest vote. Once, local elections were not national news; they were about who was best to run towns and counties. In the late sixties and seventies they became national news, a regular referendum in which the Prime Minister was applauded or slapped. It was generally the latter. Under Margaret Thatcher the Tories lost swathes of local councils in bloody electoral defeats, again and again. The result was more socialist councils, mistrusted even more by central government, which therefore, as we have seen, took still more powers away from them, which made the elections even less relevant, and fuelled more protest voting and so on. If this was not bad enough, then it was clear to Thatcher and her ministers that socialist councils were pursuing expensive hard-left policies partly because so few of the local voters were ratepayers. Too many could vote for high-spending councils without feeling any personal pinch.

One way of cutting the knot would to be to make all those who voted for local councils pay towards their cost. This was the origin of the poll tax, or community charge as it was officially known, a single flat tax for everyone. It would mean lower bills for many homeowners and it would make local councils more responsive to their voters. On the other hand, it would mean a new tax for approximately 20 million people which would be regressive. The poorest in the land would pay as much as the richest. This broke a principle which stretched much further back that the 'post-war consensus'. The idea had been knocking around for some years before it was picked up by the government and subjected to a long and intense internal debate, which we will skip, except to note that not everyone thought it was a good idea. The poll tax was sold to Mrs Thatcher by her Environment Secretary, Kenneth Baker, at a seminar at Chequers in 1985, along with the nationalization of the business rate. Nigel Lawson tried very hard to argue the Prime Minister out of it, telling her it would be 'completely unworkable and politically catastrophic'.

He was outgunned by a stream of lady-pleasers keen to prove him wrong, and indeed the tax was being discussed at the very same cabinet meeting Heseltine stalked out of during the Westland affair. It might have been less of a disaster – it might even have been successful – had it been brought in very slowly, over ten years as first mooted, or four as was then planned. But at the 1987 Tory conference there was a collective rush of blood to the head. Intoxicated by the bold simplicity of the thing, party members urged Thatcher to bring it in at once. Idiotically, she agreed. There was, to be fair, a reason for hurry. Rates, like the modern council tax, depended on the relative value of houses across Britain, which changed with fashion and home improvement. Every so often, therefore, there had to be a general revaluation to keep the tax working. Yet each revaluation meant higher rates bills for millions of homeowners and businesses, and governments tended to try to put them off. In Scotland a crisper law did not allow this. There, a rates revaluation had finally happened and caused political mayhem. It gave English ministers a nasty glimpse of what was in store for them too eventually. Scottish ministers begged Thatcher to be allowed the poll tax first. They were given their head.

Exemptions were to be made for the unemployed and low paid but an attempt by wisely nervous Tory MPs to divide the tax into three bands so that it bore some relation to people's ability to pay, was brushed aside despite a huge parliamentary rebellion. When the tax was duly introduced in Scotland, as we shall see later, it caused chaos and widespread protest. In England, the likely price of the average poll tax kept rising. Panicking ministers produced expensive schemes to cap it, and to create more generous exemptions, undermining the whole point. Capping the tax would remove local accountability; and the more exemptions, the less pressure on councils from their voters. Yet even Thatcher began to grow alarmed, as she was told that well over 80 per cent of people would be paying more. On 31 March 1990, the day before the poll tax was due to take effect in England and Wales, there was a massive demonstration against it which ended with a riot in Trafalgar Square. Scaffolding was ripped apart and used to throw at mounted police, cars were set on fire, shops smashed. More than 300 people were arrested and 400 policemen hurt. Thatcher dismissed it as mere wickedness. More than a riot, though, it was the growing swell of protest by middle-class, normally law-abiding voters who insisted they simply would not pay it, that shook her cabinet. As the Conservatives' ratings slumped in the country, Tory MPs who had opposed the tax, including Michael Heseltine's key organizer, Michael Mates, began to ask their colleagues whether it was not now time that she was removed from power.

The Final Curtain

The killing of Margaret Thatcher's political career has a dark lustre about it, like something from a book of old stories. She had conducted her premiership with a sense of vivid and immediate self-dramatization, the heroine of peace and war, fighting pitched battles in coalfields and on the streets, word-punching her way through triumphal conferences, haranguing rival leaders, always with a sense that history was being freshly minted, day by day. This is why so many insults levelled at her tended to twist into unintended compliments — the Iron Lady, La Pasionara of Privilege, She Who Must Be Obeyed, the Leaderene, the Blessed Margaret, even the Great She-Elephant. Reflected in her bloodied breastplate the eighties glowed more luridly than any other modern decade, flashing gold with the City's new wealth, sunny as the Soviets collapsed, livid in its confrontations and cruelty nearer to home. She had no sense of her own limits. The world was made anew. Her fall lived up in every way to her record. When a great leader topples, poetry requires that her personal failings bring her down. The story insists it must be more than a trip on the carpet, weariness or age. And this story's ending lives up to its earlier scenes.

There were several powder-trails that led towards the final explosion. One was the poll tax. Another was economic policy, and Europe, which had become almost the same thing. We have seen how Lawson wanted to tie the pound to the anti-inflationary expertise and reputation of the West German Central Bank, 'shadowing' the Deutschmark in the European exchange rate mechanism. In effect, he was looking for somewhere firm to plant down policy in the queasy morass of the new global financial free-for-all. Thatcher disagreed. She thought currencies should float freely, Ariel to his Caliban. She also knew that the ERM was intended one day to lead to a single European currency, part of the European Commission President Jacques Delors's plan for a freshly buttressed European federal state. Lawson, dogged, bull-like, ignored her and shadowed the German currency anyway, a fact somehow both denied yet generally known. Thatcher read about it in the newspapers. When the cost of Lawson's policy became excessive she finally ordered him to stop. He grumpily agreed but the two of them stopped talking.

Bruges in Belgium is a pretty town. Thanks to the channel tunnel and cheap flights, British people flock there for romance, beer, art and chocolate. When Margaret Thatcher rode into town in 1988, year of hubris, none of these things was on her agenda. She had come to make her definitive speech against the federalism now openly advancing towards her. The Foreign Office had tried to soften her message. She had promptly pulled out her pen and written the barbs and thorns back in again. She had not, she informed her audience, 'successfully rolled back the frontiers of the state in Britain' (a claim already anatomized) 'only to see them reimposed at a European level, with a European super-state exercising a new level of dominance from Brussels.' There was much else besides. Her bluntness much offended continental politicians and the Foreign Secretary, Sir Geoffrey Howe. Next, she reappointed as her economic adviser a lugubrious and outspoken monetarist academic, Sir Alan Walters, who was contemptuous of Lawson's exchange rate policy and said so, repeatedly. Thus she was taking on Howe and Lawson, the two Chancellors of her revolutionary years, together. A dangerous split was becoming evident at the top of government. She seemed not to care, biffing Howe about as carelessly as she always had. Nor was anyone much convinced when she told the world she 'fully, gladly, joyfully, unequivocally, generously . . . fully, fully, fully, fully' supported Lawson as her Chancellor. People said she had no sense of humour. They were wrong. It was just a slightly strange one.

Then Jacques Delors, the wry and determined French socialist, re-entered the story, with his fleshed-out plan for economic and monetary union, which would end with the single currency, the euro. To get there, all EU members would start by putting their national currencies into the ERM, which would draw them increasingly tightly together –

just what Lawson and Howe wanted and just what Thatcher did not. Howe and Lawson, Pinky and Perky, ganged up. They told her she must announce that Britain would soon join the ERM, even if she left the single currency itself to one side, for the time. She wriggled, then fought back. On the eve of a summit in Madrid where Britain had to announce her view the two of them visited her in private, had a blazing row and threatened to resign together if she did not give way. Truculently she did, and the crisis passed. But she was merely waiting. Four weeks after the summit, in July 1989, Thatcher hit back. She unleashed a major cabinet reshuffle, compared at the time to Macmillan's 'night of the long knives' in 1962. Howe was demoted to being Leader of the Commons. She reluctantly allowed him the face-saving title of Deputy Prime Minister, a concession rather diminished when her press officer, Bernard Ingham, instantly told journalists it was a bit of a non-job. Howe was replaced by the relatively unknown John Major, the former chief secretary. Lawson survived only because the economy was weakening and to lose him was thought too dangerous just then.

So the drama advanced. The atmosphere in the Commons was a combustible mix of sulphur and adrenalin. Lawson was having a bad time on all sides, including from the Labour shadow chancellor John Smith. When Thatcher's adviser Walters had another pop at his ERM policy, he decided enough was enough and resigned on 26 October, telling the Prime Minister she should treat her ministers better. She pretended to have no idea what he was on about. Lawson was replaced by the still relatively unknown John Major, who was having an interesting autumn. Around them all, the world was changing. A few days after these events, East Germany announced the opening of the border to the West and joyous Berliners began hacking their wall to pieces. Then the communists fell in Czechoslovakia. Then the Romanian dictator Ceauşescu was dragged from power. A few weeks after that, in February 1990, Nelson Mandela, a man she had once denounced as a terrorist, was released to global acclaim. In the middle of all this the Commons had witnessed an event which seemed the opposite of historic. Thatcher had been challenged as leader of the Conservative Party by Sir Anthony Meyer, an obscure, elderly pro-European backbencher much mocked as 'the stalking donkey'. It was a little like Ronnie Corbett challenging Mike Tyson to a punch-up. Yet, ominously for Thatcher, when the vote was held sixty Tory MPs either voted donkey or abstained. In the shadows, prowling through Conservative associations and the corridors of Westminster was a more dangerous creature. Michael Heseltine, no donkey, self-expelled from the Thatcher cabinet four years earlier, was looking uncommonly chipper. Tory MPs whimpered to him about the trouble they were in with the poll tax. He sympathized, trying neither to lick his lips nor sharpen his claws too obviously.

One by one, the inner core of true Thatcherites fell back. Her bone-dry Environment Secretary, Nicholas Ridley, had to resign after being rude about the Germans in a magazine interview – given, piquantly, to Lawson's son Dominic. John Major turned out to be worryingly pro-European after all. Ian Gow, one of her closest associates, though no longer in the government, was murdered by an IRA bomb at his home. Abroad, great world events continued to stalk the last days of Margaret Thatcher's premiership. Saddam Hussein invaded Kuwait and she urged President George Bush the elder towards what would become the first Gulf War – 'Don't wobble, George.' There was another summit in Rome and further pressure on the Delors plan. Again, Thatcher felt herself being pushed and dragged towards a federal scheme. She vented her contempt and anger in the Commons, shredding the proposals with the words, 'No . . . No . . . No!' And at this point the one person who could never have been expected to finish her off, did so.

For years Geoffrey Howe had absorbed her slights, her impatience, her mockery, her snarls. He had taken it all, with the rubbery fatalism of the battered husband who will never leave. Now, observing her flaming anti-Brussels crusade, he decided he had had enough. She probably tipped him over the edge by turning on him savagely and unfairly over some legislation that was not ready, but he had decided to go. On 13 November 1990 he stood up rather lugubriously in the House of Commons and did her in. His resignation statement was designed to answer the story put around by Number Ten that he had gone over nothing much at all. To a packed chamber he revealed that Lawson and he had threatened to resign together the previous year and accused her of sending her ministers to negotiate in Brussels like a cricket team going to the crease, having first broken their bats in the changing room. She was wrong over Europe, he insisted; and then threw the door open to the further leadership challenge that was now inevitable: 'The time has come for others to consider their own response to the tragic conflict of loyalties with which I myself have wrestled for perhaps too long.' Television cameras had just been allowed into the Commons. Across the country people could watch Howe, with Nigel Lawson nodding behind him, could see Heseltine's studied, icy calm, and observe the white-faced reaction of the Prime Minister herself. The next day Heseltine announced he would stand against her as leader. She told *The Times* that he was a socialist at heart, someone whose philosophy at its extreme end had just been defeated in the Soviet Union. She would see him off, of course.

The balloting system for Tory MPs required her to beat Heseltine by winning both a clear majority of the parliamentary party and being 15 per cent ahead of him in votes cast. At a summit in Paris, surrounded by many old enemies, she heard that she had missed the second hurdle by four votes. There would be a second ballot. As one of the few people in public life who could swarm all by herself, she swarmed out of the summit, somehow found a BBC microphone and announced that though disappointed, she would fight on. Then she returned with heroic sangfroid to sit through a ballet with the other leaders, who were pleasant enough to her face. While she watched the ballet, Tory MPs were dancing through Westminster in anger or delight. It was a night of softening support and hardening hearts. Many key Thatcherites believed she was finished and feared that if she fought again, Heseltine would beat her. This would tear the party in two. It would be better for her to withdraw and let someone else assassinate the assassin.

Even then, had she been in London throughout the crisis and summoned her cabinet together to back her, she might have pulled it off. But by the time she was back and taking advice from her whips the news was bleak. In what was probably a tactical mistake, she decided to see her cabinet one by one in her Commons office. Douglas Hurd and John Major had already given her their reluctant agreement to nominate her for the next round of voting but the message from most of the rest of her ministers was strangely uniform. They would personally back her if she was determined to fight but, frankly, she would lose. That would mean Heseltine. Better, Prime Minister, to stand aside and free Major and Hurd from their promises of support. Later, she was wryly amusing about the process. It looked very much as if most of them had agreed the line beforehand. The whips concurred. The cabinet were going through the motions of supporting her if she insisted, but they did not mean it, or mean her to believe it. She had lost them. Only a few ultras, mostly outside the cabinet, were sincerely urging her to continue the struggle. One was that wicked diarist and right-wing maverick Alan Clark, who told her to fight on at all costs: 'Unfortunately he went on to argue that I should fight on even though I was bound to lose because it was better to go down in a blaze of glorious defeat than to go gentle into that good night. Since I had no particular fondness for Wagnerian endings, this lifted my spirits only briefly.'[29]

So it was over. In their various ways, her cabinet were too tired to support her any longer and her MPs were too scared of the electoral vengeance to be wreaked after the poll tax. She returned to Downing Street, conferred with Denis, slept on it, and then announced to her cabinet secretary at 7.30 the next morning that she had decided to resign. She held an uncomfortable cabinet meeting with those she believed had betrayed her, saw the Queen, phoned other world leaders and then finished with one final splendid Commons performance – 'I'm enjoying this!' – vigorously defending her record. Come back, cried one emotional Tory MP. When Margaret Thatcher left Downing Street for the last time in tears, she already knew that she had successfully completed a final political campaign, which was to ensure that she was replaced as Prime Minister by John Major, rather than Michael Heseltine. She had rallied support for him by phone among her closest supporters. They felt he had not been quite supportive enough. She also harboured private doubts. So ended the most extraordinary and nation-changing premiership of modern British history.

Part Five

NIPPY METRO PEOPLE:
BRITAIN FROM 1990

Thatcher's children? By the time she left office, only a minority were true believers. Most would have voted her out had her cabinet ministers not beaten them to it. History is harshest to a leader just as they fall. She had been such a strident presence for so long that many who had first welcomed her as a gust of fresh air now felt harried. Those who wanted a quieter leader were about to get one. Yet most people had in the end done well under her, not just the Yuppies and Essex boys, but also her snidest middle-class critics. Britons were on average much wealthier than they had been at the end of seventies. The country was enjoying bigger cars, a far wider range of holidays, better food, a wider choice of television channels, home videos, and the first slew of gadgets from the computer age. Yet this was not quite the Britain of today.

More people smoked. The idea of smoke-free public areas, or smoking bans in offices and restaurants, was lampooned as a weird Californian innovation that would never come here. People seen talking to themselves with a wire dangling from one ear would have been considered worryingly disturbed. There were no Starbucks: coffee shops were still mainly locally owned places selling instant coffee, tea, fried food or cakes. Lunch had been under threat for some years in the City and the days of midday drinking were beginning to die in other professions too. The chic sandwich bar had begun to spread since the early eighties, when BLTs, avocado and blue cheese began to be regularly offered, alongside the traditional fillings of cheese, ham and egg. At a by-election outside Liverpool in 1986 a Labour activist had allegedly pointed to the mushy peas in a local chip-shop and asked for some of the 'avocado dip' too: it was a story, perhaps an urban myth, much re-told as symbolizing the gap between real Britain and the new metropolitan Britain of the south. The habit of urbanites carrying bottled water wherever they went had not yet taken off, though meaningless corporate language was already sullying business life. The ubiquitous PowerPoint presentation was in its infancy. Passengers, rather than 'customers', travelled on British Rail trains, with the double-arrow symbol which had been familiar since 1965. On the roads were plenty of flashy Ford Sierras, Austin Montegos and nippy Metros.

For a wealthy country, the mood was uneasy. An old jibe, 'public affluence, public squalor', was much heard. The most immediate worry was economic as the hangover effects of the Lawson boom began to throb. Inflation was rising towards double figures, interest rates were at 14 per cent and unemployment was heading towards two million. Over the next four years a serious white-collar recession was to hit Britain, particularly in the south, where house prices would fall by a quarter. An estimated 1.8 million people found that their homes were worth less than the money they had borrowed to buy them in the heady easy-credit eighties. During 1991 alone, more than 75,000 families would have their homes repossessed. With hindsight it is generally accepted that the Thatcher revolution reshaped the country's economy and prepared Britain well for the new age of globalization waiting in the wings, but in 1990 it did not feel quite like that.

There were other changes too. The British were fewer than they are today. The population was smaller by at least three million souls. Also, the ethnic mix of the country was simpler. Of the roughly three million non-white British, the largest groups were Indian (840,000), black Caribbean (500,000) and Pakistani (476,000), pretty much what an extrapolation from the seventies would have predicted. No serious concern was expressed politically about whether Muslims could fully integrate. In the interests of keeping an eye on troublemakers, and maintaining Britain's traditions of tolerance, a number of the most radical Islamic militants, on the run from their own countries, had been given safe haven in London. The largest white migrant group was from Ireland, which was still relatively poor. Any Poles or Russians in Britain were diplomats or refugees from communism. The term 'bogus asylum seeker' would have met with a puzzled frown. Looking to east or west, Britain was far less penetrated by overseas culture and people than she would soon become.

Britain was also about to go to war again as the junior partner to the Americans in the first Gulf conflict, which freed Kuwait from Saddam Hussein's invasion and immolated the Iraqi army's Republican

Guard. Despite British forces losing lives and the use by Saddam of human shields, the war generated nothing like the controversy of the later Iraq war. It was widely seen as a necessary act of international retribution against a particularly horrible dictator. After the controversies and alarms of the Thatcher years, foreign affairs generated less heat, except for the great issue of European federalism. There was a real sense of optimism caused by the end of the Cold War, which had resulted in the deaths of up to 40 million people around the world, and involved no fewer than 150 smaller conflicts. At last, perhaps, the West could relax. Politicians and journalists talked excitedly of the coming 'peace dividend' and the end of the surveillance and espionage secret state that had been needed for so long. The only present threat to British security was the Provisional IRA, which would continue its attacks with ferocity and cunning for some years to come. They would hit Downing Street with a triple mortar attack on a snowy day in February 1991, coming close to killing the Prime Minister and the top team of ministers and officials directing the Gulf War.

Environmental worries were present too, though a bat-squeak compared to today's panic. British scientists played a big role in alerting the world. Among the handful of Britons in the second half of the twentieth century who may be remembered centuries hence is James Lovelock. He is the scientist who in 1965 after studying the long-term chemical composition of the planet's systems, and their interaction with living organisms, developed the 'Gaia' theory. The name, from a Greek goddess, came from the British Nobel Prize-winning novelist William Golding, a neighbour of Lovelock's in Devon, during a country walk. 'Gaia' demonstrated how fragile the life-supporting atmosphere and chemistry of the planet is, an immensely complex self-regulating system keeping temperatures fit for life. Some hippies and 'New Age' mystics mistakenly thought Lovelock was saying the Earth was herself alive. He was using a metaphor but one with powerful implications for man-made climate change. At the same time as Lovelock was writing his most influential book, in the late seventies, far south the British Antarctic Survey was just beginning to notice a thinning of the ozone layer. It is said that when the first measurements were taken later in 1985 the readings were so low the scientists assumed their instruments were faulty and sent home for replacements. This led to an important treaty cutting ozone-depleting CFCs.

British influence was important at the first world climate conference in Geneva in 1979, which had appealed to nations to do more research.

By 1990, a follow-up conference attended by 130 countries focused on the growing evidence that global warming was a real threat, but no agreement was reached about what should be done. Were any senior politicians worried? One was. Two years earlier Margaret Thatcher, science-trained, had made a speech about global warming. She had been persuaded that it was a profound issue by Britain's outgoing ambassador to the United Nations, Sir Crispin Tickell, who had ironically enough got at her with worrying data during a long international plane flight. So in September 1988 she had told the Royal Society that she believed it possible that 'we have unwittingly begun a massive experiment with the system of the earth itself.' Such was the interest that no television cameras were sent to record her speech and the prime minister had to read it by the light of wax candles held over her head in an ancient hall. For most people in 1990 'the environment' or green issues meant containable local problems such as the use of chemical pesticides or the problems of disposing of nuclear waste. Books about the fate of the earth concerned themselves with nuclear weapons.

Culturally, the country was as fixated by imported American television as it would continue to be: *Baywatch* and *The Simpsons* were popular new imports. And the national self-mocking strand of comedy which would be such a mark of the next fifteen years was well established, with Harry Enfield's Wayne and Waynetta Slob joining his 'Loadsamoney' attacks on the big-bucks Thatcher years, *Spitting Image* puppetry at its most gleefully venomous, and the arrival of a new quiz show, *Have I Got News For You*. This heralded a time when interest in ideology and serious policy issues was being replaced by politics as entertainment, a stage on which humorists and hacks could prove themselves wittier than elected parliamentarians. Unsurprisingly, this would not result in a better-run country.

After a spate of transport disasters there was a widespread feeling that large investment was needed in the country's infrastructure. French and British engineers celebrated in 1990 when they met under the Channel. Mobile phone use was tiny by modern standards, mainly confined to commercial business travellers' cars and a few much-mocked City slickers carrying objects the size of a brick. The computer age was further advanced. The Thatcher years had seen a glittering waterfall of new products and applications, most of them generated in California's new 'silicon valley', a hotbed of computer inventiveness recognized by name as early as 1971. The revolutionary Apple II computer had been launched in 1977, followed by Tandys, Commo dores and Ataris with their floppy disks and basic games. The first IBM personal computer had arrived in 1981, using the unfamiliar MS-DOS operating system by a little known company called Microsoft. The Commodore 64 of the following year would become the best-selling computer of all time, though there were British computers: here, Sir Clive Sinclair's ZX Spectrum computer caught most of the headlines. Then in 1983 an IBM clone arrived, the Compaq, first of countless many, and the unveiling of Microsoft Word and Windows. A year later came the first Amstrad personal computer from the British entrepreneur Alan Sugar's electronics company and, from the US, the Apple Macintosh. A cult novelist called William Gibson introduced a new word, cyberspace.

By the end of the eighties the hot new topics were virtual reality, computer gaming – Sim City was launched in 1989 – and the exponentially increasing power of microprocessors. Computer graphics were becoming common in films, even though they were clunky and basic by modern standards. But the biggest about-to-happen event was the internet itself. The single most significant achievement by a British person in the early nineties had nothing to do with politics. Sir Tim Berners-Lee, inventor of the World Wide Web, stands alongside James Lovelock for influence above that of any politician. Today's internet is a combination of technologies, from the satellites developing from the Soviet Sputnik success of 1957, to the US military programs to link computers, leading to the early 'net' systems developed by American universities, and the personal computer revolution itself. But Berners-Lee's idea was for a worldwide hypertext – the computer-aided reading of electronic documents – to allow people to work together remotely, sharing their knowledge in a 'web' of documents. His creation of it would give the internet's hardware its global voice.

Berners-Lee was an Oxford graduate who had made his first computer with a soldering iron and cut his teeth with British firms in Dorset, before moving to the European particle physics laboratory (CERN) in Switzerland in 1980. This is the world's largest research laboratory where scientists were constantly evolving ways of communicating with one other by computer, so it is no coincidence that it was in Switzerland that Berners-Lee wrote his first program. In 1989 he proposed his hypertext revolution which arrived as 'World-WideWeb' inside CERN in December 1990, and on the internet at large the following summer.

An admirably unflashy, decent man, Berners-Lee chose not to patent his creation, so that it would be free to everyone. He could have been fabulously wealthy but preferred to live the life of a moderately salaried academic, latterly in Boston, driving a second-hand car and living quietly. He was knighted in 2004 and, two years later, warned that misinformation and undemocratic forces were spreading through the web, calling for more research on its social consequences. In the immediate aftermath of the fall of Margaret Thatcher, all this was still to come. There were articles proclaiming some kind of new computer world community taking shape, but they were confusing to most people. Would this internet be basically for scientists? Was it a new kind of telephone-cum-typewriter, or an automated library system? Nobody knew for sure. In 1990 there were no 'www' prefixes, no dotcoms.

John Ball, More Interesting than He Looks

To guide this confusing new Britain, teetering on the edge of a new spate of globalism arrived an unlikely and very English figure, a Prime Minister whose seven years in office make him one of the longer-serving of modern times but who already gets half-overlooked. John Major was not what he seemed. He appeared to be a bland, friendly loyal Thatcherite. She thought so. So did Tory MPs, who elected him their leader because of who he was not. He was not the urbane, posh, old-school Tory Douglas Hurd and he was not the floppy-haired enchanter and lady-killer, Michael Heseltine. So who was he? Major had none of Thatcher's certainty or harshness. It is a reasonable principle that when you probe the history of a normal, middle-of-the-road English person, you find it surprisingly exotic. That is the case with Major. He was a sensitive boy from the wrong part of town, from a mixed-up, rather rum family. His father was one of the music-hall artistes described much earlier in this book, a remarkable man who had been partly brought up in the United States, returning to Britain in Edwardian times to pursue a long stage career, then rampaging cheerfully round South America, marrying twice and producing two illegitimate children. His name was Tom Ball. The 'Major' was a stage name. As John Major said later he might more properly have been named John Ball, like the leader of the peasants' revolt against the original poll tax.

Major was born late. His father was already an old man, now pursuing yet another career making garden ornaments. When an informal business deal went wrong he lost almost everything and the family moved from their comfortable suburban house to a crowded flat in Brixton, which they shared with a cat-burglar, a Jamaican later arrested for stabbing a policeman, and a trio of cheery Irish tax-dodgers. The flat turned out to be owned by Major's (much older) secret half brother, though he never knew this at the time. Methodist Grantham this was not. Major, infuriated at being saddled with the name Major-Ball when he was sent to grammar school, was a poor pupil and left at sixteen. His early life was ragged and formless in shape. He worked as a clerk, made garden gnomes with his brother, looked after his mother and endured a 'degrading' time of unemployment, before eventually pursuing a career as a banker and becoming a Conservative councillor. Unlike Margaret Thatcher, his politics were formed by the inner city and he was on the anti-Powellite, moderate wing of the party. After a long search, he was finally selected as Tory candidate for the rural seat of Huntingdon and entered Parliament in 1979 as the Thatcher age began.

There he rose almost without trace, through a minor job with the Home Office, to the whips' office which, as the internal security machine of a parliamentary party, can be a useful training ground for the ambitious, to two years at Social Security. After the 1987 election Thatcher promoted him to the cabinet as Chief Secretary to the Treasury, when he haggled with ministers about their spending plans. She liked him because he had stood up to her in argument, not because he was a stooge. There followed the abrupt further promotions to the Foreign Office where he served as Foreign Secretary for all of ninety-four days, and Treasury. As Chancellor he had promoted a short-lived alternative to monetary union, the 'hard ecu', which would have been a kind of voluntary euro, running alongside the old currencies. He had then won Thatcher round to membership of the ERM, though entering as it turned out at too high a rate. By the time he suddenly emerged as a possible candidate to replace her as Prime Minister, Major was known by those who knew him for being affable, reliable, hardworking, self-deprecating and, it was assumed, as her protégé, a model Thatcherite. But to everyone outside Tory politics, he was a blank canvas. He was the least known new Prime Minister in post-war Britain as well as the youngest of the century so far. At forty-seven, he was barely a public figure.

Most Conservatives had grown sick and tired of dramatics. Here was a bloke from next door with an easy smile leading them to easier times. Chris Patten, then the brightest man in the cabinet, acted as its spokesmen when he recalled the prisoners' chorus to freedom in Beethoven's opera *Fidelio*. If only they knew what was coming. Thatcher, belatedly slightly wary, promised to be a good 'back-seat driver'. Major wanted none of her advice. He considered offering her a job, either in the cabinet or as ambassador to Washington. He decided not to. He talked of building a 'society of opportunity' and compassion, and for privileges once available to 'the few' to be spread 'to the many'. This sounds like an early try-out for the language of New Labour: Major came to believe Blair had simply swiped many of his ideas and presented them as his own, with more verve. As we shall see there is some truth in this. But Major had little time to plan his own agenda. There were immediate crises. He was quick to kill off the poll tax and replace it with a new council tax bearing an uncommon resemblance to the old rating system. He was equally quick to meet the elder President Bush and support him through the Gulf War. Above all, he had to turn straight away to confront the great hydra-headed monster that was devouring his party, the federal agenda of Jacques Delors.

If ever a place was well chosen for debating the end of a Europe of independent nation states, it was Maastricht in Holland, an attractive cobbled town nestled so close to the German and Belgian borders it is almost nationless. Here the great showdown of winter 1991 took place. A new treaty was to be agreed and it was one which made the federal project ever more explicit. There was to be fast progress to a single currency. Much of foreign policy, defence policy and home affairs were to come under the ultimate authority of the EU. A 'social chapter' would oblige Britain to accept the more expensive work guarantees of the continent and surrender some of the trade union reforms brought in under Thatcher. For a country with a weak industrial base whose economy partly depended on undercutting her continental rivals, all this would be grave. For a Conservative Party which had applauded Lady Thatcher's defiant Bruges speech, it was almost a declaration of war, in which Europe's 'federal' destiny had become made explicit and imminent. Fretting and moody in exile Thatcher saw Maastricht as a recipe for national suicide. She now believed she had been removed from Downing Street because of her stand over Europe. Hearing Major declare he wanted Britain to be 'at the heart of Europe', a mere bromide of a phrase, she added him to the long list of traitors. Her admirers hissed. He refused to rule out a single currency for all time. They became angrier still. So did she.

Major was trying to be practical, not exciting. He decided that he had no absolutist views on the single currency. One day it would happen. It had obvious business and trading advantages. But now was too soon, partly because it would make life harder for the central European countries being freed from communism to join the EU. So he was neither a 'never' nor a 'now'. Most people assumed he was glibly steering between two whirlpools, trying to keep his party united. In his memoirs, a great deal better written than most such books, he protested that he was accused of dithering, procrastination, lacking leadership and conviction. As to his true and subtle position, 'I have given up hope that this will ever be understood.' Yet at Maastricht he managed against all the odds during genuinely tense negotiations to slip Britain out of paying fealty to the EU on most of what was demanded. He and his Chancellor, Norman Lamont, negotiated a special British opt-out from monetary union and managed to have the social chapter excluded from the treaty altogether. Major kept haggling late and on every detail, wearing out his fellow leaders with more politeness but as much determination as Thatcher ever had. For a man with a weak hand, under fire from his own side at home, it was quite a feat. Major returned to hosannas in the newspapers and the widely reported remark of an aide that it was 'game, set and match' to Britain.

He was briefly a hero. He described his reception by the Tory Party in the Commons as the modern equivalent of a Roman triumph, quite something for the boy from Brixton.

Soon after this, flushed with confidence, Major called the election most observers thought he must lose. The economy was so badly awry, the pain of the poll tax so fresh, the Labour Party of Neil Kinnock now so efficiently and ruthlessly organized, that the Tory years were surely ending. Things turned out differently. Lamont's pre-election budget had helped a lot. It proposed cutting the bottom rate of income tax by five pence in the pound, which would help people on lower incomes, and badly wrong-footed Labour. Under a pugnacious Patten, now the party chairman, the Tories targeted Labour's enthusiasm for higher taxes. It was tough stuff. Patten called himself 'the liberal thug'. During the campaign itself, Major found himself returning to his roots in Brixton and mounting a soap-box – in fact, a plastic container – from which he addressed raucous crowds through a megaphone. This stark contrast to the careful control of the Labour campaign struck a chord with the media and he kept it up, playing the underdog to the Kinnock's 'government in waiting'. Right at the end, at an eve of the poll rally in Sheffield, Kinnock's self-control finally gave way and he began punching the air with delight, crying 'y'aw'right!' This is often said to have finally turned middle England against him. That seems a bit neat.

On 9 April 1992 Major's Conservatives won 14 million votes, more than any party in British political history. It was a great personal achievement, also based on people's fear of higher Labour taxes. It was also one of the biggest percentage leads since 1945, though the vagaries of the electoral system gave Major a majority of just twenty-one seats. Kinnock was devastated and quickly left front-line politics. But never has such a famous victory produced such a rotten result for the winners. Patten lost his seat in Bath and went off to become the final governor of Hong Kong, tussling with the Chinese ahead of the long-agreed handover of Britain's last proper colony. Despite the popular vote, the smallness of the majority meant Major's authority was now steadily eaten away. He has not gone down in history as a great leader of this country, but under a parliamentary system greatness is generally related to parliamentary arithmetic. What kind of revolutionary would Margaret Thatcher have been had she had a majority of twenty-one in

1979 or 1983? Nor were the economics propitious. Had Labour won in 1992 it would have been quickly tarnished too. The choice of governing in that year was what rugby players call a hospital pass. For now John Major, the delighted and much-relieved victor, had the slippery ball in his hands and was acknowledging the cheers of the crowds. Meanwhile a platoon of nasty looking, bone-crushing, twenty-stone forwards were just about to jump him.

Old Labour's Lost King

The story of modern British political life has, so far, thrown up a high proportion of nuts, or at least of unsettled people with something to prove. John Smith was not a nut. After Neil Kinnock gave up in despair following Major's victory in 1992, he was replaced by a placid, secure, self-certain Scottish lawyer with a very boring name. Today almost everyone has an interest in writing John Smith out of the history books. For the Blairites, he was the timid, grey background for the heroic drama of modernization about to unfold. For those who loved Kinnock, he was the election-losing Shadow Chancellor. For the Tories, he was an embarrassingly good parliamentary inquisitor. In politics, predictions about what will happen a month ahead are dangerous but though Smith died of a heart attack in 1994, three years ahead of an election, it is fairly safe to suggest that, after the tarnishing years of the mid-nineties, he would have become Prime Minister. Had he done so, Britain would have had a traditionalist social democratic government, much closer to those of continental Europe, and our history would have been different.

Smith came from a family of herring fishermen on the West Coast of Scotland and, though bald as a coot himself, was the son of a bristly small town headmaster known as Hairy Smith. Labour-supporting from his earliest days, bright and self-assured, he got his real political education at Glasgow University, part of a generation of brilliant student debaters from all parties who would go on to dominate Scottish politics. Back in the early sixties, Glasgow University Labour Club was a hotbed not of radicals, but of Gaitskell-supporting moderates. It was a position Smith never wavered from, as he rose through politics as one of the brightest stars of the Scottish party, and then through government under Wilson and Callaghan as a junior minister dealing with the oil industry and devolution before entering the cabinet just in time as President of the Board of Trade, its youngest member at forty.

In Opposition, he managed to keep at arm's length from the worst of the in-fighting (he and Tony Benn liked one another, despite their very different views, after working together at the Energy Department) and eventually became Kinnock's shadow chancellor. He was a good lawyer and a brilliantly forensic parliamentary operator. This won him acclaim in the Westminster village even if, in Thatcher's England, he was spotted as a tax-raising corporatist socialist of the old school. One letter he got briskly informed him: 'You'll not get my BT shares yet, you bald, owl-looking Scottish bastard. Go back to Scotland and let that other twit Kinnock go back to Wales.'[1] Smith came from a somewhat old-fashioned Christian egalitarian background which put him naturally out of sympathy with the materialist, pleasure-orientated and aspirational culture that had grown so vigorously in Thatcherite England. Just before he became leader he told a newspaper he believed above all in education because 'it opens the doors of the imagination, breaks down class barriers and frees people. In our family . . . money was looked down on and education was revered. I am still slightly contemptuous of money.'[2] This could not in all honesty be said of the man who replaced him.

Smith was never personally close to Kinnock, but scrupulously loyal. A convivial (not drunken) workaholic who ate too much, he nevertheless succeeded him by an overwhelming vote in 1992. By then he had with great good luck survived a major heart attack and taken up hill walking. The *Sun*, not always a good guide to the future, greeted his triumph with the eerily accurate and predictive headline: 'He's fat, he's fifty-three, he's had a heart attack and he's taking on a stress-loaded job.'

Though Smith swiftly advanced the careers of the brightest younger stars, Tony Blair and Gordon Brown, they swiftly became depressed by his style of leadership. He did not believe Labour needed to be transformed, merely improved. He was reluctant at first to take on the party over issues such as one-person, one-vote internal democracy. He had an instantaneous dislike of the Mephistopheles of the modernizers, Peter Mandelson, which may have been tinged with

Scottish Presbyterian homophobia. Blair, Brown and Mandelson thought Smith was smug and idle. He on the other hand was equally sure they were making too much fuss and that Labour could regain power with something of its traditional spirit. A little-known newspaper journalist called Alastair Campbell divided the party into two camps, the 'frantics', led by Brown, Blair and Jack Straw, and the 'long-gamers', led by Smith. At one point Blair was contemplating leaving politics, so despairing was he of Smith's leadership. He should, he reflected, have stuck to the law, where his elder brother was doing so well. What was there in politics for him?

Smith died of a second heart attack on 12 May 1994. After the initial shock and grieving had finished, Labour moved rapidly away from his legacy. There is, however, one part of the Smith agenda which survived intact and is a big influence on the shape of Britain today. As the minister who had struggled to achieve devolution for Scotland in the dark years of 1978–9 he remained a passionate supporter of the 'unfinished business' of establishing a Scottish Parliament and Welsh Assembly. With his friend Donald Dewar he had committed Labour so utterly to the idea in Opposition that Blair, no particular fan of devolution, found this one part of old Labour's agenda that stuck and had to be implemented later.

Black Wednesday and Party Suicide

The crisis that now engulfed the Conservative government was a complicated, devilish interaction of themes but in other ways very simple. The first thing that happened was that they lost their economic policy in a single day when the pound fell out of the European exchange rate mechanism. Major's opening words in the chapter of his book that deals with this are a fair summary: 'Black Wednesday – 16 September 1992, the day the pound toppled out of the ERM – was a political and economic calamity. It unleashed havoc in the Conservative Party and it changed the political landscape of Britain.'[3] It is worth recalling just what the ERM was and why it mattered so much in the early nineties.

Europe's old currencies, the marks, francs, lira, crowns and the rest, were supposed to move in close alignment, like a flight of mismatched aircraft in tight formation. They would stick together against outsider currencies, notably the US dollar, behaving almost as if they were one currency. Speculators would not be able to drive them apart. Eventually, they would fuse and become one, which is where the aircraft analogy falls down, because so would the aircraft. The strongest currency by far was the German Deutschmark, so the rest followed it up and down.

Like the others the pound had a narrow band of values against the mark – its own airspace, as it were – which it had to keep to, as it swept through the turbulence and storms caused by the international money markets. Once it had chosen its entry rate, the value in marks that sterling would try to maintain, the government's only steering mechanism was interest rates – plus, at the margin, protestation. What was the point of this? Dangerously, that depended on your vantage point. For Major and his government, the point was that because the German central bank had a deserved and ferocious reputation for anti-inflationary rigour, having to follow or 'shadow' the mark meant Britain had purchased a respected off-the-shelf policy. Sticking to the mighty mark was a useful signal to the rest of the world that this government, after all the inflationary booms of the past, was serious about inflation. On the continent the point of the ERM, however, was entirely different. It would lead to a strong new single currency. So a policy which Mrs Thatcher had earlier agreed to, in order to bring down British inflation, became a policy Lady Thatcher abhorred, because it drew Britain towards a European superstate. Confused? So was most of the Conservative Party.

Thus the bomb was prepared. What happened to set it off was that the US dollar began to fall because interest rates there were being cut, and pulled the pound down with it. Worse, the money flowed into Deutschmarks which duly rose; so the lead aircraft was gaining altitude, just as the pound was plunging. The government raised interest rates, up to an eye-watering 10 per cent, to try to lift the pound. But this did not work. The obvious next move was for the Germans to cut their interest rates, lowering the altitude of the mark, and keeping the ERM formation intact. This would have helped not just the pound but other weak currencies such as the Italian lira. But Germany had just reunited after the downfall of communism. The huge costs of bringing the poorer East Germans into West Germany's embrace meant a real fear of renewed inflation and all those Weimar memories. So the Germans, heedless of the pain of Britain, Italy and the rest, wanted their interest rates high. Major begged, cajoled, warned and wrote stiff letters of protest to Chancellor Kohl who would not move. He warned of the danger of the new Maastricht Treaty failing completely, for the Danes had just rejected it in a referendum and the French were now having a plebiscite of their own. None of that cut any ice either.

In public, the British government insisted the pound would stay in the ERM at all costs. The mechanism was no mere technicality. It was Major's anti-inflation strategy. Ever since as Chancellor he had told the unemployment-hit and house-repossessed British that 'if it isn't hurting, it isn't working', his credibility had been tied to the ERM. But it was his foreign policy too. British membership of the ERM showed the country was serious about being 'at the heart of Europe'. It was Major's big idea for Britain's economic and diplomatic survival. Norman Lamont, who as Chancellor was as apparently committed as Major himself, told the markets Britain would neither leave the ERM nor devalue. It was 'at the centre of our policy' and there should not be a 'scintilla of doubt'. Major then went further, telling an audience in Scotland that with inflation down to 3.7 per cent and falling, it would be madness to leave the ERM. 'The soft option, the devaluer's option, the inflationary option, would be a betrayal of our future.'

But he could hold out for not much longer. The lira crashed out of the ERM formation. The international money traders turned their attention to the weak pound and carried on selling. They were betting Major and Lamont would not keep interest rates so high the pound could remain up there with the mark – an easy, one-way bet. For in the real world, British interest rates at 10 per cent were already painfully high. On the morning of Black Wednesday, at 11 a.m., the Bank of England raised them by another two points. This would be agonizing for home-owners and business alike. But Lamont said he would take 'whatever measures are necessary' to keep the pound in the system. The sense of panic mounted. The selling went on. A shaken Lamont rushed round to tell Major the interest rate rise had not worked. But sitting in Admiralty House – Number Ten was being refurbished after the IRA mortar attack – Major and his key ministers decided to stay in the poker game. The Bank announced that interest rates would go up again, by three points, to 15 per cent, which if sustained would have caused multiple bankruptcies across the country. This made no difference either. Eventually, at 4 p.m., Major phoned the Queen to tell her he was recalling Parliament. The government cracked. At 7.30 p.m., Lamont left the Treasury with his closest advisers, including David Cameron, to announce to a throng of cameramen and bystanders in Whitehall that he was 'suspending' the pound's membership of the ERM and was reversing the first of the day's interest rate rises. Major wrote out his resignation statement for broadcast. It was the most humiliating moment for British politics since the IMF crisis of September 1976, sixteen years earlier.

If Major had actually resigned Lamont would have had to go as well. The country would have lost the two senior ministers in the middle of a terrible crisis. So Major decided to stay on, though he was forever diminished by what had happened. Lamont, always a bubblier and more resilient figure, better suited perhaps to the Regency than the fag-end of the twentieth century, announced that he had been singing in the bath after the ERM debacle, and later added to the insouciant impression by quoting Edith Piaf's song 'Je ne regrette rien'. He decided that he was delighted as the economy began to react to lower interest rates, and the slow recovery began. While others could see only endless sleet and frozen mud of unemployment, repossession and bankruptcy, he was forever spotting the 'green shoots' of economic rebirth. Perhaps it was the twitcher in him; keen bird-watchers are alert to nature.

In the following months Lamont created a new unified budget system and took tough decisions to repair the public finances but as the country wearied of recession, he became an increasingly easy butt of media derision. A few trivial incidents combined to make him something of a laughing-stock. To Lamont's complete surprise and utter shock, Major sacked him as Chancellor a little over six months after Black Wednesday. Lamont retaliated later in a Commons state- ment. The government listened too much to pollsters and party managers, he said: 'We give the impression of being in office, but not in power.' It was a well-aimed and painful blow. Major appointed Kenneth Clarke, one of the great characters of modern Toryism, a pugnacious, pro-European, beer-drinking, jazz-loving One Nation brawler, to replace Lamont. Though Lamont then moved increasingly towards full-on Euro-scepticism and never forgave Major, these three unlikely musketeers were jointly responsible for the strong economy inherited by New Labour four years later.

As to Major himself, his stony road just got flintier and steeper. In the Commons the struggle to ratify the Maastricht Treaty, hailed as such a success before the election, became a long and bloody one, conducted in late-night cabals, parliamentary bars and close votes night after night. Major's small majority was more than wiped out by the number of anti-Maastricht rebels, egged on by Lady Thatcher and her former party chairman, Norman Tebbit, now also in the Lords. Black Wednesday emboldened those who saw the ERM and every aspect of European federalism as disastrous for Britain. As John Major later wrote, it turned 'a quarter century of unease into a flat rejection of any wider involvement in Europe ... emotional rivers burst their banks.' Had not the Germans let us down again? And had lower interest rates and 'green shoots' of recovery not followed Britain's self-expulsion? If the ERM had been bad, so surely was the whole federal project? Most of the newspapers which had welcomed Maastricht were now as vehemently against it. The most powerful Conservative voices in the media were hostile both to the treaty and to Major. Lady Thatcher's new oppositionism echoed loudly through Westminster. Principle, pique and snobbery swirled together. Major's often leaden use of English, his resolute lack of panache or cool, led many of England's High Tories to brand him shockingly ill-educated and third-rate for a national leader. His own sensitivity to criticism and occasional exhibitions of self-pity simply made things worse. He lacked that layer of nerveless flesh leaders today require.

The story of the long progress through Parliament of the Maastricht bill during the autumn, winter and spring of 1992–3 is too convoluted to be recorded here. Suffice it to say that a constantly shifting group of around forty to sixty Tory MPs regularly worked with the Labour opposition to defeat key parts of their government's main piece of legislation, and that Major's day-to-day survival was always in doubt. Whenever he called a vote of confidence and threatened his rebellious MPs with an election, he won. Wherever John Smith's Labour Party and the anti-Maastricht rebels could find some common cause, however thin, he was in danger of losing. The rebels ranged from the most fastidious and high-minded MPs who were profoundly worried about the constitutional damage European Union would do an ancient parliamentary democracy, to the mischievous and the embittered. Some backbench rebels found that they were interviewed constantly on television. Their views were sought by the papers and they became very minor national characters. This can be, as the current author witnesses, dangerously intoxicating. In the end Major got his legislation and Britain signed the Maastricht Treaty but it came at appalling personal and political cost. Talking in the general direction of an eavesdropping microphone, he spoke of three anti-European 'bastards' in his cabinet – a reference to Michael Portillo, Peter Lilley and John Redwood. The country watched a divided party tearing at itself and the country was unimpressed.

By the autumn of 1993 Norman Lamont was speculating aloud that Britain might have to leave the European Union altogether, and the financier Sir James Goldsmith was preparing to launch his Referendum Party to force a national plebiscite. The next row to break was over the voting system to be used when the EU expanded, a murky matter of realpolitik which directly affected each country's leverage. Forced to choose between a deal which weakened Britain's hand and stopping the enlargement from happening at all by vetoing it, the new Foreign Secretary, Douglas Hurd, went for a compromise. In Parliament, once again, all hell broke loose. Tory rebels began talking of a challenge to Major as leader. This subsided briefly but battle began again over the European budget, and fisheries policy. Formal membership of the Tory Party was withdrawn from eight rebels. By now Smith, who had given Major some of the worst parliamentary moments of his life, had suddenly died, and had been replaced by Tony Blair. When Major readmitted the rebels, the young Opposition leader told him: 'I lead my party, you follow yours.' As with Lamont's 'in office but not in power' this caricatured the dreadful dilemma Major was in. But like Lamont's remark, Blair's struck a chord with the country.

The Age of Major

While the central story of British politics in the seven years between the fall of Thatcher and the arrival of Blair was taken up by Europe, at home the government tried to continue the British revolution. After many years of dithering, British Rail was broken up and privatized, as was the remaining coal industry. After the 1992 election it was decided that over half of the remaining coalmining jobs must go, in a closure programme of thirty-one pits to prepare the industry for privatization. This depressed or angered many Tory MPs who felt the strike-breaking effect of the Nottinghamshire-dominated Union of Democratic Mine-workers deserved a better reward, and it roused much public protest. Nevertheless, with power companies moving towards gas and oil, and the union muscle of the miners broken long since, the sale went ahead two years later. Faced with a plan by Michael Heseltine to sell off the Post Office too, Major baulked. It was a service with the stamp of Royalty on it and a long tradition. His refusal was probably good for the country. Why? Because the privatization of the railways was a catastrophe.

There has long been a problem with some politicians and railways. Perhaps it was all those Hornby models in boys' bedrooms or attics. Perhaps it was the simple romance of an industry which has beauty and complexity, which appeals to the mathematically minded in the structuring of its timetables, and to romantics in its engineering. At any rate, fiddling with the railway system became a dangerous obses-sion of governments of different colours. Thatcher, not being a boy, knew that railways were also too much part of the working life of millions to be lightly broken up or sold. She is said to have told Nicholas Ridley when he was Transport Secretary, 'Railway privatiza-tion will be the Waterloo of this government. Please never mention the railways to me again.'[4] Yet just before she resigned, under pressure from a Treasury privatization unit with too little left to do, she began to soften, and rail privatization was taken up by John Major with gusto. Trains! What could be more fun? Was not old-fashioned, curled-sandwich-serving, rail accident prone British Rail a national joke? Could not any reforming government worth its salt, brimming with nostalgia for the old days of brightly painted trains run by private companies, do better than that?

The problems with selling off an elderly, loss-making railway system on which millions of people depend, are obvious. If your first aim is to raise money, then you have to accept that fares will rise briskly, and services may be cut, as the new owners try to make a profit. This will make you less popular. If, however, your aim is to increase competition, just how do you do that? Each route has only one railway line. Different train companies can hardly compete directly, racing each other up and down the same track. Do you give up on competition and sell off all of British Rail as a single unit? The Conservatives decided against that which left them essentially with two options. They could cut up BR geographically, selling off both trains and track for each region, together, so that the railway system would end up looking much as it had in the thirties. Competition would not be direct, but it would become clear that, say, the Great North Eastern operator was offering a pleasanter and more efficient service than the company running trains to Cornwall and Devon, and in due course one might lose, and the other gain, market power. Licences could be revoked, or there might be takeovers. Alternatively, the railway could be split vertically, so that the State owned the track, some companies owned the stations, and others the trains. This could be called the Complete Horlicks option.

Under Treasury pressure to produce the maximum competition and revenue, the new Transport Secretary, John MacGregor, chose it. A vastly complicated new system of subsidies, contracts, bids, pricing (of almost everything), cross-ticketing and regulation was created, topped off when late in the day, it was decided to sell off the nation's railway tracks separately to a single private monopoly to be called Railtrack. Suddenly to get across the country could become a complicated transaction, involving two or three separate train companies. They would not, however, be left to get on with it in a new market. Trains were too important for that. A Franchise Director would be given powers over the profits and pricing, including ticket prices, of the new companies and a Rail Regulator would deal with the track. Both would end up reporting directly to the Secretary of State so that any public dissatisfaction, commercial problem, safety issue – indeed, almost everything – would be back in the lap of the politicians. If this was privatization, it was a strange and possibly pointless one, which would end up costing the taxpayer far more than old-fashioned, much-mocked British Rail. The historian of this curious tale, Christian Wolmar, dubbed it 'the poll tax on wheels'. The writer Simon Jenkins, who had sat on the British Rail board, concluded: 'The Treasury's treatment of the railway in the 1990s was probably the worst instance of Whitehall industrial mismanagement since the Second World War.'[5]

Citizens and Hoop-jumpers

As a Brixton man who had known unemployment, and as a sensitive man quick to feel slights, Major was well prepared by upbringing and temperament to take on the arrogant and inefficient quality of much so-called public service. In his early years he himself had been the plaintive figure who found 'telephones answered grudgingly or not at all. Booths closed while customers were kept waiting . . . Remote council offices where, after a long bus journey, there was no one available to see you who really knew about the issue . . . Anonymous voices and faces who refused to give you a contact name.'[6] He was making a good point. Why in a country that spent so much on public services were so many of them so bad? The answer of the Thatcher revolution was that in the end only the market is properly responsive. Yet nobody in power during the eighties or nineties, including Margaret Thatcher, was prepared to take this logic to its limit and privatize the health service or schools or road system, compensating the worse off with vouchers or cash help. Nor, under the iron grip of the Treasury, was there any enthusiasm for a revival of local democracy to take charge instead.

This left a fiddly and highly bureaucratic centralism as the only option left, one which we have seen gather momentum in the Thatcher years and which would flourish most extravagantly under Blair. Under Major, the centralized Funding Agency for Schools was formed and schools in England and Wales were ranked by crude league tables, depending on how well their pupils did in exams. The university system was vastly expanded by simply allowing colleges and polytechnics to rename themselves as universities, and a futile search began for ways in which civil servants might measure academic merit and introduce league tables there. The hospital system was further centralized and given a host of new targets. The police, faced with a review of their pay and demands by the Home Secretary, Kenneth Clarke, for forces to be amalgamated, were given their own performance league tables. The Tories had spent 74 per cent more, in real terms, on law and order since 1979 yet crime was at an all-time high, as a doleful list of high-profile murders reminded the public. Clarke's contempt for many of the police as 'vested interests' was not calculated to win them round to reform. Across England and Wales elected councillors were turfed off police boards and replaced by businessmen. Clarke's hostility to local control had been confirmed by his time as Health Secretary when, according to one department insider, he showed himself as 'a leading exponent of the Stalinist side of the Tory party. He castrated the regional health authority chairmen.'[7]

In 1993 Clarke defended his new police league tables in language that was eerily echoed by New Labour later: 'The new accountability that we seek from our public services will not be achieved simply because men of good will and reasonableness wish that it to be so. The new accountability is the new radicalism.' Accountability: once the word had implied a contest of ideas and achievements, played out in front of the voters. Now it meant something very different. Across the country, from the auditing of local government to the running of courts or the working hours of nurses, an army of civil servants, accountants, auditors and number-crunchers marched in. Once, long ago in the 1940s, Labour had been mocked for saying that the man in Whitehall knew best. Now the auditors and accountants hired by Whitehall ruled instead. Weakly, from time to time, ministers would claim that the cult of central control and measurement had been imposed by Brussels. Some had been, but this was mostly a home-grown 'superstate'.

Major called his headline policy the Citizen's Charter, though he himself did not like the name very much because of its 'unconscious echoes of Revolutionary France'. Every part of government dealing with public service was ordered to come up with proposals for improvement at grass-roots level, to be pursued from the centre by inspections, questionnaires, league tables and ultimately the system of awards, Charter Marks, for organizations that did well. Through-out, Major spoke of 'empowering' teachers and doctors, 'helping the customer' and 'devolving'. He thought his great system of regulation from the centre would not last long: it was 'a regulatory goad to raise standards . . . over time, I anticipated formal regulation steadily with-ering away, as the effects of growing competition are felt.' But how would this happen? In practice, the regulators grew more powerful, not less so. If people are paid to respond to regulators' targets and jump through hoops, they become excellent at target-practice and hoop-jumping. This does not make them wise administrators. Despite the rhetoric, public servants were not being given real freedom to manage. Elected office-holders were being sacked. Major's hopes for central regulation withering away echo Lenin, who hoped for a 'withering away' of the Soviet State, with similar success.

Small Wars, Big Questions

In December 1993 John Major stood outside the black-painted, steel-armoured door of Number Ten Downing Street with the affable Taoiseach of the Irish Republic, Albert Reynolds. He declared a new principle which offended many traditional Conservatives and Unionists. If both parts of Ireland voted to be reunited, Britain would not stand in the way. She had, said Major, 'no selfish strategic or economic interest in Northern Ireland'. Thus a long strand of Tory thinking, which was that the party was dedicated to the United Kingdom, consciously and proudly biased in its favour, was torn up. There was more. If the Provisional IRA, which had so lately bombed the very building Major was standing in front of, and murdered two young boys in Cheshire, renounced violence, it could be welcomed into the sunlight as a legitimate political party.

In the run-up to this Downing Street Declaration, the government was also conducting top-secret 'back channel' negotiations with the terrorist organization. The Provisional IRA leadership proved slippery and frustrating but in August 1994 they declared 'a complete cessation of military operations' which, though it was a long way short of renouncing violence, was widely welcomed. It was followed a month later by a Loyalist ceasefire. A complicated dance of three-strand talks, framework documents and arguments about the decommissioning of weapons followed. The road to peace would be tortuous, involving many walk-outs and public arguments. On the streets, extortion, knee-capping and occasional murders continued. But whereas the number of people killed in 1993 had been eighty-four, the toll fell to sixty-one the following year and nine in 1995. The contradictory demands of

Irish republicanism and Unionism meant that Major failed to get a final agreement, even on paper. That was left for Tony Blair, unfinished business. But Major's achievement was substantial: he was a good peacemaker.

And he made a dramatic bid for peace at home. In July 1995, tormented by yet more rumours of right-wing conspiracies against him, Major riposted with a theatrical coup all of his own, one his music-hall father would have applauded. He resigned as leader of the Conservative Party and invited all comers to take him on. He told journalists gathered in the sunshine in the Number Ten garden it was 'put up or shut up' time. If he lost, he would resign as Prime Minister. If he won, he expected the party to rally around him. This was a risk, for there were other plausible leaders. One was Michael Heseltine, who had become Deputy Prime Minister and who loyally supported Major. Another was Michael Portillo, then a pin-up boy of the Thatcherite right, whose supporters prepared a campaign headquarters for him but who decided against standing. In the event the challenger was John Redwood, the Welsh Secretary, known to many as 'the Vulcan' because of his glassy extraterrestrial demeanour but a highly intelligent Thatcherite. At a catastrophic press launch of his campaign he was surrounded by a celebratory, luridly dressed collection of supportive MPs swiftly dubbed 'the barmy army'. Major won his fight, though not gloriously. In the end 109 Tory MPs failed to back him. Nevertheless, in a clever political operation, victory was swiftly declared and he lived to be defeated finally by the real electorate two years later. By then defeat had been made inevitable by the self-destructive European war of the previous years.

Major was also a cautious warmaker. Blair would inherit not only the Northern Irish peace process but also the bubbling ethnic wars breaking out in former Yugoslavia, following the recognition of Slovenia, Croatia and Bosnia as independent states in the early nineties. The worst violence followed the Serbian assault on Bosnia and the three-year siege of its capital, Sarajevo. The term 'ethnic cleansing' was heard for the first time as woeful columns of refugees fled in different directions. A nightmare which Europeans thought had vanished in 1945 was returning, only a couple of days' drive away from London. Major asked his military advisers how many troops it would take to keep the sides apart and was told the answer was 400,000, three times the total size of the British Army. He sent 1,800 men to protect the humanitarian convoys that were rumbling south. Many British people proved ready to collect parcels of food, warm clothes, medicine and blankets, which were loaded onto trucks and driven south by volunteers. A London conference tried to get a peace deal and failed.

This new war went on, ever nastier. Many in the government were dubious about Britain being further involved. But the evening news bulletins showed pictures of starving refugees, the uncovered mass graves of civilians shot by death squads, and children with appalling injuries. There was a frenzied campaign for Western intervention. But what kind? In the United States President Clinton was determined not to risk American soldiers on the ground, but a swelling of outrage about the behaviour of the Serbs persuaded him to consider less costly alternatives, such as air strikes and lifting the arms embargo on the Bosnians. This would have put others who were on the ground, including the British, directly in the line of fire when the Serbs retaliated. There were rows between London and Washington. Hideous attacks in Sarajevo, notably a mysterious mortar strike at the market, finally provoked the Nato air strikes. In response the Serbs took UN troops hostage, including British soldiers who were then used as human shields. The Serb capture of the town of Srebrenica was followed by disgusting slaughter, and renewed demands for full-scale military intervention.

It never came. After three years of war, sanctions on Serbia and the success of Croats in fighting back, a peace agreement was finally made in Dayton, Ohio. Major was the first British Prime Minister of the post-Cold War world, grappling with what the proper role of the West should be. The Balkan wars, a result of the fall of communism, showed perfectly the dangers and limits of intervention. When a civil conflict is relayed in all its horror to tens of millions of voters every night by television, the pressure to do something, to separate the sides and succour the suffering, is intense. But mostly this requires not air attacks but a full-scale ground force, which will be drawn into the war, and must be followed by years of aid and rebuilding. Will the same voters be happy to keep paying, and keep accepting the casualties that follow? Major and his colleagues were accused of moral cowardice and cynicism in allowing the revival of fascist behaviour in one corner of Europe. This was nobody's finest hour. Yet Western leaders were wary about whether their voters would have accepted a full-scale war and the thankless neo-colonial responsibilities that would follow. They may have been right.

A Very English Coup

Tony Blair was an Establishment figure, more so than Thatcher, Major or Smith. He had been a mild teenage rebel, worn his hair long, broken school rules and imitated Mick Jagger in a rock band. His father had been brought up by a Communist on Clydeside and had suffered an early and severe stroke which brought his children uncertainty and a bump down in the world. Far more importantly, though, Blair was the son of a Tory lawyer and went to a preparatory school in Durham, then the grand fee-paying boarding school Fettes in Edinburgh, then Oxford University, and then the Bar, before becoming an MP. There was more Gothic architecture in his early history than in most volumes of Pevsner's architectural guide. Though he rebelled, the lessons of politeness, deference and a quiet knowledge about where power lay, were in place from the start. Gifted with a natural charm, infectious good humour and a great skill in acting, he was a young man whose seriousness and principle were also evident. His father's stroke had happened when he was still young: he lost his adored Irish-born mother when he was a student and turned increasingly to religion, in its activist, not contemplative form.

Much ink has been spilled about why he joined the Labour Party rather than the Conservatives. It is not a ridiculous question. Falling for a young Liverpudlian socialist called Cherie Booth sharpened his politics but he had joined Labour before he met her. There is a widespread belief that it was mere calculation. In the early eighties, the Tories were awash with bright lawyers looking for seats and political careers while Labour seemed on its last legs. If you wanted to get into the Commons and then rise, Labour offered an easier if riskier route. While this is possible, joining Labour at its lowest ebb would show uncanny prescience for a pure careerist. The likeliest explanation is simply that he believed in political action and that, though flawed, Labour's belief in social justice was nearest to the Christian social views he had formed. Once in the party, working his way through local branches in London, he displayed the full kit of soft-left beliefs of the time, being hostile to the European Community and privatization, pro-CND and high taxes, the rights of illegal immigrants and greater freedom for the press. He would ditch all of these views later but this does not mean they were insincerely held at the time; for the Labour Party of Foot's time they were considered moderate, and Blair was always opposed to the hard-left Bennite and Militant groups.

After fighting a hopeless by-election, Blair won a safe Labour seat in the north-east of England with his combination of chutzpah and charm and, in the Commons from 1983, quickly fell in with another new MP. Gordon Brown was much that Blair was not. He was a tribal Labour Party man from a strongly political family, who had barely glimpsed the crenellated English Establishment which produced Blair. Brown had been Scotland's best-known student politician and a player in Scottish Labour politics from the age of twenty-three, followed by a stint in television. Yet the two men had some things in common. They were both Christians and they were both deeply impatient with the condition of the Labour Party. For seven or eight years they seemed inseparable, working mostly from a tiny, windowless office they shared. Brown tutored Blair in the darker ways of politics, treating him like a sweetly naive kid brother. (He would learn.) Blair was also a vital sounding-board for Brown, however, teaching him what the mysterious English middle classes might be thinking. No working relationship in politics was closer. Brown summed it up in 1991: 'I think Blair could well be leader of the party after me.' Together, they made friends with Westminster journalists, together they matured as Commons performers, together they shared their frustration about older Labour politicians, together they worked their way up the ranks of the shadow cabinet.

Then Blair began to pull ahead. After the 1992 defeat he made a bleak public judgement about why Labour had lost so badly. The reason was not complicated, but simple: 'Labour has not been trusted to fulfil the aspirations of the majority of people in a modern world.' As shadow home secretary he began to try to put that right, promising (in words borrowed from Brown) to be 'tough on crime and tough on the causes of crime'. His response to the horror of the 1993 murder of the toddler James Bulger by two young boys, which provoked a frenzy of national debate, was particularly resonant. In general Blair tried to return his party to the common-sense language of morality. He drank deep from the mix of socially conservative and economically liberal messages used by the great communicator Bill Clinton and his team of 'New Democrats'.

So too did Brown. But he had a harder brief, since as shadow chancellor his job was to demolish cherished spending plans and say no to Labour MPs. Brown's support for the ERM meant he was ineffective when Major and Lamont suffered their great defeat. The Brown and Blair relationship was less close than it had been earlier but it was still strong. Together they visited the United States to learn a new political style from the Democrats. Awkwardly for Brown, it relied heavily on leadership charisma. At home Blair pushed Smith aggressively over reforming the party rulebook, falling out with him badly. Watching media commentators and some Labour MPs began to tip him as the next leader, Brown's team began to ask whether Blair was now manoeuvring and briefing against his old mentor. It was a grim time for Brown and he did not bother to reach out, or show a sunny side. Slowly but perceptibly, Brown-Blair was turning into Blair-Brown.

The days after John Smith died have produced more analysis and speculation than almost any other short period in modern British politics. But the basic story is clear. Blair decided almost immediately that he would run as leader. Brown, perhaps more grief-stricken than Blair or perhaps more cautious, hesitated. But he had assumed he would inherit and when he heard Blair's plans, he was aghast. In at least ten face-to-face meetings in Edinburgh and London, the two men argued. On Blair's side were opinion polls showing him much more popular, the support of greater numbers of Labour MPs and greater backing in the press. This was not all a plot by Peter Mandelson, as Brown people later claimed; it was a widespread assessment come to independently by many people who disagreed about other things. Crucial to the case for Blair was that he was a well-spoken Englishman who would reassure those parts of the country which were the main electoral battleground. On Brown's side were his deeper knowledge of Labour, stronger support among the unions and his more thought-through policy agenda for change. Had the two fought each other, given Labour's complicated electoral college it is impossible to say just what would have happened. Blairites say their man would have crushed and 'humiliated' Brown; Brown's people reply that his formidable campaigning skills would have taken the metropolitan Blairites by surprise. On only one subject were they both agreed. For the two modernizers to fight would be disastrous. Personal attacks would be impossible to avoid. If Brown had any hope of winning, he would have to attack Blair from the left.

So Brown came to a deal, culminating in a notorious dinner at the chic, now defunct Islington restaurant Granita. (Some sense of the cultural gap between the two men can be drawn from the fact that Brown had to go and have a proper meal afterwards.) Again, the outcome is much disputed, except that Blair acknowledged Brown's authority over a wide range of policy which he would direct from the Treasury, including the 'social justice' agenda. Did he also promise to limit his prime ministership to seven years and then make way? It would be an extraordinarily arrogant thing for one Opposition politician to say to another; the Conservatives would be in power for years yet. But probably some form of words about a transition in power was exchanged, if only to salve Brown's hurt. Looking back many years later it can be seen that the true significance of the Granita deal and the meetings that preceded it, was that it gifted Britain's mightiest government department, the Treasury, even more power than it had in the Conservative years. Blair would be, as Prime Minister, more concerned with foreign affairs than he could ever have guessed, and Brown's Treasury would become a grand Department for British Affairs, beyond its mandarins' wildest dreams. Gordon Brown would be the Treasury's final victory over George Brown.

The Killer Cows of Old England

John Selwyn Gummer, a devout Christian and environmentalist, was one of the nicest men in British politics. On a sunny May morning in 1990, he paraded his daughter Cordelia before the cameras in Suffolk and tried to persuade her to eat a beefburger. The four-year-old Cordelia was nobody's fool and absolutely refused. Gummer quickly swallowed his embarrassment, and then the cooling burger too, pronouncing it 'absolutely delicious'. He was of course trying to make a political point. There was rising disquiet about a mysterious and unpleasant disease of the brain found in cattle, which caused them to stagger, fall over and expire. It was called BSE, for bovine spongiform encephalopathy. The disease was being found all across Britain at the rate of 300 cases a week. The Ministry of Agriculture, Fisheries and Food, with Mr Gummer at its head, was more the department of farmers than the department of shoppers and it discouraged alarm about the new disease. Could it be spread to humans? At that stage the answer was no. Still, because it seemed to be spread by the use of mashed-up cow offal in feed, a kind of grisly if unwitting cow cannibalism, new rules were put in place. Farmers were told to destroy BSE-infected cattle. Gummer's stunt was intended to show how safe British beef, even in beefburgers, now was. Prior to Cordelia's rejected burger, cow brains, spleen, tonsils and gut had already been banned for human consumption.

But the problem would not go away. Among those refusing to eat British beef were the Germans, some schools, and a majority of doctors. Various other animals, including a cat, a cheetah and a monkey, died of BSE. By the mid-nineties, the government was spending tens of millions on compensation for farmers who were burning or burying their dead cattle. The line that humans could not contract the brain disease was beginning to crumble. Victoria Rimmer, a teenager from North Wales, was dying of Creutzfeld-Jakob Disease (CJD) which was closely related to BSE and said to have been caused by eating infected beef. More human cases were reported, from, amongst others, farmers, butchers and people who had had blood transfusions. It began to be clear that many slaughterhouses were not following the new rules and that some BSE-infected cattle still ended up for human consumption. The EU started to take a close interest. In March 1996 ministers admitted that a new form of CJD had been found in ten people, of whom eight had died, and that this was probably due to BSE being in food.

There was, rightly, an eruption of anger and the credibility of the department was questioned. British beef was banned by the EU. New rules about the deboning of beef before it was eaten were introduced and a massive programme of slaughtering all cows over thirty months began. Beef on the bone was off the menu and parts of the British countryside were studded with oily pyres of swollen dead corpses, an unappetizing spectacle. The slaughter was extended to 147,000 animals but Europe remained steely, and extended the ban to exported British beef outside the EU as well. 'Mad cow disease' became as emblematic of the end of the Tory years as union militancy or punk rock had been of the late seventies. The government's anger was mainly directed at continental Europe, seen as gleefully exaggerating the lethal infection in the Roast Beef of Old England in order to sell their own meat. Yet the anger might have been as profitably directed elsewhere – to the farming dominated government department that had acted slowly, the farmers who had refused to report the full extent of the disease, the sloppy slaughterhouses and, in general, a form of industrial farming that fed dead cows' brains to cows, apparently heedless of whether this was nice, safe or healthy. The science was still sketchy and the media was hysterical, but government and industry were to blame as well.

The Sword of Truth

For British voters, the Major years were remembered as much for the sad, petty and lurid personal scandals that attended so many of his ministers, after he made an unwise speech remembered as a call for old-style morality. In fact 'back to basics' referred to almost everything except personal sexual morality – he spoke of public service, industry, sound money, free trade, traditional teaching, respect for the family and law, and a campaign to defeat crime. 'Back to basics', however, gave the press a fail-safe headline charge of hypocrisy whenever ministers were caught out, and caught out they were. A series of adulteries exposed, children born out of wedlock, a sex death after a kinky stunt went wrong, rumours about Major's own affairs (truer than was realized, though the press had the wrong person) and then an inquiry into whether Parliament had been misled over the sale of arms to Iraq, were knitted together into a single pattern of misbehaviour, which got an old name, 'sleaze'.

In 1996 a three-year inquiry into whether the government had allowed a trial to go ahead against directors of an arms company, Matrix Churchill, knowing that they were in fact acting inside privately accepted guidelines, resulted in two ministers being publicly criticized. It showed that the government had allowed a more relaxed regime of military-related exports to Saddam Hussein even after the horrific gassing of 5,000 Kurds at Falluja, and revealed a culture of secrecy and double standards. Other 'sleaze' related stories were more personal. One of the more flamboyant Thatcherite MPs, the bow-tied and flippant Neil Hamilton, was accused of taking cash in brown paper envelopes from the owner of Harrods, Mohamed al-Fayed, to ask questions for him in Parliament. In a libel case which followed he vociferously denied this, but lost the action and was financially ruined. Jonathan Aitken, a Treasury minister, was accused of taking improper hospitality from an Arab business contact. He resigned to fight the *Guardian* over the claims, with 'the simple sword of truth and the trusty shield of fair play', was found guilty of perjury and served eighteen months in prison.

There is no logical link between a minister who forms improper links with a sexual partner, and a minister who forms improper links with a businessman. Never mind. All of this was expertly packaged together by the New Labour Opposition, working closely with the media. In the late nineties, sleaze was as ubiquitous and smug a word as 'spin' would be later. It set the tone of the times. One of the more dramatic episodes in the 1997 election was the overwhelming defeat of Hamilton in his Tatton constituency by the former BBC war reporter, who had been badly injured at Sarajevo, Martin Bell. Clad in his familiar white suit, helped by a decision to stand aside by the Labour and Liberal Democrat candidates, and advised by the Labour spin doctor Alastair Campbell, Bell succeeded in overturning Hamilton's enormous majority, emerging with an 11,000 majority of his own. He became Britain's first independent MP for nearly fifty years. It is worth recalling that there was a time not so long ago when it seemed that white suits, if not swords of truth, would cleanse British politics.

By the end of Major's government, it seemed that some lessons had been learned about politics in Britain, broadly defined. The European Union was perilous, a potential party-splitter. Their single currency was as toxic as our beef. There was a mood of contempt for politicians. The press had lost any sense of deference. Busy reforms directed at the health service, police and schools had produced surprisingly little improvement. The post Cold War world was turning out to be nastier and less predictable than the days of the 'peace dividend' had promised. And finally, when your luck turned, it turned dramatically. There was, in all this, material for a thoughtful and wary

Opposition to reflect on. How might the country be better governed? What was the right British approach to peace-keeping and intervention now that the United States was the last superpower left standing? How could the promises of an end to cynicism be fulfilled? But by 1997, New Labour had no time to reflect on all that. It was moving in for the kill.

Team Tony

The 1997 general election demonstrated just what a stunningly effective election-winning machine Tony Blair now led. New Labour won 419 seats, the largest number ever for the party and comparable only with the number of seats for the 1935 National government. Its majority in the Commons was also a modern record, 179 seats, and thirty-three more than Attlee's landslide majority of 1945. The swing of 10 per cent from the Conservatives was yet another post-war record, roughly double that which the Thatcher victory of 1979 had produced in the other direction. A record number of women were elected to Parliament, 119 of them, of whom 101 were Labour, 'Blair's babes'. The party also won heavily across the south and in London, in parts of Britain from which it had recently been hardly represented. Yet among this slew of heart-stopping statistics, which had Blair shaking his head with disbelief and exclaiming 'it can't be real', there were some small warning signs. The turnout was very low, at 71 per cent the lowest since 1935. Labour had won a famous victory but nothing like as many actual votes as the reviled John Major had won five years before. Still, as the sun came up on a jubilant, celebrating party there was much wet-eyed rhapsodizing about a new dawn for Britain. Alastair Campbell had assembled crowds of party workers and supporters to stand along Downing Street waving Union Jacks as the Blairs strode up to claim their inheritance. Briefly, it looked as if the country itself had turned out to cheer.

The victory was due to a small group of self-styled modernizers who seized the Labour Party, and then took it far further to the right than anyone expected. The language used tells its own story. New Labour was to be a party of the 'left and centre left', then one of the 'centre left', then the 'centre and centre left' and in Blair's later years simply of 'the centre'. Blair was the leading man in this drama but he was not the only player. He needed the support and encouragement of admirers and friends who would coax and goad him, rebuke him and encourage him, and do his will, whether he knew what they were up to or not. Who were they? There was Mandelson, the brilliant but temperamental former media boss, by now an MP. Once fixated by Gordon Brown, he was adored by Blair and returned the sentiment. Yet he was so mistrusted by other members of the team that his central role in Blair's leadership election was disguised from them under the name 'Bobby' (for Bobby Kennedy, working to Blair's JFK: modesty was never a hallmark of the inner circle).

There was Alastair Campbell, Blair's press officer and attack-dog. A former journalist, natural propagandist, ex-alcoholic and all-round alpha male, Campbell would chew the ears of everyone who criticized Blair and helped devise the campaign of mockery against Major. He behaved in private towards the Labour leader (and on one occasion was filmed doing so) with the cheery aggression of a personal trainer working over a nervous young housewife. There was Philip Gould, a working-class boy whose admiration for US political techniques knew no bounds; he would bring his focus group expertise, his polling and ruthless analysis to the party. There was Derry Irvine, the rotund, intimidating, brilliant and surprisingly sensitive Highlands lawyer who had first found a place in his chambers for Blair and Cherie Booth. He advised on constitutional change and would become Lord Chancellor. And there was Anji Hunter, the contralto charmer who had known Blair as a youth and who remained his best hotline to *Daily Mail*-reading middle England.

These people, with Brown and his team working (almost) alongside them, formed the inner core. The young David Miliband, whose father was a famous Marxist political philosopher, provided research help. They would be joined by Jonathan Powell, a diplomat who had been observing the Clintons in the United States, and whose older brother Charles had been one of Thatcher's most important aides. By the end of the Blair years, with so many others fallen by the wayside, he was undoubtedly the second most important man in Downing Street. Among the MPs who were initially close were Marjorie (better known as Mo) Mowlam and Jack Straw. The money for Blair's leadership campaign was raised from a clutch of mainly media millionaires, including Greg Dyke, later Director General of the BBC, and Michael Levy, a record promoter who would later be ennobled and later still face a police investigation and arrest on corruption charges. The first striking thing about Team Blair is how few elected Labour politicians it included. The second is how many of its original members would later fall out with him. He had a capacity to charm and pull in people whom he needed, and then to drop them briskly once they were surplus or embarrassing.

Blair had won 57 per cent of the vote in the leadership election, easily beating two more left-wing candidates, one of whom, John Prescott, was elected as his deputy. In his campaign Blair had stuck mostly to generalities about modernization and the instincts of the British people, but had sounded approving of the regime of centralized testing and quangos the Conservatives had pursued in public services. To that extent people had due warning. By the time the party congregated again for its annual conference, the Labour Party had become 'New Labour'. In his first conference speech Blair made a veiled reference to the need for an up to date statement of Labour values. What he actually meant was that he planned to scrap clause four of its constitution, which declared that public ownership of the means of production, distribution and exchange was necessary to 'secure for the workers by hand or by brain the full fruit of their industry'. Clause four, part four, was a household god for Labour, its 1918 commitment to destroy capitalism, which sat in a corner covered in cobwebs. Hugh Gaitskell had wanted to abolish it, but had drawn back and the ambition had slumbered for decades. Blair killed it. His new statement of aims began with the assertion that 'the Labour Party is a democratic socialist party' which, by then, was going it a bit. In his next conference speech Blair used the word 'new' fifty-nine times, referred to socialism just once and omitted to mention the working class at all.

Though politics is a serious business, there is an undeniably comic side to the Blair coup. With his impish grin he suddenly behaved as if everything was possible, and no political allegiance was impossible to shift. He became the playful magician of political life. He took to warmly praising Margaret Thatcher. He opened private talks with the Liberal Democrats about some grand new alliance of the centre. In Fleet Street he took to charming every rheumy proprietorial troll and crusty prophet of the right he could lay his smile on. Later he would continue the practice in government, appointing Tory statesmen to big jobs, gleefully ushering in defectors and keeping close for a while to the Lib-Dem leader Paddy Ashdown, and its elder statesman Roy Jenkins (though he would later disappoint both by his conservatism). He went to visit Rupert Murdoch's News International team in Australia and impressed them too. What manner of man was this Tony Blair? Where did he stand? Where were his limits? There were not many. In the election campaign the pro-European Blair cheerfully put his name to an article in Murdoch's *Sun*, ghost-written by Campbell, promising 'to slay the dragon' of federalism. Later relations would be so close that Murdoch would complain of the amount of time he wasted in London drinking tea with Blair and coffee with Brown. He searched out Lord Rothermere, proprietor of the *Daily Mail*, traditionally Labour's bitterest critic in the British press, and dined him privately, promising him that he abhorred high taxes, uppity unions and sleaze. It was as if, freed by winning the leadership, Blair was rattling the handle of every door in town to see if it opened. As he was on a roll and Labour was desperate to win at all costs, the traditionalists looked on in silent, helpless disbelief. Was nothing sacred? Apparently not.

Yet when it came to serious policy formation, the story was less amusing. Blair talked of his priority being 'education, education, education', of his ambition to make Britain a 'young country' and of his own belief in 'power for a purpose'. He identified the broad areas he wanted to concentrate on, but when it came to clearer proposals said little. Blair has been mocked so richly since for the airy blandness of his promises that it is worth recalling an example of the 'optimism-lite' rhetoric which was taken at least half-seriously in 1997. A few early sentences from Labour's manifesto give a flavour of this:

> I believe in Britain. It is a great country with a great history. The British people are a great people. But I believe Britain can and must be better: better schools, better hospitals, better ways of tackling crime, of building a modern welfare state, of equipping ourselves for a new world economy. I want a Britain that is one nation, with shared values and purpose, where merit comes before privilege, run for the many not the few, strong and sure of itself

at home and abroad. I want a Britain that does not shuffle into the new millennium afraid of the future, but strides into it with confidence.

Britons would stride with a purpose, and in their hands they would hold New Labour's first pledge card, a credit-card-sized rectangle of coloured cardboard. Produced in time for the election, its five pledges were rather clearer than the early rhetoric. In government Labour would cut class sizes to thirty or below for five- to seven-year-olds, by scrapping the assisted places scheme that helped people from poor families go to private schools. It would speed up punishment for persistent young offenders, halving the time from arrest to sentencing. It would cut health service waiting times 'by treating an extra 100,000 patients as a first step' paid for by cutting red tape (the last resort of political accountancy). A quarter of a million young people would be put to work through a windfall tax on the privatized utility companies. There would be no rise in income tax rates and inflation and interest rates would be kept 'as low as possible'. The last seemed entirely meaningless since no government has tried to raise inflation, but now seems like a coded reference to Gordon Brown's decision to hand control over interest rates to a committee of the Bank of England. Looking back, the pledge card revealed a lot about the strengths and weaknesses of New Labour. It was modest in promise, and costed. Its promises, however, were so simple they often turned out to be damaging in practice; the waiting times pledge was one example. And there was a yearning for numerical simplicity – all those suspiciously round numbers – which suggested the purpose of the pledges was propagandistic, not governmental, easy ideas to spoon into voters who could not be bothered to concentrate.

Most damaging of all for a campaign which so relentlessly accused the Conservatives of deceit and destroying people's trust in politics, Labour made promises which it would promptly break when it won power. It promised not to privatize the air traffic control system, but did so. It promised not to levy tuition fees for students and a year later did exactly that – and would repeat the trick with student top-up fees during the 2001 election. It promised an end to sleaze and to deception. It implied that the overall tax burden would not increase, yet it would. The most important pledges were the negative ones, coming from

Brown and his Treasury team; that there would be no increase in rates of income tax, while for two years a New Labour government would stick to the Conservatives' spending totals. Those promises were stuck to, though there were big and unmentioned stings to come.

But why were so many other pledges broken? Team Tony, the group who put together the New Labour 'project', were intelligent people who wanted to find a way of ruling which helped the worse off, particularly by giving them better chances in education and to find jobs, while not alienating the mass of middle-class voters. They exuded a strange, unstable mix of anxiety and arrogance. They were extraordinarily worried by newspapers. They were bruised by what had happened to Kinnock, whom they had all worked with, and ruthlessly focused on winning over anyone who could be won. Yet there was arrogance too. They were utterly ignorant of what governing would be like. The early success of Blair's leadership victory and his short time as Opposition leader produced a sense that everything was possible for people of determination. If they promised something, no doubt it would happen. It they said something, of course it was true. They weren't Tories, after all. The pity of all this was that they were about to take power at a golden moment when it would have been possible to fulfil the pledges they had made and when it was not necessary to give different messages to different people in order to win power. Blair had the wind at his back. The Conservatives would pose no serious threat to him for many years to come. Far from inheriting a weak or crisis-ridden economy, he was actually taking over at the best possible time when the country was recovering strongly, but had not yet quite noticed. Blair won by being focused and ruthless, and never forgot it. But he also had incredible, historic luck, and never seemed to realize quite what an opportunity it gave him.

Celebrity Life, Celebrity Death

Tony Blair arrived in power in 1997 in a country spangled and sugar-coated by a revived fashion for celebrity. It offered a few politicians new opportunities but at a high cost. The glamour industry had always been with us, under different names, but had become super-charged during the sixties when rock stars, Hollywood actors and television performers were feted by the tabloid press and a new generation of women's and urban magazines. Such interviews and profiles spread more widely during the seventies and eighties but it was not until 1988 that the shape of the modern celebrity culture became fully apparent. That year saw the first of the true modern celebrity glossies in Britain when *Hello!* magazine was launched on 17 May. It was the English-language version of the Spanish magazine *Hola!* which had already made its owner Eduardo Sanchez Junco a multi-millionaire. Its success is often credited to the exotic Marquesa de Varela, who allegedly owns 200 dogs and has four luxury homes in Uruguay, as well as New York and London. The *Hello!* formula would copied by *OK!* from 1993 and many other magazines, to the point where yards of coloured mimicry occupied newsagents' shelves in every town and village in the country. It sheds a sidelight on Britain's changing public culture.

The essence of its sweetheart deal was that celebrities would be paid handsomely to be interviewed and photographed, in return for coverage that was generally fawning and never hostile. *Hello!* allowed the flawed-famous to shun the mean minded sniping of the regular press, while it scooped up access to the most famous names, time after time. The sunny, good-time, upbeat, airbrushed world of *Hello!* was much mocked. In the real world the relentless optimism of its coverage of grinning couples and their lovely homes was inevitably followed by divorces, drunken rows, accidents and ordinary scandals. But it was hugely successful. People seemed happy to read good news about the famous and beautiful even if they knew in their hearts there was more to it than that. In the same year as *Hello!* arrived, 1988, the BBC put the Australian soap opera *Neighbours* into a prime teatime slot. At its height this show, which had been a failure on its home patch, was attracting 15 million British viewers. It too portrayed a youthful, sunny alternative to grey Britain[8] and its early stars, notably Kylie Minogue and Jason Donovan, went on to become celebrities themselves. In the same year as *Hello!* and *Neighbours*, ITV launched the most successful of the daytime television shows, *This Morning*, hosted from Liverpool by Richard Madeley and Judy Finnigan, a live magazine programme of frothy features and celebrity interviews. Daytime television had existed since 1983 when BBC One's breakfast show with Frank Bough and Selina Scott arrived alongside the independent *TVam*. These, though, were high-minded and mainstream compared to the more popular *This Morning* show, television's celebrity break-through moment.

What did this celebrity fantasy world, which continued to open up in all directions in the media through the nineties, have to do with anything else? For one thing it re-emphasized to alert politicians, broadcasting executives and advertisers the considerable if recently unfashionable power of optimism. Mainstream news in the nineties might be giving the British an unending stream of bleakness, burning cattle carcasses, awful murders and disasters on railway lines; millions turned all the more urgently to celebrity. They did not think that celebrities had universally happy lives, or always behaved well, or did not age.

But in celebrity-land, everyone meant well, everyone could forgive themselves and be forgiven, and there was always a new dawn breaking over the swimming pool. The celebrity who emoted, who was prepared to expose inner pain, enjoyed a land of power. And in eighties and nineties Britain, no celebrity gleamed more brightly than the beautiful, troubled Princess Diana. For fifteen years she was an ever-present presence. As an aristocratic girl, no intellectual, whose childhood had been blighted by a bad divorce, her fairytale marriage in 1981 found her pledging her life to an older man who shared few of her interests and did not seem to be in love with her.

The slow disintegration of this marriage transfixed Britain, as Diana moved from china-doll, whispery-voiced debutante, to painfully thin young mother, to increasingly charismatic and confident public figure, working crowds and seducing cameras like a new Marilyn Monroe. As eighties fashions grew more exuberant and glossy, so did she. Her eating disorder, bulimia, was one suffered by growing numbers of girls. When she admitted later to acts of self-harm, she sounded like teenagers and young women in many less privileged homes. When plagues and cruelties of the age were in the news, she appeared as visual commentator, hugging AIDS victims to show that it was safe, or campaigning against land-mines. Rumours spread of her affairs. Britain was now a divorce-prone country, in which 'what's best for the kids' and 'I deserve to be happy' were batted across kitchen tables. So Diana was not simply a pretty woman married to a king-in-waiting, but became a kind of Barbie of the emotions, who could be dressed up in the private pain of millions. People felt, possibly wrongly, that she would understand them. Her glance was as potent as the monarch's touch had once been for scrofula. A feverish, obsessive quality attached to her admirers, something not seen before by the Royal Family, who found all this uncomfortable and alarming. They were living symbols. She was a living icon.

After the birth of her second son Harry in 1987 Diana's marriage was visibly failing. In 1992 the journalist Andrew Morton, to general huffing, claimed to tell *Diana the True Story* in a book which described suicide attempts, blazing rows, her bulimia and her growing certainty that Prince Charles had resumed an affair with his old love, Camilla Parker Bowles, something he later confirmed in a television interview with Jonathan Dimbleby. In the December after Morton's publication John Major announced that Charles and Diana were to separate. A wily manipulator of the media, Diana became simultaneously a huntress in the media jungle, pursuing stories that flattered her, and the hunted, both haunted and haunting. Then came her revelatory 1995 interview on *Panorama*. Breaking every taboo left in royal circles, she freely discussed the breakup of her marriage ('there were three of us'), attacked the Windsors for their cruelty and promised to be 'a queen in people's hearts'. Finally divorced in 1996, she continued her charity work around the world and began a relationship with Dodi al-Fayed, son of the owner of Harrods. To many she was a selfish and unhinged woman endangering the monarchy. To millions her painful life-story and her fashionable readiness to share that pain, made her more valuable than formal monarchy. She was followed with close attention all round the world, her face and name a sure seller of papers and magazines. By the summer of 1997 Britain had two super-celebrities. One was Tony Blair and the other was Princess Diana.

It is therefore grimly fitting that Tony Blair's most resonant words as Prime Minister and the moment when he reached the very height of his popularity came on the morning when Diana was killed with Dodi in a Paris underpass after their car crashed. Blair had been woken from a deep sleep at his Trimdon constituency home, first to be warned about the accident, and then to be told that Diana was dead. He was deeply shocked, and worried about what his proper role should be. After pacing round in his pyjamas and having expletive-ridden conversations with Campbell, Blair spoke to the Queen, who said that neither she nor any other senior would make a statement. He decided he had to say something. Later that morning, standing in front of his local church, looking shattered, and transmitted live around the world, he spoke for Britain. 'I feel, like everyone else in this country today, utterly devastated. Our thoughts and prayers are with Princess Diana's family – in particular her two sons, her two boys – our hearts go out to them. We are today a nation in a state of shock . . .' As he continued, his hands clenched, his voice broke and he showed he understood why she achieved her special status: 'Her own life was often sadly touched by tragedy. She touched the lives of so many others in Britain and throughout the world with joy and with comfort. How many times shall we remember her in how many different ways, with the sick, the dying, with children, with the needy? With just a look or a gesture that spoke so much more than words, she would reveal to all of us the depth of her compassion and her humanity.'

Looking back at the words many years on, they seem strangely close to what might be said of a religious figure, someone about to be declared a saint by the Catholic Church a holy figure whose glance or touch could heal. At the time, though, they were much welcomed and assented to. Blair went on: 'People everywhere, not just here in Britain, kept faith with Princess Diana. They liked her, they loved her, they regarded her as one of the people. She was – the People's Princess and that is how she will stay, how she will remain in our hearts and our memories for ever.' These are the sentiments of one natural charismatic paying tribute to another. Blair regarded himself as the people's Prime Minister, leading the people's party, beyond left and right, beyond faction or ideology, a political miracle-worker with a direct line to the people's instincts. And in the country after his impromptu eulogy to Diana, astonishingly, his approval rating rose to over 90 per cent, a figure we do not normally witness in democracies.

Blair and Campbell then paid their greatest service to an institution which represented Old Britain, or the forces of conservatism, the monarchy itself. The Queen, still angry and upset about Diana's behaviour, wanted a quiet private funeral and wanted, also, to remain away from the scenes of public mourning in London. She stayed at Balmoral, looking after her devastated grandsons. This may well have been the grandmotherly thing to do, and the best thing for them but it could have been disastrous for her public image. There was a strange mood in the country, a frantic edge to the mourning which Blair had predicted from the first. The lack of publicly mourning Windsors, the lack of a flag at half-mast over Buckingham Palace, any suggestion of a quiet funeral, all seemed to confirm all Diana's most bitter thoughts about a cold and unfeeling Royal Family. With Prince Charles's full agreement Blair and his aides cajoled the Palace first into accepting that this would have to be a huge public funeral so the country's grief could be expressed, and second that the Queen should return to London. She did, just in time to quieten a growing mood of anger about her behaviour.

This was a generational problem as well as a class one. The Queen had been brought up in a land of buttoned lips, stoicism and private grieving. She now reigned over a country which expected and almost required exhibitionism. To let it all loll out had become a guarantee of authenticity. For some years in Britain the deaths of children, or the scenes of fatal accidents, had been marked by little shrines of cellophane-wrapped flowers, cards and soft toys. In the run-up to Diana's funeral parts of central London seemed Mediterranean in their public grieving. There were vast mounds of flowers, people sleeping out, holding placards, weeping in the streets. Strangers hugged strangers. If Blair's words in Trimdon suggested Diana was a living saint, a sub-religious hysteria responded to the thought. People queuing to sign a book of condolence at St James's Palace reported that her image was appearing, supernaturally, in the background of an oil painting.

The funeral itself was like no other before, and will never be mimicked. The capital was at a standstill. Among the lucky ones invited to Westminster Abbey, gay men in matching sado masochistic leather outfits queued up with members of the Household Cavalry, in long leather boots and jangling spurs. Campaigners stood with earls, entertainers shared programmes with elderly politicians as the worlds of rock music and aristocracy, charity work and politics, jostled together. Elton John performed a hastily rewritten version of 'Candle in the Wind', his lament for Marilyn Monroe, and Princess Diana's brother Earl Spencer made an angrily half-coded attack from the pulpit on the Windsors' treatment of his sister. This was applauded when it was relayed outside, and then disloyal clapping was heard in the Abbey itself. Diana's body was driven to her last resting place and showered with flowers all the way.

In another echo of Marilyn Monroe, Diana's death would begin a worldwide rumour that she had been murdered, either because she was pregnant by Dodi or because she was about to marry a Muslim. Wild theories about British secret service agents would ripple through cyberspace, reappearing regularly in newspapers. Those same papers, implicated in the hounding of Diana by paparazzi photographers whose work they bought eagerly, were more obvious to blame. Less was said about that. Nearly a decade later an inquiry headed by a former Metropolitan Police commissioner concluded that she had died because her driver was drunk and trying to throw off pursuing photographers; this was greeted by the conspiracy theorists as another Establishment cover-up. The Queen recovered her standing after making a grim live broadcast about her wayward former daughter-in-law. She would later rise again in public esteem to be seen as one of the most successful as well as longest-serving sovereigns for centuries. A popular film about these events sealed the verdict. Blair never again quite captured the mood of the country as he did that late summer. It may be that his advice and help to the Queen in 1997 was vital to her, as well as being, in the view of some officials, thoroughly impertinent.

What did Tony Blair take from the force of the Diana cult, and of charismatic celebrity generally? His instinct for popular culture when he arrived in power was uncanny. He too would soon launch himself onto daytime television programmes, spinning an engaging and chirpy story about his life and interests, not always accurate in every detail. The New Age spiritualism which came out into the open when Diana died, with its shrines and its charms, its wide-eyed-ness, was echoed by the influence of people such as Carole Caplin in Blair's Downing Street circle. But it went further. What other politicians failed to grasp, and he did grasp, was the power of optimism expressed by the glossy world of celebrity, and people's readiness to forgive their favourites not just once, but again and again. In celebrity-land, if you had charisma and you apologized, or better still, bared a little of your soul, you could get away with most things short of murder. Interesting. But the world of politics would prove to be a little tougher.

Days of Hope

Optimism was the only real force behind the Northern Ireland peace process. Too often, this is now remembered by one of Blair's greatest soundbites as the talks reached a climax: 'This is no time for soundbites . . . I feel the hand of history on my shoulder.' While irresistibly comic, it would be a horribly unfair thing to hold on to from one of Blair's biggest achievements. As we have seen, John Major had been tenacious in trying to bring Republicans and Unionists to the table but there had been a stalemate contributed to by both IRA bloody-mindedness and his own parliamentary weakness. Encouraged by Bill Clinton, Blair had decided in Opposition that an Irish peace settlement would be one of his top priorities in government. He went to the province as his first visit after winning power and focused Number Ten on the negotiations as soon as the IRA, sensing a new opportunity, announced a further ceasefire. In Mo Mowlam, the pugnacious, earthy and spectacularly brave new Northern Ireland Secretary, he had someone prepared to eff and blind at Unionists and coo or hug Sinn Feiners in pursuit of a deal. Mowlam was, after Blair himself, the nearest the new government had to a charismatic celebrity.

Quite soon the Ulster Unionist politicians found her a bit much, and suspected she was basically 'Green'. She concentrated her charm and bullying on the Republicans, while a Number Ten team run by Blair's chief aides concentrated their work on the Unionists. Blair would emphasize his own family's Unionist roots to try to win trust. As under Major, there were three separate negotiations taking place simultaneously. There was direct talking between the Northern Irish political parties, aimed at producing a power-sharing assembly in which they could all sit. This was chaired by former US Senator George Mitchell, and was the toughest part. There were the talks between the Northern Irish parties and the British and Irish governments about the border and the constitutional position of Northern Ireland in the future. And finally there were direct talks between London and Dublin on the wider constitutional and security settlement.

The story of the negotiations in detail is gripping but cannot be given here. Suffice it to say that this was a long, intensely difficult process which appeared to have broken down at numerous points, and was kept going mainly thanks to Blair himself. His advisers grumbled that he spent a ludicrously disproportionate amount of time on Northern Ireland, expending charm, energy, long days and late nights for months at a time. He also took big personal risks, as when early on he invited Gerry Adams and Martin McGuinness of Sinn Fein, the latter also a top Provisional IRA commander, to Downing Street. Some in the Northern Ireland Office, as well as in Unionist politics, believe Blair personally gave too much away to the Republicans, particularly over the release of terrorist prisoners. His former Northern Ireland Secretary and friend Peter Mandelson later said as much. But he spent most of his time trying to keep the Unionists with him, having moved Labour policy away from a position of support for Irish unification and in Washington, Blair was seen as too Unionist. At one point, when talks had broken down again, Mowlam made the astonishing personal decision to go into the notorious Maze prison herself and talk to Republican and Loyalist terrorist prisoners. Hiding behind their politicians, the imprisoned hard men still called the shots, at a time when this was not a metaphorical expression.

Given a deadline for Easter 1998, after last-gasp setbacks, a deal was finally struck. Northern Ireland would stay part of the UK for as long as the majority there wished it. The Republic of Ireland would give up the territorial claim to Northern Ireland, amending its constitution. The parties would combine in a power-sharing executive, based on a new elected assembly. There would be a new North–South body, knitting the two parts of Ireland together in various practical, undramatic ways. The paramilitary organizations would surrender or destroy their weapons, monitored by an independent body. Prisoners would be released. The policing of Northern Ireland, long a sore point, would be made fairer. This deal involved much pain, particularly for the Unionists. It was only the start of true peace and would be threatened frequently afterwards. The horrific bombing of the centre of Omagh a few months after the signing of the Good Friday Agreement was the worst setback. A renegade IRA splinter group murdered twenty-nine people and injured two hundred. Yet this time the extremists seemed unable to stop the rest from talking.

Once the agreement had been ratified by referendums on both sides of the border, the decommissioning of arms proved an endless and wearisome game of bluff. Though the two leaders of the moderate parties in Northern Ireland, David Trimble of the Ulster Unionists and John Hume of the SDLP, won the Nobel Prize for Peace, the agreement was to elbow both their parties aside. With electorates nervous, they lost out at the ballot box to the harder-line Democratic Unionists of Dr Ian Paisley and to Sinn Fein, under Adams and McGuinness. This made it harder to set up an effective power-sharing executive and assembly in Belfast. Yet, astonishingly, the so-called 'Dr No' of Unionism, Paisley, and his republican enemy, Adams, would eventually sit down together. The thuggery and crime attendant on years of terrorist activity has not yet disappeared. Yet because of the agreement hundreds of people who would have died had the 'troubles' continued, are alive and living peaceful lives. Investment has returned. Belfast is a transformed, cleaner, busier, more confident city. Large businesses increasingly work on an all-Ireland basis, despite the existence of two currencies and a border. Tony Blair can take a sizeable slice of the credit. As one of his biographers wrote: 'He was exploring his own ability to take a deep-seated problem and deal with it. It was a life-changing experience for him.'[9]

The Tartan Pizza

If the Good Friday Agreement changed the UK, Scottish and Welsh devolution plans changed Britain. Through the Tory years, the case for a Scottish parliament had been bubbling north of the border. Margaret Thatcher was seen as a conspicuously English figure imposing harsh economic penalties on Scotland, which considered itself inherently more egalitarian and democratic. This did not stop Scots buying their council houses (when she came to power the proportion of people living in state housing was higher than in many Eastern European countries under Communism), nor did they send back their tax cuts or fail to use the new legislation to choose which schools their children went to. But Scotland did have a public culture further to the left than that of southern England and the real action came from the respectable middle classes. A group of pro-devolution activists, including SNP, Labour and Liberal people, churchmen, former civil servants and trade unionists formed the Campaign for a Scottish Assembly. In due course this produced a 'Constitutional Convention' meant to bring in a wider cross-section of Scottish life behind their Claim of Right. It argued that if the Scots were to stand on their own two feet as Mrs Thatcher insisted, they needed control over their own affairs.

Momentum increased when the Scottish Tories lost half their remaining seats in the 1987 election, and when the poll tax was introduced there first to stave off a rebellion among homeowners about higher-rates bills. Over the next three years a staggering 2.5 million summary warrants for non-payment of the poll tax were issued in Scotland, a country of some five million people. The Constitutional Convention got going in March 1989, after Donald Dewar, Labour's leader in Scotland, decided to work with other parties. The Convention brought together the vast majority of Scottish MPs, all but two of Scotland's regional, district and island councils, the trade unions, churches, charities and many more – almost everyone indeed except the Conservatives, who were sticking with the original Union, and the SNP, who wanted full independence. Great marches were held. The newspapers became highly excited. A detailed blueprint was produced for the first Scottish parliament since 1707, very like the one later established.

Scottish Tories, finding themselves increasingly isolated, fought back vainly. They argued that 'Thatcherism' bore a close family resemblance to many of the ideas of the Scottish Enlightenment. Was not Scotland's time of greatness based on thrift, hard work and enterprise? One of the cradles of Thatcherism more recently had been in Scotland, at St Andrews University. They pointed out that if a Tory government, based on English votes, was regarded as illegitimate by the Scots, then in future a Labour government based on Scottish constituencies might be regarded as illegitimate by the English. In the 1992 election, John Major made a passionate plea for the survival of the Union. Had the four countries never come together, their joint history would have never been as great: 'are we, in our generation, to throw all that away?'. He won back a single Scottish seat. Various minor sops were offered to the Scots in his years, including the return of the Stone of Destiny, with much ceremony. In 1997, the party, which had once had a majority of seats in Scotland, had not a single one left.

So by the time Tony Blair became leader, Labour's commitment to devolution was long-standing. Unlike most of Labour's commitments this was not a manifesto promise by a single party. It had been agreed away from Westminster, outside the New Labour hub, with a host of other bodies. John Smith, whose funeral in Scotland was a great gathering of the country's establishment, united in grief, had been a particularly passionate supporter. Dewar, now in charge of the project, was Smith's great friend. Blair could not simply tear this up. He was not much interested in devolution or impressed by it, particularly not for Wales, where support had been far more muted. The only thing he could do was to insist that the Scottish Parliament and Welsh assembly would only happen after referendums in the two countries, which in Scotland's case would include a second question as to whether the parliament should be allowed the power to vary the rate of income tax by 3p in the pound. This proved to be a great service to devolution, because it entrenched the legitimacy of the parliament. In September 1997, shortly after the death of Diana, which interrupted campaigning, Scotland voted by three to one for the new Parliament, and by 63.5 per cent to 36.5 per cent to give it tax-raising powers. The vote for the Welsh assembly was far closer, indeed water thin. The Edinburgh parliament would have clearly defined authority over a wide spread of public life – education, health, welfare, local government, transport, housing – while Westminster kept taxation, defence, foreign affairs and some lesser issues. Wales's assembly had fewer powers, and no tax-raising rights. Only six Labour MPs said they would leave London and make a career in politics at home.

In 1999, after nearly 300 years, Scotland got her parliament with 129 MSPs, and Wales her assembly, with sixty members. Both were elected by proportional representation, making coalition governments almost inevitable. In Scotland, Labour provided the first 'first minister' ('prime minister' being considered too provocative a title). He was Donald Dewar, a lanky, pessimistic and much-loved intellectual who looked a little like a dyspeptic heron. He took charge of a small pond of Labour and Liberal Democrat ministers. To start with, Scotland was governed from the Church of Scotland's general assembly buildings, the forbidding gothic affair in Edinburgh. Later it would move to a new building by a Catalan architect, Enrico Miralles, who died of a heart attack at an early stage. A brewery opposite the Palace of Holyroodhouse was demolished and the complex new structure, with a roof meant to look like overturned fishing boats, was finally ready for use in 2004. It is architecturally impressive with a lightness and openness millions of miles removed from Westminster, but it was originally budgeted to cost £55 million and ended up costing £470 million, producing a vitriolic public argument in Scotland about wasted money. Dewar never lived to see it opened, collapsing and dying from a brain haemorrhage in 2000. Wales got her new assembly building, by Richard Rogers, in Cardiff Bay, in 2006 with much less controversy.

Few predictions about the Scottish Parliament proved right. It was said that it would cause an early crisis at Westminster because of the unfairness of Scottish MPs being able to vote on England-only business, particularly when the cabinet was so dominated by Scots. This did not happen, though it may yet. It was said that home rule would put paid to the Scottish National Party. Under Alex Salmond, their pugnacious leader, they were by 2007 so popular they were ousting Labour from its old Scottish hegemony. It was assumed that the Scottish Parliament would be popular in Scotland. A long and tawdry series of minor scandals, plus the cost of the building, meant that it became a butt of ridicule instead. This too may change, as Scots experience new laws it has passed. Among the policies the Edinburgh parliament has implemented are more generous provision for older people; no up-front top-up fees for students from Scotland, though English students at Scottish universities must pay; new property laws to allow Highland communities to compulsorily purchase the land they occupy; and a ban on smoking in public places. In all these Scotland has reinforced her reputation for being to the left of England, though extra taxes have not yet been levied on the Scots.

The most striking change, however, has been how quickly Scottish public life has diverged from that of the rest of Britain since the parliament was established. Scotland always had a separate legal system, schools, newspapers and football leagues. Now she had separate politics too, with her own controversies and personalities, a news agenda increasingly different from that of England. This part of post-war Britain's story is still developing. Like England's, Scotland's economy has moved steadily towards services and away from manufacturing. After many years of decline, Scotland's population has begun to rise gently since 2003, with net immigration from the rest of the UK. When large numbers of asylum seekers began arriving in Britain those who were sent to Scotland found that the Scots were considerably less welcoming than their piously democratic self-image suggested they would be. And anti-English feeling was not much quietened by home rule.

Wales too has her own politics, but feels not radically different, a change of emphasis, not direction. Scotland feels more like a different country, and London now seems a lot more than 400 miles from Edinburgh. By the winter of 2006–7 some polls showed more than half of Scots prepared to vote for independence. This may be a blip, a reaction to an unpopular government in London. There had been earlier warnings of a coming break-up of Britain, a great topic of debate from the late sixties, when the oil was discovered, right through to the final years of John Major's administration in the mid-nineties. It may be that a slow, soft separation is now taking place instead. There has been no constitutional chopper coming down to separate Scotland and England. It is more like two pieces of pizza being gently pulled apart, still together but now connected only by strings of molten cheese.

The Dawning of a New Era?

Margaret Thatcher had been a celebrity strictly on her own terms, never big on forgiveness or peace-making but always understanding the importance of optimism. Blair was learning from her. He quickly invited her back to see him in Downing Street and during his first years in office showed that he had picked up some of her bad traits too. She was unreasonably suspicious of the civil service. So was he. She was unimpressed by her first cabinet. He felt the same about his. Like her, when it might have voted him down on a pet idea, he simply went round it. Like her, he toyed with and then discarded the ideologies of intellectuals as he saw fit. With Thatcher it was the radicals of the new right, urging her to sell off hospitals or motorways. With Blair, it was the more gentle spirits urging him to adopt 'stakeholding' or 'communitarianism,' novel ways of reordering or taming capitalism. For their authors these were new political philosophies, for New Labour, briefly useful fads. Blair was no more of an intellectual than she was. He shared middle-class instincts, just like her. She took to praising him, if in qualified terms. They were really quite similar. Yet when Thatcher became Prime Minister she had years of Whitehall experience. Blair had none. She may not have enjoyed the boozy male clubbiness of Parliament but she respected the institution. Blair gave every sign of disliking the place intensely.

But the biggest difference between the two was Blair's obsession with journalism. Thatcher did her best to cope with the media, a little flattery here, a blunderbuss-blast from Bernard Ingham there. Blair during his first years in power was a fully engaged media politician. She sailed on the stuff, he swam in it. She knew who her press enemies were, and who were her friends, and more or less kept both throughout. Blair tried to make everyone his friend, and would lose almost all of them. Campbell was more powerful in the Blair court than Ingham had been in the Thatcher one. Again it was a generational thing: she had come into politics when newspapers were comparatively deferential and it was beneath a rising minister to court journalists. Blair learned the dangers fo schmoozing media people, but slowly. More a problem of his early years, his relationship with the press and his misused press briefings hurt him and his reputation badly.

One example of how, came in the debate over British membership of the euro, the single currency finally taking shape at the beginning of 1999. Though never a fanatic on the subject, Blair's pro-European instincts and his desire to be the lead figure inside the EU predisposed him to announce that Britain would join – not in the first wave, perhaps, but soon afterwards. He briefed that this would happen. British business seemed generally in favour. But, as the former Liberal Democrat leader Paddy Ashdown revealed in his diaries, Blair had a problem. According to Ashdown, Roy Jenkins told Blair in the autumn of 1997: 'I will be very blunt about this. You have to choose between leading in Europe or having Murdoch on your side. You can have one but not both.' Ouch. Pro-euro journalists went to see him and came away thinking he was on their side. Anti-euro journalists had the same experience. He had a pro-euro adviser, Roger Liddle. But he also had an anti-euro adviser, Derek Scott. The briefing and guesswork in the press was completely baffling. Lord Simon, the former BP boss now in government working on euro matters, held up a wodge of papers at one evening speech, announcing that they represented the speech about the euro that had been written for him, before putting it down and confessing that he would not bother to read it; it had been completed an hour before so the policy had probably changed. It was a joke, but meant to sting.

Gordon Brown, who had been generally in favour of the euro, munched his way through Treasury reports. For him, stability came first. He concluded that it was not likely Britain could safely enter in the first Parliament. He warned Blair. The two argued. Eventually they agreed a fudge. Britain would probably stay out during the 1997 Parliament but the door should be left slightly ajar. Pro-European business people and those Tories who had lent Blair and Brown conditional support, as well as Blair's continental partners, should be kept on board. So should the anti-euro press. The terms of the delicate compromise were meant to be revealed in an interview given by Brown to *The Times*. Being more hostile to entry than Blair, and talking to an anti-euro paper, his team briefed more strongly than Blair would have liked. By the time the story was written, the pound had been saved from extinction for the lifetime of the Parliament. When Blair discovered this he was aghast and began to phone desperately around until he reached Brown's press officer, the affable Charlie Whelan (a man Blair detested and had tried vainly to have sacked earlier in the year). Whelan was in the Red Lion public house in Whitehall and cheerfully confirmed to the Prime Minister on his mobile phone that his government's policy was indeed that Britain would not enter during the lifetime of the Parliament. As Whelan put it later, 'he was completely gobsmacked'. Blair told him to 'row back'. Whelan replied it was too late.

The chaos surrounding such an important matter was ended and patched up by Brown as he and his adviser Ed Balls quickly produced five economic tests which would be applied before Britain entered the euro. They required more detailed work by the Treasury; the underlying point was that the British and continental economies must be properly aligned first. Brown then told the Commons that though it was likely for economic reasons Britain would wait until after the next election, there was no constitutional or political reason not to join. Preparations for British entry would begin. It all gave the impression, not least to Blair, that once the tests were met there would be a post-election referendum, followed by the demise of sterling. In 1999, with tantantaras and a full-scale public launch at a London cinema, Blair was joined by the Liberal Democrat leader Charles Kennedy and the two former Tory cabinet ministers Ken Clarke and Michael Heseltine to launch 'Britain in Europe'. This was to be a counterblast to the anti-euro campaign, 'Business for Sterling'. Blair promised that together they would demolish the arguments against the euro, and there was alarmist coverage about the loss of 8 million jobs if Britain pulled out of the EU.

But this expensive, brightly coloured and crowded bandwagon was going nowhere at all. The real significance of the Red Lion kerfuffle was that the power to decide over membership of the euro passed decisively and for ever from Blair in Downing Street to Brown, whose Treasury fortress became the guardian of the economic tests. Brown would keep Britain out, something which won him great personal credit among Conservative press barons. There would be no referendum in the Blair years, however much the Prime Minister fretted. During his second administration, according to the former cabinet minister Clare Short, Blair offered Brown an astonishing deal: he would leave Number Ten soon if Brown would 'deliver' the euro. Brown brusquely rejected the offer, telling Short that he didn't make policy that way and in any case, could not trust Blair to keep his side of a bargain.

But other historic changes went ahead. Both devolution and the Irish peace process reshaped the country and produced clear results. So did other constitutional initiatives, such as the expulsion of most hereditary peers from the Lords, ending its huge inbuilt Conservative majority, and the incorporation of the European human rights convention into British law, allowing cases to come to court here. Neither produced the outcomes ministers expected. The Lords became more assertive and more of a problem for Blair, not less of one. British judges' interpretation of the human rights of asylum seekers and suspected terrorists caused much anguish to successive home secretaries; and the 'human rights culture' was widely criticized by newspapers. But at least, in each case, serious shifts in the balance of power were made, changes intended to make Britain fairer and more open.

Other early initiatives would crumble to dust and ashes. One of the most interesting examples is the Dome, centrepiece of millennium celebrations inherited from the Conservatives. Blair was initially unsure about whether to forge ahead with the £1 bn gamble. He was argued into the Dome project by Peter Mandelson who wanted to be its impresario, and by John Prescott, who liked the new money it would bring to a blighted part of east London. Prescott suggested New Labour wouldn't be much of a government if it could not make a success of this. Blair agreed, though had the Dome ever come to a cabinet vote he would have lost. Architecturally the Dome was striking and elegant, a landmark for London which can be seen by almost every air passenger arriving in the capital. Public money was spent on cleaning up a poisoned semicircle of derelict land and bringing new Tube and road links. The millennium was certainly worth celebrating. But the problem ministers and their advisers could not solve was what their pleasure Dome should contain. Should it be for a great national party? Should it be educational? Beautiful? Thought-provoking? A fun park? Nobody could decide. The instinct of the British towards satire was irresistible as the project continued surrounded by cranes and political hullabaloo. The Dome would be magnificent, unique, a tribute to daring and can-do. Blair himself said it would provide the first paragraph of his next election manifesto.

A well-funded, self-confident management was put in place but the bright child's question – yes, but what's it for? – would not go away. When the Dome finally opened, at New Year, the Queen, Prime Minister and hundreds of donors, business people and celebrities were treated to a mishmash of a show which embarrassed many of them. Bad organization meant most of the guests had a long, freezing and damp wait to get in for the celebrations. Xanadu this was not. The fiasco meant the Dome was roasted in most newspapers and when it opened to the public, the range of mildly interesting exhibits was greeted as a huge disappointment. Far fewer people came and bought tickets than was hoped. It turned out to be a theme park without a theme, morphing in the public imagination into the earliest and most damaging symbol of what was wrong with New Labour: an impressively constructed big tent containing not very much at all. It was produced by some of the people closest to the Prime Minister and therefore boomeranged particularly badly on him and the group already known as 'Tony's cronies'. Optimism and daring, it seemed, were not enough.

Squeeze, Relax: New Labour Economics

The events described so far were all, in different ways, secondary to the transformation of Britain that Blair had promised. Northern Ireland was a crisis needing solving. Scotland and Wales were inherited commitments which did not engage much of the Prime Minister's time, nor any of his passion. The Dome was also inherited, a sally of optimism and opportunism which went terribly wrong. The death of Diana was one of Macmillan's 'events', brilliantly handled. But none of this was what New Labour was really about. Its intended purpose was a more secure economy, radically better public services and a new deal for the people at the bottom. And much of this was in the lap not of Tony Blair, but of Gordon Brown. The saturnine Chancellor would become a controversial figure later in the government too but his early months in the Treasury were rumbustious, as he overruled mandarins and imposed a new way of governing. Like Blair, Brown had no experience of government and, like Blair, he had run his life in Opposition with a tight team of his own, dominated by his economic adviser (later an MP and Treasury minister) Ed Balls. Relations between Team Brown and the Treasury officials began badly and stayed frosty for a long time, rather as other civil service bosses resented the arrival of the rule of special advisers at Number Ten.

Brown's handing of interest rate control to the Bank of England was a theatrical coup, planned secretly in Opposition and unleashed to widespread astonishment immediately New Labour won. Other countries, including Germany and the United States, had long run monetary policy independently of politicians, but this was an unexpected step for a left-of-centre British Chancellor. It turned out to be particularly helpful to Labour ministers since it removed at a stroke the old suspicion that they would favour high employment over low inflation. It reassured the money markets that Brown would not (because he could not) debauch the currency. In a curious way this gave him more freedom to tax and spend. As one of Brown's biographers put it, he 'could only give expression to his socialist instincts after playing the role of uber-guardian of the capitalist system'.[10] The Bank move has gone down as one of the clearest achievements of the New Labour era – tellingly, like the devolution referendums, actions taken immediately after winning power. Brown also stripped the Bank of England of its old job of overseeing the rest of the banking sector. If it was worried about the health of commercial banks but also in sole charge of interest rates, the two functions might conflict. His speed in doing so infuriated the Bank's governor Eddie George who came close to resigning and so spoiling Brown's early period as Chancellor.

Labour won an early reputation for being economically trust-worthy. Brown was the granite-and-iron Chancellor. Then a bachelor, his only mistress was the pinched-cheeked, pursed-mouthed Prudence. Income tax rates did not move. The middle classes could relax and feel free to vote Labour a second time, as they duly did in their droves in 2001. Even when Brown found money growing on trees he did not spend it. In 2000, at the most iridescent swollen glossiness of the dotcom bubble, when Britain was erupting with childlike candy-coloured names for companies promising magical profits, when anyone would pay anything for anything allegedly digital, Brown sold off licences for the next generation of mobile phones for £22.5 bn, vastly more than they were soon worth. The fruit went not into new public spending but into repaying the public debt, £37 bn of it. By 2002 government interest payments as a proportion of its income, were the lowest since 1914. Brown's stock soared.

Another consequence of the early squeeze was more immediately controversial. What became known as 'stealth taxes', like the stealth bomber itself, made a lot of noise and did not always hit the targeted area. Stealth taxes included the freezing of income tax thresholds, so an extra 1.5 million people found themselves paying the top rate; the freezing of personal allowances; rises in stamp duty on houses and a hike in national insurance (both of which provided huge new tax streams in the Labour years); the palming off of costs onto council tax, which rose sharply; and most famously the removal of tax credits for share dividends in 1997. This was sold at the time as a sensible technical reform, removing distortions and encouraging companies to reinvest in their core businesses. In fact it had a devastating effect on the portfolios of pension funds.

By 2006, according to a paper for the Institute of Actuaries, this measure was responsible for cutting the value of retirement pensions by £100 bn, a staggering sum, more than twice as much as the combined pension deficits of Britain's top 350 companies. Pensioners and older workers facing great holes in their pension funds were outraged. What is more, Treasury papers released in 2007 showed that Brown was given ample warning of the effect. The destruction of a once proud pension industry is a more complicated story than the simple 'blame Brown' charge. The actuarial industry, rule changes in pensions during the Major years, a court ruling about guaranteed pay-outs and Britain's fast-ageing population are also part of the tale. But the pension fund hit produced more anger, directed personally against Brown, than any other single act in his time as Chancellor.

Longer term, perhaps the most striking aspect of Brown's running of the economy was the stark, dramatic shape of public spending. For his first two years he stuck fiercely to the promise he had made about continuing Conservative spending levels. These were so tight that even the former Chancellor Ken Clarke said he would not have actually kept to them had he been re-elected. But Brown brought down the State's share of public spending from nearly 41 per cent of gross domestic product to 37.4 per cent by 1999–2000, the lowest percentage since 1960 and far below anything achieved under Thatcher. He was doing the opposite of what earlier Labour chancellors had done. They had arrived in office, immediately started spending, and then had to stop and raise taxes later on. He began as Scrooge and quietly fattened up for Santa. Then there was an abrupt and dramatic shift and public spending soared, particularly on health, back up to 43 per cent. So there were the lean years followed by the fat years, famine then feast, squeeze then relax.

Prudence was a stern mistress. The first consequence of her reign was that the 1997–2001 Labour government achieved far less in public services than it had promised. During the 2001 election Blair was confronted outside a Birmingham hospital when a postmistress called Sharon Storer exploded with rage at him over the poor care being given to her partner who had cancer. Vainly he tried to stem the flow and usher her away from microphones and cameras. New Labour's choreography was usually slick but for once Blair was pinned down and harangued by someone who was no longer prepared to hear his excuses. John Prescott had promised a vast boost in public transport, telling the Commons in 1997, 'I will have failed if in five years' time there are not many more people using public transport and far fewer journeys by car. It's a tall order but I urge you to hold me to it.' Because of Prudence, and Blair's worries about being seen as anti-car, Prescott had nothing like the investment to follow through and failed completely. Prudence meant that Brown ploughed ahead with cuts in benefit for lone-parent families, angering Labour MPs and resulting in a Scottish Labour conference vote which called them 'economically inept, morally repugnant and spiritually bereft'.

Reform costs money, and without money it barely happened in the first term, except in isolated areas where Blair or Brown put their heads down and concentrated. The most dramatic programme was in raising literacy and numeracy among younger children, where Number Ten worked closely with the Education Secretary, David Blunkett, and scored real successes. But unequivocally successful public service reforms were rare. And the real drawback of the squeeze-then-relax Brown guide to fiscal fitness was that he did not entirely conform to it himself. Some new money had to be raised and it was.

One curious thing a time-traveller from the seventies might notice in the Britain of the early twenty-first century would be unfamiliar uniforms and symbols in public offices, by roadsides, in hospitals and outside schools. The men and women on security duty in the Treasury in not-quite-official caps and jackets, the badges on construction workers' jackets and helmets, the little logos of jumping manikins, bright flowers, bean-like blobs, and the new names, Carillion, Vinci or Serco, were all visual hints about the greatest change in how government was working. The name for it, public finance initiative, or PFI, was dull. Yet the change was big enough to arouse worry even outside the small tribes of political obsessives. The underlying idea was simple. It had started life under Norman Lamont, five years before Labour came to power, when he experimented with privatizing public projects and allowing private companies to run them, keeping the revenue. A group led by the Bank of America built and ran a new bridge connecting the Isle of Skye to the mainland. There were outraged protests from some islanders about paying tolls to a private consortium and eventually the Scottish Executive bought the bridge back. At the opposite corner of the country, another bridge was built joining Kent and Essex across the Thames at Dartford, the first bridge across the river in a new place for more than half a century; it was run by a company called Le Crossing and successfully took tolls from motorists.

To start with Labour hated this idea. PFIs were a mix of two things, the privatization of capital projects, with government paying a fee over many years; and the contracting-out of services – waste-collection, school meals, cleaning – to private companies, which had been imposed on unwilling socialist councils from the eighties. Once in power, Labour ministers began to realize that those three little letters were political magic. For the other thing about PFI is that it allows today's ministers to announce and oversee exciting new projects, and take the credit for them, while the full bill is left for taxpayers twenty or fifty years in the future. Today's spending on schools or hospitals is a problem that will eventually land on the desk of an education minister who is presently still at primary school, or a Chancellor who has not yet arrived at the maternity unit. This was government on tick. It was invented in Britain. And for better or worse, it is now spreading round the world. PFIs were particularly attractive when so many other kinds of spending were so tightly controlled by Prudence. At the same time large swathes of money for new schools, hospitals, prisons and the like were declared to be investment, not spending, and put to one side of the national accounts. Was this clever, or merely clever-clever? The justification was that private companies would build things and run them so much more efficiently than the State, that profits paid to them by taxpayers would be more than compensated for.

There is no doubt that sometimes this has been so, but assertions tail off into guesswork because they depend on misty unknowables – how well a modern civil service might have run such projects itself, whether the contract was drawn up tightly enough to fully protect the taxpayer, and so on. Committees of MPs certainly thought they had found incompetence and inefficiency in PFI deals. Ministers, pressed against a wall, tended to reply that since without PFIs Britain would not have got the shiny new school buildings or health centres that were so desperately needed by the late nineties, it was by definition a good thing. It was certainly a big thing. By the end of 2006 a total of £53 bn of such contracts had been signed, with another £28 bn in the pipeline, for fire stations, army barracks, helicopter training schools, psychiatric units, prisons, roads, bridges, government offices, computer programmes, immigration systems, as well as hundreds of schools and hospitals. The biggest was for the modernization of the London Underground, hugely expensive in legal fees and hugely complex in contracts. Tellingly, the peak year for PFIs was 2000, just as the early Treasury stringency on conventional spending had bitten most.

The cost of the forward contracts for running these places, sometimes half a century ahead, is hard to estimate but there is certainly over £100 bn of rent due to be paid by tomorrow's taxpayers. In the private sector lawyers, company managers and accountants began to specialize in PFIs. A whole new business sector arose. In the public sector civil servants struggled to grapple with the new skills they would need to negotiate with unfamiliar private sector partners. There is an obvious problem about defining the real risk of these projects. If a firm is commissioned to build a prized new hospital at a certain budget and falls behind, to the point where failure looms unless the taxpayer intervenes again, is it likely the hospital will simply be abandoned? Risk is a routine business idea but means something else in politics. How do you blend the culture of ministerial promises and that of construction and IT firms? Yet another white-collar industry arose to try. And by the mid-2000s the number of PFI contracts being sold on from one company to another, a booming secondary market in subcontracted government, was well over four-fifths of the total. How to keep a grip on sold on PFIs? Another mini-profession popped up to try that, too. All of it, of course, paid for by the taxpayer.

Yet, PFIs did not make quite the noise one might have expected. Most politicians from most parties reflected that one day, they too might find them useful.

The Moment of Truth

So when did Brown's great shift in policy happen? When did straightforward, on-balance-sheet, old-fashioned public spending, financed by old-fashioned taxes, return to the political agenda? And why did the great romance between Gordon and Prudence end? It occurred, appropriately, just as Brown's real-life romance with Sarah Macaulay, a very bright public relations businesswoman, was becoming public. They would marry in August 2000, six months after Prudence had been told to make other arrangements. And despite Sharon Storer's disappointment the following year, it was indeed the National Health Service which triggered the change of pace. In its first election manifesto New Labour promised to 'safeguard the basic principles of the NHS, which we founded'. It protested that under the Tories there had been 50,000 fewer nurses but a rise of no fewer than 20,000 managers – red tape which Labour would pull away and burn. Though critical of the Tory internal market, Blair promised to keep a split between those who commissioned health and those who provided it. The overall message was less fiddling and a bit more money.

Under Frank Dobson, Labour's new Health Secretary, a staunch traditionalist and the man with the filthiest sense of humour in British politics, this is what happened. There was little reform but there was, year by year, just enough extra money to buy off the winter crises. But then a quite different crisis hit the headlines. As often happens, it began with individual human stories which rapidly came together and expanded toward a general truth. First there was a particularly awful case of an old lady whose cancer was made inoperable after repeated delays. Then came a furious denunciation of his elderly mother's treatment by Professor Robert Winston, the Labour peer and fertility expert much admired by Blair. Winston said that Britain's health service was much the worst in Europe, was getting worse still, and that the government had been deceitful about the true picture. This set off something close to panic in Whitehall not only because Winston was about the most authentic witness anyone could imagine but also because he was, in general terms, right. And Labour's polling showed the country knew it. So after a difficult haggle with Brown, Blair declared on Sir David Frost's Sunday morning television show in January 2000 that the NHS badly needed more money and he would bring Britain's health spending up to the European average within five years.

That was a huge promise, a third as much again in real terms (close to what actually happened). Gordon Brown was unhappy. He thought that Blair had pre-empted his decision, had not spoken to Frost enough about the need for health service reform to accompany the money, and according to Downing Street rumour, had 'stolen my bloody budget'. Brown made up for this on the day itself when he promised that from then until 2004 health spending would rise at above 6 per cent beyond inflation every year, 'by far the largest sustained increase in NHS funding in any period in its fifty-year history' and 'half as much again for health care for every family in this country'. The tilt away from tight spending controls and towards expansion had started. There was more to come. With an election looming in 2001, Brown also announced a review into the NHS and its future by a former banker called Derek Wanless.

As soon as the election was over, broad hints about necessary tax rises began to be dropped. When Wanless finally reported, he confirmed much that the winter crisis of nearly two years earlier had shown. The NHS was not, whatever Britons fondly believed, as good as health systems in other similar countries, and it needed a lot more money. Wanless also rejected a radical change in funding, such as a move to insurance-based or semi-private health care. Brown immediately used this as objective proof that taxes had to rise to save the NHS, something Wanless felt a little uneasy about. Was he being used, in the words of one writer, as Brown's human shield? At any rate, in his next Budget of March 2002, Brown broke with a political convention which had reigned since the eighties, that direct taxes may never be put up again. He raised a special 1 per cent national insurance levy, equivalent to a penny on income tax, to fund the huge reinvestment in Britain's health.

Public spending shot up, above all on health. In some ways, it paid off. By 2006, there were around 300,000 extra NHS staff compared to 1997. That included more than 10,000 extra senior hospital doctors (about a quarter more) and 85,000 more nurses. But there were also nearly 40,000 managers, twice as many as Brown and Blair had ridiculed the Conservatives for hiring in the days when they were campaigning against red tape. An ambitious computer project for the whole NHS became an expensive catastrophe. Meanwhile, the health service budget rose from £37 bn to more than £92 bn a year. That vast investment produced results. Waiting lists, a source of great public anger in the mid-nineties, fell by 200,000. By 2005, Blair was able to talk of the best waiting list figures since 1988. Hardly anyone was left waiting for an inpatient treatment for more than six months. Death rates from cancer for people under the age of seventy-five fell by 15.7 per cent between 1996 and 2006 and death rates from heart disease fell by just under 36 per cent. The public finance initiative meanwhile meant that new hospitals were being built around the country.

If only that was the full story. 'Czars', quangos, agencies, commissions, access teams and planners hunched over the NHS as Whitehall, having promised to devolve power, now imposed a new round of mind-dazing control. By the autumn of 2004 hospitals were subject to an astonishing 100-plus inspection regimes. A great war broke out between Brown in the Treasury and the Blairite Health Secretary, Alan Milburn, about the basic principles of running hospitals. Milburn, backed by Blair, wanted more independence and competition. Brown asked how you could have competition when for most people there was just one big local hospital. If it lost the competition, it could hardly shut down. Polling suggested that in this Brown was making a popular point. Most people wanted better hospitals, not more choice. Blair's team responded that they would only get better hospitals if there was choice. A truce was eventually declared with the establishment of a small number only of independent, or foundation, hospitals. Britain was back to the old argument. Do you try to run everything from the centre, using targets as your flails and unelected quangos as your legionaries? Or do you mimic the private sector, allowing hospitals to rise and fall, expand and close?

By the 2005 general election, Michael Howard's Conservatives were attacking Labour for wasting money and allowing people's lives to be put at risk in dirty, badly run hospitals. Just like Labour once had, they were promising to cut bureaucracy and slash the number of organizations inside the Health Service. By the summer of 2006, despite that huge increase in money, the health service was facing a cash crisis. The amount of money involved was not large as a percentage of the total budget but trusts in some of the most vulnerable parts of the country were on the edge, from Hartlepool to Cornwall to London. Across Britain, 7,000 jobs had gone and the Royal College of Nursing was predicting 13,000 more would go soon. Many expensively qualified new doctors and specialists could not find work. After the great spending U-turn of 2000–2 and historic amounts of new money, it seemed that wage costs, pricey new drugs, poor management and the vast bureaucratic expense of endless 'reforms' had resulted in a health service which was irritating people as much as ever. Less fashionable health causes, such as mental health, felt left out and outside the NHS there was a vast growth in the reach of private insurance and private health. Bupa, the leading private operator, was covering around 2.3 million people in 1999. Six years later the figure was more than 8 million. This partly reflects greater affluence but it is not a resounding vote of confidence on the success of Labour's investment in the NHS.

A parallel story could be told about schools. Here too traditional socialists wanted a single system for every child, comprehensive across the country, and run directly from Whitehall (except, of course, in now-devolved Scotland and Wales). Those dangerously semi-independent institutions, the Tories' grant-maintained schools, though there were few enough of them, were abolished. In education the government did everything that enthusiasm, hard work and determination could, to improve things from Whitehall. First under David Blunkett, and then his successors, a stream of plans on every aspect of school life poured out of the department. By 2001, in a single year, 3,840 pages of instructions were being sent to schools. One headteacher settled down and counted 525 separate targets for his school. This, literal, wheelbarrow-load of paperwork no more transformed the schools than the revised NHS bureaucracy was transforming hospitals. Blair tried a new tack and returned to the idea of semi-independent schools. There were already 'specialist schools' in the state sector with say over their admissions but this was to be at a different level. Businesses, faith groups and rich local businessmen would endow part of the cost and be allowed some involvement in their 'ethos'. As with hospitals, there was great Labour resistance. Did this not mean a possible return to some kind of selection? Another great battle began and, under pressure from Labour MPs, it was written into law that such schools could not select by academic ability. Links with local education authorities were also to be kept.

Yet it seemed possible in the early years of the new century that Britain was moving back towards an educational model half remembered from long ago. Schools were being sponsored by evangelical Christians, computer companies or firms of accountants. Was this so different from the ancient schools set up by local worthies, livery companies and religious orders? Some even favoured a teaching of life's origins which edged Darwin aside in favour of the Bible. There was a great growth too in Muslim schools, closed to faithless outsiders.

The government tried to make faith schools open up a little to people from other communities but were forced to pull back. For some this was a betrayal of the idea of one nation implicit in comprehensives, a retreat to ghetto schooling. Others asked, if locally elected councillors oversaw such independent schools, and if they were restrained from being too aggressive in ramming doctrines down young throats, was that such a bad thing? Polls suggested parents were less worried about structures than lax discipline and too-easy exams. Such schools are certainly a decisive break from the direction of education in the sixties and seventies, and far nearer the dreams of Thatcher and her Conservative successors. As in health, private schools boomed.

As the public spending had begun to flow during the second Blair administration, vast amounts of money had gone in pay rises, new bureaucracies and on bills for outside consultants. Ministries had been unused to spending again, and did not always do it well. There were other unfortunate consequences. Brown and his team resorted to double and triple counting early spending increases to give the impression they were doing more for hospitals, schools and transport than they actually could. They were, rightly, roasted for it.

A fascinating insight into the problems faced by the Blair government in public service reform came in 2005 when a former spin doctor published a book. Peter Hyman, a young, serious-minded man, had worked for Tony Blair since he became leader, rising to head the Number Ten strategic communications unit. He wrote speeches, spun for him, argued with him and saw the power game at its highest, most exhilarating level. In 2003, after sweating hard at Blair's conference speech, he decided it was time to make the favoured buzzword 'renewal' personal. He resigned and became a teacher at a tough inner London comprehensive school, Islington Green. His book about the reality-jolt this produced remains one of the best texts on modern British politics available. Late on, he is arguing with a pupil about why when the Prime Minister says something, it does not just happen: 'I look him in the eye and say, "When Tony promises to deliver on education what needs to happen is that you pass your exams. How can he guarantee that? You may not even turn up for them."' Hyman reflects that his old way of doing politics, dealing frantically with 24-hour media, is useless for delivering a better school. Instead of conflict and novelty, consistency is needed; not battles but partnership. 'Now, looking through the other end of the telescope I see how unequal is the relationship between politicians and the people . . . Those at the centre relish ideas and, in the main, are bored by practicalities. Those who suggest better ways of making policy work are too often dismissed as whingers . . . Why can't politicians acknowledge that those on the front line might know more?'[11]

It is a good question. In trying to achieve better policing, more effective planning, healthier school food, prettier town centres and a hundred other hopes, the centre of government ordered and cajoled, hassled and harangued, always high-minded, always speaking for 'the people'. The railways, after yet another disaster, were shaken up again. In very controversial circumstances Railtrack, the once profitable monopoly company operating the lines, was driven to bankruptcy and a new system of detailed Whitehall control was imposed. At one point Tony Blair boasted of having 500 targets for the public sector, and later his deputy had found five times that number for local government and transport alone.[12] Parish councils, small businesses and charities found they were loaded with directives — not as many as schools or hospitals, but always more, interfering with much of what they wanted to do. The interference was always well meant but it clogged up the arteries of free decision-taking and frustrated responsible public life. Blair famously complained, early in his time as Prime Minister, that he had 'scars on my back' from trying to get reform in the public sector. Perhaps with a little less auto-flagellation and a little more conversation, both he and the country would have been happier.

Rebel British

Meanwhile the British people, the end-point of this frantic activity, proved as unpredictably stroppy as they always had been. In general, it was moral and cultural protest that took the place of the economic controversies of earlier decades. Through most of the Blair years the fox-hunting struggle engorged month after month of parliamentary time and unbelievable amounts of political energy. Polling suggested the country cared almost as little about it as the Prime Minister – plenty of people had views, but few held them strongly. Behind this, though, was the determination of animal rights activists to get something out of an avowedly radical government, while the Countryside Alliance (which expanded its campaigning to include fishing, organic food and much else) represented a feeling that part of the historic nation was being ignored, that there were people of all classes who did not fit into the New Labour world-view.

Fox hunting was a country pursuit since medieval times; the poem *Sir Gawain and the Green Knight* contains a description from around the year 1370 which is recognizable in its essentials today. By the 1670s, its rituals, red coats, language and literature were a part of British culture known around the world. Only a part, however: hunting always had its detractors. In the eighteenth century, the fox-hunting Tory squire, red-faced and stupid, was a staple of urban Whig propaganda. (The hunting nickname for the fox, Charlie, refers to the great Whig radical Charles James Fox.) Towards the end of the nineteenth century, the thunderous passage of whooping huntsmen became an emblem among radicals of oppressive aristocracy riding roughshod over the people. In Oscar Wilde's phrase they were 'the unspeakable in full pursuit of the uneatable'. Little followed from this until the arrival in the middle of the twentieth century of a militant animal rights movement, determined to frustrate hunting by using scent sprays, horns and human barriers. The first example of saboteurs at work seems to have been in August 1958 when members of the League Against Cruel Sports (which had been founded much earlier, in 1927) used chemicals to try to disrupt the Devon and Somerset Staghounds. Direct action like this began to be used against fox hunters too, with the North Warwickshire and the Old Berkeley at Amersham confronted in 1962–3. In December 1963 the Hunt Saboteurs Association was formed by a young journalist in Brixham, Devon, and the practice quickly spread.

Confrontations between hunt supporters and 'Sabs', often violent with the police in full pursuit, became a regular feature of country life from then on. Sabs would compare themselves to the hunters, needing quick wits, courage and good tactics to confuse the hounds and allow the fox or stag to escape. They were accused of thuggery. They accused the hunt supporters of being brutal to them, and many bones and noses were broken in the bracken. There was a bit of class conflict and of city-against-country in it all. Over time it became clear that while the Sabs might save some foxes, they were unable to stop the hunts, so animal rights activists turned increasingly to Parliament to get it banned. Labour voters and MPs tended to be against hunting, and the party took a £100,000 donation from the animal rights lobby before the 1997 election. When New Labour won with a massive majority it was clear that a parliamentary move to ban hunting with hounds was inevitable. With so many MPs committed, it would probably become law. This directly affected the 200,000 people who were hunting regularly and with those who watched and supported them, perhaps half a million in all. A new organization, the Countryside Alliance, was formed to campaign against a ban and held its first big rally, with 120,000 people present, at Hyde Park, six weeks after the election.

From then on pro-hunting protests were continual and varied. There were marches at Labour Party conferences, in Scotland where a separate and earlier ban was being passed, outside Parliament and in many other towns throughout Britain. People had always been on the march about something, but whereas before it had been students in duffel-coats, coalminers or left-wingers in leather jackets, this time it was ruddy-faced women in tweed skirts, farm-workers and former public schoolboys – Boden and Joden, Barbour and brogue. In the Blair years, the sound of hunting horns, the excited yelping of hounds and even the clatter of hooves became part of the backdrop of parliamentary life. After a noisy march in Bournemouth, Blair himself joined in the argument, telling his conference in 1999 that he would sweep away the 'forces of conservatism' and branding the Conservatives 'the party of fox hunting, Pinochet and hereditary peers – the uneatable, the unspeakable and the unelectable'.

This was a rare and quickly regretted Blair incursion into the language of leftism. He never much cared about hunting one way or another, and wished the issue would vanish. It did not. John Prescott, more of a class warrior than his leader, enlivened the 2001 election when a burly Countryside protester threw an egg at him during a visit to Rhyl, Wales, and was rewarded with a hefty punch. After the election Labour MPs pressed ahead while on the other side, vigils were mounted, topless women delivered petitions to Whitehall and a thousand horses rode through Leicester as part of a 'summer of discontent' in 2002. That September, the Alliance claimed more than 400,000 supporters in its biggest 'Liberty and Livelihood' protest outside the Commons, a protest which saw violent confrontations between the police and angry young men in tweed caps and waxed olive jackets.

On 18 November 2004 a law banning hunting with hounds finally passed its parliamentary hurdles. After legal challenges it became law the following February though the many loopholes, allowing riders with hounds to flush out foxes, which could then be shot, meant hunts carried on across England and Wales. The day after the ban took effect, thousands were out again and ninety-one foxes were killed. There, as in Scotland, the hunts continue and Sabs still follow with cameras, trying to find evidence of law-breaking. There have been very few prosecutions. Bloody predictions of masters of foxhounds shooting their dogs and then hanging themselves, a nightmare hanging over Labour spin-doctors for several years, were never realized. The fox hunting story can serve as a symbol for much else in the New Labour years: a long and noisy confrontation at Westminster, which in the end had surprisingly little effect on the ground.

The first intimation that protest could go further under New Labour than noisy pro-hunting demonstrations came in 2000, when a nationwide revolt by truckers against high petrol prices brought the country to a standstill. The automatic increase in fuel duty had in fact been briefly halted, but rising world oil prices and the high petrol taxes already in place meant unheard-of prices at the petrol pumps. A group of irate truckers, men who owned their own lorries, held a protest meeting in Wales and decided to mount a brief blockade of a giant oil refinery in Cheshire. They attracted widespread news coverage and an enthusiastic reaction from ordinary drivers. To begin with, Blair and his ministers concluded that it was not a serious challenge and continued with their plans. A command centre was established at Cobra, the bland meeting-room below Downing Street from where national crises are directed.

The Prime Minister himself went ahead with a tour of the English Midlands, due to end with a celebration of John Prescott's thirty years in Parliament in a Hull Chinese restaurant. On the way, officials and journalists noted V-formations of slow-moving lorries blocking motorways in other parts of the country and followed reports of petrol stations in the north of England running dry, or being besieged by queues of panicky motorists. More refineries were blockaded. Still Blair and his team insisted that nothing was really wrong and the tour would go on. He would not be diverted. By that evening, with Prescott in a Hull town hall surrounded by countryside protesters, he was getting a different message. Told that he could not be guaranteed a getaway from the splendid Chinese restaurant, he apologized to his deputy and headed for Sheffield, still insisting the show would go on. On the following morning, after overnight briefings, he gave in, turned tail and sped back to London to take charge.

Blair was generally good in a crisis and began trying to knock heads together. But this time the oil company bosses would not help him by ordering drivers of petrol tankers, who were both self-employed and sympathetic to the fuel protesters, to break through the pickets. Blair raged, threatened and begged. Now all across Britain, petrol stations ran dry. Wherever petrol remained, vast queues formed. It was all perfectly good-humoured but the crisis was spinning out of Blair's hands. Food shortages were reported. Bread was going, milk was going and the nation's egg-laying chickens were in danger. What was left of Britain's manufacturing industry was close to being forced to suspend working. Yet all tests of public opinion showed the majority of the country was with the protesters not the government. Brown repeatedly refused to pre-announce his March Budget by promising cuts in fuel taxes, in response to blackmail by two thousand to three thousand hauliers. There was private talk of bringing in the army, forcing the blockades. Panicky-sounding government papers were leaked and Blair came close to begging the protesters to stop: 'This is not on, you know. This is just not right . . .' Eventually, after health service managers had warned that people would soon die, and with even the anti-Blair press telling the protesters that enough was enough, the blockades were lifted and life returned to normal. Brown made a crabwise but generous-enough move on petrol duty in his Budget and something close to honour was restored. Yet Britain had come very close to the kind of collapse not seen since the winter of 1978–9.

The country quickly bounced back – there was no threatening undertow in the 2001 election. The combination of early Prudence and the public spending promised had played well with the electorate. John Major was succeeded as party leader by the most talented Tory of his generation, the young, bright, bald and witty Yorkshireman, William Hague. A natural Thatcherite since his schooldays and a political obsessive, he had done his best to make his leadership seem trendier and more in touch with modern Britain, donning a baseball cap and visiting the Notting Hill carnival. He was mocked for it, and learned. Hague was a man of some political experience, having been with Norman Lamont at the Treasury and later Welsh Secretary, and his greatest achievement was that he stopped a bewildered and defeated party tearing itself apart. At his best in the Commons, he had been a sparkling Opposition leader, discomfiting Blair and leading the charge on Labour 'stealth taxes', the Dome and the new issue of bogus asylum-seekers. But heavily concentrating his election campaign on saving the pound, promising voters 'we will give you back your country' and attacking the still-popular Blair as a slimy liar, he allowed New Labour to portray his party as xenophobic and nasty. By any standard, the Tory attack failed. Labour was returned with a majority of 166, having lost just six seats net, and the Conservatives, after all their energy and hard work, managed a single net gain. It was an important election because it cemented the New Labour achievement of 1997 and showed the country had moved towards Blair's agenda. Yet this general election will be remembered for one other ominous statistic too. The turnout was – just – below 60 per cent. Since Britain had first become a democracy, the public had never been less interested in voting.

Pre-Iraq Wars and Foreign Policy

The Iraq War will remain for ever the most important and controversial part of Tony Blair's legacy. But long before it, during the dog-days of the Clinton administration, two events had taken place which primed his response and explain some of what followed. The first was the bombing of Iraq by the RAF and US air force as punishment for Saddam Hussein's dodging of UN inspections. The second was the bombing of Serbia during the Kosovo crisis, and the threat of a ground force invasion. These crises made Blair believe he had to be involved personally and directly in overseas wars. They caused dark nights of self-doubt, and toughened him to criticism. They emphasized the limitations of air power and the importance to him of media management. Without them, Blair's reaction to the changing of world politics on September 11 2001 would have been different.

Evidence of Saddam Hussein's interest in weapons of mass destruc-tion was shown to Blair soon after he took office. He raised it in speeches and privately with other leaders. Most countries in Nato and at the United Nations security council were angry about the dictator's expulsion of UN inspectors when they tried to probe his huge palace compounds for biological and chemical weapons. But the initial instinct was for more diplomacy. Iraq was suffering from sanctions already; Saddam eventually allowed the inspectors back. He was playing cat and mouse, however, and in October 1998 Britain and the United States finally lost patience and decided to smash Iraq's military estab-lishment with missiles and bombing raids. In a foretaste of things to come, Blair even presented MPs with a dossier about Saddam's weapons of mass destruction. Again, at the last minute, the Iraqi leader backed down and the raids were postponed. The United States soon concluded this was another trick and, in December, British and American planes attacked, hitting 250 targets over four days. Operation Desert Fox, as they called it, probably only delayed Saddam's weapons programmes by a year or so though it was sold as a huge success. As later, Britain and the United States were operating without a fresh UN resolution. Among their publics there was a widespread suspicion that Clinton had ordered the raids to distract from his embarrassing 'Monica-gate' travails. Congress was debating impeachment proceed-ings during the attacks and did indeed formally impeach Clinton on the final day of the raids. Over this episode, however, Blair faced little trouble in Parliament or outside it.

The second bombing campaign happened as a result of the breakup of Yugoslavia in the later stages of the long Balkan tragedy that had haunted John Major's time in office. Kosovo, a province of Serbia, was dominated by Albanian-speaking Muslims but was considered almost a holy site by history-minded Serbs, who had fought a famous medieval battle there against the Ottomans. The Serbian ex-communist leader Slobodan Milosevic had made himself the hero of the minority Kosovar Serbs. The Dayton peace agreement had calmed things down in 1995 but the newly formed Kosovo Liberation Army triggered a vicious new conflict, marked by increasingly savage Serb reprisals from 1998–9. Despite the use of international monitors and a brief ceasefire violence returned with the slaughter of forty-five civilians in the town of Racak, provoking comparisons with Nazi crimes. Ethnic cleansing and the forced migration of tens of thousands of people across wintry mountain tracks produced uproar around the world. In Chicago Blair declared a new 'doctrine of the international community' which allowed 'a just war, based . . . on values'. When talks with the Yugoslavs broke down, Nato duly launched a massive bombing campaign. British and American jets attacked targets first in Kosovo and then the rest of Serbia, hitting factories, television stations, bridges, power stations, railway lines, hospitals and many government buildings.

It was, however, a complete failure. Many innocent civilians were killed and daily life was disrupted across much of Serbia and Kosovo. Sixty people were killed by an American cluster bomb in a market. An allegedly stealthy US bomber blew down half the Chinese embassy in Belgrade, causing a huge international row. Meanwhile, low cloud and the use of decoys by Milosevic's generals limited the military damage and he used the attacks to increase his ethnic cleansing massively. The death squads went back to work. Hundreds of thousands of people were on the move – eventually roughly a million ethnic Albanians fled Kosovo and an estimated 10,000–12,000 were killed. Blair began to think he might not survive as Prime Minister if nothing was done. (So Downing Street staff said at the time: if they were right, the reader will notice that Mr Blair believed he might be ousted much more often than any level-headed observer might have predicted.) The real problem was that only the genuine threat of an invasion by ground troops might convince Milosevic to pull back; air power by itself was not enough. Blair tried desperately to persuade Clinton to agree. He visited a refugee camp and angrily said: 'This is obscene. It's criminal . . . How can anyone think we shouldn't intervene?'

It would be the Americans whose troops would bear the brunt of a new war, since the European Union was far away from any coherent military structure and lacked the basic tools for carrying armies to other theatres. There was alarm in Washington about the British Prime Minister's moral posturing and it was only after many weeks of shuttle diplomacy that things began to move. Blair ordered that 50,000 British soldiers, most of the available army, should be made available to invade Kosovo. This would mean a huge call-up of reserves and if it was a bluff, was one on a massive scale, since other European countries had no intention of taking part. For whatever reason, the Americans began to toughen their language and finally, at the last minute, the

Serb parliament buckled. The Americans and Russians worked together to apply pressure and Milosevic withdrew his forces from Kosovo and accepted its virtual independence, under an international mandate. Blair declared a kind of victory. Good had triumphed over evil, civilization over barbarism. Eight months later, Milosevic was toppled from power and ended up in The Hague charged with war crimes.

First Desert Fox and then Kosovo are vital in appreciating Blair's behaviour when it came to the full-scale Iraq War. They taught him that bombing rarely works. They suggested that, threatened with ground invasion by superior forces, dictators will back down. They played to his sense of himself as a moral war leader, combating dictators as wicked in their way as Hitler; something that was underpinned by the successful, life-saving intervention in Sierra Leone in 2000. After working well with Clinton over Desert Fox, he worried that he had tried to bounce him too obviously over Kosovo. He learned that American presidents need tactful handling. He learned not to rely on Britain's European allies very much, though he pressed the case later for the establishment of a European 'rapid reaction force' to shoulder more of the burden in future wars. He learned to ignore criticism from the left and right, which became deafening during the Kosovo bombing. He learned to cope with giving orders which resulted in much loss of life. He learned an abiding hostility to the media, and in particular the BBC whose reporting of the Kosovo bombing campaign infuriated him. The Irish peace process had convinced him of his potency as a deal maker. Desert Fox, Kosovo and Sierra Leone convinced him of his ability to lead in war, to take big gambles, and to get them right.

Dubya

Most of those around the Prime Minister, certainly including his wife, had hoped that the Democrats' Al Gore would win the 2000 presidential election. Blair himself had been careful to open up early lines of communication to George W. Bush, sending diplomats to his ranch and passing a friendly message to the Texan governor via his father, ahead of the election campaign. His first phone conversation with the new President had been friendly enough but Blair was uneasy. With reason; he had enjoyed extraordinarily close relations with Clinton, an intellectual romance with the charismatic reshaper of Democratic politics which had survived their disagreements and the embarrassment of the Lewinsky affair. Bush had been elected to wipe away all that. Blair's first visit to see Bush at Camp David in February 2001 has been remembered for an uneasy photo-opportunity stroll when Blair was wearing embarrassingly tight jeans, and for Bush's awkward joke that the two of them did agree about issues – they both used the same brand of toothpaste, Colgate.

Away from the cameras, however, something more significant had happened. The two had established a relaxed private relationship which would grow into one of mutual trust, close enough to be controversial right around the world. Blair agreed to back Bush's proposed new US missile defence system, opposed by most European leaders and most Labour Party people. He would allow the upgrading of sites in Britain necessary to make it work. Bush, in turn, grudgingly agreed to support the latest British-French defence initiative to create a rapid reaction force in case of future Kosovos. More important than this bargain though, was the chemistry. Blair's aides were almost star-struck by the quality of Bush's team, particularly Condoleezza Rice, Donald Rumsfeld and Colin Powell. Blair found the new President clear, businesslike, brisk and easy to do business with – rather easier in fact than the loquacious, undisciplined Clinton. Even Cherie Blair, who had arrived on the plane still asking crossly why they had to be nice to 'these people', did her best to get on with Laura.

Those who have not met him underrate Bush's instinctive skill with people and his ability to dominate a room. Kosovo had already taught Blair the importance of sticking with the US President if he wanted to fight 'moral' conflicts. Clinton himself had told Blair to make Bush 'your best friend'. Blair decided he liked Bush (but then, did he have any choice?) and rebuked anyone from then on who described the US President as stupid or badly informed. Relations between a US President and a British Prime Minister can never be between equals, but the groundwork had been done. At the time it all seemed rather humdrum. The consequences would be awesome.

From New York to Kabul

When the al Qaeda attack on New York and Washington took place, Blair was on the point of addressing the TUC in Brighton about his public sector reforms. It seemed an important speech. Campbell had been briefing journalists that he would confront the dinosaur instincts of the unions; it would be a 'belter', and highly dramatic. Just then the 24-hour news channels, which had become a feature in every ministerial office and wherever journalists gathered, began showing repeated film of a burning building. As speculation spread about some dreadful accident involving a light plane, the second tower was hit. Blair reacted to the news like everyone else, with disbelief. He was quickly advised that this was a terrorist attack on an unprecedented scale. Whatever his failures of analysis, Blair is very fast on his feet and, as Diana's death had shown, quick to find words for moments of drama and grief. Inside the TUC there had been scenes of farce as journalists and others began taking phone calls and leaving the room. Its president rebuked them and called for order, only to find ripples of horror and speculation all round. When Blair arrived he said he was cancelling his speech, briefly described what had happened, expressed his great sympathy and support for America, and sped back to London by train with his advisers.

There, he found little preparation to defend the capital from a similar attack, which might be imminent. The airspace over London was closed, RAF jets were sent up on patrol, and the thinking began in the secure basement below Downing Street. Throughout the crisis Blair would work more closely with his military and intelligence advisers than he would with his ministers. He found he could not reach Bush by phone for more than twenty-four hours and there was a flurry of anxiety in London that the President had panicked or 'gone AWOL'. But as soon as contact was made with Bush at lunchtime on 12 September Blair was able to present not only his sympathy but also his hastily gathered briefing and thoughts about Osama bin Laden. The two resumed their mutually admiring partnership, emotionally charged by what had happened. This was a time when American flags fluttered across London, the band outside Buckingham Palace played 'The Star Spangled Banner', a carpet of flowers appeared outside the

US embassy and the Last Night of the Proms became an act of solidarity with New York. Not since 1945 had America been as popular in Britain.

By phone, Bush had promised that he was not going to act precipitously – 'pounding sand' – but told Blair he would make no distinction between the terrorists and those who harboured them. This implied first an ultimatum to the Taliban in Afghanistan and then a war. Blair agreed and made clear to the Commons soon afterwards that he believed the rules had changed, and that 'rogue states' harbouring terrorists, who might use chemical, nuclear or biological weapons, now had to choose whose side they were on. This emphatically did not mean that Iraq was to be attacked, certainly not by Number Ten's reckoning. We now know that at Camp David, four days after the September 11 attacks, Bush was advised by Donald Rumsfeld, his Defense Secretary, that he had an opportunity to attack Iraq but decided, for then, to concentrate on Afghanistan.

Nine days after the attack, in the midst of a frenzy of diplomacy, talking to the Germans, French, Chinese and Iranians, Blair went to pay tribute to the victims of what was already being called '9/11', struggling through torrential rain to the still-smoking ruins of ground zero and making an emotional cathedral oration for the British dead. In Washington afterwards, Bush told him that Iraq was for another day. Then in his speech to Congress laying out America's new 'war on terror' Bush warned that he would start with al Qaeda but not end there – another reference to Iraq. He also publicly praised Blair for showing such solidarity, turning to him theatrically, and saying: 'Thank you for coming, friend.' Congress rose to give Blair an ovation. Blair was using all his political capital, and the accumulated knowledge of the Foreign Office to help the United States, beyond the commitment of any other country and was receiving the emotional thanks of a President who now divided the rest of the world into friends and enemies. It was a high point of British prestige in America, certainly on a par with the Reagan–Thatcher age. Whether the mutual affection was truly influential is a moot point. For now, it encouraged the Americans to involve other countries in the attack on Afghanistan.

The strikes on the Taliban were launched less than a month after September 11, beginning with British submarines' cruise missiles and heavy bombing by US aircraft. Immensely destructive weaponry was dropped on al Qaeda training camps and Taliban defenders, including the notorious 'daisy-cutter' bombs. On the ground the war was conducted by the Northern Alliance and Afghan warlords, paid and supplied by the Americans and aided by Special Forces. This was a war of the twenty-first century against the nineteenth and it was over quickly, Kabul being deserted by the Taliban just five weeks after it had begun. The several thousand remaining al Qaeda Arab fighters and their Taliban hosts retreated to a cave complex near the Pakistan border, at Tora Bora, where even the Americans were unable to dislodge and capture all of them. Bin Laden, after calling for a war by the Muslim world against the West, disappeared. Throughout this, Blair had continued his diplomacy, helping win Pakistan round to the American cause and protesting to a wide range of Arab and Muslim leaders that the conflict was emphatically not aimed at Islam. In Oman, Egypt, Syria and Palestine, he and his aides assured everyone who would listen that there would be no further war against Iraq unless evidence was uncovered of a link between al Qaeda and Saddam Hussein. Meanwhile, Blair's attempts to bring the other main European leaders nearer to close support for President Bush, and to kick-start a new phase of the peace process between Israel and her neighbours, were largely unsuccessful.

During these weeks of frantic activity, Blair was trying to build support for the new 'war on terror' but also to begin to give substance to his remarkable speech at Labour's conference in October, when he suggested the ills of the globe could be addressed in the aftermath of September 11. It remains the single most important speech he made and the best reference point for his failures and successes as a foreign affairs Prime Minister. Though advisers contributed key phrases, the thrust of the speech was his own, the product of the Christian moralism he had developed as an Oxford student, a growing belief in his personal ability as a global leader, and a hot concentration of excited thinking, utterly unlike his vaguer grasp of domestic policy. The Twin Towers attack had simply been a turning point in world history, he told his party. After movingly describing the aftermath in New York, he tied war-making and aid-giving together as Bush certainly would not have done. Defeat the terrorists, was his message, and then deal with the refugees; take on poverty and the terrorism would drain away. From the slums of Gaza to Africa itself which he was already describing as 'a scar on the conscience of the world', a new world could be made:

'From out of the shadow of this evil should emerge lasting good: destruction of the machinery of terrorism wherever it is found; hope amongst all nations of a new beginning where we seek to resolve differences in a calm and ordered way; greater understanding between nations and between faiths; and above all justice and prosperity for the poor and dispossessed.'

Some laughed in disbelief; others felt their eyes mist and their hearts beat faster. Blair was in some areas specific. He promised to make the Middle East peace process a personal priority from now on. But mostly he was visionary. The starving, the wretched, the dispossessed, the ignorant, could be saved. 'This is a moment to seize. The kaleidoscope has been shaken. The pieces are in flux. Soon they will settle again. Before they do, let us reorder the world around us.' It was an undeniably powerful act of rhetoric. But was Blair already reaching too far, allowing the intoxicating moral certainty of the hour to persuade him that he could play a messianic role round the world, part Gladstone, part Gandhi? Iraq was the bloody rock which would shatter these hopes, though Blair pursued his aims doggedly in Israel and Africa too.

The Joy of Trivia

Throughout the Blair years, Alastair Campbell would berate journalists for their tiny-minded obsession with trivia rather than substance. By trivia he meant a series of scandals involving ministers and money or, less often, ministers and sex. Resignations from government punctuated the Blair years. Perhaps the most single damaging thing Tony Blair ever said was this: 'We are on the side of ordinary people against privilege. We must be purer than pure.' There were few instances of personal corruption but in trying to raise money for politics without going cap in hand to the trade unions, the Blair circle became deeply enmeshed with business and privilege, a world where favours were exchanged without anything explicit necessarily being said. The Blairs themselves enjoyed luxurious surroundings and the company of wealthy people. And after the huge endorsement of the 1997 election, lacking any restraint from a threatening opposition party, a certain swagger was soon apparent among the inner circle. From the word go, New Labour's high command, nose in the air, eyes aglitter with opportunity, was riding for a fall.

The Bernie Ecclestone affair of 1997, when the diminutive owner of Formula 1 racing around the world won an exemption from a tobacco advertising ban for his sport after giving a £1m donation to Labour, was the first rebuke to 'purer than pure'. In Opposition, Blair had been driven round the Silverstone racing circuit as the crowd waved Union Jacks at him; the two men were acquaintances.[13] The suggested link between a let-out clause in government policy for motor racing and Ecclestone's personal influence on him was hotly denied by Blair in public. Behind the scenes, he and his advisers knew how it looked. There was panic. Though nobody could finally prove wrong-doing, lies were told as Number Ten tried to cover up the detail of the story. On Campbell's advice Blair allowed himself to be interviewed by the BBC's premier attack-dog interviewer John Humphrys, to whom he made a lame half-apology and appealed to viewers: 'I hope that people know me well enough and realise the type of person I am to realise I would never do anything to harm the country or anything improper . . . I think that most people who have dealt with me think that I am a pretty straight sort of guy.' Blair got away with it at the time, just about. But a dangerous impression had been left that the fresh-faced new administration which had so vigorously attacked Tory sleaze was not quite as clean-handed as it had seemed.

If Blair could still play his public reputation for niceness, the same could not in all fairness be said of Peter Mandelson. He had revelled in his reputation as 'the sinister minister', the all-seeing, omnipresent Machiavelli of New Britain. He could be stagey, camp, bullying, charming and for a man supposed to swirl around in the dark, was rather touchingly attracted by the spotlight. It was said that his arrival in a restaurant could turn soup to ice as he passed enemies, while he could raise an ally's blood temperature with just the flicker of a smile. He was less efficient than overwrought enemies thought him. As a dark manipulator he had his Inspector Clouseau moments. Yet in the early days of New Labour, Mandelson and the people around him felt they were masters of the universe. One of his aides, Derek Draper, boasted darkly to someone working undercover for a newspaper about 'the Circle'. There were, he said (no doubt tapping the side of his nose) only 'seventeen people who count'. Perhaps the Mandelson circle was sending itself up just a little; but it was setting itself up too. Mandelson himself had a strongly developed taste for good living and had borrowed £373,000 to buy a house before the election from Geoffrey Robinson, a cheery MP and supporter of Gordon Brown's. Robinson had a fortune secreted offshore in a Channel Island tax haven, money from a long business career and also from the bequest of a Belgian widow, happily called Madam Bourgeois. In government he became Paymaster General and in due course Mandelson became Secretary of State for Trade & Industry, the job which meant he was in overall charge of investigations into – among others – one Geoffrey Robinson, the man to whom he was indebted for his West End home.

There was an obvious conflict of interest. Mandelson tried to deflect enquiries about where he had got the money. But the Brown camp both loathed him and knew the truth. So it was bound to come out. When it did so Blair was furious, not least because his close friend Peter had said nothing to warn him; nor had any of his staff. After a tearful scene with two Downing Street press officers, and Blair off-stage looking cross, Mandelson agreed that he would have to resign. The Prime Minister, though determined to see him go, then had him and his partner to stay at Chequers and gave him advice about rebuilding his life and the art of making friends. Characteristically, Mandelson's sad but noble letter of resignation and Blair's memorably moving reply were both written by Alastair Campbell. Then Robinson went too. So in due course did Charlie Whelan, Brown's press officer and the man blamed by Mandelson for revealing the story of his loan.

Had that been all it would have been bad enough. The mantra was established that nothing wrong had been done, but because of the appearance of wrongdoing, resignation was called for. But there followed a roll-call of scandals, all different in their detail, together devastating in their effect. Blair was accused of lying when he denied knowledge of any connection between a Labour donation made by Lakshmi Mittal, an Indian businessman, and his help for Mittal in trying to buy a Romanian steel company. Mandelson returned to government just ten months after his resignation and threw himself into the new job of Northern Ireland Secretary. Then came questions about whether two Indian businessmen who had helped fund the Dome had tried to obtain British citizenship via Mandelson. He was later cleared of wrongdoing but had to resign again. After Blair again showed himself entirely steely about this, Mandelson, who eventually turned up again as Britain's Commissioner in Brussels, felt badly betrayed. (Connections between ministers and business people who 'know the form' and protect one another by never explicitly asking or offering, depend on a shared culture. It is interesting that so many of the rows that broke surface concerned Asian business people. They did not know the form. They could speak English, but not Unspoken English.)

For the same cabinet minister to have to resign twice within a year was unheard-of. But in the Blair years, twice happened twice. David Blunkett, the blind, tough-talking former leader of Sheffield council who had been Blair's enforcer in education, had to resign as Home Secretary in 2004 after a row over whether he had asked his private office to fast-track a visa application for his lover Kimberley Quinn's nanny. He had not exactly rallied colleagues to his side by confiding in a journalist his derisive views on much of the rest of the cabinet, duly published in a biography to his embarrassment and their fury. Press interest in the 'nannygate' story was whipped to fever pitch by Quinn's role as well-known publisher of the Tory-supporting *Spectator* magazine and the revelation that she had had a child by him. Even Blunkett described it as the tale of the socialite and the socialist. There followed a bitter custody battle between Quinn, supported by her long-suffering husband, and the increasingly agitated Blunkett. It was a story from the wilder years of the eighteenth century and was used as the subject of a musical, which hurt Blunkett very much, as well as a television drama. He was brought back into government after the 2005 election as Work & Pensions Secretary but had to resign again after a row over shares in a DNA testing company he had purchased while out of the government. His taped diaries which were published in 2006 then revealed divisions at the heart of government before the Iraq War, his coruscating views on senior civil servants, and implied that Blair had considered sacking Brown if he failed to properly support him over it.

The Blunkett and Mandelson 'doubles' were the most celebrated resignations of the Blair years but were only part of the story. Ron Davies, the Welsh Secretary, went after 'a moment of madness' involving another man on Clapham Common. Estelle Morris, Education Secretary, went after a 'moment of sanity' – thoroughly honorably, she decided she was not up to the job. There were the Iraq resignations, first of Robin Cook, then Clare Short, the loss of a badly bruised Lord Irvine of Lairg as Lord Chancellor after Blair overruled him on constitutional reform, and the departure of Alan Milburn, Health Secretary, to spend more time with his family. Stephen Byers, a former hard leftist from the north-east of England, had been one of Blair's most trusted and loyal ministers. He was badly damaged when his special adviser Jo Moore callously emailed colleagues telling them 9/11 was a good day 'to bury bad news', not the most sensitive response to the murder of thousands. Then as Transport Secretary Byers ignited a huge row when he forced Railtrack into liquidation and took control of it back, without paying the compensation to its shareholders that straightforward nationalization would have entitled them to. They felt robbed and cheated, though Labour MPs were delighted. Byers was attacked for lying to Parliament about this, and about what he said to a meeting of survivors of the horrific Paddington train disaster about the railway's future. He resigned in May 2002.

The dirty tide washed through Number Ten too. Blair and his wife Cherie had been the butt of many attacks for the gusto with which they enjoyed free holidays at the expense of rich friends – Geoffrey Robinson, an Italian prince, Cliff Richard, a Bee Gee, and (briefly) Silvio Berlusconi, the scandal-mired Prime Minister of Italy. Cherie had been criticized frequently for free-loading more generally; though a high-paid lawyer she was unreasonably frightened of not having enough money, which presumably dated from her insecure childhood. The Blairs were less wealthy than the Thatchers (though not, in office, the Majors or the Wilsons or the Callaghans) and had failed to capitalize on the house-price boom when they sold their private north London home. Yet they and their children were looked after in two homes paid for by the State and he was well paid by the standards of ordinary Britain. Not rich only by the standards of millennial London high society, the family was comfortable. And as soon as Blair resigned he knew that through book deals, speaking fees and corporate work he could become rich beyond the dreams of avarice. None of this seemed to cut much ice.

Carole Caplin, a health and beauty trainer, had known Cherie Blair from the nineties but became more influential with her after Labour won power. Disliked by Number Ten officials who regarded her as manipulative, and her New Age views as barmy, Caplin nevertheless helped Mrs Blair develop a style and self-confidence she felt she had not had before. Particularly after her pregnancy with Leo, and then a later miscarriage, a close feminine bond was established. With Blair constantly distracted by the 'war on terror' and domestic politics, Cherie took it more upon herself to organize family plans, including financial plans. Through Caplin, she arranged to buy two flats in Bristol where her son Euan was at university, one for him and one as an investment. The deal was negotiated by Caplin's lover, a panto-mime Australian rogue and fraudster called Peter Foster. When the story broke, Cherie Blair failed to tell Campbell the full truth. Nor did she tell Fiona Miller, Campbell's partner, who had been Cherie's spokeswoman and who loathed Caplin. Nor, it seems, did her husband know the complete story either. As a result, Number Ten misled the press when stories in the *Daily Mail* and *Mail on Sunday* were put to them and were later forced to apologize. Stormy scenes erupted inside Downing Street when the link from Blair to a conman, via Cherie and Caplin, was finally established. It was a very bleak moment for the couple and media anger was only partially assuaged when at Campbell's insistence Cherie made a live televised apology, blaming her busy life and maternal pressure for what had happened. Some applauded her for a courageous performance and a life of difficult juggling. Others were unconvinced.

Britain had not become a corrupt country. But a sense of let-down, betrayal or perhaps just weary disappointment was felt by millions who had hoped for better. Why had Blair and his associates failed to show themselves purer than pure? First, by deciding to live with a system of business donations to help fund politics, they opened themselves to influence-peddling. Blair always replied that he had set up rules for the disclosure of party donations and the tightest ever code for ministerial behaviour. This was true. Yet there always seemed to be another loophole and another set of questions. By the end of his time in office his fundraiser Lord Levy had been arrested in a loans-for-peerages investigation and he was facing police questioning himself.

Second, the growth of a super-rich class of business people in

London in the two decades after the Big Bang gave some politicians a wholly unrealistic measurement of how 'people like us' live. Many did not fall for it. Brown did not. Most ministers went home to their constituencies and found themselves walking again on solid ground. But the temptation to think, 'I run the country, or part of the country, don't I deserve better?' was always present. Britain seemed to have become a society which measured success merely by money, rather than by public esteem. Finally, the way politicians were really monitored had changed. It was not the smooth expressions of warning from civil servants they had to worry about, or even tough questions from fellow MPs. A self-appointed, lively, impertinent and at times savage opposition did the job instead, a class of people courted by ministers and then despised by them: the media. After brilliantly using journalism to help discredit the Conservatives, Blair and his colleagues were themselves about to feel the rough edge of a rough trade.

Into the Furnace

Blair's biographer Anthony Seldon rightly emphasizes how worried Blair was about Saddam Hussein and weapons of mass destruction long before Bush became President, or decided to launch his war. This was not simply something Blair worried about privately. He spoke of it again and again. He was particularly worried about a nuclear-enhanced 'dirty bomb' being used by Iraqi-supported terrorists. By now his earlier experiences of Saddam, and Milosevic, and to a lesser extent Mullah Omar of the Taliban, as well as his personal contact with leaders he liked, such as Bush and Russia's Vladimir Putin, meant that for Blair foreign affairs was personal. By focusing so fully on Saddam as a man of evil, and the moral case for dealing with him, he did not focus enough on the complexities of Iraq, the country.

The hardening of views inside the White House which finally led to the decision to invade Iraq are not part of this story. In Bush's State of the Union speech for 2002 he had listed Iraq, Iran and North Korea as an 'axis of evil', sending shivers across diplomatic Europe. Attempts by US intelligence to prove a link between the secularist Saddam and the fundamentalist al Qaeda failed but this hardly halted the process of lining up Iraq as next for the Bush treatment. Blair's promises to Arab leaders about proof had no purchase in Washington. There were philosophical links between Blair's Gladstonian speech to the Labour Party and the neo-conservatives around Bush, many of whom believed that by toppling Saddam they would bring an age of democracy and prosperity to the Middle East, solving the Palestinian problem along the way. But the dominant group around Bush were not keen on grand visions. They believed first and second in toppling Saddam. They did not believe in waiting for, or depending upon, other countries, even Britain. After 9/11 this was America's war. They did not believe in UN inspectors or promises by Baghdad. Above all the hopes of some of the more intellectual US officials and of Britain's Foreign Office for a detailed plan for the reconstruction of post-war Iraq would be dashed by the hawks, Cheney and Rumsfeld at their head. 'Regime change' meant regime change. It did not mean promises to bring clean water and food to foreigners by democratic missionaries.

From the time when he visited Bush at his dusty Texan ranch at Crawford, near Waco, in April 2002, Blair knew he intended to invade Iraq. That did not end the matter, since Blair spent much of the rest of the year arguing that Bush should go via the United Nations. Without this, under British interpretations of international law, the invasion would be illegal. The UN would also give a last chance for Saddam to disarm peacefully. Keeping the international community together would make it easier to rebuild Iraq afterwards, in the spirit of Blair's conference speech. He also wanted Bush to commit to spending plenty of time on the Middle East peace process. On 7 September 2002 at Camp David Blair finally got Bush's promise to go via the UN, and Bush got Blair's promise that Britain would fight alongside America in Iraq if that route failed. Bush praised Blair for having 'cojones' – Spanish for balls. When Bush publicly confirmed his willingness to try for a UN resolution, ad-libbing in a speech to the General Assembly a few days later, Blair was delighted. But he was also locked in. He had spent his capital with Bush, and won a battle with the Washington hawks about the United Nations. But he had not persuaded anyone to take the post-war situation seriously. At the time it looked like a good deal.

It would turn out to be a rotten deal, not least because to Blair's chagrin and amazement, the United States and Britain were eventually unable to get the extra UN resolution they wanted. In the meantime the U.N. route helped keep the number of Labour's Commons rebels to fifty-six. That was still a lot. In Whitehall the Foreign Office and many ministers were growing worried about where Blair was leading them. Outside it, the anti-war movement was mobilizing. To try to win public opinion round Blair turned to a device he had used twice before, ahead of Desert Fox and after 9/11, the publication of a dossier of facts proving the case for war. This one, though, was different. The American case against Saddam was that he was a bad, dangerous guy who in the context of the new war on terror had to be taken out. The UN case was that he was failing to cooperate fully with weapons inspectors, leading to a suspicion that he was still hiding stocks of weapons of mass destruction (WMD), particularly chemical and bio-logical weapons, though to be fair some had been destroyed. To get the resolution, it was vital to concentrate on the WMD, about which as we have seen Blair had long been worried. The dossier, therefore, had to show they existed. To win round British opinion, it would have to show they were threatening to Britain too. Thus Blair laid the central case for war not on the moral cause for removing a tyrant but on narrow and unproven assertions about the condition of the tyrant's arsenal.

Blair's team had already enjoyed some success with journalists in feeding them bloodcurdling lines about the damage Saddam might wreak. There is no doubt that senior intelligence and defence people believed he had WMD but was cleverly hiding them, and that he was trying to get nuclear weapons. The trouble was that Saddam's regime of terror was so effective that there were very few sources of information from inside Iraq. Those Britain's MI6 dealt with were untrustworthy – they were after all dissidents with a strong reason to bring forward the war. Sir Richard Dearlove, the MI6 director general, brought Blair information from an Iraqi source who said he knew where chemical agent was being made – though the source was 'untried and untested'. Satellite intelligence, though used by Colin Powell at the UN, was unsatisfactorily unclear. Thus the dossier had to produce information from a vague and difficult source which was nevertheless hard-edged enough, at least at first glance, to fulfil a highly political role. It was drawn from a variety of sources, channelled through the Joint Intelligence Committee, which reported to the Prime Minister. Different texts were batted to and fro through Downing

Street, as officials questioned parts of it, and wondered whether it was sufficiently convincing. Suspicions were raised also following the publication of a second dossier in February 2003 about the background to Iraq's concealment programme, which was later dubbed 'the dodgy dossier' and proved to have been lifted without attribution from a PhD thesis found on the Internet.

Whatever the final truth about the shaping of the September 2002 dossier, something strange had happened. Suspicions had been hardened, assertions sharpened, doubts trimmed out and belief converted into proof. Nobody knew for sure what Saddam had (that was the point of the UN inspection process) but when it was published the dossier gave the impression that he had multiple weapons of mass destruction which could be ready for use in forty-five minutes and threatened, among other places, British bases in Cyprus. The forty-five-minute claim turned out to refer to some short-range battlefield chemical weapons which could not reach other countries, though maps printed in the dossier confused readers about it. And when Iraq was finally invaded, and exhaustive searches conducted everywhere, the 'weapons' never turned up. For years Blair insisted hotly that they would. He would be publicly mocked by President Putin, MPs and the world's media for this. He kept telling his critics they would be proved wrong. So far they have not been.

A tense struggle at the United Nations, with British diplomats in the lead, produced Resolution 1441, declaring that Saddam was in 'material breach' of his obligation to show he had no banned weaponry, and giving him a last opportunity to comply or face 'serious consequences'. The Iraqi leader fudged and dodged, letting inspectors back in but without offering a full declaration of his weapons. For the Americans, this was the trigger for war. For other countries, notably France, it merely meant that there should be another discussion at the Security Council about what to do. In February 2003, as British and US forces waited to attack Iraq from the south, there was a vast 'Stop the War' march through London. It was the biggest ever demonstration in the capital, a carnival of protest that put even the Suez protests in its shade. Blair, Jack Straw, the Foreign Secretary who had swallowed private doubts and resolved to loyally support his boss, with their diplomatic team were fighting desperately to get a second UN resolution agreed which would give full legal cover for the attack on Iraq. This was something Blair had told Bush repeatedly that he needed to be sure of holding his party together (and by implication, staying in power). But President Chirac of France, angry at the behaviour of Washington's hawks and worried about the impact of the war on the Islamic world generally, suggested that France would never accept a second resolution, and it collapsed. Despite everything the Prime Minister was left without the real UN cover he always thought he needed. For Blair and Straw it was a low moment.

For others, it was the last straw. Robin Cook, who as the previous Foreign Secretary had been deeply involved in Desert Fox and Kosovo, had warned the cabinet that without a second resolution he could not support this third war. He duly resigned. For the time being Clare Short, another cabinet dissenter who had publicly described Blair's behaviour as 'reckless', stayed on. In the Commons Cook, its former leader, then gave one of the most icily eloquent speeches heard in the chamber in modern times. He applauded Blair and Straw for trying so hard for the second resolution, which only showed how important it had been. Many countries, not just France, had wanted more inspections before any fighting: 'The reality is that Britain is being asked to embark on a war without agreement in any of the international bodies of which we are a leading partner – not Nato, not the European Union and, now, not the Security Council.' The US was a superpower and could afford to go it alone, but Britain could not. Iraq probably had no weapons of mass destruction 'in the ordinarily understood sense' but was in fact militarily very weak: 'Ironically, it is only because Iraq's military forces are so weak that we can even contemplate its invasion. We cannot base our military strategy on the assumption that Saddam is weak and at the same time justify pre-emptive action on the claim that he is a threat.' The British people, said Cook, possessed collective wisdom: 'On Iraq, I believe that the prevailing mood of the British people is sound. They do not doubt that Saddam is a brutal dictator, but they are not persuaded that he is a clear and present danger to Britain.' Almost uniquely, against its hallowed traditions, the Commons loudly clapped Cook as he sat down.

Blair felt he had to press ahead. Saddam had proved himself yet again untrustworthy and a liar. He had legal cover from his attorney general for the war, though it was hardly resounding, and disputed by other government lawyers, one of whom resigned. He had given his word to President Bush, who offered Blair the chance to pull out and send British troops in after the invasion, as peacekeepers. Blair turned the offer down as dishonourable and bad for army morale. He had staked his reputation on the war and felt that if he could not carry his party, he was finished as a leader. Privately, arrangements for his resignation were set in hand. In the Commons a ferocious political and media struggle began to win round doubters, emphasizing Saddam's brutality and abuse of human rights, rather than his weaponry. A backbencher and sometime left-wing firebrand, Ann Clwyd, made a particularly influential speech about Saddam's treatment of the Kurds and his use of torture. Eventually, after days of drama and one of his best parliamentary speeches ever, Blair won a majority of Labour MPs, though 139 rebelled. The overall Commons victory was never in doubt because of Conservative support, but Blair had been close to failing his private yardstick of being backed by at least half his MPs. With that overcome, the final barrier to war was lifted.

The war began on 20 March 2003 with a thunderous air attack on Baghdad, described with brutal clarity in Washington as 'shock and awe'. An early attempt by Saddam's information minister to assassinate Saddam failed. For the first weeks, calm declarations of great victories being won out in the desert by the Iraqi armed forces were broadcast almost nightly. In fact, sandstorms delayed the US advance. In Baghdad a coalition bomb killed fifty-seven people in a market-place and in Britain anger about the war grew. Yet while not quite the walkover the Pentagon had hoped, the invasion was over very quickly. By 7 April British forces had taken Basra, having surrounded it long before, and two days later the Americans were in Baghdad, first seizing the international airport and then Saddam's famous palaces. Soon his statues were being jubilantly torn down. Before the invasion, there had been speculation about Baghdad fighting to the last, surrounded by trenches of burning oil, tank regiments and possibly artillery with chemical shells – an Arab *Götterdämmerung* on the banks of the Tigris. By those standards, the war had been a great, one-sided military success. The war beyond the war would be something else entirely.

Mediaocracy

In the eighties and early nineties, Labour had been savaged by much of the press. Neil Kinnock had a terrible time. When Blair became leader the people immediately around Kinnock at the time, Mandelson and Campbell, remembered it well. Campbell had worked for the *Daily Mirror* in the dirtiest, most cynical end of the newspaper market and came away thinking that most journalists were idle liars, as well as biased against Labour. He was tribal and assumed the rest of the world was too. Mandelson, with a background in television, was a master of image, and later of the killer briefing. So it is hardly surprising that New Labour became the most media-obsessed political party in British history. We have seen how Blair opened out to Labour's traditional enemies in the press after becoming leader, and how he exploited 'sleaze' to destroy John Major's reputation. On the way to winning power, New Labour turned itself into a kind of perpetual media news-desk, with a plan for what every political headline should say every day, an endless 'grid' of announcements, images, soundbites and rebuttals, constantly pressing down on journalists, their editors and owners, fighting for every adjective and exclamation mark.

It is now incontestable that the same way of thinking was brought into power and did terrible damage to the government's reputation and that of politics generally. Bizarrely, it was assumed that rival newspaper groups with different views about say, law and order, could be kept friendly by Blair telling them what they wanted to hear – even though they would later confer. The attempted bullying of journalists, which grew much worse when some of the scandals described above began to break, was met with increasing resistance. Number Ten's news machine began to be widely disbelieved. The word 'spin' was attached to almost everything it said. Diaries published by one of the former Downing Street spin-doctors, Lance Price, show how justified this suspicion was. On the first Mandelson resignation, he notes: 'We said (quite falsely) that Peter had rung TB last night and said he wanted to resign.' Of a Sunday newspaper interview which Blair had given calling for a new 'moral purpose', Price says: 'It was totally vacuous and was made up just to give us a good story after two twelve-year-old girls were found to have got themselves pregnant. But it worked . . .'[14]

There are many other examples. Some, collected by the journalist Peter Oborne, include the smearing of Chris Patten, the former Tory chairman and Hong Kong governor for leaking intelligence reports, a false trail to deflect attention from the breakup of Robin Cook's marriage; the assertion by Peter Mandelson that the Dome would feature an exciting new game called 'surf-ball' (which never existed); and Blair's own deceptions, such as over Mandelson's own plans to become an MP.[15] While there are exceptional circumstances in which political leaders have to deceive, such as when soldiers' lives would be at risk from disclosure, or when a currency was about to be devalued, journalists came to believe the currency of truth was now devalued. Anything asserted by Number Ten, and later Blair himself, was picked over in minute semantic detail. Worryingly often, the picking-over turned out to be justified. The 'non-denial denial' became an essential phrase in reporting New Labour. At election time statistics were twisted even beyond the normal elastic rules of political debate. There was a spiral downwards. Journalists grew more aggressive in their assertions and began consigning the (disbelieved) official denials to the final paragraph of their stories. Some ministers drew the conclusion that the press was so hostile it was legitimate to use any trick or form of words to mislead them. Others complained that every time they were frank, their words were twisted and used against them: why bother? Before long a government which had arrived in office supported by almost all the national papers, was being attacked daily by almost all of them. And the papers themselves were selling fewer copies. Ultimately, cynicism is boring.

The most infamous confrontation between New Labour and the media, however, was not with a newspaper but with a broadcaster. One of the domestic consequences of the Iraq was the worst falling out between the BBC and the government since the Suez crisis. At issue was whether or not officials in Number Ten had 'sexed up' that dossier about Iraq's alleged weapons of mass destruction. As previously described, the dossier blended two cultures, the cautious, secretive, nuanced culture of intelligence gathering for internal government purposes, and the spin-doctors' culture of opinion-forming, in this case to win more of the public over to back a coming war. But the cultures did not blend, they curdled. At seven minutes after six one morning at the end of May 2003, Radio Four's *Today* programme broadcast an interview between its presenter John Humphrys and its defence correspondent, a dishevelled digger of a journalist called Andrew Gilligan. He alleged that Downing Street had 'sexed up' the dossier beyond what intelligence sources thought was reasonable, particularly in saying that weapons of mass destruction could be ready for use within forty-five minutes. Campbell quickly and unequivocally denied the truth of Gilligan's assertion and demanded an apology. Gilligan went further, in an article for a newspaper in which he named Campbell. As Iraq burned, Number Ten and the BBC began a war of their own.

In general battles between journalists and politicians do not spill real blood. There is bitterness. There may be resignations. But when the smoke clears, everyone gets up again and goes back to work. When Campbell widened his criticism of the BBC to attack it for having an anti-war agenda, he had no idea quite what he was setting off. Yet there was a certain recklessness in his mood. He confided to his diary that he wanted to 'fuck Gilligan' and wanted 'a clear win' against the corporation. On the BBC side, it would turn out that Gilligan had been loose with his words, claiming rather more than he knew for sure, so opening a flank to Campbell; nor was Gilligan frank with his colleagues. The BBC's Director Deneral, Greg Dyke, who had been hounded in the press as a Blair crony, was ferociously robust in defending the corporation against Campbell and was strongly supported by his Chairman, Gavyn Davies, whose wife was Gordon Brown's senior aide. He too was determined to demonstrate his independence.

Neither side gave way until eventually it was revealed that a government scientist with a high reputation as an arms inspector, Dr David Kelly, was probably the source of Gilligan's information. Downing Street did not name him but allowed journalists to keep throwing names at them until they confirmed who he was; a bizarre game. Because he was not involved directly in the joint intelligence committee or its work, 'outing' Kelly as the secret mole would, in the government's eyes, discredit the BBC story. Suddenly thrown into the cauldron of a media row, Kelly himself was evasive when aggressively questioned by a committee of MPs. Visibly nervous, he denied that he could have been Gilligan's informant. Yet he was. A fastidious, serious-minded man who had supported the toppling of Saddam and had served his country honourably as a weapons inspector, Kelly seems to have cracked under the strain. On a quiet July morning in 2003 he walked five miles to the edge of a wood near his Oxfordshire home where he took painkillers, opened up a pen-knife, and killed himself. This media battle had drawn blood in the most awful way. Blair, arriving in Tokyo after triumphantly addressing both houses of Congress about the fall of Saddam, was asked: 'Prime Minister, do you have blood on your hands?' He looked as if he was about to be sick.

Back home, he ordered an inquiry under a judge, Lord Hutton, which engaged the minute attention of the world of politics through the autumn of 2003. Much was revealed about Blair's informal, sloppily recorded and cliquish style of governing, and the involvement of his political staff in discussion which led to the final dossier. But with the head of the JIC and other officials insisting they had not been leant on, or obliged to say anything they did not believe, and a very strong public performance by Blair, Lord Hutton concluded Gilligan's asser tion that the government knew its forty-five-minute claim was wrong, was unfounded. The intelligence committee might have 'subcon-sciously' been persuaded to strengthen its language because they knew what the Prime Minister wished the effect of the dossier to be; but it was consistent with the intelligence at the time. Hutton decided that Kelly had probably killed himself because of a loss of self-esteem and the threat to his reputation, but that nobody else was to blame. (There was a strongly held private belief among some doctors and journalists that Kelly had been murdered but so far, not a shred of hard evidence has come to light.) Hutton attacked the BBC's editorial controls. His findings had been leaked a day early to Rupert Murdoch's *Sun* newspaper, which robustly set the political mood: victory for Blair, humiliation for the BBC. With Blair defiant and claiming complete vindication in the Commons both Dyke and Davies resigned almost immediately. Distraught employees walked out from their offices to cheer them as they left. The corporation had suffered its worst day ever. Yet the stakes were high on both sides. Had Hutton found against the Prime Minister, it would have been Blair being applauded by his tearful staff as he walked into retirement.

Feeling vindicated and as aggressive as ever about the quality of journalism, Campbell then left Downing Street. Blair had concluded that the age of spin had done them all far more harm than good. It was time, despite his personal debt to Campbell, for a new broom. A widely trusted and traditionalist press officer who had worked for Roy Hattersley, called David Hill, was appointed. Slowly, painfully, both the BBC and Number Ten moved on – although there was plenty of trouble still ahead. By his last couple of years in office, Blair had come to realize that the frantic headline-chasing and rebuttal of the early years had merely helped stoke a mood of cynicism in the press. The habits of truth-shaving, subtle deception and syntactical evasion, which had once seemed magnificently clever, had done more harm than any brief newspaper victories they might have achieved. After Iraq, one of the most common jibes made about him was simply 'Bliar'. For a Prime Minister who in his early days had been able to say that most people thought him 'a pretty straight kind of guy', it was a terrible come-down.

Always with us?

Through the New Labour years, with low inflation and steady growth, most of the country grew richer. Growth since 1997, at 2.8% a year, was above the post-war average, Britain's gross domestic product per head was above that of France and Germany, and she had the second-lowest jobless figures in the EU. The number of people in work increased by 2.4 million. Incomes grew, in real terms, by about a fifth. Pensions were in trouble but house price inflation soared, so that home-owners found their properties more than doubling in value and came to think themselves prosperous indeed. One study showed that Britain had a higher proportion of dollar millionaires than any other country. Family budgets are by definition tricky things to generalize about but by 2006 analysts were assessing the disposable wealth of the British, defined by the consultants KDP as 'the money people can really put their hands on if necessary' at £40,000 per household. The wealth was not evenly spread geographically, averaging £68,000 in the south-east of England and a little over £30,000 in Wales and north-east England. But even in historically poorer parts of the UK house prices had risen fast, so much so that government plans to bulldoze worthless northern terraces had to be abandoned when they started to become worth quite a lot. Cheap mortgages, easy borrowing and high property prices meant that millions of people felt far better off, despite the overall rise in the tax burden. Cheap air travel, which had first arrived in the seventies with Freddie Laker, gave the British opportunities for easy travel both to their traditional sun-kissed resorts and to every part of the European continent. A British expatriate house-price boom rippled slowly across the French countryside and roared through southern Spain. People began to commute weekly to their jobs in London or Manchester from villas by the Mediterranean. Small regional airports grew, then boomed.

Clever, constantly evolving consumer electronics and then cheap clothing from the Far East kept the shops thronged. The internet, advancing from colleges and geeks to the show-off upper middle classes, then to children's bedrooms everywhere, introduced new forms of shopping. It first began to attract popular interest in the mid-nineties: Britain's first internet café and internet magazine, reviewing a few hundred early websites, were both launched in 1994. The following year saw the beginning of internet shopping as a major pastime, with both eBay and Amazon arriving, though for tiny numbers of people at first. It was a time of immense optimism, despite warnings that the whole digital world would collapse because of the 'millennium bug' – the alleged inability of computers to deal with the last two digits in '2000', which was taken very seriously at the time.

In fact, the bubble was burst by its own excessive expansion, like any bubble, and after a pause and a lot of ruined dreams, the 'new economy' roared on again. By 2000, according to the Office of National Statistics, around 40 per cent of Britons had accessed the internet at some time. Cyber frenzy swept the country, and business; three years later, nearly half of British homes were connected. By 2004 the spread of broadband had brought a new mass market in downloading music and video online. By 2006, three-quarters of British children had internet access at home. Simultaneously, new money arrived. The rich of America, Europe and Russia began buying up parts of London, and then other attractive parts of the country, including Edinburgh, the Scottish Highlands, Yorkshire and Cornwall. For all the problems and disappointments, and the longer-term problems with their financing, new schools and public buildings sprang up – new museums, galleries, vast shopping complexes, corporate headquarters, now biomorphic, not straight, full of lightness, airy atriums, thin skins of glass and steel. This was show-off architecture for a show-off material culture and not always dignified, but these buildings were better-looking and more imaginative than their predecessors had been in the dreary age of concrete.

At a more humdrum level, 'executive housing', with pebbled driveways, brick facing and dormer windows, was growing across farmland and by rivers with no thought of flood-plain constraints. Parts of the country far from London, such as the English south-west and Yorkshire, enjoyed a ripple of wealth that pushed their house prices to unheard-of levels. From Leith to Gateshead, Belfast to Cardiff Bay, once-derelict shorefront areas were transformed. Supermarkets, exercising huge market power, brought cheap meat and factory-made meals into almost everyone's budgets. The new global air freight market, and refrigerated lorries moving freely across a Europe shorn of internal barriers, carried out-of-season fruit and vegetables, fish from the Pacific, exotic foods of all kinds, to superstores everywhere. Hardly anyone was out of reach of a Tesco, a Morrison's, Sainsbury's or Asda. By the mid-2000s, the four supermarket giants owned more than 1,500 superstores. This provoked a new political row about their commercial influence but it also spread consumption of goods that had once been luxuries. Under Thatcher, millions had begun drinking wine. Under Blair they began drinking drinkable wine. Their children had to borrow to study but were more likely to go to college or university and to travel the world on a 'gap year', a holiday from ordinariness which had once meant working, occasionally abroad, but which by now might mean air-hopping across South America or to the beaches of Thailand. Materially, for the majority of people, this was a golden age, which perhaps explains why the real anger about earlier pensions decisions and stealth taxes failed to translate into anti-Labour voting in successive general elections.

Not everyone, of course, was invited to the party. New Labour's general pitch was to the well-doing middle but Gordon Brown, from the first, made much of its anti-poverty agenda. Labour in particular emphasized child poverty because, since the launch of the Child Poverty Action Group, it had become a particularly emotive problem.

Labour policies took a million children out of relative poverty between 1997 and 2004, though the numbers rose again later. Brown's emphasis was also on the working poor, and the virtue of work. So his major innovations were the national minimum wage, the 'New Deal' for the young unemployed, and the working families' tax credit, as well as tax credits aimed at children. There was also a minimum income guarantee, and later a pension credit, for worse-off pensioners.

The minimum wage was first set at £3.60 an hour and rising year by year. (It stood at £5.35 an hour in 2006.) Because the figures were low the minimum wage did not destroy the 2 million jobs, or produce the higher inflation, which Conservatives and others claimed it would. Employment grew and inflation stayed low. It even appeared to have cut red tape, since the old Wages Councils had to inspect businesses more frequently than the new Inland Revenue minimum wage inspections. By the middle 2000s, the minimum wage covered 2 million people, the majority of them women. And because it was uprated slightly faster than inflation, the wages of the poor rose faster. The situation may change, particularly if unemployment worsens, but it appeared to have been an almost unqualified success, enough for the Conservative Party, which had so strongly opposed it, to embrace it under Michael Howard before the 2005 election.

The New Deal was funded by a windfall tax on privatized utility companies. By 2000, Blair said it had helped a quarter of a million young people back to work and it was being claimed as a major factor in lower unemployment as late as 2005. It was clearly less of a factor than the huge increase in the size of the state: in the Blair years, state employment grew by 700,000, funded by record amounts taken in tax. And the cost of goading, coaxing and educating people into jobs was very high. The National Audit Office, looking back at its effect in the first Parliament, reckoned the number of under 25-year-olds helped into real jobs could be as low as 25,000, at a cost per person of £8,000. All those new jobs which had to be created to help people into jobs came at a price. A second initiative was targeted at the youngest of all, the babies and young children of the most deprived families. Sure Start was meant to bring mothers together in family centres across Britain – 3,500 were planned for 2010, ten years after the scheme was launched – and help them to be more effective parents. A scheme in the United States had shown great success and Sure Start was another initiative backed in its essence by the Conservatives, though Blair himself appeared to be having second thoughts, as the most deprived families declined to turn up. He believed in sticks as well as carrots.

Abroad, the government's anti-poverty agenda concentrated on Africa. In 2004 Blair initiated the Commission for Africa which worked to persuade the world's richest countries to back a wide plan for economic, political and social reform, supported by debt relief. By then it was estimated more than 50,000 people were dying every day from famine or bad water in Africa and the continent's AIDS epidemic was wiping out much of a generation. In 2005 Brown, struggling to persuade the United States to back his plans for an international finance facility – a global piggy bank – agreed to raise Britain's aid contribution to 0.7 per cent of GDP. Washington declined to follow suit. Enormous strength was added to the campaign by Make Poverty History, one of the two biggest examples of street politics in the Blair age. Here was extra-parliamentary action which showed people's readiness to engage with politics-as-unusual, a residual idealism. There is a tradition in Britain of moral protest and practical action for famine abroad. Oxfam had started as the Oxford Committee for Famine Relief in 1942, campaigning to persuade the wartime government to lift its blockade on German-occupied Greece, where the Nazis were allowing people to starve as they diverted food to their army in North Africa. (Churchill took the view that the starvation was the fault of the occupying power and the blockade should stay – the argument was strikingly similar to those made about sanctions imposed on Saddam Hussein's Iraq in the Major and Blair years.) What made the later movement different was the fusion of celebrity, music and television to raise unheard-of sums.

It began with the Irish rock star Bob Geldof, and Midge Ure of the band Ultravox, who were shocked by news coverage of the 1984 Ethiopian famine by the BBC's Michael Buerk. They formed a thirty-strong 'supergroup' to make a fundraising Christmas single, 'Do They Know It's Christmas?' It raised £65 m and Geldof managed to persuade Margaret Thatcher to waive VAT for the famine victims. This success was followed by Live Aid, a linked global concert held in London and Philadephia in 1985. It was watched by an estimated 1.5 billion people in 160 countries, making it by far the biggest world television event to that point. Geldof continued to campaign on Africa, joining the Commission for Africa. Having sworn he would never try to repeat

Live Aid, Geldof did so in 2005 with a host of rock stars, including U2 and the (briefly) reformed Pink Floyd, breaking more records for global audience numbers. This time, though, the focus was on lobbying the richest countries, meeting as the G8 under British chairmanship at Gleneagles in Scotland.

On 2 July 2005, some 225,000 people marched in Edinburgh calling for debt cancellation to help Africa's poorest countries. A week later a £28.8 bn aid deal and a debt cancellation programme for eighteen countries, plus new guarantees to fund anti-HIV drugs, were indeed agreed at Gleneagles. Because parts of the rich world remained hostile to opening up trade to Africa, essential to helping the continent recover, some campaigners were disappointed. And the announcement was greeted with cynicism by the anti-globalization movement which was also a feature of these years. Geldof said, however, that 'never before have so many people forced a change of policy onto a global agenda' and his fellow campaigner, Bono of U2, claimed the deal would save the lives of 600,000 Africans, mostly children. The legacy of Live8 and the Commission for Africa will continue to be debated for years but it was a unique alliance between civil organizations, churches, rock musicians, actors, writers – and politicians. Both Blair and Gordon Brown were consciously trying to use the hundreds of thousands of marchers and the glamour of the rock stars to nudge other world leaders towards agreement, and they were at least partially successful. It showed what their partnership could do.

Poverty is hard to define, easy to smell. In a country like Britain, it is mostly relative. Though there are a few thousand people living rough or who genuinely do not have enough to keep them decently alive, and many more pensioners frightened of how they will pay for heating, the greater number of poor are those left behind the general material improvement in life. This is measured by income compared to the average and by this yardstick in 1997 there were three to four million children living in households of relative poverty, triple the number in 1979. This does not mean they were physically worse off than the children of the late seventies, since the country generally became much richer. But human happiness relates to how we see ourselves relative to those around us, so it was certainly real. Under their new leader David Cameron, the Conservatives declared that they too believed in the concept of relative poverty, as described by a left-of-centre commentator, Polly Toynbee. And a world of work remained below the minimum wage, in private homes, where migrant servants were exploited, and in other crannies. Some 336,000 jobs remained on 'poverty pay' rates.[16]

Nevertheless the City firm UBS believes redistribution of wealth – a phrase New Labour did not like to use in case it frightened middle-class voters – had been stronger in Britain than other major industrialized countries. Despite the growth of the super-rich, overall equality slightly increased in the Blair years. One factor was the return to means-testing of benefits, particularly for pensioners and through the working families' tax credit (which in 2003 was divided into a child tax credit and a working tax credit). This was a personal U-turn by Brown who in Opposition had opposed means-testing. As Chancellor he concluded that if he was to direct scarce money at the people in real poverty he had little choice. More and more pensioners were means-tested, eventually some 66 per cent of them, provoking a nationwide revolt and persuading the government to back down and promise an eventual return to a link between state pension rates and average earnings. The other drawback of means-testing was that a huge bureaucracy then had to track people's earnings and try to establish just what they should get. Billions were overpaid. As people getting tax credits rather than old-style benefits, did better, and earned a little more, they found themselves facing demands to hand back money they had already spent. Many thousands of civil servants were hurriedly sent to try to deal with a tidal wave of complaint, and the system became extremely expensive to administer. It was also hugely vulnerable to fraud, with gangs taking over people's identities (13,000 civil servants alone) and exploiting 'a culture of overpayment'.

In the New Labour years, as under John Major, a sickly tide of euphemism rose ever higher, depositing its oily linguistic scurf on every available surface. Passengers became customers; indeed everybody became customers. Bin-men became refuse operatives, people with mental disabilities became differently-abled. And the poor became the socially excluded. There were controversial drives to oblige more disabled (and sometimes shirking) people back into work. The 'socially excluded' were confronted by a wide range of initiatives designed to make them, in essence, more middle class. In theory, Labour was non-judgemental or liberal about behaviour. In practice, responding to the darkest areas of deprivation, an almost Victorian moralism began to reassert itself. Advice on diet, weight-loss and alcohol consumption followed earlier government campaigns on AIDS and drugs. Parenting classes were much trumpeted. And for the minority who made life hellish for their neighbours on housing estates or in the streets, Labour introduced a word which became one of its particular gifts to the language of the age, as essential as dotcom or texting, the Asbo.

The Anti-Social Behaviour Order, first introduced in 1998, was an updated system of injunctions for what earlier generations called hooligans. These had to be applied for by the police or local council and granted by magistrates. To break the curfew or restriction, which could be highly specific, became a criminal offence. Asbos could be given for swearing at people, harassing passers-by, vandalism, making too much noise, graffiti, organizing raves, flyposting, taking drugs or sniffing glue, joyriding, either offering yourself as a prostitute or kerb-crawling in your car to find a prostitute, hitting people, drinking in designated public places . . . almost anything in fact that was annoying or frightening. More bizarre-sounding ones included giving an Asbo to an entire part of Skegness to allow police arrests of troublemakers there; a 13-year-old girl being banned from using the word 'grass' and an 87-year-old man being ordered not to make sarcastic remarks to neighbours and their visitors. In one case a woman who kept trying to commit suicide was given an Asbo to prevent her jumping into rivers or canals.

Though almost every story about an unlikely-sounding Asbo as reported in newspapers turned out to have a reason behind it, Asbo-spotting became a minor national sport and there were fears that for the tougher children, they became a badge of honour. In their early years they were much mocked by Liberal Democrat and Conservative MPs for being ineffective and rarely used by local authorities, as well as being criticized strongly by civil libertarians. Since breaking an Asbo could result in a prison sentence, it meant extending the threat of prison to crimes that before had not warranted it. Yet the public when polled strongly supported Asbos and as they were refined and strengthened they were gradually used more frequently, becoming almost routine. Like the minimum wage, Bank independence and some of the anti-poverty initiatives they seemed to be a part of New Labour Britain that would stick. At the time of writing, 7,500 or so had been given out in England and Wales (Scotland followed in 2004 with its version). Was this part of a wider authoritarian and surveillance agenda changing life in the country?

The War on Privacy

At an educated guess, the British are currently being observed and recorded by 4.2 million closed circuit television (CCTV) cameras. Professor Clive Norris of Sheffield University, who did the educated guessing, has pointed out, 'That's more than anywhere else in the world, with the possible exception of China. It's one for every 14 citizens.' When they first appeared in the early nineties, gazing beadily down from a few high-security buildings, these remotely staring cameras were pointed out as novelties. They are now in almost every sizeable store, looking down at key points in most big streets, in railway and underground stations, buses, housing estates and even from the fronts of private homes. Londoners are said to be picked up on CCTV cameras on average 300 times a day; their cars are filmed and tracked by the cameras set up for the capital's congestion charge. The Home Office has spent three-quarters of its crime prevention budget on CCTV cameras and the face-recognition and 'smart' technology that goes with them. The number of mobile phones is now equivalent to the number of people in Britain; with global satellite positioning chips, they can show where their users are, and the same of course goes for GPS systems in cars (by 2007 Britons were losing the art of map-reading). There are also more than 6,000 speed cameras on British roads.

Britain's information commissioner Richard Thomas warned that the country had becoming a 'surveillance society'. He thought future developments could include microchip implants to identify and track people; facial recognition cameras fitted into lampposts; and even unmanned surveillance aircraft over Britain's towns. Thomas suggested this could lead to discrimination and harassment: 'As ever more information is collected, shared and used, it intrudes into our private space and leads to decisions which directly influence people's lives.' Certainly, if being watched makes us good and safe, the British are now the goodest, safest people in the history of the world.

Who watches all the CCTV coverage? Court cases often demonstrated that either there was no film kept, or that to spot a face took
many police officers many weeks. Though this can increasingly be
done electronically, other kinds of surveillance were being done in
person. A new force of council tax inspectors were given powers to
enter any home in England and take photographs of any room,
including bedrooms and bathrooms, on pain of a £1,000 fine for refusal
or obstruction. This was to assess improvements including patios,
conservatories and double glazing for revaluation purposes as soon as
the government gave the go-ahead for such a revaluation, which was
planned to include extra charges for people living in agreeable areas,
or who could park their cars outside their homes. It was reported in
early 2006 that discussions had taken place with the civil servant in
charge of the surveillance programme about selling on the information
his men had gleaned to insurance and mortgage companies. Paul
Sanderson, director of modernization for the tax inspectors, said he
thought privacy was 'an old-fashioned concept' and called for all the
details, including photographs, to be shown online.

If anything could be more intimate than the insides of everyone's
homes, it is their DNA, with its clues about heredity, vulnerability to
disease and much else. In 2003 the law was changed to allow the
police to take and store the DNA of anyone arrested for any imprison-
able offence, whether or not they were later convicted. Previously the
police had had to destroy the samples of anyone found innocent, or
whose case was dropped. Three years later, by which time 3.6 million
samples were being held, Tony Blair said the database should be
extended to everybody: 'The number on the database should be the
maximum number you can get' and there was 'no problem' with the
general public providing their DNA as part of the wider fight against
crime.

By then the public also knew they would be expected to give
biometric data – iris recognition and perhaps eventually DNA – for
new compulsory identity cards, due to be introduced from 2008 when
people applied for new passports. David Blunkett had promoted the
idea of compulsory ID cards despite a hostile reaction from his
predecessor Jack Straw, the Chancellor Gordon Brown, and initial
caution from the Prime Minister. But he won his fight in government
essentially because he convinced Blair the technology was becoming

safe, and that ID cards would be popular with the majority of voters. These cards would carry a range of personal information, forming yet another new database, the National Identity Register. The issue provoked rebellions in Parliament before and after the 2005 election, but seemed to have been finally resolved by a thirty-one-vote majority in the Commons in February 2006. The new cards would cost citizens at least £93 each though ministers did not initially make it an offence to fail to carry one at all times. What were they for? To combat fraud and crime, to make life easier for government, and for individuals to make it harder to lose money through 'identity fraud'. Yet compulsory ID cards would probably not have passed through Parliament had it not been for the terrorist threat.

Seven Seven

On 7 July 2005, at rush-hour, four young Muslim men from West Yorkshire and Buckinghamshire, Hasib Hussein, Mohammed Sidique Khan, Germaine Lindsay and Shezhad Tanweer, murdered fifty-two people and injured 770 more by blowing themselves up on London Underground trains and one London bus. The report into the worst such attack in Britain later concluded that they were not part of an al Qaeda cell, though two had visited Pakistan camps, and that the rucksack bombs had been constructed for a few hundred pounds. Despite government insistence that the war in Iraq – discussed below – had not made Britain more of a terrorist target, the Home Office investigation asserted that part of the four terrorists' motivation was British foreign policy.

They had picked up the information they needed for the attack from the internet. It was a particularly ghastly one, because of the terrifying and bloody conditions below the streets of London in tube tunnels and it vividly reminded the country that it was as much a target as the United States or Spain. Indeed the intimate relationship between Britain and Pakistan, with constant and heavy traffic between them, provoked fears that the British would prove uniquely vulnerable. Blair heard of the attack at the most poignant time, just following London's great success in winning the bid to host the 2012 Olympic Games. He rushed back from Gleneagles in Scotland, where the G8 summit was discussing the ambitious new aid plan for Africa, and differences between the United States and the rest over global warming.

The London bombings are unlikely to have been stopped by more CCTV coverage, for there was plenty of that, nor by ID cards, for the killers were British citizens, nor by 'follow the money' anti-terror legislation, for little money was involved. Only even better intelligence might have helped. The Security Service as well as the Secret Intelligence Service (MI5 and MI6 as they are still more familiarly known) were already in receipt of huge increases in their budgets as they struggled to track down other murderous cells. Richard Reid, the 'shoe bomber' from Bromley who tried to destroy a flight from Paris to Miami in 2001, was another example of the threat from home-grown extremists, visiting 'radical' mosques from Brixton to Yorkshire, and there were many more examples of plots uncovered in these years, though by no means every suspect finally made it to court. In August 2005 police arrested suspects in Birmingham, High Wycombe and Walthamstow, east London, believing there was a plan to blow up as many as ten passenger aircraft over the Atlantic. The threat was all too real, widespread and hard to grip.

After many years of allowing dissident clerics and activists from the Middle East asylum in London, Britain had more than its share of inflammatory and dangerous extremists, who admired al Qaeda and preached violent jihad. Once September 11 had changed the climate, new laws were introduced to allow the detention without trial of foreigners suspected of being involved in supporting or fomenting terrorism. They could not be deported because human rights legislation forbade sending back anyone to countries where they might face torture. Seventeen were picked up and kept at Belmarsh high security prison. But in December 2004 the House of Lords ruled that these detentions were discriminatory and disproportionate and therefore illegal. Five weeks later the Home Secretary, Charles Clarke, hit back with 'control orders' to limit the movement of men he could not prosecute or deport. They would also be used against home-grown terror suspects. A month later, in February 2005, sixty Labour MPs revolted against these powers too, and the government only narrowly survived the vote. Ten Belmarsh men were put under these new restraints but the battle was far from over. In April 2006 a judge ruled that such control orders were 'an affront to justice' because they gave the Home Secretary, a politician, too much power and two months later said curfews of eighteen hours a day on six Iraqis were 'a deprivation of liberty' and also illegal. The new Home Secretary, John Reid, lost his appeal and reluctantly had to loosen the orders. In other cases, meanwhile, two men under control orders vanished.

New Labour Britain found itself in a struggle between its old laws and liberties and a new borderless, dangerous world. As we have seen the Britain of the forties was a prying and regulation-heavy country, emerging from the extraordinary conditions of a fight for national survival. From the fifties to the end of the eighties, the Cold War had grown a shadowy security state, with the vetting of BBC employees, MI5 surveillance of political radicals, a secret network of bunkers and tunnels, and the suspension of British jurisdiction over those small parts of the country taken by the United States forces. Yet none of this seriously challenged hallowed principles such as habeas corpus, free speech, a presumption of innocence, asylum, the right of British citizens to travel freely in their country without identifying papers, and the sanctity of homes in which the law-abiding lived. In the 'war on terror' much of this was suddenly in jeopardy.

New forms of eavesdropping, new compulsions, new political powers seemed to the government the least they needed to deal with a new, sinuous threat which ministers said could last for another thirty years. They were sure that most British people agreed, and that the judiciary, media, campaigners and elected politicians who protested were a hand-wringingly liberal, too-fastidious minority. Tony Blair, John Reid and Jack Straw were particularly emphatic about this and on the numbers were probably right. As Gordon Brown eyed the premiership, his rhetoric was similarly tough. Against recent historical tradition it was left to the Conservatives, as well as the Liberal Democrats, to mount the barriers in defence of civil liberties.

The Waning

This book is written under the shadow of a new politics of global warming, when the British were being urged to be environmentally friendly. This author's contribution, which may save a Nordic wood or small grove of some beauty, is to resist giving a detailed account of the decade-long feud between Tony Blair and Gordon Brown. It would, apart from anything else, require at least another volume the same size as this one. But it cannot be ignored because it has affected the country itself. The feud went on from New Labour's first days in power until the last months when the Prime Minister's fingertips, white with effort, were slipping from office. Sometimes there were oases of tranquillity and good humour, for months at a time. Yet the stories of door-slamming tantrums, four-lettered exchanges, make-ups, go-betweens, public snubs and cherished policies for Britain's future being tugged back and forth like disintegrating soft toys, were repeated in Whitehall private offices, pubs and newspaper columns almost weekly. Occasionally it seemed as if Blair was on the point of sacking his Chancellor. Brown was variously reported by Number Ten to have psychological flaws, to be a control-freak, a wrecker, a traditionalist 'playing to the gallery' and disloyal whenever the Prime Minister was in real trouble. Blair, retorted the Brownites, was a vain second-rater obsessed with money and glamour, who had betrayed the Chancellor over their original deal.

In the first term, Brown was defending his huge remit as Chancellor and Blair was trying to come to terms with how brutally he was being kept out of large policy areas; how little he knew of forthcoming Budgets; and how weak was his ability to push Britain towards the euro. Brown felt the second election victory in 2001 was mostly his own work, based on the strong economy. In the second term that followed it, he began pushing for a date when Blair would leave office. Blair, turning to the 'war on terror' and Iraq, failed to concentrate enough on domestic policy. Even so, he became ever more determined to hang on until he got the reforms he wanted. A gap seemed to open between Blair's enthusiasm for market-mimicking ideas to reform health and schools, and Brown's, for delivering better lives to the working poor. As we have seen, Brown was also keen on bringing private capital into public services, but there was a difference in emphasis which both men played up. 'Best when we are at our boldest,' said Blair. 'Best when we are Labour,' retorted Brown. Over Iraq, foundation hospitals and student top-up fees, Blair thought Brown came close to leaving him at the mercy of lethal backbench revolts, disappearing off into the rhododendron bushes just when he was most needed. Brown did give his support, and rally 'his people' to help Blair out of various self-excavated holes, but the Scotsman with the ladder tended to arrive as darkness was falling.

After six years in office he felt Blair was squandering the party's reputation on gimmicks and a too enthusiastic backing for Bush. He thought Blair had lied to him about when he would step down. John Prescott intervened first during November 2003, so worried that their feud would bring down the government that he knocked their heads together – metaphorically, despite his reputation – over a dinner of shepherd's pie, telling them they would destroy the Labour Party. This produced a truce but during 2004 things worsened rapidly again. Labour was badly hurt in local elections. With Iraq still smouldering, Labour MPs began to panic about what would happen at the next election. A mix of personal and political frustration brought Blair to another low ebb. For years he and Brown had dealt with each other through a range of intermediaries meeting on neutral ground and carrying white flags. Punctuating these regular arm's-length contacts, at roughly the chilly level one might expect between a Prime Minister and Leader of the Opposition, Blair and Brown had hotter private meetings. But by now they were barely speaking and Blair was deeply depressed about his legacy, as well as private troubles.

In July 2004 four cabinet ministers were so worried he was about to resign that they jointly pleaded with him to stay on. In the autumn Prescott was involved in further talks about whether there could be a 'peaceful transition'. On one occasion he met Brown at an oyster bar by Loch Fyne in Scotland. All the tables were taken. So for an hour and a half the two men talked in a black government limousine in the carpark, surrounded by armed guards, as if they were two businessmen of Sicilian extraction planning the carve-up of criminal territories. Prescott later talked of the (tectonic) plates moving and admitted that ministers were positioning themselves for the end of the Blair years. Brown was preparing himself for his looming premiership, briefing himself on foreign affairs, reaching out to groups well outside the Treasury's normal remit. Transition teams were prepared. Surely, finally, even this soap-opera was ending?

It was not. Blair gathered together his formidable internal resources and quietly determined that he would not go after all. Immediately after Labour's conference at Brighton he returned to Downing Street to make a triple announcement. He confirmed he was buying a house (an expensive, ugly, hard-to-let house) in Connaught Square which he and Cherie would eventually use for their retirement. After a heart scare the previous year, he was going into hospital for treatment using a thin wire to correct irregular heartbeat problems. This condition, which Blair was at pains to downplay, was known only to a few close friends. Like the house purchase, it tended to focus attention on his political mortality. Hence the third announcement, a bolt from the blue. He intended to fight the forthcoming election and if elected serve a full term. But as he told the author: 'I do not want to serve a fourth term – I do not think the British people would want a Prime Minister to serve so long – but I think it's sensible to make plain my intention now.' It was an unprecedented thing to say, and caught Brown on the hop – he was on his way to a meeting in Washington. In the short term it effectively killed off speculation that Blair was about to resign. To that extent it was clever. It may also have helped Labour in the 2005 election since Blair was promising his critics he would not, like Margaret Thatcher, try to 'go on and on'.

It certainly felt like a slap in the face for Brown. Just a day earlier in Brighton the two of them had had a long, tense talk about the future in which Blair warned him that his supporters were destabilizing the government and urged him to work with him. In response to a newspaper report that he was intending to serve a full third term, Blair told Brown this was wrong. He said nothing about his heart problem. When he discovered that Blair was planning a complete third term Brown was reported to be livid. Demoted from his old role running the forthcoming election campaign, he rejected an offer to chair Labour's press conferences during it. 'There is nothing that you could ever say to me now that I could ever believe,' he was said to have told the Prime Minister.[17] But life is full of surprises. Blair discovered that pre-announcing his political mortality, however protracted, was a draining and sapping mistake, the worst purely tactical decision of his premiership. It provoked a stream of further questions – yes, but when exactly? How many years is a full term? How long does your successor get in office before a further election? If you are going, what validity do your long-term plans for the country really have? And most pertinently, do you still want Gordon Brown to take over? These questions pursued him, loud, irritating, distracting heckles. His authority was first subtly, then dramatically, weakened.

Always, there were moments of hope. After Bush declared the war over on 1 May 2003, a search began for pro-Western Iraqis to whom some authority could be given. Eventually Saddam Hussein was found hiding in a hole and taken prisoner. Some eighty other countries pledged £18 bn for reconstruction, while US and British companies worked hard on repairing infrastructure. In the south where British forces were in control, they were quick to take off their helmets, patrolling in berets and trying to build good relations with local people. To start with, this worked well. Across Iraq huge amounts of money, dollars in shrink-wrapped blocks, were sent to be disbursed locally by hastily recruited Western viceroys. The following year saw the naming of Ayad Allawi, an affable Shiite, as interim Prime Minister of Iraq. That June, the United States formally handed over sovereignty to his government and a few days later, an Iraqi court began the trial of Saddam Hussein and eventually sentenced him to death. A national assembly was chosen and a date for elections was set. In January 2005, Iraqis had their first multi-party election for fifty years, choosing a transitional government. Later a Kurd, Jalal Talabani, was sworn in as Iraq's interim President. In October Iraqis voted for a new constitution, establishing an Islamic republic. At the end of the year millions took part in the full election which by January 2006 resulted in victory going to a Shia-dominated party, though without an overall majority. These were the drumbeats of democracy and renewal, much what Blair and Bush had hoped would happen.

What had not been predicted by them was the appalling dark side of Iraq after the conflict, which completely overshadowed the reconstruction and the creation of democratic structures. A long, numbing tale of insurrection followed by religious feud, slaughters, car and suicide bombings, the killing of civilians in heavy-handed military responses, the beheading of Western hostages, the revelation of brutality by US guards at the notorious Abu Graib prison, a full-scale assault on the rebel town of Falluja, a thousand dead in a panicked stampede . . . every day brought more murders, more fighting, less hope. By 2004, child mortality had doubled compared to 1990. There was a shortage of doctors and teachers. According to the World Bank, about a quarter of Iraqi children no longer attended school. Universities reported that they were being infiltrated by Muslim militias; professors fled and female students were persecuted for failing to wear the hijab. According to the United Nations, some 750,000 people had fled their homes since the war, adding to the 800,000 refugees of the Saddam era, while an estimated 1.6 million Iraqis had moved across the borders. By 2006, electricity supply was running at below the pre-war level and only half of Iraqi homes had safe supplies of water. Baghdad was on the edge of full-scale war, her hospitals filthy and dangerous, while militias roamed the streets. The possible breakup of the country was being openly talked about. In spring 2007, the international Red Cross described the suffering of Iraqi civilians as 'unbearable and unacceptable.' According to polls most British voters wanted the troops home, whatever further mayhem was caused.

It was the same story in the United States where most voters, who had been sold the idea that the Iraq War followed on naturally from 9/11, now believed it was a mistake. Bush stopped talking about 'staying the course.' A report for a Ministry of Defence think tank described Iraq as a recruiting sergeant for Islamic extremism around the world. This reflected the view of the Washington organization which brings together America's nineteen intelligence agencies, who firmly concluded that Iraq had increased the global risk of terrorism. In December 2006 the US Iraq Study Group presented Bush with a bleak assessment of the mayhem and a series of unpalatable options, designed to slowly bring America's soldiers home while negotiating with her traditional enemies in an attempt to bring some kind of stability to the country.

So by almost any standard that can be applied, three years after the Iraq war, it looked like a catastrophe. The country was experiencing civil war. The lives of Iraqis were now even more at risk, and mostly more unpleasant, than under Saddam's dreadful regime. Terrorism had been encouraged, not defeated. Countries regarded by London and Washington as regional menaces, Syria and Iran, were stronger and more confident, not less. With 120 British military dead in Iraq, most people saw the war as the worst single mistake by a British government in recent times. Some believe that had Blair refused to give British support for the war, it would not have happened. The mood inside the White House after September 11 makes this unlikely.

Even so, having committed Britain, Blair could not stand aside from the consequences. The kaleidoscope was shaken all right. The pieces were in flux.

A Crowd of New People

One result of the long Iraqi agony was the arrival of many Iraqi asylum-seekers in Britain, Kurds, Shiites and Sunnis. This was little commented on because they were only a small part of a large migration into the country which changed it during the Blair years. It was a multi-lingual, many-religioned migration which included Poles, Zimbabweans, Somalis, Nigerians, Russians and Afghans, Australians, white South Africans and Americans, as well as sizeable French and German inflows. In 2005, according to the Office for National Statistics, immigrants were arriving to live in Britain at the rate of 1,500 a day; and since Tony Blair had arrived in power, more than 1.3 million people had come. By the mid-2000s English was no longer the first language of half the primary school children in London, and the capital boasted 350 different separate language groups.

The poorer new migrant groups were almost entirely unrepresented in politics but radically changed the sights, sounds and scents of urban Britain. The veiled women of the Muslim world, or its more traditionalist and Arab quarters, became common sights even on the streets of many market towns, from Scotland to Kent. Polish tradesmen and factory workers were followed by shops stocking up with Polish food and selling Polish magazines, and even by Polish road signs. Chinese villagers were involved in a tragedy when nineteen were caught by the tide while cockle-picking at Morecambe Bay and drowned; but many more were working in grim conditions for rural 'gang-masters' or as the then Home Secretary, David Blunkett, put it, 'as slaves'. Russian voices began to be as common on the London Underground as Irish ones. Through most of its history Britain had been abnormally open to the world, mostly imposing herself elsewhere. Now she found herself a 'world island' in a new way.

Throughout the twentieth century, Britain's foreign policy had been concerned to control the impact of outside forces on these busy, crowded islands. In its first half she had tried this by attempting to keep her imperial possessions while subduing her greatest rival, Germany. In its second half she had worked with America against the Soviet Union to preserve a system of democracy and the free market, hoping to avoid nuclear annihilation, determined to avoid European federalism. She was not a successful manufacturing country but became a popular place to do financial business. Compared to similar countries, she was unusually warlike, spending more on defence and fighting more, too. Britain had always gone out into the world. Now, increasingly, the world came to her, poor and migrant, rich and corporate, the people of Eastern Europe·and the manufactures of China. As in Victorian times, she was on the edge of newness, at the global bow-wave of change, but now it was change experienced near at hand.

Immigration had been a constant of British life. What was new was the scale and variety. Earlier modern migrations had, as we have seen, provoked a racialist backlash, riots, the rise of the National Front and a series of new laws. These later migrations were controversial in different ways. The early arrivals from the Caribbean or India were people who looked different but spoke the same language and in many cases had had a similar education to native British people. Many of the later migrants looked similar to the white British but shared no linguistic or imperial history. There were other differences. Young educated Polish or Czech people had come to Britain to earn money before going home again to acquire good homes, marry and have children in their rapidly growing countries. The economic growth of the early 2000s was fuelled by the influx of energetic and talented people, often denuding their own countries of skills, making their way in Britain as quickly as the East African Asians had before.

But there are always two sides to such changes. Criminal gangs of Albanians, Kosovars and Turks appeared as novel and threatening as Jamaican criminality had thirty years earlier. The social service bill for the new migrants was a serious burden to local authorities; towns such as Slough protested to national government about the extra cost in housing, education and other services. Above everything else, there was the sheer scale of the new migrations and the inability of the machinery of government to regulate what was happening. The Home Office's immigration and nationality department (IND) seemed unable to prevent illegal migrants entering Britain, to spot those abusing the asylum system in order to settle here, or to apprehend and deport people. An illegal and sometimes lethal trade in 'people smuggling' made it particularly hard. Even after airlines were made responsible for the status of those they carried, large articulated lorries filled with human beings who had paid over their life savings to be taken to Britain, rumbled through the Channel Tunnel.

A Red Cross camp at Sangatte, near its French entrance, was blamed by Britain for exacerbating the problem. By the end of 2002, when Blunkett finally managed to get a deal with the French to close it, an estimated 67,000 had passed through Sangatte into Britain. Many African, Asian and Balkan migrants, believing the British immigration and benefits systems to be easier than those of other EU countries, simply moved across the continent and waited patiently for their journey into the UK. Thermal-imaging devices, increased border staff and unwelcoming asylum centres were all deployed. Unknown numbers of migrants died through thirst, asphyxiation or cold; some were murdered en route. Successive home secretaries – Jack Straw, David Blunkett, Charles Clarke and John Reid – tried to gapple with the trade, introducing legislation which was criticized by civil liberties campaigners and challenged in the courts. None was much applauded for their efforts and the last of them eventually confessed that he believed his department was 'not fit for purpose'. He hived off the struggling IND as a separate agency and promised to clear a backlog of around 280,000 failed asylum-seekers still in the country within five years. Uniformed border security staff were promised, and the historic Home Office was to be split up.

Meanwhile, many straightforwardly illegal immigrants had bypassed the asylum system entirely. In July 2005 the Home Office produced its own estimate of what the illegal population of the UK had been four years earlier, reckoning it between 310,000 and 570,000 souls, or between 0.5 and 1 per cent of the total population. A year later unofficial estimates pushed the possible total higher, to 800,000. The truth was, with boxes of cardboard files still being uncovered and no national recording system, nobody had a clue. Even the Bank of England complained, asking how it could set interest rates without knowing roughly how many people were working in the country. Official figures showed the number applying for asylum falling, perhaps as former Yugoslavia returned to relative peace. Controversially, thousands were being sent back to Iraq. But there were always new desperate groups, in the Middle East or war-torn and hungry Africa: projections about the impact of global warming suggested there always would be.

The arrival of workers from the ten countries which joined the EU in 2004 was a different issue, though it involved an influx of roughly the same size. When the European Union expanded Britain decided that, unlike France or Germany, she would not try to delay opening the country to migrant workers. Ministers suggested that the likely number arriving would be around 26,000 over the first two years. This was wildly wrong. In 2006 a Home Office minister, Tony McNulty, announced that since 2004 when the European Union expanded 427,000 people from Poland and seven other new EU nations had applied to work in Britain. If the self-employed were included, he added, the real figure would be nearer 600,000. There were at least 36,000 spouses and children who had arrived too and 27,000 child benefit applications had been received. These were very large numbers indeed. The Ugandan Asian migration which caused such a storm in 1971 had, for instance, amounted to some 28,000 people. It was hardly surprising that Britain now faced an acute housing shortage and that government officials began scouring the South of England looking for new places where councils would be ordered to let the developers start building.

By the government's own 2006 figures, annual net migration for the previous year was 185,000 and had averaged 166,000 over the previous seven years. This compares to the 50,000 net inflow which Enoch Powell had criticized in his notorious 1968 speech as 'mad, literally mad'. Projections based on many different assumptions suggested the UK population would grow by more than seven million by 2031. Of that, 80 per cent would be due to immigration. The organization Migration Watch UK, set up by a former diplomat to campaign for less immigration, said this was equivalent to requiring the building of two new towns the size of Cambridge each year, or five new Birminghams over the quarter century. But was there a mood of unnecessary hysteria? As has been noted, many of the Eastern European migrants, like those from Australia, France or the United States, could be expected to return home eventually. Immigration was partially offset by the outward flow of around 60,000 British people moving abroad each year, mainly to Australia, the United States, France and Spain. By the winter of 2006–7 one policy institute, the IPPR, reckoned there were 5.5 million British people living permanently overseas – nearly one in ten of us, or more than the population of Scotland – and another half million living there for some of the year. Aside from the obvious destinations, the Middle East and Asia were seeing rising colonies of expatriate British. Who were they? A worrying proportion seemed to be graduates; Britain is believed to lose one in six graduates to emigration. Many were retired or better-off people looking for a life of sunlit ease, just as many immigrants to Britain were young, ambitious and keen to work. Government ministers tended to emphasize the benign economic effects of immigration. Their critics looked around and asked where all the extra people would go, and what spare road space, hospital beds or schools they would find to use.

Blair's Final Years

From Labour's arrival in power in 1997 right through to the 2005 election, Blair and his ministers had never been seriously worried about the Conservatives. After the heavy defeat in 2001, Hague had instantly resigned. The Conservatives then rejected the man who had seemed the obvious alternative, Michael Portillo. The son of a Spanish republican refugee and as a boy the advertising face of Ribena fruit juice, he had suffered the crippling fate of being regularly touted as a future leader from the mid-eighties, Mrs Thatcher's chosen one. But Portillo had feuded with Hague. More importantly, he was on a personal journey to a more metropolitan view of the world, had admitted homosexual affairs in his youth, and would not condescend to pretend to his party that he was anything other than socially liberal. He launched his campaign in an achingly trendy London restaurant, so the party in its first full democratic leadership vote instead chose Iain Duncan Smith. In 'IDS', a former soldier, businessman and, in Parliament, a Euro-sceptic rebel, MP for Norman Tebbit's old seat of Chingford, traditionalist Conservatives thought they had found someone who truly represented their core beliefs. Indeed they had. But they underestimated Duncan Smith's deep interest in helping the disadvantaged and, sadly, had overestimated his political skill. A thoroughly decent man, he was outclassed so badly as a speaker and on television that the Tories took fright. A growing rebellion persuaded him to resign as leader in December 2003.

A demoralized party did something rare. It chose its next leader without the customary vicious fight, returning the former cabinet minister Michael Howard to the colours. Howard had been controversial as Home Secretary but was part of the Tories' 'Cambridge mafia' and brought rivals from the liberal wing of the party back inside his leadership tent. He began brilliantly as leader, binding wounds and restoring morale. He was the first Tory leader to really worry Brown and Blair, a dangerous opponent. Like Hague, he performed well in the Commons, calling on the Prime Minister to resign over Iraq and making much of a series of Home Office scandals and failures. In 2005 his election focused on better public services and immigration. Conservative posters asked the question: 'Are you thinking what we're thinking?' Though they gained substantial numbers of seats and votes – a majority in England – the country's overall answer was 'No, not really'. Michael Howard resigned and was replaced by the bright young Old Etonian David Cameron. Taking the Tories in a green and liberal direction, he won high poll ratings and looked set, by 2007, to be the Conservative leader best placed to oust a sitting Labour government since Margaret Thatcher had the job thirty years earlier.

The Liberal Democrats might have hoped that the hugely unpopular Iraq War and the Blair government's growing reputation for illiberal and fiddly statism, would allow the third party to break through. Under Paddy Ashdown, there had been a long and fruitless courtship with Labour, ultimately made impossible to consummate by Blair's large majorities. Then the experience of the Scottish parliamentary elections turned Blair against voting reform, a key Lib-Dem demand. His old mentor Roy Jenkins wryly gave him up as a constitutional reformer of any kind, and that relationship cooled. Ashdown's successor Charles Kennedy had been the youngest MP when first elected for the Western Isles as an SDP member. He was popular with the party and the media. He took the Lib-Dems away from any proximity to New Labour and campaigned, after some encouragement, against the Iraq War. Under him the third party became a place where disaffected leftish Britons gathered, a pacific haven from Blair's bellicose certainties and the Home Secretary David Blunkett's enthusiasm for locking up asylum-seekers. In the 2001 election the Liberal Democrats won fifty-two seats and in 2005, sixty-two, a record performance. But after the heady optimism of the early eighties, they seemed to be back playing a long game. Charles Kennedy had a serious alcohol problem which could make him fuzzy and unconvincing and which, though his aides lied about it for years, eventually led to his resignation as party leader. He was replaced by Sir Menzies Campbell, a Scottish lawyer and former Olympic runner who was older but safer.

The 2005 election campaign ended with Labour's majority cut from 167 in the previous contest to just sixty-seven. For most previous prime ministers a majority of that size would have been considered handsome. Heath, Wilson, Callaghan or Major would have killed for it, and it was twenty-four more than Margaret Thatcher had enjoyed in her first, strife-ridden and tumultuous administration. But by the standards of New Labour's record the loss was a serious rebuke. The voters were noticing. But what? Blair thought they were noticing the habit of disloyalty among his MPs. Many of them thought they were noticing Blair. Certainly with so many disaffected former ministers and left-wing dissidents on the Labour benches it meant he would have an even harder time getting his own way. Then there was the further problem of his time-limited remaining tenure and the slow withdrawal of his personal authority. Brown had not been given his accustomed role in election planning but was far more involved than Blair had first intended in the 2005 fight. With their best false hearty smiles in place, and much criticized for making wild claims about the cuts planned by their Tory opponents, they had won their third mandate standing beside one another, if not hand in hand. As soon as the election was over Blair turned his mind to staying on rather longer than the Chancellor had hoped.

The latter stages of Blair's time as Prime Minister were overshadowed by the bloody aftermath of the Iraq War, and by renewed fighting in Afghanistan. After more bad local elections in 2006 he sacked his Home Secretary, Charles Clarke, who publicly protested; he demoted his Foreign Secretary, Jack Straw, and he stripped John Prescott, who had been hit by a scandal, of his departmental responsibilities. The embarrassing police inquiry into whether businessmen had been recommended for peerages as a result of offering loans to the

Labour Party drew closer to Downing Street; shortly before Christmas 2006 Tony Blair became the first serving Prime Minister to be interviewed by the police as part of a criminal investigation. He was questioned in Downing Street for two hours by Detective Chief Inspector Graeme McNulty and a colleague. This occurred on the same day as the official police report into the death of Diana was finally published, and a controversial announcement was made about rural post offices. Downing Street denied there was any attempt to bury bad news but from the outside it looked like one New Labour tradition that should have been ditched.

But would it bring forward an earlier departure? After a rocky summer in 2006 there had been an organized round of junior ministerial resignations, and demands for Blair to quit, assumed by Number Ten and most of the media to have been organized by supporters of Gordon Brown. Despite calling an open letter on the subject 'disloyal, discourteous and wrong', on 7 September the prime minister promised that the coming party conference would be his last, breaking under duress his earlier promise to serve a full term. Labour's conference, held unusually in Manchester, saw one of Blair's most eloquent speeches ever, a defiant farewell to the party which no longer wanted him, and which responded to him with largely hypocritical adulation. It did not look as if the parting would be particularly sweet, on either side. His wife was heard referring to Brown's earlier conference speech with the single word 'liar'. Soon, Blairites were attempting to persuade the young cabinet minister David Miliband to challenge Brown in a leadership contest. He was being bashful, but it was evidence of how deeply in trouble Labour now was. The polls showed Brown trailing the new Conservative leader David Cameron. Whatever this was, it was not glad confident morning again.

Britain After Blair

This history has told the story of the defeat of politics by shopping. The political visions of Attlee, and Churchill in his romantic-nostalgic mood, were overthrown by the consumer boom of the fifties. People generally wanted colour, variety and new tastes, not austere socialist egalitarianism or thigh-slapping New Elizabethan patriotism, though a large minority was drawn to each of these. In the Wilson and Heath years, politicians promised a newly scientific, planned future, all straight lines and patriotism, drawn up in Whitehall with everyone sitting down together 'backing Britain'. Their Britain collapsed and Margaret Thatcher's revolution shovelled away the rubble. Her boot-sale of state enterprise, defeat of the unions, and her abandonment of politicians' controls over money led to a new boom. The old state retreated and the consumer society advanced. Far from remoralizing the British with the Victorian values of frugality, saving, orderliness and continence as she had hoped, Thatcher gave many of us the licence and credit to behave like Regency rakes on a spree. The country went shopping again, as it had in the fifties and sixties and would again in the nineties and beyond.

The new great powers in the land were organizations that had barely been noticed before the war. In 1924 an East End barrow boy called Jack Cohen had used part of his surname and the initials of a tea supplier to market his own-brand tea under the title Tesco. Five years later he opened his first shop, then the country's first all-purpose food warehouse and in 1956, when Tony Blair was three, a self-service store. Tesco leaped ahead. In the eighties Cohen's daughter, Dame Shirley Porter, became leader of Westminster Council and, after a highly controversial 'homes for votes' scandal, left the country. By the time Blair left office, Tesco was the country's leading retailer with 1,780 stores, sales of more than £37 bn and profits of over £2 bn. It was gaining one pound in every three the British spent on groceries and there was talk of Britain becoming a 'Tescopoly'. Asda, set up by Yorkshire farmers in 1965 and now owned by Wal-Mart, the American behemoth and the world's biggest company, came second to Tesco, but was still serving more than 13 million people a week. Sainsbury's, which had originated in a Victorian dairy shop and had launched the first self-service supermarket in 1950, had sales of £17 bn, and more than 750 stores. Such companies dominated farmers and other suppliers exercised great power in planning disputes, and were becoming increasingly controversial. Meanwhile, to enjoy the consumer economy, the British were borrowing: the average adult had credit card, finance-deal and unsecured personal loans amounting to more than £4,500.

Apart from generous planning laws, the shopping boom required the 'great car economy' lauded by Margaret Thatcher, which was now restrained only by rising petrol prices and congestion. London had deployed its own congestion charge and a national debate had begun about road pricing. Car use was huge by historic standards. At the beginning of the sixties when supermarkets first took off, there were 9 million vehicles on the roads; by the mid-2000s, there were 30 million. It was not all shopping, of course. Commuting by car had become mundane and the number of journeys to school by car had doubled in ten years. By the standards of the forties or fifties, the British now led strikingly privatized lives. They mostly shunned public transport and were far less likely to shop shoulder to shoulder with neighbours, using shopkeepers they knew by name. With television, digital or analogue, and the computer boom, entertainment was much likelier to remain in the home. The British were afloat on a tide of cheap imported goods, easy credit and new labour, both skilled and unskilled. House prices had by now nearly tripled in the Blair years. But politicians, still taxing vigorously, still struggling to deliver popular and efficient public services, were not given any credit for that.

Politics shrivelled – as an activity, as a source of status, as a way of ordering life that was respected or trusted. Lady Thatcher found no truly effective way to run the public services. Nor did her successors, John Major and Tony Blair. The great middling layer of public life, the independent-minded managers of schools, hospitals and towns, who had real freedom to manage, and the self-confident local politicians who could make waves, had gone. By most measures overall crime had fallen from the late nineties, at the cost of overcrowded prisons. But violent crime was as much feared as ever, and as present on the streets of the main cities. All this had a direct effect on people's hopes and fears about the country. One commentator from a conservative-minded think tank explained the exodus of 1,000 people a day to other countries: 'People are emigrating because of a sense of hopelessness . . . nothing is ever done about the big problems like education, health, crime. There is a growing sense that politicians will never deal with the problems.'[18] That was only one voice, and others had different views, but it reminds us why the policy problems discussed at length earlier are so critical to the country's notion of its future.

Yet, at the end of this story, the need for true politics seems to have returned. Towards the end of his time in office Tony Blair unveiled a report by an economist, Sir Nicholas Stern, which he described as more important than any report to government during the New Labour years – more important, therefore, than the debate over Iraq, or pensions, peace in Ireland or the future of Britain's health service. Few questioned this bold assertion. For the report was about climate change. We have already seen how radically new waves of migration were changing Britain but they were as nothing compared to what a new climate might do. An overwhelming preponderance of scientists believed not simply that the climate was changing (there was no room left for doubt about that) but that the change was man-made and potentially catastrophic. The polar ice was melting, weather patterns were disrupted around the globe, species were disappearing and yet, as China and India advanced, the gases causing these changes continued to pour upwards. Blair had tried to persuade his partner in Iraq, George Bush, to alter in some way his hostility to carbon limits but to no avail: compared to the agreements he had won on Africa, Blair's effort on climate change had been a failure.

American self-interest overrode what to others seemed proper and fair. And there was no bigger cultural challenge to Britons' sense of proportion and fairness than the one thrown down by militant Islam. After 9/11 and the London bombings, there were plenty of angry, narrow-minded young Muslim men running amuck, either literally or in their heads. Their views, and the veiled women of Arab tradition, provoked English politicians to ask whether their communities wanted to fully integrate. Britain did not have as high a proportion of Muslims as France, but large parts of the English Midlands and the South had long-established and third-generation urban villages of hundreds of thousands of Muslim people. Muslims felt they were being watched in a new way and they were perhaps right to feel a little uneasy. In the old industrial towns of the Pennines, and in stretches of West London near Heathrow there were such strong concentrations of incomers that the word ghetto was being used by ministers and civil servants. White working-class people had long been moving, quietly, to other areas: Essex, Hertfordshire, the towns of coastal Sussex, even Spain.

They were a minority, if polling was any guide: only a quarter of Britons said they would prefer to live in white-only areas. Yet multi-culturalism, if it was defined as more than simple 'live and let live', was being questioned. How much should new Britons integrate, and how much was the retention of traditions a matter of their human rights? Speaking in December 2006 Blair cited forced marriages, the importation of sharia law and the ban on women entering certain mosques as being on the wrong side of the line. In the same speech he used new, harder language. After the London bombings, 'for the first time in a generation there is an unease, an anxiety, even at points a resentment that our very openness, our willingness to welcome difference, our pride in being home to many cultures, is being used against us.' He went on to try to define the duty to integrate: 'Our tolerance is part of what makes Britain, Britain. So conform to it; or don't come here. We don't want the hate-mongers . . . If you come here lawfully, we welcome you. If you are permitted to stay here permanently, you become an equal member of our community and become one of us.' Though Blair chose security as his ground, for others it was about more than the struggle against terrorism. Britain's strong economic growth, despite a weak manufacturing base, was partly the product of a long tradition of hospitality. The question was now whether the country was becoming so crowded – England had the highest population density of any major country in the Western world – that this tolerance was eroding. It would require wisdom from politicians and efficiency from Whitehall to keep things on an even keel.

Just the same is true of that larger threat, climate change. This threatened reshaping was physical, not demographic, the waves of water, not of people. It promised to alter the familiar splatter of Britain as she is seen from space or on any map. Nothing is more fundamental to a country's sense of itself than its shape, particularly when the country is an island. Rising sea levels could make Britain look different on every side. They could eat into the smooth billow of East Anglia, centuries after the wetlands were reclaimed with Dutch drainage, and submerge the concrete-crusted, terraced marshland of London, and drown idyllic Scottish islands and force the abandonment of coastal towns which had grown in Georgian and Victorian times. Wildlife would die out and be replaced by new species – there were already unfamiliar fish offshore and new birds and insects in British gardens. All this was beyond the power of Britain alone to deflect, since she was responsible for just 2 per cent of global emissions. Even if the British could be persuaded to give up their larger cars, their foreign holidays and their gadgets, would it really make a difference?

Without a frank, unheated conversation between the rest of us and elected politicians, who are then sent out into the world to do the bigger deals that must be done, what hope for action on climate change? It seems certain to involve the loss of new liberties, such as cheap, easy travel. It will change the countryside as grim-looking wind farms appear. It will change how we light and heat our homes and how we are taxed. All these changes are intensely political, in a way the British of the forties would have recognized. Politics is coming back as a big force in our lives, like it or not. It will require more frankness, less spin, and a more grown-up interest in policy, not scandal. Without this frankness, without trust on each side, what hope for a sensible settlement between Muslim and Christian, incomer and old timer? Without a rebuilding of strong local structures, what hope for better-run schools, councils or hospitals? Without level-headed politics, how will the future shape of the UK, if it continues, be negotiated? In the course of this history, most political leaders have arrived eager and optimistic, found themselves in trouble of one kind or another, and left disappointed. Such is the nature of political life. (Indeed, perhaps it is the nature of life.) But the rest of us need those optimistic politicians, the next leaders, the ones whom we'll laugh at and abuse. And we need them more than ever now.

The threats facing the British are large ones. But in the years since 1945, having escaped nuclear devastation, tyranny and economic collapse, we British have no reason to despair, or emigrate. In global terms, to be born British remains a wonderful stroke of luck.

Notes

Prologue

1. See Correlli Barnett, *The Collapse of British Power*, Eyre Methuen, 1972.
2. George L. Bernstein, *The Myth of Decline: The Rise of Britain Since 1945*, Pimlico, 2004.

Part One: Hunger and Pride

1. William Harrington & Peter Young, *The 1945 Revolution*, Davis-Poynter, 1970.
2. Norman Howard, *A New Dawn*, Politico's, 2005.
3. Ibid.
4. W. K. Hancock & M. M. Gowing, *The British War Economy*, HMSO, 1949.
5. All quotes from Correlli Barnett, *The Lost Victory*, Macmillan, 1995.
6. Robert Skidelsky, *John Maynard Keynes. Volume 3: Fighting for Britain*, Macmillan, 2000.
7. Ibid.
8. See Desmond Wettern, *The Decline of British Sea Power*, Jane's, 1982.
9. Vice Admiral Sir Louis le Bailly, *From Fisher to the Falklands*, Institute of Marine Engineers, 1991; and Eric J. Grove, *Vanguard to Trident: British Naval Policy since World War 2*, The Bodley Head, 1987.
10. Dan Van der Vat, *Standard of Power*, Hutchinson, 2000.
11. N. A. M. Rodger, *The Admiralty*, Terence Dalton, 1979.
12. Peter Hennessy, *The Prime Minister*, Allen Lane, 2000.
13. Quoted often but see ibid.
14. Hugh Dalton, *The Fateful Years*, Muller, 1957.
15. Story recounted to the author by Gordon Brown, who showed me the very same mahogany lavatory.

16. Alan Bullock, *Ernest Bevin, Foreign Secretary*, Oxford U. P., 1985.
17. Ibid.
18. Aneurin Bevan, *In Place of Fear*, Heinemann, 1952.
19. Dean Acheson, *Sketches from Life* (1961), quoted in Bullock, op. cit.
20. For this and further material in the following paragraph, see Paul Addison, *The Road to 1945*, Jonathan Cape, 1975.
21. George Orwell, 'England Your England', from *Inside the Whale and Other Essays*, Victor Gollancz, 1940; repr. Penguin, 1962.
22. Arthur Herman, *To Rule the Waves*, Hodder, 2004.
23. See Peter Hennessy, *Never Again: Britain 1945–1951*, Jonathan Cape, 1992.
24. CAB 134/1315 PR (56)3, 1 June 1956, reproduced in *British Documents on the End of Empire*, ed. David Goldsworthy, HMSO, 1994.
25. Labour Party, *Fair Shares of Scarce Consumer Goods*, London 1946, quoted in Ina Zweiniger-Bargielowska, *Austerity in Britain*, Oxford U. P., 2000.
26. See Susan Cooper, 'Snoek Piquante', in *Age of Austerity 1945–1951*, ed. Michael Sissons & Philip French, Hodder & Stoughton, 1963.
27. Simon Garfield (ed.), *Our Hidden Lives*, Ebury Press, 2004.
28. See Peter Hennessy, *Whitehall*, Secker & Warburg, 1989.
29. Most of this information comes from Robert Winder, *Bloody Foreigners*, Abacus, 2004.
30. See Juliet Cheetham, in *Trends in British Society since 1900*, ed. A. H. Halsey, Macmillan, 1972.
31. Jean Medawar & David Pyke, *Hitler's Gift*, Richard Cohen Books, 2000.
32. For instance in adverts warning of the dangers of VD.
33. Quoted in Nicholas Timmins, *The Five Giants*, HarperCollins, 1995.
34. Ibid.
35. Graham Payn & Sheridan Morley (eds), *The Noël Coward Diaries*, Weidenfeld & Nicolson, 1982.
36. See Gyles Brandreth, *Charles and Camilla*, Century, 2005.
37. Ben Pimlott, *The Queen*, HarperCollins, 1996.
38. Richard Chamberlain, et al (eds) *Austerity to Affluence, British Art and Design, 1945–1962*, Merrell Holberton, 1997.
39. See Maureen Waller, *London 1945*, John Murray, 2004.
40. See Paul Addison, *Now the War is Over*, BBC/Cape, 1985.
41. Zweiniger-Bargielowska, op. cit.
42. Waller, op. cit.
43. See Nigel Walker in Halsey, op. cit.

44. Peter Hitchens, *A Brief History of Crime*, Atlantic Books, 2003.
45. Timmins, op. cit.
46. For all this, Timmins, the best single account of the Beveridge report easily available.
47. See Christian Wolmar, *On the Wrong Line*, Aurum Press, 2005.
48. Barnett, *The Lost Victory*.
49. Godfey Hodgson, 'The Steel Debates' in Sissons & French, op. cit.
50. See Peter Hennessy, *Never Again*, Jonathan Cape, 1992; and Timmins, op. cit.
51. For a full description of the Prefab story, see Greg Stevenson, *Palaces for the People*, Batsford, 2003.
52. Quoted in Miles Glendinning & Stefan Muthesius, *Tower Block*, Paul Mellon Centre/Yale University Press, 1994.
53. Quoted in ibid.
54. David Hughes, 'The Spivs' in Sissons & French, op. cit.
55. Quoted in Addison, op. cit.
56. Anne Perkins, *Red Queen*, Macmillan, 2003.
57. Susan Cooper, 'Snoek Piquante' in Sissons & French, op. cit.
58. Pearson Phillips in ibid.
59. Ruth Adam, *A Woman's Place, 1910–1975*, Persephone Books, 2000.
60. Quoted in Addison, op. cit.
61. Interview, *The Stage*, 2005.
62. Dominic Shellard, *British Theatre Since the War*, Yale U. P., 1999.
63. John Osborne, *Almost a Gentleman*, Faber & Faber, 1991.
64. Arthur Miller, quoted in Terry Coleman, *Olivier: The Authorised Biography*, Bloomsbury, 2005.
65. Quoted in Max Hastings, *The Korean War*, Michael Joseph, 1987.
66. Jung Chang & Jon Halliday, *Mao: The Unknown Story*, Jonathan Cape, 2005.
67. Hastings, op. cit.
68. James Cameron, *Point of Departure*, Arthur Barker, 1967; repr. Granta Books, 2006.
69. See Jung Chang & Halliday, op. cit.
70. Tom Hickman, *The Call-Up: A History of National Service*, Headline, 2004.
71. Anthony Farrar-Hockley, *The British Part in the Korean War*, HMSO, 1990.
72. Betty Vernon, *Ellen Wilkinson*, Croom Helm, 1987.

73. B. L. Donoughue & G. L. Jones, *Herbert Morrison, Portrait of a Politician*, Weidenfeld & Nicolson, 1973.
74. Michael Frayn, and Francis Boyd of the *Manchester Guardian*.
75. Michael Frayn, 'Festival' in Sissons & French, op. cit.

Part Two: The Land of Lost Content

1. For these figures, see Anthony Sampson, *Anatomy of Britain Today*, Hodder & Stoughton, 1965.
2. For Balcon see Matthew Sweet, *Shepperton Babylon*, Faber & Faber, 2005; Michael Balcon, *A Lifetime of Films*, Hutchinson, 1969; and Charles Barr, *Ealing Studios*, Cameron & Hollis, 1998.
3. *The Macmillan Diaries: The Cabinet Years 1950–1957*, Macmillan, 2000.
4. Edward Heath, *The Course of My Life*, Hodder & Stoughton, 1998.
5. Ibid.
6. See Dominic Sandbrook, *Never Had It So Good*, Little, Brown, 2005.
7. D. R. Thorpe, *Eden: The Life and Times of Anthony Eden, First Earl of Avon, 1897–1977*, Chatto & Windus, 2003.
8. Quoted in Peter Hennessy, *The Secret State*, Penguin, 2002.
9. Hugo Young, *This Blessed Plot*, Macmillan, 1998.
10. See Alistair Horne, *Macmillan*, vol. 1, Macmillan, 1988.
11. Peter Hennessy, *Having It So Good*, Allen Lane, 2006.
12. R. A. Butler, *The Art of the Possible*, quoted in Hennessy, ibid.
13. Peter Wildeblood, *Against the Law*, Weidenfeld & Nicolson, 1955.
14. Lord Montagu of Beaulieu, *Wheels Within Wheels: An Unconventional Life*, Weidenfeld & Nicolson, 2000.
15. Tom Driberg, *Guy Burgess*, Weidenfeld & Nicolson, 1956.
16. Spike Milligan, *Adolf Hitler: My Part in his Downfall*, Michael Joseph, 1971; Penguin, 1973.
17. In a 1957 interview, quoted by Humphrey Carpenter, *Spike Milligan*, Hodder & Stoughton, 2003. The following quotes are also from this book.
18. D. R. Thorne, *Eden*, Chatto & Windus, 2003.
19. Brian Lapping, *End of Empire*, Granada, 1985.
20. Ben Pimlott, *The Queen*, HarperCollins, 1996.
21. See, for all this, Tom Hickman, *The Call-Up: A History of National Service*, Headline, 2004.

22. Thanks to Rick Richards of Christchurch and Jean Webber of Burghclere, Newbury, for this information to the author.

23. Jean-Raymond Tourneaux, *Secrets d'Etat*, Paris, 1960, quoted in Herman Finer, *Dulles over Suez*, Heinemann, 1964.

24. Quoted in Robert Shepherd, *Enoch Powell*, Hutchinson, 1996.

25. See Gerald Frost, *Antony Fisher, Champion of Liberty*, Profile Books, 2002.

26. Richard Cockett, *Thinking the Unthinkable*, HarperCollins, 1994.

27. Gillian Bardsley, *Issigonis: the Official Biography*, Icon Books, 2005.

28. See Barbara Castle, *Fighting All the Way*, Macmillan, 1993; and Anne Perkins, *Red Queen*, Macmillan, 2003.

29. See Sandbrook, op. cit.

30. Keith Middlemass, *Power, Competition and the State*, vol. 1, Macmillan, 1986.

31. Quoted in Sandbrook, op. cit.

32. Ibid.

33. Quoted in Perkins, op. cit.

34. Crossman's account, quoted in Philip Williams, *Hugh Gaitskell*, Jonathan Cape, 1979.

35. Quoted in Patrick Hannan, *When Arthur Met Maggie*, Seren, 2006.

36. Anthony Crosland, *The Future of Socialism*, Jonathan Cape, 1956; see also Susan Crosland, *Tony Crosland*, Jonathan Cape, 1982.

37. Letter of Harold Macmillan to Sir Robert Menzies, quoted in Andrew Roberts, *A History of the English-Speaking Peoples since 1900*, Weidenfeld & Nicolson, 2006.

38. James Chuter Ede, quoted in Mike & Trevor Phillips, *Windrush: The Irresistible Rise of Multi-Racial Britain*, HarperCollins, 1999.

39. Quoted in Randall Hansen, *Citizenship and Immigration in Post-war Britain*, Oxford U. P., 2000.

40. See Robert Winder, *Bloody Foreigners*, Abacus, 2004

41. Sandbrook, op. cit.

42. A. G. Bennett, quoted in ibid.

43. Phillips & Phillips, op. cit.

44. Hansen, op. cit.

45. Winder, op. cit.

46. For this, and other material here, see Hugo Young's *This Blessed Plot*, op. cit.

47. See ibid.

48. Roy Jenkins, *A Life at the Centre*, Macmillan, 1991.
49. Horne, *Macmillan*, vol. 2; also for the Birch Grove meeting.
50. Heath, op. cit.
51. Quoted in Hennessy, *The Secret State*, op. cit.
52. Hennessy, ibid.
53. Brian Lavery, *Journal of Maritime Research*: his article on Macmillan, Eisenhower and the Holy Loch affair is by far the best account.
54. Mark Amory, in his preface to *The Letters of Ann Fleming*, Collins Harvill, 1985.
55. Brian Brivati, *Hugh Gaitskell*, Richard Cohen Books, 1996.
56. Ibid.
57. For Cliveden and the following, see Derek Wilson, *The Astors*, Weidenfeld & Nicolson, 1993.
58. Harry Thompson, *Peter Cook: A Biography*, Hodder & Stoughton, 1997.
59. R. H. S. Crossman, *The Diaries of a Cabinet Minister*, Hamish Hamilton/ Cape, 1975.

Part Three: Harold, Ted and Jim

1. See Ben Pimlott, *Harold Wilson*, HarperCollins, 1992.
2. Kenneth O. Morgan, *Callaghan: A Life*, Oxford U. P., 1997.
3. Lord George-Brown, *In My Way*, Victor Gollancz, 1971.
4. Lord Rodgers of Quarry Bank, in *Dictionary of Labour Biography*, ed. Greg Rosen, Politico's, 2001.
5. R. H. S. Crossman, *The Diaries of a Cabinet Minister*, vol. 1, Hamish Hamilton/Cape, 1975.
6. Roy Jenkins, *A Life at the Centre*, Macmillan, 1991.
7. Susan Crosland, *Tony Crosland*, Jonathan Cape, 1982.
8. See Nick Timmins, *The Five Giants*, HarperCollins, 1995.
9. Hugo Young, *One of Us*, Macmillan, 1989.
10. Edward Heath, *The Course of My Life*, Hodder & Stoughton, 1998.
11. See Giles Radice, *Friends & Rivals*, Abacus, 2002.
12. Roy Jenkins, op. cit.
13. Alwyn Turner in *The Biba Experience*, Antique Collectors Club, 2004, from where much of this paragraph derives.
14. See Bob Spitz, *The Beatles*, Aurum Press, 2006.

15. *Parkinson*, quoted in Max Decharne, *Kings Road*, Weidenfeld & Nicolson, 2005.

16. Quoted in Dominic Sandbrook, *Never Had It So Good*, Little Brown, 2005.

17. Ray Davies, *X-Ray: the Unauthorised Autobiography*, Viking, 1994; see also Andy Miller, *The Kinks are the Village Green Preservation Society*, Continuum, 2003 and Neville Marten & Jeff Hudson, *The Kinks*, Sanctuary Publishing, 1996.

18. Andrew Hussey, *The Game of War: The Life and Death of Guy Debord*, Pimlico, 2002.

19. See Dave Haslam, *Not Abba*, Fourth Estate, 2005; and Robert Hewison, *Too Much*, Methuen, 1986.

20. See Brian Lapping, *End of Empire*, Granada, 1985.

21. Quoted in Pimlott, op. cit.

22. Pimlott, ibid.

23. Tony Benn, *The Benn Diaries*, Arrow, 1996 (entry in February 1966).

24. Jenkins, op. cit.

25. Barbara Castle, *The Castle Diaries*, Weidenfeld & Nicolson, 1974.

26. *The Cecil King Diaries: 1965-1970*, Jonathan Cape, 1972.

27. Philip Ziegler, *Wilson: The Authorised Life*, Weidenfeld & Nicolson, 1993.

28. Jenkins, op. cit.

29. Richard Crossman, op. cit.

30. Randall Hansen, *Citizenship and Immigration Post-war Britain*, Oxford U. P., 2000.

31. Simon Heffer, *Like the Roman*, Weidenfeld & Nicolson, 1998.

32. See Ruth Dudley Edwards, *Newspapermen*, Pimlico, 2003; and *The Cecil King Diaries*.

33. Dudley Edwards, ibid.

34. Ziegler, op. cit.

35. See Morgan, op. cit.

36. Susan Crosland, op. cit.

37. See Heffer, op. cit.

38. Ibid.

39. Roy Hattersley, *Fifty Years On*, Little, Brown, 1997.

40. See Ziegler, op. cit.

41. *The Benn Diaries*.

42. Clem Jones, quoted in Mike & Trevor Phillips, *Windrush: The Irresistible Rise of Multi-Racial Britain*, HarperCollins, 1999.

43. Nicholas Mayhew, *Sterling: The Rise and Fall of a Currency*, Allen Lane, 1999.
44. Heath, ibid.
45. Hugo Young, *This Blessed Plot*, Macmillan, 1998.
46. Quoted in Ziegler, op. cit.
47. *The Times*, 3 May 1971.
48. See Jon Savage, *England's Dreaming*, Faber & Faber, 1991.
49. See Arthur Seldon in Arthur Seldon & Stuart Ball, *Conservative Century*, Oxford U. P., 1994.
50. Robert Elms, *The Way We Wore*, Picador, 2005.
51. Bernard Donoughue, *Downing Street Diary*, Jonathan Cape, 2005.
52. Pimlott, op. cit.
53. Denis Healey, *The Time of My Life*, Michael Joseph, 1989.
54. See Young, *This Blessed Plot*.
55. Heffer, op. cit.
56. Mervyn Jones, *Michael Foot*, Victor Gollancz, 1994.
57. Richard Cockett, *Thinking the Unthinkable*, Fontana Press, 1995.
58. Letter to Anthony Seldon, quoted in Cockett.
59. See Haslam, op. cit.
60. Claire Wilcox, *Vivienne Westwood*, V&A Publishing, 2004.
61. Haslam, op. cit.
62. Healey, op. cit.
63. Quoted in Kevin Jeffreys, *Finest and Darkest Hours*, Atlantic Books, 2002.

Part Four: The British Revolution

1. See Hugo Young, *One of Us*, Macmillan, 1989.
2. Margaret Thatcher, *The Downing Street Years*, HarperCollins, 1993.
3. Quoted in Young, op. cit.
4. Thatcher, op. cit.
5. See Robert Harris, *The Making of Neil Kinnock*, Faber & Faber, 1983.
6. Denis Healey, *The Time of My Life*, Michael Joseph, 1989.
7. See Max Hastings & Simon Jenkins, *The Battle for the Falklands*, Michael Joseph, 1983; Lawrence Freedman, *Britain and the Falklands War*, Oxford U. P., 1988; Kevin Jeffreys, *Finest and Darkest Hours*, Atlantic Books, 2002; and Thatcher, op. cit.

8. Hugo Young & Anne Sloman, *The Thatcher Phenomenon*, quoted in Young, op. cit.

9. From Patrick Hannan, *When Arthur Met Maggie*, Seren, 2006.

10. Hannan, op. cit.

11. All this, and the preceding information, is taken from the fourth volume of David Kynaston's wonderful history of the City of London: *A Club No More, 1945–2000*, Chatto & Windus, 2001.

12. Interviewed in Kynaston, ibid.

13. Jill Treanor, *Guardian*, 27 October 2006.

14. Kynaston, op. cit.

15. A comparison made by Christopher Harvie in *Fool's Gold*, Hamish Hamilton, 1994.

16. Keith Aitken in Magnus Linklater & Robin Denniston (eds), *Anatomy of Scotland*, Chambers, 1992.

17. See Harvie, op cit.

18. Tony Benn, *The Benn Diaries*, Arrow, 1996 (entry for 7 January 1976).

19. Nigel Lawson, *The View from Number 11*, Bantam Press, 1992.

20. Ibid.

21. Quoted in *The Times*, 31 January 2006.

22. John Davies, *A History of Wales*, Allen Lane, 1990.

23. Martin Westlake, *Kinnock: The Biography*, Little, Brown, 2001.

24. Michael Fallon & Philip Holland, *The Quango Explosion*, Conservative Political Centre, 1978.

25. Quoted in Andrew Marr, *Ruling Britannia*, Michael Joseph, 1995.

26. Thatcher, op. cit.

27. Evan Davies, *Schools and the State*, Social Market Foundation 1993; see Marr, op. cit.

28. Simon Jenkins, *Thatcher and Sons*, Allen Lane, 2006.

29. Thatcher, op. cit.

Part Five: Nippy Metro People

1. See Andy McSmith, *John Smith: Playing the Long Game*, Verso, 1993.

2. McSmith, ibid.

3. John Major, *The Autobiography*, HarperCollins, 1999.

4. Christian Wolmar, *On the Wrong Line*, Aurum Press, 2005.

5. Simon Jenkins, *Thatcher and Sons*, Allen Lane, 2006.

6. Major, op. cit.

7. See Malcolm Balen, *Kenneth Clarke*, Fourth Estate, 1994.

8. See Mark Lawson, *Media Guardian*, 21 October 2006.

9. Anthony Seldon, *Blair*, The Free Press, 2004.

10. Robert Peston, *Brown's Britain*, Short Books, 2005.

11. All quotes from Peter Hyman, *1 out of Ten*, Vintage, 2005.

12. See Jenkins, op. cit.

13. Andrew Rawnsley, *Servants of the People*, Penguin, 2001.

14. Lance Price, *The Spin Doctor's Diary*, Hodder & Stoughton, 2005.

15. Peter Oborne, *The Rise of Political Lying*, The Free Press, 2005.

16. National Statistics website, 2006.

17. Peston, op. cit.

18. Robert Whelan of Civitas, interviewed *Daily Mail*, 3 November 2006.

Index

7/7 582–584
9/11 553–556

Abbey National 426
abortion 255, 259, 261, 262
Abortion Law Reform Association 256
Abse, Leo 254, 255, 259
Acheson, Dean 25–26
acquired immune-deficiency syndrome (AIDS) 407–410
Adam, Ruth 85
Adams, Gerry 522, 523
Admiralty, the 15
Afghanistan 554–555
Africa 39–40, 188–191, 576
agriculture xxi
AIDS (acquired immune-deficiency syndrome) 407–410
airliners 108–109
Aitken, Jonathan 508
Aldermaston 33
Allawi, Ayad 588
al-Qaeda 555
Amin, Idi 321
Amis, Kingsley 34
anarchy 330–334
Anatomy of Britain (Sampson) 168, 227
Anderson, Ian 280
Anderton, James 409
Angry Brigade 330–334
'Angry Young Men' 95
animal rights movement 544–545
anti-Americanism 141
anti-Semitism 42, 193
anti-war movement 282

Anti-Nazi League 362, 371
Anti-Social Behaviour Orders (ASBOs) 579–580
appeasement 217
Apprentice Boys of Derry 318
Arab nationalism 148–149
arms race 104–105
art colleges 268–270
Argentina see Falklands War
Arts Council 90
ASBOs (Anti-Social Behaviour Orders) 579–580
Asda 598
Ashdown, Paddy 528
Astor, Lord 'Bill' 217
Astor, Nancy 216–217
A Streetcar Named Desire 90
Aswan, High Dam 150
asylum seekers 526–527, 590–592
  see also immigration; multiculturalism
Attlee, Clement xvi, 6–8, 17–19, 25, 27, 101, 106
Austin, Herbert 169
Austin Seven 169
AWACS 402

Bailey, David 276
Baker, Kenneth 467
Balcon, Michael 119–121
Balls, Ed 529, 532
Banda, Hastings 286
Bank of England 513, 532–533, 592
Barings Bank 424
Barnett, Correlli 11, 69
Barry, Gerald 109

BBC 154, 569–572
Beadle, Hugh 289
Beatles, the 272, 273, 274, 278
Beaton, Cecil 91
Beaumont, Hugh (Binkie) 90, 137
Beckett, Samuel 100
Beeching, Richard 169, 173–174
Behan, Brendan 94
Belgrano 403
Bell, Martin 508
Benn, Tony 225, 234, 235, 293, 297, 310,
        317, 329, 370, 372, 437, 488
    domestic policy 352–353
    on the Eurodollar 423
    on Europe 350–351
    and Labour reform 393, 394–395
Bentine, Michael 144
Bentley, Derek 253
Berger, Vivian 283
Berners-Lee,Tim 481–482
Bernstein, George xxix
Bevan, Nye 23–24, 65–67, 72, 108,
        184–185, 446
Beveridge Report 63–64
Beveridge, William 40, 62–64
Bevin, Ernest 8, 20–23, 25–26, 31, 106
Bevins, Reggie 124
Beyond the Fringe 222–223
Biba 266–267, 330
Bicknell, Franklin 55–56
'Big Bang', City deregulation 424–428
'Big Brother' 275
Bin Laden, Osama 555
bio-metrics 581
Birch, Nigel 165–166
Birthday Party, The (Pinter) 99
Blackburn Technical College xxii
Black, Cilla 276
black market 80–81
Black Wednesday 489–492
Blair, Cherie 560–561
Blair, Tony 452, 488, 489, 494, 502–505,
        509, 596
    and Brown 585–588
    and Bush 551–552

and celebrity 520
and civil liberties 580–582, 584
death of Diana 517–518, 519
and the euro 528–530
final years 596–597
and fuel duty protests 546–547
and hunting 545
and Iraq 548–549, 562–567
leadership election 511–513
on multi-culturalism 601
Northern Ireland 521
and the press 528–529
resignation 586–588
and Serbia 548, 549–551
and Thatcher 527–528
'war on terror' 555–556
on weapons of mass destruction 562,
        564–565, 569–570
Blake, George 141
Blake, Peter 269
Blaney, Neil 318
Blue Streak 209–210
Blunkett, David 455, 541, 559, 581, 592
'Bloody Sunday' 335
Blunt, Antony 136–137, 140
Blunt, Maggie Joy 34
BMC (British Motor Corporation) 169–172
BNOC (British National Oil Corporation)
        437
Bono 577
Boodles Club 55
Booker, Christopher 275–276
Boothby, Lord 137
Borges, Jorge Luis 403
Bose, Subhas Chandra 37
Bosnia 500–502
Bourne, Alec 255
bovine spongiform encephalopathy (BSE)
        505–507
Boxer, Mark 276
Bowe, Collette 419–420
Bowie, David 362
Braddock, Bessie 84
Braithwaite, Rodric 209
Bramley, Ted 72

Bretherton, Russell 202
Britain Can Make It (1946) 52
British Aeroplane Company 74
British Airways 412
British Antarctic Survey 479
British Empire xviii–xix, 26–27
British Gas 431, 432, 433
British Guild of Creative Designers 84
British Housewives' League 82, 83
British Leyland 387–388
British Medical Association 66, 259
British Motor Corporation (BMC) 169–172
British Nationality Act 41
British National Oil Corporation (BNOC)
    437
British National Party *see* National Front
British Rail 68, 173, 495
British Steel 412
British Telecom (BT) 430, 432
British Transport Commission 68
Brixton 389–390
Broccoli, Albert 'Cubby' 216
Brodie, Tom *see* Glorious Glosters
Brown, George 236–237, 242–245, 292, 297
Brown, Gordon 488, 489, 503, 584, 596
    anti-poverty agenda 574–578
    and Blair 585–588
    economy 532, 533, 537–541
    and the euro 529, 530
    fuel taxes 547
    ID cards 581–582
BSE (bovine spongiform encephalopathy)
    505–507
B-Specials 316–317
BT (British Telecom) 430, 432
Buchan, Norman 181
Bulger, James 503
Bupa 465, 541
Burgess, Guy 136, 140
Bush, George 472
Bush, George W. 551–552, 562–563, 600
Butler, R. A. (Rab) 46, 122, 123, 131, 225
Butlin, Billy 86
Buxted Chickens 164
Byers, Stephen 560

Caine, Michael 277
Cairncross, John 140, 298
Callaghan, Jim 232, 241, 298, 302, 311,
    363–365
    and devaluation 294–295
    and devolution 446
    economy 366–370, 374
    and Northern Ireland 317
    and North Sea oil 433
    and trade unions 310
Cameron, David 577–578, 595
Cameron, James 104
Campaign for Nuclear Disarmament
    (CND) *see* CND (Campaign for
    Nuclear Disarmament)
Campbell, Alastair 489, 510, 556, 568, 570,
    572
cannabis 278
Caplin, Carole 560–561
Cardus, Neville 88
cars 169, 598–599
    see also Mini-Minor
Carmichael, Stokely 282
Casino Royale 213
Castle, Barbara 83, 184, 235, 292, 295,
    308–311
    pensions 353–354
    road safety 176–177
Catling, Susan 245–246
Caulcott, Tom 243–244
CCTV 581, 583
celebrity 274–277, 514–516, 520
censorship 58, 257, 258
    see also Lady Chatterley trial
Central African Federation 285–286
Central Policy Review Staff (CPRS) 406
centralism 497–499
Chamberlain, Neville xv
CERN 481–482
Chevaline 291, 354
child-centred teaching 249–250
Child Poverty Action Group 574
Chirac, Jacques 566
Churchill, Winston xv–xvii, 3, 5–7,
    121–123, 124, 125–130, 576

Churchill, Winston (*cont.*)
  on the atomic bomb 32
  on social class 45
cinema 89, 108, 119–121
Citizen's Charter 498
City, the 420–428
City Technology Colleges (CTCs) 464
civil liberties 580–582, 584
CJD (Creutzfeldt-Jakob Disease) 506
Clapton, Eric 362
Clark, Alan 474
Clarke, Charles 583
Clarke, Kenneth 492, 497–498, 530
Clarke, Otto 35
Clash, the 362
class, social 43–48, 179, 225
Clause four 511
Clayton, William 12
cleanliness 52–53
climate change *see* global warming
Clinton, Bill 501, 504, 521, 549, 550
Cliveden, Buckinghamshire 216–217
clothes 53–54, 84–85
Clwyd, Ann 567
CND (Campaign for Nuclear
    Disarmament) 182–183
  Scottish 211
  see also unilateral nuclear disarmament
coal industry 68–70
  see also miners
cocaine 278–279
Cockburn, Claud 217
coffee bars 268
Cohen, Andrew 285
Cohen, Jack 598
Cole, E. A. 136
Colonial Office 39–40, 45
Commission for Africa 576, 577
Commonwealth 202–203, 352
Commonwealth Immigrants Act 200,
    302–303
Communism 136
Communist Party of Great Britain 370
Compton, Denis 88
computers 480–482

Connery, Sean 216
Connolly, Billy 181
Connolly, Cyril 226
Conservative Party 121–124, 407, 524,
    594–595
Constitutional Convention 523–524
consumerism 50–52, 80–83
'control orders' 583–584
Cook, Frederick 173
Cook, Peter 220, 221, 222
Cook, Robin 560, 566
Cotton, Jack 168
council houses 430
Council of Industrial Design 51
council tax inspectors 581
counter-culture 281–283
  see also culture
Country Life 46
Countryside Alliance 544, 545
Cousins, Frank 133
Coward, Noël 47, 91–92, 137
CPRS (Central Policy Review Staff) 406
crack cocaine 279
Craig, Christopher 252–253
Creutzfeldt-Jakob Disease (CJD) 506
cricket 88
crime 58–60, 258–259
Cripps, Stafford 19, 20–23, 37, 70, 106
Critchley, Julian 418
Cromer, Lord 241
Crosland, Tony 187, 236, 245–246, 247,
    248, 250–251, 310
Crossman, Dick 184, 228, 235, 236,
    244–245, 291, 293–294, 310, 317
CTCs (City Technology Colleges) 464
Cuban missile crisis 208
culture xxiii–xxv, 57, 480
  see also counter-culture
Daily Express 97
Daily Mirror 568
Dalton, Hugh 13, 15, 19–20, 35, 194
Dalyell, Tam 402, 403, 446
Davies, Gavyn 570, 571
Davies, Ray 273, 281
Davies, Ron 559–560

DEA (Department of Economic Affairs) 243–245
Dearlove, Richard 564
Debord, Guy 282, 331
dept cancellation programme 577
debutantes 49
decimalization 343
decolonization 188–192
defence 107
Delors, Jacques 470
democracy, local 459–460
demography 40–42, 478
Denning, Lord 219
Department of Economic Affairs (DEA) 243–245
Desert Fox 551
Deutschmark 490
devaluation, of the pound 134, 241–242, 290–292, 294–295, 296–300
devolution 489
  Labour on 524–527
  Scotland 442–447, 523–526
  Wales 442, 447–449, 525
Devine, George 95–96
Dewar, Donald 489, 524, 525, 526
Diana, Princess 408, 516–520
Diana – the True Story (Morton) 517
Dior, Christian 84–85
directive 10/65 248
divorce 57–58, 259
Divorce Reform Act 257
DNA 581
Dobson, Frank 538
Dome of Discovery 109
domestic policy 352, 354, 459
Donovan, Terence 276
'Do They Know It's Christmas?' 576
Draper, Derek 557
Driberg, Tom 137, 140
drugs 277–279
du Cannes, Edward 357
Dulles, John Foster 128, 151–152, 158–159
Duncan Smith, Iain 594–595
Dury, Ian 269
Dyke, Greg 511, 570, 571

Ealing studios *see* Balcon, Michael
Ecclestone, Bernie 557
Economist, The 13
economy 35–36, 163–167, 290–296, 346–348, 478, 489–493, 572–579
  under Callaghan 366–370, 374
  under Churchill 130–134
  City, the 420–428
  Europe, payments to 391–392
  France 242
  under Heath 324–326
  Joseph 355–358, 406
  under Lawson 426, 458, 469–470
  under Macmillan 165
  New Labour 532–541
  and North Sea oil 438–440
  and Powell 165–166
  under Thatcher 423, 428, 458, 463–464
  United States of America 422
  wartime 10–13
  under Wilson 239, 240–245
Eden, Anthony 122–123, 125–126
  social class 179
  and Suez 145–147, 149, 152, 158
education 45–46
  New Labour 541–542
  reform 245–251
  see also faith schools; public schools
Edwardes, Michael 438
Egypt 147–148
Einstein, Albert 31
Eisenhower, Dwight 101, 128, 151–152, 158–159
electric guitars 270–271
eleven plus examination 247
Eliot, T. S. 37
Elizabeth II 48, 222–223, 289, 306
  and the death of Diana 518–519
Elizabeth, Princess *see* Elizabeth II
Ellis, Ruth 253
Elms, Robert 340–341
emigration 593–594, 599
energy 296–300
Enfield, Harry 428, 480
English Stage Company 95

Ennals, David 375
Eno, Brian 270
Enragés, Les 282
environment *see* global warning
Epstein, Brian 271
ERM 458, 470, 484, 489–493
Establishment 227
Establishment Club 223
ethnic cleansing 500, 550
Eton, Peter 145
euro, the 470–471
    Blair and 528–530
    Brown and 530
    see also 'hard ecu'
Eurodollar 422–423, 427
Europe 295–296, 326–330, 530, 593
    Benn on 350–351
    Churchill's attitude to 129–130
    Jenkins on 204, 528
    payments to 391–392
    Powell on 350
    referenda on 348–351
    Thatcher and 458–459, 470–471, 485
    Wilson and 295, 328
European Economic Community 201–207
European Exchange Rate system *see* ERM
Evans, Gwynfor 449
Evans, John 330
Everton, Marcel 313–314
Ewing, Winnie 445
Exodus 22

Fachs, Klaus 136
Fairlie, Henry 227
Fairport Convention 280
faith schools 541–542
Falkender, Lady *see* Williams, Marcia
Falklands War 398–404
Farouk 148
fashion 358, 359
Fellatio, Masochism, Politics and Love (Abse)
    255
Festival of Britain (1951) 52, 109–111
Fidler, Sheppard 77
finance, North Sea oil 437–438

Financial Times 97
First of May group 332–333
Fisher, Antony 163, 164–165
Fisher, Jack 30
fishing 327
Fleming, Ann 213–215
Fleming, Ian 213
folk music 180–182, 280
food 54–54, 82–83
football 87–88
Foot, Michael 184, 350, 394, 446, 449–450
Foot, Paul 224
Forbes, William Francis *see* Semphill,
    Master of
Ford, Henry III 325
foreign policy xxvi–xxvii, 479
    under Churchill 128–129
    under Wilson 351–352
Forster, E. M. 121
Forte, Charles 168
Fowler, Norman 410
fox hunting *see* hunting
France
    economy 242
    and Suez 153, 157–158
    uprisings in 282–283
Francis, Dai 412
Fraser, Hugh 168
Fraser, Lord 13–14
Frayn, Michael 109, 110
Free Officers Movement 148
Free Wales Army 448–449
French, Godfrey 15
Friedman, Milton 386
Frisch, Otto 31
Frognal Set 185
Frost, David 223
fuel, protests about duty 546–547
Funding Agency for Schools 464
Future of Socialism, The (Crosland) 187

'Gaia' theory 479
Gaitskell, Hugh 107, 139, 152, 185–188,
    200, 203, 214–215, 511
Galtieri, Leopold 399

gardening 89
Gaulle, Charles de 204, 296
  and Macmillan 205–206
Geilgud, John 137
Geldof, Bob 576–577
general election
  1945 3–8
  1950 105
  1970 311–315
  1992 486–487
  1997 509
  2005 596
General Strike (1926) 68
George VI 48
German Central Bank 458, 490
Ghandi, Mohandas Karamchand 36
Gibbs, Humphrey 289
Gibson, David 77
Gibson, William 481
Gilligan, Andrew 570
Gladstone, William Ewart 121
global warming 479–480, 584, 600,
  601–602
Glorious Glosters 102–103
Goldfinger, Erno 75–76
Golding, William 479
Goldsmith, James 494
Good Friday Agreement 522–523
Goodison, Nicholas 423
Goon Show, The 144–145, 220
Gorbachev, Mikhail 404
government xxv–xxvii
  and the BBC 569–572
  big 463–466
  Conservative 121–124
  post-nuclear 208–209
Gould, Philip 510
Gow, Ian 472
GPS systems 580
greyhound racing 88
Griffith–Jones, Mervyn 260–261
Griffiths, Jim 64
Grimond, Jo 227, 259, 397
Grundy, Bill 361
Guinness, Alec 137

Gulf War *see* Iraq
Gummer, Cordelia 505, 506
Gummer, John Selwyn 505–506

Hague, William 547–548
Haig, Alexander 417
Hailsham, Lord 225
Haines, Joe 240
Halifax, Lord xv–xvi, 12
Hall, Peter 92
Hamilton, Neil 508
Hamilton, Richard 270
Hammer, Armand 438
Hampstead Set 185
hanging abolition of 252–254, 261
'hard ecu' 483–484
  see also euro
Harper's Bazaar 84
Hattersley, Roy 396
Hatton, Derek 454–455
Haughey, Charles 318
Harvey, Ian 137
Hayek, Friedrich von 163
Healey, Denis 5, 232, 343–344, 346–348,
  403
  and the IMF 366–370
  Labour reform 394, 395
health 465
Heath, Edward 123, 206, 232, 248, 249,
  311–315
  Britain under 342–343
  economy 324–326
  and Europe 326–330
  and immigration 320–324
  and Northern Ireland 318
Heathfield, Peter 413
Heffer, Eric 455
Hello! 275, 515
Henderson, Hamish 181
Hennessy, Peter 131, 208
Heroin 278
Heseltine, Michael 179, 389–390, 417,
  418–419, 420, 472, 473, 500, 530
Hewitt, Patricia 451
Higgins, Terry 407

High Dam, Aswan 150
Hill, David 572
H. M. Tennant Ltd 90
Hobson, Harold 95
holidays 85–87
Holidays with Pay Act 85
Holtham, Gerald 182
Holy Loch 208, 210–211
Home, Alec Douglas- 123, 225, 226–227
homosexuality 58, 261
    legalization of 254–255
    purge of 134–139
    in the theatre 90–92
    see also AIDS
Horizon 409
Hornby, Lesley 276
housing 51, 71–75, 196–197, 466
    see also council houses; tower blocks
Housing Action Trusts 466
Howard, Michael 540, 595
Howe, Geoffrey 356, 383, 387, 427, 471,
        472–473
    on the Eurodollar 423
    and North Sea oil 435–436, 439, 440
    and privatization 429
Howell, David 439
Howells, Kim 412–413
Hulanicki, Barbara *see* Biba
human rights 583–584
Hume, John 523
humour 142–145
Hunter, Anji 510
hunting 543–546
Hunt Saboteurs Association 544
Hurcomb, Cyril 69–70
Hurd, Douglas 325, 473, 494
Hussein, Saddam 472, 507, 549, 555,
        562–567, 588
Hutton Enquiry 571
Hutton, Len 88
Hyman, Peter 542–543
Hyndley, Viscount 69

ICI 178
ID cards 581–582, 583

IEA (Institute for Economic Affairs)
        165–167
Iki, Lieutenant 29
IMF (International Monetary Fund)
        366–370
immigration 40–42, 192–195, 592–594
    Indians 300–301
    Kenyans 301–303
    Pakistani 300–301
    Powell on 302, 303–305, 321–324,
        593
    Ugandan Asians 321–323, 593
    West Indian 195–201
    see also asylum seekers; multi-
            culturalism
immigration and nationality department
        (IND) 591–592
India
    immigrants from 300–301
    independence 36–39
industry xxii–xxiii, 167–169, 177–178
    see also car industry; coal; rail system
inflation 133–134, 346–347
Ingham, Bernard 418, 420
Ingrams, Richard 221, 222, 223
Institute for Economic Affairs (IEA)
        165–167
International Monetary Fund (IMF)
        366–370
internet 481–482, 573
IQ tests 247
IRA (Irish Republican Army) 316,
        317–318, 335–337, 404, 457–458,
        479, 499–500
Iraq 104, 156, 478–479, 548–549, 555,
        562–567, 588–590
Iran, Shah of 437
Ireland, Republic of 200
    see also Northern Ireland

Irish 41–42
Irish Republican Army (IRA) 316,
        317–318, 335–337, 404, 457–458,
        479, 499–500
Irvine, Derry 510, 560

Islam, militant 600
Isle of Skye bridge 535
Israel, and Suez 153–154
Issigonis, Alec 169–172
Ivanov, Yevgeny 218

Jagger, Mick 277
Jam, the 362
James Bond 215–216
jazz 181–182
Jenkins, Roy 5, 245, 251–262, 297–298,
    310, 595
    as Chancellor 299–300
    and Europe 204, 528
    on immigration 302
    and the SDP 395–398
Jenkins, Simon 460–461, 466, 496–497
Jews 22, 41, 357
Jinnah, Mohammad Ali 38
Johnstone, Tom 444
Jones, Cliff 303
Jones, Jack 353
Jordan, model 360
Joseph, Keith 355–358, 406
Joseph Rowntree Trust 575

Kaufman, Gerald 450
Keeler, Christine 217
Kelly, David 570–571
Kemp, Alex 439
Kennedy, Charles 529, 595–596
Kennedy, John F. 422
Kennedy, Ludovic 252, 259
Kenya 190
    immigrants from 301–303
Kenyatta, Jomo 190, 301
Keynes, John Maynard 11–12, 35
Khrushchev, Nikita 145–146, 185, 208
Kilmuir, Lord 203–204
King, Cecil, and Wilson 305–307
King, John 412
*Kinks Are The Village Green Preservation
    Society, The* (The Kinks) 281
Kinks, the 272, 273, 280–281

Kinnock, Neil 75, 298, 395, 403, 413, 462,
    486
    leadership election 450–451
    and the militants 453–455
    and the miners' strike 452–453
    and Scargill 452–453
    and unilateral nuclear disarmament
        456–457
    on Welsh devolution 449
Koestler, Arthur 252
Korean War 101–104
Kosovo Liberation Army 549
Kuanda, Kenneth 287

Labour Party 7–8, 227, 407
    achievements 61–62, 105–111
    conference, 1945 5
    and devolution 524–527
    internal conflict 183–188
    public spending 429–430
    reform of 392–395
    see also New Labour; Scottish Labour
        Party

Lady Chatterley trial 259–261
Lamont, Norman 485, 486, 491, 492, 494,
    535
landowners 46–47
Laski, Harold 6
Lawson, Nigel 411, 418, 424, 471
    and the economy 426, 458, 469–470
    and North Sea oil 434, 436, 439–440
    and the poll tax 468
    and privatization 429, 432, 438
Leach, John 400
League Against Cruel Sports 544
League of Empire Loyalists *see* NF
league tables, police 498
Leathers, Lord 173
Lee, Jennie 251
Lend-Lease 10, 11
Lennon, John 280, 281
lesbianism 136
Levy, Michael 511
Lewis, C. S. 57

Liberal Democrats 595–596
Liberal Party 397–398, 407
   and the SDP 462–463
Liddle, Roger 528
LIFFE 423–424
Lilley, Peter 494
Limehouse Declaration 396
Litterick, Tom 383
Littlewood, Joan 93–95
Live Aid 576–577
Live8 577
Live and Let Die (Fleming) 216
Liverpool City Council 453–454
Liverpool Parks and Cemeteries 375
Lloyd, Selwin 153–154, 206
London 275–277
   terrorist attacks on 582–584
London Stock Exchange 425
Look Back in Anger (Osborne) 95, 96–97
Lovelock, James 479
LSD 278
Lubetkin, Berthold 75

Maastricht Treaty 484–486, 491, 493–494
MacArthur, Douglas 101
Macaulay, Sarah 537
MacColl, Ewan 93–95, 181
Macdonald, Ian 444
MacDonald, Margo 445
MacGregor, Ian 411–412
MacGregor, John 496
Maclean, Donald 136, 140
Macleod, Iain 226, 287, 302
Macmillan, Harold 24, 122–124, 129, 132,
   153, 159–163, 225–226
   on Africa 189
   attitude to spies 141–142
   on decolonization 189, 190
   and de Gaulle 205–206
   and the economy 165
   and Europe 204–207
   and nuclear weapons 208
   and Powell 161–163, 225
   social class 179
mad cow disease 505–507

Major, John 471, 472, 473, 474, 524
   and the ERM 491–493
   as Prime Minister 482–487
   and Thatcher 484
   wars 499–502
majority verdicts 258–259
Make Poverty History 576
Malawi *see* Nyasaland
Malaya 191–192
Manchester, Moss Side 389
Mandelson, Peter 456, 488, 489, 510, 522,
   530–531, 557–559, 568, 569
manufacturing 440
Mao Tse-tung 101–102
marches 316–317
Marcuse, Herbert 282
Marples, Ernie 124, 169, 174
Marshall Plan, the 16, 107
Mates, Michael 469
Mathew, Theobald 136
Matrix Churchill 507
Matthews, Stanley 87
Mau Mau rebellion 190
Maxwell Fyfe, David 136, 139, 253
Mayer, Louis B. 120
McCartney, Paul 273, 278, 280
McCullin, Don 276
McGahey, Mick 341, 413
McGuinness, Martin 522, 523
McMahan Act 31
McLaren, Malcolm 332, 359, 361, 362
McNulty, Graeme 597
McNulty, Tony 593
means-testing 578
Medium-Term Financial Strategy (MTFS)
   387, 458
Melody Maker 279
Meyer, Anthony 471–472
Microsoft 481
Middle East 351–352
Middlemass, Keith 179
migration, Jewish 22
Migration Watch UK 593
Mikardo, Ian 184
Milburn, Alan 540, 560

Miliband, David 510
Militant Tendency 370, 393, 452, 454
military xxvii–xxviii, technology 29–30
Millennium Dome 530–531, 569
Miller, Arthur 97
Miller, Jimmie *see* MacColl, Ewan
Milligan, Spike 143–144, 220
Millington, Ernest 4–5
Milosevic, Slobodan 549–551
miners, strikes 337–338, 340–341,
    411–416, 452–453
Mini-Minor 170–172
minimum wage 575
mini-skirts 277
Ministry of Agriculture, Fisheries and Food
    506
Ministry of Economic Expansion *see* DEA
Ministry of Production *see* DEA
Mitchell, George 521
Mittal, Lakshmi 558
Mitterrand, François 405
mobile phones 480, 580
Mode 269
Molotov, Vyacheslav Mikhailovich 6–7
monarchy 48–50
Monckton, Walter 130, 132
Monday Club 189
monetarism 386–391, 434–435
Montagu, Lord 135, 137–138, 139
Montgomery of Alamein 261
Moore, Jeremy 403
Moore, Jo 560
morality 57–58
Morris, Estelle 560
Morris Minor 169, 170
Morrison, Herbert 7, 8, 24–25, 39, 65–66,
    105, 109, 110, 129
Morrison, Van 280
mortgages 426–427
Morton, Andrew 517
Morton, H. V. xx–xxi
Mosley, Oswald 192–201
Mossadeq, Mohammed 148
motorbike manufacturing 178
Mowlam, Mo 510, 521, 522

Mountbatten, Louis 38, 306
Mountbatten, Philip, later Prince Philip
    49–50
MTFS (Medium-Term Financial Strategy)
    387, 458
Mugabe, Robert 284, 289
Muir, Edwin xviv–xxv
multi-culturalism 600–601
    see also asylum seekers; immigration
Murdoch, Rupert 420, 512
Murray, Len 391
music 267–274, 279–281, 358–359, 362
    see also folk; jazz; punk
music hall 142–143, 280
Myth of Decline, The (Bernstein) xxix

Nasser, Gamel Abdel 147, 148, 149–152
National Audit Office 575
National Coal Board 69, 411
National Enterprise Board (NEB) 352–353
National Front (NF) 370–371
National Health Service (NHS) 65–67,
    538–541
National Health Service Trusts 465
National Identity Register 582
National Insurance 64
nationalization 67–70, 353
National Party of Scotland *see* SNP
National Plan 244
National Service 116
National Theatre 98
National Union of Mineworkers (NUM)
    337, 411, 413–414, 415
National Union of Public Employees
    (NUPE) 375
NATO (North Atlantic Treaty
    Organization) 21–22
Neave, Airey 357, 377
NEB (National Enterprise Board) 352–353
Neighbours 515
Nehru, Jawaharlal 38
Neophiliacs, The (Booker) 275–276
New Deal 575
New Democrats 504

New Labour 452, 509–510, 511, 513–514
    economy 532–541
    education 541–542
    public spending 542
    scandals 556–562
New Look 84–85
News of the World 277
New Statesman 28, 182
NHS (National Health Service) 65–67,
    538–541
Niemasz, Hendrick 253
'Night of the Long Knives, the'
    206–207
Nixon, Richard 326
North Atlantic Treaty Organization
    (NATO) 21–22
Northern Ireland 315–319, 334–337, 404
    and Major 499–500
    peace process 521–523
North Sea, oil 438–440
Nott-Bower, John 136
Nottinghamshire, miners 414–415
Notting Hill 198–200
Novello, Ivor 91
nuclear power 177
nuclear weapons 30–33, 101, 127–128,
    208–212, 291, 404
    see also unilateral nuclear disarmament;
        weapons of mass destruction
Nuffield, Lord 169
NUM (National Union of Mineworkers)
    337, 411, 413–414, 415
NUPE (National Union of Public
    Employees) 375
Nuttall, Jeff 278
Nutting, Anthony 155
Nyasaland 286

Oborne, Peter 569
Obscene Publications Act 259
Office for National Statistics 431, 590
oil, North Sea 433–441
OK! 275
Old Vic Centre 92, 96
O'Leannain, John *see* Lennon, John

Olivier, Laurence 97, 98–99, 259
Olympics, London 36
Omagh bombing 522
O'Neill, Terry 276, 315, 316
Open University 251
Operation Desert Fox 549
Orwell, George 28, 68
Osborne, John 96–98
Owen, David 396, 397
Oxbridge 222
Oxfam 576
Oz 283

P&O 178
Paisley, Ian 523
Pakistan 38–39, 582
    immigrants from 300–301

Palestine 22
Parkinson, Cecil 424
Parkinson, C. Northcote 45
Parnes, Larry 270
Parsons, Anthony 386
Passport to Pimlico 81
Patten, Chris 484, 486, 569
pay deals 347, 374
peace process, Northern Ireland 521–523
Peierls, Rudolf 31
Penney, William 33
pensions 533–534, 578
PEP (Political and Economic Planning) 27
PFI (public finance initiative) 535–537
Philby, Kim 140, 141
Pierrepoint, Albert 253
Pike, Magnus 83
Pimlott, Ben 235
Pink Floyd 270, 577
Pinter, Harold 99–100
Pinwright's Progress 89
Piper Alpha 436
Pizzey, Erin 330
Plaid Cymru 447–449
Polaris 210, 291
Poles 42
Police, the 362

police, performance league tables 498
Political and Economic Planning (PEP) 27
politics xxviii–xxxi
Pollitt, Harry 72–73
poll tax 466–469
    in Scotland 524
Pompidou, Georges 326
Porter, Shirley 598
Portillo, Michael 494, 500, 594
potteries xxii–xxiv
pound 490–492
    devaluation of 134, 241–242, 290–292,
        294–295, 296–300, 366
poverty 574–578
Powell, Colin 564
Powell, Enoch 190, 197, 234, 313–314
    anti-Americanism 141
    and the economy 165–166
    on Europe 350
    on immigration 302, 303–305,
        321–324 593
    and Macmillan 161–163, 225
Powell, Jonathan 510
prefabs 74–75
Prescott, John 511, 531, 534–535, 545,
    546, 586
press, the 528–529
    see also spin
Price, Lance 568–569
Priestley, J. B. xxii–xxiv, 68, 182
Prior, Jim 387
privacy 580–582
Private Eye 220
privatization 428–433, 438, 460–461,
    495–497
Profumo affair 196, 217–220
Profumo, John 217–220
prostitution 58, 196
Provisional Army Council 318
'Provos' 318
public finance initiative (PFI) 535–537
public schools, influence on humour
    220–222
public spending 429–430, 542
Punch 142

punk 361–362
Pym, Francis 400

quaintness xx–xxi
Quant, Mary 277, 360
Quinn, Kimberley 559

Rachman, Peter 197
racialism 193–194
Radcliffe, Cyril 38
radio 270–271
Radio Luxembourg 267, 271
Radley, school 220–221
rail system 67–68, 173
    privatization of 495–497
Railtrack 543, 560
Railway Executive 68
rates 468
rationing 53–56
Rattigan, Terence 90–91
Ray, Robin 51
Reagan, Ronald 400, 401, 405, 456
Redwood, John 494, 500
Rees-Mogg, William 278
referenda 329–330, 348–351
Regina *v.* Penguin Books 259–261
Reid, John 584, 592
Reid, Richard 583
religion 56–57
Rent Act 197
Resale Price Maintenance (RPM) 320
Resolution 1441 565
retail 598–599
revolution 282–283
Revolutionary Socialist League 453–454
Reynolds, Albert 499
Rhodes, Cecil John 284
Rhodesia 283–290
Rice-Davies, Mandy 219
Richards, Keith 277
Ridealgh, Mabel 84
Ridley, Nicholas 472
Riley, Bridget 269
Rimmer, Victoria 506
riots 389–390

'rivers of blood' speech (Powell) 303–304
roads 172–177
Road Safety Act 167–177
Road to Serfdom, The (Hayek) 164
Robbins, Lionel 164, 165–166
Robbins Report 250
Roberts, Alfred 383
Roberts, Frank 208
Robinson, Geoffrey 558
ROBOT 131
Rock Against Racism 362
Rodgers, Bill 375, 396
Rolling Stones 280
Rolls-Royce 326, 387–388
Rooke, Dennis 431
Rooke, Pamela 360
Rosen, Tubby 72
Ross, Willie 258, 444
Rothermere, Lord 512
Rothschilds Bank 428
Roxy Music 270
Royal Navy xix, 13–16
Royal Ulster Constabulary 316
royal wedding (1947) 49–50
RPM (Resale Price Maintenance) 320
rubber *see* Malaya
Rupert Bear 283
Rumsfeld, Donald 554
Rushton, Willie 222
Russell, Bertrand 182, 259
Russia *see* Soviet Union

Said, Nuri El 123
Sainsbury's 598
Salisbury, Lord 287
Salmond, Alex 526
Saltley 412
Sampson, Anthony 168, 227
Sanderson, Paul 581
Sands, Bobby 404
Sandys, Duncan 302
Sangatte 592
satire 220–224
Saved (Bond) 257
scandals, New Labour 556–562

Scanlon, Hugh 309
Scargill, Arthur 337, 395, 411, 412–416
    and Kinnock 452–453
Schmidt, Helmut 348
Schuman, Robert 129
science 238–239
Scotland
    devolution 442–447, 523–526
    folk music in 180
    nationalism in 442–447
    poll tax 524
    see also North Sea oil
Scott, Derek 528
Scottish Labour Party 445–446
Scottish National Party *see* SNP
SDP (Social Democratic Party) 298, 328,
    407
    and Jenkins 395–398
    Liberal Alliance 462–463
SEAQ 425
Secombe, Harry 144
security xxvii, 583
Seldon, Anthony 562
Sellers, Peter 144
Semphill, Master of 29–30
Serbia 548, 549–551
SERPS (State Earnings Related Pension)
    353
services, public 534–537, 543, 599
    regulation of 432–433
Sex Pistols 361, 362
Sexual Offences Act 255
Sexual Offences Bill 254
Shakespeare, William 92–93
shareholding 430–432
Sherman, Alfred 356
Shinwell, Manny 68–69
Short, Clare 560, 566
Shrewsbury School 221
Shrimpton, Jean 276
'Sid' campaign 431
Sikorsky 417
Sillars, Jim 441, 445
Simon, Lord 528
Single European Act 458

Silverman, Sydney 252, 253
Sir Gawain and the Green Knight 544
'Situationists' 331–332
sixties, the 262–267
    see also celebrity; drugs; music
Skegness 86
skiffle 268
Skybolt, missiles 210
sleaze 507–509
'slim' *see* AIDS
Smith, Ian 287–289
Smith, John 487–489, 525
Smith, T. Dan 77
SNP (Scottish National Party) 440–441,
    443–445, 526
Social Contract 341, 343, 344, 346–347
Social Democratic Party *see* SDP
socialism 27–28, 371–372, 429–430
Socialist Workers' Party (SWP) 370, 371
Society for the Protection of the Unborn
    Child (Spuc) 255
songs 273
Soskice, Frank 300
South Georgia *see* Falklands War
sovereignty 350–351
Soviet Union 9, 404–405, 551
    Churchill's attitude to 127–128
    and Suez 152
Spaak, Paul-Henri 201–202
'special relationship' *see* United States of
    America
Special Roads Act 173
Specials, the 362
speedway 88–89
spies 139–142
spin 568–572
Spitting Image 417
spivs 80–81
Springfield, Dusty 280
Spuc (Society for the Protection of the
    Unborn Child) 255
squatting 71–73
Stalin, Joseph 104
State Earnings Related Pension (SERPS)
    353

Steel, David 256, 259, 261, 396
steel industry 70
Stern, Nicholas 599
Stewart, Donald 445
Stewart, J. L. 77
'stop the war' demonstrations 565
Storer, Sharon 534, 538
Strauss, George 257
Straw, Jack 489, 510, 565–566, 581, 584
Strawbs, the 324
strikes 132–133, 308–311, 324–325,
    373–377, 387–388
    miners' 337–338, 340–341, 411–416,
    452–453
Strummer, Joe 362
Suez 123, 145–159
Sun 571
'surveillance society' 580–582
Sure Start 575–576
SWP (Socialist Workers' Party) 370, 371

Talabani, Jalal 588
Taliban, the 554–555
tax 406, 533, 534
    fuel 546–547
    see also poll tax
Taylor, A. J. P. 182, 183
technology 480–483
    military 29–30
Teddy boys 198
television 89, 271
Templer, Gerald 192
Temple, William 4, 200
Temporary Housing Programme 74
Terrence Higgins Trust 407, 408
Tesco 598
Thalidomide 255–257
Thames Today 361
Thames Water 433
Thatcher, Denis 384, 435
Thatcher, Margaret 319, 320, 356–358,
    377, 381–392, 404–407, 457–463
    and Blair 527–528
    downfall 469–474

Thatcher, Margaret (*cont.*)
    and the economy 423, 428, 458,
        463–464
    and education 248–249, 464–465
    on the Eurodollar 423
    and Europe 458–459, 470–471, 485
    and the Falklands War 398–404
    health 465
    and Major 484
    on majority verdicts 258–259
    and the miners 411
    and North Sea oil 435–436, 440
    policy 461–462
    and the press 528–529
    and privatization 428–433, 495–497
    and the Westland Helicopter crisis
        416–420
Thatcherism 357, 434–435
That Was the Week That Was 223
theatre 89–100
Theatre of Action *see* Theatre Workshop
Theatres Act 257
Theatre Workshop 93–95
This Morning 515, 516
Thomas, Richard 580
Thompson, Harry 221
Thompson Scottish Petroleum 438
Thornycroft, Peter 165–166
Thorpe, Jeremy 207, 398
three-day working week 340–341
Tickell, Crispin 480
Times, The 71, 72, 277–278
Todd, Garfield 285, 286
tower blocks 75–79
Toxteth 389–390
trade unions 43–44, 132–133, 197,
        308–311, 337–338, 373–377, 387
transport 480
travel xx–xxi
Treasury, the 243–244
Treaty of Rome 202
Trimble, David 523
Tryweryn reservoir 448
'tripartism' 338–339
Truman, Harry S. 10–11, 101

Tull, Jethro 280
TURNSTILE 209
TVam 515
Twiggy 276
Tynan, Kenneth 95, 97
Tyndall, John 370

UB40 362
UBS 578
UDI (Unilateral Declaration of
        Independence) *see* Rhodesia
Uganda, immigrants from 321–323, 593
unemployment 388–391
Unilateral Declaration of Independence
        (UDI) *see* Rhodesia
unilateral nuclear disarmament 456–457
    see also CND (Campaign for Nuclear
        Disarmament
United Nations 102
United States of America
    economy 422
    and the Falklands War 400, 402, 403
    and Great Britain xxiii–xxv, 8–13, 108,
        213, 291–292, 423–424
    and Iraq 562–567, 589
    music 279–281, 282
    and North Sea oil 436, 437
    nuclear weapons 127–128
    and Serbia 550–551
    and Suez 156–157
    terrorist attacks on 553–556, 583
    and the Westland Helicopter crisis
        416–420
university system 250–251
Uranium 235 94
Ure, Midge 576
utilities 432, 433

Vaneigem, Raoul 331
Varela, Marquesa de 515
Varley assurances 439
Vassall, John 137
V-bombers 209–210
Verwoerd, Hendrik 189
Vicious, Sid 362

Vietnam 292–293
Vietnam Solidarity Committee 282
Vinson, Fred 12

Waiting for Godot (Beckett) 100
Walden, Brian 385
Wales
    devolution 442, 447–449, 525
    miners in 412–413
Walters, Alan 388–418, 471
Wanless, Derek 539
war xxvi–xxvii
    and Churchill 126–127
    and Major 499–502
    on terror 554, 555–556, 584
    see also Falklands War; Gulf War;
        Korean War; World War II;
        Yom Kippur War
Ward, Stephen 217–219
Watton, Harry 77
Waugh, Evelyn 46–47
Wavell, Archibald Percival 37–38
wealth, redistribution of 578
weapons of mass destruction 562,
    564–565, 569–570
Webster, Martin 370
Welensky, Roy 286, 287
Welfare State 44, 406
West Indies, immigrants from 195 201
Westland Helicopter crisis 416–420
Westwood, Vivienne 359–360, 362
Whelan, Charlie 529, 558
Whisky Galore! 81 82
Whitehouse, Mary 261
Whitelaw, Willie 410
White Panthers 282
Who, the 269, 272–273
Wigg, George 218

Wilde, Oscar 544
Wildeblood, Peter 135, 138, 139
Wilkinson, Ellen 106
Williams, Marcia 240, 344
Williams, Shirley 396, 397
Williams, W. E. 4
Wilson, Harold 68, 107, 108, 223–224,
    232, 235–240, 249, 343–345
    and Cecil King 305–307
    domestic policy 352–354
    and Europe 295, 328
    foreign policy 351–352
    and Northern Ireland 317
    nuclear weapons 291
    and Rhodesia 288–289
    style of government 307–308
    and Vietnam 292–293
Winchester Castle 134
Windscale 33
Winston, Robert 538
winter, 1947 33–35
winter of discontent 373–377
Wolfe, Billy 441
Wolfenden, John Frederick 138–139, 254
Wolmer, Christian 490
women 353–354
Wood, Kingsley 63
World Health Organization 256
World War II xv–xviii

Yarwood, Mike 346
Yom Kippur War 340
Young, Hugo 350
Young, Michael 7, 251

Ziegler, Philip 235
Zimbabwe *see* Rhodesia
Zuckerman, Solly 306

Acknowledgements

I would particularly like to thank three people who gave me an early and lasting love of history, and of good writing: my mother, Valerie Marr, and two of my teachers at Loretto School, David Stock and Peter Lapping.

This book would not have happened had I not been badgered three years ago by Peter Horrocks, now the BBC's head of television news, to write and present a television history of post-war Britain. It was his idea and I'm very grateful.

Despite a delay caused by a snapped tendon, the series was a delight to make, thanks to the wonderful team, led by Chris Granlund, the series producer, and Clive Edwards. The individual films were produced by Tom Giles, Fatima Salaria, Francis Whately and Robin Dashwood, filmed and recorded by Neil Harvey, Chris Hartley and Tim Watts, and researched by Charlotte Sacher, Jo Wade, Jo Dutton, Jay Mukoro, and Stuart Robertson. I would like to thank them all, and in the office, Rachel Bacon and Libby Hand.

The research for the book was done separately, and I take full responsibility for any mistakes I have made. That said, two people had a big influence, Philippa Harrison who hacked, shaped and re-ordered it and Peter Hennessy who, entirely out of kindness, read much of it for me and saved me from some horrible howlers.

I leaned heavily, as ever, on my wonderful agent Ed Victor, who has kept me going with gossip, suggestions, amusement and some excellent food on the way.

As with my earlier books, this owes a great debt to the London Library.

The team at Macmillan was headed by my editor Andrew Kidd, who has been endlessly patient and tolerant, and by Kate Harvey, with the excellent Jacqui Graham dealing with festivals and publicity. Josine Meijer chose the pictures.

The really tolerant people, as ever, have been my long suffering family, above all Jackie.

Andrew Marr
London, 18 March 2007

Picture Acknowledgements

Credits are by page number in order from left to right and top to bottom.

1 – Getty Images (both). 2 – Getty Images (both). 3 – The Advertising Archive; Corbis. 4 – National Portrait Gallery. 5 – Jane Bown / Camera Press; Ronald Grant Archive. 6 – Getty Images; Corbis. 7 – *Time Life* / Getty Images; Getty Images. 8 – Getty Images (both). 9 – *Illustrated London News*; Getty Images. 10 – The Advertising Archives; Popperfoto. 11 – Courtesy of British Motor Industry Heritage Trust (both). 12 – Popperfoto; Getty Images. 13 – Arnold Newman / Getty Images. 14 – Getty Images (all). 15 – *Time Life* / Getty Images. 16 – Getty Images (both). 17 – Getty Images; Petra Niemeier / Redferns. 18 – Getty Images (both). 19 – Getty Images (both). 20 – Getty Images (both). 21 – Getty Images (both). 22 – Getty Images; PA Photos. 23 – David Dagley / Rex Features; Getty Images. 24 – Getty Images; PA Photos. 25 – Peter Jordan / Getty Images; PA Photos. 26 – Michael Cummings / *Daily Express*, 6 February 1980, courtesy of the British Cartoon Archive; *Time Life* / Getty Images. 27 – P. J. Arkell; Howard Davies / Corbis. 28 – *Time Life* / Getty Images; Getty Images; PA Photos. 29 – PA Photos; Getty Images. 30 – Don McPhee / *Guardian*; Getty Images. 31 – Stephen Hird / Reuters / Corbis; AFP / Getty Images. 32 – Getty Images (both).

Visit **www.panmacmillan.com** to read more about all our books and to buy them. You will also find features, author interviews and news of any author events, and you can sign up for e-newsletters so that you're always first to hear about our new releases.